TAXATION AND ECONOMIC DEVELOPMENT

A Blueprint for Tax Reform in Ohio

ROY BAHL
Editor

BATTELLE PRESS
Columbus • Richland

Library of Congress Cataloging-in-Publication Data

Taxation and economic development : a blueprint for tax reform in Ohio
/ Roy Bahl, editor.
p. cm.
Includes bibliographical references and index.
ISBN 1–57477–015-2 (alk. paper)
1. Taxation—Ohio. 2. Ohio–Economic policy. I. Bahl, Roy W.
HJ2427.T39 1995 95-24823
336.2′009771–dc20 CIP

Battelle Press
505 King Avenue
Columbus, Ohio 43201-2693
614–424–6393
Toll Free: 1–800–451–3543
Fax: 614–424–3819

Dedicated to the memory of
Father Michael J. Lavelle
1934–1995

Father Lavelle was a member
of the Commission and
President of John Carroll University

COMMISSION MEMBERS

Frank E. Mosier
Chair of the Commission

Thomas E. Hoaglin
Vice Chair of the Commission
Banc One Ohio Corporation

Edward F. Bell
Ameritech

William W. Boeschenstein
Owens-Corning Fiberglass Corp.

Robert H. Compton
Retired Vice President
Ashland Oil, Incorporated

E. Linn Draper, Jr.
American Electric Power

Vincent A. Evers
Cincinnati Area
Board of Realtors

Arlene T. Herman
Family Services of Cincinnati

Kathleen D. Horwath
American Federation of State, County and Municipal Employees

Father Michael J. Lavelle
John Carroll University

Peggy Maltarich
RJF International Corporation

James F. Patterson
Patterson Fruit Farm

Percy Squire
Bricker & Eckler

Albert Vontz, Jr.
Heidelberg Distributing Company

Farah M. Walters
University Hospitals of Cleveland

POLICY RESEARCH CENTER
COLLEGE OF BUSINESS ADMINISTRATION
GEORGIA STATE UNIVERSITY

RESEARCH STAFF

Roy Bahl	Georgia State University	Project Director
Donald Berno	Ohio Public Expenditure Council	Fiscal History
Karl Case	Wellesley College	Telecommunications Taxes
Gary Cornia	Brigham Young University	Personal Property Tax
Philip Dearborn	ACIR	State-Local Fiscal Relations
Mary Duchi	Battelle Memorial Institute	Economic Base
William Fox	University of Tennessee	Sales Tax
Martin Grace	Georgia State University	Franchise Tax
Jorge Martinez-Vazquez	Georgia State University	Franchise Tax
Therese McGuire	University of Illinois, Chicago	General Advisor
Richard McHugh	University of South Florida	Telecommunications Taxes
David Sjoquist	Georgia State University	Property Tax
Sally Wallace	Georgia State University	Individual Income Tax
Michael Wasylenko	Syracuse University	Tax Incentives
Jack Whitmore	Ohio Public Expenditure Council	Fiscal History

INSTITUTIONAL SUBCONTRACTORS

Battelle Memorial Institute
Advisory Commission on Intergovernmental Relations (ACIR)
Ohio Public Expenditure Council

RESEARCH ASSISTANTS

Barbara Edwards
Richard Hawkins
Fitzroy Lee
Steve Maguire
Robert McNab
James Palen
Wen Tsui

STAFF

David Sandt—Director, Administration
Curtis Augustin—Systems Analyst
Dawn Baldwin—Administrative Specialist
Angela Y. Harris—Administrative Specialist
Joan Hippolyte—Administrative Specialist
Arthur D. Turner—Micro Computer Software Technical Specialist
Trudy Turner—Administrative Assistant

STAFF REPORTS[1]

No.	Title	Author
1	The Setting for Fiscal Reform: Selected Tables	Richard McHugh
2	Ohio's Sales Tax: Current Condition and Policy Options	William Fox
3	Ohio's Economic and Demographic Structure	Mary Duchi
4	Historical Review of Ohio State and Local Government Finances	Doald Berno and Jack Whitmore
5	Ohio's State and Local Individual Income Taxes: Analysis and Options	Sally Wallace, Barbara Edwards & Fitzroy Lee
6	Real Property Taxation in Ohio: Analysis and Policy Options	David Sjoquist
7	Ohio Metropolitan Area Revenues	Philip Dearborn
8a	Public Utility Taxation: Tangible Personal Property	Gary Cornia
8b	Ohio Tangible Business Personal Property: Property Taxation	Gary Cornia
9	Business Taxation in Ohio: General Franchise Tax and Taxes on Financial Institutions and Insurance Companies	Jorge Martinez-Vazquez and Martin Grace
10a	The Taxation of Telecommunications in Ohio	Richard McHugh
10b	State and Local Tax Policy and the Telecommunications Industry	Karl Case

11	The Role of Fiscal Incentives in Economic Development: How Ohio Stands Relative to Its Competitor States	Michael Wasylenko

STAFF MEMORANDA

Final Report	Title	Author
1	"Memorandum on the Combined Income Reporting	Jorge Marintez-Vazquez and Martin Grace
2	1994c. "Memorandum on the Ohio Estate Tax", November 1994.	Richard McHugh
2	1994d. "Memorandum on the Gross Receipts Tax in Ohio" November 1994.	Richard McHugh
4	1994b. "Memorandum on the Individual Income Tax Estimates", December 21, 1994.	Sally Wallace, Barbara Edwards and Fitzroy Lee

[1] Available from the Policy Research Center, College of Business Administration, Georgia State University, University Plaza, Atlanta, Georgia 30303-3083. All Staff reports and memos were provided between May and December, 1994.

CONTRIBUTORS

Roy Bahl is Professor of Economics and Public Administration, and Director of the Policy Research Center at Georgia State University. Previously he was Maxwell Professor of Political Economy at Syracuse University. He was Staff Director for the Georgia Tax Reform and has advised several states on matters of tax policy.

Donald C. Berno is President of the Ohio Expenditure Council. Previously, he was Acting Director of the Small Business Center at the U.S. Chamber of Commerce. Berno served on former Governor Richard Celeste's Economic Advisory Council and is currently serving in the same capacity for Governor George Voinovich.

Gary Cornia is a Professor and the Associate Dean over graduate programs at the Marriott School of Management at Brigham Young University. He was a member of the Utah State Tax Commission from 1983 to 1986. Currently, Cornia chairs the Governor's Tax Review Commission in Utah, and has been involved with tax studies on public utility taxation in Idaho, Utah and Wyoming.

Philip M. Dearborn is currently Director of Government Finance Research at the Advisory Commission on Intergovernmental Relations (ACIR). In addition, he lectures on government financial management at the Howard University School of Business and Public Administration. Dearborn's career includes positions as Director of Finance in the cities of Lakewood and Cleveland, Ohio; Director of Budget for Fairfax County, Virginia; Budget Analyst with the U.S. Office of Budget and Management, Financial Counselor to the Mayor of Washington, D.C.; and Executive President of the Greater Washington Research Center.

Mary Laird Duchi is Principal, Technology Management Consulting, at Battelle Memorial Institute. During the course of her 18 years with Battelle, Ms. Duchi has been a consultant to industry and all levels of government on issues related to economic development, finance, and taxation. She recently served as the socio-economic expert on a state commission to develop criteria for siting a strategically significant facility in the State of Ohio, and has led Battelle's support of the Ohio Science and Technology Council.

Barbara Edwards is a doctoral candidate at Georgia State University, concentrating in the fields of public finance, urban and labor economics. She was involved in the income tax work of the Georgia tax reform study.

William Fox is Professor and Head of the Economics Department at the University of Tennessee and Associate Director in the Center for Business and Economic Research. He recently held appointments as a Visiting Scholar for the Federal Reserve Bank of Kansas City and a Visiting Professor at the University of Hawaii. In addition, Fox served as a consultant on finance, taxation, and economic development in a number of states, and has been involved in several state tax studies.

Martin F. Grace is an Associate Professor of Risk Management and Insurance, Senior Associate in the Policy Research Center and Acting Director of the Center for Risk Management and Insurance Research at Georgia State University. Professor Grace's research areas include the regulation and taxation of the financial services industry, and he has consulted with several states on this issue.

Richard Hawkins is a doctoral candidate in economics and a Research Associate in the Policy Research Center at Georgia State University. He specializes in state and local taxation issues. He was involved in the sales tax work in the Georgia tax reform.

Jorge Martinez-Vazquez is Professor of Economics and an Associate Director in the Policy Research Center at Georgia State University. He has published numerous papers in public finance and has been a consultant for the major international organizations in over 20 countries. He led the corporate income tax work in the recently completed Georgia tax reform study.

Richard McHugh is the Director of the Center of Economic and Management Research at the University of South Florida and a Senior Associate in the Policy Research Center at Georgia State University. Previously, he was Associate Professor of Economics and Director of the Office of Research in Regional Economic Development at the University of

Missouri, and Division Leader of the Rural Economic Development Program at Iowa State University. He has also performed economic base and forecast analyses at the University of Missouri's State and Regional Fiscal Studies Unit and at Chase Econometrics.

David Sjoquist is Professor of Economics and an Associate Director of the Policy Research Center at Georgia State University. His expertise is in the areas of public finance and urban and regional economics. He led the property tax work in the recently completed Georgia tax reform study.

Sally Wallace is Assistant Professor of Economics and a Senior Associate of the Policy Research Center at Georgia State University. She formerly served as an economist in the Office of Tax Analysis at the United States Treasury. She led the work on individual income taxation for the Georgia tax reform, and also has served as consultant in the area of fiscal analysis for the governments of Guatemala, Jamaica, the Dominican Republic, Ukraine, and Uzbekistan.

Michael Wasylenko is Professor of Economics and Chairman of the Department of Economics at the Maxwell School at Syracuse University. He is widely recognized as an expert in the area of tax incentives and state tax policy for economic development. Previously, he served as Director of the Nebraska Tax Study and was a senior staff member on the Minnesota, Pennsylvania and Arizona Tax Studies. He is widely published in the areas of state and local government finance.

Jack L. Whitmore, Vice President of Research for the Ohio Public Expenditure Council, has nearly 40 years of experience analyzing state and local tax policy and practices in Ohio and the country. He began his career with the Council auditing local government financial statements and developing recommendations for improved tax and financial practices of local governments.

CONTENTS

LIST OF TABLES

LISTS OF FIGURES

LIST OF BOXES

PREFACE

The material in this book is drawn from the staff work for the Commission. The slow growth of the Ohio economy, and its changing structure, are the reasons for the existence of this review of taxation and the economy. The recommendations here, and the analysis that underlies these recommendations, have been guided by two questions: does the tax system reinforce the economic growth advantages of the state and offset its comparative disadvantages, and does the present tax system fit the present and expected future structure of the Ohio economy.

Chapter One in this book provides an overview of the work of the Commission, and a reporting of the final recommendations. A reading of this chapter will make it clear that the proposals are a blueprint for longer run reform and for a tax program that will be more investor friendly, and give the Ohio economy a better chance for keeping pace with national economic growth. Chapter Two is a tracking of the performance of the Ohio economy during the last two decades, and a review of the various projections. The remainder of this book is a tax-by-tax analysis of the current structure. Each tax chapter presents a number of reform options, all of which were placed before the Commission. The focus in all of the chapters is heavily empirical and relies on interstate comparisons.

Each chapter contains the work of the named author and does not necessarily reflect the views of the Commission. The Commission's final report is *Taxation and Economic Development in Ohio: A Blueprint for the Future*. Complete versions of each tax analysis are in the individual staff papers listed on pages vi and vii.

This project benefitted from much help and support. Tax Commissioner Roger Tracy and his staff provided assistance and information well beyond what might have been expected. Budget Director Greg Browning gave us valuable support. The Commission members worked hard to understand a great amount of technical material, and came, we think, to a sensible set of recommendations about future tax policy for Ohio. Frank Mosier, Chair of the Commission, pushed us hard on the analyses and on the alternative recommendations, and the result was a much better product. The Policy Research Center support staff at Georgia State University did their usual excellent job of putting this work together. Angela Harris prepared the Final Report, and Dawn Baldwin organized and processed this manuscript and worked on the individual staff papers.

Without all of this support and the good humor that came with it, the Ohio Project would not have been so successfully completed. And certainly it would not have been so pleasant an experience.

Roy Bahl
Atlanta, GA

FOREWORD

This work began with the appointment of a commission to study the Ohio economy and tax structure. It was prompted by the concern that Ohio's comparative advantage in attracting investment and jobs has eroded over time, and that the present tax system may exacerbate Ohio's comparative disadvantages. The hearings held across the state, the staff analyses considered by the Commission, and other studies undertaken outside the work of the Commission reinforced this concern. The Commission weighted the economic development issue heavily in coming to its recommendations. The number one priority facing the state, in our view, was to turn around a long standing pattern of losing good citizens, job opportunities and investment.

Our recommendations are laid out in the Final Report of the Commission. *Taxation and Economic Development in Ohio: A Blueprint For the Future*. This book, in addition, reports the staff research on which these recommendations were based. Each chapter spells out the problems with our system, and the options for reform that were before us. The Commission felt that there would be considerable value in making these staff analyses available as a reference document, in keeping with our view that tax reform is more a long term process than a one-shot affair. The views expressed in this book are those of the staff, though there is considerable overlap with the final report of the Commission.

The Staff, and the Commission, are greatly in the debt of many for providing the information that made this study and this book possible. We could not possibly mention all of the names here, but we must single out Commissioner Roger Tracy and his staff in the Department of Taxation. They may or may not have agreed with our conclusions, but they worked tirelessly to provide us with whatever information or data we requested, and they placed our data requests on the front burner even when other matters were pressing on their time. The result of this cooperation was that we had access to data that other tax reform commissions might only be able to hope for.

This book is dedicated to the memory of Father Michael J. Lavelle. He served as a member of the Commission, but more important he worked tirelessly for many years to improve education in Ohio. It seems appropriate to remember his wonderful career in serving others with this attempt to educate on so important a policy issue as taxation.

FRANK MOSIER
Chair of the Commission

1 Taxation and the Economy: A Plan for Reform

Roy Bahl[1]

INTRODUCTION

This Commission was established out of concern for the relationship between the Ohio economy and its tax structure. The economy has gone through a long period of slow growth relative to the rest of the nation, and though the early 1990s have seen some improvement, all signs are that this long term pattern will continue into the next century. The state's economic and population structure is changing. The Ohio of today is less of a manufacturing center and more of a producer of services, earns more income from transfer payments and less from wages, consumes more services than goods, and is home to increasing numbers of the elderly and a growing concentration of the poor.

Two major questions were central to the work of this Commission. The first is whether the present tax structure is consistent with the objective of attracting more investment and jobs to the state, and moving Ohio to a higher economic growth path. The second is whether the present tax system "fits" Ohio's new economic structure and spreads the tax burden fairly over all sectors of the economy. The evidence suggests that the present tax system is deficient on both counts. The Commission recommended a comprehensive reform (Commission 1994).

Mandate of the Revenue Commission

The mandate of the Commission was to identify a tax structure that would carry Ohio into the future. The view was never short run, and the possibility of raising or lowering taxes to match next year's budget situation was never discussed. The focus on a tax structure for the future has carried over into the recommendation of the Commission for a phasing in of proposed changes over a period of years.

Neither were politics a major concern in the deliberations of the Commission. The goal was to identify a tax system that would remove barriers to investment, raise adequate amounts of revenue, and spread tax burdens fairly. The principles of a good tax system, which drove the conclusions of this work, never included political acceptability as a criteria. One does not need to appoint a blue ribbon panel or to undertake an analytic study to identify changes that are most acceptable to elected officials.

The Commission was insistent that the proposals be realistic. In the case of every reform option evaluated, the practice in other states—neighboring states, competitor states and faster growing states—was considered. Any tax policy in practice in other states surely has met some test of feasibility, and warrants examination. The Commission decided early that it would not be responsible to ignore the experience of other states simply because some tax policy had been politically accepted or rejected in Ohio in the past. To place that constraint on the work would be to guarantee that the tax structure of the future would look very much like the tax structure of the past.

Scope of Work

The scope of work in an analysis such as this must go beyond the state government revenue system. State and Local government taxes and budgets in Ohio are inextricably linked. Virtually any changes in the state tax system effects the revenue base of local governments either because the tax base is shared (e.g., sales tax), the revenues belong to the local governments (e.g., personal property tax), or the revenues support the flow of state assistance to local governments (e.g., individual income tax). Hence the scope of this work, and these projections, must include the state and local government sector. Accordingly, the work of the Commission was concerned with state government taxes, local taxes that are administered by the State Tax Commissioner, the real property tax, and the municipal income tax. The current revenue structure under consideration here is described in Table 1-1.

There are important areas, closely related to this work, where time and resources did not permit careful study and evaluation. The effects of tax proposals on individual local governments could not be evaluated. Neither was the expenditure side of the budget studied. This is an important caveat to

TABLE 1-1
Collections for Taxes Administered by the Ohio Tax Commissioner, Real Property Taxes and Municipal Income Taxes: 1993

State-Collected Taxes	Net Tax Collections[a] Percent Distribution	Percent Distribution
State Sales and Use	3,960,181,109	18.3
Local Sales and Use	740,155,496	3.4
State Personal Income	4,719,028,442	21.8
Corporation Franchise	853,891,871	3.9
Motor Vehicle Fuel	1,121,757,345	5.2
Public Utility Excise	647,634,313	3.0
Cigarette Excise	248,492,268	1.1
Local Cigarette Excise	6,158,426	0.0
Intangible Personal Property (State Collected)[b]	13,135,362	0.1
Motor Fuel Use	52,431,813	0.2
Alcoholic Beverage Excise	45,666,720	0.2
Soft Drink Excise Tax[c]	18,278,303	0.1
Local Alcoholic Beverage	5,911,906	0.0
Horse Racing	13,749,230	0.1
Severance	9,204,102	0.0
School District Income	53,678,627	0.2
Total State-Collected Taxes	12,509,355,332	57.7
Locally-Collected Taxes	**CY 1992**	
Tangible Personal Property Taxes	1,201,218,193	5.5
Public Utility Property Taxes[d]	954,896,001	4.4
Estate Tax	220,117,148	1.0
Real Property Tax	4,676,940,872	21.6
Municipal Income Tax	2,105,904,973	9.8
Total Locally-Collected Taxes	9,159,077,187	42.3
Total Taxes Under Consideration	21,668,432,519	100.0

Sources: For state-collected taxes, data were supplied by the Ohio Office of Budget and Management. For locally-collected taxes, data were taken from State of Ohio, Department of Taxation, *Annual Report, 1993.*

[a]Gross tax collections less refunds.
[b]Taxes paid by dealers in intangibles.
[c]Effective February 1, 1993.
[d]Includes only tangible personal property taxes levied for collection the following year.

this work. Without such study it is not possible to identify an "adequate" amount of revenue to be raised from a new tax structure, or the "right" long run revenue growth. The proposals for tax reform offered in this report are revenue neutral: they should yield no more revenue in year one of the reform than would the present system. However, the Commission and the staff study recommended that the state turn soon to the development of a long-term expenditure plan, i.e., to the development of a projected capital and operating budget that is consistent with the projected long-term growth in the economy. Without such a plan, it is not possible to identify the "right" revenue growth.

WORK OF THE COMMISSION AND THE STAFF

This work is based on the principles of taxation that have driven the reform of other states and that serve as home base in most tax analyses (Ebel 1990; McGuire and Naimark 1991; Ebel and McGuire 1986). The possible objectives for tax reform were ranked and weighted by the Commission members after debate about the tradeoffs implied. Economic development and horizontal equity were identified by a wide margin as the priority objectives of the Commission. This does not mean that vertical equity, revenue stability and other important considerations have been ignored in either the analysis or the recommendations, but it does mean that economic development and fairness are emphasized in this tax reform proposal.

The Commission began its work by holding hearings across the state, and receiving written testimony from all parts of the state economy. Analytic studies were prepared, covering each major tax and the economic base. These are listed in the references. Every study considered the practice in other states vs the practice in Ohio, evaluated the present system based on the principles of "best" practice, and presented alternate reform options. The Commission weighed these choices against the objectives and priorities that were chosen and eventually voted on a reform package. This "Blueprint for Tax Reform" is presented in this chapter.

The research staff carried out technical studies, and presented these to the Commission in written and oral form. These staff studies were more or less uniform in terms of the issues covered. All were focused on the relationship between the Ohio economy and tax structure, and all were futurist in focus, i.e., where is this State's economy going, and what does this suggest about the need to reform the tax structure? Each study included (a) a description of the tax, (b) an assessment of the problems and issues, and (c) an evaluation of the reform options against the usual criteria for "good" tax practice. Interstate comparisons were at the center of all presentations. These technical studies form the basis for the chapters in this book.

PERFORMANCE OF THE OHIO ECONOMY

The slow growth of the Ohio economy, and its changing structure, are the reasons for the existence of this review of taxation and the economy. The recommendations here, and the analysis that underlies these recommendations, have been guided by two questions: does the tax system reinforce the economic growth advantages of the state and offset its comparative disadvantages, and does the present tax system fit the present and expected future structure of the Ohio economy.

OHIO'S SHARE OF THE NATIONAL ECONOMY[2]

For more than two decades, the Ohio economy has declined relative to the rest of the United States. As may be seen in Figure 1-1, the state share of national income and national population has trended down, almost without interruption.[3]

In absolute numbers, Ohio's total population has remained remarkably constant over the past twenty years. Its share of the total United States population, however, has fallen from 5.2 percent in 1969 to 4.3 percent by 1993. Ohio's share of total national income has fallen even faster, by 15 percent over the 1969 to 1991 period. In 1980, Ohio residents and workers accounted for 4.70 cents of every dollar of income earned in the United States, but by 1992, the share was only 4.05 cents. The growth in population has been slow in Ohio, largely because of outmigration. For those who have remained behind, the slower growth in the Ohio economy has left them with much less real income than their counterparts in the rest of the country.

The consequences of this history can be summed up in the slow growth in average real income described in Figure 1-2. The per capita real income level in Ohio was essentially the same as that for the nation as a whole in

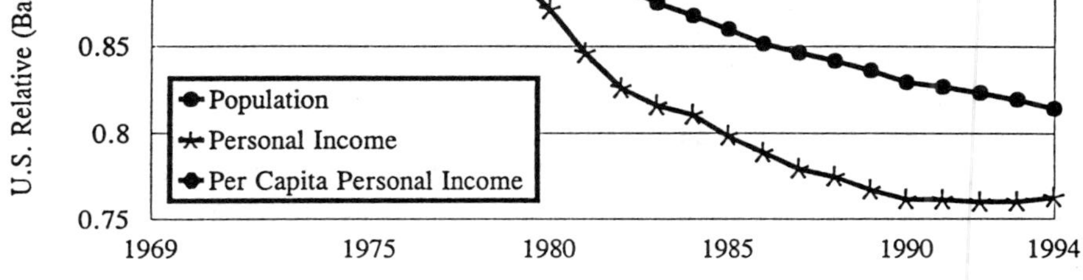

Source: Bureau of Economic analysis, *Regional Economic Information System,* 1994.

FIGURE 1-1. Ohio income, population, and per capita income.

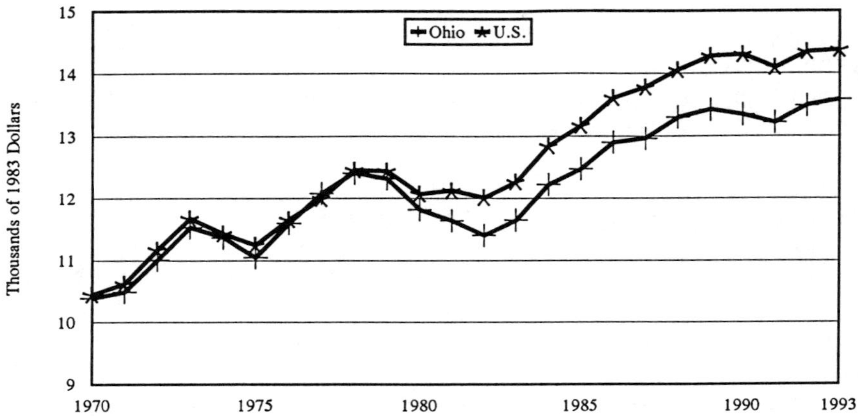

Source: Bureau of Economic Analysis, *Regional Economic Information System,* 1994.

FIGURE 1-2. Real per capita personal income.

1970, but twenty-one years later had fallen to nearly seven percent below the national average. If Ohio had grown at the national rate, even since 1980, the real income of the average Ohioan would now be about $800 higher. This gap, equivalent to five percent of the average Ohioan's income, is the real cost of the state's slow economic growth.

The early 1990s have seen some improvement, though the trend of long term decline has not been arrested. Per capita income grew at 12.6 percent in Ohio between 1990 and 1993, as compared to 11.2 percent in the nation. Non-farm employment in Ohio grew by less than one percent, between 1990 and 1994. This is a lower rate than any adjacent state and about one-fourth of the national rate over this same period (Table 1-2).

Why Has the Ohio Economy Grown Slowly?

There are many reasons for slow economic growth in Ohio. Some of these are factors that can be influenced by state policy (e.g. taxes, work rules, energy costs), and some are factors that are "uncontrollable" (e.g. international competition and weather). No reputable study has been able to provide indisputable evidence about which are most important and which are the marginal factors. The most reasonable view in the literature is that locational attractiveness is a function of a number of factors that work together to form a "climate" for doing business that is more or less favorable than that in competing states. It is this business climate, a host of situation-specific factors, and a good dose of luck that finally determines how well a state does in the jobs race (Wasylenko 1994).

TABLE 1-2
Ohio Non-Farm Employment Compared with Selected States and the United States: 1990–1994[a]

	1990	1994	1990-1994 Percent Increase
TOTAL United States	111,744.0	114,366	2.3
Ohio	4,977.7	5,001.5	0.5
Pennsylvania	5,160.9	5,217.2	1.1
Michigan	3,947.1	4,127.5	4.6
Kentucky	1,477.8	1,565.7	5.9
Indiana	2,532.3	2,645.1	4.5
West Virginia	629.7	675.4	7.3
Manufacturing			
United States	19,256.0	18,144.0	-5.8
Ohio	1,129.7	1,059.9	-6.2
Services			
United States	28,479.0	32,053.0	12.6
Ohio	1,196.9	1,318.1	10.1

Source: U.S. Department of Labor, Bureau of Labor Statistics. *Employment and Earnings*. Data are for June (non-seasonally adjusted) as reported in the September issue.

[a]Number of jobs, in thousands.

How does Ohio compare on the various indicators of business climate? Most research on the determinants of economic growth in various regions of the country point to the relative costs of doing business as a significant factor. This includes all costs, e.g., labor, land, taxes, energy, transportation, infrastructure, etc. Business investment and job creation are encouraged to the extent that the cost of doing business in Ohio is lower, especially if it is low enough to offset other disadvantages.

The information available on wage costs in Ohio shows that the wages of workers in the state are, in general, below the national average. The exception is for those working in parts of the state's important manufacturing and construction sectors, within which employee costs are somewhat higher than in the rest of the country. Energy costs are generally below the national average (although there are areas of the state with above average costs).

Overall tax costs would not, at first blush, appear to be overly high. Per capita tax collections, taxes as a share of total income, and measures of the overall tax effort in Ohio do not indicate that the average burden of taxation is onerous enough to dissuade businesses from locating in the state. However, it may be the case that some of Ohio's taxes are still too high to offset other comparative disadvantages. Moreover, broad measures of tax effort often hide subtle features of the tax system which could discourage business activity. For example, although tax collections are below average, the top corporate franchise tax rate is high, and Ohio taxes machinery, equipment and inventories at relatively high rates. It is important to remember that the strategy is not simply attracting new companies to Ohio but also holding on to that industry already in the state and encouraging its expansion. It is arguably true that Ohio's economic growth problems are less due to failure to attract new industry than to failure to hold on to the industry already in the state.

A second major determinant of economic growth in a region follows from the notion that people follow jobs and also that jobs follow people. That is, people will move to where the job opportunities are greatest and jobs will spring up around markets (people). Ohio has lost population because of the slow growth in the state's economy. The loss in population due to migration has been heavy in the younger working age groups. With the loss of families comes the loss of proximity to markets for many businesses. The outflow of people from the state fueled the downward spiral in the general level of economic activity. While it is true that Ohio's market share is declining, it is also true that Ohio is located in the heavily populated midwestern region, which holds 23 percent of the nation's income and 24 percent of its population.

A third explanation for the slow growth in the Ohio economy is that the state has specialized in manufacturing, a slow growing sector of the economy, and the fact that the service sector of the Ohio economy has grown more slowly than that in the rest of the United States The 1976-1993 growth rate in manufacturing employment in the nation averaged –0.4 percent, as opposed to –1.2 percent in the state of Ohio. In the area of services, the comparable numbers are 4.4 percent for the United States and 3.6 percent for Ohio. During the period since 1990, manufacturing employment in Ohio has continued to decline at a greater rate than in the rest of the United States (Table 1-2). Not only has the state of Ohio specialized in an economic sector which has not generated as many jobs in the nation as other sectors, but manufacturing has performed worse in Ohio than it has nationally. Neither has Ohio done as well in the service sector, in part because of the weakness in its more basic sectors, such as manufacturing, and in part because of its declining share of national income.

Finally, there are the non-economic factors (amenities), which seem to have attracted many firms to the growing regions of the country. These include factors that effect the quality of life of workers and executives, such as weather, the availability of recreational and cultural facilities, low housing costs, and less congestion. It is also true that the development of better systems of transportation and communications, and the maturing of the newer industrial regions of the country made possible the movement of large headquarters and production facilities to the south and southwest in the 1970s and 1980s. Ohio was one of the states that lost from the maturation process in the rest of the country.

The factors which are cited as a cause for the slow growth in the Ohio economy are factors which affect all states in the industrial Midwest. Much of Ohio's decline can be attributed to the fact that it is located in an area of the country which, because of the historical pattern of its development and maturation, and because of the shifting demographic trends which accompanied the development of the Southeast and Western part of the country, has not done well. It would have been truly remarkable if Ohio had stood out as an area of strong growth in the face of these broad and powerful changes in taste, technology and demography. What is troublesome, however, is that Ohio has also done poorly relative to surrounding states.

Changing Economic Structure

The economic and population structure of Ohio has changed dramatically during the last two decades. Important structural changes have occurred in what is produced, how income is earned and spent, and in the age distribution of the population. These changes all have important implications for what should be taxed in order to keep the system fair, for how high tax rates must be set to protect revenue, and for how taxes must be restructured to reinforce competitive advantage.

Employment[4]

There has been a dramatic job shift in Ohio, away from manufacturing and toward services. In 1970, 30 of every 100 jobs was in the manufacturing sector, and 17 of every 100 jobs was in services. By 1991, this position was nearly reversed: 19 of every 100 jobs was in manufacturing and 27 of every 100 jobs in services. This shift is a nationwide trend, but it has been distorted in Ohio. The gains have not been as great in the service sector and the losses have been greater in the manufacturing sector.

The losses in manufacturing employment have been widespread. Many of the industries experiencing the greatest job losses are traditional Ohio industries associated with primary metal products and industrial machinery. The state economy has reflected these losses. Manufacturing in Ohio has always been considered a basic industry, a sector which has drawn economic resources from other states and countries to Ohio. The weakness of this sector has rolled out into other sectors of the economy which directly and indirectly depend on and support the manufacturing base.

To some extent, the loss in manufacturing jobs has been replaced by an increase in service sector jobs. Two facts are noteworthy about this trend. One is that Ohio's growth in this sector has been slow whether compared to the United States or to surrounding states. The other is that service jobs are heavily concentrated in health care, education and religious activities, all of which are outside the traditional business, income, property and sales tax bases.

Sources of Income

Another factor which has affected the Ohio economy and tax base is the shift in the ways by which households get their income. Over the past few decades, the importance of "transfer income"—primarily social security, medical assistance and welfare payments—has increased. In 1970, transfer income accounted for 10 percent of total income in the nation, and 9 percent in Ohio. By 1991, this transfer income had grown to 15 percent in the nation and 17 percent in Ohio. Again, a national trend has been magnified in Ohio.

This growth in transfer income compensated for a slower growth in wage and salary payments. In 1970, Ohio residents received 68 percent of income from wages and salaries, versus 64 percent for the nation. By 1991, these shares were lower and almost even in Ohio (56 percent) and the United States (55 percent).

The shift in the source distribution of income is quite significant since transfer income does not carry the same taxpaying power as wage earnings and capital income. Medical assistance payments, welfare payments and pensions are often given preferential tax treatment. Moreover, a higher share of transfer income usually means a growing concentration of elderly population, whose consumption habits may lead to less sales and property tax revenues.

Consumption Patterns

Over time, the consumption patterns of households have shifted away from the taxed purchases of tangible goods toward the non-taxable consumption of services e.g., personal, educational and health services. In the United States, the share of total consumer expenditures for services (excluding food and housing) was 30 percent in 1976 but had risen to 43 percent by 1993. This is extremely important for the Ohio tax system, since service consumption is largely outside the sales tax base. The economic impact of this shift away from the demand for goods and toward services is not limited to domestic demand. In terms of international trade, the share of United States exports of goods and merchandise has fallen significantly relative to the exports of services (e.g., professional services). This shift has potentially important implications for the Ohio economy which relies heavily on the production of goods.

Age Distribution

Because of historical variations in birth rates, immigration, and advances in life-prolonging medical care, there are cycles in the age distribution of the population. At present, the nation is witnessing a steady aging of its population, with a growing cohort of people at or near retirement age. This national trend is even more pronounced in Ohio. The population of Ohioans aged 55 and over is much higher now than in 1970, and higher than the national share. This, in part, reflects the significant outmigration of the younger, working-age population.

This aging of the population suggests important fiscal implications over the next decade as these wage earners retire. The share of non-taxable income and consumption may grow, housing expenditures may fall, and there will be more pressure for preferential tax relief for the elderly, e.g., circuit breakers and pension income exemptions.

Central Cities[5]

The most apparent indicator of the economic decline of Ohio's central cities is the loss of population. All of the ten central cities, except Columbus, have been losing population in recent decades. Although the aggregate rate of population loss slowed from 12.3 percent between 1970 and 1980 to 4.3 percent between 1980 and 1990, four of the cities (Cleveland, Youngstown, Dayton, and Canton) still experienced a population loss of more than 10 percent in the 1980s. It seems likely that the losses are continuing in the 1990s.

The significance of population losses is determined by how those losses affect the overall well-being of the residents that remain. Unfortunately, the evidence from Ohio cities suggests that wealthier residents are leaving, a large proportion of poorer residents is remaining, and the numbers of poor are increasing. In 1990, six of the central cities had poverty rates exceeding 20 percent of their population, and two more were at 19 percent.

Youngstown's poverty rate was 29 percent and Cleveland's was just slightly less. The poverty rates in all ten cities exceeded the 13 percent national rate, as well as the 16.6 percent rate for cities over 50,000 population, and all but Columbus and Hamilton exceeded the 18 percent national rate. The statewide poverty rate for Ohio was much lower, at 12.5 percent in 1990.

Adding to this grim poverty picture, the central city poverty rates all increased between 1980 and 1990, led by Youngstown with a 10.8 percentage point increase, followed by Cleveland with a 6.6 percentage point increase.[6]

It seems clear that the outmigration from central cities has not been led by poor residents.

Another perspective on the plight of central cities can be gained by examining the incomes of city residents compared to those in the surrounding suburbs. Per capita income in all ten Ohio central cities trails that in suburbs by large margins. Only residents of Cincinnati and Columbus have incomes that reach even 80 percent of that of their suburbs, and Cleveland's per capita income is barely above 50 percent of suburban levels. In six of the ten central cities, income levels are less than three-quarters of that in the suburbs.

Population losses coupled with increasing proportions of poor residents present two potential problems for the governments of central cities, namely, higher costs required to provide services for poorer residents and a smaller revenue base from which to finance those services. The prospects are that the imbalance will grow worse and that the fiscal self-sufficiency of local governments in central cities will weaken. In the long run this will represent a potentially large claim on the revenue of the state government.

Ohio's Comparative Advantage

This picture of decline relative to the rest of the United States does not mean that Ohio is without comparative advantage. The state is home to a considerable capital stock investment by manufacturers, and a skilled manufacturing work force. It is a reasonable proposition that it is much easier to hold on to an existing economic activity than to attract a new one. Inertia can be a great comparative advantage for Ohio. Manufacturing always has played a significant role in Ohio's economic development, and it will continue to do so. Restructuring in the manufacturing sector in recent years has enhanced Ohio's competitive position.

Labor costs in Ohio are not particularly high for a unionized, industrialized midwestern state though manufacturing wages in some sectors are high. The cost of living in the state also represents a comparative advantage. Based upon surveys performed by the American Chamber of Commerce Research Associates and by the National Association of Home Builders, the cost of living is attractive, particularly for a state with many large urban areas where the living costs are typically higher (McHugh 1994a).

Human resources are also an area of competitive advantage. Educational spending and attainment are factors which are frequently cited in rankings of state business climates as one of the state's strengths. The state also has a high level of science and engineering graduate students, an indicator of the quality of the educational system and potential work force. Ohio's technology resources and the presence of several federal laboratories have also been cited as competitive advantages in various business climate studies (Duchi 1994).

Even the numbers that describe Ohio's declining national population and economic shares can be interpreted in a different light. A stable population size suggests less pressure on public expenditures, as do fewer school-aged children. Less manufacturing employment may relieve some environmental problems, and may leave the state with a less cyclical economy. Slower job growth in general can mean less pressure for increased infrastructure expenditures.

This combination of historically slow growth and comparative advantage presents two challenges to fiscal planners in Ohio. The first is to manage the budget within the constraints of slow growth. This second is to alter the fiscal structure so as to get on a higher growth path.

PROJECTED FUTURE PERFORMANCE

Where is the Ohio economy headed? This chapter presents a forecast of Ohio's economy, given anticipated changes in demography, tastes and technology.[7] These projections assume that there will be no fundamental changes in the Ohio economy, such as might be induced by a change in the international economy or a change in the state's tax structure. This forecast tells us where Ohio is headed if nothing is different in the future, not where it could be under a different policy frame.

Population

For more than two decades, the state's population has grown more slowly than population in the United States This pattern of relatively slow growth is expected to continue over the next thirty years, although the disparity in the relative growth rates between Ohio and the United States will narrow during the next century. (See Table 1-3). In each five year interval from 1995 to 2010, Ohio's population growth rate is expected to remain at 0.3 percent per year, i.e., the historical tradition of population stability will continue. This is good news on two counts: (a) there is no projection of a net outmigration substantial enough to offset natural growth, and (b) slow population growth might enable a slower growth in expenditure budgets.

The United States population growth rate will remain above that for Ohio for the next 25 years, but will slow over time, from 0.6 percent to 0.4 percent per year, narrowing the spread between Ohio and the nation. The implications of this pattern are that Ohio's share of national population will decline, bringing with it a smaller share of the national consumer market and possibly a decline in Congressional representation.

TABLE 1-3
Population Projections to 2020: Ohio and the United States

Ohio Population (Thousands)							
	1983	**1988**	**1995**	**2000**	**2005**	**2010**	**2020**
Under 18 Years	2,930	2,823	2,817	2,741	2,633	2,545	2,526
18-64 Years	6,578	6,660	6,784	6,970	7,184	7,324	7,199
65 Years and Older	1,252	1,372	1,516	1,550	1,601	1,727	2,261
Total	10,761	10,855	11,117	11,261	11,417	11,596	11,986

Average Annual Rate of Change in Ohio Population (Percentage)						
	1983-1988	**1988-1995**	**1995-2000**	**2000-2005**	**2005-2010**	**2010-2020**
Under 18 Years	-0.7	-0.0	-0.5	-0.8	-0.7	-0.1
18-64 Years	0.2	0.3	0.5	0.6	0.4	-0.2
65 Years and Older	1.8	1.4	0.4	0.6	1.5	2.7
Total	0.2	0.3	0.3	0.3	0.3	0.3

Average Annual Rate of Change in U.S. Population (Percentage)						
	1985-1988	**1988-1995**	**1995-2000**	**2000-2005**	**2005-2010**	**2010-2020**
Under 18 Years	0.3	0.5	-0.1	-0.5	-0.5	0.0
18-64 Years	1.0	0.7	0.9	0.9	0.6	-0.1
65 Years and Older	2.1	1.5	0.7	0.8	1.6	2.8
Total	1.0	0.8	0.6	0.5	0.5	0.4

Source: *BEA Regional Projections to 2040*, Volume 1, June 1990, as reported in Duchi (1994).

Note: Cohort totals may not sum to total population due to rounding.

There are expected to be important changes in the age distribution of the population, both in Ohio and the nation. In Ohio, the growth rate will increase for the 65 years old and above cohort of the population during the next 25 years. This growth rate is slightly below that for the 18-64 year old group through the year 2000. The next decade, however, will see the beginning of a rapid increase in the elderly population; the rate of growth will rise from 0.4 percent between 1995 and 2000 to 2.7 percent in the decade from 2010 to 2020.

Between the years 2000 and 2010, the Ohio population is projected to increase by 335,000 but 53 of every 100 of these additional Ohioans will be over 65 years of age. After the year 2010, all of the net growth in the Ohio population is projected to be in the over-65 age group. The same pattern will hold in the rest of the country, but it will not be so pronounced.

Another characteristic of the changing structure of the population is the anticipated decline in school-aged population. Beginning in the 1995-2000 period, the size of under eighteen years of age population is expected to decline in Ohio and in the United States. This should provide steady relief to state and local governments for school budgets and other youth-related expenditures.

Employment Growth

Job growth is projected to exceed the rate of population growth over the next decade (Table 1-4). According to these projections, about 221,000 net new jobs will be created in Ohio between 1995 and 2000. Of these, 126,000 will be in the service sector, and only 2,000 will be in manufacturing.

By comparison with other states, however, Ohio's employment growth will be slow. Employment is projected to grow at about 70 percent of the national rate until 2000 and two-thirds thereafter (See Table 1-4). Under present conditions, therefore, the outlook is for Ohio's share of national employment to fall. The sectors which will constrain Ohio's relative growth in employment are the same ones which have held it back in the past. In particular, employment growth in manufacturing is expected to be quite slow through the end of the century and then there will be absolute declines.

Most worrisome in the outlook is that the rates of decline are above those projected for all United States manufacturing (Table 1-4). This means that Ohio is losing in an area where its competitive advantages should be producing an above average performance by comparison with the rest of the country. Projections of the growth in employment by occupation also hold mixed news for Ohio. There is projected strong growth in the trade, service, and managerial occupations, and slower growth in operator, fabricator, and laborer occupations (Duchi 1994). The growth occupations are a mix of high and low wage jobs.

TABLE 1-4
Employment Projections to 2020, by Industry: Ohio and the United States

Average Annual Rate of Change in Ohio Employment (Percentage)						
	1983-1988	**1988-1995**	**1995-2000**	**2000-2005**	**2005-2010**	**2010-2020**
Agricultural Services	7.4	3.5	2.5	1.7	1.1	0.3
Mining	-4.8	-0.3	0.1	-0.2	-0.3	-0.7
Construction	6.6	0.7	0.6	0.3	0.1	-0.3
Durable Goods Manufacturing	0.7	-0.1	-0.1	-0.2	-0.2	-0.6
Nondurable Goods Manufacturing	1.2	0.2	0.3	0.0	-0.2	-0.5
Transportation, Communications and Utilities	2.1	0.7	0.6	0.3	0.1	-0.3
Wholesale Trade	2.8	0.8	0.5	0.4	0.3	-0.2
Retail Trade	3.7	0.7	0.7	0.4	0.1	-0.3
Finance, Insurance, Real Estate	3.5	0.8	0.8	0.4	0.2	-0.2
Services	4.7	2.0	1.5	1.0	0.5	-0.1
Government, Total	1.3	0.3	0.3	0.1	-0.1	-0.4
Total, Non-farm	3.0	0.9	0.8	0.4	0.2	-0.3
Farm	-3.0	-0.6	-0.5	-0.6	-0.7	0.0
Total Employment	2.8	0.8	0.7	0.4	0.2	-0.3
Average Annual Rate of Change in U.S. Employment (Percentage)						
	1983-1988	**1988-1995**	**1995-2000**	**2000-2005**	**2005-2010**	**2010-2020**
Total Employment	3.0	1.2	1.0	0.6	0.3	-0.2
Durable Goods Manufacturing	1.3	0.2	0.2	0.0	-0.1	-0.4
Nondurable Goods Manufacturing	0.8	0.4	0.4	0.1	-0.1	-0.5

Source: *BEA Regional Projections to 2040*, Volume 1, June 1990, as reported in Duchi (1994).

Personal Income

Real income will increase in Ohio over the next two decades, and it will increase faster than population. This guarantees growth in real per capita terms. The average Ohioan will be better off in real terms in 2005 than he/she was in 1995. As may be seen from Table 1-5, growth will exceed 1 percent per year for the next 15 years. This means, among other things, a greater purchasing power of residents, a greater taxpaying capacity, and perhaps a demand for more government services.

As welcome as the projection of real growth is, it must be noted that these real increases are projected to be well below that in the rest of the nation. Between 1995 and 2010, Ohio's real income will grow 15 to 20 percent below the national average rate. Thereafter the gap widens. This slow growth means that Ohio's share of national income will drop, and it will be a less attractive site for consumer-driven production and distribution.

What is more notable about this projected growth in personal income of Ohio residents are the trends in sources of income growth: earnings; dividends and rent; and transfer payments. Beginning in the 1995 to 2000 period, transfer payments will become the fastest growing component of personal income in Ohio (Table 1-6). While this shift toward transfer income is part of a national phenomena, the growth in transfer payments is not expected to exceed that for total personal income in the United States until the next century.

TAX CAPACITY AND TAX EFFORT: WHERE IS OHIO HEADED?

What are the implications of this projected slow growth in the Ohio economy for the state and local government sector? How has the state coped with slow economic growth in the past in terms of its taxing and spending decisions, and can this pattern be continued? If there is a fiscal gap ahead, what is its magnitude? What is the desired revenue-income elasticity of a reformed tax system?[8] The answers to these questions are essential inputs to determining the "right" tax reform for Ohio.

Tax Capacity and Effort

The United States Advisory Commission on Intergovernmental Relations (ACIR 1991) regularly produces estimates of the tax capacity and tax effort of states. These estimates show that Ohio's fiscal history has been one of increases in tax effort as its fiscal capacity has declined. The ACIR estimated Ohio's taxable capacity at about 4 percent above the national av-

TABLE 1-5
Real Personal Income Projections to 2020: Ohio and the United States

Average Annual Rate of Change in Ohio Personal Income (Percentage)						
	1983-1988	**1988-1995**	**1995-2000**	**2000-2005**	**2005-2010**	**2010-2020**
Non-farm personal income	2.6	1.7	1.5	1.2	1.1	0.5
Farm income	33.5	0.9	0.8	0.6	0.5	0.1
Total personal income	2.6	1.7	1.5	1.2	1.1	0.5
Average Annual Rate of Change in U.S. Personal Income (Percentage)						
	1983-1988	**1988-1995**	**1995-2000**	**2000-2005**	**2005-2010**	**2010-2020**
Non-farm personal income	3.6	2.1	1.8	1.5	1.3	1.0
Farm income	10.0	0.3	0.5	0.4	0.3	0.1
Total personal income	3.6	2.1	1.8	1.5	1.3	1.0

Source: *BEA Regional Projections to 2040*, Volume 1, June 1990, as reported in Duchi (1994).

TABLE 1-6
Projections of the Source Distribution of Personal Income,to 2020: Ohio and the United States

Average Annual Rate of Change in Sources of Income, Ohio (Percentage)						
	1983-1988	**1988-1995**	**1995-2000**	**2000-2005**	**2005-2010**	**2010-2020**
Total Earnings by Place of Work	3.1	1.6	1.5	1.2	1.0	0.5
Dividends, Interest, and Rent	2.4	2.1	1.9	1.6	1.3	0.8
Transfer Payments	1.7	1.5	1.1	1.2	1.8	2.7
Other Adjustments	5.2	2.0	2.0	1.8	1.6	1.2
Total Personal income	2.6	1.7	1.5	1.2	1.1	0.9
Average Annual Rate of Change in Sources of Income, U.S. (Percentage)						
	1983-1988	**1988-1995**	**1995-2000**	**2000-2005**	**2005-2010**	**2010-2020**
Total Earnings by Place of Work	4.0	2.1	1.8	1.4	1.2	0.7
Dividends, Interest, and Rent	3.9	2.4	2.2	1.7	1.4	0.8
Transfer Payments	2.0	2.2	1.7	1.6	2.1	2.8
Total Personal income	3.6	2.1	1.8	1.5	1.3	1.0

Source: *BEA Regional Projections to 2040*, Volume 1, June 1990, as reported in Duchi, 1994.

erage in 1977 (Box 1-1). The 1977 tax effort index, i.e., the extent to which Ohio used this capacity, was more than 20 percent below the national average. At that time, Ohio was among the lower taxing states in the United States and had traditionally been a low taxing state.

As the relative level of economic activity in Ohio declined, the state and local governments in Ohio compensated by taxing their bases more heavily. By the early 1990s, the state had a taxable capacity that was 7 percent below the national average. The use of this capacity, the level of tax effort in Ohio, was 4 percent below the national average. Between 1981 and 1991, Ohio's increase in state and local government tax burden was 112 percent—the 9th highest increase in the country during that period.[9]

From this history, one might draw two important conclusions. The first is that Ohio is still a low taxing state, and there is room for discretionary increases. The second is that the recent history of the state has been one of increasing the average tax rate to make up for the lagging economic growth.[10]

Fiscal Projections

Where is the public sector in Ohio headed under present conditions? That is, under present circumstances will there be a gap between future revenues available and future expenditure requirements? If there is a gap, what will be its size, how might it be covered, and will it lie at the state or the local government level? During the 1983-1992 period, state and local government expenditures in Ohio grew by an average real rate of 3.5 percent.[11] This is the amount of revenue growth, on average, required to provide the level of government services that the state has enjoyed over this period. To project expenditure needs forward to the year 2005, we have used a more conservative growth assumption. Our model assumes that real expenditures will grow at an annual rate of 2.5 percent per year. This is less than the historical rate, but one that is still above the projected real personal income growth in the state.

The results of this projection are described by the top curve in Figure 1-3. Real (deflated) expenditures will increase from a base of $21.7 billion in 1993 to $24.5 billion by 1998 and $29.1 billion by the year 2005. The detail of these projections are presented in the penultimate row of Table 1-7.

The question to be answered is whether adequate revenues will be generated to match these expenditure needs, or whether discretionary tax rate increases or expenditure retrenchment will be required. The revenue projections we present are based on the income elasticity of the major taxes in the system, and the projected growth rates in personal income reported in the preceding chapter. The estimated elasticities are lowest for the corporate franchise and property taxes, and higher for sales and individual income taxes. The income elasticity of each tax (the responsiveness of revenues

BOX 1-1
Measuring Taxable Capacity and Tax Effort

How does one determine whether a state is using its taxable capacity to the same extent as other states? A shorthand approach is to calculate the state and local government tax share of personal income and compare this across states. Taxes raised by Ohio state and local governments in 1992 accounted for 10.6 percent of total personal income, as compared to 11.2 percent for the U.S. average.

This shorthand approach has been criticized as an oversimplication. The Advisory Commission on Intergovernmental Relations (1991) argues that personal income is a poor indicator of taxable capacity because not all taxes used by state and local governments are levied on income and because many are not even closely related to income. The ACIR has developed an alternate measure of fiscal capacity: the yield of a Representative Tax System. The Representative Tax System is a national average set of tax bases and tax rates. Fiscal capacity is the amount of revenue a state could raise if it levied that "average" tax system on its economy. The ACIR estimated that Ohio had a per capita taxable capacity of $1936 in 1991, about 7 percent below the national average (a taxable capacity index of 93), and that it ranked 29th in the U.S. Since Ohio actually raised $1851 per capita in that year, it had a tax effort index of 96 (4 percent below the national average). By this measure Ohio's tax effort was ranked 23rd among the 50 states in 1991.

Tax Capacity

	1967	1977	1980	1985	1988	1991
U.S. Average	100	100	100	100	100	100
Ohio	100	104	97	91	91	93

Tax Effort

	1967	1977	1980	1985	1988	1991
U.S. Average	100	100	100	100	100	100
Ohio	82	78	87	103	97	96

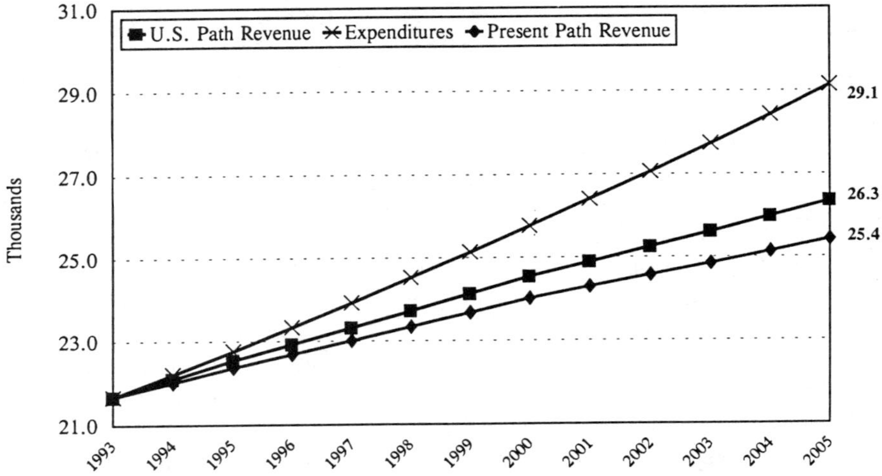

FIGURE 1-3. Ohio expenditure and revenue growth.

raised from that tax to increases in personal income) was estimated and reported in the various staff papers. It is assumed that no discretionary rate and base increases take place over this period, hence all the revenue growth is "automatic." The resulting revenue projections are shown in Table 1-7.

If the Ohio economy grows as projected by BEA, and if expenditures increase by 2.5 percent per year in real terms, a significant fiscal deficit will emerge. By the year 2005, projected revenues ($25.4 billion) will be 14.7 percent short of projected expenditure requirements ($29.1 billion). Some combination of a level of taxation that is 15 percent higher, or expenditure reduction will be required. This is a sizeable gap. If a 5-percent inflation rate is assumed, it translates into a nominal revenue shortfall of $7.2 billion, an amount equivalent to 33 percent of 1993 state and local government revenues.

The question might be asked, what is the contribution of slow economic growth to this picture? If the Ohio economy grew at the United States rate, would the gap narrow markedly? In fact, the result would be as shown in Table 1-8 and graphed as "United States path" in Figure 1-3: the gap would be reduced from 14.7 to 10.6 percent of total revenues. About one-fourth of the problem is the slow growth in the Ohio economy. The remainder is due to the relatively low elasticity of the state tax system, and to the likelihood that public expenditure demands will increase faster than personal income.

The conclusion one reaches from this analysis is that the present tax system is not going to carry public expenditure requirements into the future,

TABLE 1-7
Present Path Projected Revenue-Expenditure Gap with 2.5 Percent Real Expenditure Growth (Revenues in Millions of Dollars)

	1993[1] Actual	Income Elasticity Estimate	1998 Estimate	2005 Estimate
Major State Tax Revenues				
Personal Income Tax	$4,719	1.27	$5,208	$5,814
Sales Tax	3,960	0.97	4,273	4,662
Corporate Franchise Tax	853	0.6	895	947
Public Utilities Excise Tax	647	0.7	684	730
Other State Taxes	1,811	1.0	1,959	2,142
State Total	11,990		13,018	14,294
Major Local Tax Revenue				
Tangible Personal Property Tax	1,201	0.8	1,297	1,377
Public Utilities Property Tax	955	0.6	1,002	1,060
Local Sales Tax	740	1.0	800	875
Real Property Tax	4,677	0.8	4,982	5,361
Municipal Income Tax	2,105	0.9	2,260	2,451
Total	9,678		10,323	11,123
State and Local Total Revenue[2]	21,668		23,341	25,417
State and Local Expenditures at 2.5% Real Growth Rate	21,668		24,516	29,141
Surplus (Shortfall) as a Percent of Revenue	0.00		(5.03)	(14.65)

[1]State data are fiscal year and local data are lagged calendar year as reported in the 1993 *Annual Report* of the Commissioner of Taxation.

[2]See Table 1-1.

and the probabilities are high that tax increases are in the offing. This prospect might be avoided in several ways. One is to find a better economic performance, and to grow out of the problem. Another is to raise the elasticity of the tax system, hence to gradually raise the level of taxes. A third option is to retrench on the expenditure side, bringing budgetary outlays into line with the realities of a slower growing economy. The recommendations in this work can address the first issue only indirectly, the second issue directly, and cannot address the third issue at all.

TABLE 1-8
United States Path Projected Revenue-Expenditure Gap with 2.5 Percent Real Expenditure Growth (Revenues in Millions of Dollars)

	1993[1] Actual	Income Elasticity Estimate	1998 Estimate	2005 Estimate
Major State Tax Revenues				
Personal Income Tax	$4,719	1.27	$5,317	$6,084
Sales Tax	3,960	0.97	4,343	4,835
Corporate Franchise Tax	853	0.6	904	970
Public Utilities Excise Tax	647	0.7	692	750
Other State Taxes	1,811	1.0	1,992	2,224
State Total	11,990		13,248	14,862
Major Local Tax Revenue				
Tangible Personal Property Tax	1,201	0.8	1,297	1,420
Public Utilities Property Tax	955	0.6	1,012	1,086
Local Sales Tax	740	1.0	814	909
Real Property Tax	4,677	0.8	5,050	5,529
Municipal Income Tax	2,105	0.9	2,294	2,537
Total	9,678		10,467	11,480
State and Local Total Revenue[2]	21,668		23,715	26,342
State and Local Expenditures at 2.5% Real Growth Rate	21,668		24,516	29,141
Surplus (Shortfall) as a Percent of Revenue	0.00		(3.38)	(10.63)

[1]State data are fiscal year and local data are lagged calendar year as reported in the 1993 *Annual Report* of the Commissioner of Taxation.

[2]See Table 1-1.

State-Local Fiscal Balance

These projections point out a second problem: that Ohio's fiscal gap is largely due to a local government sector that has responsibility for important expenditure functions but is saddled with a relatively inelastic tax base. The state government in Ohio relies on the relatively elastic individual income tax and general sales tax, hence its revenues will grow in step with income and there will be some balance with growing expenditure needs. Local governments, however, use the relatively inelastic property taxes more heavily and revenues from these taxes do not automatically grow in proportion to expenditure needs (assuming that increases in expenditure demands roughly track increases in personal income). To a large extent the gaps which are projected are due to this imbalance in the expenditure and revenue elasticities.

Local governments in Ohio have used discretionary changes in effective tax rates to circumvent part of this problem, and have relied on increasing expenditure and state assistance retrenchment to cover the remainder. In fact, state assistance to local governments in Ohio has increased from 55 percent of state general revenues in 1987 to 60 percent in 1992.

What are the options for dealing with this imbalance? One is to continue the present pattern, which will increase the local government's claim on state tax revenue. Among the alternative policies are to increase the elasticity of the tax system by shifting revenue reliance away from the less elastic property taxes and toward the more elastic sales and income taxes. This would generate additional revenues for the state government to deal with the projected growth in the local fiscal gap.

GRADING THE PERFORMANCE OF THE OHIO TAX SYSTEM

Does Ohio need a tax reform? Is the present system so fundamentally out of step with good tax practice, or with the state's economic development and equity objectives, that a comprehensive restructuring is required? To answer this question the Commission adopted a set of principles to guide its evaluation of the Ohio tax system. The principles, described in Box 1-2, can be used to develop a kind of report card for the tax system.

Economic Development

It is difficult to say exactly what constitutes a tax system that is most favorable to economic development. Investors are attracted to locations that provide a high after-tax rate of return, and by certainty about the fiscal environment in which they will operate in the longer run. Those who make location choices report that they are swayed by lower taxes in some cases, a different tax structure in other cases, and better public infrastructure in still others. A great body of research on the effects of fiscal structure on economic growth has not been able to produce a hard estimate of the number of jobs lost due to higher taxes.

Another approach to linking taxation to economic development is to rely on *a priori* evidence, i.e., to evaluate the possibility that various taxes in the current system are structured so as to discourage investment in this state.

BOX 1-2
Principles Adopted by the Commission

Revenue Adequacy and Elasticity. The Commission began with a revenue-neutral proposal for restructuring, i.e., any proposed change in the system will yield the same revenue in the reform year as the present system would have yielded in that year. However, the longer term growth in revenues will be different for different reform packages. The Commission will take into consideration the need for a future revenue growth that will support the provision of government services at an adequate level.

Vertical Equity. The Commission will consider how alternate reforms will effect the distribution of tax burdens across income levels. The ability to pay taxes is one criteria that will guide the Commission in choosing among alternate reforms.

Horizontal Equity or Fairness. The Commission accepted the goal of an equal tax treatment of similarly situated individuals and businesses. To the extent possible, economic decisions should be guided by the market and not by the tax code. Where differential treatment is warranted for social, economic, administrative or other reasons, these will be explicitly recognized by the Commission.

Economic Development. The Commission seeks a reform that will be consistent with promoting a healthy growth in the Ohio economy. All reform options will be evaluated based on their potential impact on employment, earnings and investment in the state, and on the competitiveness of Ohio businesses.

Simplicity. The Commission will be guided by the objective of simplification of the tax system. The intention is to improve understanding of the system on the part of those who pay taxes, to reduce compliance cost, and to minimize administrative costs to the extent possible.

Spatial Distribution. Changes in the tax structure will have major effects on the fiscal condition of local governments. The Commission will evaluate these effects on places (of different income levels and on different types of local governments) in evaluating alternate structural reforms.

Obsolescence. The Commission will consider whether any taxes in the system are "out of step" with the present day Ohio economy.

Here the evidence is clearer that there are flaws in the state tax system that are not in the best interest of future economic development.

Net Worth Tax[12]

The net worth tax was instituted to control tax avoidance, protect revenues, and provide for a stable flow of revenue. The base for Ohio's net worth tax is the total book value of the corporation's capital, surplus, retained earnings, and reserves. The net worth component of the corporate franchise tax eliminates the possibility of complete avoidance of Ohio taxes by those who have the ability to use transfer pricing to shift tax burdens to either unprofitable subsidiaries or to lower taxing states, and by those who make no profits. It has the desirable feature of charging all companies some amount for the use of state-provided infrastructure and services. About one-third of franchise tax revenues has traditionally come from the net worth tax.

The structure of the net worth tax harms the economic development potential of the state. The list of criticisms and shortcomings of the net worth tax is a long one, and it has been a major irritant to the business community for many years.

- Taxpayers feel that the net worth tax is unfair because it puts an additional burden on those companies that have had a bad year, in terms of low income or net losses. This may be particularly damaging to new companies, which often have losses in the early years of operation.
- The apportionment formula for the net worth tax discriminates against Ohio locations.
- A third problem with the net worth tax is double taxation. This arises first because the net worth tax falls on the same assets as are taxed by the property tax. A second issue of double taxation arises when both parent company and subsidiaries located in Ohio must pay the net worth tax.
- The net worth tax may discourage investment in Ohio if the combination of the net income and net worth taxes imposes a tax burden on capital invested in Ohio that exceeds the average tax burden imposed on capital in all other states. Taxing capital investment more heavily than the average state, i.e., having a lower after-tax rate of return to capital, will drive investment away.

Sales Tax on Business[13]

The concept behind the sales tax as a consumption tax leads to the conclusion that all business purchases should be exempt and only the sale to the final consumer should be taxed. This approach results in no pyramiding of the tax. Decisions by states to tax some business purchases violate the consumption tax concept and leave policymakers without a clearly defined policy on where to draw the line on what is taxable. Moreover, sales taxation of business purchases raises the cost of doing business in Ohio, and may harm economic development. The location of retailers is unlikely to be affected, even though their costs rise, because the retailer wants to locate near the market for its goods. However, manufacturing firms and others that are producing for national markets will find it more expensive to locate in Ohio to the extent that Ohio sales taxes business purchases more than other states.

The relatively little research that has been conducted on how sales tax payments by business affect economic development, indicates that higher sales taxes reduce the number of firms in the 12 to 50 employee range, and that lower sales tax rates on business equipment purchases increase the rate of formation of small firms in a state.

Ohio exempts many business purchases from the sales tax. For example, exemption is given for purchases of products that are to be incorporated into tangible personal property through manufacture or when purchases are made to resell the item. Nonetheless, approximately 30 percent of sales tax revenues in Ohio comes from taxation of business. This percentage is not unusual in the United States The two main reasons for including business purchases in the sales tax base are the protection of revenue, and the ease of administration.

The taxation of business purchases has some disadvantages as well. Some of the more important concerns include:

- *Consumption tax concept*. Taxation of business purchases distorts the concept of the sales tax as a consumption tax, since business purchases are not final consumption.

- *Effects on vertical integration*. Businesses are discouraged from engaging in practices that otherwise would make good business sense. For example, sales taxation of business purchases encourages firms to produce their own inputs, because the sales tax payment can be reduced. Smaller firms can be hurt most by this incentive since small firms may be unable to produce their own inputs. Also, small firms may be less likely to start up if large firms are discouraged from outsourcing.

- *Uneven tax burdens*. The sales tax will pyramid as the tax is levied at several steps in the production process. As a result, the effective tax rate on goods depends on how many business purchases are in the tax base. Thus, horizontal equity is distorted by the taxation of business purchases. Further, items such as food or health care cannot be fully exempt from the sales tax because tax paid on these items will be implicit in costs of purchases by businesses.

The Tax on Inventories[14]

Arguably the most objectionable of the business taxes in Ohio is that on inventories. A consistent thread in the hearings before the Commission was that the inventory tax is a major impediment to business development in Ohio. A common complaint was "the worse my year the more inventory tax I pay." Among the major competitor states, Indiana, Kentucky, and West Virginia tax business inventories. California, Illinois, Michigan, North Carolina, Pennsylvania, South Carolina, and Tennessee do not tax inventories. In fact, most of the 50 states exempt inventories from property taxation.

There are many strong arguments to exclude inventories from the tax base. Investment in inventory is mobile, and such a tax may drive retail and wholesale distribution activities out of state. Moreover, there is an argument that inventories do not represent value in the same sense as company income or assets since they are goods in process of adding value and eventually will be taxed as final output. Finally, there is the point that a buildup of inventories may mean no more than a bad year and a diminished ability to pay taxes. It should be noted that in many local jurisdictions, enterprise zone legislation has been used to abate the personal property tax on inventories. One might take the view that with this legislation, the first steps to abolishing the inventory tax have already been taken. However, this is a very *ad hoc* approach to tax reform and leaves similar firms with quite different tax liability depending on their county of location.[15]

The tangible personal property tax in general (of which the tax on inventories is a component), might also be seen as a deterrent to state economic development. The base of the tax is capital investment, which would seem to discourage exactly the kind of activity which the state desires, and this tax discriminates against capital-intensive firms. This reasoning, and administrative difficulties, have led some competitor states (Pennsylvania and New Jersey) to remove this tax.

Insurance Company Taxes[16]

Because Ohio's 2.5 percent premium tax rate is high, Ohio insurers must pay substantial retaliatory taxes when they sell in most other states (See Box 1-3). This additional tax places Ohio insurers at a competitive disadvantage and likely reduces their out-of-state sales. Obviously, this is a major disincentive for multistate insurers to locate or grow in Ohio. Other important insurance states and neighboring states provide a more favorable climate for insurance companies that choose to headquarter in their state.

The Estate Tax[17]

The Ohio estate tax is levied according to a progressive rate schedule on the value of the estate. In addition, Ohio like most states, imposes an addi-

BOX 1-3
The Retaliatory Tax

The retaliatory tax is a unique tax applied only to the insurance industry. The tax was designed to reduce the incentive for states to tax foreign (out-of-state) insurance companies at high rates.

The tax works as follows. Suppose, for example, that Ohio has a 2.5 percent premium tax and Illinois has a 1 percent tax. Because Illinois' tax rate is lower than Ohio's, Illinois retaliates against Ohio companies operating in Illinois. This retaliation occurs by the state of Illinois taxing Ohio companies operating in Illinois the same way as Illinois companies are taxed in Ohio. Thus, Ohio companies pay 2.5 percent of their premium in taxes to Illinois, even though the Illinois rate is officially 1 percent. If Ohio decreased its premium tax rate to, say, 1 percent, Ohio companies would no longer have to pay retaliatory taxes to Illinois.

In general, the higher a state's premium to tax rate relative to tax rates in other states, the more a state's domestic companies pay to other states in premium taxes and the less the state collects in its own retaliatory tax. Thus, payments to other states by a domestic industry are tied directly to a state's own tax policy.

Source: Martinez-Vazquez and Grace (1994).

tional tax on estates. The additional tax, the difference between the calculated state tax (based upon the rate structure) and the maximum allowable Federal credit for state estates taxes, is called the "pick-up" tax.

There are two potential economic development impacts from the estate tax. First, higher estate taxes may act as a disincentive to save. Since the estate tax will take a share of a household's wealth (which has been accumulated as a result of a household's decision not to spend all that they have accumulated), the tax provides an incentive to spend from the estate, rather than to save.

Second, the state estate tax introduces an incentive for households to "shop" for a place of retirement, i.e., for tax-favored retirement homes. For elderly residents in states like Massachusetts and New York, the incentive to move can be very strong. For Ohio, this incentive exists for estate levels below about $4 million.

Horizontal Equity

In some cases the tax system has been slow to follow changes in the structure of the Ohio economy, and the structure of markets. The result is that similar businesses are treated differently from one another, and this leads to undesirable distortions in economic decisions. For example, a discriminatory tax treatment may steer investment away from a particular sector of the economy, perhaps into a less productive sector; or economic methods of doing business may be discouraged by ill conceived tax practices; or new investments may be directed to other states to avoid an unfavorable tax treatment. Electric and gas companies, telecommunications firms, and financial institutions are all subject to a different treatment than are general companies. In some cases, there are historical and economic reasons for these differences, in others it appears that the tax system has simply failed to keep pace with the changing economy. Unless there are sound reasons for differential treatment, a good tax structure should aim for an equal treatment of similarly situated firms and individuals.

Telecommunications Firms[18]

The comparison in Table 1-9, which describes the differential treatment of telecommunications firms, highlights the issue. The first row shows the tax treatment of the local exchange companies (LECs), while the second row shows the tax treatment of a private business that does not provide telecommunication services. The remaining rows show the variations in the tax treatment of alternative telecommunications service providers. Clearly, there is much diversity in how these firms are treated. Though there is not a clear statement of the rationale for this differential treatment, McHugh (1994b) has developed some implied general principles based on the current practice, as described in Table 1-9.

- The first is the distinction between the treatment of public utilities and private businesses. As a public utility, the local telephone companies (LECs) are subject to the gross receipts tax, but to neither the corporate franchise tax nor the sales tax on their services. In addition, as a public utility, the LECs are subject to the tangible personal property tax at the 88 percent listing rate. As shown on the second line, private businesses are subject to both the corporate franchise tax and the general sales tax (should their goods or services be defined as taxable) but not to the gross receipts tax. Private businesses are subject to a lower 25 percent rate on their personal property.
- Any company which is subject to the gross receipts tax will not have its services subject to the general sales tax.

TABLE 1-9
Tax Treatment of Telecommunication Services

Type of Company	Sales Tax on Services Provided	Corporate Franchise Tax	Gross Receipts Tax	Property Tax Assessed at 88 Percent	Municipal Income Tax
Local Telephone	NO	NO	YES	YES	NO
Private Business	Nur	YES	NO	NO	YES
Interexchange Companies	YES	YES	NO	YES	YES
Cellular	YES	YES	NO	YES	YES
Private Communication (CAPS Paging)	NO	YES	NO	YES	YES
Cable TV	NO	YES	NO	NO	YES
Resellers	Nur	YES	NO	YES	YES

Source: McHugh (1994b).

Nur = no uniform rule.

- Any company subject to the state corporate franchise tax will also be subject to the municipal income tax.

An evaluation based on these three general principles reveals serious shortcomings with the present system. First, the LECs are currently the only ones in the telecommunications industry still strictly defined and fully treated as a public utility (i.e., subject to the gross receipts tax and the higher personal property tax listing rate). Second, the interexchange and the cellular companies, since 1987, have not been subject to gross receipts tax but have been treated as a private company paying the franchise tax and a sales tax. Third, the private communications firms, like the CAPS and paging systems, are generally treated as a hybrid between a private company and a telecommunications firm. However, there are two gray areas: the services provided by the CAPs are not subject to the sales tax, and the CAPS and ALTS, strictly speaking, are subjected to the higher 88-percent listing rate for tangible personal property.

Fourth, cable television is subject to neither the general sales tax nor the state gross receipts tax, but is subject to local franchise taxes. Because cable companies do not provide two-

way service at this point, under Ohio law they are not classified as a telecommunications firm and they are not subject to the 88-percent listing rate. Once two-way telecommunication becomes available, however (and a major cable company has already filed with PUCO for rights to provide telecommunications service in a large portion of Ohio), cable companies would technically become subject to the higher listing rate.

In sum, the State of Ohio continues to treat its LECs as it has for years, as a regulated franchise monopoly, not subject to the Corporate Franchise Tax but instead subject to a gross receipts tax. The State's general sales tax is not levied on local telecommunications services. The LECs are also levied a personal property tax with a listing rate of 88 percent versus 25 percent for private businesses. The interexchange companies, cellular companies and other actors in the industry are subject to the corporate franchise tax, have their sales subject to the general sales tax, and also pay the differentially higher personal property tax listing rate. There are serious horizontal equities in this tax treatment of the telecommunications sector.

Public Utility Property Tax[19]

The tangible personal property of public utilities is subjected to an 88-percent assessment ratio, while general businesses are assessed at a 25 percent rate. The differentially high listing rate on personal property was justifiable in the past on the basis that, as a public utility, these firms were endowed with certain rights (e.g., access to public right-of-way) and were protected from competition through their franchise monopoly. Moreover, given the regulatory structure under which the utilities operated, the rate of return was guaranteed and differentially higher personal property taxes were not borne by the utilities.

Over the past several years, there have been encroachments on the monopoly position of some of these companies. With the onset of competition in these markets, differentially high tax rates and the horizontal inequities which they imply, will begin to have important allocative effects. The relatively high taxation of public utilities will make it more difficult to attract investment funds to the industry. This is an important issue because investment in utility infrastructure is an important economic development factor.

Also, as the tax is currently configured, the high taxation of public utilities engenders a horizontal inequity in favor of those firms not classified as public utilities but which can provide services similar to those of the public utilities. This inequity is currently most acute in the telecommunications sector where the interexchange companies (IXCs) are subject to a differentially higher tax on personal property even though they operate in a highly competitive environment.

Banks and Insurance Companies[20]

Financial Institutions. Ohio has a problem with its definition of a financial institution subject to taxation under the financial institutions tax. This definition excludes a number of bank competitors from taxation under the law. This law is based on an antiquated notion of the banking business. The statute requires that, among other things, a bank must accept deposits in Ohio before it can be taxed. As a result, banks can lower their Ohio tax liability by producing financial services outside the state (accepting deposits through the mail or by way of interbank electronic transfers) and then selling them back to Ohio residents. This discourages in-state non-depository functions and results in revenue loss and potential job loss.

There are two issues here. The first is that different tax treatment leads to different tax burdens. This is a violation of horizontal equity. By taxing all financial corporations and general corporations in a similar manner it is possible to increase the horizontal equity among competitors or potential competitors.

A second issue that has potential ramifications for horizontal equity concerns those banks owned by a holding company. Since the financial institutions tax rate is approximately three times the rate for nonfinancial corporations, a bank owned by a holding company has an incentive to transfer net worth to the parent, thus reducing the yield of the financial institutions franchise tax. Of course, this transfer may be limited by regulatory capital requirements imposed as part of risk based capital rules implemented by federal regulators. This benefits large subsidiary banks which are part of a holding company, relative to stand-alone banks.

Insurance companies. There are wide differences in the tax burdens imposed on insurance companies by Ohio's present tax structure. For example, while Ohio has a 2.5-percent premium tax rate, Ohio-based insurance companies can pay on a net worth basis. The option lowers the effective tax rate for many (but not all) Ohio insurers. Since this alternative computation is based on total rather than allocated net worth, it tends to favor single state companies with low capitalization, some of which are the largest premium writers in the state. In addition, some insurers (e.g., HMO'S, foreign fraternals) are exempt from the premium tax. This diversity in treatment produces horizontal inequities that are difficult to justify.

Gross Receipts Tax on Utilities[21]

The principle motivation for a public utilities excise tax is to tax industries which are granted "franchise monopolies". By virtue of their franchise, they are theoretically protected from competition. They are also permitted the special privileges associated with "eminent domain" and access to public right-of-ways. The levies represent an implicit *quid pro quo* for these privileges. However, there is growing encroachment upon the monopoly position of the utilities. As new providers of similar services have breached the market, the gross receipts tax has imposed some important horizontal inequities.

In the field of electricity there are several available avenues of obtaining power without relying on a provider which is subject to the public utilities excise tax. For example, there is the possibility of obtaining power through the process of cogeneration, in which a non-utility may produce power for itself and sell the excess supply to other users, bypassing the traditional power company and avoiding the gross receipts tax.

In the field of telecommunications, there are a whole host of new "bypass" firms which provide access to long distance operators (a service traditionally provided by the local exchange companies) but are not covered by the public utility excise tax. Examples include the privately owned networks (built by competitive access providers), and privately operated PBXs. The new personal communication systems permit bypass of the local exchange. The availability of the alternatives which are not subject to gross receipts taxation represent a tax-induced incentive to alter behavior, a potential (and exploited) leakage from the gross receipts tax base, and an administrative problem.

In the realm of natural gas, the exemption of interstate business from gross receipts taxation carries with it an incentive to purchase gas from out of state. FERC Order 636, issued in April of 1992, requires that natural gas companies "unbundle" the pricing of their services (that is, separate the pricing of the storage, transmission and sales of natural gas). In effect, this permits customers to purchase their natural gas from one supplier and pay the pipeline companies only for the transmission or transport of the gas. The practical impact of this, from the standpoint of the gross receipts tax, is that local customers may purchase natural gas from an out-of-state source which is not subject to the gross receipts tax. The only gross receipts taxes collected in this case would be those on the "wheeling charges" (those charges by the utility for the transport of natural gas). This provides another source of leakage from the gross receipts tax base and a disadvantage to local suppliers.

There are also inequities which arise from the combination of the exclusion of municipal electric utilities from taxation and the exemption of interstate business from taxation. While some municipal utilities produce their own power, most do not. Rather, they purchase the power wholesale from another utility. This, in itself, does not represent any sort of inefficiency or inequity. If a municipal utility purchases its power from another public utility in the state, then there is no purely tax-induced inequity since a gross receipts tax is paid by the in-state producer. However, since a municipal utility can purchase its electricity from an out-of-state provider, and all interstate business is exempt from taxation, no gross receipts tax is paid on this purchase either at the wholesale or the retail level. Since municipal utilities are also directly exempt from the excise tax, these purchases not only reduce the revenues from this tax but also impart a cost (price) advantage to municipal utilities at the expense of the investor-owned utilities.

This advantage, however, may be in part a well-defined policy of subsidizing power in communities served by municipal utilities which are disproportionately located in poorer rural communities and in central cities. There are approximately one hundred municipal electric companies, the vast majority being small and/or rural. However, there are several larger municipally-owned utilities in the state, such as those in Hamilton, Columbus and Cleveland.

Independent of the interaction between the municipal exemption and interstate exemption, municipal public utilities are given an advantage when they produce the service themselves. For example, a municipal telephone service can fully escape the gross receipts tax. The technology in the field of telecommunications has progressed to the point that a system could be built to serve a small community or to serve parts of larger areas and be competitive with the local exchange companies which are subject to the gross receipts tax. Here, too, the incentive exists to avoid the tax (by making use of the affordable alternatives) thus resulting in tax-induced changes in behavior which erodes the tax base. Although it is difficult to ascertain the precise role which the exemption from the public utilities excise tax played in the development of municipal public utilities, it is surely the case that the exemption provides an option which tilts the playing field against the investor-owned companies.

Tax Incentives and Enterprise Zones[22]

Special tax treatment of businesses by definition creates a horizontal inequity. The choice facing any state is whether to give targeted tax incentives or to provide all of the state's businesses with the lowest taxes possible. Ohio has chosen the former approach, and provides a range of tax incentives. The most important is the Enterprise Zone Program.

The Ohio Enterprise Zone Program was created in 1982. The original intent was to improve the economic development prospects in distressed urban areas of the state through the exemption of property taxes related to an investment project. Since then, the program has been extended to rural areas and the list of potential tax incentives has grown to include credits applicable to the Corporate Franchise Tax. Currently there are 247 known enterprise zones in the state. Only a few counties do not have an enterprise zone. Property tax abatement and inventory tax abatement in particular are the most used tax incentive under the enterprise zone program, with only about 10 percent of enterprise zones utilizing the franchise tax credit.

The literature concerning the impact of tax incentives on economic development has shown that these incentives have their greatest impact within a region. That is, these incentives will not have much affect on a decision to locate in Ohio versus Texas but can have a greater impact on the decision to locate in Toledo, Ohio versus Perrysburg, Ohio. The benefits of the program from one Ohio community are likely to come at the expense of another Ohio community, or a community in a neighboring state. Ohio has far more enterprise zones than most any state in the country, increasing the potential for intra-Ohio competition.

The horizontal equity problem arises because firms in enterprise zones receive preferential treatment in regards to the personal property tax. The result of this program, to the extent it works, will be to draw resources toward the 250 enterprise zones and away from other sites, or simply to give a comparative advantage to businesses included within this program.

Another problem that grows out of this practice is a complication in the intergovernmental fiscal system. When municipalities grant property tax abatements, the relief also applies to school district properties. Officials in many school districts feel that the municipal-granted tax abatements directly reduce funds for local education. Proponents of enterprise zones argue that the firms would not be in the school district at all except for the enterprise zone. While no doubt there is some truth on both sides of this argument, the asymmetry of the municipality granting a tax abatement for what is largely school district revenue does not have the ring of a well-designed fiscal incentive package.

Net Worth Tax And Debt-Equity Choice[23]

The net worth tax distorts methods of financing and encourages thin capitalization. Corporations that add to their real assets by borrowing from a bank or issuing debt will not experience an increase in their net worth tax base. However, those corporations that purchase the same real assets but finance them with new equity issues will experience an increase in the tax base by the entire amount of the investment. Thus, the marginal effective rate of taxation[24] on the same asset goes from zero, if financed with debt, to a positive rate of taxation if the asset is not exempt.

In addition, the net worth tax is horizontally inequitable because its burden depends on the structure of a business. Some business sectors require more capitalization for technological reasons and consequently a longer maturation period to profit-making. In this sense, the net worth tax can be viewed as discriminatory—favoring enterprises that are lightly capitalized, such as those in the service sector, and penalizing enterprises that are more heavily capitalized, such as those in the manufacturing sector. Both types of companies would pay the net income tax in years of good performance, but in a recession those sectors that are more heavily capitalized will pay a much higher net worth tax.

The Sales Tax Treatment of Services[25]

A major horizontal inequity in the state tax system stems from the failure to include services in the tax base (Box 1-4). The result is that consumers who purchase tangible goods and services that are in the tax net are dis-

BOX 1-4
Sales Tax and Services

The consumption of services (excluding food and housing) in the United States accounted for 43 percent of total consumption in 1993. This share has slowly and consistently grown over the past twenty years. In 1976, for example, services accounted for 29 percent of total consumption. The most noticeable decline during the period was in the purchase of nondurable goods. These goods accounted for 41 percent of total consumption in 1976 and 31 percent of consumption in 1993.

There is no general rule that describes what services states have chosen to tax. The percentage of consumption covered by the retail sales tax varies quite widely across states. The table below provides an estimate of the breadth of the sales tax base in Ohio and in surrounding states, and lists the highest combined state and local tax rate. Ohio can be characterized as having a relatively narrow sales tax base, and a tax rate that is toward the high end by comparison with its neighbors. Within the region, Indiana takes the opposite approach with a relatively broad base and a relatively low rate.

Sales Tax Base as a Percent of Personal Income and Highest State and Local Sales Tax Rate, FY91

	Base as a Percent of Income	Highest Combined Tax Rate
Ohio	36.9	7.00
Indiana	53.4	5.00
Kentucky	38.8	6.00
Michigan	46.0	6.00
Pennsylvania	30.5	7.00
West Virginia	52.9	6.00

Source: Fox (1994).

criminated against in favor of those who choose to purchase non-taxable services. Since services now constitute more than half of all consumption, the implications of not including services in the base are significant.

Ohio has continued to add services to its retail sales tax in recent years, but much consumption still remains exempt. Were all of the exempt services brought into the sales tax base, the state government could reduce its tax rate to 3.3 percent and still collect the same amount of revenue. The addition of services to the tax base adds significant scope for the improvement of horizontal equity.

Real Property Tax[26]

The real property tax is structured in such a way that it does not treat all property owners the same, even if they own properties of equal value. Under the provisions of HB 920 and subsequent legislation, separate tax reduction factors are calculated for Class 1 property (residential and agriculture) and Class 2 property (all other real property). Since price changes have been greater for Class 1 property, the effective property tax rate (i.e., the rate after application of the tax reduction factor) is lower for Class 1 property than Class 2 property.

Vertical Equity

Every state is concerned about how its tax system spreads the burden among high, middle and low income taxpayers (Minnesota Department of Revenue 1993; McGuire and Naimark 1991). The Ohio tax system gets relatively good marks on vertical equity. About one-fourth of the taxes are raised from levies that fall partly on owners of capital, the individual income tax has a progressive rate structure, and food consumption is exempt from the sales tax.

Individual Income Tax[27]

Ohio's individual income tax has several features that enhance its progressivity.

- The top marginal rate is relatively high.
- The large number of tax brackets increases progressivity.
- Retirement and senior citizen credits afford lower income retirees a relatively large benefit.

On the other hand, progressivity is dampened by a low threshold for tax payment, i.e., a large number of low income individuals are brought into the net, due to a low personal exemption and the absence of a standard deduction. The personal exemption credit mitigates this effect, especially for taxpayers with children.

The result of empirical analysis of the individual income tax, as may be seen in Table 1-10 is a progressive distribution of individual income tax burdens, rising from 0.1 percent of income at the bottom bracket to 4.7 percent at the top. These estimates exclude the local income taxes in Ohio, which are imposed at relatively steep levels, and at flat rates. The local taxes would be expected, therefore, to reduce the progressivity of the state income tax. The right column shows the distribution of burdens that would occur if every municipality and school district levied a 1 percent income tax. Again, the result is a progressive distribution of burdens, but much less than in the case of the state system.

Sales Tax[28]

The distribution of Ohio's sales tax burden is regressive when measured against current income. Households with incomes between $5,000 and $9,999 pay 2.6 percent of their income in sales taxes and households with incomes above $50,000 pay 1.3 percent of their income in sales taxes (Figure 4-8, in this volume). Thus, the burden on low-income households is almost twice as large as that on high-income households. Still, more than 60 percent of the sales tax on consumer purchases is paid by households with $30,000

TABLE 1-10
Distribution of Individual Income Tax Burdens
(Percent of FAGI)

Federal Adjusted Gross Income Class (FAGI)	Taxes as a Percent of Income (State Income Tax)	Taxes as a Percent of Income (State and Local Income Tax)[a]
Under $5,000	0.1	1.96
5,001 - 10,000	0.4	2.24
10,0001 - 15,000	0.8	2.49
15,001 - 20,000	1.4	3.14
20,001 - 40,000	2.2	4.06
40,001 - 80,000	3.1	4.98
80,001 - 100,000	3.8	5.64
Greater than 100,000	4.7	6.41
Average	2.9	4.60

Source: Wallace and Edwards.

[a]Hypothetical, see text.

or more in income. Moreover, the per household tax payment is much greater for higher-income households. For example, households with incomes over $50,000 pay nearly five times more in taxes than households with income between $5,000 and $9,999.

The regressive sales tax results from the propensity of lower-income households to spend a higher percentage of their income. In fact, families in every income class below $20,000 have higher levels of expenditure than income. Thus, the regressive sales tax is more the result of different levels of consumption relative to income than to the purchase of different "market baskets."

Some economists have argued that lifetime income is a better basis for comparing tax burdens than is annual income (Fullerton and Rogers 1993). The concept is that people set their expenditure patterns based on the overall consumption level they expect to maintain over their lifetimes. For example, people who recently lost their jobs may spend more than would be expected from their current income. Both retirees and young people consume more than is expected given their income level, because their lifetime income is greater than their current income. This reasoning has led many economists to argue that annual (or current) expenditures are a good proxy for lifetime income. Therefore, estimated Ohio sales tax burdens were compared with annual expenditures for each income category. The results show the distribution of burdens to be proportional to slightly progressive when measured against consumption rather than annual income (Figure 4-9, in this volume). By these estimates, a family with an income of $50,000 and a family with an income of $20,000 both would pay 1.8 percent in sales tax. Thus, the sales tax is not regressive when compared with lifetime income.

Property Tax Burdens[29]

The distribution of property tax burdens is a hotly debated issue in economics. Most would agree that the tax on owner occupiers is borne by them, hence the regressivity in the distribution of tax burdens depends on whether low-income owners spend disportionately more for housing, and on whether there is an assessment bias that favors those who own high value properties. An estimate of the impact of a 5-mill increase in the property tax on residential property, with and without the present system of tax credits, shows a regressive distribution of tax burdens (See Table 7-15, in this volume). For example, a taxpayer with an income of $25,000 would see an increase equivalent to 0.50 percent of income, a taxpayer with an income of $50,000 would see an increase of 0.28 percent, and a taxpayer with an income of $100,000 would see an increase equivalent to 0.21 percent of income.

The incidence of the non-residential property tax, and the incidence of a property tax that is collected from a landlord, are more difficult matters. Most would agree that the real property tax levied on businesses is shifted forward to consumers and backward to labor and to owners, with the division of the tax burdens depending on market conditions. The same is true of rented properties—the tax burden is divided between owners and renters. To the extent this tax is shifted backwards to owners, the real property tax has a progressive distribution of tax burdens. To the extent it is shifted forward to consumers and renters, it is regressive. We are unable to make an accurate estimate of this division in Ohio.

ELASTICITY

The revenue income elasticity of a tax is the percent change in revenues that occurs when income changes by one percent, exclusive of any discretionary rate or base adjustments. In general, Ohio has a relatively inelastic tax system, that is, most taxes do not automatically grow in proportion to income.

The *individual income tax* is an exception, and provides most of the buoyancy of the Ohio tax system. The overall elasticity of the state individual income tax in Ohio is 1.27, i.e., a ten percent increase in income generates a 12.7 percent increase in tax revenues (Wallace and Edwards 1994). The high elasticity is due to the combination of a low threshold and an unindexed progressive rate structure that leads to "bracket creep".

With respect to the *sales tax,* much of the revenue growth in Ohio has come from adjustments to the tax rate. An analysis of the growth in the base of the tax suggests that the elasticity is 0.97, i.e., a ten percent increase in income will lead automatically to a 9.7 percent increase in sales tax revenues (Fox 1994). The sales tax, then, would tend to support an expenditure growth that was more or less in line with income growth.

Most of the other taxes in the Ohio system are income inelastic. The estimate of the income elasticity for the real property tax for the entire period 1971 to 1992, excluding agriculture and minerals, is 0.90. The estimated elasticity for all real property over the period 1974 to 1992 is 0.78. Both estimates imply that the real property tax base grew slower than personal income (Sjoquist 1994). This inelasticity is no surprise. Ohio is a state with a slow growing population and a declining industrial base. Both of these factors suggest a lagging amount of new construction to add to the property tax base. The aging of the population is another reason why the property tax base may be growing slowly.

For tangible personal property, there appeared to be little increase in the real value of the tax base throughout the 1980s and early 1990s (Cornia 1994a and 1994b; and McHugh 1994b). In fact, real per capita assessed values have declined significantly during the past 15 years. Clearly, revenue increases from the tangible personal property tax must come primarily from discretionary rate increases.

Revenues from the gross receipts tax have grown slowly over the past decade, for several reasons (McHugh 1994d). First, the sluggish growth in these collections was due to legislated changes in the taxable base (e.g., the elimination of long distance carriers from the base of the telephone gross receipts tax and the deductibility of access charges from the taxable receipts of local exchange companies). Second, there are low income elasticities of demand for the goods which are taxed: natural gas, electric, etc. That is, the demand for these goods or services does not increase in proportion to income. Third, this is an ad valorem levy, and there has been a slow growth in the price of these goods in recent years. Since the tax is based upon the value of utility services instead of the quantity consumed, growth in prices has led to slow growth in revenues. Research has found the demand for these products to be relatively insensitive to prices. The price of these public utilities are regulated by the Public Utility Commission of Ohio (PUCO) and the number of requests for rate increases from PUCO has dwindled in recent years. Finally and most importantly, structural problems in the design of the public utility excise tax base has eroded the tax base over time as users have substituted non-taxed for taxed consumption.

Stability

The instability of revenues over the business cycle leaves state and local fiscal planners in a position of making the choice between expenditure cuts or tax increases during a time of recession. The more cyclical a state's revenue structure, the more difficult the choice, because the revenue shortfall will be greater in the contraction. In fact, the Ohio economy is cyclical, and to some extent this is amplified by the tax structure.

All sales taxes have unstable revenue growth, but it is the combination of the sales tax structure and the state's economy that determines the degree of instability. On both counts, the Ohio sales tax would appear to be highly cyclical (Fox 1994). The elasticities are lowest in recession years (FY91, FY81, FY80, and FY75), and are much higher in expansion years. The falling revenue during recessions occurs because consumers postpone expenditures on major durable goods (such as automobiles and appliances) and housing, and because businesses invest less. The impact of lower durable goods purchases is pronounced, because these items are consumed over many years, but the entire sales tax is paid when the items are purchased. The result of delayed purchase is a magnified reduction in sales tax receipts. The reverse happens during economic expansions when the purchase of durable goods and business investment goods expands rapidly. The exclusion of food from the tax base makes the Ohio sales tax base inherently less stable. Not surprisingly, most tax rate changes in Ohio (and in other states) come near the end of recessions and are intended in part to offset the very slow revenue growth that has occurred during the recession.

Annual estimates in the *individual income tax* show that the tax is cyclical, due to the effects of the business cycle on the tax base (Wallace and Edwards 1994). As the economy contracts, the growth in wages and capital income falls off more than overall personal income. In the early 1980s, for example, while personal income growth fell below 4 percent, wage and salary growth fell well below 1 percent. In the most recent recession, dividend and interest growth was less than 10 percent of personal income growth and wages grew about 50 percent less than personal income.

There is relatively little cyclical variation in personal property tax revenues (Cornia 1994a and 1994b). Purchases of new machines and equipment may be postponed in a contraction year, but this does not have a dollar for dollar effect on the overall tax base, because the latter is based on the depreciated, reproduction cost of the entire stock of machinery and equipment held by the company. Moreover, the value of the inventories may actually increase during a recession. The result, over time, has been a virtual constancy in the real value of the tax base.

The real property tax base is subject to considerable cyclical variation (Sjoquist 1994). During recessions the growth in both income and the property tax base slows. However, because of the highly cyclical nature of the construction industry, the fall off in the growth of the property tax base (new construction) is large relative to that in income, and revenue growth is slowed commensurately. The reverse is true in periods of economic expansion.

The *net worth tax* has lent some stability to the Ohio tax system (Martinez-Vazquez and Grace 1994). It serves as a revenue floor when profitability is down, and as a protection against transfer pricing practices which might otherwise drive corporate tax liability to zero. The simulation presented in Table 1-11 shows the extent to which the net worth component helps iron out cyclical variations. The two left panels show the revenue yield under the present system, and the two right panels show the yield if only the net income basis were used. The results indicate that the inclusion of the net worth tax strengthens the stability significantly, e.g., the present system led to a 10.7 percent revenue decline in 1991 whereas the system without a net worth component would have led to a 21.2 percent decline.

Administration

A good tax structure is one that imposes as little compliance cost as is necessary, as little administrative cost as is necessary and gives taxpayers confidence in the system. Usually these maxims lead to a system that is as simple as possible. To be sure, a state tax system cannot be simple in this complicated economy—there is just too much to take into account.

TABLE 1-11
Corporate Franchise Tax Liability, With and Without Net Worth Tax Component, 1988–1993

Tax Year	Total with Net Worth	Percent Change over Previous Year	Total without Net Worth: Net Income Basis Only	Percent Change over Previous Year
1988	719,430,413	---	586,959,047	---
1989	771,130,137	7.2	645,077,393	9.9
1990	728,156,622	-5.6	585,163,816	-9.3
1991	650,538,338	-10.7	461,164,160	-21.2
1992	613,496,098	-5.7	429,994,616	-6.8
1993	630,040,000	2.7	422,805,000	-1.7
Coefficient of Variation	0.083	---	0.166	---

Source: Ohio Department of Taxation, *Annual Report* and staff computations. See Martinez-Vazquez and Grace, 1994.

Businesses organize themselves in complicated ways to finance, produce and deliver goods and services, individuals have many different types of situations that require special treatment, the sales tax must reach new products where situsing is extremely difficult, and real property tax limits are a fact of today's political economy. Still, the goal is as much simplification as is possible without compromising the fairness and efficiency of the tax system.

By any grading system, however, Ohio's tax structure is unnecessarily complex, and imposes heavy compliance burdens on taxpayers. At the top of the list of problems is the net worth component of the corporate tax. Both tax options under the franchise tax—net income and net worth—must be fully computed every year despite the fact that only one will be used. The computation of the net worth tax is especially cumbersome because it requires the situsing of every component in the balance sheet based on complex rules which in some instances go back half a century.

The personal property tax presents administrative difficulties that, arguably no other business tax presents (Cornia 1994a and 1994b). In theory, every asset should be valued, depreciated and trended to an estimate of depreciated reproduction cost. A retirements list should be maintained, and the central valuation authority should keep up a valuation schedule for a great number of different types of assets. It should also maintain an active audit program. Moreover, since this is primarily a local government tax, the asset list should be kept for every jurisdiction where the firm operates. Even a moments reflection will suggest that this is a task that requires considerable investment in valuation and audit staff in the Department of Taxation.

The state individual income tax is relatively clean, but the administration of local income taxes add considerable complexity to the overall system (Wallace and Edwards 1994). In the current Ohio Code, no legislation establishes uniform guidelines for compliance with the municipal income tax throughout the state. Thus, a diversity of practices exists regarding such fundamental requirements as the forms required for filing, withholding, estimated taxes, and final payments, due dates for filing, penalties, and extensions for filing. While the administrators of the tax may be very efficient in their collection and audit procedures, there is no doubt that these differences and the apportionment calculations for business, are cumbersome. Individuals who work and reside in two different municipalities, each with a local income tax, have the added burden of multiple filing. The long tradition of this tax in terms of its use and the municipalities' autonomy would make conformity of the municipal income taxes with the state difficult, but the long-run savings to businesses and individuals would be substantial.

The real property tax is the most complex in the Ohio system largely because of the tax reduction factors and the rollback credits (Sjoquist 1994). It is arguably one of the more complex property tax systems in the United States The tax base is defined properly as full market value, but is assessed at 35 percent of market value. Increases in market values automatically result in a reduction in the effective millage rate to eliminate much of the natural growth in the property tax base, and property tax rollbacks are given in the form of credits to taxpayers. This whole process is complicated from a point of view of taxpayers, and difficult to administer and to monitor.

The quality of the state tax administration is strong. Relative to other states, staffing is highly professional, and procedures are modern. The tax structure itself is a difficult one to administer, and this puts pressure on the resources of the department, but there is no question about the ability of the state tax administration to support a modern tax system.

Obsolescence

There are some respects in which the present tax system is obsolete, i.e., it is not in step with modern realities of the economy and with generally accepted taxing practices. The following are areas where this is arguably the case:

- the failure to include a broader range of services under the sales tax base;
- the failure to recognize the competitive status of interexchange telephone companies, and the failure to give the same classification to all telecommunications companies;

- the failure to properly recognize and plan for competition in the electric utility and natural gas sectors;
- the failure to adopt combined income reporting to close off avenues for large corporations to use transfer pricing to avoid Ohio tax liability;
- the absence of a standard deduction in the state income tax; and
- the requirement of apportionment for local businesses in complying with local income taxes.

Poor Places[30]

Ohio is burdened with a heavy concentration of the poor in central cities, and with central cities that are themselves declining in population. The disparities in personal income between cities and suburbs is large and growing, suggesting a chronic fiscal problem for the central cities.

If judged by annual revenue increases, the revenue structure of cities can be said to have performed relatively well in recent years. Between 1983 and 1991, five of the seven cities for which comparable information could be obtained (Youngstown and Canton excepted) averaged annual increases in own-source revenues that were greater than inflation. Four of these cities had revenues increasing at rates exceeding those for all Ohio cities.

The apparent reason why central city revenue growth has been so robust is the heavy dependence on the municipal income tax. In Ohio, cities are permitted to tax all wages, salaries, and other compensation earned by residents and may also tax earnings by non-residents who work in the city. The income tax also applies to business net profits attributable to activities in the municipality. This relatively broad base (including resident businesses and non-resident individuals) offsets the relatively low income base of city residents, and permits the city to share in the general prosperity of the metropolitan area. Moreover, the income tax has given the city a buoyant revenue source. The average annual changes in income tax revenues compared to average annual changes in property tax revenues shows that income tax revenues increased faster in each city. With over half of their revenues from income taxes and only about 10 percent from property taxes, central cities are much better positioned to offset the adverse effects of economic disparities on their tax bases.

In contrast to city governments, central city school districts rely almost entirely on property taxes for their locally-raised revenue support. The ten central city school districts average 46 percent of their revenues from property taxes. State payments, including property tax rollback payments, provided about 49 percent, with the remaining 5 percent coming from other sources, including the school district income taxes.

The central city school districts have experienced good annual revenue growth from local taxes (principally property taxes). Among the seven cities for which comparable information could be obtained, the average annual increase between 1982 and 1991 ranged from 4.1 percent in Cleveland to 8.8 percent in Cincinnati, with four of the cities exceeding the statewide average of 7.0 percent. This good property tax performance continued through 1992 and 1993. However, the increases in property taxes were not sufficient to offset the effects of low state aid in 1992, and six of the ten cities had total revenue declines in that year.

Despite this favorable property tax growth, the central city property tax bases are not good revenue generators relative to those of the suburbs. On a per pupil basis, the central cities average only about 70 percent of the suburban bases, with Cleveland, Toledo, and Youngstown below 60 percent. This leaves the cities in a position of (a) imposing higher tax rates than the wealthier suburban systems, (b) depending on state aid to offset their weak tax bases, or (c) having lower per pupil spending. This condition will prevail as long as local school districts are heavily dependent on property taxes.

Urban county governments overlay the metropolitan areas and provide many services to residents of central cities and suburbs. Because of their broad tax bases, counties are able to redistribute revenues from the wealthier to the poorer parts of metropolitan areas. The funds are used primarily for health and social services. Many of these programs are mandated by the state and counties receive large amounts of state aid (42 percent of revenues), including pass-through federal aid. Locally, they get about 28 percent of their revenues from property taxes, another 13 percent from sales taxes, with the remaining 17 percent primarily from user charges. The county sales tax is much less important, and is not used uniformly by all urban counties. It does, however, provide an important alternative revenue source for counties that want to reduce their dependence on property taxes.

The revenue structure for urban counties is diversified, and has provided good annual average growth of revenues over the period 1983-1991. Because the counties have a broader geographic base, property tax revenue growth has far exceeded the growth rates for property tax revenues in the central cities. Overall, property taxes have provided a dependable and growing county revenue source.

Overall Evaluation of the Present System

The Ohio tax system has historically emphasized vertical equity. The individual income tax carries a progressive rate schedule, the retail sales tax exempts food, the property tax is relieved through credits, and local governments rely heavily on an income tax. It has placed less emphasis on economic development objectives. About 25 percent of the tax structure is carried by taxes on businesses—including taxes levied on income, capital invested, and machinery, equipment and inventories. About one-third of the retail sales tax is collected on business purchases. The Ohio system gets relatively good marks on progressivity, but not on investment friendliness.

A second observation about the development of the Ohio tax system is that it grew up in a piecemeal way. Past changes in the tax system have been in the nature of periodic adjustments that were driven more by the need to cover a revenue shortfall and disenchantment with the property tax than by the desire for comprehensive change that focused on the entire structure.[31] As a result, the pieces of the tax system no longer fit together as they once did, horizontal inequities have developed, and there is potentially a problem with the balance between the natural growth of revenues and expenditure requirements. The following are among the major issues

- General businesses, public utilities and financial institutions are all treated differently from one another, for reasons that made more sense in an earlier time than they do now;
- Rollbacks and credits have been added to protect the burden on property taxpayers, but these relief measures have restricted the growth in property tax revenues and are a poorly designed form of assistance to local governments;
- The overall system is not elastic enough to automatically generate sufficient revenues to meet the expenditure needs of the state and its local governments;
- There is a mismatch between the division of tax revenues between state and local governments, and the expenditure requirements of the different levels of government; and
- A substantial amount of the consumption of services remains outside the sales tax base.

A third concern is that the system is complicated, probably more than is necessary. The problem areas here are the real property tax, the net worth tax, the personal property taxes, and the municipal income tax. This complexity affects the confidence that taxpayers have in the system, and raises both the administrative and the compliance cost.

There are some significant strengths in the Ohio tax structure. In fact, this system has remained relatively free of crisis adjustments, it has produced a relatively stable flow of revenues, and it features a relatively favorable tax structure for central cities because of the municipal income tax. The level of taxes has remained below the national level.

In summary, it is not a tax system that emphasizes economic development, it is horizontally inequitable, and it is unnecessarily complex. It does not exhibit an elasticity that will support expenditure growth above that in total personal income. Its strongest features are vertical equity, stability over the business cycle, and protection of the revenue position of central cities.

WHAT ARE THE PRIORITY OBJECTIVES FOR TAX REFORM?

There is no one best tax structure for Ohio, and no single "right" way to reform the state tax structure. Any reform must be guided by the objectives to be achieved and the tradeoffs that are acceptable. The basic principles adopted by the Commission (Box 1-2) are the standard "norms" of a good tax system. This list of norms is much like those adopted by other state tax commissions, except for the economic development criteria. The Ohio Commission felt that the economic development - taxation issue warranted separate consideration because the flagging Ohio economy is the dominant issue facing the state. Another difference is obsolescence, which was included because some members felt that the Ohio tax bases and differential tax treatments no longer match the realities of the state economy.

To decide which of these principles should be emphasized, the Commission members individually ranked and weighted each of the principles. The results of this vote,[32] presented in Table 1-12, show a strong consensus. The Commission recommended a reform that emphasizes economic development and corrects the horizontal equity problems that are so pervasive in the present system.

This is not to say that other objectives, such as vertical equity or revenue elasticity are unimportant. Clearly, the fairness in the distribution of tax burdens between rich and poor people and rich and poor places are important considerations that weigh heavily in the proposed reform, as are the criteria about the future revenue performance of the tax system. But the bigger problems that drive this reform program are the declining Ohio economy and the need to avoid a future of continuous discretionary tax rate changes.

The proposals are for a change in the tax system that will be more favorable to those who invest in Ohio, thereby enhancing the general business climate, and that will create a more level playing field for all investors and consumers. Such a change in direction, or tax philosophy, is certain to raise strenuous objections from those who would like to protect the status quo. Some critics will see this change in emphasis toward economic development as a backing away from the traditional emphasis on vertical equity. The Commission did not see it this way, for the following reasons:

TABLE 1-12
Summary of the Priorities of the Commission[a]

	Ranking[b]	Weighting[c]
Elasticity	4.4	6.6
Stability	4.5	6.4
Vertical Equity	4.6	6.3
Horizonal Equity	2.3	8.6
Economic Development	1.5	9.5
Simplication/Administration	4.7	6.3
Spatial Distribution	5.4	6.4
Obsolescence	5.9	5.3

[a]13 members voted. Average rankings and weightings are presented here.
[b]Ranking: 1 (most important).
[c]Weighting: 10 (most imporant).

- If state economic development is enhanced by the tax reform, because investment in Ohio is stimulated, then the entire state population will benefit from increased jobs and real income.
- If the Ohio economy continues on its present path, the job and real income growth in Ohio will lag behind the rest of the nation and both low and high income families will suffer.
- The traditional emphasis in the tax structure has not supported a business climate that has led to an above-average growth.

Other critics will say that this program shifts the burden from "business" to individuals. This makes little sense as an argument because business taxes are ultimately paid by persons in the form of higher prices, lower wages or a lower return on their investment. A more creditable criticism would be that the shift away from business taxes could decrease the share of taxes exported to residents of other states.

Other observers, more disposed to an economic development reform, would like to argue that this shift in emphasis can be accomplished without cost or sacrifice. This also is incorrect. Tax reductions can stimulate investment but must be paid for with increases in other taxes and with the allocative and equity effects of these increases. But it is true that stronger economic growth can compensate for these problems, and the Commission's view is that the long run benefits of a stronger economy more than outweigh the short run costs.

Horizontal equity as a priority of this reform—the equal treatment of similarly situated firms and individuals—will bring winners and losers. Some firms and individuals pay higher taxes in the present system because others receive preferential treatment. These are the winners when the horizontal equity criteria drives the reform. The gratitude of these winners, however, is not likely to match the negative reaction of the losers. This is because the potential winners from reform have long since capitalized their differentially higher tax, and the potential losers have come to recognize their tax preference as a right. Moreover, many politicians have a vested interest in maintaining special tax treatments which they have championed. The Commission recognizes that tax preferences are not easily given up once they have been granted, and that proposals to enhance fairness will not be warmly received. Nevertheless, the Commission felt that bringing more fairness to the Ohio tax system is essential, and that a level playing field for investors is much preferred to the present system that causes some firms to alter behavior to avoid higher taxes.

The reform direction proposed by this Commission turns on the belief that certain changes in the tax structure can improve the climate for investment in Ohio. In fact, no research can project exactly how great this effect will be, but the basic thrust of this reform is clearly in the direction of attracting new investment to the state. A different emphasis has driven the Ohio tax structure for many years and was the view of the Commission that it is time for a change.

A BLUEPRINT FOR REFORMING THE OHIO TAX SYSTEM

How does Ohio get on a faster economic growth path, e.g., one that keeps pace with the national economy? The Commission realizes that tax restructuring alone is not the answer, because many factors have influenced those business and personal decisions that have led to slow economic growth. Still, taxes do matter, and the present tax structure is particularly hard on private investment. Unburdening the tax on investment, even in the context of a low taxing state like Ohio, can improve the business climate. The fiscal plan proposed by the Commission, therefore, emphasizes economic development.

Some will say that this is a plan that shifts taxes from businesses to people. This is simply incorrect. No matter what structure of taxation is used, people always pay the taxes imposed. Sometimes they pay in the form of higher prices for the goods they purchase, sometimes in the form of lower wages than they otherwise would have received, and sometimes in the form of lower return on their investment. It is true that the distribution of tax burdens may fall differently on families at different income levels depending on whether the final incidence is with consumers, workers, or shareholders, and it is true that some of the tax may be exported to residents of other states. But, ultimately, taxes can be borne only by people. This plan, like any restructuring, rearranges the tax burden among consumers, workers, and capitalists.

There is also an excess burden of taxation. If the tax structure has encouraged investment and consumption decisions that have led to a slower rate of economic growth in Ohio, then an additional burden has been imposed in the form of slower long run growth and fewer employment opportunities. People also bear this burden: in the form of less growth in real income than that received by other Americans, fewer job opportunities, and less expansion in public services and infrastructure. If a reform such as the one proposed here were to remove some of this excess burden and lead to an increased rate of economic growth in the state, then consumers, workers and capitalists all would benefit.

This is not a tax increase program. An important constraint that the Commission imposed on itself is that the reform program would be revenue neutral (see Box 1-5). If there is a proposal for the reduction in one tax, there must be a compensating proposal for the increase in another. The focus of this Commission is solely on restructuring.

This blueprint for comprehensive reform of the Ohio tax system carries an expectation that tax restructuring will take place over a period of years. This report lays out a new direction for tax policy in Ohio, and discusses a phasing in of the various proposed changes. Some of the changes can and should be enacted immediately, but for several reasons (discussed below), it is necessary to complete the reform on a gradual basis. Even though this reform would involve changes equivalent to no more than 15 percent of total revenues, the Commission felt that full implementation would be too great a tax shock to the Ohio political and fiscal system.

Corporate Franchise Tax[33]

Proposal: Eliminate the Net Worth Tax, and require combined income reporting for all corporations. These reforms should be adopted together, or not at all. Both could be adopted immediately. The revenue cost, if fully enacted in 1993, would have been $200 million, less the revenue gains from combined income reporting.

Currently, the Corporate Franchise Tax is levied on one of two bases: corporate income or the net wealth of corporations. The purpose of this dual base is to ensure that any corporation operating in Ohio makes some contribution to the state for the privilege of operating a business in Ohio,

BOX 1-5
Revenue Neutrality

The proposed reform is to be revenue neutral, i.e., to yield the same amount of revenue as the present system would yield. This revenue neutrality is demonstrated for various reform options using data for 1993, the latest year for which information was available on actual collections.

It should be noted, however, that revenue neutrality for one period does not necessarily mean revenue neutrality in future years. In fact, the system proposed in this reform has a greater revenue-income elasticity than the present system, hence it will automatically generate a larger flow of future revenues.

whether or not the corporation shows a profit in any particular year. The existence of the net worth component of the tax also provides stability to the revenue stream.

While the net worth component of the tax does increase the long-term expected level of revenues, it reduces the net rate of return to investment in the state. It is especially burdensome to capital-intensive and start-up companies because newer companies tend to lose money in the early stages of their development. Thus, the net worth element of the existing tax is a disincentive to new business formation and an impediment to the success of these new businesses. The Commission proposed repeal of the net worth tax.

This proposal, if accepted, would convert the corporation tax to a net income basis only. The Commission recommends no compensating change in the corporation income tax rate, because the Ohio rate is already high.

A major problem with this proposal is the revenue loss and the possibility that many firms who use Ohio services will be freed from any tax liability. In some cases these are companies with positive net income but with the wherewithal to allocate costs and revenues among subsidiaries in such a way as to avoid payment of Ohio taxes. There is reason to believe that such accounting practices are occurring at the expense of the state government in Ohio. Ohio currently has one of the highest corporate tax rates, yet receives a below average amount of revenue from this tax. The Commission proposes the requirement of combined income reporting, a method of corporate taxation already used in many states.[34] This will hold firms in the corporate tax net, enable a more fair distribution of the tax burden, and possibly increase the yield of the corporate income tax.

The Commission recommends the adoption of these two proposals as a package. If combined income reporting is not adopted, the net worth tax should be retained. By eliminating the net worth tax and requiring combined reporting, the state will remove an important disincentive to new business formation and success, reduce the expected long-term tax rate on profits, remove a tax that discriminates against capital intensive sectors, ensure that tax burdens are more fairly distributed across all firms operating within the state, and generally encourage economic development.

There are two downsides to this proposal. First, revenues from the corporate tax will be less stable when the net worth component is removed. This is because the net income base, which will now govern the tax, fluctuates more widely over the business cycle. This is an important problem for a state with a cyclical economy, but on the other hand the corporate franchise tax now accounts for less than 5 percent of total state government revenues. The second problem is that combined income reporting will require additional administrative effort, and will increase the complexity of the tax system.

TANGIBLE PERSONAL PROPERTY TAX[35]

Proposal: Eliminate the Tangible Personal Property Tax. This phaseout would take place over a number of years. The CY 1992 revenue cost would have been $1.2 billion. Eliminate the inventory tax immediately. The CY 1992 revenue cost would have been $500 million.

Currently, the state of Ohio collects a tax on the personal property of businesses (other than public utilities). The tax base is 25 percent of the market value of machines, equipment, inventories and other business movable property. The tangible business personal property tax raises a significant amount of revenue for local governments.

The Commission recommended that the tangible personal property tax be eliminated from the Ohio tax structure. This is a change that is long overdue. A state such as Ohio that is short on investment and job growth should not single out capital investments for differentially heavy taxation.

It is true that the taxation of depreciable fixed business assets is standard tax practice in the United States. There are 39 states which include tangible business personal property in their tax bases, however, many of these (e.g., Oregon, Wisconsin, Virginia, and Maryland) either exempt manufacturing machinery and equipment or treat it as real property. Of the eleven states which exempt tangible personal business assets from the tax base, Pennsylvania is a neighbor and three other states are in the same economic region (Illinois, Minnesota, and New York). Delaware, Hawaii, Iowa, New

Hampshire, New Jersey, New York, North Dakota and South Dakota are the others. The elimination of the personal property tax could prove to be an important locational advantage to Ohio.

Personal property taxes are levied on inventories in Ohio. Most states which impose the personal property tax do not tax inventories, in fact, only 16 states continue to tax inventories (these include Indiana, Kentucky and West Virginia). There are many reasons why inventories should not be taxed. The tax is inequitable, because the presence of a high level of inventories does not necessarily imply a greater ability to pay. In fact, the presence of a large inventory value may be less an indicator of wealth than an indicator that a firm had a bad year and consequently has less ability to pay. Moreover, some industries naturally require higher levels of inventory than others and are unfairly treated under this tax. Clearly, the existence of an inventory tax is a negative factor for any business considering an Ohio location for a distribution center. It acts as an offset to the locational advantages of the state. Thus, the unfairness of the tax and its negative impact for development in Ohio are two strong arguments against the personal property tax on business assets.

The personal property tax presents significant compliance problems for payers, and tax administration problems for the government. Businesses that self-report personal property, must keep detailed records on the price and vintage of all their taxable property. The State tax administration, on the other hand, is faced with a substantial job in discovering business personal property, carrying out a proper audit, and maintaining adequate valuation schedules. The personal property tax also creates administrative problems in that it is the chief reason for the existence of enterprise zones in the state. If these zones are to continue, it will be necessary to monitor their activities more closely, and this assignment will carry a significant administrative cost. Elimination of the personal property tax would eliminate much of the reason for the existence of enterprise zones.

A final, important reason to consider elimination of this tax is that the base of the tax has shown relatively little growth in recent years. However, its revenues are a mainstay of the support for financing the operations of local governments (70 percent of calendar 1992 collections went to school districts). Elimination of this tax would force a decision to move local governments (and particularly school districts) on to a tax base that is more commensurate with the growth in their expenditure needs. The elimination of the personal property tax would also lighten the administrative and compliance burden associated with the property tax.

There are desirable features to the personal property tax on business that also must be considered in evaluating the pros and cons of its elimination. Its base has grown very slowly in real terms, but this has created considerable stability, an important characteristic for a school district where fiscal planning is so important. Virtually any other replacement tax would be less stable in its revenue yield over the business cycle. Another desirable feature of the tangible personal property tax is that its burden is partly exported: to the federal government through deductibility from taxable federal income, to consumers of the final product, and to shareholders who reside in other states.

The view of the Commission was that the drawbacks of the tangible personal property tax far outweigh its advantages, and it was recommended that the tax on inventories be eliminated immediately. The revenue cost, (for calendar 1992) would be $500 million. The remaining tangible personal property tax should be eliminated over a period of five to ten years. The phasing in of this reform is required to: (a) avoid a large tax shock associated with so big a change, (b) give time to determine how the revenue loss to local governments will be replaced, and (c) give time for the differential assessment ratios for utilities to be stepped down.

Public Utility Property Tax[36]

Proposal: Eliminate the Public Utility Property Tax, bring all utilities under the corporate income tax, and reduce utility rates to reflect the tax changes. If this program had been fully implemented in 1993, the revenue cost would have been $950 million, less the corporate tax that would have been collected from the utilities. This program should be phased in over a period of years. As a first step, interexchange companies should be brought immediately into the tangible personal property tax regime for general business. All new investment by other public utilities should be assessed at the 25 percent ratio used for general business, and the assessment ratio on existing property should be stepped down over a 5 to 10 year period.

The public utility property tax introduces a serious horizontal equity into the Ohio tax system. An assessment ratio of 25 percent is imposed on the personal property of general businesses, but an assessment ratio of 88 percent is imposed on public utility property. The Commission considered both relevant questions: should there be a personal property tax at all, and should there be a differential rate on utility versus other property.

There once was an argument that public utilities should be treated differently by the tax regime: they had received a special franchise to deliver a service that had put them in a monopoly position, and their rate of return was regulated. Those reasons for different tax treatment are fast disappearing as competition comes to the electric, gas, and telecommunications sectors. However, competition is not proceeding at the same pace in all of these sectors, and there is some room for differential treatment. On the other hand, this Commission Report is meant to be a blueprint for a five to ten year program, and the state must consider the likely case that all three sectors will become highly competitive during that time period.

The first major problem with the present system is that it treats utilities different from general firms, even though in some cases (interexchange companies) the nature of the differential treatment is unclear. This policy has the effect of making it difficult to attract investment to the highly taxed sectors.

Second, some utilities are taxed differently from competing firms (especially in the telecommunications sector). Cable companies, for example, are treated differently from local exchanges. This creates an unfair situation, especially in the telecommunications sector at a time when heavy investment is being made to strengthen competitive positions.

Third, there are questions about whether such a tax should exist at all, when Ohio is attempting to increase its attractiveness to investors, to bid more capital to the state, and to expand infrastructure. By raising the cost of the investment in Ohio, the tax structure makes it more difficult to attract funds to modernize the capital stock in the utilities sector. This is an especially important issue at a time when telecommunications infrastructure has become a key consideration in the location decisions of many firms.

Fourth, the tax is inelastic in its response to income growth, and so would seem to be a weak source of revenue for funding education (which receives 70 percent of the revenues). The tax base to support education should grow in step with expenditure requirements.

There is a positive side to the public utility property tax in Ohio. It is a stable source of revenue over the business cycle. It is "invisible" in the sense that residential ratepayers do not always recognize the shifting of a substantial portion of the burden directly to them, and therefore it is seen by many as a tax without significant burden. This perception is best articulated by those who see a clear distinction between taxes on people and taxes on business. Another advantage of personal property taxes on public utilities is that they do not pose the same degree of administrative difficulty as does the tangible personal property tax. Finally, the utility taxes are in place, are understood and accepted, and their impacts have been capitalized into higher consumer prices and less investment.

The view of the Commission was that the public utility property tax should be abolished, and that public utilities should be treated as ordinary businesses with respect to the tangible personal property tax and the corporate income tax. This will lead to a tax structure that is more horizontally equitable, more conducive to economic development, and more elastic. However, it is clear that this must be a long-term program of reform, rather than a one year restructuring. This is partly because of the need to decide how the revenue lost to the local governments will be replaced, partly because of the revenue loss itself, and partly because the pace of competition is proceeding at different rates in different utility sectors.

The Commission recommended that interexchange companies be brought to parity with general companies immediately, with respect to the personal property tax. It also recommended that all new investment by public utilities be subject to the 25 percent personal property tax assessment ratio, and that this take place immediately. Third, the assessment ratio on the remaining public utility property should be stepped down from 88 percent to 25 percent over a five to ten year period, and phased out along with the tangible personal property tax. Finally, these tax reductions should be reflected in rate reductions to users.

Public Utility Gross Receipts Tax[37]

Proposal: Convert the public utility gross receipts tax to a user charge, holding public utility rates constant except for those individuals and businesses who were previously receiving a tax preference. The net revenue cost is zero.

Public utilities in the state are currently subject to a gross receipts tax (Public Utilities Excise Tax) of 4.75 percent (6.75 percent for pipelines). The tax applies to all receipts of the public utilities except those from purely interstate business. There are two major problems with this tax. One is that municipal utilities are not required to pay, creating an unfair competitive position *vis a vis* investor owned utilities, and the other is that it leaves Ohio utilities in a non-competitive position relative to competing out-of-state firms and in-state firms that are not subject to the gross receipts tax.

The Commission proposes that the gross receipts tax be replaced with a user charge on utility bills. This user charge would be either an ad valorem levy or a specific charge on the purchase of any utility service from any provider. The taxation of all purchases evens the treatment of municipal and investor-owned utilities since purchases from either provider would be equivalently taxed. The user charge also eliminates any distortions which may arise as a result of the deduction from taxable gross receipts of those receipts from purely interstate business.

It is the intention of the Commission that the switch from a gross receipts tax to a user charge not effect the gross price of utilities to consumers of the service. On the one hand, the elimination of the gross receipts tax would reduce costs. Utility prices, in principle, should fall by the full amount of the tax. On the other hand, the imposition of the equal yield user charge would push the gross prices up to their original level (less the amount now paid by those whose purchases have been outside the gross receipts tax). In practice, the PUCO would need to request a rate hearing from those affected by the switch, and there is the potential for a lag between elimination of the gross receipts tax and consequent net price reductions. The legislation authorizing the swap could, however, specifically request that the reductions take effect immediately as has been proposed by SB 120, which specifies a mandated reduction in prices for telecommunications services.

Enterprise Zones and Tax Incentives[38]

Proposal: Abolish enterprise zones, and prohibit the use of targeted tax incentives to recruit companies to Ohio. Revenues will increase, but the amounts are uncertain.

Much of the rationale for Enterprise Zones in Ohio rests on the need for relieving the property tax on inventories. Ohio is among a small number of states that still tax business inventories under the property tax. However, Enterprise Zones created all over a state are not an efficient mechanism for correcting what fiscal experts know to be poor property tax policy. Moreover, solving the problem through ad hoc agreements drawn between firms and municipalities, townships and counties is very inefficient administratively. Though Ohio's school districts receive over 70 percent of personal property tax revenues, other local governments are empowered to forgive the property tax on inventory, in most cases, without school district approval. Such a practice is disruptive to the overall system of state and local government finance in Ohio.

A major part of this tax reform plan is the elimination of the personal property tax and, in particular, the elimination of the personal property tax on inventories. Abatement of these personal property taxes is currently the most frequently used tax incentive. If either the personal property tax on inventories or on all personal property is eliminated, the primary reason for the existence of enterprise zones would be eliminated.

Some might oppose the elimination of enterprise zones on grounds that they provide a significant subsidy to low income or unemployed workers. This may not be the case. The Enterprise Zone program has only recently developed two different zone designations to target more job credits to distressed zones. There is considerable debate about whether spatial targeting is at all useful. Evidence suggests that 60 to 100 percent of the benefits of spatial targeting accrues to non-zone residents either through labor force migration into the targeted areas or simply missed targets within the area. Another important conclusion is that Ohio's proliferation of zones makes it unlikely that benefits are reaching the target population. This is because population mobility diffuses benefits among targeted zones and non-targeted areas. The Commission recommended the elimination of Enterprise Zones.

The Commission also recommended ending the practice of giving targeted tax incentives to attract firms to Ohio. This practice is inconsistent with the horizontal equity goals of this reform, i.e., creating a competitive environment and allowing the market to determine which firms will invest and expand in Ohio. But more important, the proposed reforms create a very favorable tax climate for businesses in Ohio by eliminating the more onerous taxes for investors: namely the personal property tax, the net worth tax, and the tax on inventories. This program of generally lower business taxes advantages new and existing firms to the same extent. Under a targeted incentive program for new companies, the state must make up the revenue loss with a higher tax elsewhere in the system, possibly with heavier taxes on existing businesses.

Banks and Insurance Companies[39]

Proposal: Eliminate the special taxes on banks, insurance companies and dealers in intangibles and bring all financial institutions under the corporate income tax with appropriate modifications. The 1993 revenue cost would have been approximately $66 million.

Banks, insurance companies and dealers in intangibles are each subject to special taxes that historically evolved from and reflected the distinctive nature of their operations and businesses. The Commission recommended that these special taxes be eliminated and that all financial institutions be taxed under the corporate income tax.

This reform will create a more competitive environment and encourage economic development in the state. For example, it will remove artificial distinctions between banks with and without deposits in Ohio since all companies will be subject to the same income tax. It will likewise eliminate the very different tax treatment among insurance companies. Furthermore, by putting all financial institutions on an equal footing, decisions to purchase certain types of savings instruments will not be affected by state tax policy.

Two complications arise from taxing all financial institutions under the general income tax. First, banks and other financial institutions hold a large part of their investment portfolios in tax exempt federal and state securities and their taxable income (and tax liability) is usually lower than that of the average non-financial company. One view is that this is not a problem since tax exempt securities pay lower interest rates and all taxpayers can invest in these types of securities and receive similar benefits. If the low tax liability is viewed as a problem, two options are available. One is to tax all interest from government securities (including Ohio's) received by all corporations. However, this change would interfere with the public policy underlying the exemption and may cause horizontal inequities if such interest remains exempt in other states, as most states with an income tax exempt public obligations. Another option is to tax banks and other financial institutions at a higher corporate income tax rate. This method, however, adds complexities and interferes with the goal of horizontal equity.

The second complication involves the appropriate corporate income tax apportionment formula for banks and insurance companies. The goal of equal treatment would require all companies to apportion income in a consistent manner. However, most states use a non-standard three factor formula or a single factor formula to apportion banking and insurance businesses. A single factor apportionment formula based on deposits or premiums should benefit domestic (Ohio) insurance companies and banks the same way a single sales factor would benefit all non-financial Ohio corporations. Moreover, there are reasons why the standard three factor formula may not be appropriate for both banks and insurers. For example, the Multistate Tax Commission has proposed a non-standard apportionment formula for banks. If Ohio's apportionment formula is inconsistent with the formula used in other states, Ohio's banking industry will be at a disadvantage. Similarly, a single premiums factor is used in most states where the insurance industry is subject to income taxes. Again, an apportionment method that is inconsistent with other states may put the Ohio insurance industry at a disadvantage.

While reform is clearly needed, a recommendation to bring all financial institutions under the corporate income tax must be carefully implemented in order to encourage rather than penalize financial institutions for locating in Ohio. In particular, financial institutions should be permitted the same exemption for tax exempt interest as other corporations, and the apportionment factor for banks and insurance companies should be consistent with other states and/or the Multistate Tax Commission model.

The effect of this recommendation on retaliatory taxes paid by Ohio firms must be considered. Ohio's insurance premium tax rate is among the highest in the country and, therefore, Ohio's insurance industry is at a competitive disadvantage when it sells in other states. Replacing the premium tax with a broader-based income tax should lower the effective tax, thus lowering the amount of retaliatory taxes paid by Ohio insurers to other states, while also increasing the amount of retaliatory taxes paid by out-of-state insurers to Ohio. This would not only remove the economic penalty to locate in Ohio, but would aid economic development by increasing opportunities for growth in the domestic insurance industry.

Sales Taxation[40]

Proposal: Extend the sales tax to services, immediately to a narrow category to *raise about $150 million in revenue and later to a broader category, including professional services, to gain about $600 million.*

Proposal: Give voters a choice on a ballot initiative, between the inclusion of food in the sales tax base (with a food credit for low income taxpayers), and a 1 percent increase in the sales tax rate. The extension to food, net of the credit, would produce about $400 million in new revenue, and the 1 percent increase in the rate would produce about $800 million.

The Commission proposes that a significant proportion of the tax restructuring be financed by sales taxation. Three adjustments in the sales tax might be considered.

- An expansion of the sales tax base to cover additional service consumption.
- An expansion of the sales tax base to cover food consumption, accompanied by a food tax credit for low income families.
- An increase of one percent in the sales tax rate.

The Commission proposed that Ohio voters be given a choice between the rate increase and the food/credit options.

Services

The Commission's proposal to add a significant number of service categories to the retail sales tax would improve the tax system in many ways: it would make the sales tax more fair by including more categories of consumption, it could improve the elasticity of the tax system depending on what is brought into tax, and it would yield significant revenue.

As noted above and in the background research papers, Ohio's sales tax base excludes a significant portion of the consumption of services. This is not unusual policy, though Ohio's coverage of services under the sales tax is relatively narrow. Most states do not tax a significant number of services, either because they are considered business inputs, they involve consumption of socially desirable goods, they are administratively difficult to reach, or simply because "that's the way it always has been". But these services do constitute consumption and in many cases fairness demands that they be taxed.

Most important, the inclusion of services would improve the horizontal equity of the tax system by removing tax preferences from those who consume significant amounts of services. A cursory glance at the list of exempt services in Box 1-6 should convince even skeptics about the fairness of this proposal: why should one family pay a 5 percent sales tax on its purchase of a household good while another pays no sales tax on its consumption of cable TV or income tax preparation services? Another way to view the fair-

BOX 1-6
Services Presently Exempt Under the Ohio Sales Tax

Admissions and Amusements	**Number of States Taxing**
Parimutuel events	27
Amusements, recreations, & museums	21
Billiard parlors	36
Bowling lanes	27
Cable TV services	24
Circuses and fairs - admits and games	34
Coin operated video games	20
Admission to sports events	27
Theatrical productions	31
Pinball	22
Professional sports	36
Rental of films by theaters	9
Motion picture theater admission	NA
Automotive Services	
Road service and towing (w/o repairs)	15
Parking	19
Business Services	
Outdoor ad. services	4
Media ad. representatives	3
Misc. advertising	
Newspaper advertising	4
Magazine advertising	5
Advertising agency (not ad placement)	8
Misc. business services	
Bail bond fees	7
Interior design and decorating	9
Telemarketing services/contract	6
Phone answering service(human)	10
Collection services	8
Commercial art and graphic design	20
Credit reporting services (on line)	13
Lobbying and consulting	13
Marketing	6
Packing and crating	8
Process server fees	6
Management and public relations	7
Testing laboratories	8
Computer Services	
Computer programming (application software)	34
Software-custom program-material	28
Software-custom programs-services	15
Information retrieval services	14
Mainframe access and processing service	11

continued

BOX 1-6 (continued)
Services Presently Exempt Under the Ohio Sales Tax

Construction Services	**Number of States Taxing**
General contractor service	11
Special trade contractor service	13
Misc. Contractor service	11
Water well drilling contractors	9
Finance, Insurance & Real Estate	
Service charges of banks	3
Insurance services	6
Investment counseling	6
Loan broker fees	6
Real estate services	8
Leases & Rental	
Campgrounds	27
Personal Services	
Barber and beauty shops	6
Coin operated laundries	8
Funeral services	15
Misc. services	
Dating services	10
Debt counseling	7
Tanning parlors	18
Swimming pool cleaning and maint.	15
Tax return preparation services	7
Professional Services	
Accounting	5
Legal	5
Dentistry	4
Engineering	5
Surveying	7
Medical Labs	4
Nursing and personal care facilities	4
Medical doctor services	4
Utilities Services	
Electricity (Industrial)	37
Electricity (Residential)	23
Natural gas (Industrial)	38
Natural gas (Residential)	23
Sewer and refuse (Industrial)	11
Sewer and refuse (Residential)	10
Water supply (Industrial)	20
Water supply (Residential)	12

Source: Federation of Tax Administrators, *Sales Taxation of Services: An Update*, No. 143.

ness issue is that the additional revenues raised from taxing services could be used to lower the sales tax rate on all consumption.

The revenue responsiveness of the sales tax to income growth might also be effected by the inclusion of services in the tax base. Depending on the extent to which services are included, the income elasticity of the sales tax could increase above its present 0.97 level. The consumption of medical services, for example, is growing faster than total personal income. The share of services (less housing) in total consumption in the United States grew from 30 percent in 1976 to 43 percent in 1993, suggesting that the inclusion of all services in the sales tax base would have increased the elasticity of the sales tax significantly. There are a number of other choices for inclusion, however, that are not growing as fast and would not significantly increase the income elasticity of the sales tax.

The questions to be answered are what services should be included in the sales tax base, and how should this base expansion be phased in. Certainly there are choices. The research identified 72 types of services that are not now subject to sales taxation in Ohio but are subject to sales taxation in other states (Box 1-6). It also identified the order of magnitude of revenues that could be expected from this base expansion (Table 1-13). Clearly, there is much room for base expansion.

The Commission recommended that the sales tax base be expanded to include services. Immediately, a "narrow" category of consumer type services and some professional services, can be brought into the sales tax, and can yield about $150 million (Table 1-13). Narrow base expansion includes cable television, hair salon services, coin-operated amusements, parking, laundry and dry cleaning, golf course tees, funeral services, and motion picture admittances. A second round of base broadening, carried out as the tax reductions are phased in, could raise this total to about $600 million (measured in terms of 1993 revenues). The "broad expansion" would cover selected professional (including medical) services, business services and construction services. This still will constitute only about 37 percent of the total service consumption that is presently outside the sales tax base.

Rather than recommend the exact services to be brought in at each step, the Commission proposed consideration of the following criteria in selecting services to be excluded from the tax base.

- Medical services, where taxation would impose significant hardship or compromise state social policy.

- Services that would be extremely difficult to administer because there are difficulties in determining the situs of the activity, e.g., advertising.

TABLE 1-13
Significant Ohio Servie Exemptions
(In Millions of Dollars)

	FY 1994
1. Health Care	1,172.7
2. Legal Services	157.0
3. Engineering Architecture and Surveying	60.2
4. Management Services	59.8
5. Accounting and Bookkeeping	52.3
6. Cable TV	45.0
7. Beauty Salons and Barber Shops	16.1
8. Coin-Operated Amusements	10.0
9. Auto Parking	9.9
10. Laundry and Dry Cleaning	9.3
11. Advertising and Public Relations	7.6
12. Public Golf Courses	7.4
13. Funeral Services	7.4
14. Motion Picture Theaters	4.5
Total	$1,619.2

Source: State of Ohio, *Executive Budget for the Biennium, July 1, 1993 to June 30, 1995, Book Two: Report on Tax Expenditures*, prepared by the Ohio Department of Taxation, as reported in Fox, Chapter 4 in this volume.

- Services that are direct inputs to business production and therefore would involve double taxation, and place Ohio producers at a comparative disadvantage.

Eliminating the services that meet these conditions, however, still leaves the state considerable room to expand the sales tax base.

Apart from these decision rules, the issue is not which services are best to tax, but how far the state is willing to go to make the system more horizontally equitable. Many professional services can be taxed without creating undue hardship or discouraging Ohio business, but most states have not had the political courage to bring these "hard to tax" sectors into the sales tax base. Taxing a broad range of consumer services, however unpopular, is better for economic development in Ohio than continued heavy taxation of business investment.

As fair and as reasonable as this proposal sounds, there will be vocal opposition to any proposal to remove tax preferences. There also will be questions about how to handle the distribution of the sales tax revenues among counties, since the taxation of services raises some difficult situs issues. These issues have been resolved in other states, however, and they could be resolved in Ohio. The taxation of services will place administrative burdens on the State Department of Taxation, but other states have handled these burdens, and the Commission has confidence in the ability of the Ohio administration to handle this expansion in responsibilities.

The growing share of service consumption, and the commensurate erosion of the consumption base that is presently taxed, is fact. Expansion of the sales tax base to cover the untaxed base is the only way to avoid ever-increasing sales tax rates.

Food

Food is exempt from sales taxation in Ohio and in many other states. Twenty-six of the 46 states with retail sales taxes exempt food for consumption at home. The trend generally has been for more states to exempt these items.

The taxation of food is an emotionally charged issue, and that there are strong arguments to support those who insist on the exemption of food from the sales tax: Food is a necessity that should not be taxed; lower income people spend a greater proportion of their income on food and therefore to bring food into the tax base is to make the tax system more regressive. Since a tax on food also touches every voter, there is widespread political opposition to taxing it.

But there are good, defensible reasons to include food in the sales tax base.

- Most food expenditures are made by higher income families, hence the exemption of food in the name of assistance to the low income may not be well founded;
- More than food is typically consumed at food stores hence there are administrative difficulties with the exemption;
- The differential treatment of food-at-home vs food-in-restaurants leads to many administrative ambiguities that compromise the original intent of this dichotomy;

- The food exemption leads to a lower revenue level which often is made up by a higher sales tax rate that burdens the same low income families that exemption was supposed to help;
- The inclusion of food in the tax base improves the cyclical stability of the sales tax.

The Commission believed that the case for taxing food was compelling enough that it ought to be offered to voters as an alternative to an increased sales tax rate, but recommended the inclusion of food in the sales tax base only if accompanied by a refundable income tax credit. This plan would have yielded about $400 million in additional tax revenue in 1993. All families with incomes below $20,000 would receive a $160 credit to compensate them for sales taxes paid for food. Families with an income above $20,000 would not receive the credit. While this is an efficient way to target the tax relief on the overburdened families, it would require filing a return in order to receive the cash transfer.

Sales Tax Rate

An obvious policy option for Ohio is to raise the sales tax rate. A one-percent increase in the state sales tax rate would have generated about $800 million in 1993. The additional revenue could be used either to lower other tax rates or to eliminate other taxes. There are important advantages to this approach to raising additional revenues. No one likes a tax increase, but the sales tax has proven to be less objectionable than income and property taxes; the administrative machinery is already in place; compliance costs associated with a one percent rate increase are low; and a one percent increase in the rate is revenue productive.

There are also drawbacks to a rate increase that must be reckoned with. A higher rate will magnify all the flaws presently in the system, e.g., the sales tax on business inputs, the regressivity of the present system. Border problems could arise as a result of the increase because of the increased incentive to shop in other states. Another problem is that the sales tax is not deductible from the federal income tax hence its burden is higher on itemizers than would be the case for an equal tax increase from income or real property taxes. Finally, a six percent rate would not leave Ohio as an outlier, but it would move Ohio into the higher taxing group of states.

INDIVIDUAL INCOME TAX[41]

Proposal: Convert the present individual income tax to a flat rate tax on federal tax liability. At a rate of 27.5 percent, this restructuring would have increased revenues by $850 million in 1993.

The current system of individual income taxation is burdened by three major problems. First, it is unduly complicated with nine rate brackets and four credits. This leaves open many possibilities for arbitrary manipulation by lawmakers, e.g., "change the rates", "change the bracket width", "add a new credit", and so on. In such a complicated system, the impacts of discretionary adjustments are not always clear to those who make the proposals, or to taxpayers. Second, the present system of individual income taxation brings taxpayers into the net at a low level of income. Third, to finance the Blueprint for tax reform proposed here, it is necessary to raise an additional $850 million from the individual income tax, and it is not clear how this can be done fairly under the present system (e.g., which bracket rate should be increased, should a new marginal rate be added, etc.). For these reasons, the Commission recommended a major change in the individual income tax, to a flat rate tax based on federal tax liability. The proposed flat tax would be simple, progressive and elastic.

Coupling to Federal Tax Liability

This is perhaps the simplest form of state income taxation. Taxpayers report their federal tax liability and then multiply by a single Ohio tax rate. A tax rate of 23.2 percent applied to federal tax liability (in 1993) would be revenue neutral with the present system for Ohio, and a rate of 27.5 percent applied to federal tax liability would raise approximately $850 million in additional revenue. Two states, Rhode Island and Vermont, currently use such a tax base.

This reform option would tie Ohio's individual income tax to the federal taxable income base and the federal marginal rate structure. Federal taxable income is a base which is quite different from Ohio's current tax base in many ways. Ohio's current income tax structure allows few deductions and additions to federal adjusted gross income to obtain Ohio adjusted gross income. Also, Ohio's current structure allows personal exemptions of only $650 per dependent and taxpayer(s). The result of these additions and subtractions is that Ohio brings taxpayers into the tax net at relatively low levels of income, even though certain Ohio credits mitigate this somewhat.

Under the proposed federal tax liability option, deductions from FAGI would be expanded. This reform option would allow a personal exemption of $2,350 per person (for 1993), and the greater of a standard deduction amount or itemized deductions. Itemized deductions are allowed for: medical expenses (above 7.5 percent of FAGI), home mortgage interest, state and local taxes (income and property), excessive casualty and theft losses, and some employment expenses. These deductions are adjusted annually for inflation.

Under this proposal, Ohio would implicitly be tied to the federal income tax rate structure. Currently, the federal tax rates are 15, 28, 31, 36, and 39.6

percent. The tax brackets are defined by filing status and are indexed annually for inflation.

Evaluation

This proposed change in the individual income tax would have several important effects. First, using federal tax liability as the tax base would significantly simplify the state individual income tax calculation. Taxpayers would simply multiply their federal tax liability by an Ohio tax rate to obtain Ohio tax liability.

Second, because this reform option will lead to substantially increased deductions from income for most Ohio taxpayers, adoption of this base would cause many low income families to be dropped from the rolls. Currently, for most filers, total Ohio adjustments equal their personal exemption amount of $650 per dependent plus taxpayer(s). For a family of four, total Ohio deductions are $2,600, but under this reform option, total deductions for a family of four taking the standard deduction would equal $15,600, hence families of four with incomes below $15,600 would no longer pay Ohio income tax. It is estimated that about 300,000 returns (out of 4.8 million) could have been eliminated had this reform been adopted in 1993. This would increase the vertical equity in the system, and could ease administrative burdens for the Department of Taxation.

Third, the horizontal equity of the tax would be improved due to the reduction in special income deductions (retirement income), and the elimination of the marriage penalty. The use of federal tax liability as the base of the Ohio income tax would disallow Ohio's current deductions for Social Security and Railroad Retirement Income. The simplified structure would also disallow the retirement income and senior citizen credit. However, the net benefit to retirees of the increased standard deduction and personal exemption amounts would outweigh the loss of the social security deduction and credits for most all retirees and senior citizens.

Fourth, the effective marginal tax rates would change from the current nine rates between 0.743 percent and 7.5 percent, to five effective marginal rates ranging from 3.48 percent to 9.19 percent for the revenue neutral option and 4.13 percent to 10.89 percent for the revenue enhancing option. This means that the proposed new system is more progressive than the current structure since the top effective tax rate rises from 4.3 percent to 6.03 percent. Taxpayers with incomes over $100,000 pay approximately 33 percent of the total tax liability. Currently those taxpayers pay approximately 30.7 percent of total liability. This change would put the highest individual income tax rate slightly above the highest corporate tax rate, which puts partnerships and sole proprietorships at a disadvantage relative to corporations. However, this relative disadvantage occurs for individuals with very high levels of income, over $200,000.

A comparison of the present system to an *equal yield* federal liability system shows that the top rate rises only to 5.2 percent. However, it should be emphasized that the true effects will vary by individual filer. For those individuals with very high itemized deductions, Ohio liability may be reduced substantially over their current liability.

Some will see the increased marginal rates at the top end as a problem with the proposed reform, i.e., that the result will be to make Ohio's environment less friendly to high income workers and investors. In fact, the marginal income tax rate will be high, but not significantly higher than it would have been had this reform been financed with a sur-rate on the current marginal rate schedule. The alternatives, to hold on to the high rates of tax on business investment or to ask the sales tax to carry more of the load, seemed less acceptable.

Fifth, this reform would reduce the discretion of the Legislature to adjust the income tax structure. If they remained true to the system of coupling to federal tax liability without further adjustments, they would have only one policy option to increase or reduce revenues—to change the tax rate. This is both good and bad, depending on one's point-of-view. It is bad because the state is effected by any policy actions that the federal government takes (rate changes, standard deduction increases, etc.) and can adjust to "undesirable" federal changes only by altering its single tax rate. It is good because it precludes the introduction of self-interest measures such as special deductions or credits, discretionary inflation adjustments, etc.

Sixth, the elasticity of this option is approximately 1.15, which is lower than that of Ohio's current income tax. Due to the indexation of the federal income tax, the rate elasticity of this option is lower than that of Ohio's current structure, while the base elasticity is slightly larger. This option would therefore yield a revenue source which is less volatile, and would grow faster than the growth in the economy. However, part of the very high built-in growth of the current Ohio income tax would be eliminated.

Lastly the availability of itemized deductions would encourage, to a lesser degree, the same types of behavior currently subsidized by the federal government. These types of behavior include the purchase of a home, a substantial gift to a qualified charity and relief for the burden of catastrophic health care. Deductions clearly introduce inequities, but these inequities have been found to be justified for social reasons.

Property Tax[42]

Proposal: Appoint a working group to review the system of State-Local government finance of Ohio. The charge to this study should include a review of the real property tax with an eye toward comprehensive reform.

Proposal for study: Consider a restructuring of the present real property tax that would replace the present system with a tax base of full market value, eliminate the tax reduction factor, (i.e., HB 920), freeze the dollar amounts of the property tax rollbacks, and impose an absolute millage cap. Such a program could be phased in over a five-year period and could be revenue neutral. Consideration also should be given to allowing local jurisdictions to impose differential property tax rates on land and buildings.

The Commission recognized the importance of reforming the real property tax. Reform is necessary because the tax is terribly complicated and because it may not be an adequate basis for financing the services that Ohio's local governments must deliver in the future. But the Commission had neither the time or resources to fully develop a proposal for reforming the real property tax, nor did it have the charge to study the effects of tax reform on individual local governments. It is not possible to properly evaluate alternative structures of the real property tax in isolation from analysis of the overall state assistance program for local governments, other sources of local government revenue, and school finance. The only option left open to the Commission was to strongly urge that property taxation be at the center of the terms of reference for a study group on state and local government finances in Ohio.

Both the Commission and the staff, however, did have a view on the appropriate general direction for reform. The goal of reform should be to simplify the tax, reduce the number of millage elections, and make it possible for school districts to do more efficient fiscal planning. Such changes would have to be implemented over a period of time, perhaps five years, and should be revenue neutral.

The Ohio property tax has long needed a complete reform. The problem in Ohio is less with the level of property taxation than with complexity. In fact, the Ohio property tax is so complicated that few taxpayers understand how it works or how their liability is determined. Moreover, it's revenue growth is held inelastic by "reduction factors", it is assessed at a fraction of full market value, and it includes a credit program that is a combination of property tax relief and a grant to local governments. Both features of the credit program, in fact, are poorly designed.

There are five important areas of concern, where viable reform options are open:

- Consideration should be given to increasing the assessment rate to 100 percent of full market value. This would require a reduction in millage rates to offset the increase in assessed value.
- Consideration should also be given to elimination of the tax reduction factors. This could be accomplished by freezing the factors at their cur-

rent values. New millage rates, including replacement rates, would not be subject to a reduction factor. Thus within five years, most millage rates would be freed from reduction. For any permanent or long-term millage rate, the reduction factors would be eliminated over a five-year phase-in period. During this period the tax reduction factors could be reduced by 20 percent each year, with mandated reduction in the voted millage used to keep the effective millage levy constant.

- Elimination of the 10 percent and 2.5 percent rollbacks should be considered. The funds used to finance the rollbacks would be frozen and used to offset the loss in local government revenues.
- In addition to the current 10 mill limit, a maximum property tax rate (or cap) might be considered. This could take the form of a limit on the maximum millage levy.
- The Commission recommends that consideration be given to allowing local jurisdictions the option of imposing a differential tax rate on land vs improvements. Under such a scheme, the property tax rate on land would be higher than the rate on structures, giving landowners maximum incentive to develop their properties to highest use. Such a system is used in Pennsylvania, and in several countries around the world.

Adoption of the five suggestions would have several advantages. First, it would simplify the real property tax, which is now incomprehensible to most Ohio taxpayers. Second, it would eliminate the two rollbacks, which form a poorly designed property tax relief and local government aid program. Third, it would reduce the need for local jurisdictions to seek voter approval of millage levies on such a frequent basis as is now the case. As a consequence, it would allow for a more rational budgeting process on the part of local governments. Finally by moving the tax base to full market value, the assessment process could be made more understandable.

There are many details that would have to be addressed in designing a plan with these features. For example, the state funds that are currently used to finance the rollbacks could either be used to hold each local government harmless, or be converted into a formula-based local government grant program. Likewise, going to 100 percent assessment means that the 10 mill limit will no longer be equivalent to a 0.35 percent limit, but will equal the constitutional limit of 1 percent. Thus, a decision would have to be made whether to keep the legislatively imposed 10 mill limit or lower it to 3.5 mills. Despite the difficult design problems, the Commission believed that a comprehensive reform program could be fully developed and implemented over a five-year period so that property taxes do not increase and local governments are held harmless in terms of total revenues.

Removing the tax reduction factor need not result in an increase in property taxes. Over the past twenty years voters have approved millage increases that have increased property tax revenue by about the same amount as would have occurred if the full growth in the property tax base had been taxed. The Commission believed, however, that any increases in millage rates should be approved by the voters.

There are many details that would have to be worked out before the decision could be made about the desirability of a property tax cap. Whether the cap could be exceeded by a vote of the residents is an issue for study. The value of the cap would have to be selected and a process for allocating parts of that property tax limit to each of the various local governments would have to be determined, as with the allocation of the 10 mill limit. Since the cap would require some local jurisdictions to reduce their total millage levy, alternative sources of funds would have to be found for these local governments.

THE ESTATE TAX[43]

Proposal: The Commission recommends that the Department of Taxation undertake a review of its records to re-examine the question of whether estate taxes have induced out-migration of the wealthy.

The State of Ohio has one significant policy option regarding the estate tax, specifically whether it should eliminate the extra tax on estates which is imposed in Ohio and five other states. Eliminating the tax would remove any incentive for households with estates in the range below $4 million to make a tax-based decision to move. The Department of Taxation has estimated that such a change would cost the State a significant amount of revenue (approximately $100 Million per year).

However, this revenue could be recovered if enough activity, which had presumably moved out of the state as a result of the estate tax, could be induced to stay in Ohio. There is no direct empirical evidence about the impact of estate taxes as a factor driving Ohioans out of state upon retirement. However, there is information available from the Department of Taxation's individual income tax files which might shed light on this issue.

WHO BENEFITS AND WHO PAYS?

This reform was structured to shift the emphasis in the Ohio tax system toward one that provides more encouragement to new investors and to those existing firms who would expand their business in Ohio. The blueprint developed by the Commission does exactly that, by removing existing taxes on investment in machinery, equipment, inventory, and from capital expenditures in general.

The beneficiaries of this program, to the extent it promotes economic development, are citizens of Ohio and owners of Ohio's businesses: workers who receive a higher real wage, the jobless who find work, capitalists who realize a higher return on their investment, and citizens who receive better funded public services. It seems proper, therefore, that the burden of payment for this program be spread among these beneficiaries. The blueprint proposed here calls for a combination of increased taxes on business income, individual income and consumption to pay for this program.

These reductions in business taxes would amount to approximately $2.4 billion, or 12 percent of the total revenues under consideration here.[44] This amount would be financed in some combination of the following ways:

- Increase the sales tax rate by one percent to yield about $800 million.
- Extend the sales tax base to a broad range of services, to yield about $600 million.
- Extend the sales tax base to include food with a refundable low income credit against the income tax, to yield $400 million.
- Restructure the individual income tax to yield $850 million.
- Bring all companies into the corporate net income tax, introduce combined income reporting, and eliminate tax incentive programs to increase revenues by an estimated $200 million.
- Replace the gross receipts tax on utilities with a user charge on utility bills. This will be revenue neutral, though those who have not been served by utilities subject to the gross receipts tax in the past will see an increase.

While this program will seem like a tax shock to many, the tax reductions are equivalent to less than 15 percent of revenues. The revenue shifts implied are summarized in Table 1-14, using 1993 amounts as a basis for computation.

IMPACTS ON THE TAX STRUCTURE

This blueprint emerged from the consensus of the Commission that its recommendations for tax restructuring should reflect a new emphasis on economic development and on horizontal equity. Ohio should have a tax structure that attracts investment, and one that offers the same treatment to all investors. This blueprint for long run reform will produce such a structure. The central elements in the program are a reduction in the taxation of

TABLE 1-14
A Blueprint for Tax Restructuring:
Estimated Amounts of Increase and Reduction Implied

Revenue Reductions	**Estimates Based on FY93 Collections[a] (In Millions)**
Eliminate Tangible Personal Property Tax	-1200
Eliminate Net Worth Tax	-200
Eliminate Public Utility Property Tax[b]	-950
Eliminate Gross Receipts Tax on Utility Companies	-650
Introduce User Tax on Utility Consumers	+650
Subject Financial Institutions and Insurance Companies to the Corporate Income Tax	-60
Amount Required for Revenue Neutrality	2410
Revenue Enhancing Options	
Expand Sales Tax Base Include Services, broad base Include Services, narrow base Include food, with a refundable income tax credit	 +600 +150 +400
Raise Sales Tax Rate by 1 percent	+800
Convert the Present Individual Income Tax to a Flat Rate (27.5 percent) tax on a base of Federal Tax Liability	+850
Abolish Enterprise Zones	u
Prohibit Special Tax Incentives to Attract Industry	u
Require Combined Income Reporting	u
Increase Minimum Tax on Corporations to $250	10

Source: Commission (1994).

[a]Data for personal property taxes are for CY92. Estimates marked (u) mean that revenue impact could not be estimated, but the expectation is that it will be positive.

[b]It was not possible to estimate the increase in corporate taxes from the increased coverage of utilities.

returns from capital investments, and the creation of a more competitive environment by subjecting all firms to the same tax treatment.

Economic Development

It is proposed that the net worth tax, the public utility property tax and the tangible property tax all be eliminated. This action would substantially lessen the amount of tax imposed on business machinery, equipment, inventory and capital investment in general, and increase the after tax rate of return to those who would invest in Ohio. The "price" of both capital investment and equity financing will be lowered, and there should be reduced energy costs to residential and non-residential users.

Horizontal Equity

The horizontal equity of the tax system would be improved by eliminating the differential assessment ratios for public utilities and for general business property. It would also be improved by bringing all types of companies under the general business tax, and eliminating special treatment that is presently given to certain public utilities and financial institutions. Enterprise zones and special tax incentives would be eliminated, removing special treatment now received only by beneficiaries of those programs. In addition, the switch from the public utility gross receipts tax to a user charge brings all in-state and out-of-state public utilities to the same competitive basis. Bringing services and possibly food under the sales tax would treat consumers the same, irrespective of the choices of what to buy.

Vertical Equity

The distribution of tax burdens across income classes will change with this reform, but the overall progressivity will not be worsened. The blueprint contains a package of reforms that will benefit middle and upper income families in some cases, and will benefit lower income families in other cases. The secondary effects may be even more significant. An analysis of the short run tax burden effects of the entire program, such as is presented in Table 1-15, does not take into account the benefits that will accrue in the longer run, i.e., the increase in job formation and real income growth in the state.

Nevertheless, one can point out that the short run impacts on tax burden—if this program were to be adopted in its entirety—would not compromise the vertical equity of the Ohio tax system. In fact, the proposed individual income tax reform would remove about 300,000 low income workers from the income tax rolls and would increase the marginal effective tax rate on higher income families. The shift from taxes that are deductible for federal income tax purposes to taxes that are not deductible also introduces a progressive element because itemizers (who can take advantage of these deductions) are higher income families. The elimination of the public utility property tax will benefit some utility consumers and therefore will have a progressive element. The expansion of the sales tax to include food, with a refundable credit, would protect lower income families from the increased tax.

Other changes would move in the opposite direction. This is necessary, and desirable, because one of the objectives of the reform is to increase the return to investors, who tend to be higher income. The reduction of the net worth tax is meant to increase the profitability of corporations, and to provide more rewards to those who invest in Ohio. The same is true of the reduction in the

TABLE 1-15
Tax Burden Shifts and the Blueprint for Reform: Illustrative Short Run Impacts

	Tax Burden Reductions	Tax Burden Increases
Individual Income Tax Restructuring	Approximately 300,000 low income workers would be dropped from the roll	Middle and upper income familes
Increased Sales Tax Rate	---	All consumers
Extend Sales Tax to more Services	---	Consumers of services
Extend Sales Tax to Food with Refundable Income Tax Credit	Low income families receive a rebate for food consumption	Middle and upper income consumers of food
Eliminate Net Worth Tax; Introduce Combined Income Reporting	Capital intensive firms; firms with net losses; small, start up firms[a]	Firms who avoid income tax through transfer pricing[a]
Eliminate Tangible Personal Property Tax	Capital intensive firms, and firms with heavy inventory requirements[a]	---
Eliminate Public Utility Personal Property Tax	All public utilities covered by this tax[a]; utility consumers	---
Eliminate Gross Receipts Tax on Utilities and Replace with User Charge on Consumers	---	Municipal utility company consumers; those who purchase from out-of-state companies

[a]The tax increases and reductions will be borne in some proportion by owners of the company, workers, and consumers of the products produced.

wards to those who invest in Ohio. The same is true of the reduction in the tangible personal property tax and the public utility property tax.

The overall effect of these changes on vertical equity is difficult to exactly measure. This is partly because the exact composition of the reform package is not yet known, e.g., would Ohio voters choose a sales tax rate increase or a food tax with an income tax credit, would the increase in revenues from the business sector be large enough so that the sales tax increases could be less, etc. Even with this uncertainty, however, it does not seem likely that the progressivity of the Ohio tax system would be significantly worsened by any variant of this proposed reform.

Elasticity

The elasticity of the system, i.e., its built-in revenue growth, would be increased by this package of reforms. This happens for two reasons. First, the sales and gross receipts taxes are themselves restructured in ways that lead to a greater elasticity, i.e., a greater revenue response to income increase. The sales tax can become more elastic because of the addition of services to the tax base, and the gross receipts tax becomes more elastic because all utility purchases will be included in the base. The individual income tax, on the other hand, will be less elastic than at present because it will be tied to the indexed federal tax structure.

The second reason for the increased elasticity is the shift in emphasis from the personal property taxes that have lower elasticities to more buoyant sales and income taxes. The net effect of this restructuring is that Ohio tax revenues will increase at a faster rate than under the current system, even given the same rate of growth in the Ohio economy.

Stability

Revenues under the proposed reformed tax structure will be less stable over the business cycle than under the present system. The elimination of the net worth tax and the personal property taxes drops some taxes that grow very slowly but without much fluctuation. Revenues from sales and income taxes, especially corporate income taxes, are more variable over the business cycle. The option of taxing food, if it were chosen, would add some stability to the revenue flow.

Simplification, Administrative Cost and Compliance Cost

The Blueprint for reform would lead to a simplification of the Ohio tax system. This would bring three important benefits. First, the tax structure would be less complex and more understandable by citizens. Second, it would impose less compliance costs on those who pay. Third, it would reduce the administrative effort required by the state tax administration.

- The elimination of the net worth tax and all personal property taxes will reduce administration and compliance costs by a significant amount.
- The real property tax reform would simplify the tax to a simple millage rate levied against full market value. The reduction factors and the rollbacks would be eliminated, and the tax could be understood by taxpayers.
- The individual income tax reform also would introduce a major simplification. Taxpayers will simply calculate federal liability and multiply by a single percentage rate to obtain state income tax liability.
- As many as 300,000 taxpayers would be dropped from the individual income tax rolls.

Against these simplifications, some complexities have been proposed. The extension of sales taxes to the services sector will impose some additional administrative costs on the Department of Taxation, since some services are delivered in complex ways. The same is true of the income tax credit for food consumption, which would also place an additional burden on the tax administration, and would require filing by many low income families. Additional credit filers would tend to offset one of the strong administrative features of the proposed individual income tax—the elimination of many low income families from the tax roll. Finally, there is considerable complexity associated with the requirement of combined income reporting for all corporations. The Commission felt these sacrifices of simplification to the overall goals were unavoidable, and were well within the capabilities of the Ohio Department of Revenue.

Obsolescence

The reform program eliminates some obsolescence from the tax system with three proposed changes. It recognizes competition in the public utility sector by moving utilities under the corporate income tax and by eliminating the differential treatment under the personal property tax. The extension of the sales tax to services recognizes modern consumption behavior. The adoption, implicitly, of a standard deduction and higher exemption for the individual income tax, recognizes the need for a higher tax threshold for low income workers.

Poor Places

A goal of the Commission was the protection of the fiscal condition of poor places. While the Commission was not given a mandate to work on the fiscal problems of individual local governments, or even to consider a restructuring of the general system of state-local fiscal relations, it did recognize the need to scrutinize each of its reform proposals to determine whether they would have a particularly undesirable effect on poor places. The conclusion of the Commission is that this reform would likely benefit poor places, some in the short run but perhaps all in the long run.

The main reason why the budgets of poorer central cities in Ohio have done as well as they have in recent years is the availability of the local income tax, which is levied on residents, employees, and businesses in the city. Despite the obvious gains to merging this with the state income tax (administration and compliance costs), the Commission made no recommendation for change.

The Commission's recommendations will benefit poor places in two ways. The elimination of 300,000 low income workers from the state income tax roll will benefit those locations where the working poor are clustered, and the expansion of the sales tax base to services and food will benefit counties that levy the local option sales tax (though the option of an increased sales tax rate will benefit only the state).

Finally there is the issue of abolishing the personal property tax, a mainstay of the revenue structure of local school districts. The Commission recognizes this change would result in a devastating loss for some school districts, and recommends that all local governments be held harmless for these losses until a more appropriate basis for long term financing can be worked out. The personal property tax is not a suitable way to finance local schools, and the shift to a more elastic source with a more fair distribution of revenues will be a long run benefit to education financing in Ohio.

PHASING IN THE REFORM

This Blueprint for tax reform was designed as a package. The pieces fit together to move the Ohio tax structure to a new emphasis on economic development without compromising equity, fairness and adequacy of revenue yield. Individual components of the proposal make less sense when viewed out of context. The Commission recognizes, however, that this reform cannot be implemented immediately as a single comprehensive package. There are several reasons for this, as noted in the paragraphs below.

Effect on Local Governments

The proposed reform raises major issues in state-local government fiscal relations that need to be worked out. The proposal to eliminate personal property taxes would weigh heavily on some local governments, and the proposal to expand the sales tax base would benefit others disproportionately. Similarly, the property tax simplification has potentially important effects on some local governments. The Commission was not asked to study the distribution effects of such reforms. It would be poor public policy, however, to ignore these effects or to offer patchwork solutions without careful study.

The Commission recommended that the State appoint a study group to develop a long run program for state-local fiscal relations, and for local government taxation. This group would be charged with identifying a program that is consistent with the State's goals for local government finance and is consistent with the blueprint for taxation developed here. In the interim, the Commission recommended that all local governments be held harmless from any revenue loss that resulted from this reform program. Local governments can remain unharmed through a temporary, compensating state assistance program financed from the increased state taxes resulting from this program.

State Government Expenditure Strategy

The State Government must settle on a long run expenditure program before it can decide on the growth rate it wants from its tax system. The reform program proposed here is revenue neutral but provides for a greater elasticity than the present system. The state government may want to adjust this structure depending on estimates of long-term expenditure needs.

Competition in the Public Utility Sector

The motivation for the switch away from the gross receipts tax and personal property tax with a differentially higher tax rate is growing competition. Once utility "monopolies" become competitive, inappropriate tax policy can have important allocative effects and may leave a public utility at a disadvantage relative to competitors. However, a fair question is whether all of the industries currently subject to the gross receipts tax and higher personal property taxes are now "competitive", and if not, how do they rank on the competition scale.

There are two ways of addressing the issue. On the one hand, it is certainly the case that the large bulk of the business done in these industries is still done by the public utilities. There are very few (if any) options for getting power into a house without running through the power lines of the local electric company. The same is true in the natural gas industry. However, there is competition in the purchase of the raw power or the raw natural gas. The amount of purchases from the alternative sources is still very small, but they do exist. If one wants to define a monopoly in terms of some measure of concentration of sales in a particular industry, then the utilities still look very much like a monopoly.

However, one might take the view that a monopoly no longer exits when the "monopolist" must make its pricing and production decision with an eye towards an alternative provider of the same service. This is "virtual competition". This situation exists to some degree in the electric and natural gas industries and it certainly exists in the telecommunications industry. It seems clear that the market in electric and natural gas will develop to the point that pricing and service decisions will become very sensitive to the alternative sources of service which are available.

In short, there is no easy answer to the question about the degree of competition in these industries. However, there is clearly encroachment on these markets, particularly in the telecommunications sector. A reasonable tax policy approach is to phase in the tax reform for public utilities over a period of years.

Tax Administration

Some time must be given to the Ohio Department of Taxation to organize itself to implement the new system, and to work out the inevitable transition problems. A new form of income tax is to be administered, for example, and this will require everything from new forms and instructions to a new taxpayer information service. The introduction of combined income reporting for all corporations, and the expansion of sales taxes to services both will require substantial administrative adjustments, and the switch to a user basis on public utility charges will require changes in collection procedures.

Phase One Reform

The Commission recommended that the State move to adopt a phase one reform, as a first step in implementing this blueprint for tax reform. The Phase One reform would include the following:

1. Elimination of the personal property tax on inventories.
2. Elimination of the net worth tax.

3. The requirement of combined income reporting for all corporations.
4. Reduction of the assessment ratio to 25 percent for new investment by public utilities.
5. Reduction of the assessment ratio on personal property to 25 percent for interexchange companies.
6. Replacement of the gross receipts tax on utilities with an equal yield user charge on consumers.
7. Inclusion of all financial institutions and insurance companies in the corporate tax. Abolish the special taxes on banks, insurance companies and dealers in intangibles.
8. A five year step down of the assessment ratio for public utility property from 88 to 25 percent. These reductions will be returned to rate payers in the form of rate relief.

We have not made exact projections of the amounts of revenue involved in 1995. But using 1993 estimates as a basis, we can estimate that this package would have cost about $800 million (exclusive of the gross receipts tax which will be an even swap with the user charge). There are two options for raising this additional amount. One is to introduce the individual income tax reform, with the appropriate rate. The other is to introduce a sales tax increase, with a combination of base broadening and increased rate.

Other measures that should be undertaken in Phase One include:

1. A study group on local government finance should be appointed to review the system of state local fiscal relations, and local taxation.
2. No new tax abatements should be allowed, either in the form of targeted tax incentives or enterprise zones. Existing enterprise zones should be phased out.
3. The minimum tax on corporations should be increased to $250.

During the Phase Two reform, the balance of the tax plan could be implemented. The personal property tax on utilities would be stepped down and eventually phased out, along with the non-inventory portion of the tangible personal property tax. The State Department of Taxation, the Legislature, the PUCO and the utilities should work together to make these changes over a period of time to meet the Commission's recommendations.

The revenue reductions in phase two would be paid for with increased sales/income taxes and increased business taxes as companies are phased into the corporate net income tax.

CONCLUSIONS AND LESSONS

This is a proposal for a shift in the emphasis of the Ohio tax structure toward economic development. It is prompted by a long period of slow growth in the Ohio economy relative to the rest of the nation, and by the conclusion that the state tax structure has discouraged investment in the past. Ohio has traditionally taxed businesses according to the value of their machines, equipment, inventories, structures, net worth and income. The tax structure is biased against capital intensive industries, the economic mainstay of the state, and startup firms, one of the hopes for the future.

The Commission proposed that the tax structure be changed primarily to enhance the climate for investment and to improve the horizontal equity or fairness of the system. This reform proposes to accomplish these goals by reducing taxes that have suppressed investment, job creation, and the development of necessary infrastructure. It is proposed here to eliminate the personal property taxes on business machinery, equipment and inventories. It is also proposed to eliminate the net worth tax and to replace the gross receipts tax on public utilities with an equal yield user charge. All companies would be brought under a unified corporate net income tax under this reform.

The elimination of the personal property and net worth taxes must be matched by increases elsewhere if this reform is to remain revenue neutral. The proposal is for most of the tax reduction to be made up by a combination of increased income taxation and increased retail sales taxation. The sales tax reform would include a broadening of the tax base primarily to include services and if the voters choose, an increase in the tax rate. In the area of income taxation, a shift to a flat rate tax on a base of federal tax liability is proposed.

Some will say that this is a proposal to shift taxes from businesses to people. This is simply not the case. People already pay these "business" taxes, sometimes in the form of higher prices, sometimes in the form of lower wages, and sometimes in the form of less return on their investment. This tax reform rearranges the burdens among these groups, mostly by removing tax preferences that have been given in the past and by unburdening the sectors of the economy that have been overtaxed.

Some will say that this program is too big a shock for the Ohio tax structure and the Legislature to absorb. In fact, the Commission proposals are for a change in the tax structure that affects less than 15 percent of total taxes. Moreover, a phasing in of the system is proposed to give time to accommodate the difficulties of transition, such as finding alternative sources of finance for local governments.

Some will say that this program for reform is politically naive. That it may be, because good politics was never part of the charge to the Commission.

Had it been a principle concern, the Commission likely would have recommended little change in the tax system. The charge of the Commission was to think about the long run and how Ohio might turn its economic growth path upward; toward one that matches the growth in the rest of the country. Tax policy is not the only ingredient in Ohio's economic development strategy, but it is an important ingredient, and one that needs to be put in better step with the realities of the growing competitiveness of the United States economy.

The Ohio work gives some lessons for other states, and perhaps even some guidance on how to approach comprehensive reform and how to maximize the chances of success. The following are some staff observations, possibly even principles, that are suggested by the Ohio Commission study.

1. The Commission members must become involved in the substantive analysis and Staff must present the analysis at a level that the Commission members can handle. Otherwise, a staff report rather than a Commission report will result. The Ohio Commission worked hard at substance, absorbed the analysis, and formed their own recommendations. Clearly, the final product was a Commission and not a staff report.

2. The Commission must first identify its priorities for reform, based on analysis of present data, and must build its recommendations around the priorities. The Ohio Commission members settled on economic development and horizontal equity as the driving force behind this reform.

3. The membership of the Commission is crucial to the outcome of the work. A Commission more heavily influenced by central city mayors is likely to have a quite different set of priorities than a Commission more heavily influenced by CEOs of large corporations. It is nice rhetoric to say that Commissions should be completely objective, but in reality, few capable state leaders are completely unbaggaged. Perhaps a better rule for those who appoint tax Commissions is to select members to whom they will be willing to listen. If those who appoint the Commission have a general direction for reform in mind, and see a particular problem as dominating the issues, the Commissioners should be like minded. On the other hand, the members should be open minded about alternative routes to accomplish those general objectives, and should not be wedded to any particular reform option. Finally, the Commission membership should represent a broad cross section of the state economy (business, labor, local government, the non-profit sectors, etc.) so as to insure that different perspectives on any given proposal can be gained.

The Ohio Commission did represent a broad cross section of the state economy, and did share a common concern about taxation and economic development as the key issue to be addressed. By vote, they elected this and fairness in taxation as the most important issues to be addressed, and their recommendations reflected this priority.

4. The Commission should be clear about whether its mission is long term and structural, or whether the goal is to offer a revenue package for next year. If the reform is not to be revenue neutral, the Commission mandate must include an evaluation of expenditure needs. The Ohio Commission was to produce a revenue neutral reform and the goal was to identify a structure that would carry the state into the future.

5. Property tax reform is problematic because it is usually linked with school finance. If the mandate of the Commission does not include school finance, it is not likely that a meaningful property tax reform can be structured. This problem occurred in the Ohio work, because school finance was not part of the charge to the Commission. The report contains no concrete recommendation for property tax reform.

6. Staff reports must be heavily empirical and supported by reliable data. This can help the Commission remove myths about the revenue or burden effects of certain reforms, etc. The Ohio work was heavily empirical, based on modern modeling techniques, and supported with data provided by the State Department of Taxation.

7. Staff should evaluate options, but the Commission should choose the reform. This was the approach followed in Ohio. In several instances, the Commission identified new options which staff evaluated, and all of the fiscal recommendations were generated by the Commission.

8. The time and resources allotted the Commission should be commensurate with the assignment. Staff need time to carry out the analysis and the Commission needs time to learn and to absorb the analysis. For a study of this scope, a calendar year would seem a minimum. A further complication in Ohio—that made the time constraint even more binding—was the absence of strong economic base analysis. Those who plan the study need to be realistic about the information base on which the tax study can be built, and the time needed to assemble the basic data.

9. A plan should be developed to involve the press in the work of the Commission. Hopefully, the press will objectively report the work before it takes an editorial position. The Ohio Commission did carry out

a plan to inform the press, but the press made only a modest attempt to educate the public on the tax issues under consideration.

10. Last, and first, key leadership in the state should believe in the importance of the task and in the central premise. The central premise of this report is that Ohio is a state with a weak economic outlook for the long run, and a tax system that discourages investment. It turned out that many state leaders did not share the view that Ohio was a slow growth state, or even that the taxation of investment was undesirable. Such a lack of consensus on the main issue means that the proposed reform program will not come to the fore until time reveals the basic proposition to be true or not.

ENDNOTES

1. Richard Hawkins provided valuable research assistance for this paper, and for the project in general. James Palen prepared several of the tables in this chapter.

2. McHugh (1994a) and Duchi (1994).

3. The indexes shown in Figure 1 represent Ohio's share of the United States in a given time period, relative to Ohio's share in the base period (1969 for this graph). For example, Ohio's personal income accounted for 5.34 percent of the United States total in 1969. In 1970, this share fell to 5.21 percent. The index, therefore, fell from 1.00 to .975.

4. A more detailed description of this shift is given in Duchi, McHugh, and Hawkins, Chapter 2 in this volume.

5. Dearborn (1994), and Chapter 8 in this volume.

6. By contrast, the poverty rate for the entire state, including the central cities, increased by only 1.7 percentage points over this period. The national rate declined by 0.6 percentage points.

7. These forecasts are based on projections developed by the U.S. Bureau of Economic Analysis. The projections are described in some detail in Duchi (1994).

8. The revenue-income elasticity is the percent change in revenues divided by the percent change in personal income, net of any revenue change resulting from discretionary tax rate or base adjustments.

9. Berno and Whitmore (1994), and Chapter 3 in this volume.

10. The ACIR has not made estimates beyond 1991, however, their estimates of taxable capacity have been extended here by regressing the estimated index of taxable capacity on per capita personal income and using the estimating equation to predict taxable capacity for 1992 and 1993. The results show that Ohio's taxable capacity has remained at about 7 percent below the national average.

11. These increases were computed from expenditure data taken from the Census of Governments, deflated by the consumer price index. The real increases for recent

years were 3.96 percent (1991/1992), 4.44 percent (1990/1991), and 3.06 percent (1989/1990).

12. Martinez-Vazquez and Grace (1994), and Chapter 10 in this volume.

13. Fox (1994), and Chapter 4 in this volume.

14. Cornia (1994b), and Chapter 14 in this volume.

15. Wasylenko, Chapter 9, in this volume.

16. Martinez-Vazquez and Grace (1994), and Chapter 12 in this volume.

17. McHugh (1994c).

18. McHugh (1994b), and Chapter 15, in this volume. Also see Case, (1994).

19. Cornia (1994a), and Chapter 13 in this volume.

20. Martinez-Vazquez and Grace (1994), and Chapters 11 and 12 in this volume.

21. McHugh (1994d), and Chapter 16 in this volume.

22. Wasylenko (1994).

23. Martinez-Vazquez and Grace (1994).

24. The marginal effective rates of taxation are calculated by assuming identical pre-tax rates of return for different assets and economic sectors, and calculating after-tax rates of return for each type of investment after all aspects of taxation affecting those investments has been taken into consideration.

25. Fox (1994), and Chapter 4 in this volume.

26. Sjoquist (1994), and Chapter 7 in this volume.

27. Wallace and Edwards (1994), and Chapter 5 in this volume.

28. Fox (1994), and Chapter 4 in this volume.

29. Sjoquist (1994), and Chapter 7 in this volume.

30. Dearborn (1994), and Chapter 8 in this volume.

31. Berno and Whitmore (1994), and Chapter 3 in this volume.

32. The members voted by secret ballot, and in open meeting discussed the results of the vote. Members were given the option of changing their ranking or weighting after they saw the results of the vote, but none exercised this option.

33. For a full discussion and evaluation, see Martinez-Vazquez and Grace, Chapters 10, 11, and 12 in this volume.

34. For a discussion of the problems and advantages of combined income reporting, See Martinez-Vazquez and Grace (1994).

35. For a more detailed analysis, see Cornia, Chapter 14 in this volume

36. For a more detailed analysis, see Cornia, Chapter 13 and McHugh, Chapter 15 in this volume.

37. For a more detailed analysis, see McHugh, Chapter 16 in this volume.

38. For a more detailed analysis, see Wasylenko, Chapter 9 in this volume.

39. For a more detailed analysis, see Grace and Martinez-Vazquez, Chapters 11 and 12 in this volume.

40. For a more detailed analysis, see Fox, Chapter 4 in this volume.

41. For a more detailed analysis, see Wallace and Edwards, Chapter 5 in this volume.

42. For a more detailed analysis, see Sjoquist, Chapter 7 in this volume.

43. For a more detailed analysis, see McHugh, Chapter 6 in this volume.

44. These estimates are based on 1993 data.

2 Economic and Demographic Structure

Mary Laird Duchi, Richard Hawkins, and Richard McHugh

INTRODUCTION

The State of Ohio is in the heartland of the United States. For decades it has been one of this country's major manufacturing centers; a leader in the steel, rubber, and automotive industries. In the past twenty to thirty years, however, major changes have occurred, both in the United States and world economies, altering the environment in which Ohio's industry operates, and in which Ohio's citizens live and work. In the face of those broad forces, the Ohio economy has undergone a dramatic, and not always pleasant, transformation.

This chapter provides an examination of how Ohio has been affected by, and adjusted to the changing world economy. It includes an examination and analysis of the past and current status of Ohio's industry and Ohio's population, and provides a glimpse of a future environment where Ohioans must work to meet new challenges.

Much of this analysis is accomplished by comparing Ohio's performance with the United States, the five states that border Ohio, and five states that have been identified as high growth states and competitors of Ohio. These comparisons are an integral part of several of the sections that follow including:

- Ohio's Population Structure: an examination of population growth, migration, and demographic change;

- Ohio's Economic Structure: an analysis of employment and industrial change;
- International Issues: a discussion of exports and their significance to Ohio's industry;
- Income and Its Distribution: an evaluation of changing personal income in the face of Ohio's changing economic and demographic structure;
- Regional Competitiveness: a review of studies that have evaluated Ohio's competitiveness on a regional and national scale;
- Possible Changes in the Structure of the Economy and Population in the Future: An examination of local, regional, national, and world events that will provide the environment for continued change in Ohio's economy and structure;
- Long-Term Forecasts for Ohio's Population and Economy: an examination of expectations for the future; and
- Concluding Comments.

The information in these chapters provides the basis for understanding the environment upon which the tax structure is overlaid. It also sets the groundwork for understanding how tax policy can be structured as a contributing tool in the growth of an economically competitive Ohio.

OHIO'S POPULATION STRUCTURE

Ohio is the seventh largest state in the United States, with a 1992 population of over eleven million, more than 4 percent of total United States population. Ohio is one of the largest states in the Great Lakes Region, with Pennsylvania being the only neighboring state with a larger population (Table 2-1).

Ohio's population growth has lagged that of the rest of the nation in recent years. In the early post-War period, Ohio held its ground in terms of population relative to the United States and its Midwest partners. Its annual population growth was near the United States average and exceeded that of three of its five neighboring states. More recently, Ohio has joined the rest of the Midwest pack, growing even more slowly than many of its neighbors. In fact, during the 1970-1990 time period, Ohio's rate of growth surpassed only that of Pennsylvania (Table 2-2). Ohio's population growth fared better compared to border states between 1990 and 1994, exceeding Michigan,

TABLE 2-1
Population in the United States, Ohio and its Border States, and the High Growth States, 1994
(In Thousands)

Area	**1994 Population**
United States	260,341
Ohio	11,102
Border States	
Indiana	5,752
Kentucky	3,827
Michigan	9,496
Pennsylvania	12,052
W. Virginia	1,822
High Growth States	
Arizona	4,075
California	31,431
Florida	13,953
Georgia	7,055
Texas	18,378

Source: U.S. Department of Commerce, Bureau of the Census, *Current Population Reports*, series P-25, 1995.

Pennsylvania, and West Virginia, but it still fell far behind that of the United States.

To give a better perspective on economic and demographic trends, similar information for a group of states which have enjoyed healthy expansion in recent years is also presented. Population growth data in the bottom part of Table 2-2 is also presented for five high growth states: Arizona, California, Florida, Georgia and Texas. Clearly, Ohio's recent population growth pales in comparison.

The primary cause of Ohio's low population growth in recent years has been the out-migration of its population. While Ohio was still a net destination state for migrants through 1960, net migration turned negative in the 1960s and net out-migration accelerated in the following decade (Figure 2-1).

TABLE 2-2
Population Change in the United States, Ohio and its Border States, and the High Growth States, 1950 to 1994

Area	Annual Rate of Change (In Percent)			
	1950-1970	1970-1990	1990-1994	1950-1994
United States	1.5	1.0	1.1	1.3
Ohio	1.5	0.1	0.5	0.8
Border States				
Indiana	1.4	0.3	0.9	0.9
Kentucky	0.5	0.7	0.9	0.6
Michigan	1.7	0.2	0.5	0.9
Pennsylvania	0.6	0.0	0.3	0.3
West Virginia	(0.7)	0.4	0.4	(0.2)
High Growth States				
Arizona	4.5	3.7	2.6	3.9
California	3.2	2.0	1.3	2.5
Florida	4.6	3.3	1.7	3.7
Georgia	1.5	1.7	2.0	1.6
Texas	1.9	2.1	1.9	2.0

Source: U.S. Department of Commerce, Bureau of the Census, *Current Population Reports*, series P-25, various years.

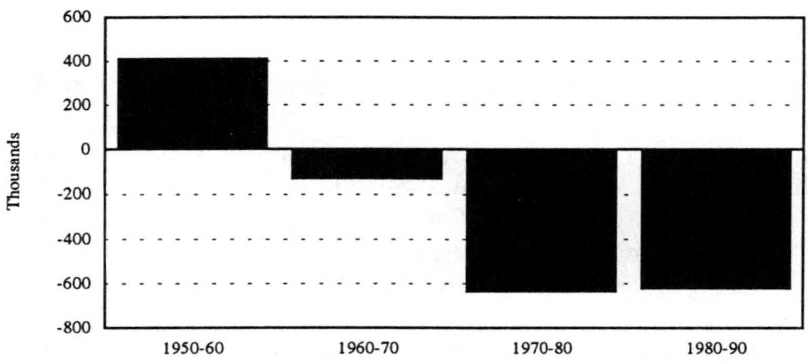

Source: Ohio Data Users Center, *Net Migration Ohio and Counties: 1980 to 1990*, May 1992.

FIGURE 2-1. Ohio's net migration, 1950 to 1990.

This pattern has been a result of the expansion of the western states and the Sun Belt, which presented Ohio with the first of several serious challenges to the state's place of preeminence in the United States economy. During the decade of the 1970s, Ohio's net migratory loss was more than 620,000 persons. This loss, the second largest loss over a decade in Ohio's history, significantly offset the population gained through natural increase (1,616,800) during the same period.

The net out-migration of Ohioans had important impacts on the total population. But given the demographic composition of the out-migrants, the migration also had an effect on the relative age distribution of the state's population. The proportion of the population that is school-age declined at the national level between 1970 and 1994, but that decline was even more pronounced in Ohio (Table 2-3). The increase in the proportion of working age population was roughly comparable at the national and state levels. A much bigger distinction has developed in the 65 years and older population category. The proportion of Ohio's population in this age group increased 4.0 percentage points over this time period (versus 2.8 percentage points for the United States). Ohio has gone from having a smaller proportion of over sixty-five residents in 1970 to a somewhat larger proportion in 1994.

The high growth states fared differently with respect to a shifting age profile between 1970 and 1994. With the exception of Florida, their under eighteen population represents a relatively large share of their population. Clearly Florida and Arizona have experienced an increase in their share of over sixty-five residents but the other high growth states are far below the average concentration for residents over sixty-five. In the forty-five to sixty-four age cohort, the high growth states again find a relatively small proportion of their population. Jointly, this profile means relatively few residents of California, Georgia and Texas have reached their peak earning years. For Ohio, a relatively large share of its population has already reached their peak earning years.

As evidence that this changing relative age distribution is partly attributable to the character of the migrants, migration patterns are shown in Table 2-4 by age group in two decades: the 1950s and the 1980s. In the 1950s, the only age groups experiencing a net out-migration were those over the age of 60, as many in this cohort moved to the sun-belt to retire. Those in prime working age groups migrated into Ohio, particularly as individuals returning from World War II came to the state for educational or employment opportunities.

In the 1980s, Ohio experienced net out-migration for *all* age groups except those aged 75 or over, for whom job opportunities are not a factor. Conversely, people in their late teens and twenties were leaving Ohio, suggesting a difficulty in retaining new entrants to the state's labor force.

Population movements also have created significant population shifts within the state's boundaries. Figure 2-2 displays the relationship between

TABLE 2-3
Age Distribution of the Population: the United States, Ohio and its Border States, and the High Growth States, 1970 and 1994 (In Percent)

Area	Under 18	18-24	25-44	45-64	65 and older
			Age Distribution -1970		
United States	34.3	11.7	23.6	20.6	9.9
Ohio	35.1	11.4	23.6	20.5	9.4
			Border States		
Indiana	35.4	11.7	23.5	19.9	9.5
Kentucky	34.6	12.2	22.7	20.0	10.5
Michigan	36.6	11.6	23.5	19.8	8.5
Pennsylvania	32.6	10.7	22.8	23.2	10.8
West Virginia	33.3	11.2	22.0	22.4	11.1
			High Growth States		
Arizona	36.4	11.9	23.3	19.3	9.1
California	33.3	12.3	25.2	20.2	9.0
Florida	31.1	10.5	22.2	21.6	14.5
Georgia	35.9	12.8	24.4	18.9	8.0
Texas	35.8	12.3	24.0	19.1	8.9
			Age Distribution - 1994		
United States	26.1	9.7	31.9	19.5	12.7
Ohio	25.7	9.7	31.0	20.1	13.4
			Border States		
Indiana	25.6	10.3	31.2	20.1	12.8
Kentucky	25.3	10.5	30.9	20.6	12.8
Michigan	26.6	9.8	31.6	19.6	12.4
Pennsylvania	24.0	9.2	30.4	20.5	15.9
West Virginia	23.5	10.4	28.6	22.1	15.4
			High Growth States		
Arizona	28.0	9.6	30.6	18.5	13.4
California	27.6	9.8	34.1	17.8	10.6
Florida	23.4	8.4	29.7	20.1	18.4
Georgia	26.8	10.3	33.6	19.2	10.1
Texas	28.8	10.4	32.1	18.4	10.2

Source: U.S. Department of Commerce, Bureau of the Census, *Current Population Reports*, series P-25, 1994.

the population living in central cities, suburbs, and rural areas, and the changes that have occurred over the last twenty years. It is evident that Ohio's population concentration in central cities is diminishing, while the proportion of population in suburbs, and rural areas are increasing.

The extent of decline in Ohio's largest cities is obvious from the data in Table 2-5. Columbus was the only large Ohio city to experience a population increase from 1970 to 1990. The city's population increased by 17.2 percent while the Ohio population increased by only 1.8 percent. At the same time,

TABLE 2-4
Trends in Ohio Net Migration, by Age Group, 1950–1990

Age Group	1950-1960 Net Migration		1980-1990 Net Migration	
	Number	Rate (%)	Number	Rate (%)
0-4	26,339	2.4	-10,355	-1.3
5-9	54,908	5.6	-9,131	-1.1
10-14	46,048	5.4	-17,807	-2.3
15-19	28,789	4.4	-79,037	-9.7
20-24	44,542	8.5	-135,726	-15.5
25-29	92,762	18.6	-88,159	-9.4
30-34	74,076	12.5	-27,903	-3.0
35-39	37,098	5.6	-42,979	-4.8
40-44	22,127	3.6	-41,368	-5.2
45-49	20,912	3.8	-26,806	-4.3
50-54	11,136	2.3	-25,001	-4.7
55-59	678	0.2	-24,420	-4.9
60-64	-5,019	-1.2	-36,170	-6.8
65-69	-17,664	-5.0	-33,167	-6.7
70-74	-11,920	-4.4	-25,499	-6.7
75+	-16,207	-4.8	2,487	0.4
Total	408,605	4.4	-621,021	-5.5

Source: Ohio Data Users Center, *Net Migration, Ohio and Counties: 1980 to 1990*, May 1992.

Akron, Cincinnati, Cleveland, Dayton, and Toledo all experienced population declines, with the biggest loss (32.6 percent) occuring in Cleveland.

Eleven of Ohio's eighty-eight counties experienced in-migration population gains from 1980 to 1990, and all were part of either the Columbus or Cincinnati Metropolitan Statistical Areas (MSAs). While these counties in central and southwestern Ohio were growing from in-migration, Cuyahoga County suffered the largest loss from out-migration, with net out-migration of over 146,000 persons.

The extent of out-migration occurring in the Cleveland area can be seen in Table 2-6. The Cleveland Primary Statistical Area (PMSA) lost population in both the 1970s and the 1980s. Moreover, the larger growth for Ohio, relative to both the Cleveland and Cincinnati PMSAs, indicates those two metropolitan areas declined in their population share over the 1970 to 1990 time period.

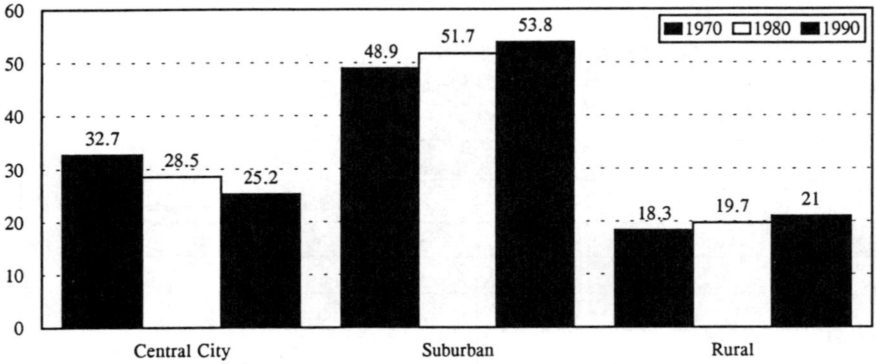

Source: U.S. Department of Commerce, Bureau of the Census, *1970, 1980 and 1990 Census of Population and Housing*, Age, Sex, Ability to speak English, and Disability Tables and authors' calculations.

FIGURE 2-2. Ohio population by Central City, Suburban, and Rural location, 1970, 1980, and 1990.

TABLE 2-5
Population Trends in Ohio and Ohio's Six Largest Cities (Population in Thousands)

	1970	1990	1970-1990 Percent Change
Ohio	10,657	10,847	1.8
Akron	275	223	-18.9
Cincinnati	454	364	-19.8
Cleveland	751	506	-32.6
Columbus	540	633	17.2
Dayton	243	182	-25.1
Toledo	383	333	-13.1

Source: U.S. Department of Commerce, Bureau of the Census, 1970 and 1990 *Census of Population and Housing*, Allocation of Selected Characteristics Tables.

Ohio's migration has impacted the age profiles of its urban and rural population. From Table 2-7, the third and fourth row give the ratio of a given age group's concentration in the urban versus rural areas. In 1970, Ohio's urban areas were more concentrated with forty-five to sixty-four year old people. By 1990, this cohort was more often found in rural Ohio. Since this group represents the largest income earners over the life-cycle, this change has implications for the ability of Ohio's local governments to raise revenue.

TABLE 2-6
Annual Rate of Population Change for Ohio and Ohio's Largest Metropolitan Areas, 1970–1990
(In Percent)

	1970-1980	1980-1990
Ohio	1.3	0.5
Cincinnati PMSA	0.1	0.4
Cleveland PMSA	-0.8	-0.4
Columbus MSA	0.8	1.0

Source: Ohio Department of Development, Ohio Data Users Center, *Ohio Metropolitan Statistical Area Population Counts and Projections by Age and Sex: 1970 to 2015*, July 1993.

Within Ohio's urban areas, the same ratio has been constructed for central cities and suburban populations. The central cities have experienced an increase in their share of young people, under thirty-five, and a decrease in their share of adults over forty-five. These changes have also changed the functional responsibilities and fiscal outlook of local governments.

Another perspective which can characterize the socioeconomic and demographic composition of Ohio's population is the poverty status of its residents (Table 2-8). Ohio has managed to stay below the United States average for the percent of its population below the poverty level. When comparing poverty rates for 1969 and 1989, however, the nation's property rate declined while Ohio's increased. In short, households who stayed in Ohio, had a relatively disadvantaged economic position. Over the same period of time, the experience of Ohio's neighboring states was mixed. The poverty rate increased for four states (including Ohio), and declined for the two most impoverished—Kentucky and West Virginia.

OHIO'S ECONOMIC STRUCTURE

Ohio has long played an important part in the industrial structure of the United States. In its prime, the state was a leader in the steel, rubber, and automotive industries. However, domestic and international events—globalization of the world economy, competition from the Sun Belt, industry restructuring, and major technological developments—deeply affected Ohio's competitive position. Today, Ohio's employment accounts for 4.5 percent of total United States employment, a decrease from 5.3 percent in 1972 (Table 2-9). Total United States employment grew by 21.6 percent between 1972 and 1982 and by 23.0 percent from 1982 to 1993. Ohio managed growth of only 5.1 percent and 18.5 percent in the same time periods.

TABLE 2-7
Distribution of Ohio's Population by Age and Type of Area, 1970 and 1990

	Under 20	20-34	35-44	45-54	55-64	65 and over
1970	0.94	1.07	0.83	0.90	1.11	1.43
1990	1.06	1.23	0.84	0.76	0.86	0.99
1970	0.92	1.12	0.95	1.04	1.07	1.09
1990	0.91	1.17	0.94	0.85	0.98	1.16
Central City 1970	36.8	21.1	10.4	11.3	9.5	10.8
Central City 1990	28.9	27.7	13.4	8.5	8.3	13.2
Urban 1970	37.9	20.5	11.3	11.8	9.0	9.6
Urban 1990	28.1	24.9	14.8	9.9	9.1	13.3
Suburban 1970	39.0	19.7	12.6	12.6	8.5	7.6
Suburban 1990	27.4	22.6	16.0	11.1	9.7	13.3
Rural 1970	41.2	18.3	11.9	11.4	8.4	8.8
Rural 1990	30.8	21.2	15.7	11.7	9.2	11.4

Source: U.S. Department of Commerce, Bureau of the Census, *1970* and *1990 Census of Population and Housing*, Age, Sex, Ability to Speak English, and Disability tables and authors' calculations.

TABLE 2-8
Poverty Rates for the United States, Ohio and its Border States, 1969 and 1989

Area	Percent Below Poverty Level	
	1969	**1989**
United States	13.3	13.1
Ohio	9.8	12.5
Border States		
Indiana	9.5	10.7
Kentucky	22.3	19.0
Michigan	9.2	13.1
Pennsylvania	10.4	11.1
West Virginia	21.8	11.9
High Growth States		
Arizona	14.9	15.7
California	10.8	12.5
Florida	16.0	12.7
Georgia	20.1	14.7
Texas	18.3	18.1

Source: U.S. Department of Commerce, Bureau of the Census, 1970 and 1990 *Census of Population and Housing,* Poverty Status in year of Families And Persons tables

Note: Poverty rate is based on money income, which is adjusted annually. The threshold for 1989 was $6,310 for one person, up to $27,942 for 9 or more persons.

The performance of the Ohio economy has been mixed relative to other states. Between 1972 and 1982, Ohio's employment grew by 5.1 percent. This slow grow exceeded three of Ohio's border states but the growth in Kentucky and West Virginia was 17.7 percent and 12.6 percent respectively.

TABLE 2-9
Total Nonfarm Employment and Employment Growth, the United States, Ohio and its Surrounding States, and the High Growth States, 1972 to 1993

Area	Total Employment (In Thousands)			Employment Growth (In Percent)		Share of U.S. Employment (In Percent)		
	1972	1982	1993	1972-1982	1982-1993	1972	1982	1993
United States	73,675	89,596	110,178	21.6	23.0	100.0	100.0	100.0
Ohio	3,938	4,139	4,905	5.1	18.5	5.3	4.6	4.5
Border States								
Indiana	1,922	2,010	2,589	4.6	28.8	2.6	2.2	2.4
Kentucky	989	1,164	1,534	17.7	31.8	1.3	1.3	1.4
Michigan	3,115	3,189	3,982	2.4	24.9	4.2	3.6	3.6
Pennsylvania	4,400	4,561	5,110	3.7	12.0	6.0	5.1	4.6
West Virginia	541	609	652	12.6	7.1	.7	.7	.6
High Growth States								
Arizona	646	1,029	1,571	59.3	52.7	.8	1.2	1.4
California	7,210	9,825	12,000	36.3	22.1	9.8	11.0	10.9
Florida	2,513	3,762	5,567	49.7	48.0	3.4	4.2	5.0
Georgia	1,695	2,202	3,106	29.9	41.1	2.3	2.5	2.8
Texas	3,884	6,274	7,479	61.5	19.2	5.3	7.0	6.8

Source: U.S. Bureau of Labor Statistics, *Employment and Earnings*, May issues.

Ohio's employment growth, relative to the United States, improved over the 1982 to 1993 time frame, but in both time periods the high growth states experienced far stronger growth. The average annual employment growth rate for Arizona was more than four times that of Ohio between 1972 and 1993, as shown in Figure 2-3.

To better understand a significant cause of the state's relatively poor economic performance, it is useful to examine the industrial structure of the state; that is, which industries employ Ohio's residents, and how the state's employment distribution differs from that of the United States and other states. In Table 2-10, the industrial employment composition of Ohio and the other states is reported.

Today Ohio's economy is still consistent with the strong manufacturing label. The most significant difference between the employment structure of the United States and Ohio is the proportion of employment in manufacturing: 16.8 percent for the United States and 21.7 percent for Ohio. Ohio's employment profile by industry is consistent with its border states (except West Virginia) which also show relatively heavy concentrations of manufacturing employment. In contrast, the employment concentration in the manufacturing sector of the high growth states is significantly lower. Only Georgia meets or exceeds the United States proportion for manufacturing employment, while Florida's manufacturing employment is a low 9 percent of its workforce.

In terms of non goods-producing sectors (excluding mining, manufacturing and construction), Ohio's share of total employment is generally lower than in the United States, although this is largely a function of its high concentration of employment in manufacturing. Ohio's share of total employ-

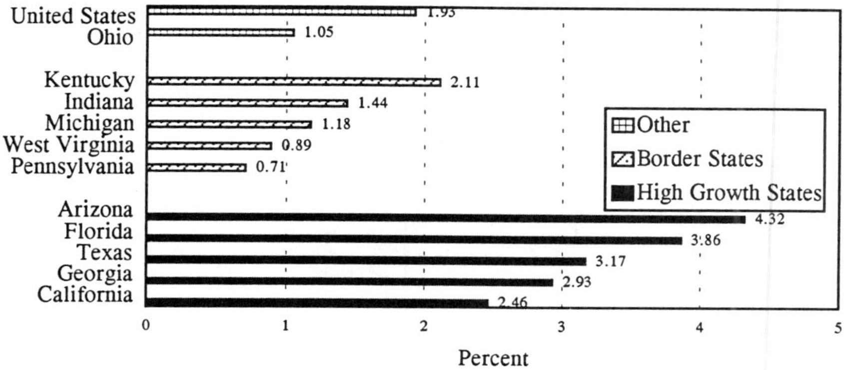

Source: U.S. Bureau of Labor Statistics, *Employment and Earnings*, May issues.

FIGURE 2-3. Annual employment growth rates, the United States, Ohio and its border states, and high growth states, 1972 to 1993.

TABLE 2-10
Proportion of Nonfarm Employment by Industrial Sector
the United States, Ohio and its Border States, and the High Growth States, 1992
(In Percent)

Industries	U.S.	OH	Border States					High Growth States				
			IN	MI	KY	PA	WV	AZ	CA	FL	GA	TX
Mining	0.6	0.3	0.3	0.2	2.0	0.4	4.7	0.8	0.3	0.1	0.3	2.3
Construction	4.2	3.7	4.3	3.3	4.6	3.9	4.4	5.3	3.9	4.9	4.0	4.7
Manufacturing	16.8	21.7	24.7	22.9	19.0	18.7	12.8	11.3	15.6	9.0	18.3	13.3
Transportation and Public Utilities	5.3	4.4	5.1	3.9	5.4	5.2	5.9	5.3	5.0	5.1	6.6	6.0
Wholesale and Retail Trade	23.2	24.0	23.5	23.7	23.5	22.8	22.9	24.8	23.3	26.4	24.9	24.1
Finance, Insurance, and Real Estate	6.2	5.3	5.0	4.8	4.2	5.9	3.9	6.2	6.5	6.6	5.4	5.8
Services	26.7	25.5	21.8	24.8	23.2	29.3	24.7	28.0	28.2	31.6	22.6	25.4
Government	17.0	15.1	15.3	16.4	18.1	13.8	20.7	18.3	17.2	16.3	17.9	18.4

Source: U.S. Bureau of Labor Statistics, *Bulletin 2320* and *Employment and Earnings*, May 1993.

ment in the wholesale and retail trade sector is higher than the United States average and higher than any of the surrounding states. Employment in the narrowly defined service sector is low relative to the United States, but is higher than any of its surrounding states except Pennsylvania. Given the concentrations of elderly in both states, this suggests that health services account for the high proportion of employment in services in these two states. The Finance, Insurance and Real Estate (FIRE) sector is similar, in that the share of total employment in this sector is low relative to the United States, but high relative to the bordering states, exceeding all but Pennsylvania. Each of the high growth states have higher shares than Ohio in this sector.

Ohio's concentration of non-manufacturing employment is particularly low in two sectors: Transportation, Communication and Public Utilities (TCPU) and Government. The share of Ohio employment in TCPU is lower than in the United States and also lower than any of the comparison states: bordering and high-growth states. The picture is essentially the same for government employment's share, where Ohio lies below the United States and all comparison states except Pennsylvania.

One convenient way to characterize and compare the distribution or concentrations of employment among industries is through the use of the "Location Quotient." The Location Quotient, or LQ, is a measure of employment concentration in a given industry relative to some standard, usually the national proportion of employment in that same industry. The LQ for a particular industry in a particular state is calculated here as a ratio, the proportion of a state's total employment in that industry to that proportion in the United States If the proportion for the state is higher than it is for the country, the LQ will be above one and would indicate a specialization or concentration of employment in that industry. For Ohio, the LQ is calculated as the ratio of the percentage in Column 2 of Table 2-10 to Column 1 of that table.

The reliance of Ohio on the manufacturing sector can be seen in Table 2-11. Only two of the broadly-defined sectors for Ohio have a higher proportion of total employment than the United States: the wholesale and retail trade sector, which is just marginally above average, and the manufacturing sector, which has an LQ of 1.29. Ohio's neighbors generally share this pattern: all are close to the national average in wholesale and retail trade while only West Virginia has a manufacturing LQ below one.

In terms of the service sectors, Ohio does not have any special areas of strength. The values for transportation and public utilities, services and finance, insurance, and real estate are all below one. With some exceptions, these low concentrations characterize the region.

The most interesting facet of this table can be found in a comparison of Ohio and its surrounding states with the rapidly growing states. The first set

TABLE 2-11
Location Quotients for Ohio and its Border States, and the High Growth States, 1992
(In Percent)

Industries	OH	Bordering States					High Growth States				
		IN	MI	KY	PA	WV	AZ	CA	FL	GA	TX
Mining	0.50	0.50	0.33	3.33	0.67	7.83	1.33	0.50	0.17	0.50	3.83
Construction	0.88	1.02	0.79	1.10	0.93	1.05	1.26	0.93	1.17	0.95	1.12
Manufacturing	1.29	1.47	1.36	1.13	1.11	0.76	0.67	0.93	0.54	1.09	0.79
Transportation and public utilities	0.83	0.96	0.74	1.02	0.98	1.11	1.00	0.94	0.96	1.25	1.13
Wholesale and retail trade	1.03	1.01	1.02	1.01	0.98	0.99	1.07	1.00	1.14	1.07	1.04
Finance, Insurance and Real Estate	0.85	0.81	0.77	0.68	0.95	0.63	1.00	1.05	1.06	0.87	0.94
Services	0.96	0.82	0.93	0.87	1.10	0.93	1.05	1.06	1.18	0.85	0.95
Government	0.89	0.90	0.96	1.06	0.81	1.22	1.08	1.01	0.96	1.05	1.08

Source: U.S. Bureau of Labor Statistics, Bulletin 2320; and *Employment and Earnings*, May 1993.

of states have a concentration of employment in manufacturing while only one of the rapidly growing states, Georgia, shows such a specialization. Also, the rapidly growing states have specific concentrations in two sectors which have grown strongly in the past twenty years: finance, insurance and real estate and several of the narrowly defined services, including personal, business, health and educational services (Table 2-12). The disparity in the overall concentration of employment in these sectors is a likely factor for explaining the recent performance of these different groups of states.

Although Ohio's level of employment in manufacturing has fallen over recent years, and in fact has fallen faster than it has in the United States, the state has not lost its position as a major concentration of manufacturing employment. The location quotient for manufacturing is presented in Figure 2-4 and shows an increase over the 1980s. The concentration in Ohio relative to the concentration in the United States is currently about equal to the 1976 level. Thus the decline in manufacturing employment was a national phenomena and not a problem unique to Ohio. Because Ohio specialized in this industry and the industry declined nationally in terms of employment, the state suffered disproportionately in terms of total employment relative to low manufacturing states but comparably to those of other manufacturing intensive states.

Examining the rate of growth in individual industries provides additional insight regarding Ohio's economic structure. Although Ohio has a higher proportion of employment in the services than most of its border states and the state's service sector is the fastest growing of all Ohio industries, the border states have generally experienced faster increases in their service sec-

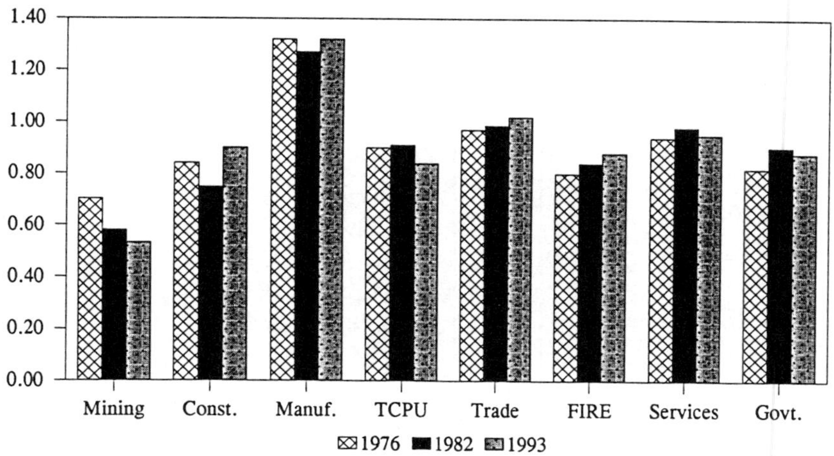

Source: U.S. Bureau of Economic Analysis, *Regional Economic Information System*, 1994.

FIGURE 2-4. Ohio employment specialization indexes, 1976, 1982 and 1993.

TABLE 2-12
Annual Rate of Growth by Industry,
the United States, Ohio and its Border States, and the High Growth States, 1980 to 1992
(In Percent)

Industries	U.S.	OH	Border States					High Growth States				
			IN	MI	KY	PA	WV	AZ	CA	FL	GA	TX
Mining	-3.9	-6.1	-1.8	-4.4	-4.5	-6.4	-6.5	-4.1	-1.7	0.0	2.1	-2.7
Construction	0.4	0.0	1.5	0.8	1.5	0.3	-2.1	0.6	0.8	-0.1	1.3	-1.8
Manufacturing	-0.9	-1.5	-0.4	-1.0	0.3	-2.8	-2.9	1.0	-0.4	0.4	0.4	-0.7
Transportation and public utilities	0.9	-0.5	1.8	0.2	1.4	0.0	-1.0	4.1	.9	1.9	3.0	1.5
Wholesale and retail trade	1.8	1.5	1.9	1.9	2.6	1.3	1.0	3.8	1.9	3.5	3.4	1.7
Finance, insurance and real estate	2.2	1.9	1.8	1.6	1.6	2.0	1.1	4.3	2.0	2.8	3.1	1.9
Services	4.1	3.4	4.2	3.5	4.4	3.6	4.1	6.3	3.9	6.2	5.7	5.3
Government	1.1	0.5	0.7	0.2	1.4	-0.4	-0.1	2.7	1.4	2.9	1.8	2.4

Source: U.S. Bureau of Labor Statistics, Bulletin 2320; and *Employment and Earnings*, monthly, May issues.

tors. As shown in Table 2-12, all border states had higher service sector growth rates than Ohio between 1980 and 1992. Furthermore, the services sectors of the high growth states grew even faster, with four out of five experiencing annual growth rates in excess of 5 percent.

Ohio, the border states, and the high growth states either lost manufacturing employment, or had small increases between 1980 and 1992. Only West Virginia and Pennsylvania experienced a sharper decline in manufacturing than Ohio. Kentucky fared well for the region with a slight manufacturing increase during the period.

Ohio's loss of manufacturing employment occurred in a diverse group of industries, including both durable and nondurable good producers. Many of the industries experiencing the greatest job losses are traditional Ohio industries who produce primary metal products and industrial machinery (Table 2-13).

For confidentiality reasons, employment data are not available on all detailed sectors but the wide range of growth rates demonstrates the different directions Ohio's manufacturing economy moved during the period. Medical instruments and commercial printing are but two examples of nontraditional Ohio manufacturers who experienced strong growth during the period.

Some high employment sectors did not fare well during the 1984 to 1992 period. Motor vehicle and equipment manufacturing (SIC 371) employed close to 100,000 people in 1984 and, its employment declined by 7.4 percent through 1992. This sector's decline was about the same as Ohio's total manufacturing decline. Metal forging firms (SIC 331) employed over 40,000 in 1992 but this represented only about 86 percent of 1984's employment. Blast furnace specialist (SIC 331) faced an extremely tough employment market, their industry declined more than 24 percent over the late 1980s and early 1990s.

In spite of Ohio's loss of manufacturing employment, manufacturing industries are still a leading source of wealth and economic output. Several of Ohio's manufacturing industries grew over the decade of the 1980s, led by plastics products which increased more than 20,000 employees, between 1983 and 1989. Those manufacturing industries with the greatest employment increases are shown in Table 2-14. Several of the industries suffered job losses with the recession of the early 1990's, but still remain important employers.

With the employment shift in the United States towards services, Ohio's relative successes and failures in both the service sector and the finance, insurance and real estate (FIRE) sectors are important. In the FIRE sectors, Ohio experienced strong growth in some areas and slow growth in others. Strong service sector growth has occurred in business services but also in repairs and personal services, see Table 2-15. The increased trend to "out-

TABLE 2-13
Employment Growth in Selected Manufacturing Industries: United States and Ohio, 1984 to 1992

SIC	Industry	U.S. Growth 1984-1992 (In Percent)	Ohio Growth 1984-1992 (In Percent)	1992 Ohio Employment (In Thousands)
	Total Manufacturing	-6.0	-7.2	1,046,964
384	Medical instruments and supplies	67.8	111.2	10,972
359	Misc. machinery, except electrical	13.0	34.4	25,603
275	Commercial printing	17.6	25.7	31,641
203	Preserved fruits and vegetables	0.1	13.2	10,295
347	Misc. metal services	3.8	12.9	10,844
382	Measuring and controlling devices	17.9	12.3	15,580
265	Paperboard containers and boxes	2.1	8.3	13,043
354	Metalworking machinery	6.0	7.9	38,818
367	Electronic components and accessories	-13.4	1.9	10,400
344	Fabricated structural metal products	-2.1	-0.6	23,654
271	Newspapers	0.6	-3.0	16,882
355	Special industry machinery	-5.1	-5.8	14,303
371	Motor vehicles and equipment	-8.1	-7.4	92,678
349	Misc. fabricated metal products	-3.6	-11.1	21,558
346	Metal forgings and stampings	-7.5	-13.9	40,064
358	Refrigeration and service machinery	-2.1	-16.4	15,338
363	Household appliances	-23.3	-16.8	14,486
362	Electrical industrial apparatus	-16.9	-19.2	14,388
356	General industrial machinery	-15.4	-19.6	23,577
331	Blast furnace and basic steel products	-24.4	-24.3	39,271
372	Aircraft and parts	8.2	-24.4	27,224
364	Electric lighting and wiring equipment	-13.0	-27.0	12,347
342	Cutlery, hand tools and hardware	-12.4	-27.5	10,008
353	Construction and related machinery	-23.8	-41.5	11,069

Source: U.S. Department of Commerce, Bureau of the Census, *County Business Pattersn*, 1984 and 1992 editions, Ohio and the United States issues, 1986 and 1994.

sourcing" by large employers over the period, however, probably accounted for some of the strong growth.

Employment growth in several FIRE sectors from 1984 to 1992 is also portrayed in Table 2-15. The state grew faster than the United States in banking, insurance agencies and real estate agency employment over the

TABLE 2-14
Ohio Manufacturing Industries with the Largest Employment Increases, 1983 to 1989

SIC	Industry	Employment Increase
3079	Plastics Products (3081-89; 3432)	20,471
3494	Industrial Components	6,950
3465	Automobile Stampings	6,018
2752	Commercial Printing Lithographic	4,739
3549	Special Machinery	3,558
3069	Industrial Products	3,133
3842	Surgical Appliances	3,076
3369	Rubber and Metal Products	2,821
3483	Ammunitions, except for Small Arms	2,532
3544	Special dies, tools, jibs and fixtures	2,505

Source: Ohio Department of Development, *Ohio Economic Competitiveness Project*, March 1993.

period. Ohio grew more slowly in security and other brokers, insurance carriers and holding companies.

Firms in the FIRE sector face different Ohio taxes specific to the type of service they perform. The rates in Ohio, as compared to other states, may account for the different employment growth patterns observed. Thus, this sector is an area where tax policy directly affects which job opportunities are available to Ohioans. Martin Grace reviews these numerous taxes in Chapter 12 of this volume and compares their levels in Ohio with similar taxes throughout the region: including retaliatory taxes in the insurance sector and the net worth taxes on banks in Ohio.

General service sector employment growth is also evident. Personal, repair and business services in Ohio grew faster than in the United States. Numerous other services, however, including medical and legal, did not keep pace with the faster national employment growth. One interesting group of services, entertainment, uniformly grew poorly. These services, including motion pictures, amusements and museums, would not be expected to expand as rapidly as the national total in a state with slow population growth.

Not only does the service sector account for the greatest number of jobs,

TABLE 2-15
United States and Ohio Finance, Insurance and Real Estate and Service Sector Employment Growth, 1984 to 1992

SIC	Industry	U.S. Growth 1984 to 1992 (In Percent)	Ohio Growth 1984 to 1992 (In Percent)	1992 Ohio Employment (In Thousands)
60	Banking	37.5	64.7	89,773
61	Credit agencies other than banks	-34.7	-44.6	17,969
62	Security and commodity brokers and services	28.1	16.4	8,017
63	Insurance carriers	26.4	16.5	65,910
64	Insurance agents, brokers and services	22.7	23.7	22,948
65	Real Estate	26.1	30.2	48,867
67	Holding and other investment companies	47.5	34.1	8,002
70	Hotels and other lodging places	25.1	8.5	35,335
72	Personal services	19.8	24.9	61,267
73	Business services	39.5	57.7	226,880
75	Auto repair, services, and garages	37.5	35.5	36,691
76	Miscellaneous repair services	23.8	39.6	19,943
78	Motion pictures	128.8	82.7	13,083
79	Amusement and recreation services	52.1	38.6	43,111
80	Health services	56.8	42.1	463,622
81	Legal services	47.5	38.4	30,336
82	Educational services	30.0	23.1	71,208
83	Social services	63.1	62.2	86,199
84	Museums, botanical, zoological gardens	112.3	83.4	3,977
86	Membership organizations	35.3	29.3	94,971
89	Miscellaneous services	-93.3	-92.8	2,502

Source: U.S. Department of Commerce, Bureau of the Census, *County Business Patterns*, 1984 and 1992 issues, Ohio and the United States, 1986 and 1994 editions.

it also generates the greatest number of *new* jobs each year. The service industry includes a number of diverse activities, including health, educational, personal and business services. In Table 2-16 it is evident that the health industry is a dominant force. The combination of several health-related services (office and clinics, nursing facilities, hospitals, home and health care services, health and allied services), accounts for over 420,000 jobs—more jobs than Ohio has in construction, transportation and public utilities, or finance, insurance, and real estate.

Growth Projections

Services are expected to be the strongest growth sector through the rest of this decade as well, accounting for one-half of the new job growth of

TABLE 2-16
Ohio Service Industries with More than 10,000 Employees in 1992

SIC Code	Service Industry	Employees
8061	Hospitals	221,410
8051	Nursing and personal care facilities	100,544
8011	Offices and clinics of medical doctors	65,787
7363	Health supply services	69,175
8661	Religious organizations	51,312
8221	Colleges and universities	42,922
7349	Building maintenance services, n.e.c.	35,562
7011	Hotels and Motels	33,556
8101	Legal services	30,336
8021	Offices and clinics of dentists	24,044
8331	Job training and related services	21,100
8711	Engineering services	21,609
7389	Business services, n.e.c.	21,139
7231	Beauty Shops	19,717
8721	Accounting, auditing, and bookkeeping	20,862
8211	Elementary and secondary school	20,970
8321	Individual and family services	19,590
7381	Detective and armored car services	18,028
8641	Civic and social associations	18,106
8631	Labor organizations	16,903
8361	Residential care	19,340
8351	Child day care services	14,708
8091	Health and allied services, n.e.c.	12,123
8741	Management services	12,011
8081	Home and health care services	14,083
7361	Employment agencies	10,647
7374	Data processing and preparation	11,054
7997	Membership sports and recreation clubs	11,198

Source: U.S. Department of Commerce, Bureau of the Census, *County Business Patterns, 1992, Ohio*. November 1994.

Note: n.e.c. is the Department of Commerce abbreviations for not otherwise classified.

about 500,000 new jobs between 1991 and 2000, as shown in Figure 2-5. Total job growth in Ohio, which had averaged 1.9 percent per year between 1970 and 1991, is expected to slow to an average of 1.2 percent annually through the year 2000 along with an expected national slowdown in job creation. This outlook for slower growth can be attributed primarily to a lower rate of labor force expansion expected over the next decade due to demographic factors.[1]

As was the case during the 1980s, health services are expected to continue their importance with respect to Ohio's employment growth, adding an estimated 91,400 new jobs between 1991 and 2000 (almost 20 percent of total job growth). Another class with rapid expected growth is business services, a component of which, computer and data processing services, is expected to be one of Ohio's fastest growing individual industries to the year 2000 with a 5.4 percent annual rate of growth.

Wholesale and retail trade will strengthen Ohio's job growth as well, with eating and drinking establishments alone adding 46,700 new jobs. Other areas of expected growth include general merchandise stores, automotive dealers and service stations, apparel and accessory stores, and miscellaneous retail stores.

Employment in the manufacturing industry is expected to hold steady over the decade, but not grow substantially. Productivity increases from additional capital investment will constrain the growth in new manufacturing jobs, in spite of expected output increases over the upcoming years. Anticipated declines in defense spending is another important factor in expected declines to the manufacture of durable goods.

Earnings

Unlike the United States, where transportation and public utilities, fol-

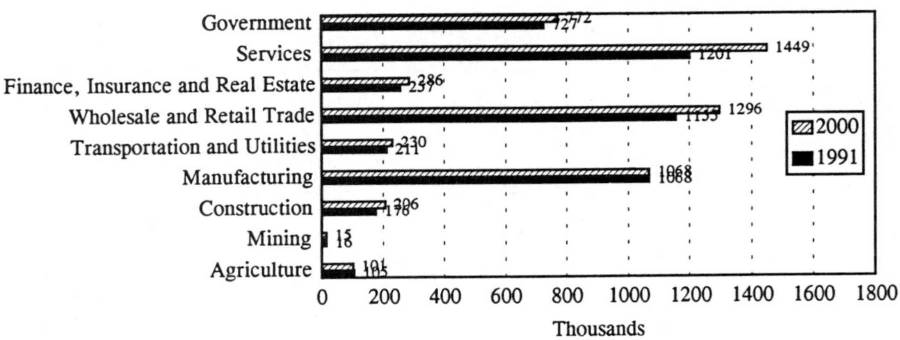

Source: Ohio Bureau of Employment Services, *Labor Market Projections, Ohio Projections,* 1991 and 2000, 1993.

FIGURE 2-5. Ohio industrial employment and projections, 1991 and 2000.

lowed by federal civilian government, have the highest average earnings of any major sector, manufacturing earnings dominate all of Ohio's sectors, as shown in Table 2-17. In fact, the average earnings for Ohio's manufacturing sector are 10 percent above the United States average. In most of the other sectors, Ohio is within 5 percentage points of the United States average, excepting mining, retail trade, and finance, insurance, and real estate. The biggest earnings discrepancy is in the finance, insurance, and real estate sector, where Ohio earnings are only 79 percent of the United States average. This figure should be interpreted with some caution, however, since this sector includes many real estate agents, whose earnings are notoriously variable in an industry with many part-time and secondary workers.

In 1970, the average Ohio worker earned five percent more than the average United States worker. The advantage has dissipated over the twenty-two year period covered by the table but manufacturing has remained strong. Significant declines have occurred in the mining, construction and transportation and public utilities sectors where earnings advantages are no longer observed.

Occupational Structure of Employment

The occupational structure of the workforce provides another perspective from which to describe Ohio's economy and to compare it with that of

TABLE 2-17
Average Earnings by Industrial Sector, Ohio and the United States, 1992

Sector	United States	Ohio	Ohio as a Percent of the U.S.	
			1992	1970
Mining	$31,223	$26,695	85	111
Construction	27,646	25,881	94	108
Manufacturing	33,010	36,471	110	109
Transportation and Public Utilities	34,007	32,466	95	101
Wholesale Trade	32,371	32,858	101	105
Retail Trade	14,239	12,878	90	98
Finance, Insurance, and Real Estate	21,151	16,640	79	91
Services	23,091	21,578	93	96
Government: Federal Civilian	33,636	35,269	105	107
Government: State and Local	25,439	24,633	97	93
Total Nonfarm Earnings	24,472	24,119	99	105

Source: U.S. Bureau of Economic Analysis, *Regional Economic Information System*, 1994.

the United States Consistent with the industrial structure of the state and its manufacturing concentration, a larger share of Ohio's population is employed as operators, fabricators, and laborers than is true of the overall United States. Further, Ohio has a slightly larger percentage than average in precision production occupations and craft and repair operations. On the other hand, Ohio has lower than average employment in the managerial and professional specialty occupations, which are among the higher earning occupations, as shown in Figure 2-6 and Table 2-18.

Overall, Ohio's occupational structure is expected to change very little over the 1990s. One significant change is the expectation of an above-average growth rate for several occupations requiring relatively higher levels of education or training, as shown in Table 2-18. The annual growth projections show increasing proportions of managerial, professional, para-professional, and technical workers. These major groups, which represented approximately one-fourth of total employment in 1991, are expected to account for two-fifths of the increase in employment between 1991 and 2000.[2] At the same time, many of the occupations that are expected to generate new jobs are among the lower paid service occupations, including food preparation, nursing aids and cashiers from Table 2-19.

The Cyclical Nature of Ohio Employment

It is important to understand the existing structure of the state's economy and the previous analysis of current and past employment structure affords us this picture. However, in addition to the long term structural direction of the Ohio economy, the cyclical nature of the economy is particularly important in the context of fiscal reform. Taxes vary in their stability over the busi-

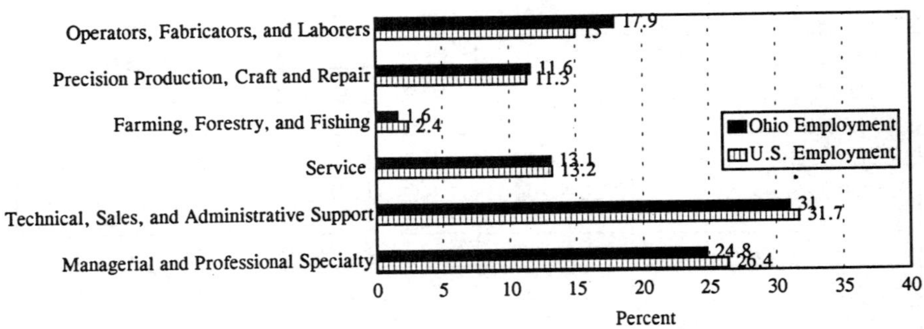

Source: U.S. Department of Commerce, Bureau of the Census, *1990 Census of Population,* Occupation of Employed Persons Tables.

FIGURE 2-6. Distribution of employment by occupation, Ohio and the United States, 1990.

TABLE 2-18
Ohio Mean Earnings by Occupation, 1989 and Projected Increases to 2000

Occupation	1989 Mean Earnings	Projected Annual Growth 1991-2000 (In Percent)
Managerial and professional specialty occupations	$29,301	1.5
Technical, sales, and administrative support occupations	15,406	1.4
Service occupations	8,031	1.5
Farming, forestry, and fishing occupations	10,107	0.1
Precision production, craft and repair occupations	22,189	1.0
Operators, fabricators, and laborers	16,425	.3

Source: Office of Strategic Research, Ohio Department of Development, July 1994; Ohio Bureau of Employment Services, *Labor Market Projections, Ohio Projections*, 1991-2000, 1993.

TABLE 2-19
Ohio Occupations with the Largest Projected Employment Increase, 1991 to 2000

Occupation Title	Projected Annual Growth
Salespersons, Retail	2,561
Registered Nurses	2,226
Cashiers	1,856
Nursing Aides and Orderlies	1,759
General Office Clerks	1,519
General Managers and Top Executives	1,454
Food Preparation and Service	1,452
First Line Supervisors, Sales	1,232
All Other Managers	1,210
Truck Drivers, Heavy	1,040

Source: Ohio Bureau of Employment Services, *Labor Market Projections, Ohio Projections 1991-2000*, 1993.

ness cycle and thus the revenue potential of certain taxes is sensitive to business cycle fluctuations.

Historically, Ohio has demonstrated high cyclical volatility. That is, Ohio's economy has reacted more strongly than the United States economy to business cycles. Somewhat less volatile experiences of the 1990s were encouraging but may not continue.

There are many different available measures for the cycle of the national or a state economy, but one of the most important and easily understood is the total number of nonfarm payroll jobs. Other measures typically cited are the unemployment rate or the level of retail sales, but each of these is considered to be fundamentally determined directly by total jobs. Therefore, we will use nonfarm payroll employment as our indicator of the length and depth of a recession's impact on the United States and Ohio economies.

Comparable local and regional employment data on a monthly basis are available only from 1976 forward. During that time period, the United States economy has experienced three recessions. In each of these recessions, the Ohio economy has performed worse than the rest of the United States. Generally, as demonstrated in Table 2-20, the Ohio economy has fallen into a recession earlier than the United States economy, it has lasted longer than the rest of the nation and it has fallen further. In the first recession, Ohio's employment level peaked earlier than the United States (five months earlier) and reached its trough later (seven months later). The drop in employment was much steeper than in the United States, falling a full 6 percent, versus just 1.4 percent in the nation.

During the second recession in the early 1980s, the peak in employment level in Ohio occurred during the same month as the country's but the state's

TABLE 2-20
Impact of Recent Recessions on Employment, Ohio and the United States

	Employment Peak Month	Employment Trough Month	Peak to Trough Length (In Months)	Employment Decrease (In Percent)
Recession I				
U.S.	March 1980	July 1980	4 months	-1.4
Ohio	October 1979	February 1981	16 months	-6.0
Recession II				
U.S.	July 1981	November 1982	16 months	-3.0
Ohio	July 1981	February 1983	19 months	-9.7
Recession III				
U.S.	June 1990	February 1992	20 months	-1.7
Ohio	June 1990	April 1991	10 months	-2.0

Source: U.S. Bureau of Labor Statistics, *Current Establishment Survey (BLS-790 data tape)*, 1995.

employment bottomed out three months later than the nation's, again indicating that the recession lasted longer in Ohio. During this event, Ohio's drop in employment was much steeper than the nation's, falling by more than three times the rate of national decline.

In the most recent recession, Ohio did not perform nearly as poorly relative to the United States as it had in the previous recessions. The peak employment month prior to this recession matched that of the nation. Interestingly, the low point in terms of Ohio employment was reached ten months prior to that in the nation as a whole. However, the drop in employment was again steeper in Ohio relative to the United States

In summary, recessions appear to have stronger impacts in Ohio than in the nation, lasting longer and bringing on deeper declines in employment. In the most recent recession, Ohio's employment decline, was greater than the United States decline, but not considerably worse, as it had been in earlier recessions.

Ohio's business cycle sensitivity is shown in Figure 2-7 with unemployment data. Note that the state's unemployment rate exceeded that of the United States during economic downturns of the mid and early 1970s, and the early 1980s. Similarly, expansions of the economy brought unemployment rates that were consistently below those of the United States Such volatility is a characteristic of an economy dominated by manufacturing employment.

Since the late 1980s, however, the state has demonstrated less volatility and Ohio's unemployment rate has been below the national average every year starting in 1991 and in ten of the last fourteen months. One could be tempted to say that the declining dominance of manufacturing in Ohio has caused a decrease in business cycle sensitivity. Other factors may have

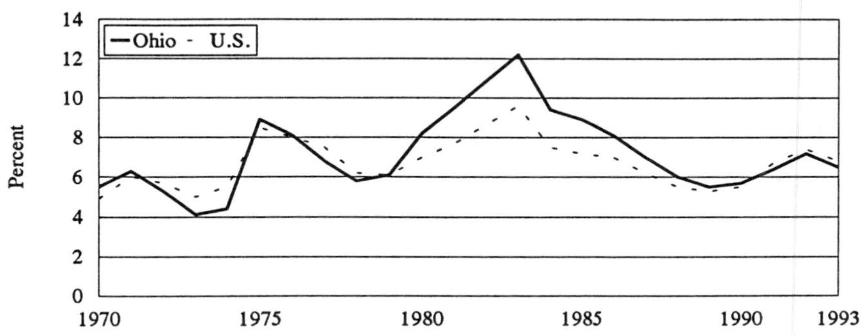

Source: Estimated in Cooperation with the U.S. Department of Labor

FIGURE 2-7. Ohio and the United States unemployment rates, 1970 to 1993.

caused this stability, however, namely, one time expansions of exports and lower concentrations of employment in the construction industry. These two ameliorating factors could well be temporary. More significantly, the Ohio economy still has above average manufacturing employment. Thus, below average business cycle sensitivity cannot be expected in the future.

Another key economic structure issue important for tax policy purposes is the number of business starts and terminations. On a national basis business failures averaged 14.5 percent of business starts in 1991 and 1992. For Ohio, the average was only slightly higher at 14.7 percent.[3] Data published by the State of Ohio provide more detail. Figure 2-8 indicates the history of starts, terminations, and net formations of new business. As can be seen in the figure, the number of new business starts consistently exceeded the terminations with the exception of the 1991 recession year where starts and failures are remarkably close. New starts have ranged from a low of about 22,758 in 1983 to a high of 28,854 in 1993. Terminations have fluctuated from a low of 17,874 in 1983 to a high of 25,365 in 1991. Net formations of new businesses has averaged about 3,300 new businesses each year since 1983. The largest number of net new businesses occurred in 1987 with more than 5,800 and the fewest occurred in 1991 when net formations were about 650 businesses. However, over the foreseeable future, an average of 3,000 to 4,000 net new businesses can be expected. Thus, the number of new businesses should not significantly change the make-up of Ohio's economy for many years.

In summary, the Ohio economy is characterized by employment specialization in manufacturing. Although manufacturing employment has declined in Ohio, this appears to be part of a national trend associated with higher productivity due to technological advances and increased competi-

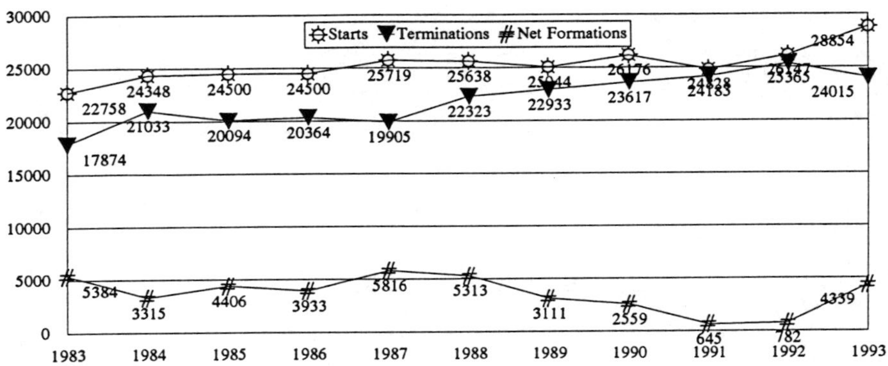

Source: State of Ohio, Bureau of Workers' Compensation, *Risk Master Files*, various years.

FIGURE 2-8. Business starts, terminations, and net formations, 1983–1993.

tion from abroad, rather than a case of general manufacturing employment migration to other regions of the country, as evidenced by the general declines in manufacturing employment in the United States overall, and in many other states. The Ohio economy is growing, although more slowly than most border states and all high growth states. Some major manufacturing sector growth successes can be cited, particularly plastics products, industrial components, and automotive stampings, each of which increased employment by more than 5,000 jobs between 1983 and 1989. The service industry has been a significant contributor to Ohio's overall job growth—with the health care industry, religious organizations, building maintenance services, and computer services each increasing employment by more than 10,000 between 1983 and 1989. The state's business cycle sensitivity has been historically high and can be expected to remain so despite a recent relatively stable recession. Finally, while Ohio has a history of new business starts, the growth has been tempered by business failures and cannot be expected to dramatically change the economic structure.

INTERNATIONAL ISSUES

Ohio manufacturers play an important role in international trade as the state ranked seventh in 1992 exports and is responsible for 4.1 percent of the country's total exports. Although Ohio's manufacturing exports are large, the focus of Ohio's industries is more national than foreign (i.e., many suppliers and customers are in Ohio). As a result, the ratio of exports to total shipments is relatively small compared to other states. Ohio ranks highly in nominal exports and export growth, but the state's export intensity (exports as a percent of manufactures shipments) is low. As shown in Table 2-21, Ohio's export intensity, defined as the share of its total manufacturing output destined for overseas markets, is below all of the "high growth states", the national average, and two of its border states.

From 1990 to 1992, Ohio's share of total exports has grown, with an annual average growth rate of 7.5 percent versus the national rate of 6.7 percent, from Table 2-22. The state's 1992 total exports of $18.3 billion were exceeded in the region only by Michigan, although Ohio's export growth rate was more than twice that of Michigan and higher than any other border state except Pennsylvania. High export growth rates are clearly one of the hallmarks of a high growth state region as all but Florida have growth rates that surpass those of Ohio and its border states. The country's two leading export states, California and Texas, are included in the "high growth state" classification.

Although 10 percent of the state's manufacturing output may seem to indicate that international trade is not an important factor driving the Ohio

TABLE 2-21
Export Intensity
(In Millions of Dollars)

State	(a) 1991 Exports	(b) 1991 Value of Manufacturers Shipments	(a)/(b) Export Intensity (In Percent)
United States	421,853	2,826,207	14.9
Ohio	16,880	174,928	9.6
Border States			
Indiana	6,438	97,282	6.6
Kentucky	3,576	53,500	6.7
Michigan	23,176	143,103	16.2
Pennsylvania	11,290	134,022	8.4
W. Virginia	1,784	12,474	14.3
High Growth States			
Arizona	5,474	22,983	23.8
California	63,113	289,613	21.8
Florida	17,595	59,275	29.7
Georgia	8,083	82,765	9.8
Texas	47,008	204,002	23.0

Source: U.S. Bureau of the Census, *Annual Survey of Manufactures*, 1992; MASSPORT Trade Development Unit, as reported by the Ohio Data Users Center, in *1992 Exports with Ohio as State of Origin of Movement*, 1993.

economy, this data masks a very important characteristic of the Ohio economy; specifically, the industry's high degree of vertical integration. Many of the input requirements for the state's export industries are filled by other Ohio firms. When these indirect effects of international trade are taken into account, the importance of trade to the state is clearly greater. And, as indicated earlier, the importance of international markets is growing more rapidly in Ohio than in the nation as a whole. In industries dominant in the Ohio economy, e.g., chemicals, primary metals, fabricated metal products, and machinery, indirect requirements are an unusually high proportion of the total value of the industry's shipments. Increases in exports of final products from Ohio also have favorable implications for other Ohio manufacturers.

TABLE 2-22
Exports by Origin, the United States, Ohio and its Border States, and the High Growth States

State	1990 (In Millions of Dollars)	1992 (In Millions of Dollars)	Growth Rate (In Percent)
United States	392,975	447,471	6.7%
Ohio	15,851	18,321	7.5
Border States			
Indiana	6,359	6,829	3.6
Kentucky	3,800	4,069	3.5
Michigan	20,919	22,454	3.6
Pennsylvania	10,431	12,071	7.6
W. Virginia	1,731	1,859	3.6
High Growth States			
Arizona	4,709	6,600	18.4
California	58,430	68,906	8.6
Florida	16,258	18,746	7.4
Georgia	7,211	8,999	11.7
Texas	41,355	49,901	9.9

Source: MASSPORT Trade Development Unit, as reported by the Ohio Data Users Center, in *1992 Exports with Ohio as State of Origin of Movement*.

Note: Export data are valued on a free alongside ship (f.a.s.) basis, which is lower than export shipment estimates based upon freight on board (f.o.b.) basis. All export data reflect shipments from Ohio ports and not necessarily goods produced in Ohio.

To understand trends in export activity in any region, it is important to understand the trade patterns for a particular region. For Ohio firms, this includes the specific destination countries, since the strength in Ohio's exports will ultimately depend on the strength of these economies.

Ohio has a broad network of trading partners; firms in the state exported to 189 countries in 1992. From Figure 2-9, however, it is evident that Canada is Ohio's overwhelming export partner. The volume of shipments to Canada comprised more than 40 percent of the value of Ohio's total exports. The state's next largest trading partners, France and Japan, are far behind Canada in this regard.

One significant difference between Ohio's export economy and the exports of the United States is the importance of Mexico. Mexico is the third largest importer of United States goods, responsible for almost 10 percent of United States exports. It ranks fifth for Ohio, and is responsible for only 3.9 percent of Ohio's exports. However, Ohio exports to Mexico have grown rapidly, increasing by more than 60 percent between 1990 and 1992.

Another important piece of information to illustrate trends in Ohio's exports is the industrial composition of the state's exports. Just five industries accounted for more than 75 percent of Ohio's exports in 1992. Transportation equipment is the most important export for the Ohio economy, from Table 2-23. It is also the leading export industry for the United States, but the country's reliance on transportation exports is not as great as it is for Ohio. As can be seen in Figure 2-10, industrial machinery, chemicals and allied products, fabricated metal products, rubber and miscellaneous plastic products, and, to a lesser extent, primary metal industries are also proportionately more important to Ohio than to the United States as a whole. Electronic equipment and instruments and related products, on the other hand, represent a higher proportion of United States exports than Ohio exports. Agricultural products-crops and food and kindred products are among the top eight export industries for the United States, but not for Ohio.

Not only do the industries in Table 2-23 dominate Ohio's exports but they have been the primary source of export growth. Exports of all Ohio industries grew by an average annual rate of 7.5 percent between 1990 and 1992.

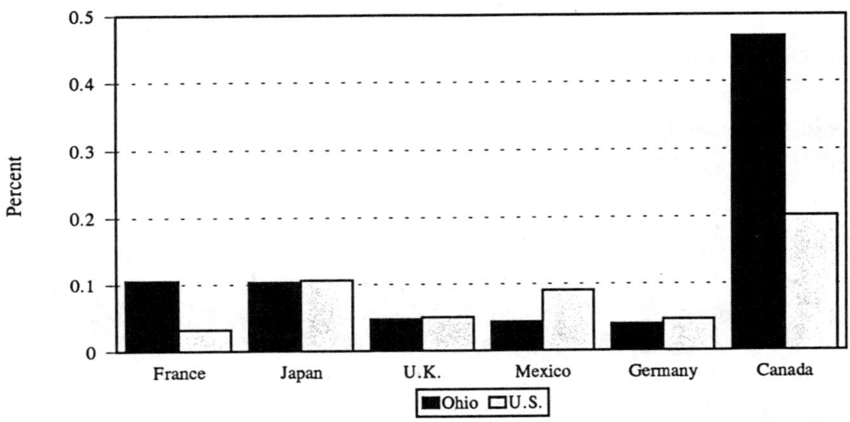

Source: Ohio Data Users Center, *1992 Exports with Ohio as State of Origin of Movement,, 1993.*

FIGURE 2-9. 1992 export share with selected export partners, Ohio and the United States.

TABLE 2-23
Ohio's Leading Manufacturing Export Industries, 1990 and 1992

Largest Ohio Export Industries	1990 Value of Exports (In Millions)	1992 Value of Exports (In Millions)	1992 Share of Ohio Exports (In Percent)	1990-1992 Growth Rate (In Percent)
Transportation Equipment	$5,405	$6,433	35.1	19.0
Industrial and commercial machinery, computer equipment	3,028	3,387	18.5	11.9
Chemicals and allied products	1,711	2,095	11.4	22.4
Electronic, other electrical equipment	924	1,067	5.8	15.5
Fabricated metal products	697	867	4.7	24.4
TOTAL	11,765	13,849	75.5	17.7

Source: Ohio Data Users Center, *1992 Exports with Ohio as State of Origin of Movement*.

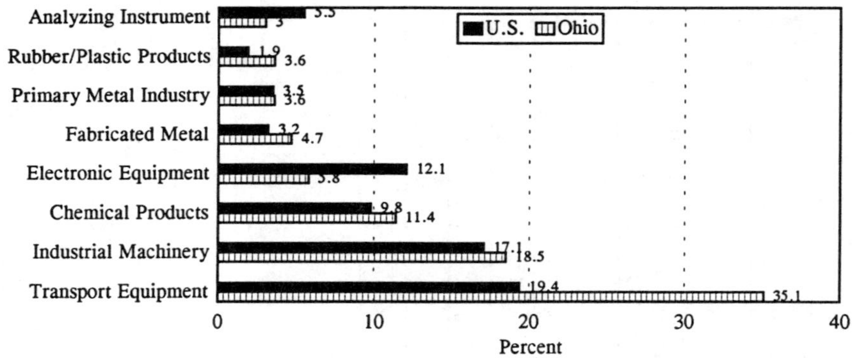

Source: MASSPORT Trade Development Unit, as reported by the Ohio Data Users Center, in *1992 Exports with Ohio as State of Origin of Movementt, 1993.*

FIGURE 2-10. 1992 top eight industry export proportions, Ohio and the United States.

During that time period, exports from three of the top five industries grew at an annual rate greater than 19 percent.

The extent to which Ohio has been able to share in the growth of the fastest growing United States export industries can be evaluated by reviewing Table 2-24. There are several industries in which Ohio has experienced growth in exports similar to that of the United States, particularly transportation equipment, rubber and miscellaneous plastics, and electronic and other electrical equipment. In fact, two of Ohio's top five export industries are among the ten industries experiencing the strongest growth in exports at a national level. The national growth rates for transportation equipment and electronic equipment averaged over 10 percent between 1990 and 1992, compared to the national average for all industries of 6.7 percent. Ohio has not been able to take advantage of expansion of export opportunities in the textile industry, particularly the apparel and other textiles, and textile mill products sectors. United States printing and publishing export growth has also far exceeded that of Ohio. Conversely, Ohio experienced high growth over the 1990 to 1992 period in several other sectors including chemicals and allied products, agricultural production-crops, metal mining, and used or second hand merchandise.

In short, exports are an important contributor to the Ohio economy. The state is also currently capturing a larger share of United States exports, moving from 8th in the United States as the state of origin for exports in 1990, to 7th in 1992, and 6th in 1993. The significance of exports in the Ohio economy can be expected to increase. The state's industries are gaining access to markets in an increasing number of countries. At the same time, the demand by export partner countries for Ohio's goods continues to grow.

TABLE 2-24
Comparison of Ohio Export Growth with the Ten Fastest Growing U.S. Export Industries, 1990 to 1992

Fastest Growing U.S. Exports	U.S. Average Annual Rate of Growth in Dollar Value of Exports, 1990-1992 (In Percent)	Ohio Average Annual Rate of Growth in Dollar Value of Exports, 1990-1992 (In Percent)
Furniture and Fixtures	26.6	5.2
Apparel and Other Textiles	26.5	-13.1
Oil and gas extraction	24.8	99.7
Nonmetallic Minerals (exc. fuels)	24.0	11.1
Rubber and Misc. Plastics	11.9	15.9
Printing and Publishing	10.3	1.9
Transportation Equipment	10.1	9.1
Textile Mill Products	10.1	.4
Electronic, other Electrical Equipment	10.0	7.4
Fishing, hunting, and trapping	9.6	33.3
All Industries	**6.7**	**7.5**

Source: MASSPORT Trade Development Unit, as reported by the Ohio Data Users Center, in *1992 Exports with Ohio as State of Origin of Movement*, 1993.

INCOME AND ITS DISTRIBUTION

As indicated in the earlier sections of this report, Ohio currently accounts for 4.3 percent of national population and 4.5 percent of national employment. However, the state accounts for only 4.1 percent of total national personal income. Ohio's growth in total personal income has fallen short of that for the United States for eleven consecutive years. As a result, Ohio has experienced a falling share of total United States personal income, from 4.7 percent in 1980, to 4.1 percent in 1992 (Table 2-25).

Ohio's sources of personal income reflect both the growing importance of transfer payments and capital income as sources of total income and, within the category of wages and salaries, the change from a manufacturing-based to a service-based economy. As recently as 1985, earnings in durable goods manufacturing were the largest source of income, (see Table 2-26). By 1990, earnings in general services had surpassed the earnings in durable goods manufacturing, increasing by 61 percent over five years. This growth resulted in services earnings comprising 17.6 percent of Ohio personal income.

One of the most significant developments in this country over the past twenty years, in terms of the sources of income, has been the growing importance of transfer payments and capital income (dividends, interest and

TABLE 2-25
Personal Income in Constant (1987) Dollars, United States, Ohio, and Border States, Selected years: 1980 to 1992

Area	Dollars in Billions				Average Annual Percent Change 1980-1992	Percent of U.S. Total	
	1980	1985	1990	1992		1980	1992
United States	2,741.5	3,130.2	3,561.9	3,655.3	2.4	100.0	100.0
Ohio	127.7	133.9	145.8	149.6	1.3	4.7	4.1
Border States							
Indiana	61.4	64.1	71.5	74.1	1.6	2.2	2.0
Kentucky	35.8	37.7	41.7	44.2	1.8	1.3	1.2
Michigan	114.1	120.0	129.9	131.7	1.2	4.2	3.6
Pennsylvania	143.0	152.9	171.9	176.5	1.8	5.2	4.8
W. Virginia	18.9	18.5	19.2	20.1	0.5	0.7	0.6
High Growth States							
Arizona	30.8	39.1	45.8	47.5	3.7	1.1	1.3
California	337.3	400.9	472.6	470.1	2.8	12.3	12.9
Florida	117.5	149.6	187.1	189.4	4.1	4.3	5.2
Georgia	55.6	71.3	85.2	89.6	4.0	2.0	2.4
Texas	171.2	207.8	218.4	232.4	2.6	6.2	6.4

Source: U.S. Bureau of Economic Analysis, *Regional Economic Information System*, 1994 and U.S. Bureau of Labor Statistics, *Handbook of Labor Statistics*, various years.

TABLE 2-26
Ohio Sources of Personal Income, 1985 and 1990

Source	Dollars in Millions		Percent of Total	
	1985	1990	1985	1990
Wages and Salaries				
Manufacturing - Durable Goods	24,818	27,468	16.6	14.4
Manufacturing - Non-durable Goods	9,951	12,306	6.6	6.5
Services	20,772	33,541	13.8	17.6
Government	13,278	18,162	8.8	9.5
Retail Trade	9,663	12,645	6.4	6.6
Wholesale Trade	6,502	8,634	4.4	4.5
Transportation and Public Utilities	6,486	8,016	4.3	4.2
Finance, Insurance and Real Estate	4,708	7,297	3.1	3.8
Construction	5,046	7,170	3.4	3.8
Farming	969	1,321	0.6	0.7
Mining	1,159	889	0.8	0.5
Other	318	528	0.2	0.3
Non Wage Income				
Transfer Payments	23,505	32,844	15.7	17.2
Rents, Interest and Dividends	22,775	30,974	15.2	16.3

Source: U.S. Bureau of Economic Analysis, *Regional Economic Information System,* 1994.

rent). Ohio has also experienced increasing significance of these non-wage income sources. In fact, Ohio has disproportionately shared in this growth. The extraordinary growth in the significance of these income sources in Ohio can best be illustrated through the use of a specialization index like that used earlier to show the concentration of employment by sector. This index is constructed as the ratio of the share of total employment (or, in this case, income) for the region relative to that same share nationally. A comparison of this index over time shows the growing significance of alternative sources of income.

The specialization index for the four major sources of income in the State of Ohio are shown in Figure 2-11. Here, the structural shift of Ohio's economy is evident. The state's reliance on transfer payments and dividends, interest, and rents has grown disproportionately in the State of Ohio (the index has increased), while the importance of wages and salaries and fringe benefits has fallen disproportionately.

The growing significance of transfer payments for Ohio is noteworthy. In

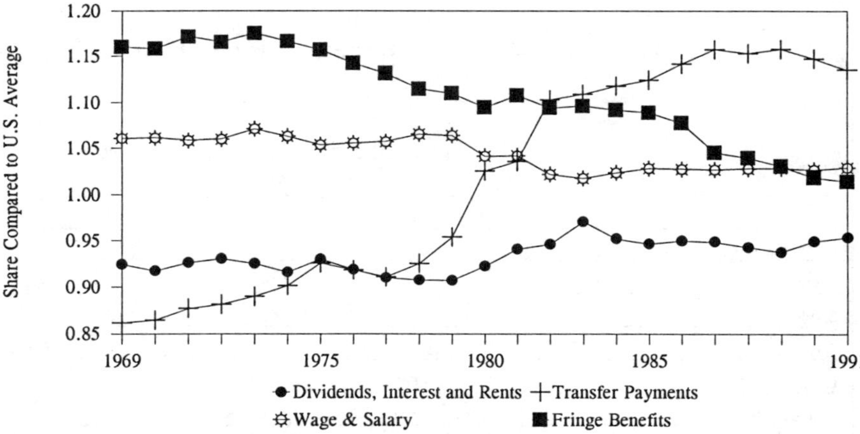

Source: U.S. Bureau of Economic Analysis, *Regional Economic Information System,* 1994.

FIGURE 2-11. Ohio income specialization index by source, 1969 to 1991.

the 1970's, the index was commonly below 0.95 meaning Ohio's residents relied much *less* heavily than the typical United States resident on transfer payments. By 1991, the state had relied much *more* heavily on this source of income. The growing importance of transfer income began to emerge in the late 1970's, when the recession hit Ohio very severely, and continued throughout the 1980's.

To understand the causes of this growth in transfer payments, it is wise to examine the component portions of total transfer payments. Transfer payments are defined as income payments to persons for which they do not render current services. Transfer payments include benefits from the social insurance funds and payment under certain other programs, including old-age survivors' payments, disability and health insurance (Social Security); hospital insurance; supplementary medical insurance; medicaid payments; unemployment insurance; government employee retirement; worker's compensation; veterans' benefits; food stamps; black lung; supplemental security income; and public assistance.[4] The components of transfer payments and their significance in Ohio's income from transfer payments is shown in Table 2-27. By far, the largest increase in transfer payments between 1970 and 1992 can be found in medical payments which have increased from 11.4 percent to 28.1 percent of Ohio's transfer payments in just twenty-two years. This is consistent with increasing health care costs being experienced nationwide, as well as with the changing nature of Ohio's population. Whereas in 1970, 9.3 percent of Ohio's population was 65 years of age or older, the population group now comprises 13.2 percent of Ohio residents.

Ohio's 1992 per capita personal income of $13,571 (1987 dollars) ranked

TABLE 2-27
Composition of Transfer Payment Income, Ohio and the United States, 1970 and 1992

Type of Transfer Payment	Percent of Ohio Transfer Payments		Percent of U.S. Transfer Payments	
	1970	1992	1970	1992
Retirement & Disability Insurance Benefit Pay	59.7	52.9	52.6	48.3
Medical Payments	11.4	28.1	15.3	29.9
AFDC	3.9	2.7	5.7	2.7
Food Stamps	1.7	2.8	1.3	2.5
Unemployment Insurance	3.9	3.8	5.0	4.7
Veterans Benefits	8.8	1.8	8.8	2.2
Other	10.6	8.0	11.3	9.8

Source: U.S. Bureau of Economic Analysis, *Regional Economic Information System*, 1994.

22nd among the states, an increase from its 25th position in 1980. In spite of its ranking, Ohio income per capita relative to the United States average has steadily declined as illustrated in Figure 1-1. In 1980, Ohio per capita income was 98 percent of the average for the United States, and in 1992 it had fallen to 94 percent as shown in Table 2-28. Ohio's personal income is also declining relative to neighboring states. Only West Virginia had slower per capita income growth than Ohio in between 1980 and 1992.

In Table 2-28, the high growth states do not show a clear advantage in real per capita income increases. For these states, total personal income and population have grown rapidly over the past decade. However, the growth may have come through increased employment opportunities in lower wage industries and occupations, accounting for the slow growth in per capita income in the face of rapid aggregate growth.

Per capita personal income among Ohio's metropolitan areas and Ohio's other areas can be compared with the same data for the United States to examine the meaning of the state's income increases for metropolitan and non-metropolitan Ohioans (Table 2-29). In 1970, Ohio's non-metropolitan area residents enjoyed a per capita personal income advantage relative to their United States counterparts. That year, the average Ohio non-metropolitan resident earned 10.6 percent more than the average United States non-metropolitan resident. By 1992, this income advantage had dropped to just 1.2 percent. Ohio's metropolitan residents were 3.6 percent behind the United States metropolitan residents in 1970 in terms of per capita income. This group also saw a decline, down to 7.4 percent behind the national average.

The distribution of per capita personal income across the state's metropolitan areas shows significant regional variation in Ohio's prosperity. Over the 1970 to 1992 time period, the Ohio metropolitan and non-metropolitan

TABLE 2-28
Real Per Capita Income,
the United States, and its Border States, and
the High Growth States, 1980 and 1992

Area	Per Capita Personal Income (1987 Dollars)		Average Annual Percent Change
	1980	1992	
United States	12,063	14,330	1.4
Ohio	11,818	13,571	1.2
Border States			
Indiana	11,183	13,091	1.3
Kentucky	9,771	11,780	1.6
Michigan	12,323	13,960	1.0
Pennsylvania	12,042	14,713	1.7
West Virginia	9,675	11,118	1.2
High Growth States			
Arizona	11,252	12,403	0.8
California	14,176	15,216	0.6
Florida	11,936	14,049	1.4
Georgia	10,137	13,221	2.2
Texas	11,942	13,141	0.8

Source: U.S. Bureau of Economic Analysis, *Regional Economic Information System*, 1994 and U.S. Bureau of Labor Statistics, periodic.

disparity increased as the non-metropolitan population averaged slightly less than a 7.2 percent increase per year. Cincinnati and Columbus led Ohio's metropolitan per capita personal income growth over the past two decades, followed by Cleveland-Akron and Dayton-Springfield. The Toledo Metropolitan Statistical Area exhibited the slowest growth, even less than non-metropolitan Ohio.

Overall, Ohio's personal income and per capita incomes have increased over the last 20 years, but these increases have been at a slower rate than most neighboring states and the United States As a result, per capita incomes in Ohio have declined relative to the United States and neighboring states. In fact, only seven of Ohio's counties have per capita incomes that equal or exceed the United States average.[5] Counties outside of Ohio's

TABLE 2-29
Metropolitan and Non-Metropolitan Per Capita Personal Income, Ohio, the United States, and Selected Ohio Metropolitan Areas, 1970 and 1992

Area	1970	1992	Average Annual Growth Rate, 1970 to 1992 (In Percent)
Ohio (Metro)	$4,153	$19,778	7.35
Ohio (Non-Metro)	3,437	15,823	7.19
United States (Metro)	4,304	21,247	7.53
United States (Non-Metro)	3,108	15,628	7.62
Selected Ohio Metropolitan Areas			
Cincinnati, OH-KY-IN	4,073	20,517	7.63
Cleveland-Akron	4,420	20,959	7.33
Columbus	3,961	19,974	7.63
Dayton-Springfield	4,160	19,411	7.25
Toledo	4,231	19,166	7.11

Source: U.S. Bureau of Economic Analysis, ***Regional** Economic Information System,* 1994.

metropolitan areas have fared the worst: their incomes advantage over the non-metro United States has eroded..

Consistent with the experience nation-wide, service income is an ever increasing percentage of Ohio personal income. Ohioans, however, are also increasingly reliant on transfer payments as a source of income—and to a greater extent than the increase experienced at the national level.

REGIONAL COMPETITIVENESS

Ohio's success in competing regionally, and nationally, is determined by a myriad of factors, many of which can in some way be affected by policies of the state government— including tax policy.

The extent to which different factors affect the competitiveness of Ohio firms was specifically investigated by three studies, which are summarized in this section:

- *Manufacturing Climates Study*, prepared by Grant Thornton;
- *1994 Development Report Card for the States*, prepared by the Corporation for Enterprise Development; and

- *The Ohio Economic Competitiveness Project*, prepared for the Ohio Department of Development.

The findings of each demonstrate that in spite of the impression of the state as unattractive, or even hostile to business, there are certain areas in which Ohio has not only a regional, but a national competitive advantage. There remain, however, other factors affecting competitiveness for which Ohio is at a decided disadvantage. The methodology and findings for each study are reviewed below, followed by conclusions of this analysis of regional competitiveness.

Grant Thornton, *Manufacturing Climates Study*

Grant Thornton, an accounting and management consulting firm, published its *Manufacturing Climates Study* for 11 years, the last issue being released in 1990. In conducting the *Manufacturing Climates Study*, Grant Thornton annually surveyed manufacturing organizations. The firms were asked to rank the importance of certain business factors to their operations. In 1990, the responses of these organizations regarding sixteen business factors were used to evaluate the manufacturing climate in each state. Each of these factors can generally be described categorized into four different groups:

- State and local government fiscal policy
- State regulated employment costs
- Labor costs
- Productivity of resources.

Based on the significance the surveyed manufacturing organizations placed on each of the factors, they were assigned individual weights shown in Table 2-30. Average hourly wage was ranked highest in importance. In fact, many of the more highly ranked factors relate to labor costs. Education, which was a newcomer to the second place ranking in 1990 (having ranked as low as eighth in 1988), reflects the increasing importance on workforce skills by employers. “Tax Effort” and “Change in Tax Effort” ranked 9th and 13th, respectively. Thus tax policy is important to businesses’ evaluations of manufacturing climate, but there are other factors that are considered to be of greater importance.

In the overall comparison between Ohio and its five border states, Ohio does not fare well, bettering only Michigan. Ohio fares just as poorly when compared with the high growth states.

TABLE 2-30
Grant Thornton Evaluation Factors
(In Percent)

Rank	Factor	Weight
1	**Average Hourly Wage** [Annual average hourly manufacturing wage]	9.14
2	**Education*** [Index comprises: average salary of teachers as ratio of average pay of all workers; student-teacher ratio (K-12); high school graduation rate; state expenditure per student for public education (K-12); and per capita higher education expenditures as a percentage of per capita income]	8.33
3	**Workers' Compensation Insurance Levels*** [Weighted average workers' compensation insurance levels per $100 of payroll for manufacturing classifications]	7.19
4	**Statutory Average Workers' Compensation Cost per Case*** [Statutory average indemnity cost per case for all disability types and fatalities under workers' compensation insurance]	7.03
5	**Percentage of Manufacturing Workers Unionized** [Unionized manufacturing employment as a percent of total manufacturing employment]	6.61
6	**Expenditure Growth vs. Personal Income Growth over Five Years*** [State and local government general expenditure growth over five years vs. personal income growth over five years]	6.24
7	**Value Added** [Value added by manufacturing process per dollar of production payroll]	6.10
8	**Fuel and Electric Energy Costs** [Fuel and electric energy costs per million BTUs for the industrial sector]	5.97
9	**Tax Effort*** [State and local government tax effort and relationship to tax capacity]	5.91
10	**Change in Average Hourly Wage over Five Years** [Percentage change over five years in annual average hourly manufacturing rate]	5.91
11	**Unemployment Compensation Trust Fund Net Worth*** [Net worth of state unemployment compensation trust fund per covered worker]	5.82
12	**Average Unemployment Compensation Benefits*** [Average unemployment compensation benefits paid per covered worker per year]	5.76
13	**Change in Tax Effort over Five Years*** [Percentage change in state and local tax effort and relationship to tax capacity over five years]	5.58
14	**Change in Unionization over Five Years** [Percentage change over five years in the unionized manufacturing work force]	5.06
15	**Debt Growth vs. Personal Income Growth over Five Years*** [State and local government debt increases over five years vs. personal income growth over five years]	4.98
16	**Manhours Lost** [Average percent of manufacturing working time lost due to work stoppages over two years involving 1,000 or more workers]	4.37
		100.00

Source: Grant Thornton, *Manufacturing Climates Study*, August 1990.
*Factor is controlled or strongly influenced by state or local governments

One striking difference between Ohio and other states is Ohio's relatively better ranking on the factors within government control. Examination of the rankings indicates Ohio is fairly strong relative to both the border states and the high growth states with respect to the following factors:

- Change in tax effort over five years

- Change in average hourly wage over five years
- Education
- Fuel and electric energy costs.

The surveys identified seven factors, including tax effort and average hourly wage, which detract from Ohio's competitiveness with respect to its neighboring states and the high growth states:

- Average hourly wage
- Tax effort
- Unemployment compensation trust fund net worth
- Percentage of manufacturing workers unionized
- Change in unionization over five years
- Value added
- Man-hours lost.

Two of these factors, tax effort and unemployment compensation trust fund net worth, are strongly influenced by state and/or local governments.

In sum, although Ohio ranked well in *change* in tax effort over five years and *change* in average hourly wage over five years, the state still ranked only 32nd in the *level* of tax effort and 48th in *level* of the average hourly wage. As a result, one can truly only consider two factors from the *Manufacturing Climates Survey*, education and energy costs, to be competitive advantages for Ohio.

Although this analysis of the manufacturing climate contains some bad marks for Ohio, there are also some favorable indicators relating to the state's future competitiveness. For example, *current* trends in wage costs and tax levels, should they continue, will leave the state more competitive in these terms. Currently, taxes may appear to be somewhat high for manufacturing firms but this factor has improved. Average hourly wages also appear to be high, but this too has improved. In a sense, the state's relative attractiveness may have turned a corner and the state may be poised to grow in the future. The improvement of the Ohio economy's performance during the most recent recession, which occurred after the Grant-Thorton survey was performed, may be evidence of the improved performance of the economy, which would support the claim that Ohio's competitiveness is indeed getting better. It should be noted, however, that this survey dealt solely with the manufacturing sector. Although Ohio remains one of the key states in the nation for manufacturing activity, the importance of this sector in terms of job production is falling everywhere. The non-manufacturing sector has recently provided, and will continue to provide in the future, the bulk of new jobs. With this national shift in mind, it is important to note that, as we saw in the personal income chapter, average annual compensation levels were high for the manufacturing sector, but lower for many others. This finding benefits workers in the sector but may serve as a deterrent to economic development, implying the conclusions of the Grant-Thornton study concern one industry which may not generate many jobs in the future anyway—manufacturing.

Corporation for Regional Economic Development, *The 1994 Development Report Card for the States*

The *1994 Development Report Card for the States* marked the eighth annual edition of this publication. Although it is designed to be an "assessment of the strengths and weaknesses of each state's economy and its potential for future growth", the more than 50 socioeconomic "index measures" on which this assessment is based provide another perspective from which to compare Ohio's competitiveness.

The Development Report Card compares the 50 states on the basis of three summary indices developed from these fifty measures.

- Economic Performance
- Business Vitality
- Development Capacity.

In addition, there is a separate rating of the ability for each state's tax and fiscal system to support long-term economic development.

Each of the three indices is comprised of three or four "sub-indices" which, in turn, are comprised of between two and eight measures each, as shown in Table 2-31. In a comparison of Ohio with its border states, and with the high growth states, Ohio ranks relatively well with respect to the "Development Capacity" index, and the sub-indices: human resources, technology resources, and financial resources. Development capacity is designed to be a measure of each state's capacity for future growth and recovery from economic adversity. Some of the measures which contribute to Ohio's relatively high ranking in development capacity are:

- High school education attainment
- Science/engineering graduate students
- Patents issued

TABLE 2-31
Corporation for Enterprise Development
Evaluation Factors

Indices	**Measures**
Economic Performance Index Measures	
Employment	Long-term employment growth
	Short term employment growth
	Unemployment rate
	Unemployment duration
Earnings and Job Equity	Average annual pay
	Average Annual Pay growth
	Health coverage
Equity	Poverty rate
	Income distribution
	Income distribution change
	Rural/urban disparity
Environmental, Social and Health Conditions	Air quality
	Superfund dumpsites
	Hazardous waste generation
	Surface water discharge
	Infant mortality
	Crime rate
	Teen pregnancy
	Heart disease
	Cancer cases
	Infectious diseases
Business Vitality Index Measures	
Competitiveness of Existing Business	Traded sector strength
	Change in traded sector strength
	Business closings
	Manufacturing capital investment
Entrepreneurial Energy	New companies
	Change in new companies
	New business job growth
Structural Diversity	Sectoral diversity
	Dynamic diversity

continued

TABLE 2-31 (continued)
Corporation for Enterprise Development
Evaluation Factors

Indices	Measures
Development Capacity Index Measures	
Human Resources	High school graduation
	High school education attainment
	College education attainment
Technology Resources	Ph.D. scientists & engineers in workforce
	Science/engineering graduate students
	Patents issued
	University research and development
	Federal research and development
	SBIR grants
Financial Resources	Commercial Bank Deposits
	Loans to deposits
	Loans to equity
	Commercial and industrial loans
	Commercial and Industrial Loans to total loans
	Venture capital investments
	SBIC financings
Infrastructure and Amenity Resources	Highway deficiency
	Bridge deficiency
	Urban mass transit availability
	Energy cost
	Sewage treatment needs
	Urban housing costs
	Health professional shortage areas
	Tourism spending
Tax and Fiscal System Index Measures	
	Total tax and fiscal system score
	Fiscal stability and balanced revenue
	Tax fairness
	Fiscal equalization

Source: Corporation for Enterprise Development, *1994 Development Report Card for the States*.

- Federal research and development
- Small Business Innovation Research grants
- Loans to deposits
- Loans to equity
- Commercial and industrial loans.

Ohio's lowest ranking is the entrepreneurial energy sub-index, one of the components of business vitality. This low ranking is derived from Ohio's poor showing with respect to new companies, change in new companies, and new business job growth. Other measures in which Ohio ranked poorly include:

- Short term employment growth
- Unemployment duration
- Air quality
- Change in trade sector strength
- University research and development
- Sewage treatment needs
- Tourism spending.

The rating of Ohio's tax and fiscal system was generally comparable to the ratings received by most of the border and high growth states. By examining the detail provided by the individual measures, it can be seen that Ohio ranked highly on fiscal stability and balanced revenue, but ranked in the lower half of states with respect to tax fairness and fiscal equalization. The latter are factors more related to equity issues and are less likely to adversely impact Ohio's overall economic development competitiveness. Here again, we see that the state of Ohio, in spite of its poor economic performance over the past two decades, is not generally regarded as having a particularly poor climate with regard to those factors affecting future economic development.

The Ohio Department of Development, *The Ohio Economic Competitiveness Project*

The project, prepared for the Ohio Department of Development by Cleveland State University, identified factors that will create either future economic opportunities or threats for existing Ohio industries. Discussion of these factors provides a framework for comparison of Ohio's current business environment with that of bordering states.

These factors include:

- State government fiscal policy
- State employment and labor regulations
- Education and technological innovation issues
- infrastructure investment policies and priorities
- Industrial energy costs
- Health care cost comparison.

State Government Fiscal Policy. Ohio's position relative to its border state for each of these factors is summarized in Table 2-32. As shown in the table, Ohio's state government fiscal policy was considered worse than Indiana and Kentucky, but better than the other three border states. This judgement was based on four factors:

- Ohio is closer to maximizing its capacity and effort for both tax and non-tax revenue sources than the majority of border states;
- The business share of total tax burden is higher in all border states except Indiana;
- State corporate income taxes per capita are lower in Ohio than in all border states, both in dollar terms and as a percent of personal income; and
- Ohio's state and local per capita tax revenues are higher than Kentucky, Indiana, and W. Virginia, but lower than Pennsylvania and Michigan.

State Employment and Labor Regulations. These regulations were recently identified as major barriers to Ohio's economic development by the Ohio Operations Improvement Task Force.[6] *The Ohio Economic Competitiveness Project,* in evaluating the conclusions of this Task Force, examined three related factors: workers' compensation claims, workers' compensation payment rates, and prevailing wage laws. They found the following:

- Ohio has more workers' compensation claims than all border states except Pennsylvania. When comparing on the basis of claims per 1000 jobs, however, Ohio's claim rate is lower than all border states except Michigan.

- Workers' compensation payment rates in Ohio are higher than all border states except Pennsylvania.
- Ohio and its border states all have prevailing wage laws and are right to work states.

As with state fiscal policy, Ohio's state employment and labor regulations were considered to be worse than Indiana and Kentucky, and better than the other three border states.

Education and Technological Innovation. The quality of education and the skills necessary to develop and operate new technologies have been recognized as important to assuring that current and future labor market needs can be met by the state's work force, thus helping to retain, expand and attract business. *The Ohio Economic Competitiveness Project* ranked Ohio and its border states on their ability to facilitate innovation in terms of both total spending, and industry spending on research and development. In both categories Ohio ranked third behind Michigan and Pennsylvania. Ohio and Pennsylvania are both leaders in state science and technology programs: Ohio, through its Thomas Edison Program, and Pennsylvania, through its Ben Franklin Partnership Program—one of the oldest science and technology programs in the country. As shown in Table 2-32, the *Competitiveness Project* ranked Ohio about equally with Indiana, Michigan, and Pennsylvania, all of which were ranked higher than W. Virginia and Kentucky.

Infrastructure Investment Policies and Programs. These programs are increasingly used by states to boost job creation and business investment. Infrastructure investment can be an important aspect of regional competitiveness. *The Competitiveness Project* reported that Ohio ranked third among border states in terms of infrastructure stock per capita, but the average annual infrastructure growth rate over the 1975 to 1988 period was actually negative, and ranked fourth among the six states compared (Table 2-33).

Industrial Energy Costs. Another comparison from the *Competitiveness Project* is energy costs. Although overall industrial energy costs in Ohio are, on average, not as high as they are in Pennsylvania and Michigan, they are above average for the region, particularly with respect to natural gas rates (Table 2-34). Caution should be exercised, however, in comparing these rates. There are significant rate variations among service territories in a given state, and economic development rates may be available to some customer classes.

Health Care Costs. The final aspect of comparison from *The Competitiveness Project* is health care costs. Data were collected showing health care costs for a number of metropolitan areas within the region; however, no data were available for West Virginia. For the remaining five, Ohio ranked in the middle.

TABLE 2-32
Ohio Economic Competitiveness Project
Comparison of Business Environment Factors

Border States	Ohio's Performance Relative to Border States		
	Better	Worse	About Same
State Government Fiscal Policy			
Indiana		●	
Kentucky		●	
Michigan	●		
Pennsylvania	●		
W. Virginia	●		
State Employment and Labor Regulations			
Indiana		●	
Kentucky		●	
Michigan	●		
Pennsylvania	●		
W. Virginia	●		
Education and Technology Innovation			
Indiana			●
Kentucky	●		
Michigan			●
Pennsylvania			●
W. Virginia	●		
Infrastructure Investment Policies and Programs			
Indiana	●		
Kentucky		●	
Michigan	●		
Pennsylvania	●		
W. Virginia	●		

continued

TABLE 2-32 (continued)
Ohio Economic Competitiveness Project
Comparison of Business Environment Factors

Border States	Ohio's Performance Relative to Border States		
	Better	Worse	About Same
Industrial Energy Prices			
Indiana		●	
Kentucky		●	
Michigan	●		
Pennsylvania	●		
W. Virginia		●	
Health Care Costs			
Indiana		●	
Kentucky		●	
Michigan			●
Pennsylvania	●		
W. Virginia	n/a		

Source: Ohio Department of Development, *The Ohio Economic Competitiveness Project, 1993*.

Other Measures of Competitiveness

The competitiveness of a region is closely related to the cost of conducting business and the cost of living in an area. Additional information on relative costs is another way of assessing the competitiveness of the Ohio economy.

The primary cost for most businesses is labor costs. Although average labor cost information has been used in those studies already cited in this chapter, average compensation data does not account for differences in the industrial and occupational characteristics of a state's work force. In other words, a proper comparison of relative costs of labor would control for industrial/occupational factors and their influence on average wage cost measures. The United States Department of Labor performs regular surveys of wage rates

TABLE 2-33
Capital Stock and Infrastructure Growth

State	Value of Infrastructure Stock Per Capita, 1988	Average Annual Infrastructure Growth Rate (%), 1975-1988
Ohio	$3,525	-0.1
Indiana	$3,114	-0.5
Kentucky	$4,157	+0.5
Michigan	$3,286	-0.5
Pennsylvania	$3,153	+0.4
W. Virginia	$4,755	+0.8

Source: Ohio Department of Development, *The Ohio Economic Competitiveness Project*, 1993.

TABLE 2-34
Industrial Energy Cost Comparison, Ohio and its Border States, 1992

State	1992 Industrial On-System Natural Gas Rate ($/MCF)	1992 Industrial Electric Rate (cents/kWh)
Ohio	$4.01	4.91 cents
Indiana	3.25	4.02
Kentucky	3.19	3.74
Michigan	4.16	5.35
Pennsylvania	4.01	6.15
W. Virginia	2.71	3.87

Sources: Energy Information Administration, *Natural Gas Monthly*, December 1992, Columbia Natural Gas of Ohio; Energy Information Administration, U.S. Department of Energy, 1992; and *Energy Users News*, January 1993, as reported in *The Ohio Economic Competitiveness Project*.

for selected occupations and industries for the purpose of inter-area comparisons. The most recent summary of these wage comparisons was prepared for 1990.[7] In that survey, wage data for three of Ohio's major metropolitan areas are included: Cincinnati, Cleveland and Toledo (see Table 2-35).

TABLE 2-35
Interarea Pay Comparison for Selected Occupational Groups, Ohio Cities and Other Midwest Cities, 1990

Occupational Group	Cincinnati	Cleveland	Toledo	Other Midwest	U. S.
Office Clerical: All	95	96	99	93.6	100
Manufacturing	95	99	106	94.9	100
Non-manufacturing	94	92	88	94.6	100
Electronic Data Processing: All	96	96	-	98.0	100
Manufacturing	-	97	-	97.0	100
Non-manufacturing	95	95	-	97.2	100
Skilled Maintenance: All	92	103	101	101.5	100
Manufacturing	93	104	103	103.4	100
Unskilled Maintenance: All	97	90	112	106.9	100
Manufacturing	97	106	129	100.9	100
Non-manufacturing	88	-	-	97.0	100

Source: U. S. Bureau of Labor Statistics, *Area Wage Surveys: Selected Metropolitan Areas*, January 1991.

Three things from the survey are clear. First, compared to the average United States metropolitan area (where the wage index equals 100), Ohio's cities are generally competitive in terms of wage rates. The exception is the Toledo area, where wage rates are somewhat higher for the skilled and unskilled maintenance personnel. Cincinnati is very competitive across the range of occupations.

Second, although competitive relative to the United States, the table shows wage levels in Ohio's areas that are indicative of the generally lower wage costs throughout the Midwest. The Midwest index, calculated as the unweighted average of compensation rates in Midwest cities in the report, are similar to those of Ohio.

Third, the wage costs for the white-collar occupations are, compared to those employed in the same occupations across the nation, lower in Ohio. With the exception of one estimate for Toledo, the state's indices are below 100. On the other hand, those working in blue collar occupations, and specifically manufacturing, are relatively highly paid in Ohio. If these higher wages are the result of high productivity by Ohio's workers, the labor costs should not interfere with the state's growth. Conversely, if bargaining table coercion is responsible for Ohio's relatively high wages for blue collar workers, the state is at a disadvantage for economic development.

Another basis for comparison of competitiveness is the relative cost of living. Lower costs of living will ultimately lead to lower wage demands. The American Chamber of Commerce Researchers Association produces a quarterly survey of the cost of living for approximately 300 metropolitan areas. From the information on Table 2-36, the cost of living in these cities is close to the national average except in the Columbus and Cleveland areas. However, in analyzing this information, one should keep in mind that the full sample of cities includes many very small communities, where the cost of living is almost always relatively low. As a result, the national average cost (an index of 100) is one formed from a sample of cities which includes smaller and generally lower cost regions. An index above 100, while indicating an above average cost of living, is not surprising for major metropolitan areas, such as Cleveland and Cincinnati. In fact, it is probably surprising that the index for these major metro areas is no greater than 104.3. Comparisons to other large metropolitan areas, particularly on the east and west coast, show these Ohio cost-of-living estimates to be relatively low.[8]

CONCLUSIONS

The studies that have been reviewed each provide different insights into Ohio's competitive position, both in its region and nationally. Although methodologies in these studies were different, some general conclusions can be drawn with respect to Ohio's competitive advantages and disadvantages.

TABLE 2-36
ACCRA Cost of Living Composite Index for Ohio Cities and Selected Regional Cities, Fourth Quarter

Ohio Cities:	Index
Akron	94.5
Cincinnati	101.0
Cleveland	104.3
Columbus	104.3
Dayton	99.1
Mansfield	97.5
Parkersburg-Marietta	99.0
Toledo	98.8
Youngstown	93.5
Other Cities:	**Index**
Indianapolis, IN	94.7
Muncie, IN	98.9
Fort Wayne, IN	94.0
Lexington, KY	99.2
Louisville, KY	91.5
Pittsburg, PA*	111.2
Erie, PA	107.6
Charleston, WV	98.0

Source: American Chamber of Commerce Researchers Association, ACCRA Cost of Living Index: Fourth Quarter, 1994.

*Data for third quarter, 1993.

Competitive Advantages. The quality of Ohio's human resources are an area of competitive advantage. The high school attainment of Ohio's population, as well as the number of science and engineering graduate students provides a strong base of human capital which can be drawn upon by business and industry. Given the ever increasing importance of a skilled workforce, Ohio's success with respect to this factor is particularly noteworthy.

Ohio's technology resources are also an important attribute. The *Ohio Competitiveness Project* noted the success of Ohio's Thomas Edison Program, and the *1994 Development Report Card for the States* identified patents issued, federal research and development, and SBIR (Small Business Innovative Research) grants as all being indicative of the strength of Ohio's technology resources. The presence of many federal laboratories, but in particular the Wright Research and Development Center and the NASA Lewis Research Center, have also provided opportunities for many supportive businesses. Lastly, should federal government's technology transfer programs improve the transfer of technology to the private sector, opportunities for business formation and growth should be ever expanding.

Competitive Disadvantages. State employment and labor regulations are Ohio's greatest competitive disadvantages. They are less a disadvantage when Ohio is compared with its border states, but become more significantly negative in national comparisons. Some of the factors that contribute to this finding are the net worth of the unemployment compensation trust fund, the percentage of manufacturing workers unionized, recent changes in unionization, workers' compensation payment rates, and man-hours lost due to work stoppages. The *Ohio Operations Improvement Task Force* and the *Ohio Economic Competitiveness Project* concur that state employment and labor regulations are major barriers to Ohio's economic development.

There is contradictory information regarding industrial energy prices, but recent data indicate that, in general, Ohio's industrial electricity and natural gas prices are higher than the majority of border states. It must be noted, however, that the variability of rates between different parts of the state, and the availability of incentive rates, can make industrial energy prices a competitive advantage in some service areas.

These competitive disadvantages, and the others that were identified earlier in this chapter, could be formidable in some competitions for new business and business growth. However, there are indications that the state leaders are increasingly aware of these issues and are searching for creative solutions, and the resources to address them.

POSSIBLE CHANGES IN THE STRUCTURE OF THE ECONOMY AND POPULATION IN THE FUTURE

The ability of Ohio's tax structure, as it now stands or as it is modified based on recommendations of the Commission to Study the Ohio Economy and Tax Structure, to meet the revenue needs of the State of Ohio is profoundly affected by the state's economic structure and vitality. The level of employment will affect personal income tax collections, industries' investment in plant and equipment will affect personal property tax collections, purchases of goods will affect sales tax collections, and so on. Although the future is unknown, anticipating some of the state, national, and international-level events that may significantly impact the health or structure of the Ohio economy provides a framework for considering the nature of that future economy and how it may affect, or be affected by, changes in the tax structure.

Twelve factors were identified in the *Competitiveness Project* as key factors which will influence Ohio's economy in the years to come. They are:

- Global auto industry restructuring
- The North American Free Trade Agreement (NAFTA)
- Defense industry conversion
- Service sector growth and restructuring
- Sustainable development (coordination of environmental constraints and economic development efforts)
- Federal government policy and spending changes
- State fiscal and tax policy changes and pressures
- State employment and labor regulations
- Education and technological innovation issues
- Infrastructure investment policies and priorities
- Industrial energy prices
- Health care costs.

The factors were discussed in greater detail in the *Ohio Economic Competitiveness Project* report. The manner in which each factor may affect Ohio's future is explored below.

Global Auto Industry Restructuring

Ohio's auto industry, because of its dominance in the state's economy, has been an important factor in the state's economic health over many decades. Although significant job losses were experienced in the early 1980's, the later half of the decade brought both domestic and foreign investments in new facilities and equipment in Ohio. The future of the auto industry is a critical issue that will be deeply reflected in the structure of the Ohio economy since it supports the existence of first, second, and third tier suppliers throughout the state. In fact, Ohio has more than 300 automotive parts plants. Therefore, changes in the auto industry are multiplied throughout the state's economy. For example, the recently announced Honda expansion of 750 employees implies a total increase of about 3,000 workers across Ohio. Corporate changes at the major American manufacturers can also be expected to have significant impacts on Ohio's job base. Ohio has benefitted greatly from investments of Japanese vehicle producers and their suppliers. The state should benefit further from recent announcements regarding additional investments in this sector in coming years.

Auto industry attraction is important, but auto industry job retention should also be a priority of Ohio policy makers during coming years. Retention is particularly important in light of high wages paid in this industry and the extent to which changes in the industry are magnified in the economy.

North American Free Trade Agreement

There is considerable disagreement on the consequences of NAFTA in Ohio, ranging from expectations of significant job exporting in major manufacturing industries to short term job losses followed by long term productivity and employment increases.

Canada and, to a lesser extent, Mexico are important trading partners. Ohio exports to Canada grew by 20 percent between 1991 and 1993, and accounted for 47 percent of Ohio's exports in 1992. Although accounting for only 4 percent of total exports, exports to Mexico increased by 29 percent over the same period. Lower tariffs under NAFTA should allow Ohio to expand the mix of products it exports; particularly by opening markets for the state's manufactured goods.

According to the Institute for International Studies in Washington, D.C., NAFTA will be responsible for an estimated 150,000 to 175,000 net job gain to Ohio over the first three years of the agreement; based on a 325,000 job gain resulting from increased export sales and a 150,000 job loss from labor force restructuring. The competitiveness of Ohio's industries and the ability of workers to meet the skill requirements of potential jobs will, in large measure, determine Ohio's ability to benefit from NAFTA.

Defense Conversion

Defense spending has been an important component of the Ohio economy for several decades. Although Department of Defense employment is higher in Pennsylvania and Kentucky, Department of Defense spending is greater in Ohio than in any of its border states by a significant margin. In 1991, prime contracts to Ohio totaled \$4.76 billion with the closest rival being Pennsylvania at \$2.95 billion.[9]

Both Ohio's manufacturing and service industries will be affected by defense conversion. The manufacturing sector can expect the greatest impact, but Ohio may not be as sensitive to defense cuts as some states. The concentration of defense activity at Wright Paterson AFB and the Defense

Construction Supply Center in Columbus add stability because these facilities are unlikely to be closed. At the same time, localized conversion impacts will be felt. For example, Mound Laboratory in Miamisburg is now transitioning from a major DOE facility with over 2,500 employees to the Mound Advanced Technology Center—a commercial operation striving to retain jobs and highly skilled people.

Service and Office Sector Growth

At the national level, service sector growth has outpaced that of the other industrial sectors. In Ohio, the same trend has been experienced with over 74 percent of the state's total jobs now provided by service-producing industries (including finance, transportation, retail and all other non-goods producing industries). Ohio has the opportunity to further benefit from the strength of its service sector, and continue or even enhance the job growth that has occurred in recent years. Expanding the extent to which services are exported to foreign markets may provide an important opportunity for growth. The export of services grew by 90 percent from 1986 to 1993, from $77 billion to $173 billion. To the extent that Ohio's domestic economic development efforts successfully promote this sector, the service sector can lead Ohio with new business location, business expansion, and new employment opportunities. Tax policy that encourages, for example, the location of corporate headquarters in the state, could play a role in the growth of this sector.[10]

Sustainable Development Policies (Coordinated Environmental and Economic Development Efforts)

Compliance with environmental regulations will be a costly burden to many Ohio firms in the coming years, constraining the availability of capital for other investments and expansion. In fact, over $671 million was invested by Ohio-based manufacturers in pollution abatement between 1982 and 1986. The result of the high compliance costs will be a conflict between environmental issues and economic development efforts. The state has the opportunity to play an active role in coordinating these conflicting efforts, and working to maximize the economic development benefits where possible.

Business opportunities—as well as expenses—will occur as a result of environmental remediation at the former Fernald Feed Materials Production Center. Waste water management must also be improved and low level radioactive waste disposal problems must be resolved at this site.

Federal Government Policy Spending Changes

In 1991, $0.99 of every federal tax dollar paid by Ohioans was returned to the state. The intensity of competition for these federal dollars can only be expected to increase, particularly given the spending cuts associated with national defense conversion. Defense outlays for 1993 comprised 5 percent of GDP and may shrink to only 3.3 percent by 1997. [11] The implications of these spending changes are uncertain but they have the potential to strongly impact Ohio's employment.

State Fiscal and Tax Policies

The recommendations of the Commission to Study the Ohio Economy and Tax Structure have the potential for a significant impact on the business environment for investment and growth in Ohio. In addition, the tax policy changes that are recommended may affect the competitive position of Ohio businesses not only with respect to border states, but with all others as well. The extent to which Ohio is able to favorably position itself will allow the state economic successes that it has not recently experienced.

State Employment and Labor Regulations

State employment and labor regulations are often cited as important factors in business decisions regarding location, relocation, and expansion. Workers' compensation costs, unemployment insurance issues, and prevailing wages have been identified by the Ohio Operations Improvement Task Force as major barriers to Ohio's economic development. The potential for these factors to adversely impact Ohio's future must be weighed against the benefits these policies offer Ohio's workers. The state may even be able to identify regulations where additional flexibility may assist employers without adversely affecting employees.

Education and Technological Innovation

For close to a decade, Ohio has been a leader in recognizing the importance of technological innovation to the economic health of the state. Ohio's Thomas Edison Program helped create several centers of excellence across the state. The Great Lakes Manufacturing Technology Center and the Great Lakes Industrial Technology Center have both played a major role in bringing together the technological resources of Ohio's universities, colleges, and federal facilities with the needs of industry. The synergy that results from these partnerships helps strengthen small as well as large businesses, and may lead to the creation of new ventures as well. Continued emphasis on education and technological innovation will assure the technological support needed to help Ohio's industry compete in the next century, and the technological position necessary to compete in the global market place.

Infrastructure Investment Policies and Priorities

The state's ability to invest in infrastructure over the coming years could have a major impact on its economy. It is important for policymakers to realize that individual infrastructure investments affect the competitive environment for business with different time schedules. Prioritizing these investments is therefore important for development.

Transportation-related infrastructure is anticipated to be an area of significant investment over the next twenty to thirty years. Ohio recently completed the first phase of *Access Ohio, Ohio Multi-Modal State Transportation Plan to the Year 2020*. The implementation of this plan has begun with planning underway for a new interstate corridor from Toledo to Portsmouth. This and other types of infrastructure investment will not only be a benefit because of the economic activity associated with construction activity, but as is the case here, the highway itself will make possible more efficient transportation of goods, and could encourage development.

Industrial Energy Prices

Industrial energy prices have fluctuated greatly over the past two decades and, in fact, can vary substantially among states. For example, the general comparative industrial natural gas rate of $4.01/MCF for Ohio is substantially higher than the West Virginia rate of $2.71/MCF and slightly lower than the Michigan rate of $4.16/MCF. General comparative data for industrial electric power rates show a similar range with Ohio at 4.91 cents/kwh and Pennsylvania at 6.15 cents/kwh.

Utility company, and the Public Utility Commission of Ohio responses to issues such as the Clean Air Act Amendments, alternative energy projects, and other initiatives have the potential to significantly influence the competitive position of these industries, as do possible changes in the tax structure affecting these industries. The impacts will be felt throughout the economy, but particularly in Ohio's energy-intensive industries.

Health Care Costs

Health care costs vary significantly across the country, resulting in differential impacts on businesses and individuals. The insurance and the health care industry both have a strong presence in Ohio. The extent to which they are impacted by the evolution of the structure of the industry, and the impacts on employers and individuals, are unknown, but will certainly affect Ohio employment and economic output.

SUMMARY

A primary conclusion to be drawn is that, by and large, Ohio has the opportunity to influence the extent to which its economy benefits or suffers from most of the events that will shape the state's economic future. There are many developments that will encourage economic expansion, such as increased exports of goods and services, new infrastructure investment, and higher production levels in the auto industry. There are threats too; such as the loss of jobs from defense conversion. The tax structure is one of a portfolio of tools that can be used to influence the environment faced by Ohio's businesses and residents.

CONCLUSION

The economic transformation which the United States economy has undergone over the past thirty years has not been kind to the Ohio economy. By virtually any standard of measurement, the growth in the Ohio economy has stagnated since the 1960s. Employment, population, income and per capita income have all fallen relative to the rest of the nation.

Much of the deterioration of the Ohio economy is attributable to broad economic forces which have transformed the nature of the United States economy, with the Ohio economy finding itself on the wrong end of these powerful forces. The slow growth in employment opportunities in manufacturing has strongly impacted the number of jobs and the state's income growth. The out-migration of prime-age workers had led to an increasingly elderly population remaining in the state, and the consequent growth in the importance of governmental transfer payments as a source of Ohio's income. The rapid development of the Southern and Western states has dwarfed the growth and opportunities which have developed in the industrial Midwest, drawing many young and educated workers out of the state.

In many ways, the experience of the Ohio economy mirrors that of much of the formerly industrial Midwest. In fact, it would have been remarkable indeed if Ohio, nestled in this stagnating region of the country and composed of an industrial structure which relied so heavily on manufacturing, would have performed well. In many ways, then, the decline of the Ohio economy should not be surprising or difficult to understand.

However, even independent of the ravages which the changing structure of the world economy has inflicted on the Ohio economy, there are other controllable factors to growth which have contributed to the decline or impeded the ability of the economy to transform in the face of these broader forces. Some of the studies cited in this chapter point to high wages and uncompetitive tax rates and labor laws which put the economy at a disadvantage.

Looking forward, the economic future holds some promise. While many of the uncompetitive features of the Ohio economy remain, there are many favorable aspects to Ohio's current business climate which may bode well for the future. Market forces, in response to the slow growth of the past few decades, have led to a reduction in the degree to which wage costs may adversely impact economic growth in the future. The level of taxes has eased relative to many other states. Ohio is making a concerted effort in the area of infrastructure development, education and training, research and development and trade development which can help Ohio's economy turn the corner. The state is in a position to share fully in the nation's future economic growth.

"Positioning itself" for the future requires many things. Ohio must assure an adequate supply of well-trained labor, provide for growth with public infrastructure and, not least, offer a tax structure which will not impede or inhibit investment and growth. Each policy is a means to an economic environment that encourages growth in existing industries but also does not impede economic transformation.

ENDNOTES

1. Ohio Bureau of Employment Services (1993).

2. Ohio Bureau of Employment Services (1993).

3. Dun & Bradstreet Corporation data.

4. U.S. Bureau of Economic Analysis (1992).

5. According to the U.S. Bureau of Economic Analysis (1994), Cuyahoga , Delaware, Franklin, Georgia, Hamilton, Lake and Medina all had per capital personal income greater than the United States.

6. See Ohio Department of Development (1993),

7. U.S. Bureau of Labor Statistics (1991).

8. The indices for some other major cities are: New York (228.3); Boston (137.7); Philadelphia (127.8) and San Diego (122.3).

9. U.S. Department of Defense (1992).

10. See Martinez and Grace (1994).

11. Wegner (1994).

3 Historical Review of State and Local Government Finances

Donald C. Berno and Jack L. Whitmore

INTRODUCTION[1]

The most recent national data on tax burden show the dramatic impact of numerous changes in state tax policy, and the changes in voted local revenue increases. In 1980, Ohio's state and local tax burden per $1,000 of income was 47th in the United States By 1991 (the most recent data available) Ohio had risen to 31st.[2] In fact, between 1981 and 1991, Ohio's percentage increase in state and local tax burden was 112 percent—the 9th highest increase in the country during that period.[3]

One of the unique characteristics of Ohio's tax policy is that while many state tax practices and policies can be adopted by a majority vote of the state Legislature, and have a large amount of natural growth, most local tax revenue sources have to be approved by a direct vote of the people. For example, the General Assembly, by a simple majority vote, has great latitude in establishing the rates and brackets for the state personal income tax. On the other hand, voters must approve (by simple majority) a local income tax rate greater than 1 percent, and it is a flat rate—there are no local brackets. While the state sales tax base is set by the General Assembly, local sales tax authorities (counties and transit authorities) benefit from any base broadenings without a vote of the local taxpayers (but any increase in the local rate above 1.5 percent must be voter-approved). And while property taxes are a local (rather than state) revenue source, the state has set strict limits on unvoted revenue growth.

STATE FINANCES

To understand how Ohio tax policy is developed, it is necessary to briefly explain the state budget process. The Administration makes revenue estimates and submits a proposed budget in January. The budget is for the fiscal year beginning July 1 of that year and continuing for the next two years, to June 30 of the second year. After the House and Senate have reviewed, modified, and approved the Administration's proposed budget, the Conference Committee looks at the total spending involved, and at the most recent revenue estimates (which have been revised in light of the most recent economic forecasts). If the proposed spending is higher than the most recent revenue estimates, then the Conference Committee makes the decision to reduce spending, increase revenues, or to undertake some combination of these two actions. The options for revenue increases are developed from suggestions provided by the technical staff from the Department of Taxation, the Office of Management and Budget, and the Legislative Budget Office.

For the past 20 years or so, Ohio's state tax structure has attempted to balance revenues from income, sales, and business taxes.[4] This approach has successfully accommodated political pressures between the Democrats (if working people pay taxes, then business must pay its share) and Republicans (if business pays too much, Ohio will not be attractive for business location and expansion).

With a few exceptions, this process has allowed Ohio to avoid "major" tax changes during the past 20 years. The first exception was the tax increases during the 1980-82 recession. Those years saw a 1 percent increase in the state sales tax rate (4 percent to 5 percent in 1981) and new brackets and rate increases for the personal and corporate income tax (1982 and 1983).

The other major exception was the state tax increase in December, 1992. The discretionary change is illustrative of the state's decision-making process, but obviously not the normal sequence of events. The Administration had implemented three spending reductions since January, 1991, but the economic recovery had not yet been reflected in state revenues. Rather than discuss revenue increases in conjunction with the FY94-95 budget, the Administration and the legislative leadership agreed to address the revenue issues during a "lame duck" session. The philosophical underpinning of the discussion was a desire to avoid rate increases in the major tax categories.[5] The exception to this philosophical base was to add a new bracket ($200,000 and over) and rate (7.5 percent) for the personal income tax. The rationale behind this was to satisfy the public belief that the rich were not paying their "fair share" of taxes, (a theme of the just completed Presidential election) and a feeling among the political leadership that this income bracket could afford to pay more.

A list of approximately 35 options was developed from the Governor's tax expenditure report (Office of Management and Budget 1995) and other sources. The consensus was that it was reasonable to expand the sales tax base, because the Ohio tax structure had not shifted to match the state's economy. The discussion then focused on which of these options had been adopted by other states, so that adoption by Ohio would not hurt our competitive position. The sales tax base was broadened to include both consumer and business services. Consumer services that would be added to the sales tax base would be discretionary (lawn care, premium cable stations, security services, etc.), so the resulting tax increase would be progressive. On the business side, the "pop tax" (now repealed by a constitutional amendment approved by the voters on November 8, 1994) and the new tax on temporary employment services were chosen to reflect economic activity, not inactivity.

This process was more tumultuous and controversial than the preceding description indicates. Early in the process, there was an agreement between the Administration and the legislative leadership to make direct sales of natural gas subject to the sales tax. The rationale was to have out-of-state natural gas producers share some of the tax burden. Several large manufacturers, who rely on the spot market and direct purchases of natural gas, successfully lobbied to have this provision removed from the final bill. Their argument was that they were saving 5 percent or so on their energy costs through direct purchases of natural gas. If these purchases were subject to a 5 percent sales tax, plus the local option sales tax, their savings would be lost, and the cost of doing business in Ohio would increase.

A second contentious issue involved imposing the sales tax on warranty services. The major impact of this tax fell on the auto industry, one of the largest employers in the state. It was adopted because the political leadership (administration and legislative) believed it was fair in the context of what business (particularly the auto industry) was paying in sales tax revenues. Although the auto sales tax is a major part of Ohio's total sales tax revenues, there is a credit given on the sales tax for the value of trade-ins. This trade-in credit is a revenue loser, and this revenue loss was replaced here.

This tax on warranty services was included in the final package, but was repealed after just one year. Upon reflection, and protests from the auto industry, it was decided that this tax was a bad precedent. Ohio was the first state in the country to adopt it. Also, the revenue it generated in just one year was close to the revenue estimate for the two year period.

Despite these policy arguments in support of a tax increase, the legislative leadership could not convince their members to vote for the bill. So, they combined the bill with the capital appropriations bill, which contained local construction projects funded totally or partially with state monies. Then the legislature was presented with one bill for a yes-or-no vote. This placed members in the politically difficult position of voting for tax increases, or voting against state-funded projects in their districts. The bill passed. It contained state funding for local capital projects, and a series of tax increases which were designed to increase state revenues by around $1 billion over the next two years.

Historical Review of State Taxation

Total annual increases in state imposed taxes range from 1.3 percent (1991) to 15.8 percent (1984).[6] The changes in real terms are 2.4 percent and 14.6 percent for those years. Personal income tax collections and sales and use tax collections range from 50 to 60 percent of total collections for any given year. This is an indication of two factors: (a) "natural growth" due to increased incomes and general inflation in prices, and (b) a combination of rate changes (for the personal income tax) and a sales tax base broadening to include more services.[7] A brief glossary of Ohio's state taxes is presented in Box 3-1.

Personal Income Tax

State personal income tax collections represent 30 percent of total state-assessed taxes, and 40.7 percent of total General Revenue Fund (GRF) taxes. It is the most income elastic tax in the revenue system (Wallace and Edwards 1994).

Ohio's Constitution authorized the state to levy an income tax in 1912. While there was a flurry of interest in the personal income tax during the 1933-1934 discussions concerning a state sales tax, the state did not exercise this option until 1971, effective January 1, 1972. The 1967 Tax Study Commission had concluded the absence of a state income tax was a detriment to the state's fiscal health. Their finding was one of the important reasons the state finally enacted the authorized tax four years later.

Ohio is one of 44 states to levy the tax.[8] Alaska, Florida, Nevada, Texas, Washington and Wyoming do not utilize this revenue source. For economic development purposes, Florida and Texas are frequently seen as competitor states.

The 1971 debate about adopting a state income tax was vocal, loud and long, according to a pamphlet titled, "A History of the Income Tax Battle,"

Box 3-1
Glossary of State Taxes and Tax Bases

ALCOHOLIC BEVERAGE TAXES: Beer, wine, mixed beverages, and liquor.

CARBONATED BEVERAGE TAX: Carbonated soft drinks and non-alcoholic beer.

CIGARETTE TAX: (1) Cigarettes. (2) Cigars, chewing tobacco, snuff, smoking tobacco, and other tobacco products — effective February 1, 1993.

CORPORATE FRANCHISE TAX: The corporate franchise tax has two alternative tax bases: (1) the Ohio net worth (book value of capital surplus, undivided profits and reserve) of the corporation; or (2) the Ohio net income (profits) of the corporation.

ESTATE TAX: The taxable estate equals the value of the gross estate less deductions.

HIGHWAY USE TAX (AXLE-MILE TAX): The highway use tax was effectively repealed January 1, 1991 by legislation relating to Ohio's entry into the interstate registration plan (IRP). The IRP is a cooperative agreement among member states to share registration revenue from interstate carriers based on mileage traveled in each state. Highway Use Tax revenues were replaced in part by a percentage of registration revenue from vehicles over 26,000 pounds (including IRP registration fees) and from a three cent surcharge per gallon of motor fuel on vehicles which were highway use taxpayers.

INCOME TAX: The amount reported as Federal Adjusted Gross Income to the U.S. Internal Revenue Service plus or minus adjustments, according to Ohio income tax law.

INSURANCE TAX-DOMESTIC: The domestic insurance tax is levied on one of two tax bases: the value of the capital and surplus of a company having capital divided into shares or the value of the surplus of a company not having capital divided into shares; the gross amount of premiums covering rises in Ohio less specified deductions.

INSURANCE TAX-FOREIGN: Gross amount of premiums received from policies for Ohio risks during preceding calendar year less specified deductions.

MOTOR VEHICLE FUEL TAX (Gasoline Tax): Gallons of gasoline, diesel fuel, and special fuels sold in Ohio.

MOTOR VEHICLE FUEL USE TAX: Fuel used by vehicles with three axles or more on Ohio highways. Taxpayers must pay tax on the difference between the fuel purchased in Ohio.

PUBLIC UTILITY EXCISE TAX: Most utilities are taxed on gross receipts from intrastate business.

SALES AND USE TAX: Retail sales and rental of tangible personal property. Selected services.

SEVERANCE TAX: The tax is levied on the weight or volume of certain natural resources extracted from the soil and water of Ohio.

published by then state representative James Thorpe. The Republican Party controlled the House 54-45 and the Senate 20-13. The Governor was Democrat John Gilligan. At the end of May, Republican Speaker Charles Kurfess pushed through a budget bill that was $1.5 billion higher than previous budgets. A 1 percent increase in the sales tax could not fund such a spending increase. The state budget year ended on June 30 with no new budget approved, and the first of eight interim budgets was approved. On July 14, the House Ways and Means Committee and the full House passed a tax package with a graduated state income tax.

When the budget bill went to the Senate, that body took two months to cut $500 million from the budget and replace the income tax with a sales tax increase of 1.5 percent. By now it was November, and the interim budgets were becoming a tool of persuasion. State employees' paychecks were threatened with delay. Welfare checks were delayed. Even legislators' paychecks were held up. Three conference committee reports containing the income tax were rejected by the Senate Republicans. Finally, on December 9, the fourth conference committee made its report, which contained the income tax. The Senate passed the bill by a 17-15 margin. The House was called to Columbus for a vote. The budget bill passed 56-42, and Ohio adopted a graduated state income tax.

In 1972, the state personal income tax generated about $1.3 billion. By the end of FY93, through rate changes, bracket changes, natural growth, and inflation, state personal income tax collections exceeded $4.7 billion.

Between 1982 and 1993, rate changes, the addition of three brackets and several changes in joint filer, elderly, and child care credits created a roller coaster effect for the individual. That is, nearly every year there was a change in rates, brackets, credits, or a combination of these. Nevertheless, the total net collections for the state increased by at least 4 percent every year except for 1986 (a 0.1 percent decrease). In real terms, the net collection increases ranged from a low of 1.5 percent in 1986 to 24.7 percent in 1984. The 1993 net collection increase, in real terms, was 7.2 percent. The major specific changes included:

- Making permanent (in 1983) the two additional brackets ($80,000 - $100,000 and $100,000 and up) temporarily imposed in 1982. The 1982 Joint Committee to Study State Taxes reasoned that rates were still low compared to other states, the income tax is a graduated structure, and those in the higher income brackets could afford to pay.

- The child care credit was established in 1988. Taxpayers with federal adjusted gross incomes of up to $30,000 could claim 25 percent of the federal child care credit on their state returns. Beginning in tax year 1993, taxpayers with federal adjusted gross incomes under $20,000 who were eligible for the federal child care credit may claim 35 percent of that credit as a state child care credit. Taxpayers with federal adjusted gross incomes between $20,000 and $40,000 who were eligible for the federal child care credit may claim 25 percent of that credit as a state child care credit.

- In 1992, a ninth income bracket (for above $200,000 of income) was added. The rate for this new bracket is 7.5 percent (effective January 1, 1993).

A history of the rate changes, exemptions, and credits beginning with 1982 is shown in the appendix to this chapter.

There has been a long-term shift in the distribution of tax liability towards the higher brackets. Taxpayers with an adjusted gross income of $30,00 or less paid 24 percent of the tax in 1985, but this dropped to 13.4 percent by 1992. Correspondingly, the taxpayers with adjusted gross incomes of $30,000 and up paid 87 percent in 1992 as opposed to 76 percent in 1985. The shift is even more dramatic when we examine the top three brackets above $50,000. The share of total income tax liability rose from 28 percent in 1985, to 63 percent in 1992.

State Sales and Use Tax

The state sales tax is the second largest source of state tax revenues. It accounts for 18.9 percent of the total from state-imposed taxes, and 38.2 percent of General Revenue Fund revenue. The history of the adoption of the state sales tax is nearly as tumultuous as that of the income tax. The Ohio Retail Sales Tax Law was passed on December 6, 1934 approved by Governor George White on December 13, 1934 and went into effect on January 1, 1935. Ohio was the 16th state to adopt a general sales tax.

In 1933, the voters approved a constitutional amendment which reduced the tax limitation on real property from 15 mills to 10 mills on each dollar of valuation. As a result, the main revenue source dropped dramatically as local government expenses, especially for "poor relief," skyrocketed as a result of the Depression. It is significant that the voters authorized the payment of old age pensions to all qualified persons 65 and over on the same day that the property taxing power of each local unit was reduced by one-third.

The sales tax had been proposed and defeated five times between January and November, 1934. A "lame duck" session was called to finally resolve the issue. This session was called after the Ohio Supreme Court ruled that the diversion of gasoline tax from roads to poor relief or any other purpose was illegal.

The purposes of the sales tax as originally passed were: (1) emergency poor relief; (2) public education; (3) state general revenues and (4) a supplement to property taxes to support local government activities. The bill also provided that some of the revenue be used to pay for state collection and administrative expenses.

The original act provided that after deducting the cost of administration and the amounts appropriated for specific purposes, 60 percent of the remainder should be distributed to the state public school fund. All remaining funds (40 percent) were to be deposited in the newly created "local government fund." Monies from this fund were allocated among counties and distributed to county auditors, who in turn provided the monies to the County Budget Commission to be distributed to local governments according to a statutory formula.

In 1939, the legislature under the guise of abolishing earmarked revenues for state subsidies, amended the state sales tax law. Beginning in that year, the 40 percent share of revenues that was allocated to the local government fund was changed to a fixed dollar amount. All remaining revenues were transferred to the state's General Revenue Fund.

The sales tax rates and the base have changed. The original rate was 3 percent, and food was included. A constitutional amendment in 1936 exempted all carry-out food from the sales tax. The rate was raised to 4 percent in 1967, and to the current 5 percent in 1981. The 1981 rate increase was a response to a sharp decrease in revenues as a result of the recession.

The economic conditions of the early 1980s and the early 1990s slowed the natural revenue growth of the sales tax.[9] Three factors came together to broaden the sales tax base. The first was slower growth. The second was the recommendations of the 1982 Joint Committee to Study State Taxes. The Committee specifically recommended taxing recreational and leisure services where appropriate. The third and final factor was the attempts of other states to include more services in their sales tax bases. The combination of these three factors led the legislature to begin broadening Ohio's sales tax base to include services. In 1983, business data processing services were made taxable. In 1987, long distance telecommunication services became taxable. The long distance carriers requested this change on the grounds that because of the deregulation of the telephone industry, they should be shifted from the public utility tax to the corporate franchise and sales tax base. In 1991, lawn care and landscaping services, as well as private investigation and security services became taxable. As mentioned earlier, the policy here was to broaden the sales tax base to include discretionary consumer purchases, and thereby improve the progressivity of the tax. In 1992, building cleaning and maintenance, extermination services, employment agencies, and personnel supply services were made taxable. This was an attempt to balance the sales tax expansion between business and consumer services.

Also, physical fitness facilities and recreation and sports club memberships were made subject to the tax. Again, these are discretionary purchases which are presumed to be made by higher-income individuals.

The vendor discount for prompt payment of the sales tax was decreased from 1.5 percent to .75 percent in 1992. This change was prompted solely by the need for revenue increases, and was contrary to the original reason for granting the discount, and to a number of national and state studies on the issue. Originally, the vendor discount was granted to compensate the vendors for the cost of, in effect, serving as the state's tax collector. Despite national and state studies which indicated that the cost of these collections ranged from 2 to 3 percent of the total sales tax collections by a particular vendor (depending on the size and number of county permissive taxes involved), the state's revenue need was so great that the discount was cut in half.

Corporate Franchise Tax

The corporate franchise tax represents 4.1 percent of state imposed taxes and 8.1 percent of the GRF. It is paid on the higher of a net worth or net income base.

The corporate franchise tax was established in 1902, with a rate of 1 mill on the value of capital stock located in Ohio. In 1971, as a part of the establishment of the state income tax, an income base was added. Some of the commentaries written on the adoption of the state personal income tax indicate that the corporate income tax was included in order to ensure labor support of the individual income tax.

There are a number of surcharges for certain industries. The major one is for "litter stream corporations." Litter stream corporations include those manufacturing or selling alcoholic beverages, soft drinks, containers, and other litter stream products. The liability is calculated on a net income and a net worth basis, and cannot exceed $10,000. The surcharge was established in 1980 for the tax years 1981 through 1986. In 1985 it was extended through 1991, and in 1987, was extended through 1993. It has since been made permanent.

The corporate franchise tax also saw a number of surcharges levied on the net worth and income bases during the recession of the early 1980s. Surcharges were imposed during 1981, 1982 and 1983, and the rates were permanently increased in 1983.

Some credits for the corporate franchise tax were created in 1992. These are credits for increased exports, new jobs created in enterprise zones, and in other areas when approved by the job credit tax authority. These credits were adopted to encourage economic development in Ohio. There is a belief among the political leadership that Ohio has to be responsive to the economic development incentives offered by other states (especially border states). These credits are also targeted at business activity that appears to have the highest growth potential (e.g., export businesses) or an ability to address social issues (e.g., decreasing unemployment in inner cities and rural areas).

Motor Vehicle Fuel Tax

The fourth major state tax is the motor vehicle fuel tax, commonly called the gasoline tax. It represents 5.4 percent of state-imposed taxes. Ohio adopted the gasoline tax fairly late compared to other states. Ohio was the 43rd state to adopt the tax, in 1925. The rate then was 2 cents per gallon. In 1993, the rate was 22 cents. The rate has increased every year since 1987 (with the exception of 1992). In 1986, the rate was 12 cents. So Ohio has experienced a 10 cent rate increase in just eight years.

The reason for these regular increases was a formula adopted by the legislature in 1981. In that year, the legislators decided that rather than discuss the need for a rate increase every year, they would develop a formula to determine the increase. The formula adds 7 cents per gallon to a figure determined by (1) the consumer price index, and (2) a consumption factor, which is the ratio of the gallons of motor fuel consumed in the second previous fiscal year to consumption in the previous year. The formula resulted in a 15 cent addition to the 7 cent base in FY93. The authority to use this formula expired after the July 1993 calculation, and all rate increases must be authorized by the Legislature.

With the exception of 0.5 percent of total gas tax collections allocated to the waterways safety fund, all the monies are distributed to state and local governments for road maintenance and construction.

There are a few exemptions and credits of particular interest. First, fuel for use on agricultural land is exempt. This exemption is justified on the basis that tractors and other farm equipment don't use the highways and roads very much. There is also an adjustment made for fuel lost through shrinkage, evaporation, and leakage. And, like many states and the federal government, Ohio has an ethanol credit.

LOCAL GOVERNMENT FINANCE

Ohio's local governments rely on three major sources of revenue: property taxes, sales and use taxes and income taxes. *The state always sets the base of these taxes, and the local voters or elected officials establish the rate.* Of these, sales and income have the most natural growth, while property tax growth is limited by the provisions of H.B. 920, and by previous practices of

Ohio law since 1925. Also, the local sales (up to 1.5 percent) and municipal income (up to 1 percent) taxes may be levied without a vote of the people. The school income tax must be approved by the voters.

Of the over $10 billion collected in total local taxes, $6.8 billion comes from property taxes; $2.2 billion from income taxes, and $824 million from sales and use taxes. An additional $114 million comes from motor vehicle license taxes, and $107 million from miscellaneous taxes.

A full glossary of local taxes is presented in Box 3-2.

Local Property Taxes

Nearly 60 percent of local government revenue ($6.8 billion) comes from property taxes. The data in Table 3-1 show the types and amounts of property taxes paid in 1993 (1992 tax year).

Real Property

The basic premise of property taxes should be that value times rate equals tax owed. Ohio's premise is a complex version of this basic rule. Ohio's current property tax laws represent a political, economic and legal evolution that has resulted in a system that is understandable to almost no one. A good deal of this complexity is the result of two laudable public policy goals: Equalization of property values within and between counties and type of property, and protection of taxpayers from unvoted tax increases. Nevertheless, Ohio's practice is quite far removed from the basic premise of property tax practice—value times rate.

In 1824, the state authorized local units of government to levy property taxes. By 1878, the legislature had consolidated all property tax laws into a general act for the assessment and taxation of property according to its true value in money. On May 10, 1910, the Legislature created the Tax Commission of Ohio, consisting of three people appointed by the Governor. This was the predecessor to the Department of Taxation. It also passed what was then commonly known as the "Smith One Per Cent Law." Today, it is called the 10 mill limit or the "inside" millage. The purposes of the Act were "to secure an equitable valuation of property for taxation by limiting the tax rate, limiting the power to issue bonds, removing certain penalties for improper valuation and amending certain sections of the General Code."

Ohio thus became the *very first state* to limit the overall property tax rate. The maximum rate of taxes levied for all purposes by taxing authorities in any taxing district upon the taxable property in the district, could not, in any one year, exceed one percent or 10 mills on each dollar of the tax valuation without a vote of the electors. Provision was made for submitting the question of additional taxes to the electors. The 10 mill limitation was increased

Box 3-2
Glossary of Local Taxes and Tax Bases

ALCOHOLIC BEVERAGES TAXES—COUNTY: Beer, wine, mixed beverages, and liquor.

INCOME TAX—MUNICIPAL: The tax is generally imposed on: wages, salaries, and other compensation earned by residents of the municipality and by non-residents working in the municipality, and net profits of business (both incorporated and unincorporated) attributable to activities in the municipality.

INCOME TAX—SCHOOL DISTRICT: A resident tax on the amount reported as Ohio adjusted gross income for state income tax purposes less the $650 personal exemption.

LODGING TAX: All transactions by which lodging in a hotel, motel, rooming house, and other lodging accommodations are furnished to transient guests.

PROPERTY TAX—PUBLIC UTILITY: Taxable value of public utility real property (land and buildings) and personal property (machinery and equipment). Real property is assessed at 35% of true (market) value. Personal property true value is based on composite annual allowances and is assessed at 88%; except for electric utility production equipment and the personal property of certain telephone companies, which is assessed at 100% of true value (50% of cost); the personal property of rural electric companies which is assessed at 50% of true value; and the personal property of railroads, which is assessed at 25% of true value.

PROPERTY TAX—REAL: Taxable value of land and buildings. Taxable value is 35% of market value, except for certain agricultural land. Counties must reappraise all real estate once every six years. Equalization adjustments are made in the third year following reappraisal.

PROPERTY TAX—TANGIBLE PERSONAL: The tax is applied to tangible personal property used in business in Ohio (machinery, equipment, inventories). Business land and buildings are taxed under the real property tax. Taxable value is determined by applying a listing percentage to the true value of tangible property. The percentage used to determine taxable value was 25% in 1993.

SALES AND USE TAX—COUNTY AND TRANSIT AUTHORITY: The County Sales Tax, Additional County Sales Tax (for special purposes), and the Transit Authority Sales Tax are applied to retail sales, rental of tangible property, and selected services. (Same base as State Sales Tax.)

TABLE 3-1
Analysis of 1993 Ohio Property Taxes (In Millions of Dollars)

Real Property Tax	Gross	Net	1992-1993 Increase	1992-1993 Percent Increase	Percent of Total
Agricultural & Residential (Class I) Taxes Levied	5,391.3				
Tax Relief H.B. 920 Tax Credit 10% General Tax Relief[1] 2 1/2% Special Tax Relief[1] Homestead Exemption[1]	-1,1620.1 -377.1 -75.3 -52.5	3,266.3	211.0	6.9	47.8
Business & Public Utility (Class II) Taxes Levied	2,066.9				
Tax Relief H.B. 920 Tax Credits 10% General Tax Relief[1]	-503.0 -156.4	1,407.5	72.0	5.4	20.6
Business Personal Property Taxes Taxes Levied $10,000 Valuation Exemption[1]	1,284.4 -78.7[2]	1,205.7	4.3	0.4	17.6
Public Utility Tangible Personal Taxes Levied	954.9	954.9	75.6	8.8	14.0
Total Property Taxes Levied Total Tax Relief	9,697.5 -2,863.1				
Total Net Property Taxes Property Taxes Per Person		6,834.3 620.0	362.8	5.6	100.0

Note: Totals may not add due to rounding.

[1]Tax loss to schools and local governments reimbursed by state.
[2]Estimated

to 15 mills in 1927 and the General Assembly exempted certain types of levies from that limitation. As a result of a constitutional amendment in 1934, the limit was again reduced to 10 mills. (This is the same constitutional amendment that led to the adoption of the state sales tax.)

There also has been a great deal of concern with the equalization features of the property tax. Prior to the early 1950s, property tax administration was a county issue with little state oversight or involvement. State oversight and involvement in local property tax administration began when the School Foundation program was first approved by the Ohio legislature. The distribution of school money was based upon the property valuation per pupil in each district. The counties discovered that the lower they kept their property values (in comparison to other counties), the more state aid they received. During the 1950s, the Board of Tax Appeals issued many orders to counties to increase their appraised values. Counties ignored the orders with the excuse that they couldn't afford the cost of reappraisal. By the early 1960's, the Legislature had passed a bill requiring that a set percentage of collections be set aside and available only to pay the cost of reappraisal. In 1965 a statute was passed that set the assessment level (by rule of the Board of Tax Appeals) not to exceed 50 percent of appraised or true market value, and the appraised value was to be as close to 100 percent of true value as possible. In 1972, the level of assessment was changed to 35 percent of true value (to take away the sting of the new state income tax). This same assessment ratio holds for real property today.

During the 1970s, industrial and commercial property was assessed at 50 percent or more of true value, while residential and agriculture property was assessed in the range of 15 or 20 percent of true value. The county auditors always made sure the total assessment for the county was at 35 percent. This was obviously a political decision rather than a tax equity decision. The Ohio Supreme Court, in the Park Investment case, ordered the Board of Tax Appeals to issue necessary orders and procedures to achieve equalization immediately (see Box 3-3). The legislators told the Board not to move too fast, they wanted to "fix" the equalization problem themselves. After the Supreme Court issued its fourth order, in 1971, it suggested that someone or some board would be cited for contempt of court if they neglected to act as directed. So the Legislature finally decided to equalize over the next six-year cycle, but added a provision that "true value" and "use value" be the same. Park Investment again asked that the law be declared unconstitutional. The Supreme Court accepted the equalization provisions, but struck down the provision relating to true and use value.

At this time, a rate of 10 mills could be levied without a vote of the people. But, as values increased, especially after the Park Investment series of cases, the dollar amount of taxes owed increased. This was largely due to an increase in property values. There was considerable unhappiness with this

Box 3-3
Park Investment Cases

In a series of decisions from the early 1960's through 1971, the Ohio Supreme Court required a substantial change in the assessment of real property in the state. Because of several court cases, commonly called the "Park Investment" cases after the company that originated the suit, the Supreme Court ruled that the Ohio Constitution requires all real property to be taxed by a uniform rule according to value. This meant that the ratio of assessed value to market value had to be the same for all classes of property and also for all counties. Because of these rulings, the real property values of homeowners and farmers increased greatly compared to the values of commercial and industrial property. Of course, this also caused a considerable shift in real property tax burdens.

These rulings required property values be updated regularly, so that the assessment-sales ratios remained relatively constant. Because rapid increases in market property values occurred in the 1970's, assessed property values rose very rapidly after 1972 as the local assessors and the Board of Tax Appeals (B.A.) attempted to maintain the 35 percent assessment ratio which had been established by the B.A. in 1972. The rapid increase in the assessed value of real property brought out hidden difficulties with the millage reduction procedures in Ohio law. Although voted millage rates were only to be reduced when *real* property values increased, the method followed also reduced the rates applied to *tangible* property values. This occurred even though the tangible property valuation may not have increased at all. Many real property owners, primarily homeowners and farmers, viewed this as an unfair shift of the property tax burden from tangible personal property to real property. They felt that since only real property valuation increases triggered the millage reductions, then only the rates for real property should be reduced.

In response to the demands of these real property owners for relief from their rapidly increasing tax bills, the General Assembly passed legislation in 1976 (H.B. 920) which limited the tax reductions resulting from increases in real property values to taxes on real property only. The bill accomplished this by reducing the voted taxes on real property through a tax credit so that the total taxes levied on real property would not exceed the taxes levied the previous year, excluding taxes on newly-constructed property. Therefore, taxes from voted millage should never increase because of inflationary increases in value. The only sources of additional revenue from real property for local governments are: (1) the increase from millage inside the 10 mill limit;(2) taxes on new construction; and (3) additional voted levies. Of course, additional revenue is also generated whenever tangible property values increase since these taxes are not reduced when values increase.

situation among Ohio taxpayers who believed that there should be a limit to property tax *revenue* increases without a vote of the electorate.

In 1925, the Legislature included in the law what was then known as the "millage rollback" provision. Millage rollback was designed to reduce the millage (tax rate) by whatever percentage was required to compensate for any increase in valuation due to reappraisal or update. There were few reappraisals from the 1925 period until almost 1960. But when Ohio moved to equalize, the equalization increases, plus the rapidly increasing true values, brought the millage rollback provisions into play. The General Assembly passed a law which created a 50 percent ceiling on the assessment level of real property. In 1972, the level of assessment was changed to a 35 percent maximum. In 1970's, when values were increasing rapidly, the legislature became concerned that the millage rollback was causing a shift in the tax load from industrial and commercial property to residential and agricultural property. The reason for the shift was that the millage rollback applied to, and was calculated based on, increases in the real and tangible personal property tax base. Personal property values were not increasing; therefore, when the total tax duplicate (personal and real) was added, and a millage rollback calculated, the rollback figure was influenced heavily by static tangible personal property values. When the millage rollback was applied to all property, the tax burden shifted substantially from tangible personal property (business) to real property (homeowners and farmers).

Therefore, in 1976, the legislature changed the millage rollback to a tax adjustment factor, and applied it only to real property. The tax reduction factor works like a credit to reduce taxes. This is the H.B. 920 that is so often criticized by local government entities. After the value of a taxpayer's property is multiplied by a voted tax rate to obtain a preliminary amount, the preliminary amount is reduced by a percentage. It equals that percentage which is necessary to offset district-wide increases in value in a taxing district caused by the reappraisal of property values. *It applies only to real property—it does not apply to personal property at all.* The net effect of this on local government revenues has been no more or less in total than the millage rollback provisions. The only difference has been that the burden has shifted to business personal property taxpayers.

There are three other issues concerning real property taxes. When the legislature adopted the state income tax in 1971, it also enacted a 10 percent rollback. After all tax reduction factors (H.B. 920) have been applied, the county reduces everyone's property tax by 10 percent. The revenue lost through this reduction is made up by payments from the State General Revenue Fund. The policy rationale for the 10 percent rollback was that since personal income tax rates had been increased, this rollback would ease some of the total tax increase on individual homeowners. Schools and the local governments who benefited from the property tax would not be harmed because the state was reimbursing them for the rollback.

In 1979, an additional 2.5 percent rollback was enacted for owner-occupied residences. The full effect of H.B. 920 and its shift of burden away from residential property to tangible property had not yet been fully realized. Also, in 1978 Hamilton County (Cincinnati) was for the first time taxed under the full 35 percent assessment ratio. In 1979, Cuyahoga County moved to 35 percent for the first time. Homeowners in these two major counties thus had major tax increases. There was a property tax revolt brewing. So the General Assembly granted an additional rollback of 2.5 percent for homeowner occupied residences.

This action by the General Assembly was immediately challenged as a violation of the constitution's uniformity clause.[10] The Ohio Supreme Court ruled that the legislature had the power to grant partial exemptions, and hence the 2.5 percent rollback did not violate the uniformity clause.

There is also a homestead exemption based on age and income that was established by a 1970 constitutional amendment. The local revenue losses from this program are also reimbursed by the state's General Revenue Fund.

These rollback provisions are becoming expensive for the state. In CY93, the cost was $740 million (including the reimbursement of $78.7 million for the $10,000 tangible personal property exemption). The Celeste Administration proposed eliminating the 2.5 percent rollback in 1983, but the legislature felt that the public had borne enough tax increases with the rate surcharges on the state income tax.[11]

The above explanation shows how Ohio arrived at its own version of value times rate equals taxes owed. To summarize, Ohio's formula is: Value (as adjusted by reappraisal) times rate (as adjusted by the tax reduction factor) equals tax owed (less 10 percent, 2.5 percent, and homestead exemption).

Taxpayers also may be confused by the different types of real property tax renewals that appear on a ballot. There are major differences between "renewal" and "replacement" levies. These differences are described below.

- *Renewal of Levy.* A renewal levy continues an existing levy as though no expiration of the original levy ever occurred. The effective rate of the old levy becomes the starting point for determining the effective rate of the new levy. For example, the voters approved an "old" levy five years ago at a rate of 3 mills. At that time this levy was placed on the tax list for the first time. Over the five years since it was first approved the "old" levy has accumulated a tax reduction factor of 17 percent. As a result, its effective rate in its last year equals approximately 2.5 mills. When the "old" levy is renewed, its effective rate in the first year of the renewal would be 2.5 mills (less any additional tax reduction factor adjustment for that year).

- *Replacement of Levy.* A replacement levy continues the nominal or voted rate of an existing levy. However, the replacement levy wipes out any tax reduction factor percentage which has accumulated since the voters approved the original levy. For example, if voters approved a 3 mill levy five years ago, and that levy has accumulated a 17 percent reduction factor, a replacement levy would impose a tax in the sixth year at an effective rate of 3 mills (less any tax reduction factor for that year only).

In the examples presented here, the difference between a renewal levy and a replacement levy is approximately one-half mill of effective rate. The replacement levy raises more taxes by wiping the slate clean of tax reduction percentages accumulated during the life of the levy which it replaces.

From a tax policy perspective, the use of replacement levies involves a serious potential for abuse and deception. Because the common or conversational meanings of "renewal" and "replacement" are so similar, the availability of the replacement levy provides a political subdivision with an opportunity (or temptation) to make voters believe that they are merely substituting a new tax authorization for one that has expired, when in fact they are authorizing a new effective tax rate.

In addition, as the "tax reduction factor" applies only to real property, use of a "replacement levy" instead of a "renewal levy" would probably result in a reduction in the tangible personal property tax rate. In the above example the *reduction would be one-half of a mill,* while real property taxpayers would receive a one-half mill increase in taxes. Thus, use of a "replacement levy" would not be of value in a school district with a high proportion of tangible personal property value. A brief history of reductions is presented in Box 3-4.

One final observation about the development of the property tax seems in order. While it has historically been the main revenue source for schools, recently other local government agencies have increased their use of property taxes as a revenue source. The effect of this has been that the property tax ballot has become more crowded as additional groups try to obtain voter approval of this funding source. In Franklin County (Columbus), for example, property tax revenues have increased over $300 million between 1988 and 1993. Six county-wide non-school levies have been approved during this period. As a result, $110 million of the $300 million increase in property tax revenues has gone to non-school activities. Also, the school share of the total property tax revenues in the county has dropped from over 64 percent to barely 60 percent. This trend is probably true in all metropolitan counties in the state, but not necessarily to the same degree. This expanded use of

Box 3-4
A Brief History of Property Tax Rate Reductions and Credit Provisions of Ohio Law (1925 to 1980)

Year Enacted	Legislative Bill Number	Purpose of New Section or Amendment
1925	Original Tax Rate	Required general reappraisals of real estate every six years in each county. The legislation also provided for the reduction of all voted levies so that the revenues produced would remain the same as before the reappraisal.
1955	(Reduction Legislation)	Voted levies for school districts cannot be reduced below minimum rate required by school foundation program.
1967	Am. Sub. S.B. 350	Amendment requiring a reduction of school district levies *only* if budget provided an amount per pupil for operation greater than 35% above the state or county average per pupil for the prior calendar year, whichever was greater. School districts in 17 counties benefited from law change. Effective for tax years 1967 and 1968.
1969	Am. Sub. H.B. 531	Amendment allowing school districts *one-half* of (State Budget Bill)additional tax revenues accruing as a result of sexennial reappraisal value increases. Change effective only until January 1, 1971. School districts in 33 counties benefited from law change. Effective for tax years 1969 and 1970 (temporary law).
1972	Am. Sub. S.B. 455	Amendment requiring school district levies to be reduced in same manner as other levies until January 1, 1978, when requirement would cease and schools would receive full benefit from reappraisal value increases. Also required annual updates of real property values to meet 35% requirement.
1975	Am. Sub. S.B. 170	Amendment removed language of Am. Sub. S.B. 455 requiring no reduction in school district levies after January 1, 1978.

Box 3-4 (continued)
A Brief History of Property Tax Rate Reductions and Credit Provisions of Ohio Law (1925 to 1980)

Year Enacted	Legislative Bill Number	Purpose of New Section or Amendment
1976	Am. Sub. H.B. 920	New section requiring a real property tax credit system to compensate for additional taxes generated by increases in valuation due to reappraisal or equalization of real property. Annual updates of real property value removed—changed to three-year updates.
1980	Am. H.B. 1238[(a)]	Required the classification of real property into two classes—residential/agricultural property and non-residential/non-agricultural property, and a separate but uniform reduction in the taxes levied against the real property in each of the two classes. Prior to 1980, only one percentage reduction applied to all of the real property in a taxing district.

(a) Result of Constitutional Amendment approved by voters 11/4/80. Legislation effective 12/19/80.

property tax revenues should present some interesting policy questions for the future. These questions include: (1) Should other taxing authorities be added to the list of activities allowed to utilize property taxes? (2) If yes, does this make it more difficult for school districts to gain voter approval of their levies? (3) Is it appropriate for taxing authorities with high growth costs (aging, for example) to rely on a low-growth revenue source (property taxes)?

The long-term growth in real property tax revenues is described in Tables 3-2 and 3-3. The aggregate increases over the 1983—1993 period in both Class I and Class II property, exceeded both the rate of inflation and the rate of personal income growth. These revenue increases, however, have not been adjusted for discretionary changes.

Tangible Personal Property

Ohio's practice of taxing tangible personal property is unique among the industrial states and in the country. As a result, it has been criticized by the

TABLE 3-2
Total Real Property Taxes Charged, 1983 through 1993
(In Millions of Dollars)

Total Taxes Charged[1]				
		Increase		Personal Income Increase
Collection Year	Amount	Amount	Percent	Percent
1983	2,718.4	---	---	---
1984	2,825.2	106.8	3.9	9.4
1985	2,964.7	139.5	4.9	5.5
1986	3,137.4	172.7	5.8	5.0
1987	3,384.9	247.5	7.9	4.5
1988	3,689.2	304.3	9.0	6.6
1989	3,997.6	308.4	8.4	6.4
1990	4,276.1	278.5	7.0	5.7
1991	4,593.1	317.0	7.4	3.3
1992	5,034.6	441.5	9.6	6.3
1993	5,335.0[2]	300.4	6.0	4.4
Increase 1983-1993		2,616.6	96.3	74.0

Source: Computations by The Council from Ohio Department of Taxation, Tax Analysis and Local Government Distribution Division data.

Note: As noted in the previous discussion, Ohio state law limits the "natural growth" in real property tax revenues. Thus, the revenue increases in the above chart are the result of major discretionary increases in the voted property tax rates.

[1]Prior to state government reimbursements for real property tax relief.
[2]Estimated

reports of the 1967 Ohio Tax Study Commission and the 1982 Joint Legislative Committee to Study State Taxes. In fact, the Joint Legislative Committee stated:

> "The Committee is convinced that the tangible personal property tax imposes an unreasonable burden on business taxpayers because it is levied without regard for ability to pay. Therefore, the Committee believes this tax ought to be repealed."[12]

The Committee immediately concluded that the revenue implications of repeal meant it should not be attempted without some revenue replacement program(s).

While there has been a long-standing concern about the adverse impact

TABLE 3-3
Increases in Real Property Taxes Charged, By Class of Property: 1983–1993 (In Millions of Dollars)

	Class I Agricultural and Residential Real Property Taxes[1]			Class II Business and Public Utility Real Property Taxes[1]		
		Increase			Increase	
Collection Year	Amount	Amount	Percent	Amount	Amount	Percent
1983	1,967.1			751.3		
1984	2,034.9	$67.8	3.5	790.3	39.0	5.2
1985	2,130.2	95.3	4.7	834.5	44.2	5.6
1986	2,245.5	115.3	5.4	891.9	57.4	6.9
1987	2,421.0	175.5	7.8	963.9	72.0	8.1
1988	2,595.9	174.9	7.2	1,093.3	129.4	13.4
1989	2,815.3	219.4	8.5	1,182.3	89.0	8.2
1990	3,003.7	188.4	6.7	1,272.4	90.1	7.6
1991	3,245.4	241.7	8.1	1,347.7	75.3	5.9
1992	3,552.1	306.7[2]	9.5	1,482.5	134.8	10.0
1993	3,771.1	219.0	6.2	1,563.9	81.4	5.5
Increase 1983-1993		1,804.0	91.7		812.6	108.2
Percent Increase: Consumer Price Index Ohio Personal Income (estimated)			45.0 74.0			45.0 74.0

Source: Computations by The Council from Ohio Department of Taxatation, tax analysis and Local Government Distribution Division Data.

Note: "Taxes Charged" is different than tax liability. Tax charged is before the tax relief of 10 percent, 2.5 percent and homestead exemption reimbursements. Thus, the liability owed from a parcel of property will be less than the taxes charged. The state reimburses schools and local governments for the revenue lost from tax relief measures.

[1]Prior to state government reimbursements.
[2]Largest increases in Ohio history

of the tangible personal property tax, the legislature has been reluctant to address the problem because of the revenue implications for local governments. In 1993, for example, business tangible personal property taxes were $1.2 billion, or 17.6 percent of total collections. (The addition of $954.9 million in public utility tangible personal property taxes makes a total of over $2.1 billion, over 31 percent of total property tax collections). All of this money goes to local governments.

As an acknowledgment of the adverse impact of this tax on the business community, and to minimize the impact of eliminating the tax, the legislature has taken the approach of reducing the assessment ratio over time. Revenues from this source still increase each year because of value increases and locally approved rate increases, but at a much slower rate. The assessment ratio is now at 25 percent, down from 35 percent in 1982. No further assessment ratio reductions have been approved by the legislature. An exemption for the first $10,000 for tangible personal property values was created in 1983. This represented an effort by the legislature to compensate for the burden on small businesses, and was also an effort to ease the rate increases on the corporate franchise tax. The revenue loss from this exemption is reimbursed to the local governments ($78.7 million in CY93).

Public Utility Tangible Personal Property

Public utility tangible personal property taxes are $954.9 billion (14 percent of total property taxes collected). They are exempt from the adjustments of H.B. 920. This property is assessed at 88 percent of true value, as compared to 35 percent for other types of business tangible personal property. Electric utility production equipment and the personal property of telephone companies are assessed at 100 percent of true value, the personal property of rural electric companies is assessed at 50 percent of true value.

Any changes in this category of property taxes will have to include careful consideration of the impact on the local taxing districts. About 30 percent of public utility tangible personal property is located in 12 school districts, 40 percent of the total is in 30 school districts, and 50 percent of the value is in 50 school districts (less than 10 percent of the 611 school districts).

Local Income Taxes

There are two types of locally imposed income taxes: municipal and school district (a third type, a joint municipal/school income tax, has been authorized by the legislature but has been approved by just one local authority). Ohio is one of the heaviest users of this tax in the country. Ohio's combined state and local personal income tax burden, either per capita or per $1,000 of income, is at or near that of the top ten states in the country.

Municipal Income Tax

Ohio is one of eleven states that levy a municipal income tax.[13] This tax is imposed on wages, salaries, and other compensation earned by residents of the municipality and by non-residents working in the municipality; *and* on net profits of business (both incorporated and unincorporated) attributable to activities in the municipality. Two other states (Georgia and Arkansas) grant such taxing authority to their municipalities, but none have chosen to levy this tax. Also, three states levy a payroll tax on employers.

The municipal income tax has been used in Ohio since 1946. Toledo was the first city in Ohio, and the second city in the country (after Philadelphia) to use the tax. The sparse written history on this tax indicates that Toledo was facing financial difficulties after World War II, and the property tax, with its (then) 15 mill limitation was not providing sufficient revenue to fund city operations. The sales tax was not available because of the constitution's preemption doctrine. The state constitution permitted the state to levy an income tax. Despite some discussion of adopting an income tax during the 1933 sales tax debate, the state had not yet implemented an income tax, so theoretically the income tax was the only major revenue stream available to the city. After Toledo voters approved the tax, the Ohio Supreme Court ruled that although the Ohio Constitution contained a preemption clause, the state had not enacted an income tax, so the local government entities were allowed to use local income taxes as a revenue source.[14]

Once Toledo adopted the tax, and the Supreme Court approved its use at the local level, other cities began to approve it in a fairly rapid fashion. Not only were income tax levies easier to implement (they could be adopted without a vote in many cases), the income tax held the potential of higher natural growth rates to fund city operations. By 1957, the city income tax was so widely used that the legislature passed the Uniform Municipal Income Tax law, which established statewide regulations.

A municipality may impose a rate of up to 1 percent without a vote. In 1992, the actual rates ranged from .25 percent to 2.5 percent. A total of 519 cities and villages levy this tax. 1992 collections were over $2.1 billion. This is more revenue than 14 states collected from their state income tax. Any changes in the collection process will have to consider the impact on the ten largest cities in the state. In 1993, half of the municipal income taxes are collected in these ten cities. The other 509 cities and municipalities collect the remaining revenues (Berno and Whitmore 1994).

School District Income Tax

Ohio has the broadest tax base for, and widest usage of, the school district income tax in the country. Pennsylvania (Philadelphia and Pittsburgh), Iowa (59 districts), and Kentucky (Jefferson County) are the only other states to use this revenue source for their school finances. This tax was first adopted in 1981 as an amendment to the state budget bill. The 1982 Joint Committee to Study State Taxes raised several concerns, including comments that the bill authorizing this tax did not come before the Ways and Means Committee of either the House or the Senate.[15]

The differences between the municipal income tax and the school district income tax are very important. First, the school district tax is levied against total income. The municipal tax is levied only against compensation. Second, the school district income tax is *not* paid by corporations (but it is paid by types of business entities—sole proprietorships, partnerships, etc — where income flow through to the individual tax return). Third, the municipal income tax may be imposed at a rate of up to 1 percent without a vote of the people. The school district income tax must be approved by the voters at any rate. The tax is paid by residents of a school district on the amount reported as Ohio Adjusted Gross Income less the $650 personal exemption. It is levied on individuals and estates residing in a school district. *The tax is not levied on corporations.*

The school district income tax can be levied for either a finite or an unlimited period of time. Rate options are in one quarter of one percent increments, and current rates are from 0.5 percent to 1.75 percent. As of June, 1994, 101 districts (nearly 20 percent of the districts in the state) levy the tax. The revenue is withheld by the employer, and remitted to the state Department of Taxation (DOT) along with state income tax withholding. The DOT then distributes the revenues back to the districts, less 2 percent for administrative expenses. The equivalent in property tax millage of income tax collections can be used toward 20 mill eligibility for state aid. (The school income tax may also be enacted with reductions in property taxes.) Taxpayers 65 or older are allowed a $50 credit against the amount of school district income tax due. Only one credit is allowed per return.

The revenue collected from this tax has jumped from $3.7 million to $53.7 million in just 3 years.

This taxing authority was first enacted in 1979 in order to provide an additional local revenue source for schools. The authority was repealed in 1983 (as recommended by the Joint Committee) after six districts had approved it. One district voted to repeal its income tax in 1987. The authority was restored in 1989, with the $50 senior credit. Municipalities oppose this authority because it infringes on their "revenue stream" and violates an informal agreement whereby schools were allowed property tax revenues, and the cities used income taxes as their major source of revenue. The policy behind the adoption of this authority is unclear, other than the need for increased revenues for public education.

Joint Municipal/School Income Tax

Recent legislation allows school districts to request municipal officials to place a joint municipal/school income tax on the ballot for voter approval. Liability for the tax would be similar to that for the municipal income tax. Municipal officials may refuse to place the tax on the ballot. The first two attempts at this taxing authority were on the November, 1994 ballot. The city of Euclid and Euclid School District now have the only joint income tax in the state.

County and Transit Sales and Use Tax

The county sales tax was the result of a 1967 Ohio Tax Study Commission. The members believed that if—and they stressed "if"—an additional revenue source was necessary to finance county government, the sales tax would be most appropriate.[16] The Commission was concerned about competitive and "cross-border" issues and believed that a county was a large enough geographical area to minimize that problem.

The authority to levy this tax was actually part of a "local permissive tax package" passed in 1967. The components of this package, all recommendations of the Tax Study Commission, were: the piggyback sales tax, a real estate transfer tax, a utilities service tax and a motor vehicle license tax. Of these four options, the only one which has not been adopted by any county is the utilities service tax.[17]

The local sales tax is used by seven neighboring industrial states. It is the third largest revenue source for local governments—behind property and income taxes. The local sales tax can be levied at a rate up to 0.5 percent by the county commissioners. Anything over that rate must be approved by the voters.

The first county to levy the tax was Lake County, in 1969. As recently as 1982, only 57 of Ohio's 88 counties levied this tax. As of August, 1994, 86 of the 88 counties use the sales tax (the exceptions are Butler County and Stark County).

The tax base is the same as for the state sales tax. Therefore, whenever the state broadens its sales tax base, the counties benefit. Over time, the General Assembly has also allowed county commissioners and voters greater latitude in deciding how sales tax revenues may be utilized. Formerly, these revenues were only for the county's general revenue fund. Now, they may be used for Regional Transit Authorities, county permanent improvements, convention facility notes or bonds, implementation of emergency phone (911) systems, and operation or maintenance of a detention facility.

While the county sales tax is levied on a county-wide basis, in 1974, the legislature granted regional transit authorities the right to levy the tax if the voters so approved. Since 1975, five transit authorities have used this revenue source: Cleveland, Miami Valley, Central Ohio, Lake County and Summit County.

INTERGOVERNMENTAL FISCAL RELATIONS

Intergovernmental fiscal transfers occur on two levels: Federal revenues to the states, and state revenues to local governments. During FY93-94, federal aid to Ohio state government was over $6.3 billion. Total state revenues were nearly $21 billion that year. State government distributes over $7.4 billion to local governments.

Ohio has an involved, complex system of state and local shared revenues. Two themes dominate this structure. The first is a desire to have uniform administration and collection of certain revenue sources. This is best shown by the Motor Vehicle Fuel Tax structure. The second is the desire by the General Assembly to protect local governments from revenue losses as a result of changes in the state tax code.

There are also constitutional provisions that establish this structure (Berno and Whitmore 1994). The first provision is that 50 percent of the state personal income tax collections must be returned to the county of origin. This is accomplished through the property tax rollback and state foundation aid to local schools. The second is the pre-emption doctrine discussed above in the municipal income tax section. An Ohio Supreme Court decision in 1947 allowed municipalities to impose an income tax because the state had not utilized that taxing power. On the other hand, since the state had adopted the sales tax, legislation was necessary to create the county sales tax.

The major state-local fiscal programs include (with 1993 numbers): the school foundation formula ($3 billion), property tax reimbursements ($740 million), and several local government funds ($792.7 million).

School Foundation Formula

By far the largest component of state aid to local governments involves the school foundation formula. State aid is comprised of two parts: state aid to schools (per formula grant), and reimbursements from the state for the 10 percent, 2.5 percent homestead exemption and the $10,000 tangible personal property exemption.

For FY92-93, the SF-12 distribution was over $3 billion (including $569.3 million in lottery profits). State aid from the SF-12 is divided into two broad categories: basic program aid of nearly $2.4 billion, and what is called categorical aid (over $1.6 billion).

The basic aid is based on applying 20 mills against the total property valuation. For FY93, it is designed to provide at least $2,817 for each pupil. This figure is established by the General Assembly and changes every year. The state guarantees that no district will receive less money than in the past three years, and gives districts extra money based on the poverty level of their enrollment. These two figures are the basic program aid of $2.395 billion.

Categorical aid provides money for specific types of students and transportation. The additional revenue distributed through these activities is $1.66 billion.

The state provided an additional $600,000 for miscellaneous programs. The total is nearly $4.5 billion of state revenues to local schools.

Property Tax Reimbursements

Property tax reimbursements are one of the major features of Ohio's intergovernmental fiscal system. They are one of the best examples of the Legislature's desire to protect local governments from fiscal harm that result from state changes in fiscal policy. They have also been created as a way of reducing the total tax burden on individuals when the state has increased other types of taxes (particularly the income tax).

Property tax reimbursements were over $740 million in 1993, a $375 million increase (103.1 percent) over 1983. In percentage terms, this is the third fastest growing line item in the state General Revenue Fund budget. Almost 80 percent of the increase ($300 million) was for general tax relief that was not based on "need." This does not include the $2.1 billion in property tax reductions due to the effect of H.B. 920. These reductions are not reimbursed to the local governments by the state. This $2.1 billion is a savings to the taxpayer and a revenue loss to local governments.

The property tax reduction programs that are reimbursed by the state to local governments include: 10 percent to all real property taxpayers ($533.5 million reimbursed to local governments, 73.2 percent of the 1993 total); 2.5 percent to homeowner occupied real estate ($75.3 million, 10.2 percent of total), the $10,000 valuation exemption for tangible personal property (over $78 million, 10.2 percent of the total), and the homestead exemption ($52.5 million, 7.1 percent of the total).

The 10 percent reimbursement was created in 1971 to ease the burden of the newly implemented state income tax. The General Assembly felt that because many taxpayers were already feeling tax increases as a result of the Park Investment series of cases, and the (then annual) reappraisals that were occurring, it was politically appropriate to offer some form of tax reduction along with the state personal income tax. It was determined that the new state revenues generated by the income tax would be sufficient to reimburse the local governments for this 10 percent reduction.

These thoughts established the precedent for the 2.5 percent reduction for homeowner-occupied real estate, which was established in 1979. This rollback compensated for unexpected homeowner property tax increases as a result of equalizing residential property at the 35 percent level.

The $10,000 tangible personal property exemption is the most recent reimbursed property tax reduction program. It was established in 1983 for two reasons. First, the tax increases which were taking place at that time were imposing new burdens on business in conjunction with the recession. Second, the Joint Committee to Study State Taxes had recently released its report acknowledging the burdens that the tangible personal property tax imposed on business. This exemption was a way to help business, and by reimbursing local governments, basically to hold them harmless.

The homestead exemption program was a 1970 constitutional amendment, implemented by legislation in 1971. Homeowners who are disabled, or 65 or over, and meet certain income requirements are eligible. The amount of homestead exemption tax relief is determined by the income of the owner-occupants. The maximum income limit was $8,000 in 1973 and is now $16,500. In 1991, the homestead exemption was extended to surviving spouses by constitutional amendment. In 1993, the number of homestead exemptions granted was 253,646, a decrease of over 100,000 exemptions since 1983. The average per capita property tax reduction has increased from $151 to $207 (37.1 percent).

State and Local Government Funds

The implementation of the state sales tax resulted in the first earmarking of state tax collections for distribution back to local governments. The State Local Government Fund was established in 1934 to disburse 40 percent of state tax collections back to local governments.

Today, the State Local Government Fund is composed of 4.6 percent of the state sales, use, personal income, public utility, and corporate franchise tax collections. The amount which is allocated to each municipality which levies an income tax is determined in proportion to its share of all municipal income tax collections in the state. The budget bill for the 1994-95 biennium temporarily lowered the State Local Government Fund's percentage share of the five tax sources from 4.6 percent to 4.2 percent. This lower percentage is in place from July 1, 1993 through June 30, 1995.

About $445.8 million was allocated to the State Local Government Fund in 1993, a 3.8 percent increase over 1992. In addition to the revenues received from the State Local Government Fund, each county's undivided local government fund also receives five-eighths of the taxes paid by dealers in intangibles in the county. These combined revenues are then distributed by the County Budget Commission to eligible subdivisions within the county (municipalities, townships, park districts, and the county government itself).

Library and Local Government Support Fund

This fund was established in 1986 to replace the locally collected intangible property tax, which was repealed in that year. This fund is comprised of 6.3 percent of the preceding month's personal income tax collections. The budget bill for the 1994-95 biennium temporarily reduced this share to 5.7 percent during the period July 1, 1993 through June 30, 1995. The total amount distributed to the counties for the calendar year 1993 was $284,700,000.

State and Local Government Revenue Assistance Fund

This fund was established in 1989 to allow local governments to share some of the revenue increases the state had enjoyed because of the rate increases, and to help them with the slower growth in their local revenue sources. This fund is comprised of 0.7 percent of state sales, use, personal income, public utility, and corporate franchise tax collections. As with the other local government funds, the percentage share of the five tax sources was temporarily reduced from 0.7 percent to 0.6 percent for FY94 and FY95. The amount allocated to each county is determined each year based upon the county's population compared to the total population of the state. The population used is the more recent of either the latest Federal estimated census figures or the latest decennial census figures that include population totals as of June 1 of the preceding year. The total amount distributed in CY93 was over $59.2 million.

STATE AND LOCAL GOVERNMENT DEBT

State and local government debt has grown rapidly over the past 14 years, but is still relatively low compared to other states. The total state and local government debt outstanding is $28.9 billion. Total state government debt increased $7.7 billion dollars (222 percent) from FY79 through FY93, to a new high of $11.1 billion. Ohio local government debt increased $10.9 billion dollars (186 percent) from 1979 through 1993, to a total of $16.8 billion.

STATE GOVERNMENT DEBT

In contrast to the federal government, the bonded debt of Ohio cannot be used for operating deficits, but is reserved for capital improvements. State government debt falls into two broad categories: General Obligation bonds, which are backed by the full faith and credit of the state, and Special Revenue bonds, which have pledged income derived from user fees and rentals on the acquired or constructed assets to pay the debt service.

At various times since 1921, Ohio voters, in 13 constitutional amendments (the last adopted in 1993), have authorized general obligation debt for the construction and improvement of state facilities and highways, research and development of coal technology, and local infrastructure improvements. In practice, General Obligation bonds are retired over periods of 10 to 35 years.

As of June 30, 1993, $2.74 billion in general obligation debt (excluding Highway Obligations and Infrastructure Bonds) had been authorized by constitutional amendments, of which $2.47 billion had been issued and $74.4

million was outstanding; the authorization to issue $232.5 million had expired. Coal Research and Development bonds may be issued as long as the outstanding principal amount does not exceed $100 million.

Highway Obligations may be issued as long as the outstanding principal amount does not exceed $500 million. The aggregate of General Assembly authorizations as of June 30, 1993 for Highway Obligations was $1.6 billion, of which $1.34 billion had been issued and $330.6 million was outstanding. Additional Highway Obligations may be issued from time to time, as authorized by the General Assembly, as outstanding Highway Obligations are retired.

A 1987 constitutional amendment authorized the issuance of $1.2 billion of general obligation bonds for infrastructure improvements, of which no more than $120 million may be issued in any one year. As of June 30, 1993, the General Assembly had authorized $600 million of these bonds to be sold, of which $480 million had been issued and $432.5 million was outstanding; the authorization to issue $120 million had expired.

Primary users of the special revenue bonds include the Treasurer of the State for the Ohio Department of Development's Economic Development Financing Division and the Ohio Building Authority. A more detailed analysis of the state's debt follows.

State Government Long-Term Financing and Capital Improvements

Ohio has engaged in major capital construction of highway and non-highway facilities, beginning with constitutional amendments passed by the voters in 1953 and 1955. These capital programs have resulted in the construction and improvement of public school classrooms, higher education facilities, and highways. Construction has generally been financed by the issuance of long-term bonds, which are retired over periods of 10 to 35 years, because the high costs of such projects could not be funded from current revenues. This allows payments for the bonds to be spread over the useful life of the facilities and allows the taxpayers who benefit from the facilities to pay the construction costs on an equitable basis. These capital improvements are financed by three methods: (a) general obligation bonds; (b) revenue or special obligation bonds; and (c) current revenues.

General Obligation Bonds. Since 1953, many improvements have been financed through the issuance of general obligation debt, which is backed by the full faith and credit of the State of Ohio. Revenues from almost any tax enacted by the legislature can be pledged. This type of debt must be authorized by the voters in a constitutional amendment.

The Commissioners of the Sinking Fund, of the Governor, Auditor, Treasurer, Attorney General, and Secretary of State, oversee the issuance and retirement of general obligation debt. Capital improvements programs financed by the currently outstanding general obligation debt include improvements, development, public improvements, highway construction, and coal research and development.

The Treasurer of the State of Ohio has been authorized to issue general obligation debt for local government infrastructure improvements.

Revenue or Special Obligation Bonds. Revenue or special obligation bonds finance a specific project or group of related projects, with debt service paid by revenues from, or fees charged for the use of the facilities constructed, rather than by the full faith and credit of the state. Special authorities and commissions have been established by Ohio law with the authority to issue revenue bonds. These include the Ohio Turnpike Commission, the Higher Education Facilities Commission, the Underground Parking Commission, the Ohio Housing Finance Agency, the Ohio Air Quality Development Authority, and the Ohio Water Development Authority. The construction funds raised by these authorities, and the funds necessary to make the debt service payments on their obligations, are handled apart from the state treasury.

Some types of revenue bonds were issued pursuant to Section 2i, Article VIII of the Ohio Constitution, which was approved by the voters on November 5, 1968. These bonds have been issued by the Director of Natural Resources, the Ohio Public Facilities Commission, and the Ohio Building Authority. These bonds constitute a special type of bonded debt in that appropriations for the lease rental payments are made from the General Revenue Fund; these are the primary source of debt service payments, rather than user fees.

Economic Development Bonds. Some special types of bonds have been issued by the Treasurer of the State to finance economic development in the state. The debt service on those bonds is paid from the liquor profits earned by the Department of Liquor Control. The Treasurer has also issued state economic development revenue bonds for economic development purposes and the debt service costs are paid by repayments of economic development loans made from the Facilities Establishment Fund. The Treasurer is also issuing additional economic development revenue bonds on which the debt service costs will be paid by the corporations that receive the proceeds of the bonds, but the bonds will also be backed by the repayments of loans made from the Facilities Establishment Fund in the State Treasury.

The Department of Development has issued industrial development revenue bonds, and the debt service costs are paid solely by the corporations that receive the proceeds of those bonds.

Certificates of Participation. The Department of Administrative Services has been a participant in the issuance of Certificates of Participation for the installation of a State Micro-Wave Communications System and for computer equipment for the use of various state agencies. The costs of the

Certificates of Participation are paid from charges to agencies that use the system and equipment.

Current Revenues. A variety of capital improvements are financed from current or accumulated revenue rather than by the issuance of long-term debt. Most of the current revenue used to fund these projects is from the General Revenue Fund. Revenue from other funds such as the Highway Safety Fund, the Wildlife Fund, the Waterways Safety Fund and the Public School Building Fund is also used for capital improvements, as is some of the revenue from funds in the Federal Special Revenue Budget Fund Group.

Trends and Levels of Dept

The presentation in Table 3-4 summarizes the state debt paid by state funds and paid by non-state funds. This analysis excludes certain long-term obligations, presented in Table 3-5.

Ohio's credit standing has seen a steady long term drift downward, possibly reflecting the slow growth in the state economy. Ohio's bond rating history is described in Box 3-5.

Local Government Debt

The ability of Ohio's local governments to issue and repay debt is controlled by the State Constitution. Basically, local governments cannot issue debt without voter approval, or without otherwise ensuring a fixed income stream sufficient to cover interest and principal. The levels of local government debt are described in Table 3-6.

TAX REVENUES AND ECONOMIC DEVELOPMENT

A variety of factors influence the relationship between the economy and government revenues. The most obvious are rate changes and/or base increases. Another is how the natural growth in taxable income, due to inflation and normal growth factors, influences revenue increases. A factor which may have just as large an influence is how individuals and businesses respond to the tax system, i.e., financial adjustments they may make to minimize tax liability for one year or shift liabilities to another year.

While some of the above factors are not measurable, it is helpful to examine the economic growth rate, tax base and tax rate changes, and the trends in state and local government revenues in Ohio.

TABLE 3-4
Ohio State Debt Outstanding by Type of Issue: June 30, 1993

Debt Paid from State Funds	Outstanding Amount (In Millions of Dollars)	Percentage of Total
General Revenue Fund:		
Higher Education	1,885.0	39.5
Prisons	699.4	14.7
Mental Health	484.3	10.2
Buildings	574.8	12.1
Infrastructure	432.5[1]	9.1
Parks and Recreation	102.8	2.1
Development	32.9[1]	0.7
Coal Research	36.0[1]	0.7
Juvenile Corrections	62.5	1.3
Other	17.8	0.4
Total Paid from General Revenue Fund Directly or by Lease Rental Payments	4,328.0	90.8
Highway Revenue Funds: Highway Obligations	330.6[1]	6.9
Liquor Profit Funds: Economic Development	110.3	2.3
Total Debt Paid-State Funds	4,768.8	100.0

Debt Paid From Non-State Funds	Outstanding Amount (In Millions of Dollars)	Debt Paid From Non-State Funds	Outstanding Amount (In Millions of Dollars)
Ohio Water Development Authority	987.5	Development-Industrial Revenue Bonds	358.3
Ohio Air Quality Authority	1,630.6*	Public Higher Education	262.5
Housing Authority	2,441.0	Private Higher Education	266.1
Hospitals	318.2	Other	5.8
Ohio Enterprise Bond Program	105.7		
Total Paid From Non-State Funds			6,375.7
Total Paid From State Funds			4,768.8

Source: Ohio Office of Budget and Planning, *Ohio Comprehensive Annual Financial Report*, 1994 and Ohio Municipal Advisory Council, *Compendium of Municipal Debt*, 1994.

[1]Voted Debt—Backed by full faith and credit of state.
[2]Outstanding 1/1/93

TABLE 3-5
Excluded Long Term Debt Obligation

General Long-Term Obligations	
Ohio Expositions Commission/Pepsi-Cola/ Celeste Center	$5.8
Ohio Department of Transportation/Panhandle Rail Line Project	8.5
Total General Long-Term Obligations	*$14.3*
Other Long-Term Obligations	
Compensated Absences	$224.1
Lease Agreements	7.0
Judgements, Settlements, and Claims	105.2
Litigation Liabilities	21.1
Worker's Compensation Obligation	442.2
Required Contribution to the Great Lakes Protection Fund	4.6
Total Other Long-Term Obligations	*$804.2*

Source: Ohio Office of Budget and Management, various reports.

Box 3-5
Bond Rating History For Selected Ohio Issuers

Highway Obligations

Standard & Poor's	AAA since before 1974
Moody's	AAA from 1974 to November 1979 AA since November 1979

General Obligations

Standard & Poor's	AAA until January 1982 AA since January 1982
Moody's	AAA until November 1979 AA since November 1979

Ohio Public Facilities Commission and Ohio Building Authority

Standard & Poor's	AA until November 1979 A+ from November 1979 to April 1982 A from April 1982 to September 1989 A+ from September 1989 to present
Moody's	AA until November 1979 A from November 1979 to October 1993 A1 from October 1993 to present

The top half of Table 3-7 shows changes in selected economic indicators: the national Gross Domestic Product, Ohio's Gross State Product, employment, and earned income. The bottom half of the chart shows major changes in state and local tax practices (base and rate changes), and changes in major revenue sources at the state and local levels.[18] There were only two

TABLE 3-6
Increases In Ohio Local Government Debt
(In Millions of Dollars)

	Gross Outstanding Debt	14 Year Increase		Percentage of Total State and Local Debt - June 20	
Government Entity	**Amount**	**Amount**	**Percent**	**1993**	**1979**
Local Governments CY 1993:					
Counties	6,755.5	5,789.9	600	24.2	10.3
Municipalities	5,832.3	3,133.2	116	20.9	28.9
Schools	2,259.8	785.0	53	8.1	15.8
Special Districts	1,922.1	1,184.1	160	6.9	7.9
Townships	28.8	22.9	388	--	--
Total Local Government Debt	16,798.5	10,915.1	186	60.1	62.9

Source: Ohio Office of Budget and Management, *Ohio Municipal Advisory Council.*

periods when revenues actually declined. The first, in 1986, was a 0.1 percent decrease in state personal income tax revenues. That year shows a slower than normal economic growth rate at the national and state levels (United States GDP and Ohio GSP), and a correspondingly lower increase in employment and earned income. In that year, the Legislature enacted a 5 percent personal income tax rate reduction. The second, in 1991, was due to the decrease in state sales tax revenues. That year was the end of the 1990-91 recession, and saw a decrease in Ohio's private sector employment and the second lowest earnings increase (2.3 percent) during the period examined. Also, there was no state rate increase or state base-broadening. More generally, the economy and tax revenues have grown.

A different analysis has been carried out to show the relationship between private sector employment growth and the changes in tangible personal property values. The Ohio Public Expenditure Council compiled changes in private sector employment from the Ohio Bureau of Employment Services annual reports. These changes were then compared to tangible personal property value reports filed by the county auditors with the state Department of Taxation. The county reports have adjusted the tangible personal property values for abatements and for changes in taxable value (state law reduced the assessment value 1 percent a year during this period). The Public Expenditure Council then adjusted all the reported tangible personal property taxable values for the tax years 1981 and 1986 to the 27 percent assessment rate of 1991. *These values do not include changes in public utility tangible personal property values.* Therefore, they reflect the changes in business investment (machinery, equipment, inventories, furni-

TABLE 3-7
Selected Economic and Tax Revenue Data for Ohio
(Current Dollars)

	1980*	1981*	1982*	1983	1984	1985	1986	1987	1988	1989	1990**	1991**	1992	1993
U.S. Gross Domestic Product	+8.9%	+12.1%	+4.5%	+7.6%	+11.5%	+7.1%	+5.3%	+7.0%	+8.0%	+6.5%	+5.5%	+3.1%	+5.2%	+5.4%
Ohio Gross State Product	+3.4%	+9.0%	+0.6%	+7.1%	+11.9%	+5.9%	+5.0%	+5.9%	+6.9%	+5.8%	+4.3%	+2.3%	N/A	N/A
CPI	+13.5%	10.3%	+6.2%	+3.2%	+4.3%	+3.6%	+1.9%	+3.6%	+4.1%	+4.8%	+5.4%	+4.2%	+3.0%	+3.0%
Ohio private employment	-3.2%	-1.3%	-4.9%	-0.5%	+5.4%	+3.0%	+2.4%	+2.8%	+3.0%	+2.6%	+1.1%	+1.1%	-1.8%	+1.6%(e)
Ohio Earned Income	+4.3%	+5.8%	+0.5%	+4.4%	+10.7%	+6.0%	+4.5%	+5.6%	+7.4%	+5.4%	+5.2%	+2.3%	+6.9%	+4.4%

	1980	1981	1982	1983	1984	1985	1986	1987	1988	1989	1990	1991	1992	1993
State Law Changes		Sales Tax Rate +1% to 5%	50% tax hike •2 new income tax brackets	40% tax hike		5% annual rate reductions						•sales tax expanded	•sales tax expanded •1 new bracket	
Local Rate/tax Changes		6 School income taxes	57 Cos. with sales tax	58 Cos. with sales tax	TPP 35% ratio reduced 1% a year; $10,000 exempt	68 Cos. with sales tax 3 RTA's		78 Cos. with sales tax 3 RTA's		Franklin County RTA tax • School income tax adopted	85 Cos. with sales tax 4 RTA's	5 RTA's		101 schools levy income tax; 87 Cos. sales tax
State personal income tax revenues	+19.8%	+9.1%	+9.6%	+58.6%	+26.1%	+11.7%	-0.1%	+15.9%	+4.5%	+16.1%	+4.5%	+4.0%	+3.0%	+7.9%
Local personal income tax revenues	+6.9%	+12.1%	+7.8%	+7.9%	+13.4%	+8.8%	+6.3%	+7.6%	+9.1%	+7.7%	+4.4%	+3.7%	+5.9%	+4.1%
State sales tax revenues	+1.3%	+13.6%	+10.8%	+10.0%	+15.9%	+10.0%	+9.1%	+6.5%	+8.3%	+6.4%	+4.8%	+0.4%	+5.0%	+5.9%

continued

TABLE 3-7 (continued)
Selected Economic and Tax Revenue Data for Ohio
(Current Dollars)

	1980*	1981*	1982*	1983	1984	1985	1986	1987	1988	1989	1990**	1991**	1992	1993
Local sales tax revenues	+7.2%	+17.0%	+16.9%	+11.6%	+16.8%	+16.8%	+14.0%	+11.1%	+17.9%	+10.4%	+6.4%	+7.5%	+9.2%	+11.7%
Local property tax revenues	+5.8%	+7.7%	+8.7%	+4.7%	+2.0%	+4.8%	+6.1%	+7.1%	+7.9%	+7.5%	+7.7%	+6.4%	+7.9%	+5.6%
Tax burden per $1,000 income	47th	48th	43rd	32nd	28th	31st	29th	29th	33rd	32nd	30th	31st	31st	N/A

Sources: GDP, GSP, CPI and Ohio earned income data from U.S. Department of Commerce, *Survey of Current Business*, August 1994; Ohio employment from Ohio Bureau of Employment Services; tax changes selected by Council staff; tax revenues from Ohio Department of Taxation *Annual Reports*; tax burden per $1,000 personal income from *Government Finances* (various years). Annual percentage change calculations by Council staff.

* January-July 1980, July 1981-November 1982 are recession periods ** July 1990-March 1991 is recession period.

ture and fixtures) and private sector job changes. The results by county are listed in Table 3-8. There are slightly different relationships in the 5- and 10-year changes.

To better describe this relationship across counties, we have regressed property values against private sector employment. The regression coefficient for the 1986-1991 period is 2.49393. This means that for each 1 percent increase in private sector employment, there is a 2.49 percent increase in tangible personal property values. The regression coefficient for the 1981-1991 period is 1.927002. This means that for each 1 percent increase in private sector employment, there is a 1.93 percent increase in tangible personal property values.

This is important to the property tax revenues of state and local government. Tangible personal property values are not affected by the adjustment factors of H.B. 920. Tangible personal property is the only segment of Ohio's property tax structure that operates on the basic formula: the product of value and rate is revenue. Therefore, value increases, even if the tax rate does not increase, represent tax revenue increases for local governments which rely on property tax revenues.

This also indicates that, depending on the composition of the property tax base for a particular taxing district, the judicious use of tax abatements should not harm local governments. The tangible personal property values used in this analysis are the actual taxable values, and have been adjusted for the abatements and the assessment rate reductions.

The authors are confident that this beneficial impact of private sector employment growth also applies to other tax revenues: real property, sales, and income. Unfortunately, because of the many changes in rates and bases of the income and sales taxes, and the nuances of real property tax practices, the data are not available to show this conclusively.

A final way to look at the relationships between the economy and tax revenues is to consider the share of earnings which is devoted to federal, state and local taxes. While the federal tax burden has decreased slightly over the past 10 years (from 75.4 percent to 69.7 percent of total taxes), the state and local burden, as a percentage of total tax burden, has increased from 24.6 percent to 30.3 percent (Table 3-9). The total state and local tax increase of 98.5 percent over ten years is more than double the 45.4 percent increase in the Consumer Price Index and well above the 73.2 percent increase in Ohio's personal income.

Among the various types of state and local taxes, the largest increases have been where Ohio has had the highest rate increases—in the state personal income tax, the state sales and use tax, and the motor vehicle fuel tax.

TABLE 3-8
Analysis of Employment and Adjusted Business Tangible Personal Property Value Changes, by County, for 1981–1991

		1981 to 1991						1986 to 1991					
		Private Sector Employment				Adjusted Tangible Personal Property Values		Private Sector Employment				Adjusted Tangible Personal Property Values	
Economic Region	County	Percent Chg	Rank	Percent Chg	Rank	Percent Chg	Rank	Percent Chg	Rank	Percent Chg	Rank	Percent Chg	Rank
I-75	Union	105	1	8,417	13	251	3	51	2	5,525	13	43	29
I-75	Warren	89	2	13,825	6	228	4	46	3	9,231	7	82	8
River	Holmes	59	3	3,466	32	86	32	28	7	2,034	35	40	35
I-75	Clemont	57	4	10,918	9	28	78	24	9	5,757	11	19	67
Mid-State	Madison	53	5	2,468	38	198	6	54	1	2,483	26	192	2
I-75	Shelby	53	6	7,220	16	257	2	39	4	5,819	10	161	3
I-75	Greene	50	7	9,741	10	122	14	24	8	5,693	12	63	11
I-75	Clinton	45	8	4,195	25	176	7	30	6	3,173	22	114	4
River	Jackson	42	9	2,331	41	109	19	10	39	740	58	37	39
Lake	Geauga	42	10	6,229	19	161	8	14	26	2,584	25	58	13
I-75	Logan	41	11	3,620	31	390	1	34	5	3,193	21	345	1
I-75	Wood	39	12	9,419	11	84	35	14	23	4,148	17	43	27
Lake	Medina	36	13	8,380	14	111	18	19	15	4,999	15	57	16

continued

TABLE 3-8 (continued)
Analysis of Employment and Adjusted Business Tangible Personal Property Value Changes, by County, for 1981–1991

		1981 to 1991						1986 to 1991					
		Private Sector Employment				Adjusted Tangible Personal Property Values		Private Sector Employment				Adjusted Tangible Personal Property Values	
Economic Region	County	Percent Chg	Rank	Percent Chg	Rank	Percent Chg	Rank	Percent Chg	Rank	Percent Chg	Rank	Percent Chg	Rank
Mid-State	Franklin	35	14	120,615	1	122	15	12	29	50,966	1	46	24
Lake	Huron	34	15	5,369	21	125	12	15	18	2,833	23	53	17
Mid-State	Delaware	31	16	4,029	28	103	22	16	17	2,297	28	49	20
River	Carroll	30	17	1,106	52	96	23	8	49	370	68	42	31
I-75	Ottawa	30	18	2,744	36	205	5	6	61	637	62	11	75
I-75	Paulding	29	19	752	63	50	64	18	16	518	64	30	47
I-75	Preble	29	20	1,638	43	89	30	12	32	758	56	12	73
I-75	Fulton	28	21	3,146	33	152	9	15	19	1,876	38	100	5
Lake	Portage	28	22	6,719	17	96	24	20	13	5,072	14	40	34
I-75	Hancock	28	23	6,294	18	107	21	10	40	2,715	24	35	41
I-75	Wyandot	27	24	1,443	46	61	55	3	73	175	72	30	49
I-75	Williams	26	25	3,077	35	91	29	12	30	1,594	41	66	10
Lake	Sandusky	21	26	3,866	30	72	40	9	45	1,909	36	34	44
I-75	Auglaize	21	27	2,429	39	93	28	15	21	1,833	39	41	32

continued

TABLE 3-8 (continued)
Analysis of Employment and Adjusted Business Tangible Personal Property Value Changes, by County, for 1981–1991

		1981 to 1991						1986 to 1991					
		Private Sector Employment				Adjusted Tangible Personal Property Values		Private Sector Employment				Adjusted Tangible Personal Property Values	
Economic Region	County	Percent Chg	Rank	Percent Chg	Rank	Percent Chg	Rank	Percent Chg	Rank	Percent Chg	Rank	Percent Chg	Rank
I-75	Darke	20	28	2,424	40	108	20	12	28	1,582	42	42	30
Lake	Lake	20	29	12,560	7	120	16	14	24	9,237	6	58	14
I-75	Mercer	18	30	1,956	42	64	52	20	11	2,138	32	58	15
I-75	Champaig	18	31	1,262	48	135	11	10	44	745	57	68	9
I-75	Hamilton	18	32	71,088	2	64	53	8	52	34,113	2	29	50
Mid-State	Licking	17	33	5,195	22	58	57	11	36	3,458	19	8	81
River	Highland	17	34	993	56	85	34	11	34	713	60	29	53
Mid-State	Morrow	16	35	556	67	70	42	3	70	122	75	12	72
I-75	Putnam	16	36	1,026	54	84	36	4	67	310	69	40	37
I-75	Henry	16	37	1,200	51	70	43	11	33	918	52	29	51
River	Morgan	15	38	497	68	96	25	-4	85	-137	82	52	18
I-75	Allen	15	39	6,142	20	60	56	4	68	1,830	40	14	70
Mid-State	Pickaway	15	40	1,348	47	74	39	10	43	846	51	40	33
Mid-State	Fayette	15	41	890	60	46	66	12	27	764	55	25	58

continued

TABLE 3-8 (continued)
Analysis of Employment and Adjusted Business Tangible Personal Property Value Changes, by County, for 1981–1991

		1981 to 1991						1986 to 1991					
		Private Sector Employment				Adjusted Tangible Personal Property Values		Private Sector Employment				Adjusted Tangible Personal Property Values	
Economic Region	County	Percent Chg	Rank	Percent Chg	Rank	Percent Chg	Rank	Percent Chg	Rank	Percent Chg	Rank	Percent Chg	Rank
River	Brown	15	42	563	66	52	62	10	38	417	67	28	55
I-75	Miami	15	43	4,122	26	96	26	7	53	2,256	29	50	19
Lake	Erie	14	44	3,867	29	52	63	7	56	2,067	34	30	48
Lake	Wayne	14	45	4,104	27	71	41	8	51	2,409	27	34	42
I-75	Montgom	14	46	30,576	3	67	48	3	71	7,819	9	8	79
River	Tuscaraw	13	47	3,125	34	69	45	9	47	2,129	33	29	52
I-75	Butler	13	48	8,989	12	34	73	6	64	4,044	18	43	28
River	Athens	11	49	980	58	144	10	12	31	1,044	48	44	26

Source: Ohio Public Expenditure Council.

TABLE 3-9
Estimated Federal, State, and Local Tax Collections in Ohio (In Millions of Dollars)

			Increase		Percentage of Total	
Ohio Tax Collections	**1982**	**1992**	**Amount**	**Percent**	**1982**	**1992**
Federal Taxes	$33,428.0	$49,838.3	$16,410.3	49.1	75.4	69.7
State and Local Taxes	10,904.1	21,640.7	10,736.6	98.5	24.6	30.3
Total Estimated Tax Collections in Ohio	$44,332.1	$71,479.0	$17,146.9	61.2	100.0	100.0
State and Local Tax Collections:						
Personal Income-State	$1,243.6	$4,403.8	$3,160.2	254.1	11.4	20.3
Municipal Income (Est.)	1,.045.0	2,050.0	1,005.0	96.2	9.3	9.5
Sales and Use	2,036.5	4,417.2	2,380.7	116.9	18.7	20.4
Real Estate and Public Utility Real Property	2,226.8	4,383.3	2,156.5	96.8	20.4	20.3
Business Personal Property	880.0	1,184.7	304.7	34.6	8.1	5.5
Motor Vehicle Fuel	527.0	1,128.8	601.8	114.2	4.8	5.2
Public Utility Personal Property	420.0	877.6	457.6	109.0	3.9	4.0
Unemployment Compensation	566.9	841.3	274.4	48.4	5.2	3.9
Corporate Franchise	637.0	814.1	177.1	27.8	5.58	3.8
Public Utility Excise	496.9	582.5	85.6	17.2	4.6	2.7
Insurance	149.6	274.9	125.3	83.8	1.4	1.3
Cigarette	198.6	230.4	31.8	16.0	1.8	1.1
Estate	104.0	206.3	102.3	98.4	0.9	0.9
Alcoholic Beverage	43.4	70.0	26.6	61.3	0.4	0.3
Highway Use and Motor Fuel Use	46.0	57.5	11.5	25.0	0.4	0.3
School Income	0.0	37.6	37.6	100.0	0.0	0.2
Intangible Personal Property	239.9	11.6	-228.3	-95.2	202	0.0
Other	42.9	69.1	61.1	61.1	0.4	0.3
Total Estimated State and Local Tax Collections	$10,904.1	$21,640.7	$10,736.6	98.5	100.0	100.0
Increase in Consumer Price Index Increase in Ohio Personal Income				45.4 73.2		

Source: Ohio Department of Taxation, *Annual Report*; Ohio Department of Taxation (1994).

CONCLUSIONS

- Ohio's state and local tax structure is much better (in terms of fairness, equity, etc.) than in the early 1960's. But there is still room for improvement. Constitutional provisions frame much of Ohio's state and local tax structure. Therefore, some reforms may first require approval by the voters of a constitutional amendment, then implementation by the legislature.
- Ohio has a long history of ensuring that local governments (especially

schools) are "held harmless" by tax changes. This "hold harmless" approach could be an impediment to reform efforts. It has stymied tangible personal property reform since the late 1960's.

- The legislature tends to act only in times of real or perceived economic "crisis" or court decisions.
    - Economic conditions played a major role in the adoption of the state sales tax, the state personal income tax, and the tax increases of the 1980's and 1990's.
    - The Ohio Supreme Court decisions in the Park Investment cases during the late 1960's led to a much fairer and equitable local property tax structure.
- Additional local taxing authority (municipal and school income taxes, local option sales tax, etc.) granted to Ohio's local governments and school districts have reduced the reliance on the local property tax as a means of financing local governments.
- Ohio's state and local tax structure has not fully responded to changes in the nature of business activities in the state. Public utility taxation has not fully responded to judicial and federal regulatory changes which have increased competition for public utilities, especially in the telecommunications. The same applies to changes in financial services—banks, insurance companies, savings and loans, etc. The changes in the nature of manufacturing have made the tangible personal property tax even more onerous than in the past. Finally, the change in the economic base to more of a service industry orientation has been viewed by state policymakers as a problem rather than an opportunity as they face increasing pressures on government spending and taxpayer concerns of an increasing tax burden.
- Future improvements in Ohio's tax structure will require compromise by the vested interests involved. There will be "winners" and "losers" as Ohio solves the problems existing in the tax structure, be it fairness, equity or practices that discourage economic development. Prime examples of the necessary compromises could be real property tax relief based on need, rather than the current flat rate, and the repeal of the personal property tax.

APPENDIX
STATE AND LOCAL TAX CHANGES BY TYPE OF TAX

STATE
ALCOHOLIC BEVERAGE TAXES

Tax Base

Beer, wine, mixed beverages, and liquor.

History of Major Changes

1933 Beer and malt beverages taxed at $1.00 per barrel.

1934 Liquor gallonage taxed at $1.00.

Rate on bottled beer and malt beverages set at 0.75 cents per six ounces.

1935 Mixed beverages taxed at 10% of retail price.

1939 Mixed beverages taxed at 40 cents per gallon.

Wine tax revised as follows:

Wine less than 14% alcohol	.12 cents per gallon
Wine, 14% to 21% alcohol	.30 cents per gallon
Vermouth	.60 cents per gallon
Sparkling wine and champagne	$1.00 per gallon

1959 Sales of wine and mixed beverages subject to sales tax.

Beer tax increased to $2.50 per barrel.

1967 Beer and malt beverages subject to sales tax.

1969 Liquor gallonage tax increased to $2.25.

Mixed beverages increased to 80 cents.

Wine tax increased as follows:

Wine, less than 14% alcohol	.24 cents per gallon
Wine, 14% to 21% alcohol	.60 cents per gallon
Vermouth	.75 cents per gallon
Sparkling wine and champagne	$1.25 per gallon

1981 Temporary tax increases on beer, malt beverages, wine, and mixed beverages during the period January-June 1981.

1982 Credit against taxes for Ohio brewers and wine producers.

Two cents excise tax increase on wine per gallon.

Three cents per gallon of wine earmarked for grape industries.

Repeal of distinction between "beer" and "malt beverages."

Tax on beer in containers of 12 ounces or less changed to 0.125 cent per ounce.

1986 County sports facility liquor tax authorized.

1989 Barreled beer rate increased $1.00, to $3.50 per barrel.

1990 County sports facility alcoholic beverage tax authorized. County sports facility liquor tax amended.

1992 Alcoholic beverage and liquor gallonage rates increased.

STATE
CARBONATED BEVERAGE TAX

TAX BASE

Carbonated soft drinks and non-alcoholic beer.

HISTORY OF MAJOR CHANGES

1981 Soft drinks tax enacted on only pre-mix and post-mix.
1982 Tax ruled unconstitutional and repealed as of December 31.
1991 Tax on carbonated soft drinks and non-alcoholic beer enacted.

STATE
CIGARETTE TAX

TAX BASE

1. Cigarettes.
2. Cigars, chewing tobacco, snuff, smoking tobacco, and other tobacco products — effective February 1, 1993.

HISTORY OF MAJOR CHANGES

Year	Change	Total Tax Rate Per Pack of 20 (amount in cents)
1931	Tax enacted	2
1956	1 cent rate increase	3
1959	2 cents rate increase	5
1967	2 cents rate increase. Cigarettes made subject to sales tax	7
1969	3 cents rate increase	10
1971	5 cents rate increase. Cigarettes exempted from sales tax	15
1981	1 cent rate decrease. Cigarettes made subject to sales tax	14
1983	Tax changes to a per cigarette rate of 0.7 cent	14
1986	Counties authorized to levy permissive cigarette tax for funding the building of a sports facility.	
1987	0.2 cent per cigarette increase.	18
1991	All cigarette tax revenues to be allocated to the General Revenue Fund when capital improvement bonds are retired in 1992.	
1992	As of January 1, 1992, taxpayers no longer allowed 30 days credit on purchases of tax stamps or meter impressions.	
	0.3 cent per cigarette increase	24
	17% of the wholesale price.	

STATE
CORPORATE FRANCHISE TAX

TAX BASE

The corporate franchise tax has two alternative tax bases:

1. The Ohio net worth (book value of capital surplus, undivided profits and reserve) of the corporation; or
2. The Ohio net income (profits) of the corporation.

HISTORY OF MAJOR CHANGES

1902 Enacted at rate of 1 mill on value of capital stock located in Ohio.

1959 Rate increased to 3 mills.

1967 Rate increased to 4 mills.

1969 Rate increased to 5 mills.

1971 Income base added; 4% on first $25,000 of net income, 8% on income over $25,000.

1978 Credit allowed for certain tangible property taxes.

1980 "Litter" rates enacted for tax years 1981 through 1985.

Additional rates for all corporations except litter stream corporations: 0.14 mills on net worth; or 0.11% on the first $25,000 or income; 0.22% on income over $25,000. Maximum tax: $5,000. Additional rates for corporations manufacturing or selling "litter stream" products: 0.28 mills on net worth; or 0.11% on the first $25,000 of income; 0.44% on income over $25,000. Maximum tax of $10,000.

1980 15% surcharge imposed for tax year 1981.

1981 Increase in regular corporate rates: 5.5 mills on net worth; 4.6% and 8.7% on net income; minimum tax of $150.

Financial institutions exemption repealed; 6.5 mill rate on net worth for tax years 1982 and 1983.

5.75% surtax imposed for tax year 1982.

1982 5.75% surtax for tax year 1983.

1983 Increase in regular corporate rates: 5.82 mills on net worth; 5.1% and 9.2% on net income; surtax of 5.4% on net income rate; minimum tax reduces to $50.

Increase in financial institutions rates; 15 mills on net worth; additional tax of 6.47 mills on savings and loans and 1.54 mills for other financial institutions for tax years 1984 and 1985.

1985 Litter tax rates continued through 1991.

Surtax on net income reduced to 2.7% in 1987, repealed in 1988.

"S" corporations exempted from corporate franchise tax for year 1987 and thereafter.

1986 Decrease in regular corporate tax on net income top rate to 8.9% effective 1988; lower bracket doubled to first $50,000 of net income effective 1989. Litter tax rates codified.

1987 Long distance telephone companies subject to corporate franchise tax effective tax year 1988.

Litter tax rates continued through 1993.

1989 Corporations undergoing "F" reorganizations subject to tax.

1991 Income transferred, and certain costs and expenses paid to passive income corporations, are subject to tax.

1992 Credit for increased exports.
Credit for new jobs created.
Railroad are explicitly subject to corporate franchise tax effective tax year 1993.
Litter tax rates extended to 1995. (Now continued indefinitely.)

STATE ESTATE TAX

Tax Base

The taxable estate equals the value of the gross estate less deductions.

History Of Major Changes

1893 First Ohio death tax enacted — an inheritance tax levied on individual successions to property within the state.

1968 Inheritance tax repealed and an estate tax levied on taxable value of the estate.

1975 Surviving spouse exemption increased from $20,000 to $30,000.

1979 Resident decedent estates with gross value under $5,000 exempted from filing returns.

1981 Resident decedent estates with gross value under $20,000 exempted from filing returns and all previous general and family exemptions doubled in amount.

1983 Tax credit and marital deduction adopted, family and general exemptions repealed, and resident decedent estates with gross value under $25,000 exempted from filing returns.

1989 Effective July 1, 1991, marital deduction changed to greater of $1 million or one-half the adjusted gross estate value.

1991 The scheduled increase in the marital deduction limit to the greater of $1 million or one-half the adjusted gross estate value is repealed. The current marital deduction limit is retained for estates with dates of death through June 30, 1993, with unlimited marital deduction after this date.

STATE HIGHWAY USE TAX (AXLE-MILE TAX)

The highway use tax was effectively repealed January 1, 1991 by legislation relating to Ohio's entry into the international registration plan (IRP). The IRP is a cooperative agreement among member states to share registration revenue from interstate carriers based on mileage traveled in each state. Highway Use Tax revenues were replaced in part by a percentage of registration revenue from vehicles over 26,000 pounds (including IRP registration fees) and from a three cent surcharge per gallon of motor fuel on vehicles which are highway use taxpayers.

STATE INCOME TAX

TAX BASE

The amount reported as Federal Adjusted Gross Income to the United States Internal Revenue Service plus or minus adjustments, according to Ohio income tax law.

HISTORY OF MAJOR CHANGES

1912 Constitutional amendment authorized income taxes.

1972 Personal income tax enacted.

Up to $4,000 exempted from adjusted gross income for retirement benefits.

1972 Tax credit of $25 per return for taxpayers over 65 years of age.

1973 Joint filer credit on joint returns where both spouses earn more than $500 of wage income.

1974 Removal of the $3,000 personal exemption limitation.

1975 Value of each exemption increased from $500 to $650.

1978 Income tax credit for home improvements.

1979 Income tax credit for installation of a solar, wind, or hydrothermal energy system (expired after tax year 1985).

1982 Two new income tax brackets added above $80,000 of income for 1982 and 1983.

Temporary withholding surcharge of 50% from July 1982 through March 1983.

1983 The two brackets enacted in 1982 made permanent.

Temporary withholding surcharge increased from 50% to 90%, made permanent effective March 1.

For each $650 personal exemption a taxpayer may claim an additional $350 exemption or $20 credit.

Tax credit for taxpayers over 65 years of age increased to $50.

Joint filer credit increased over two years.

$4,000 retirement income deduction replaced by a sliding scale for retirement income credit.

1984 One-time special tax refund of 2.03% of tax year 1983 liability (minimum of $7).

Title II Social Security and Tier I Railroad Retirement benefits exempt from taxation.

1985 Rates reduced from 1984 level by 4% for 1985, an additional 5% for 1986, and an additional 5% (total of 15%) for 1987 and thereafter.

1986 Maximum rate reduced to 6.9%; other rates reduced by 7% in 1987 and 8% in 1988 from rates enacted in 1985.

1987 Home improvement credit repealed.

1988 Income tax checkoff for qualified political parties established.

Child care credit implemented.

1989 Accelerated employer withholding schedule implemented.

Tier II Railroad Retirement benefits exempt from taxation.

$20 personal exemption credit allowed for all taxpayers.
Additional $350 exemption eliminated.
Joint Filer Credit capped at $650.

1990 Basis of the joint filer credit is changed to Ohio adjusted gross income.

1991 Child care credit expanded beginning in tax year 1993.

1992 Ninth income bracket (above $200,000 of income) to be taxed at 7.5 percent beginning in 1993.
Job creation credit enacted.
Export credit enacted.

1993 Withholding payment requirements amended.

STATE INSURANCE TAX—DOMESTIC

Tax Base

The domestic insurance tax is levied on one of two tax bases: the value of the capital and surplus of a company having capital divided into shares or the value of the surplus of a company not having capital divided into shares; the gross amount of premiums covering rises in Ohio less specified deductions.

History Of Major Changes

1830 4% property tax on dividends paid by insurance companies.

1852 Insurance companies required to list real and tangible property and money and credits for taxation.

1933 Changed to a franchise tax on the smaller of the following:
0.2% of capital and surplus;
1.67% on premiums.

1971 Franchise tax rate changed to smaller of the following:
0.3% of capital and surplus.
2.5% of gross premiums.

1981 Tax rate on capital and surplus increased to 0.6%.

1989 Establishment of the Ohio Life and Health Guaranty Association; 100% tax credit to participating insurers.

STATE INSURANCE TAX—FOREIGN

Tax Base

Gross amount of premiums received from policies for Ohio risks during preceding calendar year less specified deductions.

History Of Major Changes

1830 4% tax on profits from premiums (minimum $50).

1852 Value of gross premiums subject to property tax.

1888 Supplemental tax on gross premiums that, when added to the property tax, would produce 2.5% value of gross premiums.

1902 Direct 2.5% tax on gross premiums.

STATE
MOTOR VEHICLE FUEL TAX

TAX BASE

Gallons of gasoline, diesel fuel, and special fuels sold in Ohio.

HISTORY OF MAJOR CHANGES

Year	Changes	Total Tax After Change
1925	2.0 cents per gallon tax enacted	2.0 cents
1927	1.0 cent per gallon increase	3.0 cents
1929	1.0 cent per gallon increase	4.0 cents
1933	1.0 cent per gallon reduction	3.0 cents
1947	1.0 cent per gallon increase	4.0 cents
1953	1.0 cent per gallon increase	5.0 cents
1959	2.0 cents per gallon increase	7.0 cents
1981	3.3 cents per gallon increase	10.3 cents
1982	1.4 cents per gallon increase	11.7 cents
1983	0.3 cent per gallon increase	12.0 cents
1987	2.7 cents per gallon increase	14.7 cents
1988	0.1 cent per gallon increase	14.8 cents
1989	3.2 cents per gallon increase	18.0 cents
1990	2.0 cents per gallon increase	20.0 cents
1991	1.0 cent per gallon increase	21.0 cents
1992	No Change	21.0 cents
1993	1.0 cent per gallon increase	22.0 cents

STATE
MOTOR VEHICLE FUEL USE TAX

TAX BASE

Fuel used by vehicles with three axles or more on Ohio highways. Taxpayers must pay tax on the difference between the fuel purchased in Ohio and consumed in Ohio for the excise tax equal to the motor vehicle fuel tax rate. The surtax is paid on all gallonage consumed in Ohio.

HISTORY OF MAJOR CHANGES

1982 Excise tax equal to the motor vehicle fuel tax rate enacted.

1991 Three cents per gallon surtax enacted.

STATE
PUBLIC UTILITY EXCISE TAX

TAX BASE

Most utilities are taxed on gross receipts from intrastate business.

HISTORY OF MAJOR CHANGES

1894 Enacted.
1911 Present type of tax structure established.
1935 1% rate increase for certain utilities.
1938 Rate increases for certain utilities.
1963 Advance payment system inaugurated.
1966 All revenue allocated to General Revenue Fund.
1970-71 Rates increased from previous 3% to 4% for most utilities.
1977 Advance payment system altered for gas, pipeline, and electric companies.
1979 Advance payment system altered for remaining utilities except freightline and equipment companies.
1980 Rates temporarily increased for 1981 (from 4% to 5% for most utilities).
1981 Rates temporarily increased for 1982 (from 4% to 4.5% for most utilities).
Charter-city credit repealed.
5.55% surtax imposed on 1982 liability.
1982 Temporary rate increase for 1983 (from 4.25% to 4.5% for most utilities).
5.55% surtax imposed on 1983 liability.
1983 Temporary rate increase for 1983 (from 4.5% to 5.0% for most utilities).
Permanent rate increase for 1984 and thereafter *from 4.25% to 4.75% for most utilities.
Advance payment system altered.
1987 Long distance telephone companies exempted from public utility excise tax.
1990 Public utility excise tax on freightline and equipment companies repealed as of tax year 1990.
1991 Legislation passed granting a one dollar per ton credit beginning tax year 1995 to electric companies using pollution control devices for burning Ohio coal.
Credit established for telephone companies with a lifeline program of rate discounts for low-income, elderly and disabled persons.
Railroads exempted from tax as of tax year 1992 by court decision.

STATE
SALES AND USE TAX

TAX BASE

Retail sales and rental of tangible personal property. Selected services.

HISTORY OF MAJOR CHANGES

1935 Enacted at 3%.

1936 Food for human consumption off the premises exempted.

1962 Use of sales tax stamps discontinued.

1967 Rate increased to 4%. Cigarettes and beer made taxable.

1971 Cigarettes exempted.

1981 Rate increased to 5%; cigarettes, repairs, and other selected services made taxable. Credit for trade-ins on new motor vehicles.

1983 Business data processing services made taxable.

1987 Exempted food stamp purchases.
Long distance telecommunications service made taxable.

1989 Investment coin and bullion purchases exempted.

1990 Credit for trade-ins on new or used watercraft.
Tangible personal property primarily used in manufacturing operations exempt (replaces manufacturers' direct use exemption).

1991 Lawn care and landscaping services, and private investigation and security services, made taxable.

1992 Building cleaning and maintenance, exterminating, employment agencies, and personnel supply services made taxable.
Physical fitness facilities and recreation and sports club memberships subject to tax.
Vendor discount decreased to 0.75% of tax collections.
Tax exemption for property used in making retail sales defined more narrowly.
Property and third part labor used to fulfill a warranty or service contract are taxable.
Tax exemption for food service operators narrowed.
Qualified property use in research and development is tax exempt.

STATE SEVERANCE TAX

Tax Base

The tax is levied on the weight or volume of certain natural resources extracted from the soil and water of Ohio.

History Of Major Changes

1972 Tax became effective.

1983 Tax rates increased on oil and natural gas.

1985 Rate on coal temporarily increased by two cents per ton for reclamation and defaulted areas special account.
Rate on coal permanently increased by three cents.

1989 Rate on limestone, dolomite, sand, and gravel increased by one cent per ton.
Tax of one cent per ton on clay, sandstone, shale, conglomerate, gypsum, and quartzite became effective.

COUNTY ALCOHOLIC BEVERAGES TAXES

Tax Base

Beer, wine, mixed beverages, and liquor.

History Of Major Changes

1986 County sports facility liquor tax authorized.

1990 County sports facility beer, wine, and mixed beverage tax authorized.
Voters of Cuyahoga County enact county tax on beer, wine, and liquor.

MUNICIPAL INCOME TAX

Tax Base

The tax is generally imposed on:
Wages, salaries, and other compensation earned by residents of the municipality and by non-residents working in the municipality, and net profits of business (both incorporated and unincorporated) attributable to activities in the municipality.

History Of Major Changes

1946 Toledo enacted first tax.

1957 General Assembly enacted Uniform Municipal Income Tax Law establishing statewide regulations.

1987 A municipality cannot initiate a tax on intangibles income. Taxes already in effect may continue through tax year 1988.

1992 Municipalities may grant job creation credits.

SCHOOL DISTRICT INCOME TAX

Tax Base

A resident tax on the amount reported as Ohio adjusted gross income for state income tax purposes less the $650 personal exemption.

History Of Major Changes

1979 General Assembly granted school districts authority to levy an income tax solely for repaying a state loan (no school district ever used this authority).

1981 Current law enacted.

1983 Certain provisions of the law were repealed so that no additional school districts could enact the tax. Any school district enacting the tax prior to August 3, 1983 could continue to levy the tax (six did so).

1986 Tax for Licking Valley Local S.D. repealed effective 1987.

1989 General Assembly reinstated provisions of the law allowing additional school districts to levy the tax.
$50 senior citizen credit allowed.

1990 Equivalent property tax millage of income tax collections can be used toward 20 mill eligibility for state aid.

1991 Income taxes can be levied for a finite period of time in addition to continuing.
Clarification of taxation of state retirement income.

1992 Permanent income taxes may be enacted in the same issue as reductions in permanent property taxes.

LOCAL LODGING TAX

TAX BASE

All transactions by which lodging in a hotel, motel, rooming house, or other lodging accommodations are furnished to transient guests.

HISTORY OF MAJOR CHANGES

1967 Municipal and township lodging tax of up to 3% permitted.

1980 County lodging tax of up to 3% permitted; municipal and township lodging tax of up to 6% permitted if county tax is not in effect.

1985 Permitted a county to enact an additional 3% lodging tax between July 15, 1985 and October 15, 1985 for convention center construction.

1988 Convention Facilities Authority permitted to levy an additional 4% lodging tax between June 29, 1988 and December 31, 1988 for financing a new convention or sports center.

1992 Counties permitted to levy an additional 1.5% lodging tax between December 22, 1992 and March 21, 1993 for financing an educational or cultural center in the county.

PROPERTY TAX—PUBLIC UTILITY

TAX BASE

Taxable value of public utility real property (land and buildings) and personal property (machinery and equipment). Real property is assessed at 35% of true (market) value. Personal property true value is based on composite annual allowances and is assessed at 88%; except for electric utility production equipment and the personal property of certain telephone companies, which is assessed at 100% of true value (50% of costs); the personal property of rural electric companies which is assessed at 50% of true value, and the personal property of railroads, which is assessed at 25% of true value.

HISTORY OF MAJOR CHANGES

1910 Public utility property assessed by newly-created state tax commission.

1939 Public utility property assessed by Tax Commissioner.

1941 Assessment level for personal property of rural electric companies reduced from 100% to 50%.

1963 Certified air pollution control facilities exempted.

1965 Certified water pollution control facilities exempted.

1973 Certified noise pollution control facilities exempted.

1979 Personal property of railroads assessed at same level as non-utility tangible property.

1982 Public utility real estate (except railroads) assessed by county auditors.

1985 70% of the value of production plant equipment of electric companies is apportioned to the taxing district in which the property is physically located. Remaining value is apportioned to each taxing district based on the percentage of the total cost of transmission and distribution property in each district.

1989 For production equipment at an electric utility plant whose cost exceeds $1 billion, the amount in excess of a specified level of value is apportioned according to the distribution base.

True value of public utility personal property is based on composite annual allowances, and taxable value of most public utilities is assessed at 88% of true value.

True value of electric production equipment statutorily defined as 50% of original cost.

REAL PROPERTY TAX

Tax Base

Taxable value of land and buildings. Taxable value is 35% of market value, except for certain agricultural land. Counties must reappraise all real estate once every six years. Equalization adjustments are made in the third year following reappraisal.

History Of Major Changes

1851 New constitution required taxation of all property by uniform rule (but expressly authorized exemption for certain property classes, e.g., churches, schools, etc.).

1902 End to state property tax levies for general fund.

1910 Culmination of reform movement leading to creation of single State Tax Commission to supervise local property tax administration.

1925 First statutory requirement for six-year reappraisal cycle.

1927 Statute set aggregate tax limit of 15 mills on each dollar of tax valuation except for taxes approved by voters (1% of true value since 1933).

1931 Constitutional amendment limited levies without voter approval to 1.5% of true value.

1933 Constitutional limit of 1% of true value on non-voted levies.

1934 Statute reduced aggregate tax limit from 15 mills to 10 mills.

1939 State Tax Commission replaced by Department of Taxation; a Board of Tax Appeals (BTA) which supervised real property tax administration, and a

Tax Commissioner assuming functions with respect to public utility property.

1965 First statutory requirement that real property be assessed at no more than 50% of true value, with actual percentage to be established by uniform rule by Board of Tax Appeals.

1971 Enactment of 10% rollback and first legislation authorizing homestead exemptions.

1972 BTA rule setting tax value at 35% of true value to be implemented by all counties as they complete their sexennial reappraisal cycle, with annual adjustments to maintain the 35% level.

1973 Top bracket of the homestead exemption increased from $8,000 to $10,000.

1974 Legislation authorized valuation of agricultural property according to current use (1973 constitutional amendment).

1975 Homestead exemption extended to permanently and totally disabled homeowners.

1976 Real property tax credits provided; real property valuations updated every three years; and State Department of Tax Equalization created.

Definition of "total income" for homestead exemption amended to exclude disability benefits paid by the Veterans Administration and other branches of the armed services, and social security income increases after December 31, 1975. The limit of each homestead exemption income bracket increased by $1,000 (except the highest bracket).

1977 School districts must have an effective rate of 20 mills (before 10% rollback) to be eligible for state aid.

1978 Closing date for payment of first half real property taxes changed.

1979 A 2.5% tax rollback on residential property is granted.

Solar, wind, and hydrothermal energy systems are exempt from real property taxes.

Upper income limit of the homestead exemption set at $15,000; three $5,000 income brackets created.

1980 Separate percentage reduction factors applied to two classes of real property (combined value of residential and agricultural property and value of all other real property).

1983 Department of Tax Equalization eliminated and all of its functions transferred to the Department of Taxation.

1986 The limit of each homestead exemption income bracket increased by $1,500 beginning in tax year 1988.

1991 Homestead exemption extended to surviving spouses of homestead exemption recipients (1990 constitutional amendment).

1992 Definition of real and personal property revised.

COUNTY TANGIBLE PERSONAL PROPERTY TAX

Tax Base

The tax is applied to tangible personal property used in business in Ohio (machinery, equipment, inventories). Business land and buildings are taxed under the real property tax.

Taxable value is determined by applying a listing percentage to the true value of tangible property. The percentage used to determine taxable value was 25% in 1993.

HISTORY OF MAJOR CHANGES

1931 Tangible property separated from real property and intangible property; tangible property tax limited to property used in business (based on 1929 amendment to Ohio Constitution).

1967 Listing percentages applied to property used in agriculture gradually reduced from 50% until property is exempt in 1973.

Listing percentages applied to inventories and restaurant property gradually reduced from 70% to 50% by 1971.

1971 Listing percentages for inventories gradually reduced from 50% to 45% by 1973.

Listing percentages for furniture and fixtures gradually reduced from 70% to 50% by 1976.

1976 Starting in 1977, whenever annual revenue growth conditions were satisfied, listing percentages were to be reduced by 2 percentage points each year until reaching 35%. Revenue growth conditions were satisfied in 1977 and 1978, reducing listing percentages for inventories from 45% to 41% and listing percentages for all other property from 50% to 46%.

1978 Revenue growth conditions were removed for further annual reductions in listing percentages to the 35% level.

Credit against the corporate franchise or personal income tax allowed for certain tangible property taxes paid on manufacturing machinery and equipment. The credit is effective through 1993.

1983 Starting in 1984, whenever annual revenue growth conditions are satisfied, listing percentages are to be reduced by one percentage point each year until reaching 25%.

Exemption enacted for first $10,000 of taxable value.

1985 Growth condition removed from law—annual reductions made automatic until reaching 25% level in 1993.

1992 Definitions of real and personal property revised.

SALES AND USE TAX
COUNTY AND TRANSIT AUTHORITY

TAX BASE

County Sales Tax Additional County Sales (for special purposes) Transit Authority Sales Tax	Retail sales and rental of tangible property. Selected services.

Retail sales and rental of

History Of Major Changes

County Sales Tax

1967	General Assembly granted power to counties to levy the tax at 0.5% rate.
1969	Lake county was the first county to levy the tax.
1982	Counties authorized to levy the tax at 0.5% or 1%.
1986	Counties authorized to levy an additional 0.5% tax for specific purposes subject to voter approval.
1987	County sales tax or additional sales tax may be levied at 0.25% increments.
1992	Counties authorized to levy an additional 0.25% or 0.5% tax to implement and operate a county 9-1-1 system.

History Of Major Changes

Transit Authority Sales Tax

1974	General Assembly granted power to transit authorities to levy the tax at following rates: 0.5%, 1%, 1.5% subject to voter approval.
1975	Greater Cleveland Regional Transit Authority adopted tax at a 1% rate.
1980	Miami Valley R.T.A. and Central Ohio Transit Authority adopted tax at a 0.5% rate.
1985	The 0.5% rate for Central Ohio Transit Authority expired.
1987	Transit authority sales tax may be levied at 0.25% increments.
1988	Lake County Regional Transit Authority adopted tax at a 0.25% rate.
1989	Central Ohio Transit Authority adopted tax at a 0.25% rate.
1991	Summit County Metro Transit Authority adopted tax at a 0.25% rate.

ENDNOTES

1. A more detailed version of this paper can be found in Berno and Whitmore (1994).

2. *Government Finance* (various years). One could state, but never be able to accurately prove, that some of this "burden" is exported to other states. The 1992 preliminary report shows Ohio's tax burden per $1,000 of income is 32nd.

3. *Government Finances*, (various years). This is due to slower changes in the denominator (Ohio personal income) rather than above-average increases in the numerator (revenues).

4. Author's interview with House Speaker Vern Riffe, September 29, 1994

5. Author's interview with R. Gregory Browning, Director of Office of Budget and Management, September 22, 1994.

6. This includes all state-imposed taxes. Locally imposed taxes include property taxes, municipal and school income taxes, local option sales taxes, hotel/motel lodging taxes, the motor vehicle license tax, and several smaller taxes.

7. More detail on these trends is provided in Berno and Whitmore (1994).

8. Advisory Commission on Intergovernmental Relations, *Significant Features of Fiscal Federalism* (1994).

9. The long-term elasticity is estimated to be less than unity by Fox (1994).

10. *Swetland v. Kinney*, 62 Ohio State 2nd 23.

11. Author's interview with Dean Conley, former Chairman of the House Ways and Means Committee, September 9, 1994.

12. Final Report and Recommendations of the Joint Committee to Study State Taxes, December, 1982, pg. 1.

13. Advisory Commission on Intergovernmental Relations, *Significant Features of Fiscal Federalism* (1994).

14. *Angell v. City of Toledo, et al.,* 153 Ohio State 179. Interestingly, on the same day, in the case of *Zimmer v. Hagerman,* 153 Ohio State 187, the Court held that Dayton's creation of a municipal income tax was invalid. The Court reviewed the language of the city charter, which stated, "Unless authorized and approved by a vote of the people, the City Commission shall levy no tax outside of the limitations set forth . Thus, the city could implement a municipal income tax only after a vote of the electorate.

15. *Final Report of the Joint Committee*, p. 9.

16. 1967 Ohio Tax Study Commission, *Final Report*, p. XXI.

17. Under this provision, County Commissioners may impose a "utility service tax" on charges for utility services rendered to businesses at a rate not to exceed three percent. The tax on utility services to all other customers cannot exceed two percent. The law requires that the utility tax on businesses must be 50 percent greater than the charges to all non business customers.

18. Ideally, an analysis of this type would show quarterly economic changes on the top part of the chart, and the corresponding quarterly revenue changes on the bottom of the chart. Unfortunately, tax payment dates don't allow such an analysis. Several major state revenues (the corporate franchise tax and the public utility excise tax, for example) are concentrated in the first half of the calendar year (and second half of the state fiscal year). Also, real estate property tax revenues are paid twice a year (June 20 and December 31). Tangible personal property taxes (over 17 percent of total property taxes) are due April 10 and September 20.

4 Sales Tax: Current Condition and Policy Options

William F. Fox

INTRODUCTION

Ohio was the fifteenth state to adopt a sales tax when it did so in 1935.[1] Ohio followed the initial state, Mississippi, by only three years. The neighboring states of Indiana, Michigan, and West Virginia all preceded Ohio, enacting their sales taxes in 1933. Since these early beginnings, the sales tax has grown to be the second largest state government tax in Ohio, yielding $4.47 billion in FY94. Ohio local governments began imposing a sales tax, termed a permissive tax, in 1969. The permissive sales tax is the third largest revenue source for all local governments and the second largest for counties, raising $824 million for all local governments in calendar year 1993.

This chapter provides a comprehensive analysis of Ohio's sales tax. After the introduction, the first major section is a description of the sales tax structure, including consideration of the tax base and the tax rate. The following section describes Ohio's reliance on the sales tax. Issues such as the amount of revenues, tax elasticities, and a comparison with other states are discussed. The third section evaluates several topics regarding the consumer portion of the sales tax, including equity and border tax effects. Next is a discussion of the sales tax as it is imposed on business purchases. Then a section composed of major policy issues is presented. Broadening the base, raising the rates, taxing not-for-profits, and other topics are analyzed. Finally, the issues and options raised in the paper are summarized.

The Commission to Study the Ohio Economy and Tax Structure is proposing the sales tax as a revenue source where substantial new tax revenues could be raised to allow for reform in other areas of the tax structure. Specifically, the Commission proposes raising the sales tax rate, broadening the sales tax base to include food, and expanding the sales tax to include certain additional services. The general notion of broadening taxation of services is consistent with the proposals of recent tax study commissions in other states. However, the Ohio proposal of explicitly increasing the relative importance of the sales tax has not been a theme in most other reports and reflects the heavy emphasis that the Commission has placed on designing a tax structure that enhances the competitive environment of Ohio.

OHIO'S SALES TAX STRUCTURE

This section describes the existing Ohio state and local government sales tax structure. The tax base, tax rates, and application of the use tax are all discussed.

Defining Ohio's Tax Base

Ohio's sales tax, like that in nearly every state, was initially developed as a tax on purchases of tangible personal property. The sales tax is levied on all transactions involving tangible personal property, unless sales of an item are always exempt regardless of how the item is used (such as with food for consumption off the premises), the sale is to an entity that is always exempt (such as the Federal or state governments), or a certificate of exemption is presented.

Two categories of exemptions are given from the sales tax. The first set, called exceptions from the sales tax, is given to reduce pyramiding and to make the tax more consistent with a tax on consumption, thereby preventing the tax from being a turnover levy against all transactions. Exceptions are given:

- when the consumer purchases tangible personal property for exempt purposes, including for resale of the purchased product;
- to incorporate the product into tangible personal property for sale through manufacture, assembly, processing, or refining;
- to hold the product as security for performance;
- to incorporate the item in magazines distributed as controlled circulation publications;

- to use the thing transferred primarily in manufacturing;
- seven other exceptions.2

The second set, called exemptions, is granted for organizations and products that the Legislature has determined should not be subject to tax or for which taxation would be unconstitutional. Exemptions from the tax are given for:

- the Federal Government;
- the State of Ohio and its political subdivisions;
- the sale of food for consumption off the premises where sold;
- the sale of newspapers and magazine subscriptions delivered by second class mail;
- the sale of motor vehicle fuel that is subject to the motor vehicle fuel tax;
- the sale of natural gas, electricity, water and steam;
- casual sales;
- the sale of items by churches or nonprofit organizations operated exclusively for charitable purposes, provided that the number of sales days does not exceed six per year;
- transportation;
- 38 other categories.[3]

In recent years Ohio has joined a number of other states in expanding the sales tax beyond tangible goods by including a number of specified services. These enumerated taxable services include:

- washing, waxing, cleaning, polishing, or painting a motor vehicle;
- industrial laundry cleaning services;
- automatic data processing, computer services, or electronic information services;
- specific telecommunications services;
- landscaping and lawn care services delivered by persons with $5000 or more in annual sales;
- building maintenance or janitorial services by persons having $5000 or more in annual sales;

- private investigation and security services;
- area code 900 telephone calls;
- employment services (with exceptions);
- employment placement services;
- exterminating services;
- physical fitness services and recreation and sports clubs;
- production of written or graphic material;
- repair and installation services;
- production of tangible personal property for consumers who furnish the materials.[4]

Consumers are legally liable for the Ohio sales tax. The vendor collects the tax on behalf of the state. About one-third of the states, like Ohio, impose the tax on consumers, about one-third on vendors, and about one-third impose mixed responsibility.[5] The tax is incident at the time of sale, regardless of when payment occurs. Thus, a vendor can sell a product and be required to remit the tax, even though the vendor may not receive sales tax revenues from the consumer for a considerable time. In these cases, the vendor can be thought of as lending the tax payment to the state, or alternatively, lending the payment to the consumer.

Vendors are provided some payment for collecting the sales tax. They are permitted to retain 0.75 percent of their sales tax collections as compensation for prompt payment of the tax. Vendor's compensation has been very common around the United States Due and Mikesell (1994) report that 26 of the 45 sales taxing states allow a discount to vendors for timely payment. Thirteen of the states allow greater discounts than Ohio. In 10 other states, the compensation rates depend on the size of firms, and small firms may receive greater compensation than in Ohio. Many states, including Ohio, have reduced the discounts in recent years. Pressure to reduce vendor's compensation is likely to continue because states can effectively collect additional revenues without the need to raise tax rates or to broaden the base to an untaxed service. Some businesses argue that the compensation is lower than the costs that firms bear in collecting the tax. Whether this is true or not, the compensation probably is closer to adequate for larger retailers than for smaller firms or for firms with complicated tax issues.

A side issue involves the remittance of tax by motor vehicle dealers. All motor vehicle dealers remit the sales taxes they collect to county clerks of court without any deduction for the 0.75 percent discount. New car dealers typically claim the discount on vehicle sales against the tax they collect on their non-motor vehicle sales (such as repairs and parts sales). However, used car dealers usually have no taxable sales other than motor vehicles and therefore must apply to the DOT for vendor compensation. The state permits the clerks to retain 1.0 percent of collections (a so-called "poundage fee"), so the clerks benefit from collecting taxes before the 0.75 percent discount. The clerks would receive slightly smaller poundage if car dealers were able to remit tax to the clerks net of the discount. The existing system, however, raises the administrative costs for both the DOT and the dealers. A mechanism should be designed so that the dealers pay the clerks 0.75 percent less and the clerks are permitted to keep a slightly higher percentage of collections to offset any revenue losses.

The Use Tax

A use tax is levied on consumers who store, use, or consume tangible personal property or realize in the state the benefits of the property.[6] The use tax operates as a companion to the sales tax in all states imposing a sales tax, and is levied at the same rate as the sales tax. The use tax is imposed with the intent of ensuring that tax is collected on taxable goods and services consumed, used, or stored in Ohio, regardless of whether the purchase was made inside or outside the state. However, consumers receive a credit for sales taxes already legally paid in another state. The combination of the sales and use taxes results in tax liability generally being determined in an amount equal to that imposed where the good or service is enjoyed rather than where it is purchased.[7] Thus, the tax system is intended as a levy at the destination, not at the origination of goods and services. The use tax is not imposed when the Ohio sales tax is collected, nor when the same property or service is exempt from the sales tax. Nonresident tourists are exempt from the use tax, but not from the sales tax. In the remainder of this chapter, the term sales tax refers to both the sales and use taxes, unless otherwise noted.

Tax Rate

Ohio law permits sales taxes to be levied by the state, counties, transit authorities, and resort areas.[8] The state levies a 5.0 percent tax. The tax was originally enacted at 3.0 percent, and was increased to 4.0 percent in 1967 and to 5.0 percent in 1981. Counties and transit authorities each can impose taxes in 0.25 percent increments up to 1.5 percent, and resort areas can levy a tax in 0.5 percent increments up to 1.5 percent. The maximum state and local sales tax rate is currently 8.0 percent.[9] The highest combined actual tax rate, 7.0 percent, is levied in Cuyahoga County. Transit taxes are levied only in Franklin, Lake, Summit, Montgomery, and Cuyahoga Counties. The average effective local government tax rate was 0.93 percent in 1993, up from 0.3 percent in 1972.[10]

The actual Ohio tax liability is drawn from a schedule of tax brackets that are written directly into tax law.[11] The bracket shows the amount of taxes due for each level of expenditures. Forty-two states establish brackets, either by statute or administrative regulations (Due and Mikesell 1994, p 35). Application of the brackets often results in an effective tax rate a little greater than the legislated percentage, since the brackets tend to round the tax liability up to the next cent. The bracketed tax raises the compliance cost for businesses since they must track each sale to determine their total tax liability. Ohio is one of only ten states (even though other states use brackets to set individual liabilities) that seeks to collect the actual amount collected by firms, as opposed to accepting the tax rate times the sales (Due and Mikesell 1994, p. 36).

OHIO'S RELIANCE ON THE SALES TAX

Ohio's state government collected \$4.47 billion in sales taxes in 1994 (Table 4-1). State sales tax collections have risen at a compound annual 8.5 percent rate since 1972. The sales tax raises 31.0 percent of total tax revenues, second to the 36.4 percent generated by the income tax (see Figure 4-1). The share of revenues raised by the sales tax has been relatively constant in recent years.

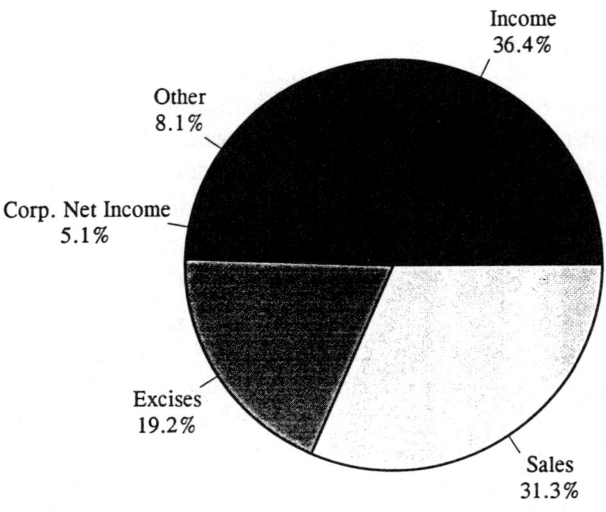

Source: U.S. Department of Commerce, Bureau of the Census, *State Government Finances: 1992.*

FIGURE 4-1. Ohio state government tax collections, 1992.

TABLE 4-1
Ohio State and Permissive Sales Tax Collections, 1972–1994

	State Sales Tax Revenues (000)	Percent Change	Income Elasticity	Permissive Sales Tax Revenues[1] (000)	Percent Change	Income Elasticity
1972	$ 744,947	---	---	$ 45,353	---	---
1973	816,538	9.61	0.91	52,252	15.21	1.44
1974	888,026	8.76	0.83	59,193	13.29	1.27
1975	933,427	5.11	0.66	58,697	-0.84	-0.11
1976	1,023,761	9.68	1.13	66,269	12.90	1.51
1977	1,140,345	11.39	1.11	73,040	10.22	0.99
1978	1,295,674	13.62	1.18	87,098	19.25	1.67
1979	1,429,931	10.36	0.94	97,596	12.05	1.10
1980	1,449,041	1.34	0.14	107,220	9.86	1.06
1981	1,640,984	13.25	0.28	115,644	7.86	0.87
1982	1,814,397	10.57	0.74	219,420	89.74	14.23
1983	2,000,330	10.25	0.81	239,548	9.17	2.55
1984	2,307,038	15.33	1.94	293,668	22.59	2.86
1985	2,552,036	10.62	1.40	323,559	10.18	1.34
1986	2,783,058	9.05	1.86	391,042	20.86	4.28
1987	2,965,013	6.54	1.45	408,747	4.53	1.01
1988	3,209,870	8.26	1.43	454,159	11.11	1.93
1989	3,414,140	6.36	0.91	535,551	17.92	2.55
1990	3,578,923	4.83	0.87	591,073	10.37	1.87
1991	3,564,879	-0.39	-0.09	629,065	6.43	1.40
1992	3,741,206	4.95	1.08	675,977	7.46	1.64
1993	3,960,181	5.85	1.02	737,999	9.18	1.60
1994	4,468,000	12.82	---	824,000	11.65	---
Annual Average Growth		8.48	---	---	14.09	---
Long-Term Elasticity		---	0.97	---	---	1.39

Source: Ohio Department of Taxation and author's calculations.

1. Permissive tax rates are for the preceding calendar years beginning in 1991.

Local governments received $824.0 million in sales taxes in 1993. Local government revenues have grown at a compound annual 14.1 percent rate since 1972 (Table 4-1).[12] As a result of the rapid growth, permissive sales taxes grew from 5.7 percent of total local government tax collections in 1972 to 15.7 percent in 1993.

Sales tax revenue growth occurs because of increased purchases as the economy rises and because of policy decisions to raise the sales tax rate or to expand the sales tax base. Ohio state and permissive sales tax increases shown in the table can be attributed to both. The state sales tax rate was increased from 4.0 to 5.0 percent in 1981. Numerous base expansions have been enacted during the past 13 years as well. For example, cigarettes, repairs, long distance telecommunications services, employment services, and numerous other services have become taxable. On the other hand, the sales tax base was reduced when the value of trade-ins for new automobiles and for new and used watercraft was exempted.

The major reason that the permissive taxes have experienced a higher growth rate than the state's is increases in the number of counties and transit authorities imposing sales taxes, combined with increases in the legislated tax rates. Forty-three counties and one transit authority imposed the tax in 1978, and eighty-six counties and five transit authorities imposed the tax in 1992 (Table 4-2). As a result the effective tax rate has nearly tripled since 1978. Note that the county share of permissive taxes has risen from less than two-thirds to nearly four-fifths of total collections during these 15 years.

The rapid growth in collections has resulted in Ohio's sales tax revenues tending to rise as a share of personal income (Figure 4-2). Revenues from the state and permissive taxes rose from 1.7 percent of personal income in 1972 to 2.2 percent in 1993. However, the share of income paid in sales taxes in 1993 is slightly below the pre-recession level reached in 1989 and 1990. Tax collections also have grown in per capita terms (Table 4-3). Per capita state collections have risen more than five-fold during the past two decades. Most of the change can be attributed to inflation, but per capita sales tax receipts are up 56.2 percent once the effects of inflation are subtracted out. Per capita permissive tax collections have grown much more dramatically than have the state's.

Tax Elasticities

The income elasticity of taxes is the best way to judge the ability of a tax to generate sufficient revenues over a number of years. The elasticity is calculated as the percentage change in tax revenues divided by the percentage change in personal income. A value of 1 indicates that tax revenues grow at the same rate as personal income. A value less than 1 indicates that tax revenues grow more slowly than income (described as inelastic) and a value greater than 1 indicates that revenues grow more rapidly than income (described as elastic). The desired elasticity for a state tax system needs to be

TABLE 4-2
Statistics on Permissive Sales Taxes, 1978–1992

	Revenues (000)			Number of Governments Levying		Percent of Collections		Average Effective Tax Rate
	Total	County	Transit	County	Transit	County	Transit	
1978	$144,221.6	$92,690.3	$51,531.2	43	1	64.27	35.73	0.34
1979	154,784.7	102,580.9	52,203.8	51	1	66.27	33.73	0.34
1980	166,628.1	107,416.6	59,211.5	54	1	64.46	35.54	0.37
1981	214,939.7	125,177.7	89,762.0	55	1	58.24	41.76	0.35
1982	230,883.7	139,424.8	91,458.9	56	3	60.39	39.61	0.60
1983	262,668.7	161,752.0	100,916.7	61	3	61.58	38.42	0.60
1984	306,937.0	194,441.3	112,495.7	63	3	63.35	36.65	0.64
1985	358,630.4	240,528.2	118,102.2	76	2	67.07	32.93	0.63
1986	408,751.4	306,739.0	102,012.4	74	2	75.04	24.96	0.70
1987	454,159.3	349,343.0	104,816.3	79	2	76.92	23.08	0.69
1988	535,551.2	422,585.0	112,966.3	83	3	78.91	21.09	0.71
1989	591,073.4	469,448.9	121,624.4	85	3	79.42	20.58	0.78
1990	629,065.1	487,891.8	141,173.3	83	3	77.56	22.44	0.83
1991	675,977.1	522,182.3	153,794.7	86	5	77.25	22.75	0.88
1992	737,998.6	575,867.4	162,131.2	86	5	78.03	21.97	0.90

Source: Ohio Department of Taxation and author's calculations.

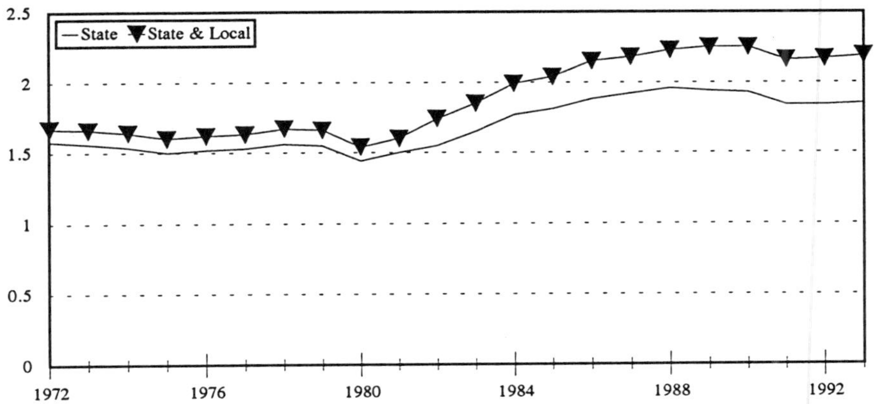

Source: Author's calculations.

FIGURE 4-2. Sales tax collection as a percent of personal income.

TABLE 4-3
Ohio Per Capital Sales Tax Collections

Year	Per Capita State Collections	Inflation-Adjusted State Collections	Per Capita Permissive	Inflation-Adjusted Permissive Collections
1972	$ 69.32	$ 69.32	$ 4.22	$ 4.22
1973	75.84	72.73	4.85	4.65
1974	82.48	73.24	5.50	4.88
1975	86.67	70.03	5.45	4.40
1976	95.20	72.07	6.16	4.66
1977	105.87	75.36	6.78	4.83
1978	120.03	79.88	8.07	5.37
1979	132.41	81.59	8.76	5.40
1980	134.13	75.11	9.93	5.56
1981	152.11	77.58	10.72	5.47
1982	159.38	75.79	20.40	9.70
1983	186.29	84.25	22.31	10.09
1984	214.83	93.01	27.35	11.84
1985	237.71	99.29	30.14	12.59
1986	259.32	104.34	36.44	14.66
1987	275.51	107.31	37.98	14.80
1988	297.21	111.02	42.05	15.71
1989	315.28	112.43	49.46	17.64
1990	329.46	112.22	54.41	18.53
1991	325.86	105.46	57.50	18.61
1992	339.46	106.05	61.34	19.17
1993	357.06	108.28	66.54	20.18

Source: Ohio Department of Taxation and author's calculations.

consistent with the pattern of expenditure growth, but an elasticity near 1 for the overall tax system often is seen as an appropriate norm.

Elasticities are most informative if they reflect the growth pattern in revenues from natural expansion in the economy, without any change in the tax structure. Much of Ohio's revenue growth has come from policy changes in the tax rate and base. Elasticities were calculated here after actual state tax collections were adjusted appropriately to offset the revenue effects of rate changes that took place in 1981.[13] The estimated elasticity still is affected by the frequent base changes that took place during the 1980s and 1990s.

Unfortunately, the background data necessary to extract effects of base changes from the tax revenue data are unavailable. The likely effect is that the elasticity is somewhat overstated.

The long-term elasticity from 1972 until 1993 was estimated to be 0.97, meaning revenues grew slightly more slowly than income.[14] An inelastic sales tax in Ohio is consistent with the findings of other research on the sales tax, though sales tax elasticities normally are found to be lower than the Ohio estimate (Fox and Campbell 1984). All sales taxes have unstable revenue growth, but the tax base structure and the state's economy determine the degree of instability. Elasticities can be estimated annually to judge the volatility of tax revenue growth. Annual Ohio elasticities evidence that the sales tax is highly cyclical. The elasticities are lowest in recession years (FY91, FY81, FY80, and FY75), and are much higher in expansion years (see Figure 4-3).

The falling elasticity during recessions occurs because consumers postpone their expenditures on major durable goods (such as automobiles and appliances) and housing, and because businesses invest less. The impact of lower durable goods purchases is pronounced, because these items are consumed over many years but the entire sales tax is paid when the items are purchased. The result is a magnified reduction in sales tax receipts. The reverse happens during economic expansions when the purchase of durable goods and business investment goods expands rapidly. The relatively high elasticities during the mid-1980s illustrate the effects of a strong economic

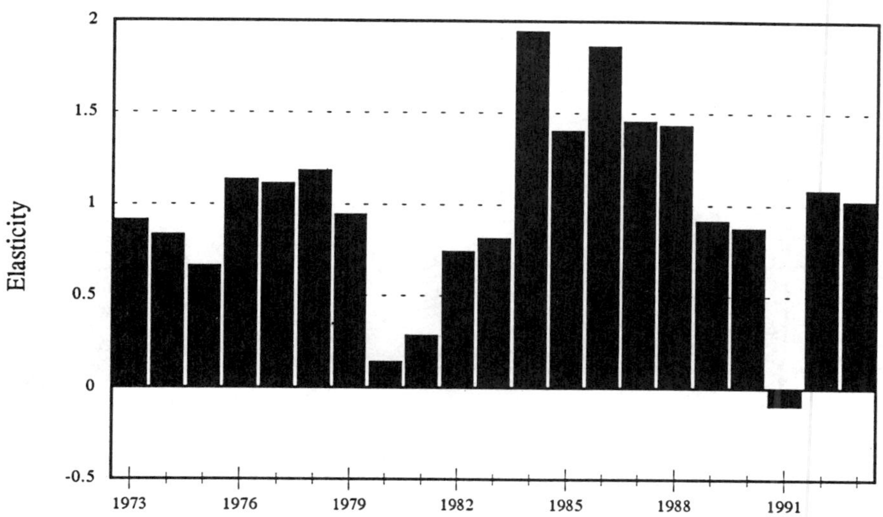

Source: Author's calculations.1973

FIGURE 4-3. Ohio state government sales tax elasticity.

recovery on sales tax revenues. Not surprisingly, most tax rate changes in Ohio and other states come near the end of recessions and are intended in part to offset the very slow revenue growth that has occurred during the recession (see Figure 4-4).

The pattern of elasticities means the sales tax is very volatile. The growth in tax collections falls during recessions, both because personal income growth slows and because sales tax revenues grow more slowly relative to the economy. Similarly, the increase in revenues during an economic expansion is a function of better income growth and a higher elasticity. Notice that revenue growth has ranged from a 0.4 percent decline in 1991 to a 15.3 percent rise in 1984. Ohio's cyclical sales tax means unstable revenue growth and therefore more difficulty in financing public services during recessions. Further, unstable revenues are less predictable, making it more difficult to budget expenditures.

Dye and McGuire (1991) found that narrow-based sales taxes and broad-based sales taxes have about the same long-term growth pattern. In the context they developed, this is comparable to finding that the elasticities are about the same. However, narrow-based taxes, like Ohio's, have much greater variability than broader-based taxes. Thus, Ohio's unstable tax structure is similar to what would be expected. The exemption of food from the base is an important reason for instability. Dye and McGuire found that food consumption is the most stable part of the tax base.

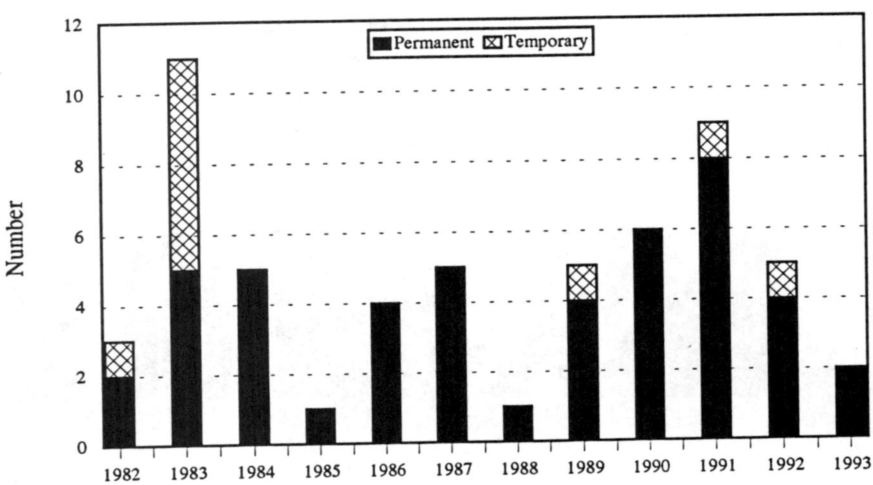

Source: National Conference of State Legislatures

FIGURE 4-4. Number of sales tax rate changes, all states.

Local government elasticities were calculated without adjustment for rate and base changes, meaning the estimated values are much higher than would result from natural economic growth.[15] Elasticities in almost every year were much greater than 1 (see Table 4-1).

Sales Tax Vendors

Sales tax collections are received in a number of different forms, both according to who collects the tax and to the way the tax is legally imposed (Table 4-4). About 70.2 percent of state receipts comes from the vendors' sales tax, which is sales tax revenues that are collected by vendors and submitted to the Department of Taxation (DOT). The payments may be made monthly or semi-annually, depending on the size of vendor sales. Another 8.9 percent is use taxes that are paid either by sellers or consumers. A small number of large businesses pay the sales tax due on their purchases directly

TABLE 4-4
Sales and Use Tax Collections by Type of Payment

Type of Payment	1993	Percent Distribution
Vendors Sales Tax	$2,778,195,919	70.15
Sellers Use Tax	258,699,392	6.53
Direct Payment Sales Tax	144,449,892	3.65
Consumers Use Tax	95,549,842	2.41
Sales and Use Tax Assessments and Penalties	92,628,696	2.34
Attorney General Sales and Use Tax Collections	25,201,589	0.64
Liquor Sales by Department of Liquor Control	14,254,990	0.36
Tax on Casual Watercraft Sales	9,752,182	0.25
Tax on Motor Vehicles and House Trailers	541,448,608	13.67
Net Total	3,960,181,110	100.00
State's Share of Total Collection		84.29
County and Regional Transit Authority Sales Tax	737,998,644	15.71
Grand Total	$4,698,179,754	100.00

Source: Ohio Department of Taxation.

to the DOT. These direct payments are 13.7 percent of collections. The sales tax on motor vehicles, watercraft, and house trailers is paid through the County Clerks of Court and represents 13.7 percent of total receipts. The Department of Liquor Control collects sales taxes on liquor sales and remits 0.4 percent of the total collections. Finally, assessments and penalties are 2.3 percent of the total receipts.

Sellers are required to collect and remit the use tax if they have substantial nexus with the state. Substantial nexus is defined as maintaining a business, having employees regularly in the state for purposes of conducting business, using a person in the state for purposes of receiving or processing orders, making regular deliveries of tangible personal property in the state by means other than common carrier, belonging to an affiliated group that has one other member with substantial nexus, renting or leasing tangible personal property to consumers in the state, registering with the Secretary of State to do business in the state, or having other contacts with the state that require the firm to collect and remit use taxes.

The DOT tracks revenues for a number of different vendor categories. The data represent sales for vendors, and are not for specific types of goods. For example, apparel stores do not represent all apparel sales, since clothing also is sold in department stores, specialty stores, and others. A summary of 1992 data is provided in Table 4-5. Autos, trailers, and boats are the largest share of the tax base, representing almost 18 percent of total taxable sales.[16] Restaurants are responsible for 9.1 percent and department stores for 8.0 percent of taxable sales. Grocery stores are responsible for 4.8 percent of taxable sales, because they sell many non-food items.

Taxable sales are only 31.1 percent of gross sales because of exemptions and exceptions from the tax.[17] This percentage does not represent the share of consumption that is taxable, since many sales may be exempt because they are purchases by businesses or by charitable organizations. Note that 91.2 percent of department store sales are taxable, but only 8.6 percent of sales by farm equipment dealers. One important implication of substantial untaxed sales is that auditing is more difficult because justifications for exemptions must be examined more carefully.

Taxable sales per vendor averaged $281,000, but the range across categories of vendors is very large. Department stores averaged $40.6 million and furniture repair establishments averaged only $44,800. Costs of administering the tax tend to be larger relative to collections for smaller firms.[18] Note that companies with more than one location that file as a single vendor (such as certain retail chain stores) are counted as only one vendor in the data. This results in a much higher sales per vendor figure than if each separate location was counted independently as a vendor.

TABLE 4-5
Sales Tax Collection by Vendor Category, FY 1992
(Dollar Amounts in Thousands)

Business Classification	Taxable Sales	Percent of all Taxable Sales	Gross Number of Sales Vendors		Taxable Sales Per Vendor	Taxable Sales as of Percent Gross Sales
Autos, Trailers, Boats (1)5	$11,773,493	17.95	$20,821,782	5,503	$2,139	56.54
Restaurants	$5,944,564	9.06	$9,834,830	20,492	$290	60.44
Department Stores	$5,232,056	7.98	$5,734,329	129	$40,559	91.24
Construction Materials	$4,667,827	7.12	$20,556,128	9,710	$481	22.71
Unclassified	$4,255,597	6.49	$26,136,645	47,168	$90	16.28
Apparel	$3,243,963	4.95	$3,887,699	7,057	$460	83.44
Grocery Stores	$3,120,228	4.76	$13,054,125	4,524	$690	23.90
Specialty Stores	$2,173,219	3.31	$5,066,047	28,345	$77	42.90
General Merchandise	$2,047,395	3.12	$5,246,699	4,970	$412	39.02
Variety Stores	$1,984,901	3.03	$2,768,220	478	$4,153	71.70
Household Supplies	$1,885,031	2.87	$7,772,124	4,675	$403	24.25
Antiques	$1,730,210	2.64	$3,207,641	11,300	$153	53.94
Appliance	$1,468,049	2.24	$4,602,243	4,679	$314	31.90
Telecom & Comp Serv	$1,414,426	2.16	$2,495,670	1,376	$1,028	56.68
Drug Stores	$1,257,826	1.92	$5,142,853	1,320	$953	24.46
Filling Stations	$1,217,645	1.86	$11,863,168	3,392	$359	10.26
Other Food Stores	$1,194,334	1.82	$7,884,337	10,200	$117	15.15
Auto Rental	$1,132,455	1.73	$1,508,034	1,823	$621	75.09
Paper Companies	$1,023,896	1.56	$6,405,755	5,832	$176	15.98
Other	$892,117	1.36	$10,925,669	10,381	$86	8.17
Auto Parts	$815,746	1.24	$4,125,831	4,854	$168	19.77
Medical & Scientific	$763,872	1.16	$4,038,469	3,894	$196	18.91
Garages	$748,128	1.14	$1,237,181	7,878	$95	60.47
Book & Newsstands	$716,384	1.09	$1,449,395	2,907	$246	49.43
Other Trade Equipment	$686,367	1.05	$1,498,424	4,739	$145	45.81
Hardware Stores	$655,887	1.00	$1,123,137	1,081	$607	58.40
Tire, Batteries	$563,888	0.86	$3,481,635	1,946	$290	16.20
Industrial Equipment	$539,768	0.82	$7,009,794	2,983	$181	7.70
Nurseries & Garden	$502,808	0.77	$1,027,929	5,697	$88	48.91
Heating & Cooling	$281,203	0.43	$1,378,309	1,424	$197	20.40
Lawn Care	$261,626	0.40	$402,637	3,368	$78	64.98
Farm Equipment	$257,952	0.39	$3,017,832	1,370	$188	8.55
Private Investigation	$202,354	0.31	$297,226	659	$307	68.08
General Stores	$195,539	0.30	$1,062,002	302	$647	18.41

continued

TABLE 4-5 (continued)
Sales Tax Collection by Vendor Category, FY 1992
(Dollar Amounts in Thousands)

Business Classification	Taxable Sales	Percent of all Taxable Sales	Gross Number of Sales Vendors		Taxable Sales Per Vendor	Taxable Sales as of Percent Gross Sales
Dry Goods	$153,551	0.23	$245,843	399	$385	62.46
Machinery	$135,924	0.21	$1,440,246	881	$154	9.44
Tools & Implements	$130,559	0.20	$1,250,443	1,435	$91	10.44
Furniture Repair	$89,156	0.14	$286,681	1,989	$45	31.10
Construction Cont	$75,091	0.11	$727,271	927	$81	10.33
Marine Equipment	$67,236	0.10	$307,440	644	$104	21.87
Airplanes	$54,934	0.08	$609,178	307	$179	9.02
House Trailers	$21,118	0.03	$293,000	466	$45	7.21
Totals	$65,578,323	100.00	$211,223,901	233,504	$281	31.05

Source: Ohio Department of Taxation and author's calculations.

Notes: Gross sales = taxable and non-taxable sales
Number of vendors = number of accounts
(1) Taxable sales calculated as tax revenues divided by .05. Truck and auto dealers are categorized here as well.

COMPARISON OF OHIO'S SALES TAX WITH OTHER STATES

Ohio is just below average in reliance on sales taxes as a state revenue source.[19] First, the 31.0 percent contribution of the sales tax to Ohio tax revenues is below the average state's 32.8 percent (Figure 4-5). Ohio is in the middle of neighboring states in use of the sales tax. Second, Ohio collects a smaller percentage of personal income in sales taxes. The average state raises 2.2 percent of personal income with the state sales tax, versus Ohio's 1.9 percent (Figure 4-6). Ohio is lowest among nearby states in the share of personal income paid in sales taxes. There has been a general tendency among states, including Ohio, for the percent of personal income paid in sales taxes to rise. Higher tax rates have been the most important reason for the rising share of income paid in sales taxes, since the base has tended to fall relative to income (see discussion below).

Ohio's state sales tax rate is the same as the median state's tax rate, 5.0 percent. Ohio's combined state and maximum permissive rate is higher than any bordering state, except Pennsylvania (see Figure 4-7). However, only Cuyahoga County has a 7.0 percent rate and the combined state and local rate is 6.0 percent in most Ohio counties, so Ohio's rate generally is in line

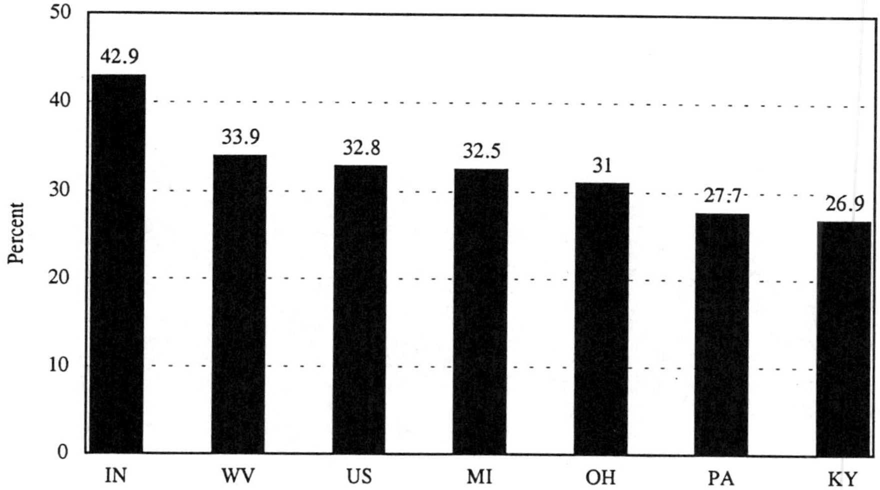

Source: U.S. Department of Commerce, Bureau of the Census, *State Government Finances: 1992.*

FIGURE 4-5. General sales tax collections as a percent of total tax collection, 1992.

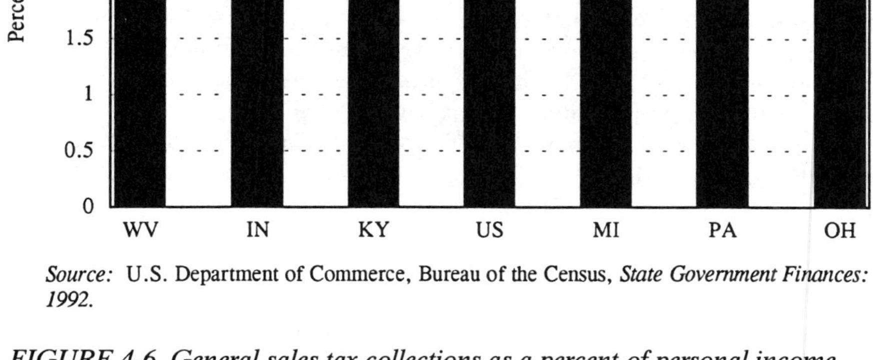

Source: U.S. Department of Commerce, Bureau of the Census, *State Government Finances: 1992.*

FIGURE 4-6. General sales tax collections as a percent of personal income, 1992.

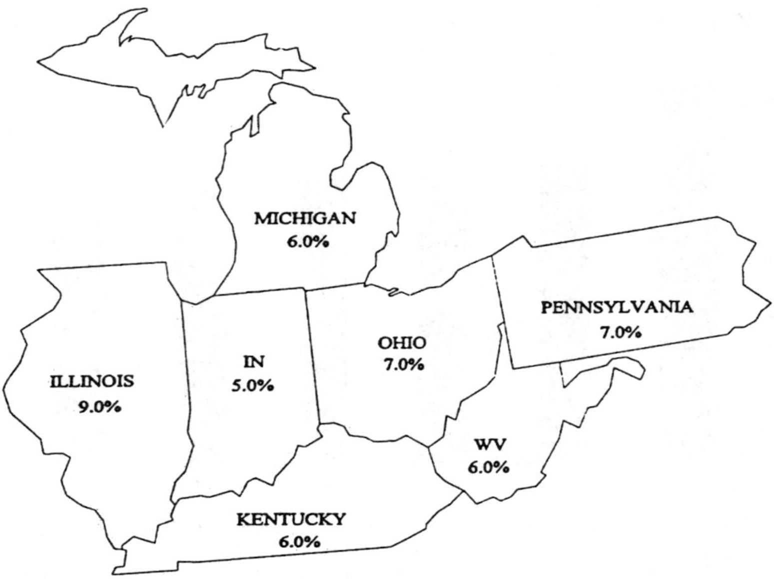

Source: Advisory Commission on Intergovernmental Relations, *Significant Features of Fiscal Federalism*, Volume 1, 1993.

FIGURE 4-7. Highest sales tax rates.

with its neighbors. Twelve states have higher maximum rates than Ohio and six states have the same rate (Table 4-6).

Comparisons of tax bases across states are more difficult because of definitional differences. One means for comparing states is to examine the implied tax base as a percent of personal income.[20] In FY91, Ohio's sales tax base was equal to 36.9 percent of personal income (see Table 4-6). Using this measure, only Pennsylvania has a narrower tax base among the neighboring states and Ohio has the eleventh narrowest base in the United States There has been a general trend downward in the sales tax base as a share of personal income, suggesting that sales tax bases are declining, not expanding. In 1981, the Ohio sales tax base was 38.9 percent of personal income. Rapid growth in untaxed services is one reason for the relative decline in the tax base.

Changes that have been enacted by Ohio in the state sales tax rate and the base are consistent with changes that have been occurring in other states. State sales tax rates were raised at least 57 times in the United States between 1982 and 1993, though Ohio has not raised the state rate since 1981 (see Figure 4-4). Also, a strong trend has been underway in Ohio and other states to add selected services to the base. Expansions of the base to services

TABLE 4-6
Sales Tax Base as a Percent of Personal Income and Highest State and Local Sales Tax Rate, FY 1991

State	Sales Tax Base as a Percent of Personal Income	Highest State and Local Sales Tax Rate
Alabama	41.64	9.00
Alaska	0.00	---
Arizona	65.43	7.00
Arkansas	64.45	6.50
California	45.80	8.50
Colorado	43.75	7.50
Connecticut	36.13	6.00
Delaware	0.00	0.00
Florida	54.21	7.00
Georgia	58.11	6.00
Hawaii	132.77	4.00
Idaho	50.90	5.00
Illinois	28.43	8.75
Indiana	53.43	5.00
Iowa	52.02	6.00
Kansas	48.33	6.90
Kentucky	38.77	6.00
Louisiana	52.62	10.00
Maine	47.01	6.00
Maryland	28.54	5.00
Massachusetts	28.27	5.00
Michigan	46.03	6.00
Minnesota	39.08	7.50
Mississippi	56.05	7.00
Missouri	48.27	7.23
Montana	0.00	0.00

continued

TABLE 4-6 (continued)
Sales Tax Base as a Percent of Personal Income and Highest State and Local Sales Tax Rate, FY 1991

State	Sales Tax Base as a Percent of Personal Income	Highest State and Local Sales Tax Rate
Nebraska	44.81	6.50
Nevada	55.88	7.00
New Hampshire	0.00	0.00
New Jersey	30.46	6.00
New Mexico	84.13	6.25
New York	35.52	8.50
North Carolina	50.96	6.00
North Dakota	47.79	5.50
Ohio	36.88	7.00
Oklahoma	43.96	8.50
Oregon	0.00	0.00
Pennsylvania	30.49	7.00
Rhode Island	33.28	7.00
South Carolina	53.13	6.00
South Dakota	55.56	6.00
Tennessee	53.88	8.50
Texas	44.50	8.25
Utah	58.60	6.25
Vermont	31.02	5.00
Virginia	35.92	4.50
Washington	74.98	8.20
West Virginia	52.92	6.00
Wisconsin	42.32	5.50
Wyoming	74.18	5.00
District of Columbia	48.40	6.00

Source: U.S. Department of Commerce, Bureau of the Census, *State Government Tax Collections: 1991*, Series GF191-1, ACIR (1993), and author's calculations. The most current rate is used for Michigan.

states to add selected services to the base. Expansions of the base to services are discussed below.

EVALUATING THE CONSUMER SALES TAX

Economists have traditionally evaluated the sales tax as a consumption tax. The presumption is that the tax is a levy intended to be paid by households on their consumption, even though the tax may be collected by businesses. A consumption framework is useful and will serve as a basis for much of the evaluation that follows. Nonetheless, the sales tax base deviates from consumption by households in a number of important ways. First, the sales tax continues to be primarily a tax on the purchase of tangible goods, not on all consumption. Despite Ohio's recent efforts to broaden the tax base to selected services, only a series of itemized services are taxed. Major omissions include health care, housing, and professional services. Second, the tax normally is levied on transactions, not on consumption (though the combined sales and use taxes are closer to representing a consumption tax). Consumption occurs when an item is actually enjoyed, and the transaction occurs when the item is purchased. A major difference arises with the purchase of durable goods. For example, the sales tax is levied at the time an automobile is purchased, but the consumption benefits from the vehicle may be received over many years. Another difference is that the DOT will not be able to collect taxes on many out-of-state purchases by residents, even though the purchases may be taxable under the use tax.

Third, businesses are defined as the consumer for many purchases. Manufacturers' purchases are exempt if they are incorporated "into tangible personal property to be produced for sale."[21] However, except for a number of other exclusions and exemptions, purchases by manufacturers and other businesses are taxable. Ray Ring (1989) estimated that 30 percent of the sales tax in Ohio was paid by businesses or tourists in 1979. The estimate for Ohio sales taxes paid by business is lower than the national average estimate of 41 percent. Still, based on Ring's estimate Ohio businesses pay about $1.4 billion in sales taxes to Ohio state and local governments. Further, Ring's analysis used 1979 data, so it reflects tax law prior to recent reductions in exemptions for retailers.[22] Businesses may be expected to pay a larger share of the sales tax today. Despite the importance of business sales tax payments, the following analyses of equity and border tax effects are couched in terms of the sales tax as a consumption tax. A separate section on issues associated with imposing the sales tax on businesses is presented below.

EQUITY

Equity has two dimensions, vertical equity and horizontal equity, that allow examination of fairness in different contexts. Vertical equity refers to the distribution of tax burdens across people with different incomes. Horizontal equity refers to the relative tax burdens of people with similar incomes. Ohio's sales tax will be examined in terms of each concept in this section.

Equity is best evaluated in terms of the final incidence of the tax, after taxes have been shifted. Taxes imposed on businesses can be shifted to consumers through higher product prices, to workers or other input suppliers through lower wages, or to owners through lower profits. Unfortunately, there is little information on who actually bears the sales tax. Therefore, no attempt is made in this discussion to allocate tax burdens that are initially incident on business.

Vertical Equity. Vertical equity, or the degree of fairness for people with different incomes, must be measured in the eye of the beholder. Some feel that taxes should be progressive, some believe they should be proportional, and others feel they should be regressive. A tax is described as progressive if the percentage of income paid in taxes rises as income goes up, as proportional if the percentage of income paid in taxes is the same for all income levels, and as regressive if the percentage of income paid in taxes falls as income rises. Higher income households probably pay more tax dollars than do lower income households, regardless of whether the tax is progressive or regressive. Thus, discussions about whether taxes should be progressive or regressive actually are centered on how fast the tax burden should rise with income, not whether it should rise. This section contains a description of the vertical equity characteristics of the sales tax. The normative decision of whether the tax is fair is left to the reader.

The Consumer Expenditure Survey (CES) reports data on how consumers in different income brackets spend their available resources. For example, the CES shows how much money consumers in the $5,000 to $9,999 income bracket spend on apparel for men and boys, major appliances, health insurance, and dairy products. Data drawn from the CES were used to determine the sales tax liability for Ohio residents in different income brackets.

The first step in the analysis of tax burdens was to classify each category of expenditures as taxable or non-taxable. The second step was to estimate the tax liability for all taxable expenditures. The 5.0 percent state sales tax rate was used in the analysis, so the incidence analysis is based on the state tax only.[23] Finally, tax payments for each category were summed and divided by the average income in the bracket to determine the percentage of income paid in taxes for each bracket.[24]

Households in the category earning less than $5,000 annually represent a very diverse group. For example, retired individuals, full-time students, people who have lost their jobs, and the long-term poor may all be classified in this category. Many households in this category may have substantial capacity to purchase that is not reflected by their income. One evidence is that the average annual expenditures for the category are more than four times greater than the average income. Thus, this category is not included in the comparisons of tax burdens given here.

The analysis of expenditure patterns evidences that Ohio's sales tax is regressive when compared with current income. Households with incomes between $5,000 and $9,999 pay 2.60 percent of their income in sales taxes and households with incomes above $50,000 pay 1.33 percent of their income in sales taxes (Figure 4-8). Thus, the burden of low-income households is almost twice as large as for high-income households. Still, the bulk of tax payments is made by higher-income households (Table 4-7). More than 60 percent of the tax is paid by households with $30,000 or more in income. Also, the per household tax payment is much greater for higher-income households. For example, households with income over $50,000 pay nearly five times more in taxes than households with income between $5,000 and $9,999.

The regressive sales tax results from the propensity of lower-income households to spend a higher percentage of their income. The percentage of income that is spent, as opposed to saved, falls as income rises. In fact, every category with income below $20,000 has higher expenditures than income. Thus, the regressive sales tax is more the result of different levels of con-

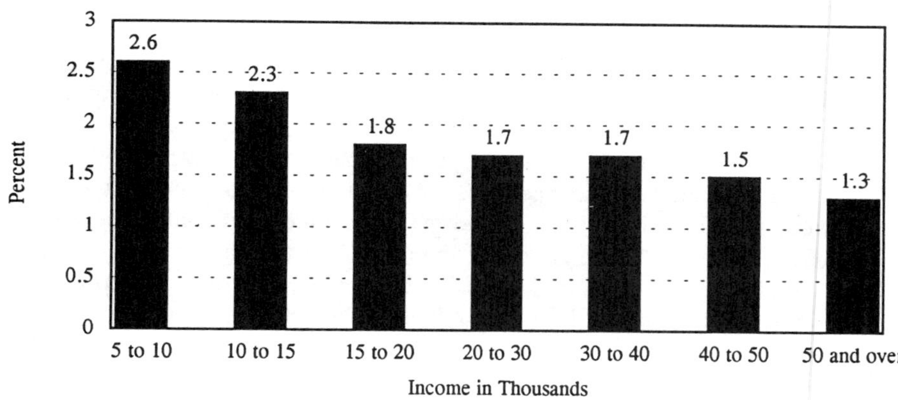

Source: U.S. Department of Labor, *Consumer Expenditure Survey, 1990-91* and author's calculations.

FIGURE 4-8. Ohio state sales tax collections as a percent of income: annual income basis.

TABLE 4-7
Ohio Sales Tax Payments by Household Income

Income Bracket	Total Tax Payment (Millions)	Per Household Tax Payment
Less than $5,000	$67.3	$225.35
$5,000 to $9,999	$105.3	$249.35
$10,000 to $14,999	$156.2	$361.54
$15,000 to $19,999	$170.0	$402.16
$20,000 to $29,999	$427.0	$539.13
$30,000 to $39,999	$476.9	$728.99
$40,000 to $49,999	$452.5	$843.05
$50,000 and above	$916.9	$1,222.73

Source: Consumer Expenditure Survey and author's calculations.

sumption relative to income than of different patterns of spending across income groups.

Some economists have argued that lifetime income is a better basis for comparing tax burdens than is annual income. The concept is that people set their expenditure patterns based on the overall consumption level they expect to maintain over their lifetimes. The consumption level depends on expected income over one's lifetime rather than for a single year. For example, people who recently lost their jobs may spend more than would be expected from their current income. Both retirees and young people consume more than is expected given their income level, because their lifetime income is greater than their current income. Poterba (1989) has argued that annual (or current) expenditures are a good proxy for lifetime income. Therefore, estimated sales tax burdens were compared with annual expenditures for each income category. The distribution is proportional to slightly progressive when the tax burden is compared with consumption instead of annual income (see Figure 4-9). Thus, the sales tax is not regressive when compared with lifetime income.

Improving Vertical Equity. As noted above, equity is in the eye of the beholder, and some may feel the sales tax burden is fair because people are taxed according to what they take from the economy in consumption or because they are taxed proportionately relative to lifetime income. Others may think it is unfair because the tax burden is regressive when compared to current income. If the tax burden is regarded as unfair, a frequent question is

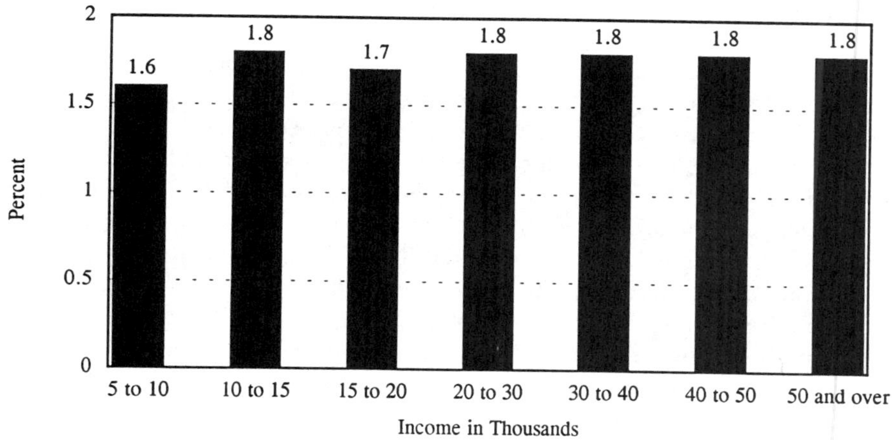

Source: U.S. Department of Labor, *Consumer Expenditure Survey, 1990-91* and author's calculations.5 10 10

FIGURE 4-9. Ohio state sales tax collections as a percent of expenditure: lifetime income basis.

how can the tax be made more fair? A major point to remember is that the sales tax's regressiveness compared with current income results from the propensity of lower-income households to spend more relative to their income, not from the pattern of expenditures. Households in the $5,000 to $9,999 income bracket spend the same or a greater percentage of their income than do higher-income households on essentially all consumption categories. The only consumption categories where higher-income households consistently spend a larger percentage of income are mortgage interest, floor coverings, new and used cars,[25] vehicle finance charges, entertainment, and insurance. Thus, the sales tax's regressiveness against current income will not be eliminated by exempting certain categories of consumption that are consumed heavily by low income residents, unless the tax base is to be a very narrow assortment of items. Food and utilities already are exempt, and the tax remains regressive relative to current income. Similarly, broadening the base to additional services is unlikely to result in any significant improvements in equity.

Second, an appropriate response to concerns about fairness of the sales tax is that the wrong issue is being raised. A strong case can be made that the issue is whether the overall Ohio tax burden is fair, not whether each separate tax is fair. With this perspective it can be argued that changes in the sales tax base are a clumsy means to enhance equity because the benefits of exempting items from the base cannot be targeted to the intended group. High-income taxpayers benefit from sales tax base exemptions just as do low-income taxpayers. The result is that changing the tax base can be a very expensive means (in terms of lost revenues) to reduce tax burdens for low income households. Perceived unfairness in the tax system can be overcome more efficiently through taxes levied directly on people, such as the income tax, because the benefits can be targeted to the desired beneficiaries.

One method for improving equity is to combine characteristics of the sales and income taxes. For example, the sales tax could be broadened to include exempt items, such as food and utilities. Then, the tax rate can be lowered and an income tax credit equal to the sales tax paid on these necessary taxable items can be given to reduce any perceived equity problems. This system can make the overall tax burden less regressive (or more progressive) against current income if all households are given the same value of credit, because the tax burden for low income households would not rise while the burden for high income households goes up. The effects of such a policy are estimated and included in the section below on issues in the sales tax.

Horizontal Equity. Horizontal equity is the second highest priority of the Commission. Taxes are horizontally equitable when people with the same ability to pay have the same tax liability. Thus, a horizontally equitable sales tax would impose the same tax burden on all people with the same level of consumption.[26] The sales tax will score well on horizontal equity only when essentially all consumption is taxable. Otherwise, wide variation in tax liabilities will occur as people make different decisions about which items to consume. A horizontally equitable sales tax would be imposed on all household consumption, including:

- All household consumption regardless of where purchased (in-state, out-of-state, mail order, etc.)[27]
- All household purchases regardless of what source of income finances the purchases (food stamp income, social security income, labor income, etc.)
- All household purchases regardless of the vendor (government, hospitals, not-for-profit enterprises, etc.).
- All goods and services (food, health care, clothing, etc.)

Despite these guiding principles, exemptions and exclusions for certain expenditures are granted because of high administrative or compliance burdens associated with the tax, perceived vertical equity problems, constitutional or legal restrictions, and political judgements. All of these exemptions and exclusions violate horizontal equity and make the tax less "fair," though other goals may be met.

The sales tax fails on horizontal equity grounds because most household consumption is exempt. Expenditure patterns given in the CES indicate that between 32.7 percent (by households earning less than $5,000) and 38.5 percent (by households earning between $30,000 and $39,999) of expenditures are for sales of taxable commodities. In other words, Ohio exempts much more of consumption than it taxes. As a result, tax burdens differ simply because of how people choose to spend their resources. Large exempt expenditure categories include health care, food, gasoline, personal services, and most housing expenditures. Thus, for both low income and high income households, those that are relatively heavy consumers of housing, food, health care, and so forth will have lighter tax liabilities than those that are heavy consumers of clothing, automobiles, reading materials, and household supplies.

The best way to reduce horizontal inequities is to broaden the sales tax base to the maximum extent possible. Other goals of the tax structure, such as vertical equity, can then be achieved better through other means.

Effects of Taxes along Ohio's Borders

Tax structures must be set with recognition that all taxes distort behavior in some way. One of the challenges of designing tax structures is to balance the consequences so that the overall effects are acceptable. The effects of taxes on economic development are a primary distortion that is of concern to all states when they design tax structures and is a major concern of the Commission to Study the Ohio Economy and Tax Structure. One dimension of the economic development issue is the effect of taxes along state borders. The states on each side of the border are worried about the loss of economic activity and the loss of tax revenues if people (or businesses) cross the border to buy on the opposite side.

The use tax can reduce border effects because the use tax combined with the sales tax means a liability is due on most consumption regardless of whether the purchase is made inside or outside of Ohio. The use tax is incident on many purchases out-of-Ohio, and results in collection of taxes on automobiles and many purchases by large businesses. However, the ability to collect the use tax is very limited on many purchases by Ohio residents, since there is no practical means for the DOT to collect the tax on numerous transactions.[28]

A number of people have raised the issue of border taxes in testimony before the Tax Commission. For example, Art Arnold, State Manager of Border Ohio Business Coalition Against Taxes, presented testimony in May noting the advantages that Ohio has received as Pennsylvania and Michigan have changed their tax structures in Ohio's favor. Much of the testimony has focused on the effects of selective sales taxes, such as on alcohol and cigarettes, and on where people shop rather than on effects of sales taxes.

The quantitative effect of taxes on the location of sales is the important issue. A number of factors go into determining the effects that taxes have on where sales take place. First, taxes matter only to the extent that the rates or base definitions differ between states. No incentive to cross the border exists unless one side of the border has lower effective tax rates than the other. In fact, the costs of traveling across the border, including travel costs and the value of people's time, must be larger than the tax differentials before any advantage is reaped from going to a lower tax area. Further, the greater the differential in effective tax rates, the larger the effect on the location of sales.

Second, the closer that shopping alternatives and people are to the border, the greater the effects will be. The smaller the distances, the more likely that the tax differentials will be greater than the cost of traveling from one state to another. Walsh and Jones (1988) found that sales in West Virginia border counties are affected by tax differentials with other states, but sales in interior counties are unaffected.

Third, the entire tax structure, rather than a single tax, must be evaluated to determine what effect taxes have on the location of sales. The sales tax is the first tax that most analysts consider when trying to understand whether taxes will shift the location of sales, but most other taxes must be considered as well. The effect that other consumption taxes, such as cigarette and alcohol taxes, have on prices can be an important consideration as consumers decide where to shop. Higher property taxes and corporate income taxes can raise the cost of doing business in a state. The greater costs can be reflected in higher prices that can offset any advantage that results from lower sales taxes. Even higher personal income taxes can lead to greater business costs if firms must pay higher wages to compensate for the additional income tax liabilities that workers incur on one side of the border relative to the other. Again, higher business costs can be reflected in higher product prices.

Fourth, taxation and expenditures are linked, and a reduction in taxes to make Ohio more competitive along state borders will lead to lower service levels. Lost benefits of infrastructure, education, or other services could be more detrimental than the gains from lower taxes.

Empirical research on the effects of tax differentials along state borders supports the expectation that taxes affect where people shop. Research over the past several decades has consistently demonstrated that consumers will cross state borders to purchase in lower sales tax jurisdictions.[29] A one percent sales tax differential has been found to reduce spending in the higher tax area by between one and ten percent. As note above, the effects occur only in the localized area near the state borders. The effect on border sales of taxes other than the sales tax has not been as consistently demonstrated.

Ohio's current state and permissive sales tax rate is the same as neighboring states (except Indiana). In addition, Ohio tends to have a narrower tax base. Thus, the Ohio sales tax should not create undue burdens along the state's borders. Increases in the rate or broadening the base to services, both of which are proposed by the Commission, have the potential to create greater border problems but these effects must be evaluated in a broader context. First, border effects can be limited by establishing taxes properly. For example, negative consequences from broadening the sales tax to services can be reduced by taxing on the basis of destination rather than origination. Second, the gains in terms of keeping the sales tax rate low to attract consumers along the border must be weighed against the consequences that will result from alternative ways to raise the same revenues. The overall effects on economic development of the Commission's proposal to reduce business taxes and raise sales taxes may be positive, even if some employment and sales losses occur along the border. The overall effect is positive if the gains from industries benefiting from lower business taxes and in areas away from the border are greater than any losses along the border.

Third, the entire range of taxes must be evaluated to measure the border effects. Cigarette tax rates are high in Ohio compared with Kentucky, Indiana, and West Virginia and low compared with Michigan and Pennsylvania.[30] Some cigarette purchases are likely to be shifted from Ohio to the lower tax states as a result, and consumers likely will buy some other items while purchasing inexpensive cigarettes. On the other hand, Ohio surely attracts some cigarette sales from Pennsylvania and Michigan. Vedder, Klingaman and Galloway (1992) examined the effects of cigarette taxes on the location of sales along Ohio's border with Kentucky. They took a survey of automobiles located in the parking lots of vendors on both sides of the border and spoke with retail merchants. Their conclusions were that Ohio experienced significant sales losses as a result of the cigarette tax differential and that consumers purchased other items when they bought low-priced cigarettes. All of this suggests that Ohio's state and permissive sales tax rates and selective sales tax rates should be watched carefully to ensure that no significant problems develop relative to other states. About 30 percent of the state's economic activity is in border counties, so it is important to be very aware of border effects.

Issue 1: Should Ohio's state and permissive sales tax rates be reduced in an attempt to attract cross border sales?

Option 1: Leave the tax rate unchanged.

Option 2: Lower the tax rate.

TAXING BUSINESS WITH THE SALES TAX

Whether the tax structure is consistent with attracting more jobs and investment was one of two basic research questions addressed by the

Commission. Thus, business concerns about the sales tax were a very important issue for analysis. Businesses raise two major objections to being taxed on their purchases. First, businesses are concerned about how much they pay in taxes. Obviously firms would like to minimize their tax liabilities. Second, businesses are disturbed by the compliance costs associated with the sales tax. High compliance costs can ensue as firms seek to determine what purchases are taxable and as they go through the audit process.

Many of Ohio's larger firms are audited every three years, but on all three years' tax payments. Businesses believe that a tendency exists within the DOT to evaluate the audit process in terms of how much revenue is generated, rather than by whether the tax is being administered evenly and appropriately. Also, businesses believe that evaluating the success of audits by how much revenue is raised makes the audit process much more antagonistic and makes it much harder to reach reasonable outcomes from the audit. One consequence is substantial litigation over tax liabilities. The DOT recently adopted a managed audit approach. Both the taxpayers and the DOT are very optimistic that the managed audit system will improve the process.

Ohio exempts many business purchases from the sales tax. For example, exemption is given for purchases of products that are to be incorporated into tangible personal property through manufacture or for purchases made on items to be resold. Nonetheless, approximately 30 percent of sales tax revenues in Ohio comes from taxation of business. Two reasons for including business purchases in the tax base can be easily identified.

- *Revenues.* Revenues are probably the most important reason why the sales tax base includes so many business purchases. Taxing business purchases broadens the tax base and allows more revenues to be collected with a given tax rate. Alternatively, the overall sales tax rate can be kept lower with business purchases in the base. Further, sales tax payments by businesses are hidden from the consumer/taxpayer perspective. The consumer does not realize what is happening when prices are raised to reflect the higher costs that businesses bear when their purchases are sales taxed. This pyramiding of taxes means the effective tax rate is higher than the stated rate.

- *Administration and Compliance.* Determining whether a purchase is made by a business or by a consumer can be very difficult. For example, both a carpenter and a consumer can go to a hardware store to buy a hammer. Total business exemption allows easy opportunities for tax evasion, because the carpenter may be purchasing the hammer for use at home rather than for use on the job. On the other hand, taxation of business purchases creates a number of thorny administrative and compliance problems. Some of these are outlined below.

Taxation of business purchases has some disadvantages as well. Some specific concerns include:

- *Consumption tax concept.* Taxation of business purchases distorts the concept of the sales tax as a consumption tax, since business purchases are not final consumption.
- *Effects on vertical integration.* Businesses are discouraged from engaging in business practices that otherwise would make good business sense. For example, sales taxation of business purchases encourages firms to produce their own inputs, because the sales tax payment can be reduced. Smaller firms can be hurt most by this incentive since small firms may be unable to produce their own inputs. Also, small firms may be less likely to start up as large firms are discouraged from outsourcing. The use of temporary employment services in Ohio may be a case where firms are discouraged from engaging in efficient behavior. Sales taxation of temporary employment services discourages firms from using temporary agencies, hurting the demand for temporary services.
- *Uneven tax burdens.* The sales tax will pyramid as the tax is levied at several stages in the production process. As a result, the effective tax rate on a particular good is a function of how many of the transactions between businesses that occur in production of a good are in the tax base. Thus, horizontal equity is distorted by taxation of business purchases. An example of tax pyramiding is given in the appendix. Further, items such as food or health care cannot be fully exempt from the tax because the sales tax will be implicit in costs of purchases by businesses delivering these products.
- *Economic development.* Sales taxation of business purchases raises the cost of doing business in Ohio. The location of retailers is unlikely to be affected, even though their costs rise, because the retailer wants to locate near the market for its goods. However, manufacturing firms and others that are producing for national markets will find it more expensive to locate in Ohio to the extent that Ohio taxes business purchases more than other states. Relatively little research has been conducted on how sales tax payments by business affect economic development. Fox and Murray (1990) found some evidence that sales taxes reduced the number of firms in the 12 to 50 employee range. Bartik (1989) determined that lower sales tax rates on business equipment purchases increase the start up of small firms in a state.

Business Production Exceptions

The concept behind the sales tax as a consumption tax leads to the conclusion that all business purchases should be exempt and only the sale to the final consumer should be taxed.[31] This approach results in no pyramiding of the tax. Decisions by states to tax some business purchases violate the consumption concept and leave policy makers without a clearly defined policy on where to draw the line on what is taxable.

Ohio altered its exceptions from the sales tax for manufacturing in 1990 and for retail firms in 1993. Until 1990, Ohio permitted manufacturing firms an exception for the purchase of any items that were directly used in the production process. The legislation now sets exceptions based on primary use rather than direct use. Examples of how the former and current exceptions differ are that repair tools and certain safety materials are now taxable, but would not have been taxable prior to the change. Though the change in the manufacturing exception was intended to be revenue-neutral, the courts have interpreted the exception more broadly than was anticipated when the legislation was passed. The exception for retail firms was narrowed. Examples of items that are now taxable, but were formerly exempt, include point-of-sale equipment, such as cash registers, cooling units in super markets, and mannequins. Printed advertising and packaging materials remain exempt.

Direct use exemptions are still allowed for certain industries. The legislation for public utilities says an exception is granted if the thing transferred is used "directly in the rendition of a public utility service." Similar wording is used for the printing industry. The direct use exemption allows lower tax burdens on these industries than they would bear if their exemptions were structured in the same way as the manufacturing exemption.

Most states, including Ohio, exempt many business purchases of capital equipment to reduce the negative consequences of the sales tax on economic development. States have been moving aggressively to reduce the taxation of business capital purchases. California, Minnesota, and Texas recently passed legislation to phase out or eliminate their taxation of capital. These purchases already were exempt in Illinois, but the state passed a tax credit against the corporate income tax for sales taxes that would have been paid on the purchase of capital equipment, if the capital equipment purchases were taxable. Thus, Illinois not only exempts the purchases but also subsidizes them.

Ohio allows exemptions for purchases of packaging material and equipment by manufacturing and retail firms.[32] The courts have construed the exemption rather broadly to include a nearly integrated approach to the entire packaging process. The exemption saves both manufacturing and retail firms considerable taxes and is regarded as very important to the industries. Nonetheless, some narrowing of the exemption can be considered as a policy option.

Many representatives of the Ohio manufacturing industry would like to see a broadening of the existing exception to an integrated plant concept. The idea is that all purchases necessary to a facility's operation would be exempt. This approach would substantially lower manufacturing tax payments, and firms feel it would be easier to comply with because determination of what is taxable would be simpler. The current approach is viewed as selecting various components of a manufacturing facility for exception. For example, a large new piece of equipment may be exempt, but the cooling towers associated with the equipment may not be exempt. The DOT believes the existing law is a quasi-integrated plant approach. The difference between the current law and an integrated plant concept can be seen by where the exemption begins. Under existing law, the exemption begins at the point in the production process where the item is committed to the process that will transfer the item purchased into tangible personal property for sale.

A border-type problem arises with one area of production exemptions. Ohio law imposes the use tax on items that are stored in the state. Therefore, under Ohio law the use tax is incident on tangible personal property that is stored first in Ohio warehouses (so that tax has not been paid on the items in other states). The State of Ohio won a recent court case with Norandex affirming its authority to tax the storage. Some firms are threatening to move their warehouses from Ohio if the tax continues to be imposed. The storage of promotion and advertising materials is one use that business is very concerned about. Ohio could enact a temporary storage exemption to lessen the impact of taxing items that are merely passing through Ohio. However, failure to tax the storage of tangible property opens a wide opportunity for firms to avoid the tax or to pay the tax after a considerable time period.

The decision of where to draw the line for business exemptions is a tradeoff between revenues on the one hand and effects on equity, economic development, and business practices on the other. Administration is less of a concern because close decisions on what is taxable must be made wherever the line is drawn. States use different approaches to exemptions, but have generally been able to find reasonable ways to administer the tax wherever the line lies.

Issue 2: Should the production exemptions allowed for business purchases be changed?

Option 1: Leave the production exemptions alone.

Option 2: Broaden the exemption to the fully integrated plant approach.

Option 3: Broaden the exemption to all business purchases.

Option 4: Narrow the exemptions granted to public utilities and the printing industry.

Option 5: Narrow the exemptions granted to manufacturing further.

Option 6: Narrow the exemption for packaging materials.

Option 7: Pass a temporary storage exemption for tangible personal property stored briefly in Ohio.

Taxation of Temporary Employment Services

Ohio taxes the purchase of employment services. The services include both placement services and provision of personnel, such as is done by temporary employment agencies. Taxation of personnel provision is raising about $31.0 million annually and taxation of placement services is raising about $6.0 million annually, based on data for January 1993 through March 1994.

Businesses can be thought of as purchasing two separate activities when personnel provision services are bought from a temporary employment agency. One is the placement service associated with identifying and hiring prospective employees, and the other is the actual provision of personnel. Taxation of placement services can be justified in the same way as taxation of other purchases by businesses. However, the tax on employee compensation is comparable to a payroll tax and can be expected to have greater negative implications than the tax on placement services. A sales tax equal to 5 percent or more of labor costs will discourage the use of employment agencies and prevent firms from setting up their employment structures in the most efficient manner. Firms can avoid the tax by merely hiring workers directly, rather than through agencies.

An alternative structure to the one currently used in Ohio is to tax the services provided by employment agencies other than the actual provision of workers. Pennsylvania imposes a tax on employment services in this way. Employment agencies can be taxed on a base that is defined as total revenues minus direct payments to employees (wages plus taxes directly on employees plus fringes). The base would represent the charge for the placement service. However, the value of this charge is a highly sensitive and confidential component of employment firms' business. An alternative would be to presume that a fixed percentage of billings represents the value of the service and to levy the tax on the fixed percentage. The charge represents about 20 percent of total billings by temporary employment agencies.

Perhaps the biggest objection to altering the tax structure is the lost revenues, that could be around $25 million annually, based on about 20 percent of the value of temporary employment services representing the placement service. However, revenues should not be the driving force behind every decision about what to tax, and the logic of the tax structure should be given heavy weight in this decision.

Issue 3: How should Ohio treat employment services for tax purposes?

Option 1: Exempt all employment services

Option 2: Tax the value of services provided by employment agencies, but not the charge for direct labor. Measure the service based on the actual charges of the employment firm.

Option 3: Tax the value of services provided by employment agencies, but not the charge for direct labor Measure the service based on an average of actual charges by employment firms.

Option 4: Tax the full value of employment agency charges.

ISSUES IN SALES TAXATION

This section is a policy analysis of a series of topics that are important in the design of Ohio's tax structure. The issues include determining the taxable value, taxing services, taxing food and utilities, increasing the sales tax rate, setting permissive sales tax rates, taxing not-for-profits and governments, and taxing mail order sales.

DETERMINING THE TAXABLE VALUE

Two issues in setting the taxable value of items in the tax base can be identified. First, the price at which items are sold must be set. The issue may seem straightforward, but in some cases firms may be able to state the price for their product in two parts. One part is any tangible property that is sold and the other part is the labor input. Only the tangible property may be taxable in some circumstances. One small example of this practice already has arisen in Ohio. As a norm, the good or service delivered must be viewed as a unitary activity, and the taxable price must be defined as the total amount charged for the unitary activity, unless a very clear case can be made for why these activities are separated. Otherwise, the revenue loss will be substantial, the potential for avoidance very broad, and the ability to audit taxes reduced.

Second, the taxable value of many business purchases is based on each item's cost. Businesses believe the DOT is seeking to levy the tax on a fully loaded cost that includes the direct, indirect and overhead costs. Using the fully loaded cost as the taxable value is consistent with other business practices and raises more revenues, but entails more compliance costs for taxpayers.

Issue 4: What is taxable value?

Option 1: The full cost of any transaction.

Option 2: The tangible goods portion of the transaction.

Option 3: The direct cost of a purchase.

TAXING SERVICES

The Commission listed the issue of whether Ohio's system of taxes fits the new economic structure as the second major research question, along with effects of the taxes on jobs and business. The major shift in Ohio towards a services-based economy raises the question of whether the Ohio sales tax, that exempts most services, fits the new economy (Duchi 1994;McHugh 1994a). The Commission proposed broadening the sales tax to a series of services to raise about $150 million now and broadening the tax later to a series of other services, including professional services, to raise about $600 million. Recent studies of the Arizona, Minnesota, and Nevada sales taxes led to the conclusion that the sales tax should be expanded to personal services, but not to services that are heavily used by business (Ebel 1990; Ladd and Weist 1991; Mikesell 1986).

Broadening the sales tax base to include services has been the subject of much discussion in recent years, both in Ohio and in other states.[33] The quest for new revenue sources and efforts to slow the rise in sales tax rates are the driving forces behind the new attention that taxing services has attracted. Nonetheless, the idea of taxing services is not new since several states have a long history of taxing most or all services. For example, Hawaii taxes essentially all services and New Mexico, South Dakota and Iowa also tax a wide range of services. All of these states included services in their bases at least two decades ago.

The lesson drawn from experience across the United States during the past decade is that significant new base expansions to services are very difficult to pass into legislation. Florida enacted the most dramatic legislation when it introduced broad-based taxation of services in 1987.[34] The legislation was repealed after just six months. Many other states, including Texas, Indiana, Arkansas, Wisconsin, Illinois, Connecticut, and Nebraska, have carefully considered a broad-based expansion of the sales tax base to services but have failed to pass corresponding legislation.

States have managed to pass small, piecemeal expansions of the base to services. Ohio has been very aggressive in adding services to the tax base during the past several years (see Table 4-8), though the base remains narrow because the newly taxed services tend to be small relative to total service's consumption. Many other states have added services as well. Twenty-eight states added selected business services, 27 added personal services, 11 added amusements, 9 added repairs, and 8 added utilities to their bases between 1990 and 1992.[35] For example, Kentucky included equipment rentals and leases in the base; Connecticut included repairs, health clubs, car washes, landscaping, and others; Maryland included cellular and beeper services, custom calling features, pay-per-view television, and building cleaning; and Kansas imposed a 2.5 percent tax on construction services.

Should Services Be Taxed? A decision to include services in the base should be made after separately weighing the advantages and disadvantages for each service. The advantages and disadvantages apply to specific services

TABLE 4-8
Number of Services Taxed in Ohio, by Category: 1990 and Current

Category	Services Taxed in 1990	Services Currently Taxed	Change: 1990-Current
Agricultural Services	0	1	1
Industrial and Mining Services	0	0	0
Construction	0	0	0
Transportation	1	1	0
Storage	0	0	0
Utilities	6	8	2
FIRE	0	0	0
Personal Services	4	6	2
Business Services	4	13	9
Computer Services	2	2	0
Automotive Services	3	3	0
Admissions and Amusements	1	2	1
Professional Services	0	0	0
Leases	1	1	0
Fabrication, Repair and Installation	12	12	0
Miscellaneous	0	0	0
TOTAL	34	49	15

Source: Inter-Office Communication from Christopher W. Hall to Ronald A. Mucha, Ohio Department of Taxation, June 16, 1994.

to differing degrees, so taxation of services will be appropriate in some cases but not in others. The advantages often given for taxing services include:

- *Horizontal equity.* Taxation of services means a greater percentage of consumption is in the tax base, so horizontal equity is enhanced. Services represent 54.3 percent of personal expenditures across the United States, versus 14.2 percent for durable goods and 31.4 percent for nondurable goods.
- *Vertical equity.* Vertical equity may be improved by inclusion of services that are heavily consumed by higher-income households. However, we noted above that any increases in tax progressiveness will be limited. The reason is that the Consumer Expenditure Survey evidences that consumption of few services is progressive.36 Siegfried and Smith (1991) conclude that the sales tax on business services also will be regressive if the tax is shifted forward into higher consumer prices.
- *Efficiency.* The sales tax raises the price a consumer pays for taxed goods proportionately by the tax rate, thereby making taxed goods relatively more expensive than untaxed goods. The increase in the relative price of taxed goods distorts the economic efficiency that results from allowing private market prices to decide what goods consumers will buy. The expectation is that consumers will respond to price differences by reducing their purchases of taxed goods and raising their consumption of untaxed goods. For example, consumers in Ohio are expected to eat at home more and to go out to eat less than they would do without effects of the tax. Taxing services takes away the price advantage that many services have received in the past from the tax system.
- *Revenues.* Broadening the tax base to include new items allows a state to either increase its revenues or decrease its tax rate. Essentially all states use the opportunity of taxing new services to increase revenues, because states generally will not go through the political strife necessary to tax services just to lower the tax rate imposed on already taxed goods (though a case could be made to follow such a policy). However, the amount of new revenues available from expanding the base to services is smaller than many expect. Goods consumed in the production of services generally are taxable today as an indirect way to tax part of the service. Direct taxation of services probably would be accompanied by production exemptions for some goods consumed in production of services, similar to the exemptions that exist for production of goods. Also, production exemptions would be allowed for some services consumed in the production of goods. Therefore, the new revenues from

taxing services are lower than the apparent increase in the tax base times the existing tax rate.

- *Revenue growth.* Consumption of services has grown much more rapidly than consumption of goods. On the surface this seems to suggest the sales tax would be more revenue-elastic compared with income if services were in the base. However, effects of services on the growth pattern are highly dependent on which services are taxable. Dye and McGuire (1991) examined a set of services that might be added to the sales tax base. They found that personal services, such as cleaning, clothing repair, other repairs, and beauty services, grow more slowly than existing tangible goods tax bases. Recreation services, such as admissions to certain amusements and club memberships, grow somewhat faster than the existing tax bases. Personal business services, such as investment counseling, bank service charges, and legal services, grow much more rapidly than existing tax bases. Personal and business services also tend to make the tax base more erratic, though recreation services are even more stable than food purchases.
- *Political salability.* Broadening the sales tax to services often can be sold as loophole closing. On the other hand, elimination of tax preferences can be very difficult to enact through the political process.

A number of disadvantages also result from taxing services, including:

- *Administrative and compliance.* More service vendors will need to file returns and comply with the tax. The state will bear both implementation costs, associated with registering new vendors and making decisions on specifically how the new tax would operate, and monitoring costs. Research evidences that the sales of service vendors are smaller on average than goods vendors so, to the extent that administrative costs are fixed per vendor, the collection costs for raising a given amount of revenues will rise. Also, administrative and legal determination of exactly what is taxable will need to be made for an entirely new set of taxable items. Contentious issues remain, but generally widespread agreement exists on how to apply the sales tax to goods. Similar agreements must be reached for a new group of taxable items if services are to be taxed.37 Most vendors will bear additional compliance costs as well, with the greatest costs being incurred in the early years of expansion of the base to services.
- *Economic development and border effects.* Border effects can arise because of rate divergences along the borders or because items are taxed in one state but not in another. Broad-based taxation of services will result in a substantial number of services being taxed in Ohio, but not

in neighboring states. The result can be a significant incentive for services to be produced outside Ohio, either in neighboring or in other states. Production of many services, and particularly those consumed by businesses, can be shifted easily outside the state, meaning the impact can be a considerable loss of service production. However, this problem can be avoided by taxing services where they are consumed, not where they are produced.

- *Taxation of business.* Many services are purchased substantially more often by businesses than by consumers. Examples are legal services, computer services, and employment agencies. Including these services in the base in a relative sense moves the tax away from being a consumption levy and towards a tax on business. Pyramiding of the sales tax will increase as some services are taxed. Thus, if the intent is to tax consumption, a tax on services that also are consumed by business must be carefully structured so as to avoid taxing many business purchases of services. Nonetheless, not taxing services only because a portion of the base would be business purchases places a higher standard on the taxation of services than on the taxation of goods, and is inconsistent with the taxation of goods.
- *Equity.* Some believe that equity will be harmed if services such as health care are taxed. The feelings expressed often are concerns that a tax on health care is a tax on misery, suffering and misfortune. Certainly, in some circumstances a tax on health care purchases would be a tax on expenditures that cannot be avoided, but such an argument cannot be made for exemption of cosmetic and other voluntary health care purchases.

Two complicated problems arise with taxation of services. The first is situsing where the service is delivered. As discussed below, the goal is to tax the services where the benefits are enjoyed, not where the service is produced. Services that are produced and consumed in Ohio, such as when a Cleveland attorney provides services for a Cleveland resident, create no unusual problems. Similarly, there are no conceptual difficulties in identifying where a service is taxable if the benefits are enjoyed at a single location in Ohio and the service is produced in another state. The biggest problem is determining that the transaction has occurred because there may be no easy way to identify such transactions. The situsing problem is more complicated in several other circumstances. For example, when a person in New York places a telephone call to someone in Illinois that passes through Ohio.[38] Another situsing problem occurs when a single entity purchases a service from an unrelated company for use in more than one state. Examples include the purchase of an economic forecast that may be used by several divisions of a company in different states and the purchase of computer information services offered via terminal to locations in different states. Alternative solutions include taxing the service where it is billed, taxing the service where the predominant user is sitused, sharing the tax base equally among all states where the service is consumed, and apportioning the tax base using a formula.

The situsing problem is compounded for the permissive tax because taxation on a destination basis, as is encouraged in this chapter, requires identifying the county in which consumption of a service takes place. Destination taxation is important because it reduces the effects that the tax has on where firms produce services. Services produced and consumed in the same county or produced out of state and consumed in a single county present no unusual situsing problems. However, services produced in one county and consumed in another require tracking each purchase to determine which county is entitled to the revenues. Tracking the purchases creates compliance and administration problems and some service providers have argued that they have no way to track where consumption occurs. Services produced in one place and consumed in multiple counties exacerbates the problem because decisions must be made on how much revenue to collect (since different rates may apply) and which county gets the tax revenues. One solution that has been discussed in Ohio is to impose a single permissive rate on the consumption of all taxed services (see the section on permissive taxes below) in Ohio. The single rate solution solves the problem of how much revenue to collect and reduces any effects of the tax on where the production of services takes place. However, this solution does not solve the problem of tracking consumption and determining which county gets the permissive tax revenues.

The second problem is defining the service. Again, in many cases this may not be difficult. In other cases, such as banking, insurance, and consulting, there are many difficult issues. For example, separating the information content from telecommunications can be very difficult, but is necessary if they are taxed differently. Even defining pet grooming can be trying.

Services That Could Be Added to the Tax Base. An estimate of revenues that could be obtained by broadening the tax base to a series of services is presented in Table 4-9. A broader listing of exempt services, and states where the services are taxable, is given in Box 1-6, in this volume. Ohio could reduce its sales tax rate to about 3.3 percent and still collect the same revenues if all of the expansions listed in the table were brought into the tax base.[39]

The major exemption is for health services, representing nearly three-fourths of the total value of exemptions listed in Table 4-9. Health services are exempt in most states with only Hawaii and New Mexico taxing the service (Due and Mikesell 1994). Prescription drugs are exempt in all states, except New Mexico which allows an income tax credit instead. A strong case

TABLE 4-9
Significant Ohio Service Exemptions

		FY1994	FY1995
1.	Health Care	$1,172.7	$1,477.0
2.	Legal Services	157.0	193.8
3.	Engineering, Architecture, and Surveying	60.2	72.4
4.	Management Services	59.8	70.8
5.	Accounting and Bookkeeping	52.3	64.0
6.	Cable TV	45.0	53.9
7.	Beauty Salons and Barber Shops	16.1	19.8
8.	Coin-Operated Amusements	10.0	12.2
9.	Auto Parking	9.9	12.3
10.	Laundry and Dry Cleaning	9.3	11.8
11.	Advertising and Public Relations	7.6	8.7
12.	Public Golf Courses	7.4	9.6
13.	Funeral Services	7.4	8.2
14.	Motion Picture Theaters	4.5	5.3
	TOTAL	$1,619.2	$2,019.8

Source: State of Ohio Executive Budget for the Biennium, July 1, 1993 to June 30, 1995, Book Two: Report on Tax Expenditures, prepared by the Ohio Department of Taxation.

can be made for taxing certain health care services, such as voluntary cosmetic surgery and braces put on teeth for cosmetic reasons. In fact, the consumption of health care services is regressive (Bohm and Craig 1987) suggesting that exemption of health care contributes to making the sales tax more regressive. However, the main reason that health care normally is exempt is because of arguments that taxing health care is inequitable since it would be a tax on misery. Further, much of the sales taxation of medical services could become a higher cost for business since a significant share of health care expenditures are financed by insurance, and businesses pay much of the cost of health insurance. In any event, expansion of the sales tax base to include health care services is very difficult politically, particularly at this time when health care reform is receiving substantial attention.

Exemption of legal services results in a loss of $193.8 million during FY95. The case for exempting legal services often is made because business purchases much of the service, the tax would be imposed on the constitutional right to counsel, most of the service is provision of labor so that taxation of legal services would be comparable to a payroll tax, or Ohio lawyers would be placed at a competitive disadvantage. None of these arguments appears to strongly compel full exemption of legal services from the base as long as the tax is placed on consumption of legal services in Ohio rather than on production of legal services.

A number of services that are purchased almost exclusively by businesses are on the list, including engineering, architecture, and surveying; management services; accounting and bookkeeping services; and advertising and public relations. Exemption for each of these services can be argued because none represents consumption by households. Still, the basis for exemption is not greater than for many other business purchases that already are taxed.

Recreation services, such as cable TV, coin-operated amusements, public golf courses, and motion picture theaters, are on the list. Legitimate justifications for exemption of these services are difficult to identify, though Tennessee imposed the sales tax on coin-operated amusements several years ago and has found the tax difficult to administer. The history of the tax structure and the politics of broadening the base explain these exemptions.

Several personal services, such as beauty salons and barber shops and laundry and dry cleaning services, are exempt. Again, exemptions for these are difficult to justify.

Construction services are not on the list of estimated revenues but represent another area where considerable revenues can be raised. The value of construction work in Ohio during 1987 was $18.1 billion. As with many services, construction materials often are taxable, so some of the service already is taxed indirectly. However, adding the labor component of construction to the base would represent a significant expansion of the sales tax to construction. A sales tax on the labor component of construction services would have raised $273.7 million during 1993.

Transportation services also could be considered for inclusion in the base. Production type exemptions may be appropriate for certain shipping activities related to retailing and manufacturing activities. However, other transportation could be added to the base.

Ohio taxes interlata telephone services that originate or terminate and are billed in Ohio, and taxes cellular services. Intralata and local telephone services are not in the tax base but could be. No substantial reasons for exempting local telephone service from the tax can be given, except for the existence of the public utilities excise tax. A decision to impose the sales tax on local telephone services needs to be handled simultaneously with a decision on the public utilities excise tax.[40] WATS like telephone service also is exempt. A number of states have chosen to grant a similar exemption because of concerns that intensive users of 800 services will choose to locate in another state. Mail order companies, reservation systems, and businesses like Chemical Abstracts are examples of the types of firms that may choose a location to avoid a tax on 800 services.

Companies performing consumer credit reporting are exempt by statute, but firms performing credit reporting for businesses are taxable. The exemption is stated by type of firm, rather than by type of service. A problem arises for firms that do credit reporting for both businesses and consumers, because these firms are not paying the tax on their business credit reporting either. Firms doing business credit reporting only are placed at a disadvantage because they must collect sales taxes on their services and then compete with firms that are not collecting the tax. Horizontal equity for businesses argues that all firms delivering the same services should be subject to the same tax. This can be accomplished by broadening the base to all credit reporting or by changing the exemption to apply to consumer credit services, rather than to a particular type of firm. One lesson that can be learned from this problem is that exemptions should be granted for the activity that is to be favored rather than by the type of vendor.

Guidelines for Taxing Services. A comparison of the advantages and disadvantages seems to suggest that base expansion should continue. The specific service tax structure is very important to developing a tax system that is conducive to a healthy Ohio economy and that is also logically consistent. The guidelines that follow are intended to minimize any distorting effects of taxing services, but they also will reduce the amount of revenue raised. Service taxation would not raise as much revenue as reported in Table 4-9 if these guidelines are not followed. The specific guidelines are:

- *Use destination rules.* Services should be taxed where they are consumed, not where they are produced. Thus, legal services consumed by Ohio businesses and Ohio residents would be taxable in Ohio, regardless of whether the attorneys delivering the service are located in Cincinnati or Chicago. A destination basis would eliminate any incentive for either Ohio or non-Ohio purchasers to buy services from outside of Ohio. However, the destination basis raises administrative and compliance problems for the tax because service providers must be able to track consumers of their services. Hawaii taxes services on an origination basis (i.e., where services are produced) but is able to do so because of the large distances involved. Other states would severely disadvantage their service industries with such a strategy.

- *Allow liberal interfirm exemptions.* Services should be exempt from sales taxation if they are directly used in the production of another good or service. The physical test rules that often are used to determine if a purchase is exempt do not work with services.

- *Exempt purchases from a firm set up solely to sell services to another firm.* This exemption allows businesses to establish subsidiaries without the direct influence of tax considerations. Taxation of direct purchase arrangements can lead to vertical integration.

- *Exempt business purchases of labor.* The tax can be imposed on business purchases of services, but not the direct purchase of labor. For example, the purchase of landscaping services could be taxable, but the purchase of workers' time to do landscaping should be exempt. Obviously, very careful rules must be designed to prevent firms from avoiding the tax by simply saying they are buying workers' time rather than purchasing a service.
- *Track business practices to ensure that service taxes do not become overly influential in the operation of business activities.* The structure of business is constantly changing, and the state must be prepared to alter its tax structure to encourage efficient business operations.

Issue 5: Should the sales tax base be expanded to additional services?

Option 1: Tax medical services.

Option 2: Tax legal services.

Option 3: Tax business services.

Option 4: Tax recreation services.

Option 5: Tax personal services.

Option 6: Tax additional construction services.

Option 7: Tax local telephone services.

Option 8: Tax transportation services.

Option 9: Tax all credit reporting.

Option 10: Tax all business credit reporting.

Is a Separate Law Necessary for Taxing Services? Expansions of the sales tax to services have been undertaken with changes in Ohio's existing sales tax legislation. Some have expressed the opinion that services should be taxed with a separate tax law, rather than fitting services into the existing sales tax law. The main argument for having separate tax laws is that taxation of services and taxation of tangible personal property are very different from an administrative perspective. Separate laws could be established to recognize these differences.

The tax law should be established to operate effectively in legal, administrative, and compliance terms. Economics has little to contribute to this debate. The key issue from an economics perspective is that the unique characteristics of services be considered when the tax law is designed. Two of these unique characteristics are that production of many services can be located a long distance from the point of use (particularly banking services and many business services), and that services normally cannot be seen once they are used in production. The rules governing application of taxes to services must be established differently to account for these characteristics.

Taxing Food and Utilities

Food and Utilities are exempt from sales taxation in Ohio and in many other states. Twenty-six of the forty-six states[41] taxing sales exempt food for consumption at home, and 29 exempt electricity and natural gas used for residential consumption.[42] The trend generally has been for more states to exempt these items, though this has not been true exclusively. One state, Tennessee, initially exempted food in 1984 but reinstated the tax on food before the exemption took effect. In 1992 Maryland broadened taxation of food to include ready-to-eat food in grocery stores, certain snack foods, and sales by college and hospital cafeterias. California recently broadened the sales tax to include certain snack foods.

The Commission proposed expanding the sales tax to include food consumption, combined with a food tax credit against the income tax to limit any effects on regressiveness that would hurt low income households. Advantages of taxing food and utilities include:

- The administrative and compliance costs of the tax would be lessened because fewer difficult decisions would be necessary on what is taxable.
- The sales tax rate could be reduced, meaning the distortions that taxes make in business and consumer behavior could be lessened.
- The overall tax burden could be made more progressive, depending on how the policy change is structured.
- Tax policies aimed at making taxes more progressive could be aimed directly at the people who are the intended beneficiaries, rather than at all groups.
- The system would be more horizontally equitable because the tax system would impose less of a penalty on people who choose to eat in restaurants versus those who eat at home.
- More sales tax revenues could be raised from nonresidents.

Border problems are one potential disadvantage of taxing food. Indiana, Kentucky, Michigan, and Pennsylvania all exempt food from the sales tax. Ohio residents would have an incentive to cross the border to shop for groceries if Ohio taxed food. On the other hand, the revenues from taxing food and utilities could be used to lower the tax rate, and this could improve Ohio as a place for other shopping. Vedder, Klingaman and Galloway (1992) examined the number of food store employees in counties along the West Virginia and Ohio border. They concluded that Ohio gained a significant number of workers because West Virginia residents do considerable food shopping in Ohio. Based on this study, taxation of food in Ohio could cause Ohio stores to lose the sales currently being attracted from West Virginia and to lose food sales to other states along the border.

Taxing food for consumption off the premises where it is purchased is unconstitutional in Ohio. Therefore, taxing food is an option, but is not easily viable since a constitutional amendment would be necessary to expand the base to include food. The Commission addressed this issue by proposing that voters be given a choice between broadening the tax base to food or raising the sales tax rate.

Several types of estimates were made of the sales tax revenues that could be obtained from broadening the sales tax to include currently exempt food and utility purchases. First, an estimate was made of the additional revenue that could be raised from the base expansion. Approximately $700 million would be generated from taxation of currently untaxed food and another $478 million from taxation of utilities (Table 4-10, Column 1).[43] The assumption in this calculation is that no existing taxes on utilities are reduced when the tax base is broadened to utilities. Second, an estimate was made of how much the sales tax rate could be lowered so that the base expansion was revenue-neutral. The tax rate could be 3.8 percent if both utilities and food are taxable, 4.2 percent if only food is taxed, and 4.4 percent if only utilities are taxed (Table 4-10, Column 2).

TABLE 4-10
Tax Rates and Revenues with Food and Utilities Taxable
(Dollar Values in Millions)

	1 1993 Revenue at 5% (millions)	2 Revenue-Neutral Tax Rate	3 1993 Revenue with Tax Credit ($15,000-$19,999)	4 Revenue-Neutral Tax Rate with Credit ($15,000-$19,999)	5 Revenue-Neutral Tax Rate with Credit ($10,000-$14,999)
Food	$ 700.1	4.23	102.0	4.77	4.72
Utilities	$ 478.1	4.44	40.1	4.91	4.90
Food & Utilities	$1,178.2	3.82	142.1	4.69	4.63

Source: Author's calculations.

Broadening the base and lowering the rate have several important implications (see Figure 4-10). One observation is that the tax burden for all income groups rises, even though the change is revenue neutral. The reason is that the lower tax rate must be shared with business, so the consumer's share of the tax rises. This result evidences that base expansion reduces the business share of the tax unless the business share of newly taxable items is at least as great as the average business share of the existing tax base. Second, the relative increase is greater for lower income residents. Therefore, the change makes the tax structure more regressive against current income. Adding utilities alone also would make the structure more regressive (not illustrated).

An alternative is to impose the tax on food and/or utilities and to give a refundable credit against the income tax for sales taxes paid on these items.[44] The credit is intended to offset the increase in sales taxes paid by lower-income households, while still obtaining the benefits of having food and utilities in the base.

The tax credit first was assumed to equal the tax increase from broadening the base that is imposed on households earning $15,000 to $19,999. Thus, the average household in the $15,000 to $19,999 bracket is unaffected by the base-broadening since the income tax credit equals the sales tax hike. In general, lower income households will be better off because they receive a higher valued credit than the amount they spend on food and utilities. In general, higher-income households will be worse off because they pay more sales taxes on food and utilities than they receive back through the credit. The net effect of these tax changes is shown in Table 4-11. Relatively little additional revenue (Column 3) or little decrease in the tax rate (Column 4) can be achieved because most of the revenue is used to finance the tax cred-

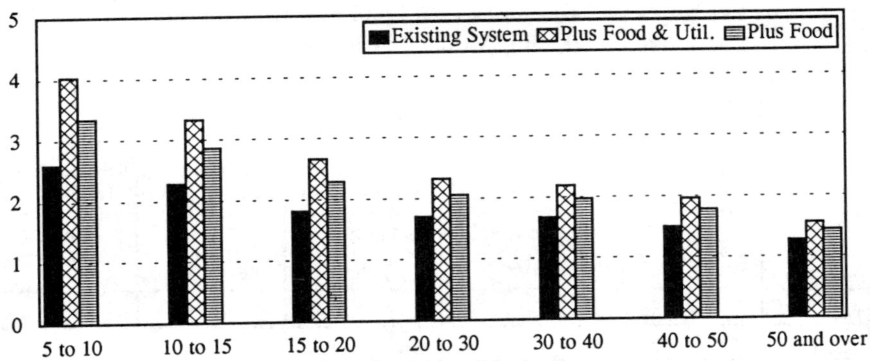

Source: U.S. Department of Labor, *Consurer Expenditure Survey*, 1990-91 and author's calculations.

FIGURE 4-10. Ohio state sales tax collections as a percent of before-tax income.

TABLE 4-11
Equity Implications of Taxing Food and Utilities and Granting an Income Tax Credit

Income Group ($)	Sales Tax Increase ($)	Income Tax Credit per Person ($)	Net New Tax per Person ($)	Effective Sales Tax Rate with No Policy Change(%)	Effective Rate after Policy Changes (%)
Less than 5,000	51.26	62.13	-10.87	6.78	6.11
5,000-9,999	63.01	62.13	0.88	2.60	2.62
10,000-14,999	62.13	62.13	0.00	2.28	2.28
15,000-19,999	64.00	62.13	1.87	1.81	1.84
20,000-29,999	61.28	62.13	-0.85	1.70	1.69
30,000-39,999	59.77	62.13	-2.36	1.67	1.65
40,000-49,999	69.74	62.13	7.61	1.49	1.54
50,000 or more	68.61	62.13	6.48	1.27	1.30

Source: Author's calculations.

its.[45] Businesses get a very small tax rate reduction if the additional base is used to lower the rate. The policy change would improve vertical equity since low-income households would get a tax cut and high-income households would have a small tax increase. Also, there would be fewer distortions in decisions, easier sales tax administration and compliance, and increased taxes paid by nonresidents.

An alternative calculation was made with the credit set equal to the increase in taxes paid by households in the $10,000 to $14,999 bracket. In these calculations a larger tax rate reduction can be achieved with a revenue-neutral tax policy (Table 4-11, Column 5). The reason is a smaller income tax credit is given because the credit is based on expenditures by a lower-income household. The calculations are demonstrated in Table 4-11 and are illustrated in Figure 4-11. Note that all calculations in Table 4-11 are made using a 4.63 percent tax rate. First, regressivity of the tax is slightly reduced at the upper end by the broader base and the tax credit. Regressivity would be reduced more if the tax credit were phased out for higher-income households. Second, the tax burden of some middle-income households actually falls because the lower sales tax rate and income tax credit save these households more money than is generated by taxation of their food and utilities.

Many states provide special treatment of utilities under the sales tax, with 28 states specifically exempting residential utilities from the tax (see Table 4-12).[46] Some disagreement may exist on the definition of exemptions from

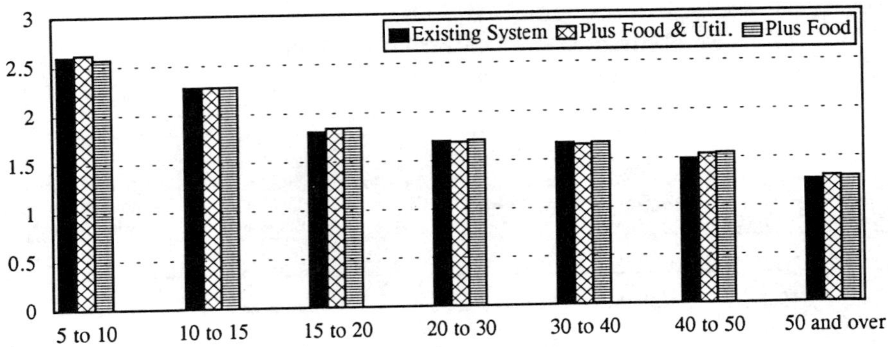

Source: U.S. Department of Labor, *Consumer Expenditure Survey*, 1990-91 and author's calculations.

FIGURE 4-11. Ohio state sales tax collections with credit as a percent of

the sales tax. Definitions selected by staff at the ACIR are accepted in Table 4-12. Thirty-one states either impose a gross receipts tax on public utilities in lieu of the sales tax or in addition to the sales tax. The gross receipts rates reported in Table 4-12 normally are the highest imposed on each type of utility. States often have other industry specific taxes on utilities besides the gross receipts tax, and these are not reported in the Table.

Issue 6: Should food for consumption at home and residential utilities be taxable in Ohio?

Option 1: Tax neither food nor utilities.

Option 2: Tax food taken off the premises.

Option 3: Tax utilities.

Option 4: Broaden the base and lower the sales tax rate to achieve a revenue neutral change.

Option 5: Broaden the base and give a refundable income tax credit to offset equity effects.

Increasing the Sales Tax Rate

The Commission proposed raising the sales tax rate by 1 percent to finance other tax relief that is part of the overall Commission plan. A one percent rate increase would generate about $935 million in FY95. As proposed

TABLE 4-12
Sales and Gross Receipts Taxes on Utility Services, All States

State	Sales Tax on Residential Utilities	Sales Tax on Telecommunications Services	Gross Receipts Utility Tax
Alabama	X	X	E,W,G 2% Tele 3.7%
Alaska	NS		
Arizona			Tele 2.3%
Arkansas			
California	X	X	Tele 0.69%
Colorado	X		
Connecticut	X		E,W,G,P 5%
Delaware	NS		4.25%
Florida	X		E 2.5% Tele 2.5%
Georgia			
Hawaii	X		5.885%
Idaho	X	X	
Illinois			E,G 5% Tele 5%
Indiana			
Iowa			
Kansas	X		
Kentucky	X		
Louisiana		Limited	2%
Maine	X		
Maryland	X		2%
Massachusetts	X		
Michigan			
Minnesota			
Mississippi	X		
Missouri	X		
Montana	NS		Tele 1.8%
Nebraska			
Nevada	X	X	
New Hampshire	NS		E,G 1% Tele 5.5%

continued

TABLE 4-12 (continued)
Sales and Gross Receipts Taxes on Utility Services, All States

State	Sales Tax on Residential Utilities	Sales Tax on Telecommunications Services	Gross Receipts Utility Tax
New Jersey	X		7.5% Tele + 2%
New Mexico			Interstate Tele 4.25% E,G,W 0.5%
New York	X	Partial	W,G,E 4.25% Tele 3.8%
North Carolina			E,G 3.22% W 4.0% Tele 3.22%
North Dakota	Limited		Tele 2.0%
Ohio	X	X	4.75%
Oklahoma	X		Rural E 2%
Oregon	NS		Rural Tele 6.0%
Pennsylvania	X		5.0%
Rhode Island	X		E 4.0% G 3.0% Tele 6.0%
South Carolina	X		
South Dakota			Rural E 2% Rural Tele 5%
Tennessee	X		G 1.5% W,E, 3.0%
Texas	X		E,G,W 1.997%
Utah	Limited	Partial	0.3%
Vermont	X	X	
Virginia	X	X	E,G,W 2%
Washington	X		E 3.62% G 3.6% W 4.7%
West Virginia	X		E 2.0% G 4.29 W 4.4% Tele 4%
Wisconsin			E 3.19% Tele 7.9%
Wyoming			0.3%

Source: ACIR (1993) and Commerce Clearing House, *State Tax Guide*.

X = Exempt, NS = No sales tax, E = Electricity, G = Gas, W = Water, Tele = Telecommunications, P=Power.

by the Commission, the additional revenue can be used to lower other tax rates and to eliminate other taxes.

The policy effects of replacing another tax with a higher sales tax rate depend on the specific changes that are enacted. Politically, there does not appear to be a maximum sales tax rate that states have reached that suggest Ohio would encounter major objections to a higher sales tax rate. The highest combined state and local rate is imposed in Louisiana at a 10 percent rate. Thus far no significant backlash has occurred in states with higher rates than Ohio. Further, Ohio has not raised its sales tax rate since 1981, though rates have been raised 57 times by other states since 1982. However, there have been many increases in Ohio permissive sales tax rates since 1981.

Without examining the specifics of the Commission's overall recommendations, several points can be made. A higher rate would increase the distorting effects of the sales tax in terms of what and where consumers buy. For example, the negative incentive effects of high taxes rise more than proportionately with the tax rate.[47] Incentives to evade the tax and to shop in other states would rise. Other effects, including those on equity, economic development, and administration and compliance, would depend on the revenue source replaced with the sales tax revenues. Any negative effects on administrative and compliance effects would be small because it would be less costly to raise more revenues by raising the rate than by broadening the base.

Issue 7: Should the sales tax rate be raised and the revenues used to lower other tax rates or to replace other taxes?

Option 1: Leave the tax rate unchanged.

Option 2: Raise the tax rate.

Option 3: Lower the tax rate.

Permissive Sales Tax

Thirty-two states, including Ohio, permit local governments to impose sales taxes. At least 29 of these states allow local governments flexibility over the tax rate imposed, within some limits. Some states also permit local option on the tax base. Flexibility on the tax rate and base allows local governments to better tune their tax structures to the wishes of local residents and to generate sufficient revenues to provide the services demanded by residents.

A concern here is the complexity that multiple local rates and bases create for business and the DOT. There is no question that multiple bases within a state create substantial problems for taxpayers and collectors. Ohio, fortunately, has chosen not to allow local governments control over the tax base, but sets the local base the same as the state base. One result is that expansions of the state sales tax base also broaden the base for counties and transit authorities, so local governments are indirect beneficiaries of any decisions to broaden the state sales tax base.

Ohio does allow each county and transit authority to set its own local rate (see Table 4-13). Multiple rates beget fewer problems than multiple bases. Businesses must collect and report taxes for all of the different locations where they operate, and DOT must collect and tabulate revenues for every local government regardless of whether local rates are the same or different, because local governments receive revenues based on the situs of sales. Thus, little administrative advantage results from identical rates unless the revenues are distributed on some basis other than situs.

A problem with multiple rates is that consumers and businesses may purchase items in low-rate jurisdictions to avoid the tax. In Ohio, situs for the permissive tax normally is determined where the vendor is located for tangible property and at the location where the service is enjoyed for services. Purchasers can lower their tax burden by buying tangible goods where the rates are low, since the rule is on an origination basis. Purchasers cannot lower their services tax liability since the liability is levied on a destination basis.

Some have suggested that a flat tax rate should be imposed across all counties for the services component of the permissive sales tax. The flat rate

TABLE 4-13
Ohio Permissive Tax Rates, June 1993

Tax Rate	Number of Counties
0%	1
0.5%	6
0.75%	5
1.0	59
1.25	5
1.5	11
2.0	1
Total	88

Source: Ohio Department of Taxation.

would lessen the compliance burden that arises from tracking where services are consumed. A different means for distributing revenues to local governments would need to be developed if services are not tracked to the location where they are enjoyed. A flat tax rate would lessen the local government's flexibility.

Issue 8: Should a flat tax rate be imposed on behalf of local governments?

Option 1: Allow local governments flexibility to impose differential permissive tax rates.

Option 2: Allow local governments flexibility over the tangible goods tax rate, but not the services tax rate. Impose a flat rate permissive tax on services.

Option 3: Impose a flat tax rate for tangible personal property and services on behalf of local governments and distribute the revenues using a formula.

TAXING NOT-FOR-PROFITS AND GOVERNMENTS

Both taxation of purchases and sales by governments and not-for-profits are important issues that must be considered.[48] Ohio exempts both not-for-profits and governments from payment of taxes on their purchases.[49] Recent legislation exempted all 501-C-3 corporations. Exemption of not-for-profits represents a subsidy for the activities of these organizations, equal to the foregone tax revenues of state and local governments. The subsidy can be justified either on humanitarian grounds or as a quid pro quo for services that the public sector otherwise would need to deliver. The justifications imply that the exemptions for not-for-profit organizations should be granted only in circumstances where the state finds the activity sufficiently meritorious. However, the exemption statute only requires that nonprofit organizations be "operated exclusively for charitable purposes in this state." Thus, the tax subsidy provided by the state is available rather broadly. The amount of tax savings and the activities receiving the savings are determined mostly by the not-for-profit organizations rather than through the public process. Direct state funding for the activities of nonprofit organizations may be a better way to provide subsidies if financial contributions by Ohio are deemed appropriate.

One reason for concern about the role of not-for profits is that the number of not-for-profits and their contribution to the economy are growing very rapidly. For example, the share of national income originating in the nonprofit sector grew from 3.3 percent in 1960 to 4.4 percent in 1985.

The availability of exemptions for the many not-for-profit organizations may need to be examined on a regular basis to ensure that the tax savings are appropriate and that the organizations are worthy of public support. Several states, California, Hawaii, Louisiana, South Carolina, and Washington, provide no exemption for purchases by not-for-profits (Mikesell 1992). A law that sunsets all exemptions at regular intervals can be one way of ensuring reconsideration of the status of such organizations.

Issue 9: Should nonprofit organizations be granted exemption from the sales tax on their purchases?

Option 1: Leave the exemption unchanged.

Option 2: Allow an exemption only for organizations deemed to be performing sufficiently worthy activities.

Option 3: Eliminate the exemption.

In Ohio, not-for-profits must collect taxes on their sales unless they sell on six or fewer days during the calendar year. Similar legislation exists in most states, with not-for-profits exempt on casual sales and taxable otherwise (Mikesell 1992). The existing Ohio exemption is intended to avoid taxation of casual sales by not-for-profits, and appears acceptable. However, compliance with the tax for organizations selling on more than six days appears to be relatively poor and the DOT has chosen not to aggressively pursue the revenues. The state can consider making a clear determination of how aggressively to seek the revenues, and whether there is a clear intent to tax sales by not-for-profits. "Sales of services provided by the state or any of its political subdivisions..." are exempt.[50] The tax is intended to be paid by consumers, so a justification based on the character of the vendor seems inappropriate. The federal government is exempt on constitutional grounds.

Issue 10:Should the sale of services by the state and its political subdivisions be taxable?

Option 1: Leave the exemption unchanged.

Option 2: Tax the sale of services by the state and its political subdivisions.

Mail Order Sales

Taxation of mail order sales is consistent with the concept of taxing all consumption that occurs within a state. Failure to tax the sales places in-state firms at a disadvantage relative to mail order sales, costs the state lost revenues, and creates horizontal inequities. The Advisory Commission on

Intergovernmental Relations (1994) recently estimated that Ohio could raise an additional $116.3 million in 1994 if currently untaxed mail order sales could be brought into the tax base. This represents about 2.5 percent of current sales tax collections.

The states were aggressive in seeking to tax mail order sales until the 1992 Supreme Court decision in the Quill Corporation v. North Dakota case indicated that mail order firms cannot be required to withhold sales tax payments unless the firms have substantial nexus in the state. Ohio remains aggressive in seeking to tax mail order sales in cases where firms have nexus. Ohio should participate actively as new mechanisms to tax mail order sales are pursued. Federal legislation or an agreement between the states and direct marketers could permit taxation of the sales, but neither option looks likely in the near term.

APPENDIX

SALES TAX PYRAMIDING[51]

As discussed in the body of the paper, an ideal sales tax would be imposed only on purchases for final personal consumption. However, no state's sales tax meets this ideal. Minnesota's tax base includes many items which are not purchased for consumption, but rather to produce goods or services which ultimately will also be subject to sales tax. The Minnesota sales tax exempts purchases of materials consumed in production of personal property[52] and capital equipment for new and expanding manufacturing facilities.[53] However, most other non-service business inputs are taxable, and a few business services. Studies have estimated that between 43 and 47 percent of Minnesota's sales tax base consists of producers' goods, rather than consumption items.[54]

A sales tax on business inputs causes the sales tax to **pyramid** or **cascade**, resulting in an effective tax burden on the ultimate product in excess of the statutory rate. How pyramiding occurs can be most easily explained with an example:

> **Example**
>
> The example traces the imposition of sales tax on each stage of the production process for a hypothetical consumer product, a Widget kitchen gadget. Widget Inc. manufacturers the widgets and we assume that the wholesale price of the widgets is $10 each.
>
> To keep matters simple, the example is limited to three stages of production and distribution: (1) the production of capital equipment and supplies used by the manufacturer; (2) the manufacture of the product; and (3) retail distribution. In the real world, there are many more stages of production and distribution to which the sales tax applies.

Stage 1 — production of capital equipment and other supplies used by the manufacturer. As part of its manufacturing process Widget Inc. uses machinery and equipment (stamping and assembly machines) purchased from Capital Equipment Corp. It buys raw materials and other supplies (everything from office supplies, furniture, and computers) from a variety of other suppliers. In making the stamping and assembly machines, Capital Equipment must pay sales tax on all of its purchases of goods and supplies, except the materials consumed in production and exempt capital equipment.[55] Assume that 40 percent of the total price of Capital Equipment Corp.'s products consists of purchases (inputs) subject to the sales tax. For simplicity, assume this is true for all of Widget Inc.'s other suppliers. Thus, the price charged to Widget Inc. for its supplies includes an indirect or hidden sales tax equal to 2.6 percent of the price (40% of inputs taxable X 6.5% sales tax rate = 2.6%).[56]

Stage 2 — manufacturing of the widgets. As stated above, we assume that the wholesale price of each widget is $10. Assume further that raw materials, labor, and profit comprise $6 and that the cost of the capital equipment and other equipment and supplies is $4. Under the sales tax, Widget Inc's purchases of its raw materials and labor are exempt, but its purchases of capital equipment (assuming it is replacement equipment) are taxable, as are the other supplies. The $4 of capital equipment and other supplies includes $.25 of direct sales tax (i.e., $3.75 + 6.5% sales tax = $4) per widget paid by Widget Inc.

However, to measure the full impact of the sales tax, we must account for the sales tax paid at Stage 1. In Stage 1, we assumed that Widget Inc.'s taxable suppliers prices included 2.6 percent of indirect sales tax they had paid. Thus, the $3.75 cost of capital equipment and non-consumable supplies included a hidden sales tax component equal to $.10 (i.e., $3.65 x 2.6% = $.10) paid by Capital Equipment Corp. and the other suppliers and built into the $3.75 price. Thus, the $10 wholesale price of a widget includes a total indirect sales tax of $.35 ($.10 paid by Widget Inc.'s suppliers and $.25 paid by Widget Inc. itself).

Stage 3 — distribution and retail sale. Following our widget to its final sale to a consumer, Retail Co. resells the widget to purchasers for use in their kitchens at $15. Of the $5 markup, assume $1 covers items on which Retail Co. must pay sales tax. The $10 wholesale price of the widget is exempt as a purchase for resale, but Retail Co's purchases of cash registers, display cases, office supplies, and so forth are not. This $1 included $.06 of sales tax which Retail Co. paid depending upon Retail Co.'s suppliers' cost structures, and the $.94 sale price also included hidden sales tax, but we ignore that for the sake of simplicity.

Final accounting. The consumer who buys a widget for $15 pays explicit sales tax of $.98 ($15 price X 6.5 % sales tax = $.98). However, the $15 price itself includes indirect sales taxes of $.41 ($.10 paid by Capital Equipment Corp. and other suppliers; $.25 paid by Widget Inc.; and $.06 paid by Retail Co.). Absent this, the price would have been $14.59 and the sales tax $.95. Thus, by the taxation of inputs in the production process, the actual effective sales tax rate is 9.5 percent ($.98 in nominal tax paid + $.41 in hidden tax/$14.59 sale price net of indirect tax). In effect, by taxing inputs in the production and distribution chain the tax has pyramided or cascaded, yielding a 45 percent increase in the effective rate over the statutory rate.

Note that the 9.5 percent effective rate in the example is a hypothetical rate. Actual effective rates will vary dramatically from one product to another, depending upon the amount of vertical integration, the types of supplies and equipment used, and other factors. Some of the pyramided taxes will be from sales taxes imposed by other states when materials and products used in the production process are made outside Minnesota.

ENDNOTES

1. Berno and Whitmore (1994) provide a very interesting review of the history of Ohio's adoption of the sales tax.

2. See Ohio Revised Code 5739.01.

3. See Ohio Revised Code 5739.02.

4. See Ohio Revised Code 5739.01.

5 Due and Mikesell (1983) report that 13 states impose the tax on vendors, 17 on consumers, and 15 on a hybrid of consumers and vendors.

6. Ohio Revised Code 5741.02.

7. Purchase and consumption of goods and services occurs in the same rate in many cases.

8. The resort area tax is a gross receipts tax levied on certain business activities, and not a sales tax. The tax is imposed on the business firm, not the consumer, and has no corresponding use tax. Only Kelly's Island imposes the resort area tax.

9. The resort area tax is not included in this total.

10. Calculated as the permissive sales tax revenues divided by state sales tax revenues times 5 percent.

11. See Ohio Revised Code 5739.025 for the brackets.

12. Some of the growth in permissive tax collections results because two different data series are used to create the history. The series used for 1972 through 1981 reveals a lower growth level than the series for the more recent years, 1982 through 1993. Thus, all growth patterns that are calculated over the entire history are exaggerated by this shift.

13. The rate was 4.0 percent until 1980, 5.0 percent from January 1, 1981 through June 30, 1981, 4.0 percent from July 1, 1981 through November 14, 1981, 5.1 percent from November 15, 1981 through November 25, 1981, and 5.0 percent from November 26, 1981 through the present.

14. The elasticity is 0.98 if calculated by regressing the log of sales tax revenues on the log of personal income.

15. Elasticities calculated on data that are not adjusted for rate and base changes often are called buoyancy coefficients.

16. Sales taxes collected on the sale of autos, trailers, and boats are remitted to the Clerks of Court and are not received directly by the DOT. Taxes on other types of sales by these dealers are remitted to the DOT. Both are included in this category in Table 5.

17. Gross sales may be understated, so taxable sales may be an even lower percentage of total sales.

18. Administration cost differences across firms of varying sizes are lessened because small vendors are allowed to file less frequently. As of February 14, 1994, 287,331 sales tax filers were reported, of which 48.8 percent filed semi-annual returns.

19. Comparisons across states and tax sources are based on Census of Governments data so that constant definitions are used.

20. The implied tax base is defined as the tax revenues divided by the tax rate.

21. Ohio Revised Code 5739.01E2.

22. Ring is currently updating his estimates, and his preliminary numbers show little change in the share of Ohio's tax paid by business. However, the new analysis depends on data from 1989, before Ohio's changes in manufacturing and retailing exemptions.

23. The effective sales tax rate will be higher than 5.0 percent in cases where business purchases used in delivery of the good or service are taxable and when these business payments of the sales tax are passed forward to consumers through higher product prices. The effective rate also will be higher because of permissive taxes.

24. Expenditure data for the Midwestern region were used to approximate Ohio's expenditure pattern. A single expenditure category in the CES may include purchases that are taxable and purchases that are non-taxable. For this reason, it was necessary in some cases to assume a percentage as taxable.

25. The value of new car trade-ins is exempt in Ohio. The effect of the exemption is to make the tax more regressive, given the consumption pattern for new autos.

26. Alternatively, horizontal equity may be defined in terms of income. In this case, the tax would be horizontally equitable if all people with the same income paid the same sales tax.

27. As noted above, expenditures and consumption are not identical. The most important reason is that expenditures for major durable goods (such as automobiles and washing machines) and housing normally are made when the items are acquired, but the consumption takes place over many years.

28. The DOT receives information from tax departments in other states on purchases by Ohio residents. The information normally is obtained when a tax department does an audit and discovers that Ohio residents purchased items. The DOT bills Ohio residents for the use tax when it is made aware of such transactions.

29. See Fisher (1980), Fox (1986), and Mikesell (1970).

30. Commerce Clearinghouse,(1994b).

31. A value added tax concept could be used, where the contribution added by firms is taxable at each stage of the production process. One approach to imposing value added taxes allows a credit at each stage for taxes paid earlier in the production process, so the value added tax also is effectively levied on a base equal to the sale to the final consumer.

32. See Gall and Ellman (1992) for a comprehensive discussion of Ohio's treatment of packaging, and a comparison of Ohio's exemption with that available in a number of other states.

33. See Fox (1992) for a series of articles on sales taxation of services. Also, See Hellerstein (1988) and Fox and Murray (1988).

34. See Hellerstein (1988) for review of the Florida tax.

35. Ohio Department of Taxation, (1994).

36. Bohm and Craig (1987) reach a similar conclusion.

37. See Fox and Murray (1988) for a discussion of the key issues associated with administration and compliance.

38. The call should not be taxable in Ohio since the benefits are not enjoyed in Ohio. Further, in Goldberg v. Sweet (488 U.S. 252 1989) the Supreme Court decided that

a call could be taxed in the state in which the call was either originated or received and in which it was billed.

39. The data available for estimating potential sales tax revenues from untaxed services make it very difficult to make precise calculations. Actual receipts can be higher or lower than anticipated. Recent Ohio experience with sales tax base expansions can illustrate the point. For example, estimates for lawn care and landscaping services were $8.9 million for 1992 and $10.3 million for 1993, versus actual collections of $10.6 million and $17.2 million. For private investigation and security services, the estimates were $14.3 million and $18.8 million, versus actual collections of $7.5 million and $9.5 million.

40. See McHugh (1994b) for a detailed examination of telecommunications taxation in Ohio.

41. The District of Columbia is counted as a state in these statistics.

42. See ACIR (1993), Table 29.

43. The estimates are based on expenditures reported in the 1990/91 Consumer Expenditure Survey (CES). The aggregate level of spending in the CES, including that for food and utilities, was shifted up under the assumption that total consumer spending on sales-taxable items equals 70 percent of 1993 state sales tax collections.

44. Gold (1992) provides an in-depth discussion of the relative merits of exemption from the base versus granting credits.

45. The tax credit is the amount of revenue necessary to prevent a tax increase for the 15,000-$19,999 household. The credit equals expenditures for food and utilities times the tax rate in the case where additional revenues are raised (Column 3). The credit is reduced because of the lower rate in the revenue-neutral tax rate case (Column 4).

46. See McHugh (1994c) for discussion of Ohio's gross receipts tax on public utilities.

47. Economic burdens of taxes rise proportionately to the square of the tax rate.

48. See Mikesell (1992) for further discussion.

49. Ohio Revised Code 5739.02(B)(01&12).

50. Ohio Revised Code 5739.02(B)(22).

51. Taken from "Tax Policy Principles and Minnesota's Sales Taxation of Capital Equipment," (1993).

52. See Minn. Stat. § 297A.25, subd. 9 (1992). Note that this exemption is not available to producers of taxable services, such as car washes, building cleaning services, and so forth.

53. Minn. Stat. §§ 297A.03, subd. 16; 297A.25, subd, 42 (1993 Suppl.).

54. See Minnesota Department of Revenue, (1989)(47 percent producer goods). This study used 1979-80 data and thus does not reflect the major changes which were made in the Minnesota sales tax during the 1980s and 1990: the expansion of the tax to include more services and the exemption of some capital equipment — changes in the composition of purchases (e.g., toward more purchases of services).

55. Minn, Stat. §§ 297A.03, subd. 16; 297A.25, subd. 42 (1993 Suppl.).

56. Note also that the raw materials that Widget Inc. buys include some component of indirect or hidden sales tax. For simplicity, the example ignores this effect.

5 State and Local Individual Income Taxes: Analysis and

Barbara Edwards and Sally Wallace[1]

INTRODUCTION

The individual income tax is an important revenue source for the state and local governments in Ohio. In FY93 state government individual income tax collections yielded $4,718 million in revenue and accounted for approximately 37 percent of all state tax revenue in Ohio, above the national average of approximately 32 percent.

Ohio is one of 14 states where local governments impose an income tax, and it is relatively unique with respect to the use of income taxation by the state, the municipalities, and the school districts. In Ohio, local government income tax revenues represented approximately 21 percent of local government revenues in FY92,[2] as compared with a United States average of only about 4.5 percent.[3] In FY92, state and local government income taxes combined accounted for approximately 31 percent of total state and local tax revenue in Ohio, while they accounted for 21 percent of state and local tax revenue nationwide.

Ohio adopted its state government individual income tax relatively recently—in 1971 (effective in 1972). Conversely, the city of Toledo adopted its income tax in 1946 and the first school district income tax was adopted in 1982 (effective in 1983). The municipal income tax tradition is very strong, which may help to explain the differences in tax structure and administration between the state and municipal income taxes. This strength may also explain in part the current lack of coordination in the administration of the municipal income taxes among local governments in Ohio.

This chapter presents a full analysis of the individual income tax in Ohio and in the United States In the first two sections, we discuss the principles of individual income taxation and summarize the structure of the individual income tax in Ohio. The third section discusses Ohio's reliance on the tax and its performance over time, and compares the Ohio income tax to that in a number of other states. The fourth through sixth sections discuss local income taxation, in Ohio and in the nation. The seventh section summarizes the effects of state and local income taxes in Ohio on its residents. The analysis leads to a set of concerns regarding Ohio's current individual income tax structure:

- the state's reliance on the individual income tax at a time when the base is changing may lead to problems down the road;
- the complexity of the three-tiered structure of the income tax;
- the elasticity of the tax;
- the vertical and horizontal equity of the system;
- interstate competition; and
- specific issues related to exemptions, credits, deductions, indexation, and coupling to the federal system.

In the eighth section of this chapter, we present microsimulation model results for a variety of reform options that target the "ills" of the current tax system, and analyze the effects of such reforms on Ohio. The final section summarizes the recommendation of the Commission regarding the individual income tax.

PRINCIPLES OF INCOME TAXATION

The Ohio state income tax was first imposed in 1972. At that time, 41 other states had already imposed some form of state income tax, so Ohio was a relative late-comer in the use of the state individual income tax. Hawaii was the first state to impose an income tax (in 1901), and Connecticut is the most recent state to impose a broad-based income tax.[4] To date, 43 states and the District of Columbia impose some form of state income tax: 41 states and Washington, D.C. use a broad-based tax, and two states use a limited base.[5]

"Why have an income tax?" One basic idea underlying justice in taxation is that individuals should be taxed in accordance with their "ability to pay."[6]

The ability of individuals to pay is measured by "comprehensive" income, typically defined as the combination of the value of all liquid and non-liquid income, i.e., as accretions to wealth.[7] In this context an income tax comes closer to taxing people according to their ability to pay than perhaps any other tax, which is a principal reason why the individual income tax is a mainstay in most tax systems.

Although widespread in use, the income tax has been debated on a number of fronts including: equity (vertical and horizontal), economic efficiency, elasticity and growth, administration and compliance, and economic development.

Proponents would list the following reasons for having an individual income tax:

1. Ability to pay is an accepted basis for taxation. Tax payments in accordance with ability to pay can reflect society's view of an equitable distribution of tax burdens. Income is a convenient measure of ability to pay. The other tax principle, the "benefits principle," says that taxes should be paid commensurate with the benefits received from public expenditure. For many public goods, it is practically impossible to measure individual valuation of the benefit from public goods. Additionally, benefit taxes may be argued to be less equitable than taxes based on ability to pay.[8]

2. It is income-elastic, i.e., its revenues grow naturally in proportion to income. Reliance on the income tax means that during periods of economic expansion legislators and governors are less likely to have to return to the voters to ask for rate increases and base expansion.

3. It can be relatively neutral in its effects on economic decisions, thus reducing distortions in the economy. If a tax system is designed to heavily tax some forms of income and lightly tax other forms of income, taxpayers will naturally move their income-generating activities to the lightly taxed sector. This behavior imposes a cost on society, since the movement of investment from one type of activity to another decreases the total production in the economy. If the income tax structure does not allow preferential treatment of various forms of income, this cost to society is reduced.

4. It is deductible at the federal level, thus reducing the overall burden on Ohio's residents. By itemizing on their federal returns, Ohio taxpayers can deduct the total value of their state and local tax payments. These deductions will lower their federal income tax liability by 1 minus their federal tax rate, effectively shifting state and local taxes to the federal government. This lowers the "cost" of state and local in-

come taxes. Property taxes can also be deducted, but sales taxes cannot.[9]

5. The efficiency of audit procedures is increased due to federal cooperation in information sharing. The federal government makes its tax return data available to state and large local governments.
6. The use of an income tax enables state and local governments to impose lower tax rates for all other taxes.

Those who are less taken with the virtues of the individual income tax also make strong arguments:

1. Because it is income elastic, revenues may decline during economic downturns. In difficult economic periods, the revenue from an elastic tax will grow much slower, thus adding to a state's fiscal stress during a difficult time.
2. The tax may have high marginal rates for some tax brackets which may discourage higher-income individuals from investing in Ohio, living in Ohio, and locating their businesses in Ohio. If higher-income individuals are faced with very high individual income tax rates relative to those in neighboring states, the individuals may locate "across the border" in another state. This effect could cost Ohio revenue and potential long-term economic development.
3. Bracket creep due to inflation results in potentially increased tax burdens with no change in real income. A progressive rate schedule may guarantee that taxes will grow faster than income. Individuals may see this as unfair since their real income (spending power) has not increased, but their tax liability has. This tax structure would leave individuals with less real disposable income.
4. The tax is often used to give special preferences to certain groups based on some criteria other than equity, thus disrupting the equity and efficiency advantages of the tax. Examples are differential treatment of the elderly, married taxpayers, homeowners, etc.
5. Taxpayers feel that compliance with the tax is cumbersome and expensive. The more difficult the tax forms and filing requirements, the more incentive there is for non-compliance with the tax system.
6. The tax requires a costly administrative effort. The administrative costs include mailing forms, answering taxpayers' questions, processing tax returns, and auditing taxpayers—all of which are costly. Also, the more complicated the tax structure, the more costly the administrative procedures.

Each of these issues has strong theoretical justifications associated with them. We now turn to a more complete discussion of each.

EQUITY

When one speaks of equity, we may refer to vertical or horizontal equity. The first refers to how the tax burden changes as income increases and the second refers to how "like" individuals are treated. Tax burden may be measured many ways, but the most commonly used measure is a ratio of tax paid divided by total income (Phares 1980; Aaron 1965).

Vertical equity. Regarding vertical equity, tax structures can be described as regressive, proportional, or progressive, depending on how the percentage of income paid in taxes varies with the level of income. With a regressive tax, the percentage of income paid in taxes decreases as income increases. The social security tax is generally considered a regressive tax since a portion of the tax is phased out at high incomes. Taxes on goods that are consumed disproportionately more by lower income individuals are also regressive.

A proportional tax remains a constant percentage of income, regardless of the level of income, i.e., a flat-rate income tax. Proportional taxes are thought to be among the easiest to administer, due to the lack of tax brackets. (A proportional tax is also more economically efficient, as discussed later.) A few states do use a flat individual income tax rate (Connecticut, Indiana, Illinois, Massachusetts, Michigan, New Hampshire, Pennsylvania, and Tennessee use flat rates on various income bases), but most states use some form of progressive taxation.

Under a progressive tax rate structure, the average tax rate (tax/income) increases as income increases. Such a structure places an increased burden of payment on individuals with higher incomes, effectively redistributing income from higher-income individuals (in the form of higher taxes) to lower-income individuals (in the form of services, financed through progressive taxation). Many states and the federal government use a progressive individual income tax rate structure.

The objective of progressive taxation is to redistribute income or welfare among citizens. Note that the ability-to-pay ideal defines income as a basis for taxation. While the ability to pay principle supports a progressive income tax structure in certain circumstances, it does not define the appropriate degree of progessivity.[10] The amount of redistribution done through the income tax is in large part a policy decision determined by the preferences of the population.

Many have argued that a progressive income tax should not be used by state or local governments. Musgrave (1959) claimed that redistributive policies should be carried out by the central or national government. In his view, almost any redistributive policy by state or local governments would cause individuals to move from one state or jurisdiction to another.[11] This migration would effectively cancel the intended outcome of the redistributive policy. As wealthy individuals move out of a region, the remaining relatively poor residents are forced to pay all of the tax. The evidence on migration is discussed later.

Even with these strong theoretical arguments against progressive state and local taxation, many state governments have relied heavily on progressive income taxes for many years. Slemrod (1986) summarized some of the reasons for states' reliance on progressive income taxes. As he points out, the residents of different states simply have different preferences for redistribution; some people want more equality in the distribution of income in their state. Also, as pointed out by Oakland (1983), because of regional cost-of-living differences, the same dollar transfers given by the national government will have a less equalizing impact in high-cost states and regions than in lower-cost states and regions. Therefore, states as well as the federal government are justified in trying to equalize incomes.

Break (1980) also pointed out that state and local governments may effectively carry out redistributive policies, within reason. He points out that if state or local governments get very far away from the "average" with respect to redistributive policies, the policies may become ineffective. So, there is some support for progressive taxation at the state level. At the same time, all of these arguments suggest that, as the jurisdiction size gets smaller, the use of a progressive income tax is fraught with difficulties due to migration and homogeneity of the population.[12] These issues are particularly relevant in Ohio where heavy use is made of the local income tax.

Many instruments are used to affect the degree of progressivity in income tax structures nationwide. These include: (1) personal exemptions, (2) standard deductions, (3) graduated statutory rate structures, (4) various bracket widths, (5) credits (6) phase-outs of deductions, and (7) coupling to the federal tax. Standard deductions create a floor for taxation; any filer with taxable income below the standard deduction (or zero bracket amount) has no tax liability. Standard deduction amounts are often adjusted for filing status (single, head of household, or married), and the amounts are often increased for elderly and/or blind taxpayers.

Personal exemptions may also influence the overall progressivity of a state's individual income tax. Most states offer some personal exemption, i.e., a deduction from income based on the number of family members and/or filing status. Very large exemptions, such as those in the state of Connecticut, keep the lowest-income individuals out of the tax net, but also provide some relief to any tax filer.[13] Depending on the level of standard deduction and personal exemptions, the first non-zero marginal tax rate may occur at a low or high level of income.

Under a graduated marginal statutory rate structure, income is grouped in tax brackets, with each tax bracket facing a higher marginal tax rate. For example, under a graduated structure, the first $10,000 may be taxed at 2 percent, the next $10,000 at 3 percent, and so on. While most states use multiple tax brackets, eight states use eight or more tax brackets. Missouri and Montana use the largest number of brackets (10), which can increase the progressivity of a tax.

Other factors can change the progressivity of a tax, even when the tax structure utilizes many tax brackets with relatively high rates. These include: itemized deductions (which benefit high-income individuals relative to low-income individuals), income adjustments (for retirement savings), tax credits for certain types of investment, tax credits for low-income filers or the elderly, and income exemptions (for tax-exempt interest, pensions, etc.). The use of the deduction for Individual Retirement Accounts (IRA) presents a good example of the effect of adjustments on the progressivity of the income tax. In 1986 (the height of IRA contributions) contributions (and therefore deductions) were largest for the middle and upper income groups (Internal Revenue Service 1988), which effectively reduced the progressivity of the rate schedule.

Horizontal equity. Horizontal equity refers to the "equal treatment of equals." In taxation, horizontal equity requires that "equally situated" taxpayers pay the same level of tax. The definition of "equals" is a very difficult concept. Although two individuals may have the same level of income, their family situations, consumption patterns, health problems, work-related expenses, etc. could vary significantly.

Does income alone define "equals?" There is no easy answer to this question.[14] For purposes of individual income taxation, state governments and the federal government usually measure "equals" based on income, with some allowances to control for differences in family size (by personal exemptions) and unplanned consumption (by medical and catastrophic deductions). Federal itemized deductions have existed in some form since 1913, and many states comply with these deductions effectively accepting the federal government's definition of acceptable differential treatment of individuals.

Personal exemptions serve as a way to compensate tax filers with children for the costs associated with the children. In effect, the personal exemptions for dependents say that a childless married couple earning X dollars a year has a different tax-paying capacity from a married couple with two children earning the same amount of income per year.[15] Additional deductions and exemptions (such as home mortgage interest deductions and retirement exemptions) disrupt the horizontal equity of a tax system. Thus, few states come close to treating equals equally.

INFLATION AND INDEXATION

Each year, individuals are faced with higher overall prices due to inflationary forces in the economy. As the general price index grows, the costs of consumer items increase. If wages and salaries do not grow as quickly as the overall price level, consumers are faced with a decrease in real income. If a state's tax structure is not indexed for inflation, increases in consumers' income may be met with an increase in their tax liability resulting from a greater portion of their income being taxed in brackets with higher marginal rates. This is referred to as "bracket creep."

The effect of inflation on tax liabilities will be magnified as nominal income and inflation grow and as the number of tax brackets and rates increases. As real after-tax income is eroded due to inflation, the basic progressivity of the income tax changes. More and more individuals are forced into higher-income tax brackets. Although inflation has slowed considerably since the early 1980s, "bracket creep" is still a real phenomenon. The 1981 federal tax reform (ERTA) established indexation at the federal level beginning in 1985. The federal government indexes tax brackets, personal exemptions, and standard deductions. This costly provision reduced federal revenues by approximately 60 billion in 1990 (Steurle 1992). The following states use some form of indexation: Iowa (standard deduction and tax brackets); California, Maine, and South Carolina (personal exemptions and tax brackets); Arizona, Nebraska, and Oregon (personal exemptions); Montana (personal exemptions, tax brackets and standard deduction); and North Dakota, Rhode Island, and Vermont (standard deductions and personal exemptions through coupling with federal income tax liability) (ACIR 1994).

SIMPLICITY OF THE SYSTEM AND COUPLING

A basic tenet of tax theory is that a tax should place as small a compliance burden on individuals as possible (Musgrave and Musgrave 1984). A state's tax structure may be more or less complex due to the number of brackets, tax rates, personal exemptions, standard deductions, credits, and income exemptions. The complexity of a state's tax structure affects taxpayers and tax administrators alike. The more complex a tax structure, the higher the probability of error on the part of the taxpayer, and the higher the cost of tax administration at any level of government.

One way to simplify a state's individual income tax system is to couple with the federal government. *Coupling* refers to the states' use of federal income tax calculations for state individual income tax calculations. In general, the "closer" the coupling of a state structure to the federal income tax, the fewer the calculations on the state income tax form.[16]

Starting with calculations of federal taxable income and tax liability, a closely coupled state income tax requires few additional computations to arrive at the state income tax liability of the taxpayer. While a complete coupling of the two systems is nearly impossible, some states go all the way to define their tax base as federal tax liability.[17]

The two most closely coupled types of state individual income tax systems calculate state tax liability based on: (1) a percentage of federal income tax liability or (2) a percentage of federal taxable income. In 1993, three states based their taxes on the taxpayer's federal income tax liability: North Dakota (14 percent), Vermont (28-34 percent), and Rhode Island (27.5 percent).[18] Colorado's income tax is levied at 5 percent of federal taxable income.

A third level of coupling is to base the state tax on the federal definition of adjusted gross income. In this case, the taxpayer starts his or her state taxable income calculation with federal AGI and then makes adjustments, as needed, to comply with state regulations. This level of coupling allows the states more flexibility in tailoring the individual income tax structure to meet the needs and preferences of the state and its citizens. This flexibility comes at a cost, however. As the degree of coupling with the federal regulations decreases, the compliance cost to the taxpayer increases. The administrative costs also increase as the level of coupling decreases. These differences between the federal and state regulations also increase the probability of taxpayers inadvertently submitting erroneous data.

Most states use federal AGI as their starting point and allow deductions from federal AGI. Many states require additions to income. Credits and additional income exemptions add another degree of complexity to most state income tax systems. Many state individual income tax forms are as lengthy as those of the federal government, yet they require different calculations.

Federal law allows states which couple their systems closely with the federal income tax requirements to delegate their individual income tax administrative and collection responsibilities to the federal government (Sunley and Walz 1986). To qualify, the state must levy either a flat or graduated tax rate on federal taxable income or a flat tax rate on federal income tax liability. Such an arrangement would significantly reduce the administrative and compliance costs associated with the state individual income tax. The state would forgo the administrative costs of levying and collecting the tax, as well as the costs of audits to ensure compliance with the state tax requirement. The taxpayer would prepare and submit only one tax return and would be subject to audit by only one government agency. Businesses would report amounts and remit collections for both the federal and state income taxes to only the federal government. The federal government would then remit the taxes paid on behalf of the state's citizens to that state.

One disadvantage to the state that results from delegation of administrative responsibilities to the federal government is that the state government has no control over the requirements for individual income taxes; the state is "held hostage" to federal changes. An extensive change in federal regulations could cause shortfalls in anticipated revenues from state individual income taxes. Additionally, as the federal government would not receive any portion of state revenues collected in the delinquent payment of state taxes, the federal government has little incentive to pursue individuals delinquent on state tax payments. Another objection to this system is that the state would possibly lose some employment associated with income tax administration.

However, if a state is closely coupled to the federal system, there is less room for state legislatures to "tinker" with the structure. Some individuals would consider this a positive aspect of coupling, as the politicians can only adjust rates in this case. No state has yet chosen this system of individual income tax administration.

Compliance and Administrative Costs

Economists classify the costs of implementing a tax into two categories: (1) compliance and (2) administrative. Compliance costs of individual income taxes include costs of record keeping, costs of remitting payments to the government on behalf of the taxpayer, any professional or legal fees spent to ensure compliance with governmental requirements, and costs of understanding the requirements. Administrative costs of an individual income tax system include governmental expenditures for collecting and administering the tax, including the costs of auditing individuals and businesses. Both administrative and compliance costs should include direct expenditures, such as legal fees or salaries of government workers, as well as any indirect costs, such as overhead and utilities.

From administrative and compliance viewpoints, efficiency in collection and administration are desirable as a means to control the money and time outlays of taxpayers and the government. The most efficient system for administering a state individual income tax would be for the state to couple its system closely with the federal individual income tax system and delegate responsibility for collection and administration to the federal government. Such a system would result in no incremental record keeping for either the state government or the taxpayer. However, as discussed in the previous section, no state has chosen that option due to its inherent disadvantages, which include loss of state control. State individual income taxes which are not based on federal requirements will produce higher compliance and administrative costs. As a general rule, as differences between state and Federal income tax regulations increase, efficiency decreases and compliance and administrative costs increase.

Two alternative ways to gauge the magnitude of administrative costs of the state individual income tax are to consider these costs (1) relative to the revenue collected from the tax and (2) relative to administrative costs for other taxes. Slemrod and Soren (1984) estimated the costs of collecting federal income taxes to be approximately 0.5 percent of revenue collected. While no comparative data are available on the exact costs of administration of state individual income taxes, there are likely to be economies of scale in the collection of tax revenues. This would suggest that administrative costs for state individual income taxes would be larger than the federal cost of 0.5 percent. Additionally, compared to the sales tax, which generates a large share of total revenue for some states, administrative costs of the individual income tax are high.[19] Part of the reason for the higher administrative costs is the greater number of returns necessitated by the individual income tax.

Slemrod and Soren (1984) estimated that compliance costs averaged $275 per household in 1982, or 1.4 percent of all household income in 1982, for filing and payment of federal, state, and local individual income taxes nationally. Compliance costs on a nationwide basis were estimated at a total of $17 billion to $27 billion in 1982. Although no estimate of the cost of complying with state individual income tax requirements is available, the incremental costs associated with filing these returns increase as differences increase between the state and federal requirements.

One way to examine the differences in compliance costs between different states' requirements is to look at the complexity of instructions for completing the individual income tax forms. Urbancic (1992) examined the 1990 tax instructions used by 14 southern states and the District of Columbia.[20] Based on an index meant to measure the educational achievement levels necessary to complete the forms, the states ranged in difficulty from high school senior level (South Carolina) to post-graduate level (North Carolina). Using the Flesch Reading Ease Formula, which measures the relative readability of the forms, all states measured at least "fairly difficult." Both results indicate that simpler verbiage and sentence construction are needed in the tax return instructions to more closely match the reading and comprehension skills of the average taxpayer. This simplification would allow taxpayers to complete the required forms in less time and with less assistance, thus reducing compliance costs.

STABILITY AND ELASTICITY

Elasticity. The income elasticity of any type of tax refers to the responsiveness of tax revenue to changes in income. Elasticity is measured as the percent change in tax revenue divided by the percent change in income, and can be broken into two parts: the rate elasticity and the base elasticity. We can define the elasticity calculation as follows:

$$\frac{\textit{Percent Change in Tax Revenue}}{\textit{Percent Change in Personal Income}} = \frac{\textit{Percent Change in Tax Revenue}}{\textit{Percent Change in Taxable Income}} \times \frac{\textit{Percent Change in Taxable Income}}{\textit{Percent Change in Personal Income}}$$

Any tax can be more or less elastic, depending upon the tax rate structure and the tax base. The more elastic a revenue source, the more the revenue increases (decreases) as income increases (decreases). In general, the state individual income tax is a relatively elastic revenue source.

There are a number of components of an individual income tax structure which make the tax more or less elastic. They include the following:

- *The tax base.* If the tax is applied to a base that is growing faster than overall income the tax will be very elastic.
- *The graduation of the tax rate.* The higher the successive statutory tax rates, the larger the increase in revenue as individuals move "up the tax rates" in response to income increases. The effect is amplified in the absence of indexation.
- *The standard deduction amounts or zero bracket amounts and personal exemptions.* The use of standard deductions and exemptions can increase the elasticity of the tax. This occurs because a growth in income can push individuals over the standard deduction amount, so that the change in their tax liability increases dramatically. The effect of these exemptions and deductions on the elasticity depends on the growth in income over the threshold, relative to the overall growth in income.

Under a flat-rate tax structure with no "floor" or standard deduction, the only gain in tax revenue comes from growth in income. If total personal income in the economy grows by 5 percent, and the tax base includes all forms of personal income, income tax revenue will increase by 5 percent.

Stability. A number of authors have pointed out the "double-edged sword" regarding revenue growth and revenue stability. A tax with a relatively high elasticity leads to high revenue growth during economic upturns, but also leads to low (or negative) growth during downturns (Dye and McGuire 1991). While state individual income taxes have generally been found to be more elastic than sales taxes, Dye and McGuire (1991) pointed out that revenue growth and variability do not have to go hand-in-hand. A flat-rate income tax can be more stable and faster-growing than a sales tax with a narrowly defined base, as long as the individual income tax base is itself broad.

The income tax *is* at least somewhat variable. It is cyclical in nature due to the importance of wage and salary income and capital income (dividends, interest, and capital gains) to the tax base. During downturns in the economy, layoffs and permanent increases in unemployment will decrease wages and therefore decrease taxable income. While unions could at one time mitigate the loss in wages, they have increasingly negotiated for other compensation in lieu of salary increases, much of which is *not* taxable. Part-time workers and second wage earners, which are both increasing shares of the labor force, are also frequently laid off during recessions.

The data in Table 5-1 demonstrate the variability of United States state income tax collections over the period 1981-1991. In general, income tax revenues vary more from year to year than personal income. While part of this variability is due to the cyclical nature of the income tax base, part of it is due to discretionary changes in the federal and state income tax structures. While it is difficult to discern a strong pattern, an analysis of historical data suggests that the variability (e.g., the year-to-year fluctuation in the income tax) is decreasing. If we compare this to the year-to-year fluctuation in the sales tax, we find that while the income tax has been more variable over time, it has become less so vis-a-vis the sales tax.

Economic Development and Migration

The effect of income taxes on economic development is a highly contro-

TABLE 5-1
Growth in Real Individual Income Tax Revenue and Personal Income

Year	Percent Change in Real State Individual Income Tax Revenue	Percent Change in Real Personal Income
1981	-0.05	1.36
1982	5.28	0.07
1983	5.54	3.18
1984	13.48	5.48
1985	4.26	3.43
1986	4.08	4.35
1987	8.99	2.13
1988	0.96	2.93
1989	5.74	2.55
1990	2.63	1.16
1991	-0.80	-0.18

Source: Authors' calculations.

versial subject. A vast amount of literature has been devoted to analyzing the effects of tax incentives on economic growth and labor migration.[21] Most economic studies conducted over the past twenty years have found that a variety of factors contribute to economic development within a region. In general, studies conclude that taxing policies, especially relative to those in surrounding areas, can affect economic development and growth. Consistency of tax policies and tax trends within an area is thought to have a positive impact on development. However, the importance of specific factors in location decisions varies between different industries.

Carlton (1979) examined the location choices of firms in three manufacturing industries: plastic products, electronic components, and electronic transmitting equipment. His results indicated that wages, technical expertise, proximity to similar companies, and energy costs were the primary factors influencing location decisions. Tax rates and policies had little impact on the firms' location decisions.

Plaut and Pluta (1983) constructed a model based on data from 1967-1977 to explain the effects of business climate, taxes, and expenditures on manufacturing growth in the 48 contiguous states. Results from their analysis suggest that high tax effort appears to have a negative effect on employment growth. They concluded, however, that the role of taxes was less important than market factors (i.e., land, labor, energy, etc.) and climate variables.

Bartik, Becker, Lake, and Bush (1987) provided further support of the conclusions of Plaut and Pluta. Bartik et al. concluded that the primary factor affecting the location of the Saturn plant near Nashville, Tennessee was the lower overall projected production costs of that location relative to other sites considered by General Motors. Although their study included state and local taxes as one component of total cost, the primary determinant appeared to be the lower labor costs of the area.

Munnell (1990) suggested that high levels of local public services relative to those of other regions positively affect economic development within a region. If tax increases fund local infrastructure and services, such as education, public safety, transportation networks, local utilities, etc., they can positively affect development. However, increased taxes to redistribute income reduce the attractiveness of, and development in, a region.

For Minnesota's tax reform effort, Wasylenko and McGuire (1985) conducted a nationwide study covering the period 1973 through 1980 to determine the effect of taxes on the employment growth within different industries. Their results indicated that lower percentage changes in tax effort over time positively affected employment growth rates. An analysis of specific industries showed that the individual income tax burden significantly affects employment growth in wholesale and retail trade, and in finance, insurance, and real estate services. Their study concluded that the relatively high individual income tax in Minnesota deterred employment growth, but that any reduction of the income tax should not come at the expense of education, a factor found to positively affect employment growth rates.

McGuire hypothesized that the harmonization of different state tax systems in the 1980s may explain the more recent findings that taxes have no significant impact on employment growth (Wasylenko and McGuire 1987; Wasylenko 1989). They conclude that "stability in taxes and tax policy, and rational, predictable decision-making on the part of the state government, may be more important than the level of taxation."

The effects of individual income taxes on labor migration are even less clear. While the general tax incentives' literature suggests that within regions, taxes matter somewhat to businesses, the labor migration literature concludes that some combination of taxes and services affect migration decisions. In general, it is the total level of state and local taxes relative to the level of services that affects migration within a regional area. Fox, Herzog, and Schlottman (1989) found that the individual income tax does affect an individual's decision to enter a metropolitan area, but once the person is there, the tax has little impact on the decision to leave that area. Herzog and Schlottman (1986) tested the effect of changes in the deductibility of state and local taxes on metro area migration. There, they found that out-migration from a metro area was also positively affected by increases in the average state and local tax rate. Aronson and Swartz (1973) found that individuals moved into an area if the public service benefits outweighed the incremental tax cost. Wallace (1995) finds that the state individual income tax does not exert much influence on migration decisions nationwide, but has a stronger effect within a region.

A summary of the current migration literature suggests that average individual income taxes may affect labor migration, but the impact is stronger within a region and even among metropolitan areas. The effect of state individual income taxes on state-to-state migration has not really been thoroughly studied. Additionally, as in the general economic incentive literature, the effect of the income tax on the migration decision is found to be considered along with other taxes and public services.

Voter Response

While not a "principle" of taxation, it is very important for policy makers to know how voters will respond to a particular tax. No one likes to face a new tax, but if revenue needs to be raised from some tax, which tax would the voters choose to increase? The United States Advisory Commission on Intergovernmental Relations (ACIR) polls a sample of adults each year to determine their attitudes toward governments and taxes. Since 1973, a pattern has emerged regarding responses to the question, "Which do you think is the worst tax—that is, the least fair?" Nationwide, the property tax wins the prize of being the least liked state-local tax and the federal income tax is the least liked tax overall. The percent of individuals judging the state individual income tax to be the worst tax has averaged 10 percent, with years when the response was as low as 8 percent and as high as 12 percent (ACIR 1993).

The state of Michigan recently ran one of the most explicit tests of the voters' tax preferences, pitting the state's sales tax and income tax against each other. In an effort to raise an additional $4.2 billion in revenue, the voters faced the choice of a large increase in the sales tax rate increase (from 4 percent to 6 percent) and a 50-cent cigarette tax increase, or an income tax increase.[22] The taxpayers voted for the sales and cigarette tax increases. The relative "dislike" of the taxes will obviously be affected by the voters' perception of the fairness of certain taxes in each state, as well as individual states' tax rates.

Differential Taxation of Income

Almost all taxes distort economic decisions, because most taxes change the relative prices of goods, investment, and even labor.[23] When prices change, individuals must adjust their consumption, and end up consuming a bundle of goods that is different than the one that they would have consumed in the absence of taxes. In economic terms, this less-preferred bundle of goods decreases a person's welfare (or utility). This decrease in utility is referred to as "excess burden." Another basic tenet of good tax policy is that, given some notion of the equity of a tax system, the excess burden of the system should be minimized.

Individual income tax structures that give special tax preferences to different types of income, or that apply different tax schedules to various types of income are inefficient—that is, they impose excess burdens. Take, for example, the pre-Tax Reform Act of 1986 treatment of capital gains income. The federal government effectively exempted 40 percent of capital gains income from taxation. Corporate tax credits such as the investment tax credit, and various depreciation schemes worked with the preferential treatment on the individual income tax side to reduce the cost of investment. Fullerton and Mackie (1989) show that the cost of capital was significantly lower pre-Tax Reform Act of 1986, so that we could expect the TRA 86 changes to induce some behavioral changes in terms of investment decisions.

Some inefficiency in the tax structure is "allowed" in the name of equity and economic development. In fact, some of the most efficient taxes are highly inequitable so, in the name of fairness, some inefficiency is allowed.[24] Inefficiencies arise in the attempt to expand business in a state. By offering tax credits and abatements to firms that create new jobs or investment, the tax system treats separate forms of investment differently. In response, investors change their form of investment, and a welfare loss to society may result.

In summary, the equity, efficiency, and economic development goals of a system may actually be competing goals. For this reason, policy makers need to decide which goals are most important and then concentrate on minimizing the negative impacts of the remaining attributes. The Ohio Commission set the issue of Ohio's lagging economy as the primary focus of study. The remainder of this chapter is designed to analyze Ohio's current tax structure and potential changes to it, paying particular attention to the interaction between the income tax structure and Ohio's economy.

STRUCTURE OF THE STATE GOVERNMENT INCOME TAX

All residents of the State of Ohio are required to file an individual income tax return unless they fall into the following categories:

- The only source of income is retirement income, and the retirement income credit is equal to or greater than the income tax due before the credit.
- The filer is eligible for the senior citizens credit, and the credit is equal to or greater than the income tax due before the credit.
- The filer's federal adjusted gross income is less than \$3,350 (singles under 65 years of age), \$7,875 (singles over age 65), \$6,500 (married couples filing jointly under 65 years of age), or \$9,875 (married couples filing jointly over the age of 65).
- The total value of the filer's exemption is greater than Ohio adjusted gross income.
- In some cases, residents of Indiana, Kentucky, West Virginia, Pennsylvania, and Michigan who work in Ohio may not have to file an Ohio income tax return.[25]

Individuals who file a joint federal tax return are required to file a joint Ohio individual income tax return. All tax returns are due to the Ohio Department of Taxation by April 15 of each year, although extensions are allowed.[26]

The data in Table 5-2 summarize the calculation of Ohio's state individual income tax. The Ohio state income tax uses federal adjusted gross income (FAGI) as the base for the state tax computation.[27] From FAGI, Ohio

TABLE 5-2
1994 Structure of Ohio State Income Tax

FEDERAL ADJUSTED GROSS INCOME

Add		*Subtract*	
1.	State and local bond interest (except Ohio governments).	1.	Federal interest and dividend exempt from state tax..
2.	Federal bond interest exempt from federal tax but subject to state tax.	2.	Disability and survivor's benefits.
3.	Accumulation distribution from a complex trust.	3.	Compensation earned in Ohio by residents of reciprocity states.
		4.	Social Security and Railroad Retirement benefits in FAGI.

equals:

OHIO ADJUSTED GROSS INCOME

Subtract
Personal exemptions of $650 per person.

equals:

OHIO TAXABLE INCOME

Rate Schedule:

Ohio taxable income	Tax Rate
$0-5,000	0.743%
5,000-10,000	1.486%
10,000-15,000	2.972%
15,000-20,000	3.715%
20,000-40,000	4.457%
40,000-80,000	5.201%
80,000-100,000	5.943%
100,000-200,000	6.900%
over 200,000	7.500%

equals:

TAX BEFORE CREDITS

Subtract
Personal exemption credit of $20 per person.
Senior citizen credit of $50.
Retirement income credit.
Child and dependent care credit.
Joint filer credit for two working spouses (graduated based on income with a maximum credit of $650)

equals:

OHIO PERSONAL INCOME TAX LIABILITY

Subtract
Credit for income earned in or taxed by another state.

equals:

OHIO NET PERSONAL INCOME TAX LIABILITY

individual income taxpayers are allowed to make various adjustments as described in Box 5-1.[28]

Adding and/or subtracting these adjustments from FAGI yields Ohio adjusted gross income (OAGI). Taxpayers are then allowed a deduction equal to the total number of personal exemptions claimed multiplied by $650. The

BOX 5-1
Ohio State Income Tax Adjustments to Federal Adjusted Gross Income

The deductions from federal adjusted gross income include (to the extent included in FAGI):

- federal interest and/or dividends exempt from state tax;
- compensation earned in Ohio by residents of neighboring states;
- state and/or municipal income tax overpayment;
- disability and survivor's benefits;
- gains from the sale of exempt Ohio state and local government bonds and Ohio public obligations;
- wage and salary expenses not otherwise deducted due to the federal targeted jobs credit;
- Social Security and Tier I, Tier II and Supplemental Railroad Retirement benefits;
- interest on Ohio Public and Purchase Obligations;
- increase in value of nonrefunded or used tuition credits;
- refund or reimbursements of prior-year federal itemized deductions;
- repayment of income reported in a prior year; and
- self-employed health insurance costs.

The following additions to federal adjusted gross income must be made:

- interest and/or dividends on U.S. obligations that are exempt from federal taxation but not exempt from state taxation;
- interest and/or dividends on obligations of any state or political subdivision except Ohio;
- accumulation distribution from a complex trust;
- losses from the sale or exchange of Ohio Public Obligations which were deducted in determining federal adjusted gross income; and
- federal interest and dividends subject to state taxation.

number of exemptions is equal to that reported on the filer's federal tax form, with a few exceptions:

- Ohio does not have additional exemptions for elderly or blind taxpayers;
- children may be claimed as dependents on their parent's return as well as on their own return; and
- Nonresidents and part-year residents may deduct the $650 for each exemption.

Subtracting the total value of the exemptions (the number of exemptions times $650) yields Ohio taxable income (OTI). OTI is then subject to the following tax schedule:

Ohio Taxable Income	**Tax Liability**
0–$5,000	.00743(OTI)
$5,000–$10,000	$37.15 + [.01486(OTI-$5,000)]
$10,000–$15,000	$111.45 + [.02972(OTI-$10,000)]
$15,000–$20,000	$260.05 + [.03715(OTI-$15,000)]
$20,000–$40,000	$445.80 + [.04457(OTI-$20,000)]
$40,000–$80,000	$1,337.20 + [.05201(OTI-$40,000)]
$80,000–$100,000	$3,417.60 + [.05943(OTI-$80,000)]
$100,000–$200,000	$4,606.20 + [.069(OTI-$100,000)]
Over $200,000	$11,506.20 + [.075(OTI-$200,000)]

Once the tax liability has been calculated, the taxpayer is allowed a number of personal credits as shown in Box 5-2.[29]

EVALUATION AND ANALYSIS OF THE STATE INDIVIDUAL INCOME TAX

This section evaluates the Ohio individual income tax in terms of its growth, the state's reliance on the tax, the elasticity of the tax, the equity and efficiency of the tax, and its potential effects on economic development. The section also compares Ohio's individual income tax to its neighbors and to comparison states. The "comparison group" includes: Arizona, California, Florida, Georgia, Indiana, Kentucky, Michigan, Pennsylvania, Texas, and West Virginia.

BOX 5-2
Ohio State Income Tax Credits

Retirement income credit. This credit is allowed for retirees who are the recipients of retirement benefits, annuities, or other pension distributions included in OAGI (not including Social Security, Tier I or II Retirement, Supplemental Railroad Retirement, or Dual Railroad Retirement benefits). The credit is computed as follows:

Amount of qualifying retirement income (total combined amount if non-single filer)	*Retirement income credit*
less than $500	$ 0
$500 to less than $1,500	$ 25
$1,500 to less than $3,000	$ 50
$3,000 to less than $5,000	$ 80
$5,000 to less than $8,000	$130
more than $8,000	$200

Lump-sum retirement credit. Some lump-sum distributions received on account of retirement from a qualified retirement plan may be eligible for this credit. The lump-sum distributions may be attributed as income under the rules included in Section 5747.05 of the Revised Ohio Code. Once the income has been attributed, it is subject to the same schedule as that for the retirement income credit detailed above.

Senior citizen credit. This credit is available to individuals aged 65 or older. The credit is a flat $50 credit per return (joint filers can receive only $50 total in credit).

Lump-sum distribution credit. Individuals who received lump-sum distributions from a pension or retirement plan are eligible for this credit. This credit allows a taxpayer to increase the value of the senior citizen credit by a multiple of his or her expected remaining years of life. Retirees cannot take both the senior citizen credit and the lump-sum distribution credit.

Child and dependent care credit. This credit is available to individuals with less than $40,000 in Ohio adjusted gross income. For filers with Ohio AGI of less than $20,000, the credit is equal to 35 percent of the federal child and dependent care credit reported on federal form 1040 or 1040a. For filers with Ohio AGI from $20,000 to less than $40,000, the credit is equal to 25 percent of the federal credit.

continued

BOX 5-2 (continued)
Ohio State Income Tax Credits

Exemption credit. All filers are allowed a credit equal to the number of exemptions claimed multiplied by $20. For example, a single filer with no dependents would be allowed a $20 credit and a single filer with one dependent would be allowed a credit worth $40.

Joint filing credit. This credit is allowed for joint filers, who each have at least $500 of Ohio adjusted gross income, not counting income from capital or royalties. The credit is a percent of tax liability after the credits above are taken. The percent is between 5 and 20, depending on Ohio taxable income. The maximum credit allowed is $650.

Resident credit. This credit is allowed for Ohio residents who had income subject to tax in another state or in D.C. The credit is calculated as Ohio tax liability after joint filing credit times the percent of out-of-state income included in Ohio adjusted gross income and taxed by the other state. (This credit is not allowed for income earned by Ohio residents in Indiana, Kentucky, West Virginia, Michigan, or Pennsylvania.)

Nonresident and part-year resident credit. This credit is allowed for income not earned or received in Ohio. The credit apportions the income received in Ohio and adjusts Ohio tax liability accordingly.

Business-related credits. Credits are allowed for jobs creation, increased export sales, and new investments, along with a few additional credits.

Donations. Once all credits have been calculated, they are subtracted from Ohio tax liability. Tax liability is compared to withheld and estimated payments, and the taxpayer can then calculate the amount of the refund or payment due. The individual income tax form also allows for donations to the following charities:

- nature preserves, scenic rivers, and endangered species protection; and
- conservation of endangered and other wildlife species.

RELIANCE, ELASTICITY, AND STABILITY

Reliance. Even through the economic downturns of the 1980s, real state government income tax revenues have grown in most years, nationally and in Ohio. Also, state governments' individual income tax revenues have grown as a percent of all state tax revenues over time nationwide. Growth in reliance on the tax in Ohio has been mostly stable since the mid-1980s although the trend has been upward through time. Data for the 1990s suggest that the national trend of growth in reliance declined slightly in the early 1990s, but has begun to pick up again (Wallace and Edwards 1995). The data presented in Figure 5-1 show that state individual income tax revenue in Ohio comprises a larger percentage of tax revenue than in any of the comparison states. Two of Ohio's neighbors, Indiana and Kentucky, use the individual income tax to a similar degree.

What are the reasons for this heavy reliance and the growth in reliance on the individual income tax in Ohio? To answer this question we must look at the relative growth in other revenue sources, the general trends in the economy, and discretionary changes that have been made to the various taxes in the state.

Discretionary Changes. Changes to the corporate franchise and public utilities excise taxes may have reduced their relative growth somewhat in the late 1980s, which would have led to an increase in individual income tax revenue as a percent of total state tax revenue. Increases in the top individual

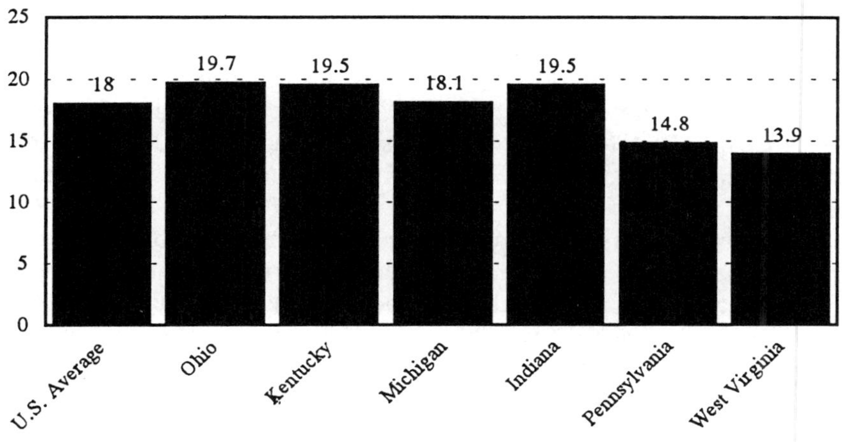

Source: ACIR, 1994.

FIGURE 5-1. State individual income taxes as a percent of total revenues, 1991.

income tax rate may also have increased reliance on the tax. While these changes may be part of the story of the growth in the importance of the individual income tax as a revenue source, further analysis suggests that the natural growth or elasticity of the tax may also account for its increased revenue importance. We turn to the elasticity next.

Elasticity. Early studies of the elasticity of states' individual income taxes shows that the elasticity of Ohio's tax is greater than the average for all states. Feenberg and Rosen (1986) estimated that the elasticity of Ohio's state government individual income tax was 1.73 in 1983, compared with a national average of 1.54.

Our analysis of the elasticity of Ohio's state individual income tax is based on the tax's structure as of 1993. Using the Ohio Microsimulation Model we calculated the change in individual income tax revenue due to a given change in the income of all filers.[30] We estimate that the rate elasticity of the current structure is high—approximately 1.5. However, taxable income is growing slightly slower than personal income in Ohio, which leads to a smaller base elasticity. This lower growth is mainly due to the growth of transfer and medical payments as components of personal income. The majority of these payments are *not* included in taxable income. We estimated that, if overall personal income grows by 10 percent, taxable income will grow by only 8.5 percent. The overall elasticity of the state income tax is approximately 1.27—still relatively elastic, but less than the pure rate elasticity.[31]

Stability. The elasticity of the income tax is variable from year to year, due to statutory changes to the tax and to changes in the economy. Annual estimates of the elasticity show that the tax is cyclical, and therefore tends to swing with the business cycle. Layoffs, business losses, and poor dividend growth during economic downturns decrease taxable income and, therefore, decrease income tax revenue growth. When the economy recovers, individuals are called back to work, business losses lessen, and dividend growth increases. All of these changes serve to increase income tax revenues when the economy "picks up."

One way to quantify the variability of the tax relative to other taxes is through the pattern of quarterly collections. During economic downturns the quarterly collections of sales and income taxes fall, and then increase during expansionary periods. When quarterly sales tax collections are analyzed, the income tax is *more* responsive to downturns in the business cycle then the sales tax. However, the income tax collections recover more quickly from the downturns than does the sales tax.

The pattern of this variability does appear to be changing. While the variation in quarterly income tax collections was greater than that of the sales tax through the early 1980s, the variability in income tax collections more recently is about the same as that for the sales tax. This was especially true throughout the most recent recession. This result is most likely due to a relative stabilization in the largest component of the income tax base—wages and salaries. This trend will likely continue—that is, the income tax elasticity will become more stable at a *lower* elasticity. This is true in other states as well, since an increasing share of personal income growth occurs for nontaxable income.

EQUITY, EFFICIENCY, AND TAX STRUCTURE

Ohio's individual income tax has a larger number of tax brackets and tax rates than most states, suggesting that the income tax is more progressive than in other states. However, while the highest income earners are taxed at a relatively high rate, the average state individual income tax rate in Ohio is lower than that in the comparison states for individuals with income under $170,000.[32] A recent study by the National Conference of State Legislatures analyzes states' individual income tax revenue per $100 of personal income. In their ranking, Ohio's state government personal income tax is $2.25 per $100 of personal income, which is lower than 27 other states that impose the income tax, and below the national average of $2.44 for states that impose an individual income tax.

The overall equity and efficiency of a tax structure is a function of all components of the tax law. All of Ohio's comparison states except Pennsylvania start their state individual income tax computations with FAGI. In Pennsylvania, taxpayers start with a comprehensive income definition that includes most items included in FAGI. In overall structure, Ohio's income tax is very similar to that found in the comparison states.

One of the largest differences among states is found in the amount of pension, retirement, and Social Security income exclusions allowed. Most states, including Ohio, exempt all Social Security income. Many states also allow a variety of other pension and retirement income exclusions and credits for the elderly; seven of the eight comparison states allow a direct pension exclusion for retirees as the data in Table 5-3 shows.

Ohio allows two credits to retirees and/or senior citizens, for a total credit for up to $250. At the highest marginal tax rate in Ohio, this credit is equivalent to a maximum income exclusion of $3,334. For low-income retirees, this credit may be as generous as any state's exclusion. However, for high-income retirees, this is a less generous exclusion than is found in many states. Ohio has been part of the national trend to exclude larger and larger portions of retirement income.[33]

All else held equal, the exclusion of retirement income may eventually decrease a state's individual income tax elasticity, as retirement income grows as a percentage of overall personal income. Pension benefits are difficult to measure, but aggregate data show that public retirement benefits

TABLE 5-3
Individual Income Tax Structural Issues, Ohio and Comparison States: 1993

State	Conformity to Federal Code	One or Multiple Schedules	Marriage Penalty Avoided	Itemized Deductions	Special Retiree Credit or Exemption	1993 Maximum Pension Exclusions: Social Security	Private	Military	Federal	State/ Local
Ohio	Federal AGI	1	No	None	Yes	Full	None	None	None	None
Indiana	Federal AGI	1	Yes	Very limited	Yes	Full	None	$2,000	$2,000	None
Kentucky	Federal AGI	1	Yes	Most federal	Yes	Full	None	Full	Full	Full
Michigan	Federal AGI	1	Yes	None	No	Full	$7,500	Full	Full	Full
Pennsylvania	Items determined by state law	Multiple	Yes	None	No	Full	Full	Full	Full	Full
West Virginia	Federal AGI	Multiple	No	None	No	Federal amount	$8,000	$2,000	$2,000	$2,000
Arizona	Federal AGI	Multiple	Yes	Most federal	No	Full	None	$2,500	$2,500	$2,500
California	Federal AGI	Multiple	Yes	Most federal	Yes	Full	None	None	None	None
Florida	————	————	N/A	————	————		————	N/A	————	
Georgia	Federal AGI	Multiple	Yes	Most federal	No	Full	------------$10,000 maximum combined---------			
Texas	————	————	N/A	————	————		————	N/A	————	

Sources: ACIR, (1994). Ohio Department of Taxation, (1994).

State notes: Ohio also allows a retirement credit and a senior citizen credit.
Indiana federal pension exclusion must be offset against the Social Security exclusion.
West Virginia places a ceiling of $8,000 on all exclusions for filers 65 years of age or older.
California allows a tax credit for filers 65 years of age or older.

grew by 8 percent from 1988 to 1989, and private pension benefits grew by almost 9 percent per year from 1985 to 1989.[34] This strong growth will continue as the retiree population expands. States that effectively exempt this income from taxation may face a decline in individual income tax revenue growth as this income source grows.

Aside from revenue concerns, one fundamental issue related to the exclusion of pension income is that it adds horizontal inequities to a tax structure. If two individuals each receive $15,000 in income in a given year, but one receives the income as wages from a full time job and the other receives it as income from a retirement plan, why does one pay tax and the other not pay tax? Two similar individuals are treated very differently in such a case, which may not be considered fair.

Of the comparison states, five offer a dependent deduction and two offer a credit; Ohio offers both. Ohio's deduction amount is low relative to the comparison states—and low relative to the United States The relatively low dependent exemption deduction and the lack of a standard deduction mean that Ohio has a larger percentage of potential taxpayers in its tax net than some other states. Ohio's state income tax structure puts taxpayers into the tax net at a relatively low level of income when compared to all states. However, it is on par with other states in the region. As we will see, the distributional effects of the lack of a standard deduction and the low personal exemption are mitigated somewhat by the relatively low marginal tax rates for the lowest tax brackets and the personal exemption credit. The decrease in the administrative costs of filing low-income returns that owe very little tax liability may warrant a standard deduction and expansion of the dependent exemption in a state like Ohio.[35]

Michigan, Indiana, and Pennsylvania all impose one tax rate on all taxable income in their states. This accounts for 50 percent of the states nationwide that use a flat tax rate structure for the individual income tax.[36]Ohio's top tax bracket starts at a higher level of income than any of the comparison states, with the exception of Arizona and California. Additionally, with nine tax brackets, Ohio has the second largest number of brackets in the country. Ohio's top tax rates also run high relative to the nation, while its lowest are among the lowest in the country.[37] At the top end, this may influence to the migration of top income individuals. While the burden of all taxes and the services provided should be considered, by itself the individual income tax imposes a relatively high burden on high-income individuals. Coupled with the state's reciprocity agreement with nearby states, this may encourage these individuals to take up residence in the neighboring states.

Many of the comparison states allow additional deductions from income in the calculation of state taxable income. These deductions are typically some portion of federal itemized deductions. Ohio and four of its comparison states allow few or no itemized deductions, which simplifies the income tax structure somewhat. Since the federal government allows itemized deductions, the use of all federal itemized deductions would not be terribly complex, but most states require some adjustment to federal itemized deductions. These adjustments would be another compliance burden placed on the taxpayer.

Many states across the country have different tax schedules for married filers, single filers, and head of household filers. The effect of having different schedules is to impose some level of horizontal equity in the system, by keeping the tax liability of two individuals filing as a married couple "equal" to that of two separate individuals filing separate tax forms, and vice versa. This equity is very difficult to achieve with other than a flat-rate tax.[38]

Typically, the use of a single tax schedule imposes a "marriage penalty" on married couples. Some states reduce or eliminate the marriage penalty through the use of different tax schedules for married couples. These tax schedules have brackets which are wider than those for singles. Other states allow married couples to file separately on the same return, which keeps the tax liability of married couples the same as the tax liability of two single filers. Individual income tax structures that use a flat tax rate do not impose a marriage penalty.

Ohio and one of its comparison group, West Virginia, impose a marriage penalty. Due to the penalty, Ohio's structure is not horizontally equitable: a married couple typically pays more in tax than two equally situated single individuals. Ohio does allow a joint-filer credit of up to $650. While this mitigates the problem somewhat, most married couples still see a higher tax liability than similarly situated single filers.

Married taxpayers can file separate returns in Ohio if they file separate returns with the federal government. Nationally, most married couples do not file separately for federal purposes since the tax liability associated with filing separately is greater than that associated with filing jointly. However, for Ohio taxpayers, the additional federal income tax liability associated with filing separately is more than offset by the decrease in Ohio tax liability for a growing number of couples. As these couples move to separate filing, the overall Ohio tax liability of these couples decreases.

If the household unit is considered the basic unit for taxation, then no preferential treatment should be given to married couples. In this case, a household that earns any given amount of income should be taxed the same, whether married or not married. This has been given as the justification of Ohio's structure. However, not forcing couples to file jointly allows some "households" to file as separate units to reduce tax liability. Also, the presence of the joint-filer credit reduces the "household as a taxpaying unit" justification for the single rate structure.

Finally, many states offer a variety of credits for the elderly, non-resident filers, low-income earners, business expansion, etc. As discussed above, Ohio has credits for the elderly, joint filers, dependents, personal exemptions, non-residents, and residents earning income in other states, as well as a few business credits. Ohio is not out of line with the comparison states in terms of the number of credits allowed, but some of the credits are quite different from those used in other states.

For one, Ohio allows a personal exemption deduction *and* a credit. The personal exemption credit is an additional allowance equal to $20 multiplied by the number of exemptions claimed. In effect, it is an additional personal exemption that could be added to the personal exemption deduction. In fact, having both a credit and a deduction serves to complicate the form for taxpayers. Ohio joins many other states in offering a credit for the care of dependent adults. Over one-third of all states allow such a credit.[39] This credit is an attempt to relieve some of the costs associated with the care of elderly parents as well as children.

Summary of Ohio State Government Income Tax

The following list summarizes the performance of Ohio's individual income tax, on its own merits and relative to other states:

1. The individual income tax is an important source of revenue and its importance has grown over time.
2. The individual income tax is an elastic tax. It is cyclical, but has stabilized somewhat in recent years.
3. The declining variability in wages will tend to stabilize revenue growth, but at a slower pace.
4. The tax base of the individual income tax is similar to that in other states.
5. Ohio's state individual income tax structure is most different from the comparison states in the following ways:
   - The top marginal tax rate is relatively high.
   - More low-income individuals are brought into the tax net, due to relatively low personal exemptions and the lack of a standard deduction. The personal exemption credit mitigates this effect, especially for taxpayers with children.
   - Ohio has a relatively large number of tax brackets, which increases progressivity.
   - Ohio has a significant marriage penalty.

- Ohio does not allow itemized deductions which reduces the complexity of the tax structure, but the credits Ohio allows increase its complexity.
- Ohio's retirement and senior citizen credits afford lower-income retirees a relatively large benefit.

More Distributional Considerations

Although Ohio's effective income tax rate structure is progressive, it is somewhat difficult to compare progressivity among states through tax rates alone. Instead, we calculated the tax burdens of "representative taxpayers" at three different income levels for all of the comparison states. The representative taxpayers have the following characteristics: all use the states' standard deductions if available; married couples file jointly and have two dependents, the married retirees are both 65 or older and have a combination of pension income, Social Security income, and other income; and the single retirees have the same characteristics. Finally, the income for all representative taxpayers is included in federal adjusted gross income, with the exception of retirement and Social Security income, which is treated in accordance with each state tax code for purposes of this exercise.

The data in Table 5-4 show the tax burdens for the representative taxpayers in Ohio and the comparison states. By representative taxpayer filing status, the tax burdens among the states can be summarized as follows:

Singles. For the $25,000 taxpayer, Ohio's tax structure yields a lower tax burden than all the comparison states. As income increases to $50,000 for the representative taxpayer, the tax burden in Ohio remains relatively low, but two other states are lower. Once the taxpayer reaches $100,000, the tax burden in Ohio is the median tax burden. Although Ohio's tax burden is not the largest for the $100,000 representative taxpayer, the difference between the tax burdens of the representative taxpayer having the lowest income and the one with the highest is relatively large. Of the comparison group, only California has a greater increase between the tax burdens of the low-income filer and the highest- income filer.

Married-joint. For the $25,000 taxpayer, Ohio's individual income tax structure imposes a larger tax burden than that of only two other states. As income increases, the relative burden of tax in Ohio does not increase significantly. The representative taxpayers earning $100,000 pay less state individual income tax in only three other states than they do in Ohio.

Single retirees. The treatment of retirees is very different from state to state, as shown by the tax burdens of the representative taxpayers. For the relatively low-income retiree, Ohio's tax burden is the second lowest of the comparison group of states. For the retiree with $50,000 in income, Ohio's

TABLE 5-4
Comparison of State Individual Income Taxes and Tax Burdens

Singles		Ohio	Kentucky	Pennsylvania	Indiana	Michigan	Arizona	California	Georgia	West Virginia
25,000	tax	620	1178	700	816	1053	794	675	1082	968
	burden	2.48%	4.71%	2.8%	3.26%	4.21%	3.18%	2.7%	4.33%	3.87%
50,000	tax	1803	2741	1400	1666	2203	2059	2863	2582	2055
100,000	tax	4548	5741	2800	3366	4503	4684	7513	5402	5245
	burden	4.55	5.74	2.80	3.37	4.5	4.68	7.51	5.40	5.25
Married joint										
25,000	tax	362	1118	700	714	764	345	339	700	580
	burden	1.44	4.47	2.80	2.86	3.06	1.38	1.36	2.80	2.32
50,000	tax	1384	2681	1400	1564	1914	1834	1222	2200	1695
	burden	2.77	5.36	2.80	3.13	3.83	3.67	2.44	4.40	3.39
100,000	tax	4026	5681	2800	3264	4214	3876	4222	5200	4695
	burden	4.03	5.68	2.8	3.26	4.21	3.88	4.22	5.20	4.70
Single retirees										
25,000	tax	147	941	140	606	478	574	370	190	500
	burden	.59	3.76	.56	2.42	1.91	2.30	1.48	.76	2.00
50,000	tax	1293	2291	490	1371	1513	1564	2166	1532	1575
	burden	2.59	4.58	.98	2.74	3.03	3.13	4.33	3.66	3.15
Married retirees										
25,000	tax	28	793	140	572	382	308	---	80	420
	burden	.11	3.17	.56	2.29	1.53	1.23	---	.32	1.68
50,000	tax	1030	1933	280	1252	1302	1068	622	1180	1485
	burden	2.10	3.87	.56	2.54	2.60	2.14	1.24	2.36	2.97

Source: Computed by authors.

tax burden is still relatively low. For all states, the tax burden of single retirees is much lower than that of non-retired singles.

Married retirees. Again, Ohio places a very low tax burden on the $25,000 representative married retired couple. The tax burden for married retirees earning $50,000 is also relatively low in Ohio.

The information presented in Table 5-4 is based on case studies, but it does give us some information on the progressivity of Ohio's tax structure relative to the comparison states. The average tax burden on most of our representative taxpayers is lower in Ohio than in many of the comparison states. Ohio's tax rate structure is such that very high-income individuals (over $100,000 of income) face higher rates in Ohio, but the average person faces a relatively low tax burden from the state is individual income tax.

While the basic structure of the Ohio individual income tax is fairly clean, there is some room for simplifying the system. The high top marginal tax rates may also cause concern regarding the migration of high-income individuals. The lack of a standard deduction and the relatively low personal exemption amount may bring more low-income individuals into the tax net than is administratively worthwhile. The retirement credit is effectively a reduction in tax liability aimed at low-income retirees. Finally, the state individual income tax is progressive, but the average rate of tax measured by the average tax burden is relatively low.

Any or all of these issues could be addressed with various tax structure changes. However, these changes should be made in the context of policy decisions relating to the overall progressivity of all the taxes, economic development goals, and the desired efficiency of the overall system. Before outlining specific policy options for the state income tax, we turn to an analysis of the local income taxes in Ohio.

LOCAL INCOME TAXATION

Local income taxes are an important source of revenue for local governments in eleven states. While the arguments *against* local income taxes are quite similar to those against state government income taxes, the arguments for local incomes taxes are a bit different. Most importantly, the benefits principle of taxation potentially applies more to local income taxes than to state income taxes, as explained below.

The ACIR (1988) summarized Rodgers' (1987) list of the objectives of local non-property taxes:

- to obtain additional revenue while avoiding higher property taxes;
- to broaden the distribution of the local tax burden to include more of those who benefit from local public services;

- to make the tax structure more flexible with respect to local circumstances;
- to make the tax structure more responsive to rising costs and service demands; and
- to reduce relatively high tax rates in overlapping jurisdictions, all of which employ a property tax.

While the last three objectives generally apply to taxes at the state level as well, the first two issues relate more to the concerns of local governments.

In an era of increasing concern over the heavy use of property taxes, local governments have looked to alternative revenue sources. Although taxpayers may pay the same amount in property tax as they would in an equal-yield income tax, since the property tax is very visible (you receive an annual property tax bill) some taxpayers feel that it is a worse tax than the income tax (ACIR 1993). Additionally, the use of the property tax for public school funding has increasingly come under fire, since it has been shown to be counter-equalizing. Finally, residents (particularly of central cities) have felt the pinch of a reduction in property values due to the general decline of the inner cities. Employment-based income taxes can supplement dwindling property tax revenues in these cities.

Local income taxes are justified in large part by the benefits principle of taxation. While for a large number of services it is nearly impossible to determine the value of the benefits received by each individual, local governments tend to use flat-rate taxes to pay directly for government services. Taxes at local levels of government tend to be aimed at payments for specific services, and much less at income redistribution.

What about the benefits received by individuals who come into a city to work during the day, and then return to the suburbs after work? These people receive benefits from the city such as roads, police and fire protection, public transportation, etc. However, if the only tax that is levied in the city is the property tax, these commuters pay nothing for the benefits that they receive. An income tax based on place of employment would be one way of paying for benefits received. The problem is that it is still nearly impossible to determine how each commuter values the services received. By imposing an income tax based on place of employment, the city government is able to receive some compensation from users of services, although the government certainly cannot match the tax exactly with the value of the services. A local income tax based on employment is therefore a benefit tax, or a charge for services in a local jurisdiction used by commuters.

Residence-based income taxes may also be viewed as direct payments for services, as the benefits principle would require.[41] Flat-rate local income taxes are imperfectly designed benefits taxes, as a single tax rate does not capture the diversity of benefits accruing to individuals.[41] However, while a progressive local income tax could be rationalized by the ability-to-pay principle, especially for public goods such as education, progressive taxes are not often used.[42]

Local income taxes can be very simple, so that the administration and compliance grades of the tax are good. From the administration and compliance perspective, a local income tax that is coupled with the state government's income tax may well be a "better" tax than the property tax. The flat-rate structure of most local income taxes also wins high marks from the viewpoint of economic efficiency. Since many local governments have chosen flat-rate income taxes, the local income tax is least effective in the area of redistribution. Progressive taxes would likely induce more migration than a state income tax, as the cost associated with moving among school districts and cities is smaller than that associated with moving among states.

The next two sections discuss Ohio's municipal and school district income taxes in detail.

MUNICIPAL INCOME TAXES

Overview

In 1939, Philadelphia became the first municipality in the United States to adopt an income tax. No other major cities enacted income tax ordinances until after World War II. Toledo and Columbus adopted their ordinances in 1946 and 1947, respectively, making them the second and third major cities in the nation to adopt the tax. With cities seeking alternative revenue sources over the years, the income tax has become popular with local municipalities in some states as a revenue source that will provide growth. Through 1970, 52 cities with 50,000 or more inhabitants had adopted a city income or payroll tax; twenty of these are located in Ohio. The adoption dates of the individual income tax for major cities in states for which comparisons are made in this study can be found in Table 5-5.

Currently, eleven states have municipalities which impose local income taxes; two other states allow the adoption of the tax by local municipalities, but do not currently impose local income taxes; three states have cities which tax the total payroll within the city. Rates range from a low of .0056 percent to a high of 4.96 percent (imposed by Philadelphia on residents of that city). The rates for taxes imposed in larger cities in states used in this comparative study are shown in Table 5-6. Tax bases typically consist of a combination of wages and salaries and capital income. Ohio is relatively unique in its use of a local tax on corporate net income.

TABLE 5-5
Chronological Listings of City Income and Payroll Tax Adoptions, Selected Cities

Year	City	Year	City
1939	Philadelphia, Pennsylvania	1960	Hamilton, Ohio Owensboro, Kentucky
1946	Toledo, Ohio	1962	Akron, Ohio Detroit, Michigan
1947	Columbus, Ohio	1964	Penn Hills Township, Pennsylvania
1948	Altoona, Pennsylvania Erie, Pennsylvania Louisville, Kentucky Scranton, Pennsylvania Springfield, Ohio Youngstown, Ohio	1965	Flint, Michigan Saginaw, Michigan York, Pennsylvania
1949	Dayton, Ohio	1966	Chester, Pennsylvania Harrisburg, Pennsylvania Mansfield, Ohio Wilkes-Barre, Pennsylvania
1952	Lexington, Kentucky Warren, Ohio	1967	Cleveland, Ohio Cleveland Heights, Ohio Euclid, Ohio Grand Rapids, Michigan Parma, Ohio
1956	Covington, Kentucky	1968	Abington Township, Pennsylvania Kettering, Ohio Elyria, Ohio Lakewood, Ohio Lansing, Michigan Lorain, Ohio Pontiac, Michigan
1957	Bethlehem, Pennsylvania	1969	Reading, Pennsylvania
1958	Allentown, Pennsylvania	1976	Los Angeles, California San Franscisco, California
1959	Lima, Ohio Lancaster, Pennsylvania	1986	Indianapolis, Indiana

Source: Sjoquist, Wallace, Edwards, and Murphy (1993).

Within Ohio, 519 municipalities collected income taxes for calendar year 1992. Many municipalities levy income taxes at rates of one percent or below. State law requires that municipalities levy a flat rate on all income earned within the jurisdiction.[43] One reason for the predominance of these rates is that state regulations permit municipalities to implement an income tax at a rate of up to one percent without voter approval. Thus, over 50 percent of the municipalities which levy the tax impose rates in this range; of these, one municipality levies a rate as low as .25 percent, while over 93 percent levy a one-percent rate. Approximately 15 percent of the municipalities levy income taxes of 2.0 percent or more within their jurisdictions; the remaining municipalities, or approximately one-third of the total, levy rates ranging from 1.13 percent to 1.8 percent, with a high proportion imposing a 1.5 percent rate.

Summarizing and aggregating some data reported by the individual mu-

TABLE 5-6
Local Income Tax Rates: Selected Cities (Over 125,000)[1] as of May, 1994

City	Percent Tax Rate	City	Percent Tax Rate
Ohio[2]		**Michigan**	
Akron	2.00	Detroit	
Cincinnati	2.10	residents	3.00
Cleveland	2.00	nonresidents	1.50
Columbus	2.00	Flint	
Dayton	2.25	residents	1.00
Toledo	2.25	nonresidents	0.50
Youngstown	2.00	Grand Rapids	
		residents	1.00
Pennsylvania		nonresidents	0.50
Philadelphia		Lansing	
residents	4.96	residents	1.00
nonresidents	4.3125	nonresidents	0.50
Pittsburgh			
residents[3]	2.875	**Kentucky**[5]	
nonresidents	1.00	Lexington-Fayette	
		Urban County	
California[4]		Government	2.50
San Francisco	1.00 to 1.50	Louisville	
		residents	2.20
		nonresidents	1.45

Source: Commerce Clearing House, (1994) ACIR, (1994).

[1]Excludes cities in Alabama, Maryland, Missouri, New Jersey, New York, and Oregon.
[2]Does not include school district taxes. School district rates range for 0.5% to 1.25%.
[3]Includes 1.875 school district tax levied on residents only.
[4]Payroll expense tax levied within the city. Rates vary by size of business, as measured by payroll dollar value.
[5]Local school boards levy a county tax on wages and net profits.

nicipalities provides a clearer idea of which areas collect the highest proportion of municipal taxes. In general, the main municipality in an urban area levies the highest tax in that area. For instance, in the Cincinnati area, the city of Cincinnati levies a rate of 2.1 percent; three suburbs impose rates of 2.0 percent; other municipalities in the urban area levy lower rates. Another observation about these urban areas is that looking at information only for the cities can be misleading for those urban areas which encompass many different municipalities. In Cleveland, for instance, the city's portion of total local income tax collections represents less than 50 percent of the collections for the entire urban area.

While the municipal income tax has been most important to municipalities which have populations greater than 500,000, it has grown in importance for a number of cities. Looking at the contribution of the tax to the finances of individual cities over time provides a clearer understanding of the importance of the tax. The data in Table 5-7 show income tax revenues for the seven largest cities in the state of Ohio, for fiscal years 1977-78 and 1990-91. In terms of total local tax collections, the income tax gained in importance from the 1970s to the most recently reported period. When the tax is

TABLE 5-7
The Importance of the Municipal Income Tax

	Fiscal Year Collections - 1977-78			Fiscal Year Collections - 1990-91		
City	Income Tax Amount	Percent of Total Taxes	Percent of Own-Source Revenue	Income Tax Amount	Percent of Total Taxes	Percent of Own-Source Revenue
Akron	$27,241	69.8	44.9	$68,933	74.4	43.9
Cincinnati	71,576	67.6	45.3	168,981	75.5	41.4
Cleveland	57,538	56.9	33.2	212,986	77.3	53.3
Columbus	62,549	81.9	50.1	232,405	85.8	54.4
Dayton	39,414	78.4	55.6	84,978	83.8	43.7
Toledo	38,177	76.5	45.8	107,980	86.0	57.6
Youngstown	12,475	75.9	43.2	26,645	86.4	62.9

Source: U.S. Department of Commerce, (1978 and 1991).

measured as a percent of own-source revenues, however, no trend is evident. In some cities, such as Cleveland and Youngstown, the tax gained in importance as a revenue source; in other cities, such as Akron and Cincinnati, more reliance is placed on other revenue sources. While the growth trends in the tax changed over time, it is obvious that this revenue source is *extremely* important.

Comparisons of individual cities within the state to cities outside the state can also provide insight into the importance of the tax. The data in Table 5-8 present a comparison of some measures of the importance of the tax among the seven major cities in Ohio and cities in other states included in this study. Income taxes as a percent of total revenues of the municipalities are, in general, highest in the Ohio cities. This fact further emphasizes the importance of these taxes to Ohio's municipalities. Per capita income taxes reflect the average amount paid by each individual residing within a municipality. Using this measure, Philadelphia's rate results in the highest tax per capita. This result is expected because, as noted earlier, Philadelphia's tax rate is significantly higher than that of other cities. Compared to other cities, Ohio's cities have among the highest per capita municipal income taxes. Caution, however, must be exercised in drawing conclusions from this measure, for at least three reasons. First, as noted earlier, the amounts include corporate as well as individual income taxes. As most cities in other states do not levy local corporate income taxes, Ohio's amounts will be significantly higher. Second, city income taxes are levied on individuals employed within the municipality, as well as on the city's residents. A city with a high level of employment but a low population relative to an otherwise comparable city will have higher per capita income taxes than its counterpart. Finally, the pattern of the tax burden associated with all state and local taxes may be different from that for a single tax.

HISTORY OF THE TAX

In 1946, Toledo became the first city in Ohio to impose a municipal income tax. While the Ohio Constitution grants broad powers to the municipal governments in the state, the wording did not explicitly define the right to levy income taxes as within the purview of the municipal governments.[44] In 1948 a taxpayer challenged the legality of the tax in the court case Angell v. City of Toledo et. al.[45] The Supreme Court of Ohio addressed two issues in making its decision on the case in March, 1950. The court first dealt with the issue of whether the city's charter granted it the power to assess and collect an income tax. The second issue related to the right of the city to tax nonresidents who work and receive their pay in Toledo. The court ruled that, in the absence of a state income tax, municipalities have the power to levy and collect an income tax until the state preempts the municipalities.

TABLE 5-8
Local Income Tax Effects: Selected Cities (Over 125,000)*
for the Fiscal Years 1990 and 1991

City	State	Total Revenues 1990-1991	Income Taxes 1990-1991	Income Taxes as % of Total Revenues	Population 1990	Per Capita Income Taxes 1990-1991
San Francisco	CA	$3,145,862	n.a.	n.a.	723,959	n.a.
Lexington	KY	214,016	$58,969	27.6	225,366	$26.17
Louisville	KY	282,723	86,559	30.6	269,063	32.17
Detroit	MI	1,965,307	274,625	14.0	1,027,974	26.72
Flint	MI	358,627	21,647	6.0	140,761	15.38
Grand Rapids	MI	196,753	26,396	13.4	189,126	13.96
Lansing	MI	285,519	20,351	7.1	127,321	15.98
Akron	OH	214,496	68,933	32.1	223,019	30.91
Cincinnati	OH	647,184	168,981	26.1	364,040	46.42
Cleveland	OH	734,999	212,986	29.0	505,616	42.12
Columbus	OH	606,895	232,405	38.3	632,910	36.72
Dayton	OH	263,156	84,978	32.3	182,044	46.68
Toledo	OH	253,732	107,980	42.6	332,943	32.43
Youngstown	OH	63,663	24,645	38.7	95,732	25.74
Philadelphia	PA	3,426,957	974,524	28.4	1,585,577	61.46
Pittsburgh	PA	402,011	40,113	10.0	369,879	10.84

Source: U.S. Department of Commerce, (1993 and 1991).

*Excludes cities in Alabama, Maryland, Missouri, New Jersey, New York, and Oregon.

Further, the court stated that the levying of taxes on nonresidents did not violate the due process clause because a direct fiscal relationship exists between the taxes paid to and the benefits received from the municipality in which the taxpayer is employed.

The major provisions of the Ohio code regarding municipal income taxes originated in 1957.[46] The regulations relate to such topics as the determination of income subject to tax, the use of uniform rates for income taxes and definitions of income to be exempted from taxation, such as military pay. Prior to this date, no restriction existed regarding the highest income tax rate a municipality could levy. The imposition of the one-percent limit on the tax rate without voter approval probably had the most far-reaching effect on the development of municipal income taxes in Ohio. Without such a limit, the average tax rate levied by municipalities would undoubtedly have risen above the current level.

In 1971, the state adopted an income tax. To avoid any question regarding the invalidation of municipal income taxes, the state also included an express provision in the code enacting the state tax that stated, in part, "The levy of this tax on income does not prevent a municipal corporation from levying a tax on income."[47] Nonetheless, the issues of double taxation and preemption by the state of the municipalities' powers to levy income taxes were raised in *Village of Ottawa Hills v. Joelson*.[48] The Supreme Court ruled that the state had clearly and specifically disclaimed any intention to preempt the powers of the municipalities to levy income taxes. Regarding the question of the legality of double taxation, the Ohio Constitution does not specifically restrict the state and municipalities from levying taxes on the same base. The court found that, as the state and each municipality are separate taxing authorities, double taxation is not an issue.

The latest development in the area of municipal income taxes is a revision to the Ohio code effective April 16, 1993, which allows two municipal corporations occupying the same territory to levy a joint income tax, subject to voter approval. The primary intent of this revision to the code is to provide an additional funding source for school districts. The code requires that the proportion of the municipal income tax paid to the school district shall not be less than twenty-five percent of the revenue generated by the tax. The voters' ballot shall specify the tax rate and the proportion of taxes to be provided to the school district. To date, no municipalities had voted on the issue. However, the citizens of Lakewood and Euclid will have voted on the issue in the November 1994 election. In neither case do the local school districts currently levy a separate income tax. The municipal income tax rates in Lakewood and Euclid are 1.5 and 2 percent, respectively. If the agreement between the cities and their respective school districts provided the school districts with the minimum percentage allowed by law (twenty-five percent of the total income tax) and if the two cities chose to maintain their effective rates at the same level, the rates would be 2.0 and 2.67 percent, respectively.

Compliance and Administration

In the current Ohio Code, no legislation establishes uniform guidelines for compliance throughout the state. Thus, a diversity of practices exists regarding such fundamental requirements as the forms required for filing withholding, estimated taxes, returns, due dates for filing, penalties, and extensions for filing. The Ohio Society of Certified Public Accountants is addressing these issues and has submitted testimony to the Commission that advocates more uniformity in these requirements, because the current diversity places a large burden on members of their organization and the taxpayers who operate in more than one municipality.

One area in which the state does not impose restrictions, but which could make a significant difference in the revenues of a municipality, relates to tax credits. When an employee resides in one municipality and is employed in another jurisdiction, the question arises regarding to which jurisdiction local income taxes should be paid. In general, the tax is paid to the municipality in which employment occurs. If the municipality in which the individual resides also levies an income tax, the taxpayer must ascertain whether that municipality permits credits for taxes paid in other municipalities.

Practices regarding credits vary widely throughout the state. In most cases, 100 percent credit for taxes paid in one jurisdiction can be applied to tax liabilities in another jurisdiction. However, in some cases, a lesser percentage or even no credit is allowed. One possible way for a municipality to increase its revenues without seeking voter approval for a rate increase is to change its requirement regarding credits for taxes paid in other municipalities. Additionally, as no state regulation exists regarding credits for taxes paid to local governments in other states, no uniformity exists regarding the granting of credits to either residents of other states or individuals residing in Ohio but employed in another state. To illustrate the diversity of practices regarding tax credits, of the ten municipalities administered by the City of Columbus, nine allow 100 percent credit, with the remaining municipality offering no credit (Dorrian 1993). This pattern of diversity repeats itself throughout the state.

In some instances, a single municipality administers its income tax. However, significant economies of scale can exist with the administration of the tax. Thus, a lower cost per dollar of taxes collected can result from combining with other municipalities to administer income taxes. This cost advantage has resulted in the development of numerous governmental and quasi-governmental units throughout the state. Some of these administrative groups, such as the ones operating in Columbus and Cleveland, originated because a large city formed a group to administer its local income tax and contracted with nearby municipalities to perform the service for them. These groups remain part of the city government, but perform services on a fee basis for the other municipalities they serve. In other cases, a number of municipalities joined together to organize a group to administer their taxes. The Regional Income Tax Agency (RITA) was formed in 1971 under such an organizational structure. A closer examination of some practices employed in the municipalities administered by the City of Columbus, the City of Cleveland, and RITA will provide a clearer understanding of the diversity of administrative and compliance requirements existing across the state.

The City of Columbus collects a municipal income tax for itself, as well as for ten other municipalities (Dorrian 1993). On a monthly basis, the city collects and distributes each municipality's tax receipts, plus interest earnings, less a collection fee. Table 5-9 shows the requirements for remittance of withholding by employers as stated in Columbus' local ordinance. Considering that the determination of such amounts is at the discretion of the local municipality, employers operating in numerous municipalities must be aware of the details of each ordinance to ensure compliance.

The City of Cleveland enacted its income tax ordinance in 1966 and included in that ordinance a provision authorizing the establishment of a central collection facility on behalf of the municipality. That agency, the Central Collection Agency (CCA), began collecting taxes in 1967 for 14 member communities. Over the ensuing four years, 49 additional municipalities contracted with CCA to provide collection services for them (CCA 1993). Disagreements regarding the distribution of revenues to members of CCA resulted in a cancellation of the agreements between the City of Cleveland and most member communities in 1971. Approximately 40 communities left

TABLE 5-9
Requirements for Remittance of Withholding by Employees
City of Columbus, Ohio

Remit...	If taxes withheld in the prior calendar year were...	OR	If taxes withheld for any month in the preceding quarter were...	Due date for remittance...
Quarterly	less than $1,200		less than $101	No later than the last business day of the month following the end of each quarter
Monthly	$1,200 to $11,999		$101 to $1,000	Within fifteen days after of the close of each calendar month
Semi-monthly	$12,000 or more		$1,001 or more	Within five banking days after the fifteenth and the last day of each month

Source: City of Columbus, Ohio, General Operating Fund Resources, (Dorrian , April, 1993).

CCA to form RITA. The remaining communities continued to contract with CCA for their income tax administration. Other communities joined CCA in the ensuing years; in 1993, CCA administered taxes for 42 communities. The administration of CCA remains part of the City of Cleveland. The cost of the service to member communities is based on the overhead costs of the agency, and, for most communities, is approximately two percent of the taxes collected. CCA collects and distributes funds by wire transfer to the member communities each month. Any funds held by CCA are invested daily by the City of Cleveland Treasury, with interest paid to the member communities. As practices for municipalities change over the years, CCA must have the flexibility to adjust to these changes.

The filing requirements for member communities are uniform, which enabled CCA to produce one instruction booklet and form for filing the tax returns for each year. Nonetheless, sufficient diversity exists within the group to necessitate some instructions specific to the different municipalities. For instance, filing requirements vary according to the gross rentals received within different municipalities. Additionally, the diversity of tax rates in effect and tax credits serves to complicate the filing process.

In 1971, when the group of cities and villages decided to sever their connection with CCA and form their own organization to administer their municipal income taxes, the group initially organized a Regional Council of Governments to administer the tax. RITA now collects taxes for approximately sixty different communities and actively recruits additional municipalities to contract for its services. RITA bases collection fees on its operating costs, and notes that its operating costs have decreased from 2.59 percent of collections in 1984 to 1.72 percent in 1993 (RITA, 1994). As with CCA, RITA developed one form for all individuals residing or employed within any of its member communities. This form and its instructions also contain numerous exceptions by municipality which can complicate the filing process for the individual taxpayer, as well as add complexity to the administration of the taxes.

While the administrators of the tax may be very efficient in their collection and audit procedures, there is no doubt that the differences in filing requirements, tax rates, tax bases and the apportionment calculations for business are cumbersome. Individuals who work and reside in two different municipalities, each with a local income tax, have the added burden of multiple filing. The long tradition of this tax in terms of its use and the municipalities' autonomy may make conformity of the municipal income taxes difficult, but the long-run savings to businesses and individuals would be substantial.

Differential Effects of Taxation on the Individual

To more clearly illustrate the effects of the municipal income tax on individuals working and residing in different municipalities, in Table 5-10 we show examples of the tax calculation for six different individuals. All individuals have Ohio taxable income of $25,000, but some individuals have different residence and/or employment locations, as well as income from different sources.

Example 1. The individual resides and works in Cleveland. Income is derived solely from wages. In this instance, the calculation is straightforward for the taxpayer in that the Ohio AGI is multiplied by the tax rate for Cleveland, 2%. The resulting tax liability is $500.

Example 2. This individual also resides and works in Cleveland. However, $10,000 of this individual's Ohio AGI represents dividend income; the remaining income is derived from wages earned. The calculation, in this instance, is only slightly more complicated than in the first example and results in a tax liability of $300 for the taxpayer.

Example 3. This individual resides in Plain City, but works in Cleveland. Plain City grants no tax credit; therefore, earnings are subject to full taxation in both municipalities. The calculation of the liability for taxes in Cleveland is the same as that performed by the individual in the first example. However, rather than calculating the tax solely for Cleveland, the taxpayer must also calculate the tax for Plain City. As Plain City does not grant a tax credit for taxes paid to other municipalities, the individual is also liable

TABLE 5-10
Examples of Municipal Income Tax Calculations

	Residence: Cleveland Employment: Cleveland		Residence: Plain City Employment: Cleveland		Residence: Cleveland Employment: Plain City	
	Example 1	Example 2	Example 3	Example 4	Example 5	Example 6
Ohio AGI	$25,000	$25,000	$25,000	$25,000	$25,000	$25,000
Less: Dividends	0	10,000	0	10,000	0	10,000
Municipal Taxable Income	25,000	15,000	25,000	15,000	25,000	15,000
Municipal Tax Rate (Employment)	2.0	2.0	2.0	2.0	1.0	1.0
Municipal Tax Liability (Employment)	500	300	500	300	250	150
Municipal Tax Rate (Residence)	n.a.	N.a.	1.0	1.0	2.0	2.0
Municipal Gross Tax Liability (Residence)	n.a.	N.a.	250	150	500	300
Less: Credits for Other Municipalities	n.a.	N.a.	0	0	125	75
Municipal Net Tax Liability (Residence)	n.a.	N.a.	250	150	375	225
Total Municipal Income Tax Liability	$500	$300	$750	$450	$625	$375

Source: Computed by authors.

for payment of taxes to Plain City of $250. In comparison to the individual in the first example, this taxpayer must pay municipal taxes that are 50 percent higher on the same income. This higher tax payment is directly attributable to the taxpayer's residing in a municipality which does not allow a credit on taxes paid to other municipalities.

Example 4. This individual is very similar to the individual portrayed in the previous example. However, $10,000 of his income is derived from dividends, which reduces the municipal taxable income in both municipalities to $15,000. Again, a comparison of this individual to the individual with equivalent taxable income who lives and works in Cleveland reveals that additional taxes of $150, or taxes which are 50 percent higher, are paid by the individual.

Example 5. In this example, the individual resides in Cleveland, but works in Plain City. Cleveland grants a tax credit of 50 percent for taxes paid in another municipality. As the tax liability is initially calculated on income based on the individual's employment location, the individual first applies the one percent rate to taxable income to determine the tax owed to Plain City. In the calculation of the tax liability for Cleveland, the individual's city of residence, the individual will take a 50 percent credit for taxes paid to Plain City. Total tax liability for the individual is less than that owed by the individual who resides in Plain City, but works in Cleveland. However, as Cleveland grants only a 50 percent credit for taxes paid to other municipalities, this individual's total tax liability is 25 percent higher than that of the individual who resides and is employed in Cleveland. One further observation is worth noting for this individual. If the individual moved to Plain City, his municipal tax bill would decrease by $375 annually. Although this amount may not seem significant, consider an individual having twice or thrice the taxable income of this individual. Over a period of years, savings in taxes paid would be significant.

Example 6. This individual is similar to the one portrayed in Example 2, with the one change in the individual's place of employment. Again, the 50 percent tax credit provided by Cleveland results in the individual paying higher taxes than if the individual resided in Cleveland. As seen in example 5, this individual could also save taxes by relocating to Plain City from Cleveland.

These examples give the reader an indication of the extent of variation in local income tax liabilities among municipalities in Ohio. While the place of employment may be less open to the individual's choice, the place of residence certainly is more flexible. As employment opportunities grow in the suburbs, the municipal income tax may "pull" on central city residents, which may cause an increase in out-migration from the central city.

Comparisons of Taxation on Individuals between States

The data in Table 5-11 allow an evaluation of the effect of differences in

TABLE 5-11
State and Local Individual Income Tax Liabilities:
Comparisons of Selected Ohio Cities with Cities in Neighboring States

		State and Local Individual Income Taxes for Different Income Levels[1]					
		Single Individual			Married, Filing Jointly[3]		
City	Local Tax Rate[2]	$25,000	$50,000	$100,000	$25,000	$50,000	$100,000
Cincinnati	2.1	1,145	2,853	6,648	887	2,434	6,249
Lexington	2.5	1,803	3,991	8,241	1,743	3,931	8,181
Louisville	2.2	1,728	3,841	7,941	1,668	3,781	7,881
Cleveland	2.0	1,120	2,803	6,548	862	2,384	6,149
Erie	1.0	950	1,900	3,800	950	1,900	3,800
Dayton	2.25	1,182	2,928	6,798	925	2,509	6,399
Indianapolis	0.7	991	2,016	4,066	889	1,914	3,964
Toledo	2.25	1,182	2,928	6,798	925	2,509	6,399
Detroit	3.0	1,748	3,610	7,335	1,459	3,321	7,046
Fort Wayne	0.7	991	2,016	4,066	889	1,914	3,964
Youngstown	2.0	1,120	2,803	6,548	862	2,384	6,149
Pittsburgh	2.875	1,419	2,838	5,675	1,419	2,838	5,675

Sources: Commerce Clearing House (1994). ACIR (1994).

[1]Based on Federal Adjusted Gross Income (AGI) levels of $25,000, $50,000, and $100,000.
[2]Includes county and city income tax rates.
[3]Married, Filing Jointly represents couples with two dependent children in the household.

income tax requirements between Ohio and its neighboring states, as well as between Ohio's cities and the closest major cities in other states. The table reflects calculations for single and married individuals filing joint returns. While the taxes differ in most cases between single and married individuals filing joint returns, in few instances does the "low state" change for any income category. In fact, the only instance in which the level of income makes a difference in determining which city has lower taxes is when Youngstown is compared to Pittsburgh. In that example, the taxpayers having taxable income of $25,000 and $50,000 would pay lower taxes in Youngstown. At the $100,000 income level, however, the individual would pay lower income taxes in Pittsburgh.

Regarding the other comparisons presented, the taxpayers would pay lower income taxes in Cincinnati than in either Lexington or Louisville.[49] When comparing Cleveland with Erie, state and local income taxes are lower in Erie. The comparison of Indianapolis with Dayton shows a lower tax liability for the taxpayers residing in Indianapolis. In the comparisons made for Toledo, the taxes paid by individuals residing in Michigan are higher than those of the Toledo residents. However, the individuals living in Fort Wayne would pay significantly lower taxes than residents of either Toledo or Detroit.

SCHOOL DISTRICT INCOME TAXES

Overview

Only a few states within the United States, Iowa, Pennsylvania, and Ohio, levy a school district income tax.[50] As of December 31, 1994, 101 school districts within Ohio had adopted a school district income tax, with rates varying from .5 percent to 1.75 percent.

From a geographic perspective, the largest concentration of school districts which have initiated the tax is in the relatively rural western part of the state. For example, Darke County, which borders Indiana, has school district income taxes in six of its seven school districts. Paulding County, which also borders Indiana, imposes the tax in all of its school districts. Further, the tax has primarily been implemented in the rural areas of the state rather than in the major metropolitan areas. For example, none of the 31 school districts in Cuyahoga County (Cleveland) and none of the eight districts in Lucas County (Toledo) levy the tax; only one of the 22 districts in Hamilton County (Cincinnati) levies the tax; two of the 16 districts in Franklin County (Columbus) levy the tax.

To obtain school district income, an adjustment is needed if the taxpayer resided in a different school district for some portion of the year to which the return applies. Additionally, if that school district imposes an income tax, the taxpayer would need to file two school district income tax returns—one for each school district. School district taxable income results from the deduction of personal exemptions from school district income. The only other necessary adjustment is for taxpayers who are senior citizens. For taxpayers 65 years of age or older, a credit of $50.00 per return is allowed.

HISTORY OF THE TAX

As noted in the section regarding Municipal Income Taxes, the municipal income tax provides the primary own-source revenue for most municipal governments. In 1981, despite opposition from municipal representatives, support of a school district income tax by school district representatives resulted in the Ohio General Assembly authorizing a school district income tax.[51] This legislation allowed local school districts to impose a tax on the incomes of all residents and the estates of residents, subject to voter approval within the school district. Unlike the municipal income tax, procedures for levying the school district tax were clearly defined in the legislation, which would result in a more uniformly administered tax throughout the state. The legislation detailed the steps a school district must take to determine what rate would meet its needs and defined the duties of the Tax Commissioner in that process. The legislation also specified that the collection and administration of the tax would be the responsibility of the state.

The school district income tax was not an overwhelmingly popular tax from its inception. During the ensuing two years, only six school districts obtained voter approval to levy the tax. Five of those school districts are located in the west central part of the state; the remaining district, the Licking Valley Local School District, is located near the center of state.

Three principal factors resulted in the repeal of the tax by the legislature effective July 1, 1983. First, the tax created compliance problems for employers because the employers were required to know in which school district their employees resided and whether any of those employees were subject to the tax. Second, the state had recently raised the state income tax rates, resulting in more revenue at the state level. Thus, the state had sufficient money to fund local educational expenditures. Third, the opposition to the tax met with little resistance from school district officials. Less than one percent of the school districts had implemented the tax and, with adequate funding from the state, little interest in such a tax existed in the remaining school districts.

Under the 1983 provisions of the repeal, the six school districts which had enacted a school district income tax could retain the tax as a revenue source, but could not change any local ordinance provisions related to the tax. During this period, the tax rate levied by these districts varied from .5 percent to one percent. Effective in tax year 1987, the tax for the Licking Valley Local School District was repealed, leaving only the five school districts located in the west-central portion of the state with a school district individual income tax. Thus, as a result of the repeal of the statute, no new school districts were added and no tax rate increases occurred during the period 1984 to 1989.

The question now arises, "What happened in the late 1980's to cause school districts to reconsider the benefits of a school district income tax?" First, the leveling off of property values during the 1980s resulted in a low growth rate in property tax revenues. During this same time, union demands resulted in increases in the salaries and wages of school district employees, the major component of school district operating expenditures. School districts required additional revenue to meet these expenses. State laws regarding property taxes require school districts to obtain voter approval of millage rate increases. Over time, voters became resistant to the requests of the school boards for increases in the property tax. In at least one instance, a school district placed a property tax increase on the ballot in more than ten separate elections without obtaining voter approval for higher rates. These factors, coupled with increased concern regarding uniform educational funding throughout the state, caused some school district administrators to voice opposition to continued reliance on the property tax as the primary funding source for education. To many school districts, the personal income tax appeared to be the best alternative to the property tax. In inflationary or growth periods, individuals' salaries would increase, thus providing revenue growth, even under a flat-rate system. This renewed interest in alternative funding for education resulted in a reinstatement of the provisions of the original law in 1989. Tax collections began in 1990 for school districts which obtained voter approval during 1989. The prospects of a more stable revenue source resulted in a significant increase in the number of school districts requesting voter approval of the tax. During the period November, 1989 through August, 1990, 154 proposed school district income tax ordinances were placed before the voters. While a significant number of these proposed regulations were defeated, the number of school districts levying income taxes increased from five in 1989 to 101 at the present. The data in Table 5-12 summarize the number of issues successfully passed from 1989 through May, 1994. While the number of issues approved in the last two years declined significantly, proposals for school district taxes continue to be placed before the voters.[52]

Performance of the School District Income Tax

1984 through 1989. Analysis of data for the years 1984 through 1989 can provide an indication of the revenue effects of the tax on the five school dis-

TABLE 5-12
Approvals of School District Income Taxes

Election Year	Issues Passes
1989	17
1990	30
1991	25
1992	15
1993	5
1994	4

Source: State of Ohio, Department of Taxation, (1994).

tricts which had a tax. The data in Table 5-13 provide a comparison of the net tax collections with the percentage changes from year to year. Data reported by the Ohio Department of Taxation cover fiscal years rather than calendar years, whereas the income tax is imposed on a calendar year basis. Thus, 1984 data represent collections from July 1, 1983 through June 30, 1984. Due to this difference between the periods covered by the reports and the actual tax collections, the data for the three school districts which implemented the tax in 1984 reflect only payments made within the first six months of 1984. While this is a major factor causing the significant increase

TABLE 5-13
School District Income Tax Collections
For the Years 1984 through 1989

Year	Net Collections	Percentage Increase/(Decrease)
1984	$456,289	
1985	1,202,352	163.51
1986	1,357,013	12.86
1987	1,331,861	(1.85)
1988	1,152,242	(13.49)
1989	1,187,562	3.07

Source: Ohio Department of Taxation, (1985-1989).

in net collections from 1984 to 1985, one other factor must be noted. Some individuals were unaware that they owed a school district income tax until after the end of the first tax year. In some cases, this uncertainty regarding filing and payment requirements may have persisted for considerably longer. Based on experiences recounted by some school board administrators and the state, tax collections can take up to eighteen months to reflect full compliance and administration.[53]

This implementation problem also explains some of the increase in net collections from 1985 to 1986. The repeal of the tax by the Licking Valley Local School District effective in 1987 resulted in a decrease in net tax collections for part of 1987 and 1988. Thus, analyzing the aggregate data for the school districts is compounded by many factors. Even in this relatively stable time period, enough changes occurred to make comparisons between years to determine the possible growth in revenues meaningless. Analysis of the changes between 1988 and 1989 show a 3 percent increase in revenue occurred, providing an indication of the revenue potential of the tax.

Two conclusions can be drawn from looking at these data. First, the implementation period is lengthy for school district income taxes due to a lack of awareness of the tax on the part of employers and employees. As the school districts do not follow county boundaries, many individuals do not know in which school district they reside. With the small number of districts levying a tax, distribution of public information regarding the tax is primarily the responsibility of the local government. Second, it is difficult even to study the effects of the school district income tax. To most clearly discern the effects of the tax, we need data related to the taxable earnings of residents of a particular school district over a long period of time. Aggregate statewide data will generally not be suitable for analysis, due to changes in the number of districts levying the tax as well as changes in tax rates in different districts. The final part of this section presents an analysis of growth in collections for a few selected school districts.

Performance of the school district income tax—the longer term outlook. To provide an idea of the performance of the tax as a revenue source over time, the data in Table 5-14 reflect tax collections in three of the districts which adopted the school district tax during the period 1981 through 1983. The other two districts increased their rates within the last two years, which causes their data to be incomparable between periods. From this information, one conclusion that is reinforced by this view of three "stable" tax systems is that school district income taxes can vary significantly from one year to the next.

Administration and compliance. Current legislation leaves no latitude for administration of the school district income tax. The state provides all administration of the tax, including mailing forms to individuals, processing returns, collecting withholding and estimated tax amounts, remitting the tax

TABLE 5-14
School District Income Tax Performance

	Fiscal Year 1992	Fiscal Year 1993		Fiscal Year 1994	
School District	Amount	Amount	Increase/ (Decrease)	Amount	Increase/ (Decrease)
Arlington	$270,473	$292,582	8.2%	$291,974	0.2%
McComb	382,261	362,788	(5.1)	487,793	34.5
Anna	247,961	246,919	(0.4)	278,341	12.7

Source: Ohio Department of Taxation (1992-1994).

(less an administration fee charged by the state[54]), and conducting audits for noncompliance.

During the initial years of the school district income tax, the small number of school districts did not necessitate a separate group to administer the tax. With the growth in the number of districts imposing the tax, however, the Tax Commissioner formed a separate group to handle the administration. The improved level of service to school districts provided by this administrative body caused one school district official to remark, "We are pleased by the level of service provided by the state." Improvements continue each year, with more detailed verification of school district tax returns to data provided on state income tax returns.

When the state remits payments to the school districts, information regarding the number of returns filed, the amounts provided through withholding by employers and the amounts provided by estimated returns filed by individuals accompanies the payments. This information assists the school district in understanding the sources of revenue and helps the school district project revenues for future periods. However, the school district receives no information regarding individual taxpayers. While the school district officials recognize the need for privacy regarding income levels, some school district officials believe that information regarding who has filed a return for a particular year would be useful. In many cases, school officials have better knowledge of the local area than the state has and the school district could assume a more active role in policing compliance with the tax. An additional source of frustration to school district officials is that they receive no feedback from the state on reports regarding questions about non-compliance by some school district residents.

The law requires employers to withhold taxes from individuals' pay for the school district tax and remit those amounts to the state. This requirement applies to all employers, even those outside the state of Ohio, if they employ individuals who reside in a school district that imposes the tax. The first problem to be overcome is educating the employers about the requirement to withhold school district income taxes. As noted earlier, until 1990 the tax had applied only to individuals living in five school districts in the western part of the state, making the widespread use of the tax a fairly recent phenomenon. A second problem caused by this requirement is that employers must identify taxpayers who are subject to the tax before they can process withholding for them. Additionally, as rates vary between school districts, withholding rates may vary among employees within a firm. Although the booklet distributed by the state containing the withholding rates for employers is easy to use, the booklet is quite lengthy as separate withholding amounts apply for different tax rates by school district. Currently, six different rates exist throughout the state. When employers are located in other states, the uniqueness of this type of tax is even more evident in the confusion that results from the withholding requirement.

One strong incentive to employers to withhold the tax is that the state can hold the company liable for the payment of the employees' taxes if the employer refuses to withhold and remit amounts for school district taxes. The only exception that exists to the employers' withholding rule is for the federal government. Currently, the federal government's payroll personnel maintain that no obligation exists for the federal government to withhold the tax. This refusal compels federal employees to file estimated taxes to ensure that no penalties and interest accrue to them.

From a taxpayer viewpoint, implementation of a school district tax causes the most problems for retired and self-employed individuals. These individuals must not only file a different form at the end of the year, but, provided that the combined Ohio and school district tax liability exceeds $300, they must remit quarterly estimated payments. The school district officials receive the largest number of complaints from both of these groups of individuals, because of the additional burden that compliance imposes on them.

When individual taxpayers received their school district income tax return and instructions for 1993, the eight-page booklet contained detailed instructions related to the filing of the tax. While calculation of the tax is relatively straightforward for individuals who remain a resident of one school district for the entire year, complexity is added when the taxpayer moves from one tax district to another within the calendar year. In those cases, the individual must file a separate income tax return for each of the two different school districts. The individual is allowed to claim his full personal exemption deduction on both forms, but must claim withholding based only on the district for which the withholding amount was reported.

The future of the school district income tax. Almost one-sixth of the school districts in the state have adopted a school district income tax. While the rush to adopt the tax appears to have waned, that situation could change if more school districts feel the squeeze from the lack of revenue growth during periods of rising costs and incomes. The main advantage seen by proponents of the tax is the built-in growth mechanism of the tax—as long as income grows and out-migration does not cause a significant decline in the taxpayer base. Additionally, the tax is viewed as having a less painful collection method for those individuals who have withholding done by the business for which they work. The primary disadvantages relate to the problems with compliance and administration of the tax. While property is relatively immobile, individuals are likely to move, which causes higher administrative costs for tracking their movements to ensure taxes are paid.

As previously mentioned, a new variation of local income taxation was added to the list of options available to municipalities and school districts. This variation allows the school districts and the municipal governments to levy a single combined tax and divide the tax collections between themselves to satisfy their funding needs. As this tax form could potentially replace two taxes (the existing school district and municipal taxes) with a single tax, there would be one less governmental body involved in the taxing process, one less set of regulations with which to be familiar, and one less set of forms to file. However, due to the existing structure of school districts, this hybrid form could not totally replace the school district income tax, because of the overlapping jurisdiction of municipalities within school districts and the multiplicity of school districts in some municipalities.

COMBINED EFFECTS OF STATE AND LOCAL INCOME TAXES

The combination of individual income taxes at the state, municipal, and school district levels puts Ohio's state and local government reliance on the income tax above the average for the nation. The data in Figure 5-2 show the individual income tax as a percent of total state and local government revenue for the comparison states and the United States As the data show, Kentucky is the only comparison state with a higher reliance on the tax. One reason for the relatively high tax burden is the imposition of local income taxes. The percentage increase in the tax burden is especially large for low-income groups, as the local income tax rates are the same for all filers.

An additional consideration for the individual income tax relates to the burden of compliance. It is obvious from the information presented above that the individual income tax compliance burden placed on individuals in Ohio can be very large. Some individuals must file up to five tax forms: federal, state, municipality of employment, municipality of residence, and school district. If someone moves between cities in a given year, the problem is even worse! Businesses must keep records of business activity among municipalities in the state, and apportion their income accordingly. The taxes

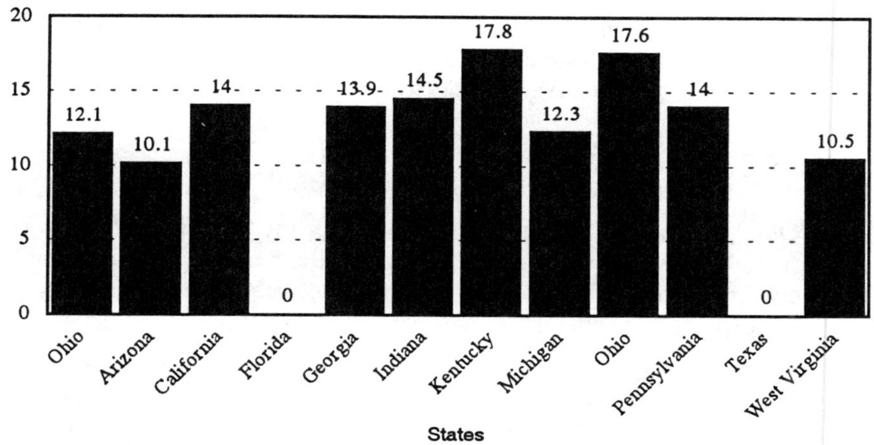

Source: ACIR, 1994.

FIGURE 5-2. State and local individual income taxes as a percent of total state and local revenues.

are administered by different agencies and the state, and the filing requirements vary among municipalities.

The combined tax and compliance burden of the state and local individual income tax structure in Ohio is relatively unique. However, as noted in the next section, these burdens may be a cause for concern in Ohio.

ISSUES AND CONCERNS

The results of the preceding sections point to four sets of issues for the individual income tax in Ohio: reliance on the tax, vertical equity, complexity of the overall system, and specific problems with the tax code. The choices that the Commission faces regarding the income tax are driven by these issues and the changes in Ohio's economy. Each of the major issues, concerns, and options can be summarized as follows.

Reliance on the Tax

Concerns:

1. The tax is elastic and it has also been found to be variable and responsive to downturns in the economy. A heavy reliance on the tax could cause instability in revenue flows through the business cycle.

2. The individual income tax base is heavily concentrated in wage and salary income, with smaller shares of the base coming from capital and retirement income. Wages tend to be cyclical, although less so than capital income.

Concerns as they relate to changes in Ohio's economy:

1. Ohio's economy itself is cyclical, although the growth in the service sector may slowly decrease the effects of the business cycle on Ohio's economy. In the near term, however, the effects of the business cycle are expected to remain strong.
2. The composition of personal income in Ohio is changing, as it is nationwide. The increase in the share of transfer income has been larger in Ohio than in the nation. This trend along with the increase in private pension income will decrease the elasticity of Ohio's income tax. At the same time, it will decrease the volatility of the tax base.

What could be done to alleviate the problems:

1. General diversification of the revenue structure to insulate it from the business cycle.
2. Expansion of the income tax base to stabilize elasticity.

Specific options:

1. Elimination of credits (senior citizen, retirement, personal exemption for all filers).
2. Elimination of income exclusions (Social Security, Railroad Retirement).
3. Inclusion of interest on state obligations.
4. Elimination of double dependent exemption for filers with unearned income.

VERTICAL EQUITY

Concerns:

1. Low-income individuals come into the tax net quickly.
2. The state's top marginal tax rate is high relative to neighboring states and the United States and the addition of municipal and school district income taxes increases this difference.

Concerns as they relate to changes in Ohio's economy:

1. Low income growth in Ohio implies a larger percentage of poor individuals coming into the tax system. This may increase the cost of administration for a group that adds little revenue to the system.
2. Ohio may be handicapped in attracting higher-income employees. Ohio's increased competition for new and expanding businesses includes the attraction of high-income individuals. Municipalities within Ohio may find themselves competing more against one another for high-income individuals as problems with the property tax as a revenue source grow.

What could be done to alleviate the problems:

1. Take the low-income individuals out of the tax net.
2. Reduce the total tax burden for high-income employees.

Specific options:

1. Create a zero-bracket amount, which would effectively make income less than some amount (say, $5,000) non-taxable, and eliminate the personal exemption credit.
2. Create a standard deduction amount based on filing status and eliminate the personal exemption credit.
3. Means-test the personal exemption deduction and/or credit.
4. Index the income tax system so that nominal income increases are not subject to higher tax rates.

Complexity of the Overall System

Concerns:

1. The three-tiered structure of income taxation imposes a heavy burden on taxpayer compliance and on state and local administration.
2. The individual income tax has become slightly more complicated with the addition of credits and brackets over time.

Concerns as they relate to changes in Ohio's economy:

1. The fiscal pressures faced by state and local governments, particularly with respect to the property tax, may necessitate heavier use of taxes such as the local income tax. Given the current complexity of the in-

come tax structure, taxpayers may be less willing to utilize the income tax more.

2. The aging of Ohio's population could increase the cost of the senior citizen and retirement credits.
3. The growth of new (particularly small) business may be influenced by the complexity of the local income tax in Ohio, since there is such diversity in tax structure and administration.

What could be done to alleviate the problems:

1. A general simplification of the system.
2. Reduce the credits for the state government income tax.
3. Move toward more conformity in the local income tax structure and administration.
4. Reduce the number of tax brackets.

Specific options:

1. Eliminate the personal exemption credit, the senior citizen credit, and the retirement credit, and replace with one means-tested credit.
2. Eliminate the jobs credit and export credit.
3. Couple the state income tax closer to the federal structure. Piggyback the local income taxes off of the state income tax (this could be done with or without state administration of either local tax).
4. Create a flat-rate tax structure.

Specific Problems with the Tax Code

Concerns:

1. Joint filers face a significant marriage penalty, but joint filers have also discovered the increased benefits of filing as singles.
2. Dependents are allowed to claim a personal exemption deduction whether or not their guardian claims them.
3. The use of both a dependent exemption and a dependent deduction.

Concerns as they relate to changes in Ohio's economy:

1. As joint filers discover the benefits of filing as singles, the income tax revenue is made more unstable at a time when stability is needed.

2. The double allowance of the dependent exemption further erodes the tax base at a time when revenue is needed.

What could be done to alleviate the problems:

1. Change the rules on filing status. While forcing couples to file jointly under the current rate structure is horizontally inequitable, such a move would stabilize the revenue from these individuals. Creating a new schedule which does not impose a marriage penalty may alleviate some of the horizontal inequity of the current structure.
2. Eliminate the ability of dependents to claim their own exemption when claimed by a guardian (this can be means-tested).

Specific options:

1. Create a married filing jointly tax structure.
2. Allow couples to file separately on a combined return.
3. Create a new schedule for married filing separately.
4. Eliminate the dependent exemption for dependent filers.

What Are the Options to Retain Revenue Neutrality?

Enactment of many of the options listed above would cause a change in individual income tax revenue. While it is typically easy to find a way to offset revenue gains from some of the options, it is much more difficult to find increased revenue from the income tax (or any tax). Additionally, revenue losses from changes in the structure of other taxes may need to be offset by increases in the individual income tax.

The following are some options for individual income tax revenue increases or reductions as offsets to other changes, some of which have been listed above. This list is by no means exhaustive, it simply represents some of the obvious choices:

Revenue increases:

1. Increasing the top statutory marginal tax rate.
2. Creating new tax brackets within some of the widest current brackets and applying new statutory marginal tax rates (especially the bracket for income between $100,000 and $200,000).
3. Elimination of any or all of the credits.
4. Elimination of the personal exemption.

5. Elimination of the current income exemptions.

Revenue reductions:

1. Creation of a standard deduction or a zero bracket amount.
2. Increase in the personal exemption amount.
3. Reduction in the top marginal tax rate.

What Have Other States Done?

A number of states have been grappling with issues similar to those faced by Ohio. In fact, as the information in Table 5-15 shows, states have made a number of adjustments in the structure of their state government income taxes over the seven years from 1986 to 1993. Since 1990, in the comparison

TABLE 5-15
Summary of Changes to the Individual Income Tax Structure Selected States: (1986–1993)

State	Year of Change	Description of Change	Estimated Effect (In Millions of Dollars)
Michigan	1986	Reduced tax.	$301 decrease for 1986; $445 decrease for 1987.
Pennsylvania	1986	Reduced tax.	$94 decrease for 1987.
Arizona	1987	Avoided "windfall" by providing a special deduction.	
California	1987	Revised personal income tax; lowered marginal rates.	
Georgia	1987	Avoided "windfall."	
Indiana	1987	Kept "windfall."	$50 increase for 1988.
Kentucky	1987	Kept part of "windfall."	$25 increase for 1988.
Ohio	1987	Increased tax revenue by raising taxes on part-year residents and repealing home improvement credit.	$21 increase for 1988.
Pennsylvania	1987	Increased tax relief for poor.	$11 decrease for 1988.
West Virginia	1987	Restructured tax and avoided "windfall."	
Arizona	1988	Increased tax by placing limit on deduction for federal tax payments and eliminating gas tax deduction.	$35 increase for 1989.

continued

TABLE 5-15 (continued)
Summary of Changes to the Individual Income Tax Structure Selected States: (1986–1993)

State	Year of Change	Description of Change	Estimated Effect (In Millions of Dollars)
Kentucky	1988	Authorized tax amnesty program.	
Michigan	1988	Reduced tax.	
Michigan	1989	Applied tax to lottery winnings.	$10 increase for 1990.
Ohio	1989	Revised personal exemptions and credits.	$10 increase for 1990.
West Virginia	1989	Revised tax treatment of state and federal pensions.	Less than a $1 increase for 1990.
Arizona	1990	Eliminated exemption for various contributions to pension funds (mainly public service funds); conformed to federal code.	$9.6 increase for 1992.
California	1990	Imposed temporary new top rate of 10% for taxable income in excess of $100,000 (single), $400,000 (joint). Increased alternative minimum tax rate from 7% to 8.5%. Extended sunset date for carry forward of NOL attributable to taxable years beginning after 1/97. Disallowed deductions of NOL for taxable years beginning 1991 and 1992. Conformed to federal code and limited certain itemized deductions for high-income taxpayers. Phased out personal and dependent exemption credits for high-income taxpayers. Limited temporarily eligibility for renters' credit to low-income taxpayers (repealed at end of 1995 tax year). Eliminated deduction for cosmetic surgery. Allowed exclusion up to $5,250 for employer-provided education assistance and extended for graduate courses. Extended provision allowing deduction of 25% of the cost of health insurance purchased by self-employed individuals. Reduced deduction from $15,000 to $35,000 for providing access to the disabled. Required withholding for personal income tax purposes at a flat rate of 6% for supplemental wages. Required quarterly estimated payments on income derived from estates and trusts.	$2,310 increase for 1992.

TABLE 5-15 (continued)
Summary of Changes to the Individual Income Tax Structure Selected States: (1986–1993)

State	Year of Change	Description of Change	Estimated Effect (In Millions of Dollars)
Georgia	1991	Enacted tax credit for low-income persons.	Effective for 1992; $30 decrease for 1993.
Ohio	1991	Modified certain provisions (e.g., reduced interest on NOL carrybacks). Accelerated withholding.	$17.9 increase for 1992.
Pennsylvania	1991	Increased rate from 2.1% to 2.8%; imposed temporary 0.3% surcharge from 7/91 through 6/30/92; increased basic poverty exemption from $6,300 to $7,000; increased dependent exemption to $2,000 for each dependent.	$1,359 increase for 1992.
Arizona	1992	Increased personal exemption from $2,000 to $2,100. Increased elderly exemption from $1,500 to $1,750. Reduced medical expenses deduction floor from 7.5% to 6.5%. Lowered estimated payment threshold from $100,000 to $70,000.	$6.2 decrease for 1993.
Georgia	1992	Modified treatment of capital gains on sale of personal residence.	$28 decrease for 1993.
Kentucky	1992	Conformed to federal tax treatment of high-income taxpayers.	$5.2 increase for 1993.
Pennsylvania	1992	Eliminated 0.3% surtax because of previously enacted legislation; rate drops from 3.1% to 2.8%. Restored special poverty exemption to previous status.	$422 decrease for 1993.
West Virginia	1992	Modified withholding for distributions to nonresidents by partnerships, S corporations, estates, trusts, etc.	$3 increase for 1993.
Arizona	1993	Increased personal exemption from $2,100 to $2,300. Increased elderly exemption from $1,750 to $2,100. Accelerated phaseout of limitation on medical expense deductions; for 1993, allowed deductions exceeding 4% of income (down from 5%), with full deduction phased in by 1995.	$10.6 decrease for 1994.
Georgia	1993	Conformed to federal IRC.	$1.5 decrease in 1994.
Ohio	1993	Added a new tax bracket of 7.5% for Ohio taxable income above $200,000; previous top rate was 6.9% (enacted in the 12/92 special session). Accelerated employer remittance of withholding to conform to federal requirements.	$16 decrease in 1993; $78.6 increase for 1994.
West Virginia	1993	Increased standard deduction for low-income taxpayers filing under federal head-of-household.	No effect for 1994; $4.9 decrease for 1995.

Sources: ACIR (1990-94) and Commerce Clearing House (1990-94).

states, the number of changes that have led to individual income tax revenue decreases is similar to the number that have increased revenues. Nationally, 12 states have made changes that have increased individual income taxes, while four have made changes that decrease revenues from the tax (Gold, 1993). The information presented in Table 5-16 shows that a few relatively minor adjustments have been passed by state legislatures in 1994.

TABLE 5-16
Current Developments—Income Tax Legislation in Selected States as of June, 1994

State	Description of Change	Status	Effective Date
Arizona	Reduced tax rates in all brackets; enacted additional modifications for 1993; re-defined Internal Revenue Code.	Approved	6-29-94 or prior year, as noted in Regulation.
	Provided filing requirement for gross income amount.	Approved	Tax years beginning after 12-31-93.
	Medical savings account provisions enacted.	Approved	6-29-94.
California	Constitutional amendment setting minimum amount of renter's credit.	Rejected	
	Disaster relief for Northridge earthquake victims and Southern California fire victims.	Approved	Tax years beginning on or after 1-1-94.
	Exclusion provided for cost-share payments received by forest landowners.	Approved	Tax years beginning on or after 1-1-94.
Georgia	Lottery prizes subject to withholding.	Approved	Tax years beginning on or after 1-1-94.
	Lottery prizes includable in taxable nonresident's net income.	Approved	3-29-94.
	Deductions for dependents and retirement income increased; exemption for withholding of wages for dependents raised.	Approved	7-1-94.
	"Periodic Payment" defined and withholding requirements amended.	Approved	Tax periods beginning on or after 1-1-94.
	References to Internal Revenue Code updated.	Approved	4-5-94.
Indiana	IRC provisions updated; research credit amended; riverboat building credit enacted.	Approved	Various dates.
Kentucky	Innocent spouse may qualify for relief from state income tax liability.	Approved	90 days after adjournment of session.
	Reference to Internal Revenue Code updated.	Approved	Tax years beginning after 12-31-93.
	Credits prioritized.	Approved	Tax years beginning after 12-31-93.
	Enacted Limited Liability Company Act.	Approved	7-15-94.
Michigan	Revised income tax rate (lowered rate because of increase in sales and use tax rate).	Approved	5-1-94.
Ohio	Limited Liability Company Act follows federal guidelines.	Approved	7-1-94.
West Virginia	Personal income tax terms conformed to federal tax meaning.	Approved	Tax years beginning after 12-31-92 to extent allowed by federal income tax law.

Source: Commerce Clearing House (1994).

Summary of Issues and Concerns

The set of concerns and options discussed above are very much interrelated. For example, if the main concern is to reduce the complexity of the tax system, this may be done in such a way that reduces vertical equity by imposing a flat tax rate or in a way that increases vertical equity by allowing a significant standard deduction in lieu of all credits. Each specific potential change to each suggest an effect on the equity, stability, and/or elasticity of the system, and the final section of this report examines the effects of some actual changes in the income tax structure on the equity, elasticity, and revenue yield of the income tax.

POLICY OPTIONS

This final section analyzes a sample of changes to the individual income tax. These examples are meant to illustrate some options that face the Commission. They address simplicity and horizontal and vertical equity, and each has elasticity and revenue implications as discussed (see Table 5-17). The options and their policy concentrations (in parenthesis) are as follows:

Option #1: increasing the dependent exemption to the federal level (equity);

Option #2: doubling the joint filer credit (equity);

Option #3: instituting a standard deduction equal to the federal standard deduction (equity, administration);

Option #4: creating a new 6.6 percent tax bracket for income of \$100,000-\$150,000, and 6.9 percent for \$150,000-\$200,000 (equity, elasticity);

Option #5: coupling of Ohio's tax base to federal adjusted gross income (compliance, administration);

Option #6: application of a flat-rate tax structure coupled with federal AGI as the tax base (compliance, administration, efficiency);

Option #7: indexing the tax brackets and personal exemption (equity, administration);

Option #8: coupling the local income taxes to the state income tax (compliance, administration);

Option #9: eliminating all credits (simplicity, compliance);

TABLE 5-17
Taxes Paid as Percentage of Federal Gross Income
Current Law, Options 1, 2, 3,
Fiscal Year 1991
(All Numbers in Thousands Except Percentages)

		Current Law-Taxes Paid		Option 1-Taxes Paid		Option 2-Taxes Paid		Option 3-Taxes Paid	
Original Federal AGI Class	Federal AGI	Amount	As Percent of Fed AGI	Amount	As Percent of Fed AGI	Amount	As Percent of Fed AGI	Amount	As Percent of Fed AGI
Under$ 5,000	1,549,561	1,246	0.1	2,485	0.2	1,246	0.1	9	0.0
$5,000 - 10000	4,488,794	16,244	0.4	15,669	0.3	16,194	0.4	2,242	0.0
10,000 - 15000	7,157,951	54,453	0.8	42,951	0.6	54,030	0.8	19,959	0.3
15,000 - 20,000	9,267,227	121,050	1.3	96,347	1.0	118,887	1.3	60,894	0.7
20,000 - 40,000	41,843,692	935,032	2.2	790,184	1.9	897,923	2.1	670,350	1.6
40,000 - 80,000	47,791,203	1,483,812	3.1	1,315,083	2.8	1,350,297	2.8	1,246,488	2.6
80,000 - 100,000	6,866,139	260,617	3.8	242,417	3.5	251,530	3.7	234,796	3.4
Over - 100000	28,737,861	1,339,756	4.7	1,308,436	4.6	1,318,115	4.6	1,296,411	4.5
TOTAL	147,697,427	4,212,212	2.9	3,813,572	2.6	4,008,221	2.7	3,531,149	2.4

continued

TABLE 5-17 (continued)
Taxes Paid as Percentage of Federal Gross Income
Current Law, Options 1, 2, 3,
Fiscal Year 1991
(All Numbers in Thousands Except Percentages)

Original Federal AGI Class	Federal AGI	Current Law-Taxes Paid		Option 4-Taxes Paid		Option 5-Taxes Paid		Option 6-Taxes Paid		Option 7-Taxes Paid	
		Amount	As Percent of Fed AGI	Amount	As Percent of Fed AGI	Amount	As Percent of Fed AGI	Amount	As Percent of Fed AGI	Amount	As Percent of Fed AGI
Under $5,000	1,549,561	1,246	0.1	1,246	0.1	1,259	0.1	45,172	2.9	1,217	0.1
5,000 - 10,000	4,488,794	16,244	0.4	16,244	0.4	16,547	0.4	129,333	2.9	15,689	0.3
10,000 - 15,000	7,157,951	54,453	0.8	54,454	0.8	55,323	0.8	277,020	2.9	116,604	0.7
15,000 - 20,000	9,267,227	121,050	1.3	121,050	1.3	123,299	1.3	277,020	3.0	116,604	1.3
20,000 - 40,000	41,843,692	935,032	2.2	935,032	2.2	956,663	2.3	1,171,623	2.8	915,009	2.2
40,000 - 80,000	47,791,203	1,483,812	3.1	1,483,813	3.1	1,501,474	3.1	1,338,153	2.8	1,463,830	3.1
80,000 - 100,000	6,866,139	260,617	3.8	260,612	3.8	269,559	3.9	210,545	3.1	257,784	3.8
Over - 100,000	28,737,861	1,339,756	4.7	1,315,376	4.6	1,404,121	4.9	870,757	3.03	1,331,022	4.6
TOTAL	147,697,427	4,212,212	2.9	4,187,823	2.8	4,328,244	2.9	4,253,714	2.9	4,146,151	2.8

Source: Authors.

Option #10: coupling the state income tax to federal taxable income (simplicity, compliance); and

Option #11: coupling the state income tax to federal tax liability (equity, simplicity, compliance).

To see the effects of changes in the current tax structure, the first seven policy options were simulated. The simulations are based on the Ohio Microsimulation Model.[55] A sample of 15,870 tax returns are used as the base data set for the simulation model.

Option #1: Increasing the dependent exemption of $650 to the federal level of $2,350 and eliminating the personal credit reduces individual income tax receipts by about 9 percent. There is a small increase in the tax burden of the lowest income group due to the loss of the credit. All other income groups see a reduction in their tax burdens. The size of the reduction in the tax burden increases as we move up to the $40,000-$80,000 income group, making for a less progressive tax structure. The natural growth of the structure under this alternative will not be greatly affected.

Option #2: Doubling the tax rate for the joint filer credit decreases individual income tax receipts by about 5 percent. Under this policy alternative, all taxpayers experience a reduction in tax liability. The reduction in the tax burden is the greatest for middle to upper income taxpayers. This change will actually increase the elasticity of the system *slightly,* as the marginal decrease in the graduated credit rate is larger when the tax rates are increased.

Option #3: Instituting the 1993 federal standard deduction decreases individual income tax receipts substantially—by approximately 16 percent. This change removes taxpayers in the lowest income bracket from the tax roll. Progressivity is increased over the present tax structure as all income groups, except the lowest, experience an increase in their tax burdens. This change will increase the elasticity of the system if the growth in income is such that more individuals come into the system at the new standard deduction level than at the current law threshold.

Option #4: Change the tax brackets to incorporate a new bracket: $100,000-$150,000 at 6.6 percent and $150,000-$200,000 at 6.9 percent. This change reduces the individual income tax receipts by .5 percent. All of the reduction in revenue comes from a reduction in the tax liability of the taxpayers in the top income bracket, resulting in a tax structure that is slightly less progressive than the present one. The tax structure will also be more elastic as a result of this change.

Option #5: Using the federal AGI as the tax base (no Ohio adjustments or deductions, but retain credits) increases the individual income tax receipts by about 2.7 percent. There is a slight increase in the tax paid by filers in all income groups, although the largest increases occur in the top income groups. This reflects a loss in the deduction for Ohio state and local bond interest and a reduction in the exemption of Social Security and Railroad Retirement income. This option leads to a slight increase in progressivity in the system, along with simplification of the system. In general, this change would increase revenue growth in particular due to the taxation of Social Security benefits.

Option #6: A revenue-neutral flat rate on Ohio AGI (no credits, etc.) would apply a 3 percent tax rate to all Ohio tax filers. The tax structure is certainly less progressive in this case, but it is a much simpler system. The elasticity of the system would decline under this option.

Option #7: A simple scheme would index the tax brackets and personal exemption amount for Ohio. As an example, we simulated the effect of a 3 percent inflation adjustment in the tax brackets and personal exemption. The effect of this adjustment is a rather small revenue loss (approximately 2 percent). The indexation reduces the burden primarily for lower-income individuals, but reduces elasticity.

Option #8: One option for local governments is to "piggyback" local taxes on the state tax structure. As an example, it is estimated that property tax revenues account for $4.7 billion of school district financing. An individual income tax rate of approximately 3.5 percent on Ohio taxable income would account for approximately $4.9 billion in additional revenue. The flat structure would be relatively *regressive,* however.

Option #9: The data in Table 5-18 summarize the revenue implications associated with eliminating certain credits and exemptions from the system. The figures are produced in the State of Ohio Tax Expenditures Budget. As seen there, the elimination of the three retirement-related credits and exemptions would increase revenue by $225 million in FY 94. The personal exemption credit alone accounts for more than half of the senior citizen-related credits.

Option #10: This option would require Ohio taxpayers to apply one tax rate to their federal taxable income. A rate of 4.75 percent would be revenue neutral. The effect of this option is to take a relatively large number of taxpayers off the tax roles due to the relatively high federal

TABLE 5-18
Revenue Effects of Elimination of Certain Credits and Income Exclusions

Credit or Exclusion	Revenue Effect FY 94
Social Security and Railroad Retirement	+$66.4 million
$20 Personal Exemption Credit	+$174.5 million
$50 Senior Citizen Credit	+$33.5 million
Joint Filer Credit	+$209.2 million
Retirement Income Credit	+$125.1 million

Source: Ohio Department of Taxation, (1992).

deductions and exemption amounts. However, applying a single rate to federal taxable income will lower the overall progressivity of the tax system.

Option #11: This option would require Ohio taxpayers to apply one tax rate to their federal tax liability. A rate of 23.2 percent would be revenue neutral. This option would effectively couple Ohio to the federal taxable income base and the federal marginal tax rate structure. As with option #10, this option would take a large number of taxpayers off the tax roles due to the larger exemptions and deductions allowed under this coupling option. The progressivity of the system would also be enhanced due to the progressive federal rates. The current federal marginal rates are 15, 28, 31, 36, and 39.6 percent. Under this option, the top Ohio marginal tax rate would be 10.098 percent—which is relatively high. The commission also considered this coupling option with a 27.5 percent tax rate which would raise revenue by approximately $850 million in 1993. This revenue enhancing option would create a new top rate of 10.89 percent.

These policy options are meant as examples of types of changes for consideration by the Commission. There are many other specific options, but the options should be designed with a specific purpose in mind. The three main issues for the Commission to respond to regarding the Ohio individual income tax structure are (1) the reliance on a cyclical tax which may be stabilizing, but also declining in elasticity; (2) the vertical equity of the system: since the current statutory marginal tax rate is relatively high, there is not much room for an increase, while individuals get into the tax net quickly; and (3) the overall compliance and administration burdens of a three-tiered tax structure.

The commission recommended the option of coupling the state income tax to federal tax liability, using a flat rate of 27.5 percent. This recommendation would do four things: (1) simplify the current individual income tax structure, (2) increase the progressivity of the current structure and (3) decrease the number of Ohio state income tax filers, and (4) increase revenue by approximately $850 million in 1993.

CONCLUSION

The Commission concluded that the current structure of the Ohio state individual income tax is overly complicated with nine rate brackets and four credits and brings too many low income people into the tax net. The Commission's recommendation to couple directly to federal tax liability would simplify the structure of the income tax as taxpayers would use calculations from their federal tax returns to compute Ohio tax liability. The recommendation would also remove a significant number of taxpayers (approximately 300,000 returns) from the tax rolls, reducing administrative costs and compliance costs for low income individuals. Finally, the recommendation retains the progressivity of the state income tax, and actually increases the top marginal tax rates under the option to increase income tax revenue by $850 million for 1993. This option will also reduce the volatility of the income tax revenue due in large part to the indexation that is implied by coupling to federal tax liability.

By itself, the Commission's recommendation for the income tax fits in well with their priorities of vertical equity and stability. There was concern regarding the economic development aspects of the high top marginal tax rates. As noted in this chapter, high marginal tax rates may discourage individuals from living in the state. However, significant increases in the marginal tax rates are greatest for only the very high income individuals, of whom there are relatively few. Also, the overall set of recommendations is aimed at reducing the cost of doing business in Ohio, so the impact of the income tax recommendation should be considered along with those other recommendations.

This individual income tax recommendation could be considered radical, especially when compared with the changes that other states have adopted over the last decade. While it makes the Ohio income tax cleaner, neater, and easier to comply with, it makes Ohio vulnerable to the changes that the United States Congress makes to the federal income tax. Given the current mood of Washington, these changes at the federal level could be very significant, and would impact Ohio directly due to this coupling option. This loss in autonomy over the tax structure should be carefully weighed against the benefits of reducing complexity of the tax structure. At the same time, this proposal reduces the State Legislature's ability to "tinker" with the Ohio state income tax code—which some individuals, businesses, and policy makers would consider a positive change.

The Ohio Legislature did not adopt this income tax reform option in the 1994-95 legislative session, but tax reform does not frequently occur very quickly. The process of reforming a major revenue source like the individual income tax is difficult. Debate over this proposal needs to consider both the positive and negative aspects of coupling to the federal structure. The time may not be right to trust that Washington itself will make informed, well thought out decisions regarding tax policy. The radical reform proposals being discussed in Washington have significant ramifications for a state that is closely coupled to the federal income tax. However, the recommendation of the Commission has raised the prospect of simplifying the individual income tax structure in Ohio, and it can therefore serve as a starting point for future tax reform debate in Ohio.

ENDNOTES

1. According to the Advisory Commission on Intergovernmental Relations and Commerce Clearing House, local income taxes are imposed by cities, counties, and/or school districts in eleven states, and employer payroll taxes are imposed in three states. Arkansas and Georgia also have provisions for the use of local income taxes, but neither state currently imposes the tax.
2. These figures include individual income and business income taxes.
3. Connecticut adopted an income tax on capital in 1969, and in 1991 the state expanded the income tax to wages and salaries (ACIR, 1994).
4. Tennessee and New Hampshire impose a tax on dividends and interest only; Alaska, Florida, Nevada, South Dakota, Texas, Washington, and Wyoming do not impose a state individual income tax. Alaska repealed its state income tax in 1979 (ACIR, 1994).
5The roots of this concept date back to the sixteenth century, as pointed out in Musgrave (1959).
6. This is referred to as the Haig-Simons definition of comprehensive income (Simons, 1938). Alternate definitions have been discussed by other authors; see for example Goode (1977). The term "ability" was translated as "property" in colonial America (Musgrave, 1959). It may be taken literally as income *potential* versus actual income.
7. For a classic discussion of these issues see Musgrave(1959).
8. In 1992, 27.5 percent of Ohio taxpayers claimed itemized deductions on their federal returns. These filers claimed over $6 billion in Ohio state and local taxes paid (Internal Revenue Service, 1994). At an average federal marginal tax rate of 25% for itemizers, approximately $1.5 billion in Ohio state and local taxes was "shifted" to the federal government.
9. Mills (1921) stated that the just distribution of tax shares occurs when all individuals contribute to the common good so as to incur equal sacrifice. Musgrave (1959) presented a comprehensive history of thought on this theory.

10. Oates (1968) reiterated Musgrave's view of the redistributive policies of state and local governments.
11. When the smaller jurisdiction refers to a sub-state local government, not only a progressive income tax, but a non-zero local income tax can induce migration.
12. In 1993, Connecticut's personal exemption was $12,000, but the state did not allow a standard deduction (ACIR, 1994).
13. Feldstein (1976), among others, argued that horizontal equity should be measured in terms of welfare, or utility. Under this measurement, individuals with equal utilities before the imposition of a tax should have equal utilities after the imposition of a tax. Utility, as a definition of satisfaction or well-being of the taxpayers, is extremely difficult to measure and as such does not offer a practical solution to this problem.
14. An alternative interpretation is that society views children as a social benefit and, therefore, "rewards" the taxpayer who has children.
15. There are certainly other ways to simplify a state tax system (such as levying a flat rate on wage income, or all measurable income with no deductions, exemptions, etc.), but the coupling method has become popular among the states.
16. Because some differences between federal requirements and state requirements exist, full coupling is not possible. For example, the U.S. Constitution expressly forbids states from generating tax revenue on interest earned on U.S. obligations. As these amounts are taxable at the federal level, the taxpayers must adjust their taxable amounts to exclude these earnings from taxable income.
17. ACIR, (1994). Vermont allows an earned income tax credit that differs from that of the federal income tax, and also applies a 3 percent surcharge on tax liability between $3,400 and $13,100 and a 6 percent surcharge on liability over $13,100, which is reflected in the rate stated.
18. Due and Mikesell (1983) estimated that the average cost of sales tax administration was 0.73 percent of state sales tax revenue in 1979-81. As a comparison, anecdotal evidence suggests that the administration of the municipal income tax is 2 to 5 percent of municipal income tax revenue.
19. The states included: Alabama, Arkansas, Delaware, Georgia, Kentucky, Louisiana, Maryland, Mississippi North Carolina, Oklahoma, South Carolina, Tennessee, Virginia, and West Virginia.
20. Among the authors who analyzed the effects of fiscal variables on economic development are Bartik (1991), Wassmer (1992), and Wasylenko and McGuire (1985)
21. For a summary, see *The Economist* (1994).
22. Head taxes or poll taxes do not distort decisions because these taxes are imposed as a fixed amount on all individuals, regardless of income, consumption, age, investment, etc.
23. As mentioned earlier, a poll tax or head tax is very efficient, but since it is a set dollar tax per person, low-income individuals pay a much larger percentage of their income for the tax than do high-income individuals.
24. If the only source of Ohio income for residents of these states is wages, salaries, tips, and/or commissions, that income is not subject to Ohio income tax.
25. According to Section 5747.08 of the Revised Ohio Code.
26. Federally adjusted gross income is defined by the U.S. Internal Revenue Code as gross income (Section 61 of the Code) except for exempt income (Sections 101-135 of the Code), minus adjustments (Section 62 of the Code). Income includes: wages and salaries, other compensation, interest and dividend income, income from farms and sole proprietorships, royalties, alimony, annuities, partnership income, etc. Exempt income includes: some life insurance proceeds, some annuities, bequests, certain fringe benefits, etc. The adjustments to income include: individual re-

tirement income contribution (IRA), alimony payments, jury duty pay remitted to an employer, lump-sum distributions included in gross income, self-employed pension contribution, non-reimbursed moving expenses, etc.

27. The information regarding exemptions, deductions, brackets, rates, and credits has been taken from the Ohio Revised Code Sections 5747.01-5747.99 and the 1993 Ohio Income Tax Return and Instructions.

28. Business owners may be allowed additional credits for certain properties and energy systems (see Ohio Revised Code, Sections 5747.051-5747.053), as well as export sales and jobs credits.

29. This model is discussed in the Technical Appendix to Wallace and Edwards (1995). It was provided by the Ohio Department of Taxation, and modified and re-estimated by the Commission staff at the Policy Research Center. A comprehensive tax incidence model built by the Policy Research Center staff incorporates this income tax model as one component, with other components added for consumption, property, and capital taxes.

30. As a comparison, William Fox (1994) estimated the sales tax elasticity in Ohio to be .97, and Feenberg and Rosen's 1983 estimate of the sales tax elasticity was less than one. Both of these estimates show that the sales tax elasticity is significantly lower than that of the individual income tax.

31. See McHugh (1994) for more information.

32. For example, Georgia recently passed legislation that will raise the total retirement income exclusion to $14,000.

33. 1993 *U.S. Statistical Abstract*, tables 592 and 595.

34. For low-income filers, Ohio's exemption/credit system and West Virginia's standard deduction/credit system yield very similar net tax liabilities.

35. The three other states are Massachusetts, Illinois, and Connecticut (ACIR, 1994).

36. Aside from the states with no individual income tax and Delaware's zero bracket structure, Iowa's first bracket tax rate is the lowest (.5 percent). Montana has the highest top marginal tax rate, 11 percent for income over $100,000 (ACIR, 1994).

37. Sunley and Walz (1984) presented a summary of this issue.

38. National Conference of State Legislatures (1994).

39. While residence-based income taxes may be useful as a benefit tax for some services, they are *not* the answer to the school financing issue. High-income areas tend to have large residential property tax bases. In many cases, switching from property taxes to income taxes does not equalize school expenditures among school districts. In fact, Sobul (1993) showed that the variation in total income among school districts is only slightly lower than the variation in total property value (.46 for income versus .53 for property). He concluded that statewide use of a school district income tax would not make school financing any more fair than under the current system.

40. For some services, the valuation of the service may be a constant percentage of income. For example, basic sanitation services may be worth the same percentage of income for wealthy people as they are for less well-off individuals.

41. New York City is among the cities using a progressive local income tax.

42. Chapter 718, "Ohio Revised Code."

43. Article XIII, Section 6 permits the General Assembly to provide for the organization of cities and incorporated villages and *"restrict their power of taxation...so as to prevent the abuse of power."* Article XVIII, Section 13 specifies that *"laws may be passed to limit the power of municipalities to levy taxes..."* Article XVIII, Section 3 grants municipalities the authority *"to exercise all powers of local self-government and to adopt and enforce..., as re not in conflict with general laws*

44. Reference: 153 Ohio State 179.

45. Chapter 718, Municipal Income Taxes, Ohio Revised Code.
46. Ohio Revised Code, Section 5747.02, Am. Sub. H.B. 475.
47. 45 Ohio App. 2d 176, 341 N.E. 2d 611.
48. A comparison between Indianapolis and Cincinnati is also justified because Indianapolis is approximately the same distance from Cincinnati as the two Kentucky cities used for the comparison. However, as Indianapolis is compared with Dayton, that comparison is not shown explicitly in the table.
49. Due to the large number of local income taxes levied and their complexity, no clear indication of the number of school districts levying an income tax in the state of Pennsylvania is available.
50. Ohio Revised Code, Chapter 5748.
51. As noted earlier in the section regarding municipal income taxes, a new hybrid form of municipal taxation was approved by the legislature in 1993. Under this legislation, a school district and the municipality of which it is a part can propose to the voters an income tax, the proceeds of which they will share on a predetermined basis. The first test of voter acceptance of this new form of taxation occurred in November, 1994 when two municipalities place the issue on their ballots.
52. Based on interviews with Mr. Staller, Wellington Exempted Village School District, Mr. Davis, Oberlin City School District, and the Ohio Department of Taxation.
53. The fee was recently reduced from 3% of tax collections within a school district to 2.5% of collections.
54. This simulation model is discussed in detail in the Technical Appendix to Wallace and Edwards (1995). The model was developed by the Tax Analysis and Local Government Distributions Division of the Ohio Department of Taxation and re-estimated by the staff of the Policy Research Center.

6 The Estate Tax

Richard McHugh

OVERVIEW

The Ohio Estate Tax is a levy on the taxable value of the estates of Ohio residents. The tax is also placed on that portion of a nonresident decedent's estate which is attributable to Ohio (i.e., real and tangible personal property having situs in Ohio and intangible property used in business in Ohio).

The revenues from the estate tax are divided between the state and the municipal corporation or township in which the tax originates. Sixty-four percent of the revenues go to the local governments with the remainder going to the state General Fund. In calendar year 1992, the estate tax raised a total of $220 million. In terms of contributions from all state and local revenue sources, it is the ninth most important tax in the state, raising approximately the same amount as the Cigarette Excise Tax.

TRENDS IN ESTATE TAX COLLECTIONS

Total estate tax collections in Ohio over the most recent eleven years are reported in Table 6-1. As can be seen, the revenues from this source are very volatile, increasing by more than 10 percent in four of these eleven years and decreasing in another three years. Given this volatility, analysis of a consis-

TABLE 6-1
Estate Tax Collections in Ohio: 1983–1993

Year	Total Estates	Gross Estate ($000)	Taxable Estate ($000)	Tax Collections ($000)	Percentage Change In Collections (%)	Effective Rate (%)
1983	25,416	3,718,748	2,493,658	99,587		4.0
1984	22,041	3,608,671	2,532,913	102,257	2.7	4.0
1985	19,528	3,776,676	2,773,659	106,377	4.0	3.8
1986	18,490	3,493,083	2,642,965	95,972	-9.8	3.6
1987	20,663	4,169,655	3,186,795	119,809	24.8	3.8
1988	20,342	4,471,889	3,455,245	135,009	12.7	3.9
1989	20,954	4,908,091	3,771,512	151,596	12.3	4.0
1990	20,630	4,783,013	3,662,907	143,680	- 5.2	3.9
1991	20,249	4,908,668	3,779,527	150,382	4.7	4.0
1992	21,781	5,421,848	4,270,108	175,130	16.5	4.1
1993	23,015	5,688,761	4,371,392	174,922	-0.1	4.0

tent trend is difficult. Changes in revenues from any one point in time to any other will be sensitive to the choice of the base year. In general, however, the revenues from this source have grown at a rate which exceeds the rate of increase in total state and local revenues and the rate of increase in personal income over this period of time.

The overall strength of this tax as a source of revenue is illustrated in Table 6-2. In terms of the growth in the numbers of taxable estates, one source of the growth in revenues, it is difficult to easily characterize the trend. This is, in part, a result of the difficulties one has when a base year for analysis must be chosen. Looking first at the longer 1983 to 1993 period, we see that the growth was slow relative to population growth. This is attributable to a very high number of taxable estates in 1983 (see Table 6-1). Over the shorter 1986 to 1993 period, a period during which the number of taxable estates grew more steadily, estates grew very rapidly, increasing 24.5 percent. Over those same years the total population in Ohio increased just 2.7 percent.

In terms of total estate tax revenue, the growth was higher than the rate of growth in personal income in both periods. In the longer 1983 to 1993 period, estate tax revenue grew 75.6 percent while personal income grew 68.4 percent. In the shorter, more "stable" period, from 1986 to 1992, the growth

TABLE 6-2
Growth in Ohio Estates, Estate Taxes, Personal Income and Population

Growth Population	Growth in Estates
2.6% (1983-1992)	-9.4% (1983-1992)
2.7% (1986-1992)	24.5% (1986-1992)
Growth in Personal Income	**Growth in Estate Tax Revenue**
68.4% (1983-1992)	75.6% (1983-1992)
38.3% (1986-1992)	82.3% (1986-1992)

in estate tax revenue far exceeded the growth in personal income (82.3 percent versus 38.3 percent).

In this more recent period, the growth in estate tax revenue is attributable to three factors: the growth in the number of estates, the growth in the average value of an estate and the growth in the average tax rate applicable to the estate. As indicated, the growth in total taxable estates was very high over this period. At the same time, the average value of a taxable estate grew a bit more rapidly than per capita personal income, from $143,000 in 1986 to $190,000 in 1993, a 37.1 percent increase over those years. Per capita personal income grew by 34.7 percent over those years.

The last component of growth is the growth in the average effective tax rate on taxable estates. While the average rate applicable to estates was 3.6 percent in 1986, it grew to over 4.0 percent in 1993, a greater than 10 percent growth in the effective tax rate. This growth in the effective rate is attributable to the growth in the average taxable estate value in conjunction with the progressive nature of the estate tax rates.

STRUCTURE OF THE TAX

Among the fifty states, there are two general types of death taxes: Inheritance taxes and Estate taxes. The Inheritance Tax is a progressive tax on the receipts (inheritance) from an estate. The rates are structured so that those who are more closely related to the deceased (brothers, spouses, etc.) pay lower rates than those more distantly related (e.g. cousins) or those not related at all (e.g., friends). An estate tax, on the other hand, is levied upon the taxable value of the estate *before* distribution. Like the inheritance tax, the rates imposed are also progressive.

Thirty-five states impose the estate-type death taxes. Ohio is one of these states. In Ohio, the rate structure is:

Taxable Estate of:	**Tax Rate Imposed:**
Not Over $40,000	2% of Taxable Estate
$40,000 to $100,000	$800 plus 3% of excess over $40,000
$100,000 to $200,000	$2,600 plus 4% of excess over $100,000
$200,000 to $300,000	$6,600 plus 5% of excess over $200,000
$300,000 to $500,000	$11,000 plus 6% of excess over $300,000
Over $500,000	$23,600 plus 7% of excess over $500,000

Ohio allows a credit of $500 for each estate, effectively exempting the first $25,000 of the estate from taxation. These rates have not changed in over twenty years.

In addition to the taxes computed using these statutory rates, Ohio, like most states, imposes an additional tax on estates. This additional tax is directly related to the tax liabilities computed under the Federal Estate Tax. The Federal Estate Tax is also a progressive levy on the value of the taxable estate.[1] Under the Federal Estate Tax, each return is allowed a credit for state estate taxes paid up to a maximum credit set by Federal statute. Since Federal liabilities are reduced by the state credit dollar for dollar by higher state estate taxes up to the limit, the state can impose additional taxes up to the maximum credit without "costing" the estate any additional total taxes (federal plus state). The credit effectively allows each state to take a pre-specified amount of Federal liability for its own use. This additional tax, the difference between the calculated state tax (based upon the state-specific rate structure) and the maximum allowable Federal credit for state estate taxes) is called the "pick-up" tax. It is called this since it allows the state to "pick up" the difference between the tax computed based upon the state's marginal rates and the maximum credit. All states avail themselves of this option. In fact, most states impose only a tax equal to the maximum credit (the "pick-up" tax) only and do not bother to specify a separate rate structure.

To illustrate the calculation of the pick-up tax, a $5 million estate might owe state estate taxes of $500,000 (calculated on the basis of the state specific rates) and $2 million in Federal estate taxes, with a maximum state tax credit of $800,000. If the state imposes additional taxes up to the $800,000 credit (a $300,000 pick-up tax), federal net-of-credit revenues would fall by the same amount as state revenues increase and total taxes paid would not change. Notice that with or without the $300,000 "pick-up" tax, total estate taxes paid on the estate will equal $2.5 million.

The rationale for the Federal Government's establishment of the generous tax credit for state estate taxes was to allow states to gain revenue from these estate taxes without leading to inducements for individuals to relocate upon retirement or in anticipation of death. That is, the Federal Government wanted to avoid a "bidding war" for wealthy retirees. Since most states would impose the same effective tax—that equal to the maximum federal credit for state taxes paid—there would be minimal estate tax-induced reason to relocate.

Of the 35 states which impose a graduated state estate tax, 28 levy only a pick-up tax (that is, the state tax is simply defined to equal the maximum allowable credit. Seven states define their own, independent tax structure which may impose a tax higher than the maximum allowable credit. Ohio is one of seven states which imposes this additional tax.

Of these seven states, two of the extra levies are small local government excises. Michigan imposes a 0.5 percent levy on the estate for county governments in Michigan. Virginia allows local governments to impose a tax equal to one-third of the amount of the state's tax on the probate of the wills. The other states levying the independent state estate tax are: Massachusetts, Mississippi, New York, Oklahoma and Rhode Island.

The average tax rate on estates in Ohio and the other states levying this separate tax at the state level are shown in Table 6-3. This table also shows the average effective estate tax rate based upon the "pick-up" tax alone in the second column. The true Ohio tax rate (regular tax plus pick-up tax) would equal the rate shown in the Ohio column so long as the rate is above the pick-up tax rate and would equal the pick-up tax rate when the Ohio rate is below that rate (these latter cases are shown as the bolded entries in column 2). The taxes imposed under the Ohio estate tax are the lowest among that group of states imposing the extra levy.

The Ohio tax raises additional revenue (that is, tax rates are above the maximum Federal credit) for estates less than $3,600,000. Above this level, however, the rate structure does not impose any additional burden. That is, in these ranges, total taxes paid in Ohio are the same as in all states imposing the simple "pick-up" tax (including popular retirement destination states such as Arizona and Florida).

The Ohio Department of Taxation estimates that the revenues generated by the independent Ohio rate structure, affecting those estates below $3.6 million, are approximately $100 million per year. In other words, were the state to eliminate its independent rate structure, as 28 states have done, it would lose $100 million per year. This large revenue loss will occur since the vast majority of estates are below the taxable estate level at which the pick-up tax becomes effective (i.e., the independent state rate is above the maximum Federal Estate Tax credit). As shown is Table 6-4, 98.3 percent of estates have taxable value below $1 million.

TABLE 6-3
Effective Tax Rates on Taxable Estates:
States with Estate *and* "Pick-up" Tax

	Effective Tax Rate (%)					
Gross Estate Value	U.S. "Pick-up"	Ohio	Massachusetts	Mississippi	New York	Oklahoma
$500,000	2.7	5.0	9.5	3.0	4.3	4.9
$1,000,000	3.7	5.8	10.7	3.9	5.4	5.9
$2,000,000	5.2	6.4	12.4	5.3	7.4	6.9
$3,000,000	6.2	6.6	13.2	6.4	8.7	7.3
$4,000,000	**7.2**	6.7	13.7	7.3	9.8	7.6
$5,000,000	**8.0**	6.8	14.1	8.1	10.8	7.8
$6,000,000	**8.6**	6.8	14.5	8.7	11.7	8.0
$7,000,000	**9.2**	6.8	14.7	9.3	12.4	8.1
$8,000,000	**9.8**	6.9	14.8	9.8	13.4	8.2
$9,000,000	**10.3**	6.9	15.0	10.3	13.8	8.3
$10,000,000	**10.8**	6.9	15.1	10.8	14.4	8.3

TABLE 6-4
Distribution of Taxable Estates: 1993

Net Taxable Value	Number of Estates	Cumulative Returns	Average Net Gross Value	Average Taxable Value
Under $40,000	3,272	14.2%	$55,488	$153
$40,000 to $100,000	8,182	49.8	93,627	1,089
$100,000 to $200,000	5,779	74.9	175,194	3,776
$200,000 to $300,000	2,237	84.6	288,109	8,188
$300,000 to $500,000	1,884	92.8	470,414	16,179
$500,000 to $1,000,000	1,279	98.3	838,395	33,722
Over $1,000,000	382	100.0	2,946,678	135;492
	23, 015	---	---	---

THE ALLOCATIVE IMPACTS OF THE STATE ESTATE TAX

There are two potential economic impacts from the estate tax. Economists argue, first, that higher estate taxes act as a disincentive to save. Since the estate tax will take a share of a households accumulated wealth (which has been accumulated as a result of a household's decision not to spend all that they have earned), the tax provides an incentive to spend from the estate. Second, the statewide estate tax, to the extent it varies across jurisdiction, introduces an incentive for households to "shop" for a place of retirement, and move to a tax favored destination.

Regarding the first point, it may be true that the estate tax introduces a disincentive to save. However, this disincentive is attributable almost exclusively to the tax's existence at the Federal level. The Federal estate (or, actually, "transfer" tax, since the Federal tax now combines the estate tax with the old gift tax) sets the general level of such taxation from which the states merely diverge to a greater or lesser degree. This differential, as can be seen, is usually quite small relative to the general level set by the Federal government and these differentials will not cause significant changes in consumption and savings behavior of households.

What the state estate taxes *can* induce is an incentive to choose tax-favored retirement homes. This happens only at those levels of estates and among those states for which there is a rate structure separate from the maximum credit. Looking back at Table 6-3, and keeping in mind that the effective rate of estate taxation in most states is equal to the United States column (defined to equal the maximum credit, or the "pick-up" tax), it is clear that for states like Massachusetts and New York, the incentive to move can be strong. However, for Ohio, this incentive exists only for estate levels below about $3.6 million dollars.

The amounts of the differential tax at various estate levels are shown in Table 6-5. Clearly, the differences are very small relative to the size of the estates. However, this differential affects the vast majority of estate tax returns and may in the aggregate, affect retiree behavior, an issue addressed here.

POLICY OPTION

The state of Ohio has one significant policy option regarding the estate tax, specifically whether it should eliminate the separate tax on estates which it imposes and use only the pick-up tax, as in most other states. Eliminating the tax would remove the incentive for households with estates in the range below $3.6 million to make tax-based decisions to move.

There have been no direct empirical tests of the proposition that estate taxes have been a major factor in driving Ohioans out-of-state upon retirement. However, there is information available from the Department of Taxation's income tax files which might shed some light on this issue. Information on the income tax returns of part-year residents can reveal the income of persons who have moved into or out of the state during any tax year. The Ohio Department of Taxation provided these tabulations for 1991 and 1992. They are shown in Tables 6-6 and 6-7.

Looking specifically at the older taxpayers in 1991 (those above the age of 65), it can be seen that the number of persons moving out of the state exceeded the number moving in, by a very small margin (3,186 moving out versus 3,162 moving in). In the following year, more elderly people moved in than moved out (2,659 moving in versus 2,622 moving out).

TABLE 6-5
Additional Estate Tax from the Ohio State Structure

Gross Estate Value	Extra Tax from Ohio Structure
$1,000,000	$22,040
2,000,000	24,680
3,000,000	11,320
4,000,000 and up	0

TABLE 6-6
1991 Part Year Residents by Income and Migration Pattern

Income	Migration	All Taxpayers	Taxpayers Avg. Income	Older Taxpayers	Taxpayers Avg. Income
Under $5,000	Moved In Moved Out	3,542 2,713	$3,076 3,005	66 63	$3,257 3,518
$5,000 to $10,000	Moved In Moved Out	6,052 4,665	7,508 7,572	284 214	7,733 7,674
$10,000 to $15,000	Moved In Moved Out	5,537 4,838	12,441 12,481	401 339	12,497 12,665
$15,000 to $20,000	Moved In Moved Out	4,551 4,173	17,420 17,430	377 372	17,525 17,497
$20,000 to $40,000	Moved In Moved Out	10,909 11,014	28,925 29,161	1,029 977	28,776 28,723
$40,000 to $80,000	Moved In Moved Out	9,166 9,733	55,923 55,908	691 816	55,399 55,244
$80,000 to $100,000	Moved In Moved Out	1,836 1,880	89,059 89,224	127 135	89,059 88,702
$100,000 to $200,000	Moved In Moved Out	2,646 2,531	132,350 130,735	142 199	132,911 132,759
$200,000 to $500,000	Moved In Moved Out	505 505	279,414 284,799	36 50	293,866 308,169
Over $500,000	Moved In Moved Out	72 130	1,066,986 1,414,152	9 21	586,297 1,687,760
Total	Moved In Moved Out	44,816 42,182	39,367 44,290	3,162 3,186	40,468 54,944

Notes: Represents 86,998 part year filers out of 95,410. The others had errors in their returns and are not in our working files.

Older taxpayers identified by value in credits equal to allowable amounts for the Senior Citizen Credit, the Retirement Income Credit or both.

At higher income levels (defined as those making $100,000 or more per year), those most likely to have been affected by the estate tax, there is an excess of those moving out than those moving in. In 1991, 270 taxpayers whose head of household was 65 years old or older and who made $100,000 per year moved out of the state, with only 187 households with similar demographics moving in, a difference of 83 households. In 1992, 213 of these households moved out versus 164 moving in, a difference of 49 households. If we redefine our measure of "at risk" households as high earning elderly households to include those making $80,000 per year or more, the differ-

TABLE 6-7
1992 Part Year Residents by Income and Migration Pattern

Income	Migration	All Taxpayers	Taxpayers Avg. Income	Older Taxpayers	Taxpayers Avg. Income
Under $5,000	Moved In Moved Out	4,243 2,875	$2,870 2,846	75 66	$3,357 3,329
$5,000 to $10,000	Moved In Moved Out	5,827 4,441	7,539 7,564	246 207	7,944 7,774
$10,000 to $15,000	Moved In Moved Out	5,057 4,282	12,417 12,431	354 261	12,531 12,434
$15,000 to $20,000	Moved In Moved Out	4,046 3,783	17,416 17,394	313 304	17,594 17,532
$20,000 to $40,000	Moved In Moved Out	10,152 9,812	28,924 29,015	813 769	28,576 28,994
$40,000 to $80,000	Moved In Moved Out	7,779 8,007	55,914 55,673	599 688	55,822 55,602
$80,000 to $100,000	Moved In Moved Out	1,620 1,473	89,086 88,963	95 114	88,515 88,851
$100,000 to $200,000	Moved In Moved Out	2,198 1,819	132,257 131,168	126 152	133,872 131,288
$200,000 to $500,000	Moved In Moved Out	392 399	277,312 283,921	36 52	285,717 279,667
Over $500,000	Moved In Moved Out	58 65	792,846 981,755	2 9	814,389 744,674
Total	Moved In Moved Out	41,372 36,956	36,442 38,911	2,659 2,622	39,868 46,638

Notes: Represents 78,328 part year filers out of 98,030. The others had errors in their returns and are not in our working files.

ences between those moving out versus those moving in grows to 91 households in 1991 and 68 households in 1992.

Clearly, there are a very small number of households who might be considered "at risk" of being induced to leave the state for pure estate tax reasons. Suppose we were to assume that the entire difference in the number moving out versus moving in was the result of the estate tax differential and that these individuals could be induced to stay in Ohio simply by eliminating the differentially higher estate tax? Could the state hope to recover the $100 million it raises from the rate reductions?

To illustrate the quantitative issue, for the state to make up for the loss in revenues of $100 million from the estate tax rate reductions and the presumed retention of 49 households in 1992, each household would need to generate approximately an additional $2 million in tax revenues, through increased estate tax revenues, sales tax revenues, income tax revenues, etc. The average income levels of households in this range of income is approximately $225,000. For the state to benefit from this action, each household would need to generate, in state and local tax revenues alone, an amount equal to approximately nine times that amount of income! The numbers for 1991 are similar. Clearly, it would appear that there would be little to gain, in terms of revenue or increased economic activity, from such a policy move.

There are several caveats. First, this analysis assumes that the estates of elderly households moving into the state are equal to that of those moving out. If the estates of those moving out of Ohio are, on average, larger than that of those moving in, then the impact of tilting the tax laws to induce the wealthier to move to (or stay in) Ohio, the returns could be greater. However, analysis of this option is not possible because of the absence of data.

Second, and related, we used information on the income level of those moving into and out of the state as a basis for the identification of the at risk group. The best information would be that on the values of the estates. While there is a positive correlation between annual income levels and total estates, it is a less than perfect fit. A household with low reportable income may have a substantial estate if the estate is held in non-taxable bonds or non income-earning assets, such as a residence.

CONCLUSION

The estate tax, although not typically thought of as one of the major sources of revenue to state and local governments, raises a significant amount in Ohio, approximately $200 million per year. Over the next few decades, as the baby boom generation ages, the importance of this revenue source will grow.

The state estate tax is unique in that it is the one tax for which the Federal Government has provided states with significant tax-raising capacity without introducing distortionary differences from state rates. This has been accomplished through the introduction of a generous tax credit on Federal Estate Tax returns for taxes raised at the state level.

While the majority of states use the maximum allowable credit as both a floor and ceiling for state estate taxes (through the use of the "pick-up" tax alone), Ohio is one of five states which impose an estate tax and which also employ a tax rate structure which could impose taxes above the maximum Federal credit. The Ohio extra tax raises approximately $100 million per year from this extra levy, primarily on estates valued at approximately $4.6 million or less. At higher estate values, the state tax rate is equivalent to the rate imposed in virtually all other states (with only Massachusetts and New York having higher rates on estates above $6 million).

ENDNOTES

1. The definition of taxable estate differs between the Federal Government and the State of Ohio. The Federal Government provides for an exemption for the first $600,000 of the estate ($1.2 million for a married couple). Ohio provides a credit of $500, the equivalent of a $25,000 exemption at the 2 percent initial tax rate. The definition of taxable estate also differs from that of the Federal Government in that the value of life insurance is not taxable in Ohio although taxable under the United States Tax Code.

7 Taxation of Real Property

David L. Sjoquist[1]

INTRODUCTION

Throughout the United States the property tax is an important source of revenue for local governments, comprising 63 percent of local government general revenue. It is the mainstay for schools; nationally 81 percent of locally raised revenue for schools comes from the property tax.[2] Because it generates such large revenues, and does so with a base which in the short run is generally immobile, the property tax has endured despite the criticisms leveled against it and its unpopularity among taxpayers. However, reliance on the property tax has declined in relative importance over several decades, although it has seen a resurgence since the early 1980s.

The property tax has changed substantially over the centuries.[3] Some of the major changes in the property tax over the pass several decades have been: to narrow the base by excluding more and more categories of property, e.g., intangibles, household personal property, inventories, and manufacturing equipment;[4] to impose controls on property tax rates and the growth of assessed values, such as was accomplished by Proposition 13 in California,[5] and; to provide state-funded property tax relief, such as is provided by property tax circuit breaker programs.

Recent changes, proposed or enacted, continue these trends. Recently proposed exemptions include low-income housing (Tennessee), surviving spouse of a disabled property owner (California), hospitals (Pennsylvania), nursing homes (New Jersey), and blueberry bushes (Georgia). One exception was Kansas, which considered making exemptions harder to obtain. A number of additional states have considered limiting the increase in the assessed value of property; for example, a proposal in Washington would limit the annual percentage increase in property taxes for certain retirees to the growth in social security payment. Recently, several states have considered general property tax reduction programs, many tying the reduction to school financing. These states include Michigan, Wisconsin, Idaho, South Carolina, Vermont, South Dakota, Minnesota, Iowa, Arizona, and Montana.

Proposals for the reform of the property tax are numerous and many, perhaps most, have been made repeatedly over an extensive period of time. Reeb and Tomson (1985) provide a history of property tax reform proposals from the mid-19th century to the present. They note that reform suggestions focus on improved assessment of property, issues of inequities, and considerations of what types of properties should be taxed. An earlier review of Ohio's real property tax and suggestions for reform can be found in the report of the 1967 Ohio Tax Study Commission.

The structure of the property tax differs from country to country and across states, sometimes rather substantially.[6] Almy (1973, p. 175) states it well:

> In the United States, "the" property tax is composed of fifty-one separate state-level property tax systems: each subject to numerous legal and extralegal local variations and each changing in some fashion over time—through constitutional revision, enactment of statutes and ordinances, changes in administrative procedures, court decisions and changes in the capabilities of tax administrators.

Thus, while there are similarities, each state's property tax system is unique.

There are, as with all taxes, advantages and disadvantages with the property tax.[7] One advantage is that the property tax provides a balance to the tax structure. There are three classes of taxes: those on the sources of income, e.g., the income tax; those on the use of income, e.g., sales tax; and those on wealth, e.g., the property tax. Income, consumption, and wealth are all measures of ability to pay.[8] To rely on just one type of tax would accentuate the undesirable behavioral responses to the incentives or disincentives inherent in that tax, e.g., the income tax's effect on work behavior. Thus, a balance between the three types of tax sources is desirable.

The property tax is thought to be well suited for local government. First, within small jurisdictions the ability of taxpayers to shift the location of income and purchases is high relative to property. Second, it is hard to hide property, at least real property, from taxing authorities, making that aspect of tax administration easier. Third, differential property tax rates between jurisdictions do not pose the administrative problem that would exist if all jurisdictions had different sales tax rates. Fourth, it is easier to adjust property tax rates at the margin than, say, sales tax rates, in response to shifts in economic conditions.

There are four principal difficulties with the property tax. First, it is not popular, as evidenced by the surveys conducted by the Advisory Commission on Intergovernmental Relations (ACIR). In 1993, 25.7 percent of the respondents to the ACIR survey said they thought that the property tax was the worse tax. Second, and related to the first, the tax is frequently considered unfair and inequitable. Because property tax liability depends upon the *estimated* value of one's property, large differences in property tax liability can exist between owners of property of equal value as a result of different estimates of value. Third, many individuals believe that the property tax is a regressive tax, i.e., one for which low-income households, especially the elderly, pay a larger amount relative to their income than do high-income households. This is an issue on which there is much disagreement, and which is discussed later. Finally, the property tax provides a strong disincentive toward investment in housing and business capital, and the inter-jurisdictional differences in tax rates within urban areas lead to distorted land-use patterns.

This chapter, however, focuses just on the taxation of real property in Ohio; the taxation of tangible personal property and public utility personal property are treated in separate chapters. The objectives of the chapter are to:

- evaluate the administration of the property tax, the features of the tax, and the behavior of the tax base and rates relative to the economy;
- offer options for improving the functioning of the real property tax in Ohio.

While the chapter does not provide a comparative analysis of property taxation in the United States, differences between Ohio and other states in the characteristics of the property tax are noted. A glossary of terms specific to Ohio's property tax is included as Appendix A.

PROPERTY TAXES IN OHIO: COMPARISONS AND TRENDS

This section presents data on how Ohio's reliance on the property tax compares with other states and how it has changed over time. Table 7-1 presents comparisons with ten other states and the United States average; changes over time are shown in Tables 7-2 and 7-3.

TABLE 7-1
Property Taxes in Ohio in Comparison with Other States: FY91

	Property Tax Per Capita	Property Tax Per $1000 Of Income	Property Tax As A Percent of Own Source Revenue	Property Tax As A Percent of Total Taxes	School District Percent Of Property Taxes
Ohio	$540.7	$30.4	20.8	29.2	67.2
Arizona	660.2	39.8	23.5	33.0	51.9
California	639.4	30.7	19.3	28.0	28.4
Florida	687.7	36.2	24.2	37.5	43.1
Georgia	506.4	29.0	19.3	28.2	51.2
Indiana	570.8	33.2	22.2	32.8	56.5
Kentucky	276.5	17.7	11.3	16.0	35.1
Michigan	892.7	47.9	29.7	42.4	67.1
Pennsylvania	561.9	29.1	21.7	29.8	64.5
Texas	679.4	39.4	26.7	38.7	57.9
West Virginia	272.6	19.0	11.3	16.7	68.1
United States	666.3	34.8	22.5	32.0	41.5

Source: U.S. Bureau of Census, *Government Finance: 1990-91*, Series GF/91-5. U.S. Government Printing Office, Washington, DC, 1993.

These tables are based on property tax revenues as reported by the Bureau of Census, *Government Finances* series; the latest year available being FY90-91.[9] These data include all forms of property taxes, including those on real property, tangible personal property, utility personal property, and intangibles. While the subject of this chapter is real property, national data breaking out the different sources of property tax revenue are not available. Thus, this section presents data that include all sources of property tax revenue.

COMPARISONS WITH OTHER STATES

Property taxes in Ohio in FY91 were $540.70 per capita and $30.40 per $1,000 of income. As may be seen in Table 7-1, Ohio's reliance on the property tax is below the national average, and is less than in 7 of the 10

TABLE 7-2
Property Taxes per Capita and per $1000 of Income in Ohio and the United States: FY69 to FY91

Year	Property Taxes Per Capita In Real Terms (1987 = 100)		Property Taxes Per $1000 Of Income	
	OHIO	U.S.	OHIO	U.S.
1969	$503	$515	$38.3	$40.0
1970	504	521	40.2	41.3
1971	502	532	40.6	42.6
1972	496	552	39.3	43.2
1973	470	544	36.2	41.5
1974	440	515	34.1	39.8
1975	422	499	34.0	39.5
1976	434	512	33.7	39.5
1977	451	518	33.8	39.2
1978	416	506	30.4	36.8
1979	401	448	28.9	32.1
1980	395	424	28.8	30.3
1981	383	446	27.8	29.7
1982	403	433	29.9	30.5
1983	417	448	30.6	31.2
1984	416	457	29.3	30.7
1985	401	467	27.9	30.8
1986	410	483	28.1	31.2
1987	414	500	28.3	31.99
1988	425	518	28.5	32.6
1989	442	532	29.0	32.6
1990	457	554	29.6	33.4
1991	465	573	30.4	34.8

Source: Bureau of Census, *Government Finances*, various years. U.S. Government Printing Office, Washington, DC.

TABLE 7-3
Property Taxes in Ohio as a Share of Other Revenue: FY69 to FY91

Year	Property Taxes As A Percent of State and Local Own Source Revenue	Property Taxes As A Percent of Total State and Local Taxes	Property Taxes For Schools As A Percent of Total Property Taxes[a]
1969	37.5	47.9	N.A.
1970	36.5	47.2	N.A.
1971	36.1	47.3	N.A.
1972	33.5	43.0	N.A.
1973	30.4	39.1	N.A.
1974	29.5	38.6	N.A.
1975	28.6	37.9	68.6
1976	28.6	38.2	68.3
1977	29.6	38.9	67.5
1978	26.8	35.2	66.9
1979	25.5	33.9	65.7
1980	25.5	34.7	64.8
1981	24.4	33.7	64.1
1982	24.3	33.7	64.7
1983	23.3	32.3	66.0
1984	21.6	29.8	65.9
1985	20.1	28.1	68.2
1986	20.1	27.9	67.8
1987	19.7	27.4	68.3
1988	20.4	28.1	68.2
1989	20.4	28.1	68.0
1990	20.7	28.4	67.8
1991	20.8	29.2	67.2

Source: Bureau of Census, *Government Finances*, various years. U.S. Government Printing Office, Washington, DC.

[a]Data or allocation of property taxes are not available annually before 1975.

property tax is below the national average, and is less than in 7 of the 10 comparison states on a per capita basis, and less than in 6 states on a per $1,000 of income basis.

These data predate the recently adopted changes in Michigan's school finance scheme. In Michigan, two-thirds of the property tax was used for school purposes; the recently adopted plan will cut the use of property taxes for school purposes in half.[10] Applying this change to 1991 taxes would have reduced property tax revenue in Michigan to $595 per capita and to around $31.20 per $1,000 of income, still above the level for Ohio.

About 20 percent of Ohio's (state and local) own source revenue is derived from property taxes, while about 29 percent of total (state and local) taxes are from property taxes. On both scores Ohio is below the national average and below 6 of the 10 comparison states. The data in Table 7-1 suggest that Ohio does not put an undue burden on the property tax as a source of revenue, relative to either other states or other sources of revenue.

In Ohio over two thirds of property tax revenue goes to support schools.[11] This is higher than all but one of the comparison states. There is nothing inherently wrong with this current arrangement in which schools rely on property taxes, counties rely mainly on the sales tax, and municipalities rely on the income tax. Some even believe it is a desirable division of tax bases.[12] However, to the extent that the property tax base grows more slowly than the sales and income tax bases,[13] and that there are restrictions or barriers on the use of the property tax in Ohio (e.g., the need to vote on outside millage and the tax reduction factor),[14] schools are in a more difficult position vis-a-vis other local governments in generating increased revenue. (The issues of the growth of the property tax base and the tax reduction factor are discussed below.) A fundamental issue that Ohio should address is whether it is desirable to have schools so heavily reliant on the property tax, particularly a tax whose use is so restricted.

Changes in Property Taxes Over Time

Beginning in 1970, property tax revenues per capita begin to fall, and from 1970 until 1981 per capita property taxes in *real* terms fell by 24 percent (Table 7-2). But since 1981, the trend has been upward, and by 1991 per capita property taxes in real terms reached the level of 1973.

Property tax revenues relative to income tracks that of property taxes per capita. In 1969 property taxes were 3.8 percent of income while in 1991 they were 3.0 percent although most of the decrease during the two decades occurred during the 1970s. Thus, over the two decades property taxes have not increased either in per capita terms, adjusted for inflation, or as a percent of income.

With the exception of the large increase in 1982 in Ohio, the changes in Ohio's property tax revenue match the pattern of change in the United States. Relative to the average for the United States, property taxes in Ohio are now lower than in 1969, although over the period property taxes in Ohio relative to the United States have varied substantially.

Figure 7-1 shows the change since 1970 in property tax charges by class of property, unadjusted for inflation, based on Ohio Department of Taxation data. These data are based on charges, i.e., tax liability after the tax reduction factor and rollbacks, and not actual revenue collected. The growth in total property tax revenue over the period is the result mainly of the growth in property taxes on real property; taxes on personal property did not change much over the period.

Property taxes as a share of own source revenue declined from 1969 until about 1987 but have increased slightly since that time (Table 7-3). This pattern matches the pattern of change nationally, although the decrease in relative reliance on property taxes in Ohio has been substantially greater than

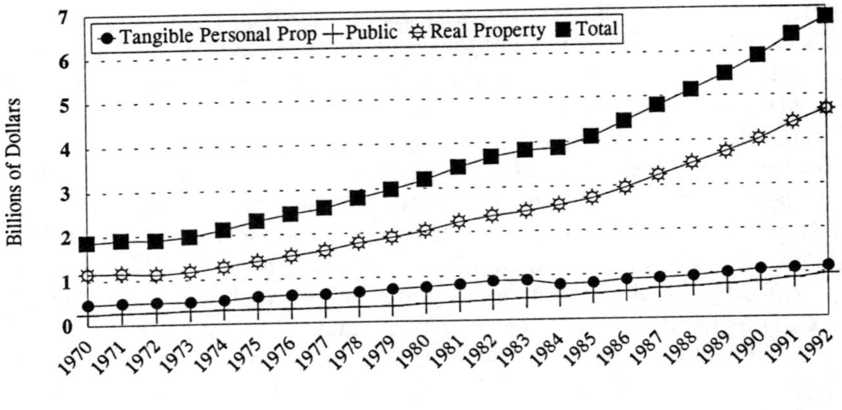

Source: Ohio Department of Taxation

FIGURE 7-1. Actual property tax charged by class of property, tax years 1970—1992.

for the United States A similar pattern exists for property taxes as a share of total taxes. School districts share of property tax decreased between 1975 and 1982, followed in 1982 by an increase.[15]

Finally, Table 7-4 shows how the use of the property tax among all types of local governments in Ohio has changed since 1976. The data in this table are in nominal terms.

CONCLUSIONS

The data presented above show that Ohio's reliance on the property tax is modest, both relative to other states and other sources of revenue. For example, both in per capita terms and as a percent of income, Ohio's property taxes are below the national average. Likewise, Ohio's property taxes as a share of own-source revenue and of total taxes are less than the national average. There is nothing to suggest that there is a need to reduce the property tax in order to get it "back in line" with the rest of the country.

While property taxes per capita and as a percent of income have increased during the past decade, they have grown less rapidly than the national average. And, in terms of their importance relative to other sources of revenue, property taxes in Ohio have declined. Thus, there is nothing in the historic pattern to suggest that property taxes are growing out of control.

The property tax in Ohio has been and continues to be principally a tax for education, with over two-thirds of property tax revenue going to local school districts. The obvious reason for this is that other local governments

TABLE 7-4
Nominal Property Tax Revenue in Ohio by Type of Jurisdiction
(in Million of Dollars)

Year	State Government	Total Local Government	County	Municipalities	Townships	Special Districts	School Districts	Total
1976	98	2292	298	239	57	64	1632	2390
1977	108	2560	311	310	66	71	1800	2668
1978	119	2532	342	268	76	70	1775	2652
1979	132	2660	378	275	85	86	1834	2792
1980	142	2892	425	298	102	98	1967	3034
1981	147	3024	466	315	110	97	2033	3171
1982	159	3585	514	340	125	111	2293	3744
1983	109	3704	563	351	142	130	2515	3813
1984	114	3878	605	366	158	114	2631	3992
1985	15	4001	621	357	162	119	2741	4016
1986	17	4223	666	371	174	134	2876	4240
1987	16	4444	712	387	181	115	3046	4460
1988	13	4778	779	403	196	131	3267	4791
1989	13	5180	857	428	218	145	3530	5193
1990	8	5584	919	464	233	173	3793	5592
1991	10	5905	1016	473	254	186	3974	5916

Source: Bureau of Census, *Government Finances*, various years. U.S. Government Printing Office, Washington, D.C.

are able to rely on income and sales taxes, while nearly all locally raised revenue for school districts is derived from the property tax. (Some school districts use an income tax (Wallace 1995, in this volume). As will be discussed below, various features of the property tax in Ohio make it undesirable as a sole tax source for the local financing of a service that requires growing expenditures.

INCOME ELASTICITY OF THE REAL PROPERTY TAX BASE

One measure of the long-term growth potential of a tax is the income elasticity. To estimate the income elasticity for the real property tax data for the period 1971 to 1992 was used. The reported assessed values must be adjusted for changes in the definition of the tax base, e.g., changes in the legal assessment ratio. In the case of the real property tax base, the only major changes made since 1970 were to adopt a current use value for agriculture (1974) and to reduce the maximum assessment rate from 50 percent to 35 percent (1972).[16] There were other minor adjustments in the definition of the property tax base, but most of these involved properties that were added to the tax exempt category, especially tax abatements.

To account for the changes in the treatment of agricultural land, we made two separate adjustments and calculated the elasticity under each adjustment. First, we excluded all agricultural property from the calculations.[17] Under the alternative, we included agricultural property but restricted the estimation from 1974 to 1992 since the treatment of agriculture changed in 1974.

One issue to be addressed is whether to adjust for differences over time in the actual assessment ratio.[18] This decision is based on whether one considers the year-to-year variations in the actual assessment ratio to be inherent to the property tax, in which case no adjustment should be made, or a correctable error, so that the reported property tax base should be adjusted for differences over time in the actual assessment rate. We have adopted the assumption that the base should be adjusted for differences in the actual assessment rate. Thus, in each year the reported assessed value is divided by the calculated assessed value to sales price ratio to obtain an estimate of fair market value. This calculation also adjusts the reported assessed value for the change in the legal assessment rate from 50 percent to 35 percent in 1972.

Data was not available to make adjustments for the minor changes in what constitutes taxable property, but it is not likely that these changes would have much effect on the estimated elasticity. For example, in 1992, tax abatements reduced the assessed value by 1.6 percent. However, ignoring these changes will result in a slight underestimate of the income elasticity.[19] The elasticities were estimated by regressing the logarithm of the assessed value of real property, adjusted for differences over time in the assessment rate, on the logarithm of total personal income, with a first order autoregressive correction.

The estimate of the income elasticity for the real property tax base for the entire period 1971 to 1992, excluding agriculture and minerals, is 0.90; the estimated elasticity for all real property over the period 1974 to 1992 is 0.78.[20] Both estimates imply that the real property tax base grew slower than personal income. The difference in the two elasticities reflects the slower growth in the value of agricultural land.[21]

Because of the possible lag in the effect of an increase in income on property values, the elasticity was estimated using income lagged one period; the resulting elasticity for the period 1971 to 1992 is 0.82, which is somewhat smaller than the value presented above.

There are several published estimates of the income elasticity of property tax bases for the United States and specific states.[22] The earlier work of Netzer (1958) and others, e.g. Hogan (1960) and Kurnow (1963), suggested that the income elasticity of real property in the United States was close to unity. Odden and Vincent (1976) report an elasticity of 0.5 for Missouri and 0.4 for South Dakota, while Berney and Frerichs (1973) report an income elasticity of 1.07 in 1961 for Washington. Mikesell (1978) finds an income elasticity for Indiana of 0.513, but an elasticity of 0.271 when controlling for the assessment process.

McLoone (1966) estimated elasticities for all 48 contiguous states with the following results, as reported in Netzer (1966, p. 189):

Elasticity	**Number of states**
0.85 and above	8
0.75 - 0.84	15
0.65 - 0.74	13
less than 0.65	12

The United States average was 0.79, with a range of 0.47 to 1.08. McLoone also notes that the elasticity of agricultural property is lower than for other types of property. Anderson (1992) reports an income elasticity of the residential property tax base for Michigan of 0.94 for urban areas and 0.64 for rural areas. However, when factors affecting the residential property tax base are controlled for, he obtains income elasticities of 0.68 for urban areas and substantially smaller estimates for non-urban counties that depend upon the agricultural intensity of land use in the county. On the other hand, Sexton and Sexton (1986), using a structural model, i.e., controlling for factors other than income, obtain elasticities of 1.53 for Kansas and 1.17 for

Minnesota. Bowman (1990) reports an income elasticity for Nevada of 2.18 for the five-year period 1982 to 1987.

Clearly, the value of the income elasticity varies across states. The literature suggests several factors that affect the value of the elasticity. First, different types of property have different elasticities; for example, rural areas have lower elasticities than urban areas (Anderson 1992), and business property has a lower elasticity than residential property (McLoone, as reported in Netzer, 1966). Thus, the make-up of the state affects the value of the elasticity. Other factors that have been found to affect the income elasticity are population and property tax rates (a faster growing population and a higher property tax rate lower the elasticity (Anderson 1992)). There has not, however, been a serious study to explain the source of variation in elasticities across time or space.

There is substantial variation over time in Ohio in the annual income elasticities (Table 7-5). Although the annual elasticities vary from year-to-

TABLE 7-5
Year-to-Year Income Elasticities for Real Property Tax Base

Year	Elasticity[1]
1972	0.83
1973	0.87
1974	0.95
1975	1.22
1976	2.56
1977	1.12
1978	0.37
1979	0.35
1980	2.52
1981	0.32
1982	0.56
1983	-0.17
1984	0.01
1985	0.47
1986	0.55
1987	0.55
1988	2.92
1989	0.88
1990	1.21
1991	1.21
1992	2.60

[1]Elasticity is calculated as the percent change in property tax base, excluding agriculture, from the previous year divided by the percentage change in state personal income from the previous year.

year, there is no tendency for the elasticity to increase or decrease over this period.[23] The annual elasticities are generally less than one, i.e., income generally grew faster than property values. Furthermore, fluctuations in the growth of taxable values is greater than the fluctuations in the growth of income. Although the growth in taxable values fluctuates, that does not mean that the entire base fluctuates widely from year-to-year; as was seen in Figure 7-1, the total base does not change much from year-to-year.

Growth in the real property tax base results from increases in the value of existing property and from new construction. Prices of existing property increase with increasing family income and population. But the magnitude of the change in demand for existing property differs over the business cycle. For example, as the economy moves out of a recession, consumer confidence grows and individuals are able to replace their savings, but the demand for housing remains pent up. Eventually consumers seek expanded housing, leading to an accelerated increase in demand for housing beyond the annual increase in income. The fluctuation in the growth rate of real property also may result from the lumpiness with which non-residential construction projects are initiated and completed, and the highly cyclical nature of the residential construction industry. Grebler and Burns (1982) find, for example, that the number of fluctuations in total construction exceeds that of the economy in general, and that there is increasing volatility of private construction.[24] Thus, short-run decreases in the growth of income because of recessions can produce large year-to-year changes in the growth rate of the property tax base. The relationship between income changes and changes in the property tax base over the business cycle produces year-to-year elasticities that are also cyclical.

Large values (greater than 2.0) of the elasticity are found in 1976, 1980, 1988, and 1992, while small values are found in 1978, 1979, 1981, 1983 and 1984. While not a perfect fit, the smaller values are associated with the economic recessions, while larger values are associated with economic expansions.

Annual income elasticities for the sales tax for Ohio are presented by Fox (1995) in this volume. The correlation between the year-to-year sales tax elasticities and the year-to-year property tax elasticities is very small. In part, this is due to the much larger annual fluctuations in the year-to-year income elasticity for the property tax, but also because of the very different pattern of change during the period 1982 to 1987.

To compare the variability in the real property tax base and in the sales tax base we calculated for each tax the sum over the period 1974 to 1992 of the absolute value of the difference between the annual percentage change in the tax base and the average annual percentage change in the tax base. This sum was divided by the number of years in the data series. The resulting values are 3.57 for the real property tax base and 3.46 for the sales tax base. These numbers are the average variation around the trend and imply that the real property tax base is slightly more variable than the sales tax.[25]

Although the property tax base is not as stable as the sales tax base, property tax revenue may well be more stable in most states. One of the advantages of the property tax is the ability to adjust the millage rate to even out fluctuations in the base. The property tax rate is usually set by the jurisdiction after the property tax base is determined, allowing for a more stable revenue source. In Ohio, however, most local jurisdictions are not able to adjust (upward) the millage rate without a referendum. Thus, property tax revenue will vary with the property tax base.

THE REAL PROPERTY TAX BASE IN OHIO

Changes in the composition of the real property tax base in Ohio over the periods 1974 to 1984 and 1984 to 1993 are shown in Table 7-6. Note first that the residential component of the base increased from 61 percent to nearly 68 percent, and second, that the growth in the total base is due mainly to increases in the value of residential and commercial property. When the increases are adjusted for inflation, only the residential and commercial components have positive growth rates; agriculture and industrial property declined in real terms.

Information on the property tax base and collections for 1993 for real property is presented in Table 7-7. The tax "levied" refers to the tax liability before the application of the reduction factor, while tax "charged" is the liability after the reduction factor but before the 10 percent and 2.5 percent rollbacks and the homestead credit. The effective tax rates differ by property class because the reduction factors differ by class. Class 2 property (commercial and industrial) pays a somewhat higher rate than Class 1 property (residential and agricultural), 55 mills versus 50 mills. These millage rates translate to effective tax rates on fair market value of 1.50 and 1.65 percent, respectively, assuming an actual assessment ratio of 30 percent. (See below for a discussion of the actual assessment ratio.)

Tables 7-8 through 7-10 focus on the level and change in the real property tax base from 1974 through 1993. Table 7-8 illustrates the levels of the real property tax base per capita in 1993 for Ohio counties. Statewide the real property tax base per capita was $10,010. However, the mean of county base per capita was $8,408, implying that smaller counties, measured by population, have lower per capita bases than do larger counties. There is substantial variation in the per capita base across counties, as seen in Table 7-8; the range is from $4,924 to $17,789, a ratio of 1 to 3.61. The coefficient of variation (the ratio of the standard deviation to the mean) is 0.28, which is modest. The real property tax base per capita is highly correlated with per capita

TABLE 7-6
Changes in the Composition of the Real Property Tax Base

	1974		1984		1993		Annual Growth Rates					
							Nominal Dollars			Constant Dollars[a]		
	Base (millions)	Share (%)	Base (millions)	Share (%)	Base (millions)	Share (%)	1974-84	1984-93	1974-93	1974-84	1984-93	1974-93
Residential	$18,268.1	60.98	$45,969.5	65.33	$74,796.3	67.80	9.67%	5.56%	7.70%	0.72%	0.90%	0.80%
Agricultural	2,958.4	9.88	5,942.1	8.45	5,724.4	5.19	7.22	-0.41	3.54	-1.52	-4.81	-3.10
Industrial	2,752.7	9.19	4,973.1	7.07	6,574.8	5.96	6.09	3.15	4.69	-2.56	-1.40	-2.02
Commercial	5,932.7	19.80	13,314.1	18.92	23,084.8	20.93	8.42	6.31	7.41	-0.43	1.62	0.53
Mineral	46.4	0.15	161.9	0.23	139.3	0.13	13.31	-1.66	5.96	4.07	-6.00	-0.83
Total	29,958.3	100.00	70,360.7	100.00	110,319.6	100.00	8.91	5.12	7.10	0.03	0.49	0.24

Source: Ohio Department of Taxation and author's calculations.

[a]Price index was the CPI, shelter component.

TABLE 7-7
1993 Real Property Tax Base and Taxes Levied and Charged
(Thousands of Dollars)

	Base		Levied		Charged		1 -Reduction Factor	Tax Rate	
	Total	Share	Total	Share	Total	Share		Levied	Charged
Class 1	74,091,384	72.25%	5,391,263	72.29%	3,771,117	70.69%	0.699	0.073	0.051
Class 2	28,457,243	27.75%	2,066,880	27.71%	1,563,871	29.31%	0.757	0.073	0.055
Total	102,548,627	100.00%	7,458,143	100.00%	5,334,988	100.00%	0.715	0.073	0.052

Source: Ohio Department of Taxation (PD-23 No. 50 August 4, 1993) and author's calculations.

TABLE 7-8
Real Property Tax Base Per Capita: 1993

Per Capita Property Tax Base	Number of Counties
less than $5,000	1
5,000 - 5,999	10
6,000 - 6,999	13
7,000 - 7,999	19
8,000 - 8,999	17
9,000 - 9,999	8
10,000 - 10,999	8
11,000 - 11,999	4
greater than $12,000	6
$10,010 $ 8,408 $ 8,068	Statewide mean County mean County median

Source: Ohio Department of Taxation and author's calculations.

income; the simple correlation coefficient between per capita real property tax base and per capita income across counties is 0.85.

The range across school districts of total property tax base per student in 1993 was from $16,210 to $426,432, producing a ratio of 1 to 26.3.[26] Sobul (1993) reports that the coefficient of variation across school districts in 1991 for total property tax base per student was 0.51, which is higher than for the real property tax base per capita at the county level. Sobul also reports that the coefficient of variation in property tax base per student has increased over time. This result is consistent with our analysis, below, of the growth in the base across counties.

As expected, the counties with the highest value of per capita tax base are in the urban areas, i.e., those in the Cleveland, Columbus, Akron, and Cincinnati areas. The smallest values are in the counties in the southern and eastern part of the state, i.e., those near the border with West Virginia and Kentucky.

Table 7-9 shows the change, in nominal terms, in the real property tax base per capita for the two periods 1974 to 84 and 1984 to 93. During the first period the real property tax base, statewide, increased by nearly 134.9 percent. This compares with an increase in the shelter component of the Consumer Price Index (CPI) of 134.2 percent. In the second period, the statewide base increased by 56.8 percent, while the shelter component of the

TABLE 7-9
Change in Real Tax Base

1974 - 1983		1983 - 1994	
Percent Change	**Number of Counties**	**Percent Change**	**Number of Counties**
60 - 99	11	greater than 0	2
100 - 139	20	0 - 14.9	11
140 - 179	28	15 - 29.9	21
180 - 219	16	30 - 44.9	27
220 - 259	7	45 - 59.9	11
greater than 260	6	60 - 74.9	7
		75 - 89.9	5
		greater than 90	4
134.9%	Statewide change	56.8%	Statewide change
163.4%	County Mean	39.0%	County Mean
161.6%	County Median	33.6%	County Median
134.2%	Change in Consumer Price Index (shelter)	50.1%	Change in Consumer Price Index (shelter)

Source: Ohio Department of Taxation and author's calculations.

CPI increased by 50.1 percent. Thus, in both periods the base increased only slightly faster than prices, reflecting the lack of economic growth in the state. In the first period, the base in the less-populated counties increased faster, while in the second period, more-populated counties increased faster. Economic conditions during the first period were hard times for urban areas, while the economic recovery during the second period provided a better environment. During the second period, there were two counties that experienced an actual decrease in the real property tax base.

Table 7-10 shows the percent of the real property tax base that is residential, and by deduction, the percent that is non-residential.[27] Between 1974 and 1993, the percent of the real property tax base, statewide, that was residential, increased from 60.1 percent to 67.8 percent. While there is a substantial range across counties in the percent residential, the bulk of the counties in 1974 were in the 40 percent to 70 percent range, and in 1993, in the 50 percent to 70 percent range. Counties in the urban areas of the state are those with higher percent residential. The large increases in percent residential occurred in the western part of the state, particularly the north-

TABLE 7-10
Residential as a Percent of Real Property Tax Base

Percent Residential	1974 Number of Counties	1993 Number of Counties
20 - 29.9	1	0
30 - 39.9	14	1
40 - 49.9	21	7
50 - 59.9	23	18
60 - 69.9	26	41
70 or more	3	11
Mean percent	60.1%	67.8%

Source: Ohio Department of Taxation and author's calculations.

western part. For most counties the change in the percent of the base that is industrial is negative. The decline in the percent of the base that is manufacturing activity reflects the decline in manufacturing in the state and is concentrated in the northeastern and middle parts of the state.[28]

THE APPRAISAL OR ASSESSMENT OF PROPERTY

The appraisal process involves the discovery and valuation of property. In Ohio, the County Auditor is responsible for determining the value of each parcel of land and improvements within the county, with the real property of railroads being assessed by the state. The Ohio Department of Taxation oversees the entire process.

The property tax is unlike most other taxes in that the property tax bill is determined by the local government. Other taxes are largely self assessed; for example, each individual calculates his or her own income tax liability.[29] For the property tax, the government determines the taxable value of the property and calculates the amount due. The accuracy of the assessments plays a major role in determining the fairness of the property tax; equivalent property assessed at different values is inherently unfair. For this reason, the administration of the property tax, and in particular the appraisal process, is an important aspect of property taxation.

Local Involvement in The Appraisal Process

The county auditors, who are elected, are responsible for determining the assessed value of every property in their respective county. The Tax

Commissioner provides oversight of the assessment process. Values are set as of January 1, with taxes normally paid in the following year.

Each county is required to appraise each piece of property at its market value every six years, a process known as the sexennial re-appraisal.[30] Counties are on a rotating cycle. This sexennial re-appraisal requires a site inspection of every parcel within the county. Because of the manpower required to conduct such an appraisal, most counties contract with independent appraisal firms to perform this work. The state maintains extensive control over this process. It has a list of 12 approved appraisal firms with which the counties can contract, although most of the re-appraisals are done by 5 or 6 firms. The terms of the contract are spelled out by the state, and the actual contract must be approved by the state.

In general, counties provide the firm with a list of properties maintained on the county's computer. Representatives of one appraisal firm that were interviewed stated that the records maintained by the counties in Ohio were very good, which made the appraisal process relatively easy. The result is that the per parcel cost of the appraisal process is low relative to many other states.[31] Generally, the list of properties contain most new construction and changes in existing property, and an accurate list of owners.

Unlike some states, Ohio requires that the County Auditor receive a copy of any change in ownership of a parcel. This allows the Auditor to maintain an accurate record of ownership. New construction is relatively easy to track in those counties that require building permits. The Auditor receives a copy of the permit and records the change. Changes such as renovation are more difficult to track since they may be done without obtaining a building permit. By driving through the county, the Auditor and staff can frequently observe new construction and major renovations. In rural areas, the construction of out-buildings does pose a problem. By requiring a site inspection of every parcel every six years, all, or nearly all, of the new construction and renovations that have been missed by the Auditor through the checking of building permits and other methods are found and recorded.

During the third year after the sexennial re-appraisal, the Auditor is required to adjust property valuation for changes that have occurred. This triennial update involves adjusting "classes" of property for changes in market conditions. For example, if there is evidence from sales data that the price of a certain type of property or property within a certain subdivision has changed, the Auditor will adjust the valuation of all of the property within that class of property or area. The types of property include residential, industrial, etc, but may also include property in a certain value range.

Many counties rely on computer assisted mass appraisal systems (CAMAs) to perform this triennial re-appraisal.[32] In addition, many counties contract with private firms to conduct the triennial update.

In non-sexennial and triennial years, the County Auditor will add new construction to the property list and change valuations of existing property because of renovations and other physical changes. The Auditor may, but is neither required to, nor can he be directed by the Tax Commissioner, adjust valuations based on changes in market conditions.

The appraisal process is financed by earmarked revenue. A share of property tax collections within the county is allocated directly to the County Auditor for the purpose of administering the real property tax. The revenue for the real estate assessment fund is determined as follows:

Amount of Collection	**Percent Earmarked**
First $100,000	3.5
Next $3 million	1.375
Next $3 million	1.0
Next $143.9 million	0.75
On sums over $150 million	0.6

The amount generated for this fund is sufficient for most counties to perform the appraisal function with a high level of quality. Some counties with small property tax bases do not receive sufficient revenues from this source and either have to supplement with general county funds or perform the administrative function at a somewhat lower quality.

Role of The State in The Assessment Process

The state plays an important role in the appraisal process. The Tax Commissioner oversees the administration of the property tax and by law has substantial powers regarding the administration. The primary function of the Tax Commission, vis-a-vis the real property tax, is to assure that all property in the state is uniformly assessed. If the Tax Commissioner determines that a county has not appropriately appraised the property within the county at either the triennial update or the sexennial re-appraisal, he can require the County Auditor to change the values of all real property by a given percent, but cannot require the county to redo the appraisals. He exercises substantial control over the selection of and the nature of the contract with private appraisal firms.

In order to evaluate the appraisal, the Tax Equalization Division of the Department of Taxation prepares a sales ratio study every six months. This study compares the sales value of property to the assessed value, and thus allows the Tax Commissioner to determine whether the appraisal and updates produce uniform assessments which equal the required 35 percent of fair market value.

Evaluation of The Appraisal Process

By all accounts, the appraisal process of real property works well in Ohio, and certainly with more professionalism and state control than in the pre-Park Investment case period.[33] The state exercises control over the assessment process and constantly monitors the quality of assessment by collecting data on sales and comparing the sales price of a property to the appraised value of the property.[34]

The administrative procedures are similar, in many ways, to those used in other states. However, there are some unique aspects. The level of state control is stronger, and with 88 assessing districts, i.e., counties, the assessing process is more centralized than in many states. A six-year re-appraisal cycle, however, is longer than in most states.

Sales-assessment Ratio

The sales-assessment ratio (i.e., the value of the ratio of total assessed value on properties that have been sold to the aggregate sales price for these properties) for sales within the first six months for each of the past five years, is as follows:

Year	Ratio of Assessed Value to Sales Price (Percentage)
1992	30.09
1991	30.52
1990	30.05
1989	28.96
1988	30.27

Source: Ohio Department of Taxation

The ratio of assessed value to sales value has hovered around 30 percent, not the legally required ratio of 35 percent. A ratio of assessed value to sales value of 30 percent when the legally required rate is 35 percent is acceptable, but a ratio closer to 33 percent should be achievable.

There are at least two potential explanations why the actual assessment ratio is less than 35 percent. First, for a given year, some of the sold properties are in counties that have just completed an update or a re-appraisal while other counties are two years beyond that. However, there is very little difference in the value of the ratio of assessed value to sales price for those different classes of counties. Consider those counties that have just completed a re-appraisal or update, those that have completed it one year ago, and those that completed it two years ago. The average of the ratios of assessed value to sales value for the three classes of counties for the first six months of 1992 are 30.9 percent, 30.4 percent, and 29.7 percent, respectively. In other words, there is not much of a decrease in the ratio the longer the time from either an update or re-appraisal.

The second explanation focuses on the appraisal process. Appraising property is difficult and not an exact science. To the extent that appraisers assign values that are greater than fair market value, owners will appeal in order to lower the appraised value, while they do not request an increase in value if the appraisal is too low. Appraisers would like to minimize appeals and thus they have an incentive to appraise property a little bit low.

There is also variation of the ratio across counties, but the variation is not substantial. For the first six months of 1992 the values of the ratio ranged from a low of 25.97 percent to 33.50 percent. However, the bulk of the counties have ratios that are close to 30; 45 of the 88 counties have ratios greater than 29 but less than 31, and 57 have ratios greater than 28 but less than 32.

A major concern with the assessment process is the inequities in the assessment rates across parcels within taxing jurisdictions. Just as there are variations across counties in the assessment to sales ratios, there are variations across parcels within a county. Judging the quality of a re-appraisal should not be restricted to comparing the aggregate assessment to sales ratio to the legally required 35 percent or even the sales-assessment ratios across classes of property. There are standard measures of the variation or dispersion in sales-assessment ratios across parcels, and professional standards exist as to what are acceptable values for these measures. Ohio statute does not require the Tax Commissioner to calculate any measure of dispersion. State statute does require a sales ratio study and specifies general parameters to be used in the construction of the assessment to sales ratio. Ohio Code Annotated §5715.33 does allow the Tax Commissioner to require the triennial update if in the Tax Commissioner's opinion such property has been unequally or improperly assessed.

The coefficient of dispersion (COD) is one standard measure of the variability across individual parcels within a county in the ratio of assessed value to sales value.[35] A COD of 0.20 or less is considered an acceptable level.[36] In 1992, the CODs for residential property ranged from 0.11 to 0.25, with 20 counties having CODs greater than 0.20. Of the counties with a COD greater than 20, only 5 had recently gone through a re-appraisal or update. These numbers suggest that the variation in assessment ratios within the counties are relatively small and that the state generally meets the minimum standard, but improvements could be made.

There have been numerous studies that have explored the cause of intra-area variations in assessment rates.[37] Schroeder and Sjoquist (1976), and others, find that the actual assessment rate varies inversely with property values, a practice some authors associate with conscious behavior on the part of tax assessors. In addition, Schroeder and Sjoquist find that there is greater variation in actual assessment rates the fewer the sales of property within an area. Borland and Lile (1980) find that there is greater uniformity the higher the property tax rate, and hypothesize that the relationship is driven by the higher probability of appeals the higher the tax rate.

Shannon (1973) and Gaffney (1973) argue that the lack of uniformity of property assessment is the cause of the general dislike for the property tax, and that the dislike of the property tax has lead to efforts at tax relief. They argue that more attention needs to be paid to improvements in the assessment of property, a call made by many students of the property tax.

Frequency of Appraisal

A related assessment issue is the frequency of the re-appraisal and updates. A six-year interval between re-appraisals is long; a three-year cycle is more common.[38] Certainly, the assessment of property would be more accurate if counties conducted a re-appraisal more often than every six years. There are three arguments that are generally advanced for doing so. First, inequities across property owners that arise because of assessment lags are reduced. This was discussed above and therefore not discussed here. Second, the potential inequities across school districts in local fair share (qualifying millage) would be reduced. Third, owners are not hit with the "shock" of a large tax increase every three years.

Variation across jurisdictions in the actual assessment ratio has implications for the equity of school aid. In order to qualify to receive state education funds, a school district must levy at least 20 mills; such a requirement is commonly referred to as local fair share. Consider three school districts, A, B, and C. Assume that District A's property is assessed at 35 percent, District B's property is assessed at 26 percent, and District C's property is assessed at 33 percent. For every $1,000 of fair market value of property within the school district, there should be $350 of taxable value. ($350 equals the fair market value times the legal assessment rate of 35 percent.) A 20 mill tax on $350 would yield $7.00 in taxes, which is what District A would contribute to the basic school aid grant, i.e., it is the required local fair share or qualifying millage. With an actual assessment rate of 26 percent, the taxable value of the $1,000 property would be $260, and a 20 mill tax would yield $5.20, which is what District B would contribute. With an actual assessment ratio of 33 percent, the 20 mill tax rate would yield $6.60, which is the contribution that District C would make. District A contributes $1.80, or 34.6 percent more than District B, and District C contributes $1.40, or 26.9 percent more than District B.

This is an inequity. District C's local fair share for every dollar of fair market value is 26.9 percent higher than for District B. This is the maximum

This is an inequity. District C's local fair share for every dollar of fair market value is 26.9 percent higher than for District B. This is the maximum degree of inequality using the actual variations in county level assessment rates. For most counties the degree of inequality will be much less. However, the magnitude of the variations in assessment rates presented above are for counties. It is very likely that the variations in assessment rates across school districts are larger, since variations are generally greater the smaller the unit of analysis.

One way to correct for this inequality is to use sales-assessment ratios to adjust the value of the district's assessed value so that the adjusted assessed value is 35 percent of fair market value.[39] For example, suppose that the state calculates a sales-assessment ratio of 30 percent for a jurisdiction with reported taxable value of $100 million. Without any adjustment, this district would be required to contribute $2 million in order to qualify for school aid. But since the $100 million is only 30 percent of fair market value, the state would adjust the $100 million taxable value by dividing it by 0.30 to get the true fair market value, which would be $333.33 million. The $333.33 million would then be multiplied by 0.35 to get the corrected taxable value, or $116.67 million. Twenty mills on $116.67 million would yield revenue of $2.33 million, which would be the required local fair share.

While easy to do in concept, administratively it is difficult. First, it would be necessary to conduct a sales-assessment ratio study for each one of the 611 school districts. It would probably be impossible to do that with a sufficient degree of accuracy such that the study would hold up to serious challenges. It would be possible to use the county-level sales-assessment ratio and apply it to all school districts within the county. But without knowing more about the variation within the county, i.e., the variation across the school districts, it is not clear whether adjusting taxable values would actually reduce inequities in school district local fair share contributions. Furthermore, one-third of the school districts cross at least one county line making use of county-level sales-assessment ratios even more problematic.

Despite the problems, Texas does conduct an equalization study for over 1000 school districts (Sherill and Whorton 1991). New Jersey also uses an assessment-sales ratio study to equalize grants to schools. However, Bogart (1991) found its use to be very deficient and unreliable.

Second, conducting a sales-assessment ratio study takes time. For example, the sales-assessment ratios for the first six months of 1992 have just become available. Thus, it would be necessary to adjust the taxable value for 1995 using a ratio based on 1992 data. Because assessed values will have been adjusted during that time, either because of a third-year update or a reappraisal, using three year old data is not likely to correct the current degree of under-assessment.

The third issue regarding the frequency of assessments is the effect that infrequent re-appraisals have on the size of the increase in an individual owner's property tax bill after an update or re-appraisal. While large changes in property taxes no doubt occur as a result of the three-year cycle, the evidence does not suggest substantial changes in assessed values in the aggregate as a result of updates or re-appraisals. For example, for the counties that conducted an update in 1993, the increase in aggregate assessed value for residential property was 14.3 percent (see Table 7-11 for the distribution.) Thus, on average, property owners could potentially experience a maximum increase in their tax bill of 14.3 percent. This 14.3 percent increase overstates the actual increase that an average owner will likely experience since it includes new construction, and, in addition, the tax reduction factor offsets part of the effect of the increase in actual property taxes. But this does not mean that within counties much larger increases in the values of some properties do not arise, increases that result in large increases in property taxes despite the tax reduction factor.

The assessment process would be improved by more frequent re-appraisals and updates. One option is to go to annual re-appraisals.[40] Despite the benefit of removing inequities that arise from periodic re-appraisals, conducting a re-appraisal every year would add substantially to the cost of administering the property tax. Judging from the relatively small variations across counties in the ratio of assessed value to sales price, including the small variation over the three year re-appraisal, updating cycle, there does not seem to be a substantial need for an annual re-appraisal. But an alternative that might be considered is to go to a four-year re-appraisal cycle with an update in the second year.

TABLE 7-11
Percent Increase in Residential Taxable Values: 1992 to 1993[a]

Percent Change	Number of Counties
less than 5	1
5 - 10	6
10 - 15	15
15 - 20	12
20 - 25	7
Total	41

Source: Ohio Department of Taxation and author's calculations.

[a]Restricted to counties that either updated or reappraised in 1993.

A second option is to do more frequent updates. During the two years between re-appraisals and updates, the counties do not have to adjust property values. In particular, the state cannot require a county to update assessed value other than in the third year.[41] An update is much less costly than a re-appraisal; a re-appraisal by a private firm would cost $7 to $9 per parcel, while an update would cost $0.75 to $2.00 per parcel.[42] Many, perhaps most counties, have the ability to do computerized mass appraisals, which is what is generally done in the third-year update. Thus, it is reasonable from a financial perspective to allow the state to require updates more frequently than every three years.

The authority to require updates between the triennial update and the sexennial re-appraisal might be restricted to counties for which there is evidence of large increases in value, say 10 percent, or of large intra-county inequities in the sales-assessment ratios. Thus, an alternative to requiring every county to do annual updates is to allow the Tax Commissioner to require more frequent updates in those counties whose assessments appear out of line. However, as was noted above, obtaining timely information on either price changes or inequities will be difficult.

When property prices increase slowly, there is less need for a short re-appraisal cycle. Since inflation is currently low relative to other recent periods, e.g., the late 1970s, the increase in inequities that are likely to arise in most counties as a result of infrequent re-appraisals or updates will be relatively small. Thus, granting authority to the Tax Commissioner to require more frequent updates in those counties that are experiencing more rapid increases in property values might be a more cost effective procedure than mandating updates in every country.

Qualifications

There are no requirements regarding training or experience in property appraisal of either the County Auditor or employees of the auditor or appraisal firms. The state might consider establishing minimum standards that the County Auditor and employees must have. These standards might require minimum levels of formal and/or on-the-job training in appraisal practice. Twenty-eight states in 1985 required certification for assessors (Clatanoff 1986).

The County Auditor is an elected official, while the responsibility for property tax assessment is an administrative job. In more populated counties, the Auditor delegates the responsibility for property tax assessment. Given that the assessment function is an administrative one, and that there are potential political pressures to adjust assessed values, e.g., as was apparently done in the pre-Park Case era, an appointed property tax administrator might be more appropriate. However, Bowman and Mikesell (1989) find that for at least one measure of assessment performance, assessment uniformity, there is no significant difference between appointed and elected assessors.

The Assessment Rate

Ohio currently assesses all real property at 35 percent of value, either fair market value or current use value in the case of agricultural land.[43] The legal assessment rate, however, has no real bearing on the actual tax paid, provided other components of the property tax system are appropriately set. For example, a 10 percent tax on a parcel assessed at 35 percent of value yields the same tax as a 3.5 percent tax on the same parcel assessed at 100 percent of value.

The selection of the legal assessment rate is arbitrary. However, given the complexity of the property tax in general and in Ohio in particular, by adopting an assessment rate of 100 percent, one of the complications can be eliminated.[44] Twenty-three states assess property at 100 percent of value Clatanoff 1986), and it is the rate that has been recommended by many students of the property tax.[45]

In order for a change in the assessment rate from 35 percent to 100 percent not to affect actual property taxes, other components of the tax system, in particular the millage rate, must be changed. Other changes, for example, the state's school aid formula, are also necessary. The state's basic grant program for schools requires a local fair share, which is the amount of revenue generated by a 20 mill property tax on the actual assessed value. If the state set the legal assessment rate at 100 percent and reduced the required local fair share to 7 mills, the revenue that would be generated would be the same as with a tax rate of 20 mills and a legal assessment rate of 35 percent.

The so called 10 mill limit, which is the legislative maximum tax rate that can be levied without holding a referendum, could be adjusted by reducing all inside millage by 65 percent so that the total mill limit would be 3.5 mills. Alternatively, the 10 mill limit could be retained as is, which would mean that the inside millage would actually be 1 percent of value, which is the constitutional maximum tax rate. The 10 mill limit is discussed in more detail below. Since tangible public utility property is assessed at 88 percent, it would be necessary to make appropriate changes in the treatment of this property, either applying a higher millage rate or increasing the assessment rate to 251 percent.

Treatment of Agricultural Land

Beginning in 1974, owners of land devoted exclusively to agricultural use could request that the County Auditor value the land on the basis of its that was being taxed on a current use basis is converted to non-agricultural use, then the owner must pay the amount of tax savings for the past three years. Programs that allow agricultural land to be assessed on a current use basis or at a lower assessment rate exist in almost all states (see Clatanoff 1986).

Farms located adjacent to growing urban areas have property values that are much higher than equivalent farm land in rural areas. If the "urban" farm land was assessed at the price it would command for residential or commercial development, the taxes would be substantially higher than on farm land in rural areas. It is argued that because the higher taxes reduce the farmer's cash flow, the farmer may be forced to sell the farm. Thus, the argument is that current use value assessment protects the farmer from being forced off his land.

Farm property tax relief programs have been the subject of many studies. Studies of the effect of use-value assessment on the retardation of farm land conversions have found the impact to be slight.[47] Ladd (1980) is particularly critical of use-value assessments, arguing they are blunt instruments as policy tools with respect to land use decisions, have adverse distributional effects, and result in inequities.

Aaron (1975) calls for a repeal of the preferential taxation of farmers, arguing that preferential treatment should not affect the timing of the development of land and that the preferences are inequitable. Wunderlich (1992) presents the arguments in support of special treatment of agricultural land, while Simeral (1989) presents a defense of Ohio's program; the arguments for special treatment are essentially the ones presented above.

As the urban community sprawls toward the farmer's land, the value of that land increases, and the farmer accumulates large unrealized capital gains. Furthermore, the special tax treatment of agricultural land should be reflected in still higher values for the land, i.e., any tax advantage is capitalized into land prices. Thus, if the owner sold the agricultural land to another farmer, the beneficiary of the special tax treatment would be the current owner, not the new owner. This is consistent with Anderson and Bunch (1989), who find that tax relief for agricultural land is capitalized into land values.

Keeping property taxes down on "urban" agricultural land provides an incentive for the farmer to hold on to the land and to continue farming it. But the land has become more valuable for other uses, which is why its price has increased. Thus, the current use value program results in inefficiency in the use of land; it is not being used in its most productive activity.

To determine the current use value of a tract of agricultural land in Ohio, the appraiser uses the income approach to appraisal.[48] In simple terms the estimation works are follows. First, based on soil type, drainage conditions, erosion, and slope, the productivity of the farm is determined. Based on the productivity of the farm, the potential amount and mix of each of several crops is determined, and using a five-year average of crop prices, the cost of seed, etc., the net income of the farm is determined. Finally, using an interest rate to discount the stream of net income, the present value of the land is estimated.[49]

The Ohio program is essentially designed to protect farmers located adjacent to expanding urban areas, not as a general property tax relief program for farmers. There is evidence, however, that the procedure used to determine current use value provides property tax relief to all farmers. Agricultural land that has no alternative use, i.e., land that if sold would continue to be used for agricultural purposes, should have a fair market value that is equal to current use value. Thus, in rural counties, the current use value of agricultural land should be close to the fair market value.[50] However, such is not the case, as can be seen in Table 7-12 and Figure 7-2. In both urban and rural counties, as measured by the percent of the population classified as rural, the current use value is substantially less than the fair market value. For countries with 50 percent or more rural population aggregate current use value is only about 27 percent of aggregate fair market value.

The estimated value of the property is sensitive to the capitalization rate used. The capitalization rate used in Ohio is based largely on the current interest rate on a 30-year loan with a 25 percent down payment. In the calculation of market value the assumption is made that the current interest rate will exist for all time. Part of the problem with the selected capitalization rate is that anticipated inflation is not taken into consideration, which results in a capitalization rate that is too high and current use values that are too low. As noted above, the estimated current use value is the ratio of annual net earnings to the capitalization rate. The expression assumes that net

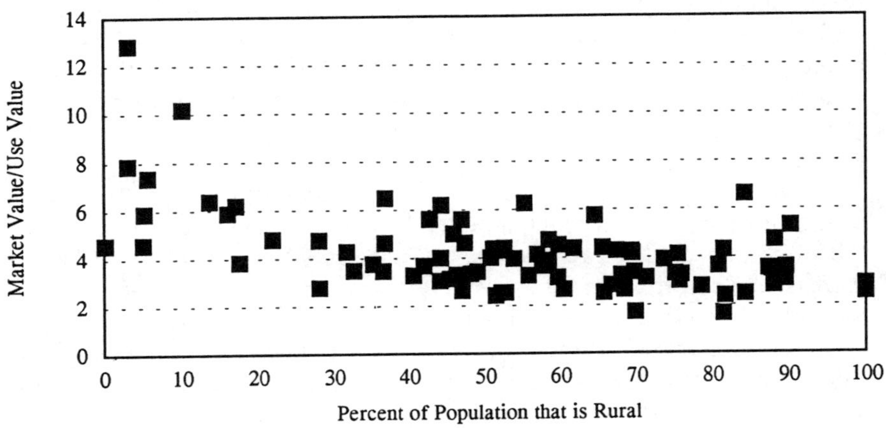

FIGURE 7-2. Agricultural assessment comparison of market value to use value.

TABLE 7-12
Comparison of Current Use Value to Market Value, 1993

County	Current Agri. Use Value ($)	Fair Market Value ($)	% Rural Population	County	Current Agri. Use Value ($)	Fair Market Value ($)	% Rural Population
Noble	3,369,500	8,199,930	100.00	Delaware	19,844,780	123,660,410	55.21
Morgan	5,411,700	13,523,600	100.00	Van Wert	31,116,750	122,669,200	53.78
Vinton	1,123,430	3,187,070	100.00	Fayette	29,441,470	74,552,740	52.73
Holmes	14,699,900	77,576,420	90.27	Tuscarawa	12,971,930	56,883,280	52.52
Brown	15,802,220	56,107,420	89.63	Athens	3,618,560	9,103,440	52.18
Morrow	18,262,290	55,743,970	89.56	Ashland	13,889,750	59,425,660	51.75
Putnam	31,534,970	148,347,360	88.23	Belmont	3,327,590	7,983,690	51.41
Meigs	2,494,760	6,992,070	88.09	Fairfield	23,064,020	100,694,950	51.34
Adams	13,581,270	46,925,680	87.80	Huron	19,809,840	85,767,730	51.11
Paulding	22,861,180	80,069,000	87.42	Seneca	32,183,960	128,369,280	50.78
Gallia	5,899,230	14,481,860	84.39	Clinton	23,092,280	78,532,240	48.98
Geauga	5,097,680	33,530,550	84.32	Defiance	23,539,390	78,176,900	48.08
Monroe	4,583,460	10,867,560	81.73	Ashtabula	10,319,430	47,677,260	47.25
Preble	25,114,700	107,428,920	81.56	Marion	29,003,630	76,014,300	46.98
Pike	11,089,890	17,970,180	81.54	Clermont	12,179,590	67,767,220	46.89
Carroll	6,499,690	23,482,840	80.88	Sandusky	27,154,710	89,146,510	46.22
Harrison	3,765,440	10,360,600	78.62	Licking	20,685,580	103,194,190	45.83
Darke	42,880,740	140,043,480	76.01	Lawrence	4,267,200	13,301,870	45.35
Pickaway	30,266,990	90,049,810	75.74	Portage	7,154,780	44,115,510	44.15
Perry	4,405,160	18,020,250	75.54	Auglaize	25,202,190	100,511,960	44.12
Ottawa	14,319,300	47,351,910	75.20	Jefferson	1,888,010	5,696,580	44.07
Hocking	1,999,390	7,732,990	73.66	Medina	14,660,280	82,117,810	42.66

continued

TABLE 7-12 (continued)
Comparison of Current Use Value to Market Value, 1993

Logan	23,593,160	73,937,650	71.30	Miami	29,359,700	107,075,550	41.97
Gurnsey	12,189,670	20,719,720	69.90	Hancock	44,794,390	145,439,640	40.56
Union	30,627,280	102,894,850	69.77	Warren	18,065,120	116,538,580	36.77
Henry	33,801,210	140,207,840	69.48	Crawford	19,326,820	88,830,770	36.75
Knox	14,115,880	59,851,950	69.33	Wood	50,935,220	175,115,940	36.51
Champaign	27,496,070	72,266,850	68.48	Erie	12,446,120	46,437,490	35.15
Ross	23,343,630	62,348,460	68.38	Allen	26,126,380	90,492,620	32.68
Highland	19,572,720	63,504,610	68.07	Richland	16,518,000	70,362,730	31.70
Muskinglum	8,709,670	37,138,150	67.37	Clark	27,574,280	76,184,340	28.13
Madison	32,868,810	92,690,490	66.79	Trumbull	6.962,480	32,985,170	28.05
Williams	20,804,250	52,310,410	65.78	Stark	15,998,720	76,235,290	21.97
Coschocton	9,577,260	42,006,500	65.58	Greene	25,386,910	97,078,160	17.55
Mercer	30,221,840	172,755,670	64.54	Butler	19,707,840	121,821,930	17/13
Wayne	23,893,710	104,285,610	61.80	Mahoning	5,998,720	31,503,720	16.05
Washington	6,787,590	18,017,940	60.49	Lorain	11,266,250	71,713,450	13.63
Columbian	8,778,060	39,593,510	59.75	Lake	2,376,800	24,141,600	10.16
Jackson	2,421,450	7,644,260	59.67	Summit	2,543,546	18,653,510	5.67
Fulton	28,269,130	133,238,820	58.47	Lucas	11,967,880	69,982,510	5.23
Shelby	24,496,290	94,223,960	58.44	Montgomery	19,644,280	89,605,600	5.07
Scioto	6,685,890	24,337,900	57.52	Hamilton	3,391,615	43,458,216	3.19
Wyandot	25,002,230	102,398,370	56.91	Franklin	17,239,950	135,113,980	3.15
Hardin	30,421,980	98,299,590	55.74	Cuyahoga	602,120	2,755,470	0.17

Source: Ohio Department of Taxation and *1990 Census of Population*.

earnings will not increase over time, i.e., it assumes there will be no inflation. The capitalization rate, however, is based on the current market borrowing rate, and this market interest rate reflects anticipated inflation. If the numerator is expressed in real terms, then the denominator should also be expressed in real terms, which means subtracting the expected inflation rate from the borrowing rate.[51]

One option for changing the current use value calculation is to use a different capitalization rate, one that would correlate actual agricultural land sales and current use value estimates. Another option is to use an alternative approach to determining current use value, namely, to rely on sale prices of farm land that remains as farm land and that does not have alternative uses. Estimating current use value can then be based on comparative sales data, much like how residential property is appraised. This does not necessarily mean totally replacing the current procedures, since even with the use of comparative sales data, it is necessary to adjust for variations across farms in their quality or productivity.

Exempt Property

Like all other states, Ohio exempts certain property from real property taxation. In 1992, the estimated taxable value of exempt property was $17.3 billion, which is 14.5 percent of the total of taxable and exempt real property.[52] There was substantial variation across the counties in the percent of real property that is exempt; the range was from a low of 6.5 percent (Holmes County) to 72.2 percent (Pike County). In 1986, exempt real property was $12.7 billion, which was 11.1 percent of the total of taxable and exempt property. Over the last six year period the value of exempt real property increased by 36.1 percent while the value of taxable real property increased by 35.7 percent.

Table 7-13 shows the taxable value of real exempt property by type of exemption in 1986 and 1992 and the change over that period.[53] Outside of government property, the value of exempt property for charitable institutions, churches, and tax abatement programs are of similar magnitude. While there has been an increase in all categories, by far the largest is in tax abatement programs, which more than tripled within the six-year span. If real taxable value, tax abatement and other tax exempt property increase at the same rate as over the past six years, then in six years, total exempt property will have increased by nearly $5 billion. Whether the new legislation (SB 19) will retard the growth in tax abatement programs such as CRA and enterprise zones remains to be seen.[54]

It should be noted that these data are based on information from the counties' tax records and are thus based on the appraisals made by the counties or the appraisal firms they hire. Conversations with representatives of

TABLE 7-13
Tax Exempt Real Property by Type of Property

Tax Exemption	Taxable Value (Millions of Dollars) 1986	1992	Percent Change
Federal Government	$841.1	$1,167.0	38.7
State Government	1,442.7	1,729.1	19.8
Local Governments[a]	5,911.6	6,827.7	15.5
Private Schools[b]	844.1	1,340.1	58.8
Charitable Institutions	1,437.3	1,963.4	36.7
Churches	1,626.2	1,977.5	21.6
Cemeteries/Monuments	127.6	160.7	25.9
Other	NA	556.1	NA
Subtotal	12,230.6	15,721.6	28.5
Community Urban Redevelopment Corp	187.0	404.0	116.0
Community Re-Investment Areas	187.9	802.0	326.8
Tax Investment Financing	47.7	216.4	353.7
Urban Renewal	48.7	129.3	165.5
Other (including enterprise zones)	20.8	75.9	264.9
Subtotal	492.0	1,627.6	230.8
Grandtotal	12,748.6	17,349.2	36.1

Source: Ohio Department of Taxation.

NA: Not available; for 1986, the "other" category was not provided.

[a]This category includes counties, municipalities, boards of education and conservancy and park districts.
[b]This category includes schools, colleges, academies.

an appraisal firm indicated that the firm does try to do a thorough job of appraising exempt property. However, since this property is not taxable, there is little reason to spend much time appraising it. Thus, the data may be only a reasonable estimate of the actual value of exempt property.

The value of tax exempt property increases over time because of increases in value due to price increases, new construction, the expansion of the governmental and non-profit sectors, adoption and expansion of exemption programs such as the tax abatement programs, and more liberal interpretations of the real property tax exemption statutes by the courts. Tax abatement programs in Ohio are considered in detail by Wasylenko (1995) in this volume, and thus we focus on the other categories of real property tax exemption.

There are three ways of classifying property for exemption: the use of the property, for example, for charitable purposes; the ownership of the property, for example, by a non-profit organization, and; special characteristics of the property, for example, where it is located or its historic value. As with most states, Ohio classifies most real property tax exemptions on the basis of the use to which the property is put.

The Ohio Constitution (Article XII, section 2) states that, "general laws may be passed to exempt burying grounds, public school houses, houses used exclusively for public worship, institutions used exclusively for charitable purposes, and public property used exclusively for any public purpose . . ." The legal descriptions of real property tax exempt property are contained in several places in the Ohio Code, principally in chapter 5709.

Coriell (1992) argues that over time in Ohio the interpretation of this provision has been broadened in many ways by both the courts and the state legislature. She presents several examples of court rulings liberalizing the interpretation of tax exempt property. She also argues that the state legislature has allowed exemption on the basis of ownership rather than use, a practice which the courts have upheld. In an opinion written by the Cincinnati City Solicitor it is argued that court decisions regarding tax exempt property suggests that it may be constitutional for the General Assembly to exempt all improvements in real property from taxation.

Coriell (1992, p. 266) states that the Ohio statutes are "full of contradictions and inconsistencies," and cites several examples. For example, a state educational institution is able to lease space to a for-profit organization and yet not pay property taxes on the space, while a private firm conducting the same business would be subject to the property tax. Coriell cites another example in which one non-profit was allowed to exempt the parking lot used by the employees while another non-profit was not.

A particular concern regarding property tax exemptions is the loss of tax revenue. As the magnitude of exemptions expand, the millage rate needed to collect a given revenue must increase. But, as noted above, non-governmental exempt property is a relatively modest percent of the total taxable and exempt property. However, Mullen (1990) finds that property tax exemptions are a significant source of fiscal stress for local jurisdictions.

Pfister (1976) presents an evaluation of the traditional justification for property tax exemptions and concludes that the traditional justifications are no longer valid.[55] The two principal purposes for property tax exemption are: 1) to promote some particular activity or behavior considered socially desirable by providing a subsidy, and 2) to protect the sovereignty of particular governments. Other more specific arguments for exemption include:

- a government unit gains nothing from taxing its own property;
- certain exemptions can reduce the regressivity of the property tax; and
- certain exemptions might yield more in benefits to the community that costs.

Pfister argues that these justifications have no validity today. For example, one reason for exempting certain non-profit activities is that otherwise the government would have to provide the social services. However, generally it is the state government that would have to provide the social service, while it is local government that loses the tax revenue yet must deliver local services to the exempt property. Federal and state properties are exempt because of a Supreme Court ruling in 1819, in which the dictum, "the power to tax is the power the destroy," was the principle on which the ruling was made. But it is no longer likely, Pfister argues, that local governments can destroy state and federal governments with the property tax.

There is a very long history of exempting property in Ohio and the rest of United States. And, while it is hard to envision eliminating these exemptions, at least in mass, consideration should be given to the purpose for these exemptions, and how the law should be changed accordingly. Exemptions are a "back door" way of providing support to certain activities. It would make for more rational budgeting if all property was subject to taxation and the budget process used to decide which properties or activities should receive a direct subsidy. One option that the state should consider is to conduct a thorough study of this issue and develop recommendations for specific changes in the constitution and state statues.[56]

MILLAGE REFERENDA AND TAX REDUCTION FACTORS

Calculating the gross property tax liability involves the application of millage rates and the tax reduction factors to the assessed value. As in many states, increases in millage rates must be voted on. What is unusual is the tax reduction factor, an element of the Ohio property tax that adds greatly to its complexity.

MILLAGE RATES

From the reported sales-assessment ratios it appears that currently property is assessed at about 30 percent of value. The effective millage rate (calculated as the ratio of real property tax revenue divided by total assessed value) is 50 mills. Thus, real property is being taxed at 1.75 percent of fair market value or current use value in the case of agriculture. The Ohio constitution limits property taxes on all property to 1 percent of value, a provision first passed in 1911 as part of the Smith Act and a part of the constitution for a long time (Ohio Constitution XII §2).[57] The constitution does allow for additional taxes beyond the 1 percent limit if a proposal for a property tax levy is approved by a majority of the electors voting within the taxing jurisdiction or when it is provided for by the charter of a municipal corporation. In 1933, the General Assembly interpreted the constitution to mean that 1 percent was the same as 10 mills, which would be the same if property was assessed at 100 percent of value. However, with property assessed at 35 percent of value, the 10 mill limit is actually a limit of 0.35 percent of value.

There are two types of millage rates, inside and outside. The inside millage refers to the 10 mills that can be levied without voter approval.[58] With the exception of charter cities, of which there are about 140, all other millage levies must be voted upon. The voted, or outside millage rates are approved for specific purposes and durations. Millage rates are passed to fund or enhance specific programs, including general support for schools. This means that much of the property tax revenue is earmarked for specific budgetary items. Since the local governments have other sources of revenue, they can substitute one source of funds for another. Thus, property tax millage that is approved for one service can potentially replace other funds being used to finance that service.

The voted millage can be for a fixed number of mills, or to raise a given amount of revenue each year, such as a levy imposed to finance the payment of the principal and interest on a bond issue. In the latter case, the millage rate is set each year to yield the necessary revenue.

The General Assembly has approved a list of types of levies that local governments can put before the voters. Authority differs between types of jurisdictions regarding what types of levy referenda can be held. Most levies can be imposed for a period of up to five years, but there are exceptions for which a longer period is allowed. School districts may hold referenda on three general types of levies: operating levies, permanent improvement levies, and bond issues. There are five different kinds of operating levies: regular operation levies for current expenses, emergency levies, millage incremental tax levies, dollar incremental tax levies, and replacement levies.

REDUCTION FACTOR

In 1925, the Ohio state legislature passed the first millage rollback law.[59] The provision of the 1925 law required re-appraisals of real property every six years but that taxable property value on all taxable property be reduced so that in the aggregate the re-appraisal would not result in an increase in property tax revenue. This law applied to all property, real and personal, and required that the value of all types of property be reduced by the same percent.

In 1976, Ohio passed a new law (HB 920) that replaced the 1925 statute. This new law was also designed to prevent automatic increases in taxes due to increases in prices, i.e., inflation. However, the new law provided that the rollback would apply only to real property, not personal property. HB 920 also imposed the triennial updates of assessments.

HB 920 was caused in part by the fallout from a series of court rulings known as the Park Investment cases. In these decisions, the Ohio Supreme

Court found that property was not being taxed uniformly, and in particular, that commercial and industrial property was being assessed at a much higher percent of fair market value than residential and agricultural property. In order to equalize the percentage assessment at 35 percent, commercial and industrial property had to be reduced from an actual assessment rate of about 40 percent while residential and agricultural property had to be increased from levels reportedly as low as 15 percent. Consequently, property taxes were shifted from nonresidential to residential property. The resulting political outcry led to HB 920.

Because during the late 1970s residential values were increasing faster than commercial and industrial values, action was taken to separate the two classes of property. A constitutional amendment was *approved* that *allowed* for two classes of property, but only for the purpose of *fully* eliminating any effect of increases in the value of property. In 1980, legislation was passed that *required* that the rollback be calculated separately for residential and agricultural property (Class 1) and for all other real property (Class 2).

HB 920 reduces the effective voted millage rate through what is known as the tax reduction factor. The reduction factor works as follows. For simplicity for the moment ignore the distinction between types of millage rates, e.g., inside millage and voted millage, ignore the difference between types of real property, i.e., residential and non-residential, and assume that there is only one government, say a county government, i.e., ignore schools, municipalities, etc. Suppose that the county has a millage levy that was approved by the voters in 1990 and that it conducts a sexennial re-appraisal. The increase in the total assessed value within the county consists of new construction, including renovations, and price increases of existing property. The reduction factor is designed to limit the increase in property tax revenue to that which results from new construction only.

The state government calculates the ratio of (a) the increase in taxable value resulting from price changes from the time the millage levy was passed to (b) the new assessed value including the price increase. This ratio is known as the tax reduction factor. The approved millage levy is multiplied by one minus the tax reduction factor to obtain the effective millage levy. The resulting product of the effective millage levy and the new assessed value yields the gross tax liability. The difference between the product of the voted millage times the new assessed value (i.e., the tax liability in the absence of any reduction factor) and the tax liability is know as the tax reduction credit.

The property tax revenue that is generated by the effective millage levy equals what could be obtained if the voted millage levy was applied to the 1990 assessed value plus any new construction since that time. HB 920 produces essentially the same result as the 1925 law, with two exceptions. First, under HB 920 personal property taxes are based on the approved millage levy, not the effective levy. Second, there is a differential effect between the two classes of real property.

Consider the following specific example, maintaining the simplifying assumption listed above. Suppose that the county in 1990 has a property tax base of $100 million and it voted a millage rate increase of 5 mills. Thus, in 1990, the county collects $0.5 million from this millage levy. In 1993 a re-appraisal is conducted, and the assessed value increases to $120 million. Suppose that $5 million of the $20 million increase is due to new construction and $15 is due to price increases of existing property. HB 920, in effect, will allow the county to add only the $5 million to its tax base, and therefore the county can only collect $0.525 million in 1993 from the 5 mill levy. To arrive at this value, the following calculations are made. First, divide $15 million (the price increase of existing property) by $120 million (the new assessed value), to obtain 0.125. This tax reduction factor is subtracted from one to yield 0.875, which is then applied to (multiplied by) the 5 mill property tax levy to obtain an effective rate of 4.375 mills. Applying 4.375 mills to the new assessed value of $120 million yields revenue of $0.525 million.

If the entire $20 million increase in assessed value had been due to price increases, then one minus the reduction factor would have been 0.833 (one minus $100 million divided by $120 million). Multiplying the 5 mills by 0.833 yields 4.167 effective mills, which applied to $120 million assessed value, yields a revenue of $0.5 million. In other words, there would be no increase in revenue as a result of the increase in the fair market value of existing real property.

There are several complicating aspects to the calculation and application of the reduction factor. First, separate reduction factors are calculated for every voted millage levy. Since the intent is to restrict the growth in revenue from the time the millage levy is adopted, separate tax reduction factors must be calculated for every millage levy, of which there are thousands. Second, certain millage levies are not subject to the tax reduction factor, including inside millage, millage authorized by the charter of municipalities, fixed dollar millage, and taxes to make bond payments. In addition, the tax reduction factor cannot reduce the total current operating school millage rate below 20 mills or below 2 mills for joint technical schools.

A further complication occurs when school district voters approve replacement levy. Although the new levy may be the same millage as the existing levy, the new millage starts fresh in terms of the tax reduction factor. For example, if the existing millage was 7 mills and one minus the tax reduction factor was 0.8, the effective millage would be 6.3 mills. If a replacement millage of 7 mills is voted in, the calculation of the tax reduction factor starts anew, so that no tax reduction factor is applied in the first year. Thus, the effective millage would be 7 mills. Note that the procedure for a renewal levy is different. A renewal levy is considered a continuation of the existing levy and so the reduction does not start anew, but continues from the point the levy was first adopted.

For each millage levy, separate tax reduction factors must be calculated for each of the two classes of property. Class one includes residential (housing of 4 units or less in which the owner lives) and agricultural, and Class two includes all other real property.

The property tax for an individual parcel is a combination of the millage levies and reduction factors for all jurisdiction in which the parcel is located. Suppose that a parcel is located in three jurisdictions that levy a property tax. Suppose that the school district has an inside millage of 5 mills and two outside millage levies, one for 2 mills and one for 12 mills. Assume that the county has an inside millage of 3 mills and one outside millage of 15 mills, while the municipality has an inside millage of 2 mills and one outside millage of 12 mills. Suppose that one minus the reduction factors for the two school millage levies are 0.50 and 0.45, respectively, while one minus the reduction factors for the county and municipality levies are 0.75 and 0.67, respectively. Suppose that the appraised value of the parcel is $150,000, so that the assessed value with an assessment rate of 35 percent is $52,500. The property tax for this parcel will be $1,873.73, and is calculated as follows:

School district:	5 mills * $52,500	= $262.50
	2 mills * 0.50 * $52,500	= $ 52.50
	12 mills * 0.45 * $52,500	= $283.50
County:	3 mills * $52,500	= $157.50
	15 mills * 0.75 * $52,500	= $590.63
Municipality:	2 mills * $52,500	= $105.00
	12 mills * 0.67 * $52,500	= $422.10
Total		$1,873.73

Without the reduction factors, the property tax payments would have been $2,677.5. But of course, without the reduction factor, the outside millage rate would undoubtedly be less.

The reduction factor reduces the millage rate for the jurisdiction so that *aggregate* revenue does not increase as a result of changes in the price of property in the *aggregate*. Thus, an individual parcel of property that increases in value by the average for the jurisdiction will not experience any increase in property taxes. However, parcels that increase in value by a greater percentage than the average will experience an increase in property taxes, while the parcels that increase at a lower rate will have a reduction in property taxes.

EVALUATION

Ohio has one of the earliest and one of the most restrictive property tax limitations programs in the county, at least until California voted in Proposition 13. Currently, non-voted millage is effectively restricted to 0.35 percent of fair market value, compared, for example, to the 1 percent limit in California. However, California does not allow property taxes to exceed 1 percent of value even by referendum.

There are several points to be made regarding the tax reduction factor. First, the reduction factor controls, but does not eliminate, the growth in property taxes due to increases in prices of property. For example, since the tax reduction factor does not apply to inside millage, revenue will increase as assessed values increase.

Second, since the reduction factor applies only to real property, not personal property, there is a shift in tax burden from real property to personal property as a result of the reduction factor. As the voted millage rate is increased, the total approved millage rate is applied to personal property, while only the effective millage rate is applied to real property. This shift has been offset, at least in part, by the decrease in the assessment rate for personal property. But since the assessment rate for personal property has reached its target of 25 percent, personal property will begin to bear a greater burden of the property tax if there are no further changes in personal property taxation.

Third, the reduction factor restricts the growth in nominal revenues, not real revenues, i.e., it does not allow for any adjustment for inflation. In order to increase property tax revenue beyond what the inside millage and new construction will yield, voters must approve additional millage. This means, that if the cost of providing government services has increased because of inflation, it is necessary to go to the voters if the government is to provide the same level of service. The original rollback provision was adopted in 1925, and for the next several decades inflation was not an issue. After World War II, inflation begin to increase, reaching double digits in the late 1970s. A program of tax limitations adopted in 1925 does not fit the current economic environment in which inflation of 3 to 5 percent per year is normal.

One of the main issues is the effect of the property tax limitation on the growth in property tax revenue. There are two schools of thought regarding tax and expenditure limitations. One view is that elected officials respond to the wishes of the voters, and thus that taxes and expenditures will be the same under a representative and a direct democracy. An alternative view is that self-interested bureaucrats, the political process, and other forces result in expenditures, and thus taxes, that exceed the desires of the public.[60] Studies of the effect of tax and expenditure limitations, e.g., Joyce and Mullins (1991) and Mullins and Joyce (1994), suggest that their effect is not to control the level of spending but to substitute one tax source for another or to shift spending to another governmental level. Preston and Inchiowski (1991) find that state limitations on property taxes do reduce the growth in property tax revenues but that the magnitude of this reduction depends critically on the features of the limitation. As a case in point, a study of Arizona's expenditure and property tax limitations found that they did not affect the level or reliance on property taxes (Fisher and Gade 1991).

Levin (1977) reports that for the period 1942 and 1975, Ohio property taxes per capita were slightly below the national average, but that the growth in property taxes between 1942 and 1967 closely paralleled the national growth rate. Between 1967 and 1975, the growth in property taxes in Ohio was less than the national rate of increase.

Regarding the more recent period, i.e., post HB 920, it was noted above that total property taxes, i.e., personal property as well as real property taxes, per $1000 of income, have tracked the pattern for the United States. In other words, relative to the United States, property taxes have not fallen in Ohio. Of course, it is possible that in the absence of the reduction factor, property taxes would have increased relative to the rest of the states.

There are two studies that have analyzed the growth in property tax revenue for school purposes in Ohio. Sobul (1992) performed two calculations. First, he took the 1975 operating tax rates and applied them to the 1990 taxable values, with tangible personal property reassessed at 35 percent of value. He compared the result with actual 1990 collections and found that statewide there was no difference between the two numbers. In other words, if the tax rates and the personal property assessment rate had been frozen in 1975, and if there had been no tax reduction factor, then the revenue that would have been generated would have been the same as was actually raised. Thus, automatic increases in revenue due to new construction, etc., plus increases in voted millage offset the effect of the tax reduction factors. He also showed that the amount collected in 1990, statewide, after adjusting for inflation was slightly above the revenue raised in 1975.

Levin and Driscoll (1994) performed the same calculation and obtained similar results, i.e., that actual collections of property taxes for school purposes have kept up with inflation. Levin and Driscoll also looked at five separate school districts and found that while some districts did offset inflation, others did not; it depended upon whether the district was willing to vote for additional millage.

Another way to study the effect of the tax reduction factor is to see how the growth in expenditures per student in Ohio compares to the growth elsewhere. In 1969-70 and 1979-80, Ohio spent less than the average in the United States; in particular, in those two years, Ohio's expenditures per student were 10.5 percent and 8.7 percent less than the average for the United States, respectively. By 1990-91, expenditures per student in Ohio were equal to the national average. While the pattern is mixed when making comparisons across the states, generally Ohio's school expenditures per student increased faster than in other states that had about the same per student expenditures at the beginning of the period.

This increase could be due to an increase in the state share of education funding, which has increased. However, local expenditures per student in Ohio increased faster than the average for the United States. In fact, expenditures per student adjusted for inflation increased by 46.5 percent between 1979-80 and 1990-91, or 3.9 percent per year.

While the results of the research of Sobul and Levin and Driscoll have shown that property tax revenues have increased at a rate that offsets inflation, student enrollment in the state has declined. This has resulted in an increase in per student expenditures adjusted for inflation. Sobul shows that while approximately half of the school districts kept up with inflation in terms of total property tax revenue, nearly 73 percent did so on a per student basis.

The evidence certainly suggests that despite the tax reduction factor, total (statewide) property taxes for education in Ohio have at least kept pace with inflation. Part of the growth in school district property tax revenue occurs automatically, i.e., with no tax rate increase. There are several sources for this automatic growth. First, increases in the real property tax base from new construction result in additional revenue with no tax rate increase. Second, increases in personal property are not subject to the reduction factor, although the assessment ratio on most personal property has been reduced from 50 percent in 1976 to 25 percent in 1993.[61] Third, the tax reduction factor cannot reduce the millage rate for schools below 20 mills. Thus, school districts at the 20 mill limit receive automatic revenue increases equal to 20 mills times the total increase in property values. In 1992, more than 200 school districts were at the 20 mill floor for either Class 1, Class 2, or tangible property, and that, therefore, generate additional revenue based on the full value of the increase in taxable value.[62] Fourth, inside millage is not reduced.

The difference between the actual increase in school property tax revenue and the automatic increase is due to voter approved millage rate increases. It is not possible to determine exactly how much of the actual increase in the post HB 920 period is due to automatic increases and how much is due to millage rate increases; data are not readily available that split out increases in taxable property between new construction and increases in value. Nor is there information on the extent of fixed dollar levies. However, probably 40 to 60 percent of the increase in property taxes between 1975 and 1992 is accounted for by automatic increases, while the rest is the result of voter approved increases in millage levies to offset the tax reduction factor (see Exhibit A).

The reduction factor has necessitated that local governments, particularly school districts, go to the voters to ask for millage rate increases in order to generate the revenue needed to offset cost increases due to inflation, man-

EXHIBIT A
Estimation of Automatic Increase in School Property Tax Revenue

Assumptions:

Personal Property is 25 percent of the total property tax base.

New construction is 15 percent of the increase in the real property tax base.

Twenty percent of property tax base is a taxed at the 20 mill minimum.

The taxable value of real property increases by $1 million.

Voted millage is 63 mills in year 1 and the effective millage is 52 mills.

I. First, calculate taxes assuming no change in effective millage, i.e., voters approve levy increases to offset the tax reduction factor.

	Taxable Value (1000s of dollars)		Effective Millage Rate	Taxes		
	Real	Personal		Real	Personal	Total
Year 1	1,500	500	52	78,000	36,500	114,500
Year 2 assuming no change in millage rates	2,500	750	52	130,000	54,750	184,750
Change	1,000	250	0	52,000	18,250	70,250

II. Calculate automatic increase, i.e., assume no change in voted millage.

1. Inside millage times real property base increase:
   10 mills × $1,000,000 = $10,000

2. Personal property millage rate (inside + outside millage) times increase in personal property:
   73 mills × $250,000 = $18,250

3. Outside millage times new construction:
   63 mills X $150,000 = $9,450

4. (Qualifying millage less inside millage) times increase in non-construction value of real property times 20 percent:
   (20–10) × $850,000 × .20 = $1,700

Total automatic increase equals $39,400.

III. Automatic increase divided by full increase:
$39,400/$70,250 = 56.1 percent

dates, etc. (As noted above, statewide school districts have been able to increase expenditures per student faster than inflation, as measured by the consumer price index. However, the cost of education is very labor intensive and thus the cost of education may have increased faster than the consumer price index.) There are several problems that arise from such a process.

The first is that it is costly. Levin and Driscoll (1994) reported that there have been 5,474 school operating millage referenda and another 2,300 capital or bond levies referenda over the past 17 years. While only about 45 percent of these referenda pass, about 75 percent of the districts eventually win approval for the millage levy (Sobul 1991). The jurisdiction must pay for more referenda and must spend time trying to educate the public, which given the complexity of the system is not easy.[63] If going to the voters were a rational process with informed voters, then a direct decision by the voters on the level of expenditures would be reasonable.

While no hard evidence exists, conversations with various individuals suggest that there is something of a game that goes on between the voters and the school districts. Voters may believe that the school district proposes a levy which is either more than is needed or is proposed before it is needed. Thus, voters reject the levy the first time around. School boards, on the other hand, expect that the voters will reject the levy the first time it is proposed and so the boards propose a levy before it is needed or for more than is needed, fully expecting to have to go back to the voters. The result of such a process is what is observed, namely that school districts must go to the voters more than one time to get the millage levy approved.

The uncertainty regarding the outcome of the referenda makes budgeting difficult. If the referenda is not approved, then cuts have to be made, only to be replaced after the second or third referenda passes. It also appears, from the evidence presented by Levin and Driscoll (1994), that there are variations across districts in the voters' willingness to approve added millage.

Ohio is in litigation over its school funding procedures. The lower court in its ruling against the state cited the reduction factor as contributing to the inequity in the current funding of education. In order to maintain the level of expenditures in real terms, most school districts must go to the voters to obtain millage rate increases. While voters statewide have approved increases that are sufficient to keep real local expenditures on education constant, many districts have been unable to obtain such voter approval. Levin and Driscoll (1994) show that there are variations across the state in the ability of school districts to obtain voter approval for millage rate increases. This results in increasing inequality in revenues per student.

The tax reduction factor has had a small effect on the equity of property taxes. Within a taxing jurisdiction, personal property, Class 1 real property, and Class 2 real property pay different effective rates on fair market value, which is clearly an inequity. For any parcel within one of these categories, however, property taxes as a percent of fair market value is the same within any taxing jurisdiction. The value of the tax reduction factor will vary across jurisdictions depending upon the mix of new construction and increase in value of existing property. For equal voted millage rates, parcels of the same fair market value may have different effective tax rates, i.e., property taxes divided by fair market value, depending upon the jurisdiction in which the parcel is located. But this is no more inequitable than having different millage rates in each jurisdiction.

The effect of the tax reduction factor on property tax incidence is less clear. If the tax reduction factor was eliminated (but not the levy limitation), some local jurisdictions may choose a property tax rate that is higher than its current effective rate with the tax reduction factor in place. If property tax rates increase more in low-income communities than in high-income communities, then property taxes as a percent of income will increase for low-income households relative to high-income households, making the property tax more regressive.[64] But, of course, there is nothing on which to base a conjecture of the effect of removing the tax reduction factor. Thus, it is not possible to state how the distribution of property tax payments across income classes might be affected by eliminating the tax reduction factor.

Conclusions Regarding Tax Reduction Factor

The analysis of the tax reduction factor must be considered in conjunction with the limitation on inside millage; we assume here the existence of a 10 mill limit. The tax reduction factor has not prevented property tax increases on real property. School property taxes on real property have increased at a rate exceeding inflation since 1975, in part because the tax reduction factor does not apply to all millage levies, and in part because voters have approved new levies that offset the effect of the tax reduction factor. However, in the absence of the tax reduction factor property taxes might have grown even faster. For example, the tax reduction factor has no doubt encouraged local jurisdictions to adopt other sources of revenue. To the extent local governments have turned to sales and income taxes, property tax growth has been limited. However, total property taxes per $1000 of income increased faster in Ohio during the post HB 920 period than the average for the United States. Thus, while the tax reduction factor may have restrained the growth in property taxes, the evidence suggests otherwise.

The tax reduction factor has resulted, in effect, in a tax classification scheme with different millage rates on personal property, residential property, and non-residential property.[65] Beyond that, the tax reduction factor results in no other inequities within a taxing jurisdiction. Nor are there inter-jurisdictional inequities introduced by the tax reduction factor.

The tax reduction factor adds greatly to the complexity of the system, and has perhaps generated inefficiency as jurisdictions have tried to cope with the process and its timing effects on the budget. Furthermore, the tax reduction factor has direct effects on the local financing of education. The state should be careful not to allow concern over the level of property taxes to have undesired consequences for the level of funding for education. These are two separate and distinct issues.

There are several alternatives for revising the tax reduction factor:

1. The state could eliminate the reduction factor entirely. Because the millage rates are set based on the reduction factor, it would be necessary to roll back the voted millage rates if total revenue is not to increase as a result of the elimination of the tax reduction factor. The state would have to mandate or declare that all voted outside millage rates will have to be reduced to the current effective rate, i.e., the voted millage rate times one minus the reduction factor. Thus, if the reduction factor was 0.46 and the millage rate was 65 mills consisting of 6 inside mills and 60 outside mills (and thus an effective millage rate of 39 mills), then with the elimination of the reduction factor, the millage rate would be reduced to 39 mills, consisting of 6 inside mills and 33 outside mills. Additional increases in the millage rate would require a referendum, unless the 1 percent limit were repealed, but revenues would increase automatically with increases in the value of property.

   The adoption of the tax reduction factor was in response to rapid increases in property taxes due to high inflation, especially for real estate. At present, inflation is more modest. But eliminating the reduction factor does eliminate the control voters have over large automatic increases in property taxes due to high levels of inflation. Of relevance here is the finding for Indiana by Mikesell (1978) that reassessments do not result in an increase in the property tax levy, i.e., local governments reduce millage rates to offset the increase in assessed value. However, Bloom and Ladd (1982) find that cities in Massachusetts, but not towns, do take advantage of reassessment to increase property tax levies. Ladd (1991) finds that before 1975 local governments in North Carolina did make use of reassessments to increase property tax levies, but not since 1975. Thus, the evidence is mixed on whether eliminating the tax reduction factor will result in automatic increases in property tax revenues beyond what would otherwise be expected.

2. A second option is to allow for an adjustment in the reduction factor for inflation while maintaining some control over automatic increases.[66] For example, rather than eliminating all price-related increases in the assessed value, the state could allow for an increase equal to the change in the consumer price index (CPI), or some fraction of the change in the CPI, or the change in the CPI up to some maximum. This option allows for expenditures to increase with infla-

tion, but still retains some control over the increases that would result from large increases in real estate prices. Implementing this option, however, would likely require a constitutional amendment since the constitution allows for a reduction factor for the entire increase in assessed value due to price increases, not fractional increases.

3. Since the property tax is used mainly for school purposes and schools districts rely almost entirely on property taxes, concern over the reduction factor is essentially a concern over education funding. One option is to impose the control directly on education expenditures per student rather than on property taxes. Voters could be asked to approve a base expenditure level per student. This base amount would be allowed to increase each year to adjust for inflation, mandates, etc., where the allowable increase would be set each year by some state-level body. Increases in the expenditures per student beyond the allowed increase would require a vote of the residents of the district. The millage rate would be set each year so as to raise the approved level of revenue.

   It would take some work to design the details of such a system, particularly making allowance for unexpected changes in enrollment, and to allow for the timing differences between setting the millage rate and the actual expenditures. But essentially it would work the same way as the fixed revenue voted millage, the only difference being that the revenue would be revenue per student, not total revenue.

CREDITS

There are three tax credits that apply to the real property tax, a 10 percent rollback, a 2.5 percent rollback, and a homestead credit, that serve to reduce the gross tax liability. The 10 percent credit was adopted as a real property tax relief program in 1972 at the time the state adopted the income tax; the credit applies to all real property. In 1993 the total 10 percent rollback amounted to $531.5 million. A second credit or rollback of 2.5 percent applies only to property that is owner occupied, and was adopted in 1979. In 1993 the 2.5 percent credit amounted to $75.3 million.

There is a third property tax credit program which is a homestead credit restricted to owner occupied housing in which the owner is at least 65 years of age, permanently and totally disabled, or a surviving spouse of an eligible homeowner. The credit is means tested and is equal to the gross millage rate (i.e., before any tax reduction factor) times an amount determined from the following schedule:

Total Income of Owner and Spouse	**Credit is the Lesser of**
$6,500 or less	$5,000 or 75 percent of taxable value
$6,501 to 11,500	$3,000 or 60 percent of taxable value
$11,501 to 16,500	$1,000 or 25 percent of taxable value

There is no credit if income is over $16,500. There are four other states (Indiana, Minnesota, Oregon, and Wisconsin) that provide credits equal to some percentage of gross property tax.[67]

Income for the homestead credit is defined as federal adjusted gross income plus social security and railroad retirement benefits, retirement, pension, annuity, or other types of retirement payments or benefits not included in federal adjusted gross income, and interest on federal, state, and local government obligations. Disability benefits paid by the veteran's administration or a branch of the armed forces are excluded, as well as, beginning in 1976, increases in social security benefits effective after a person receives the homestead exemption for the first time.

For such a small relief program, the definition of income is complex. While it is inequitable to allow someone with large nontaxable income to benefit from the program, these income items are not subject to the income tax. If it is fair to include these non-AGI items in determining eligibility for the homestead exemption, they should be included for income tax purposes as well.

In 1993, the homestead credit amounted to $52.5 million. Because the homestead credit is means tested and the income levels have not changed for several years, the total amount of homestead credit has fallen over time.

The state reimburses local governments for the revenue that is lost because of the credits. The Ohio Department of Education reimburses the schools for their share of the tax credits, while the Tax Commissioner reimburses all other local governments. The county auditors are paid to administer the program; the payment in 1993 was $2.6 million.

The three credit programs are a substantial reduction in property taxes. In 1993, they amounted to a reduction of 14.2 percent of property taxes. Of course, the state had to raise an additional $661.9 million dollars in revenue to finance it. To put it in perspective, $661.9 million is the amount that would be raised by a sales tax rate of 0.7 percent.

Consider first the 10 percent tax rollback, ignoring for the time being the 2.5 percent and homestead credits. Consider a property owner who faces a 50 mill property tax rate. With the 10 percent credit, the individual effectively pays a property tax of 45 mills. From the perspective of the local government, it receives property tax revenue from the property owner equal to 45 mills on the assessed value of the property and a grant from the state equal to 5 mills times the assessed value of the property. From the perspective of the owner, he or she can be thought of as paying a property tax of 50 mills with the state providing a transfer (credit) to the property owner equal to 5 mills on the assessed value. While the state does not actually make the payment to the individual, the outcome is the same whether the owner pays 50 mills to the local jurisdiction and gets a credit directly from the state, or pays 45 mills and the local government gets a payment from the state. Thus, the credit programs can be considered as either a grant to the local government or as a transfer to property owners.

The current credit program is essentially an open-ended entitlement program; the more property tax revenue raised by the local jurisdiction, the more the state pays. As it currently operates, the annual cost to the state is not under the control of the state.

From the perspective of a program of grants to local governments, the program is designed such that the state government gives the local jurisdiction $1 for every $9 the local government raises locally. Thus, it rewards those jurisdictions that raise more property taxes, providing an incentive to use property taxes. This means that those jurisdictions that rely heavily on sales or income taxes are penalized.

As a grant program to local governments, no consideration is given to the fiscal condition of the local jurisdiction. Since the two rollback programs provide transfers, either to the local government or the owners, equal to a constant percent of taxes paid, and since wealthy districts raise more property taxes, the grants go to districts that are less in need. There are many alternative designs for a grant program to local governments that might be considered. A grant program could be designed in which the size of the grant depends inversely on available resources, measured, for example, by property wealth or income per capita, and directly on need, measured, for example, by the expenditures needed to provide some standard set of services with a certain level of quality. Much work has been done at trying to design such a system (see Ladd and Yinger 1989). Since nearly 70 percent of property taxes is raised by school districts, the funds for schools could be rolled into the school funding formula.

If the rollback program was eliminated, local governments would be expected to increase local taxes to make up for the loss in state funds. However, without the grant program, the cost to the local taxpayers for each $1.00 of expenditures will now cost $1.00 rather than $0.90.[68] Thus, the local government is not expected to increase taxes to make up fully for the loss of grants. It is also expected that local governments would attempt to adjust the current revenue mix away from property taxes to other revenue sources.

As relief programs to taxpayers, there are issues of equity and need inherent in the current rollback programs. First, the credit program provides property tax relief to all property owners, not just residential property owners, although only the 10 percent credit applies to nonresidential property. The issue of whether nonresidential property should receive the same reduction as residential property is a difficult one. It is not appropriate to talk about equity between individuals and businesses, and the notion of ability to pay does not apply to businesses.[69] On the other hand, taxing residential property at a lower rate than commercial and industrial property could lead to misallocation of resources.

Second, the current credit program provides the same percentage relief to individuals regardless of income except for the current homestead credit, which is similar to a circuit breaker program. The homestead credit program is rather modest both in terms of who is eligible and the amount of relief that is provided.

Table 7-14 presents estimates of how the magnitude of the three property tax credit programs vary across income classes for homeowners. For the 10 percent and 2.5 percent programs, the average credit across income classes is relatively constant up to the higher income classes. The credit is a smaller percent of income for higher income classes, but the bulk of the credits go to higher income individuals; over 60 percent goes to households with income over $30,000.

If the desire or intent is to provide property tax relief to individuals, i.e., to residential property, an alternative to the 10 percent and 2.5 percent credit programs now in place is to adopt a means tested relief program in the form of a circuit breaker.[70] This would essentially expand the current homestead exemption credit, which is a form of a circuit breaker. While the focus here is on residential circuit breakers, similar programs could be designed for businesses.

INCIDENCE OF THE PROPERTY TAX

With the exception of the corporate income tax, the incidence of the property tax is the most unsettled question in tax incidence analysis. The literature refers to the "old view" and the "new view" of property tax incidence.[71] Under both views, the property tax on land is borne by the owner of the land at the time the tax is imposed. Since the supply of land is perfectly inelastic, the owner can take no action to avoid the tax. An individual who purchases the land after the tax has been imposed will offer a lower price to compensate for the higher taxes he will now have to pay. In other words, the increase in the tax will be capitalized into the price of the land.

The two views differ on who bears the burden of the tax on improvements. The old view held that the property tax on structures increased the prices of goods and services and thus the tax was borne by consumers. Thus, in the case of the property tax on housing the occupant (either the owner in the case of owner occupied housing or the renter) bears the burden, while the tax on nonresidential property is born by consumers of the product produced in the facility, much like a sales tax. Since the value of housing as a

TABLE 7-14
Property Tax Rollbacks and Homestead Credits (Homeowners Only)

Income Class (000s)	2.5% and 10% Rollback		Homestead Credit	
	Average Credit	Class As Percent Of Total	Average Credit	Class As Percent Of Total
0	$114.91	0.4	$318.80	3.6
< 1.0	93.10	0.2	144.40	1.3
1 - 2.5	108.17	0.4	217.35	3.9
2.5 - 5.0	112.81	1.4	342.95	21.6
5.0 - 7.5	104.41	2.4	269.43	31.8
7.5 - 10.0	89.51	2.4	138.74	18.4
10.0 - 12.5	87.83	2.6	82.16	12.3
12.5 - 15.0	85.72	2.5	29.25	4.2
15.0 - 17.5	87.04	2.8	16.07	2.6
17.5 - 20.0	87.20	2.8	-0-	
20.0 - 25.0	93.60	6.3	-0-	
25.0 - 30.0	98.08	6.7	-0-	
30.0 - 35.0	102.63	7.2	-0-	
35.0 - 40.0	109.23	7.3	-0-	
40.0 - 50.0	120.34	13.9	-0-	
50.0 - 75.0	146.22	22.7	-0-	
75.0 - 100.0	191.85	8.5	-0-	
100.0 - 150.0	248.27	5.4	-0-	
> 150.0	346.70	4.1		

Source: Author's estimates based on *1990 Census of Population and Housing, Public Use Micro Sample.*

share of income is smaller the greater the income, the property tax was considered highly regressive.

The new view is that the owners of capital bear the burden of the property tax on structures and equipment. If the stock of improvements and equipment is fixed, at least relative to the labor force, then if a uniform tax is imposed on the value of all capital throughout the economy, capital owners are unable to shift the tax burden unto either the consumer of goods and services or labor. Thus, the owners of capital bear the burden. However, property tax rates vary between jurisdictions. In response to the differential tax rates, capital will migrate from high tax jurisdictions to low tax jurisdictions. For example, consider rental units. If the tax rate is low in one jurisdiction, more rental units will be built there. This will lower the rent on units in that jurisdiction, and correspondingly, raise the rent in the higher tax jurisdictions. Thus, the new view holds that the return to capital falls as a result of the tax on capital, but consumers face differential prices across jurisdictions, some paying more and some less. On average, consumers bear no burden.

The basic theory inherent in the new view is generally accepted. However, the specific conclusion of the new view depends upon the value of several parameters. The debate regarding the incidence centers on these value of these parameters.

The theory applies to the question, what is the incidence of a national property tax? The answer we get will be different if we ask, what is the incidence of an increase in the property tax rate within one jurisdiction? If the jurisdiction is small relative to the market for capital, then we can assume that the price of capital will not change. In response to the higher tax rate, capital will have an incentive to leave the jurisdiction. In order to retain the capital, the price of land or labor must decrease or the price of the product must increase. What happens depends upon the responsiveness of the various factors of productions and consumers to changes in taxes and prices. If labor is relatively mobile and if close substitutes are available to consumers, then the price of land will fall as demand for it decreases. But it is also possible to build a case for either the consumer or labor bearing part or all of the increase in the tax.[72] In all cases, however, the tax on owner occupied housing is born by the owner.

Despite this uncertainty regarding the incidence, the commonly adopted assumption is that an increase in property tax rates will be passed along in the form of higher prices. For owner occupied and rental housing, this means that the occupant will bear that part of the tax increase. For other goods and services, part of the tax is exported to consumers in other jurisdictions, while the remainder will be born by consumers in the form of a broad based sales tax.

We calculated the incidence of a statewide 5 mill property tax (effective rate) on housing, owner occupied and rental. The calculations were based on the *1990 Census of Population and Housing, Public Use Micro Sample*. The data provide information on income, property taxes paid by owners, and rent paid by renters. We had to make an assumption regarding the proportion of rent that is accounted for by property taxes which we took to be 12 percent of rent. We present results showing the effective tax rate (tax payments within the class divided by income within the class) both with and without the reduction in the tax payments for the 10 percent and 2.5 percent rollbacks, and homestead credit. Table 7-15 presents the results of the calculations. As can be seen, such an increase in the property tax is highly regressive, with or without the various credits.[73] The difference between the effective tax rate with and without the credits is somewhat larger for lower income households, due to the homestead credit, but for most income classes the difference in the effective rates is about the same. The effect of the credits is thus to slightly reduce the regressivity of the property tax.

There are few studies that have examined the incidence of the residential property tax in isolation, so there is no professional consensus as to the accuracy of these assumptions and calculations. Three studies which address the incidence of the residential property tax come to different conclusions. Setting aside the burden on the lowest income class due to data problems,

TABLE 7-15
Incidence of a 5-Mill Increase in the Property Tax Rate: Residential Only

Income Class	Effective Tax Rate	
	With Credit	Without Credits
1,001 - 2,500	5.27%	5.58%
2,501 - 5,000	1.97%	2.11%
5,001 - 7,500	1.31%	1.45%
7,501 - 10,000	0.99%	1.09%
10,001 - 12,500	0.81%	0.88%
12,501 - 15,000	0.70%	0.74%
15,001 - 17,500	0.63%	0.66%
17,501 - 20,000	0.54%	0.57%
10,001 - 15,000	0.47%	0.50%
25,001 - 30,000	0.39%	0.42%
30,001 - 35,000	0.33%	0.36%
35,001 - 40,000	0.29%	0.32%
40,001 - 50,000	0.25%	0.28%
50,001 - 75,000	0.21%	0.24%
75,001 - 100,000	0.19%	0.21%
100,001 - 150,000	0.18%	0.20%
150,001 and higher	0.15%	0.17%

Source: Author's calculations based on *1990 Census of Population and Housing, Public Use Micro Sample*

Netzer (1966) and Harmon (1989) find rough proportionality, ACIR (1973) and Folkman and MacDonald (1993) find fairly sharp regressivity. The studies are not strictly comparable due to differences in coverage, methodologies and definitions.

The Minnesota Department of Revenue (1993) recently published a detailed and extensive study of the incidence of Minnesota taxes. For the property tax on residential property, the study found that the property tax was relatively proportional, with a somewhat larger effective tax rate at the lowest income class and the middle income class. The results are driven by the assumption that landlords bear a large proportion of the tax on rental property. This result is consistent with other studies based on the new view that capital bears the burden of the property tax.

A further issue regarding the incidence is the use of annual income on which to compute effective tax rates. Since income varies from year-to-year, it is more appropriate to measure incidence on the basis of average income over several year, perhaps even one's lifetime. Fullerton and Rogers (1993) conducted such a study and found that for the property tax, the effective tax rate was U-shaped, i.e., decreasing over lower incomes and increasing over higher incomes, when income was measured on the basis of lifetime income. Metcalf (1994) also estimated the lifetime incidence of the property tax and concluded that it is regressive. Clearly, there is no consensus regarding the incidence of the property tax. However, it does appear that the residential segment is regressive, while the entire property tax for a state is close to proportional.

CIRCUIT BREAKER PROGRAM[74]

INTRODUCTION

The presumed regressivity of the tax on residential property has been used to justify the institution of relief schemes designed to blunt the burden of that tax on lower income taxpayers. Most states have enacted some policy designed to provide progressive relief of property taxes imposed on households. This section presents several circuit breakers plans as an alternative to the current credit programs. The characteristics of circuit breaker plans in other states are summarized and the effects of several particular plans which could be implemented in Ohio are simulated. A summary of the features of the circuit breaker programs in other states is provided by the ACIR (1993). Ohio's homestead credit does qualify as a circuit breaker, but it is a very simple and minor program.

A property tax circuit breaker is a property tax relief program that reduces the tax burden, or effective tax rate, of the residential property tax. If the property tax burden for a household exceeds a certain threshold, a portion of the excess is relieved, usually by a refundable credit on the taxpayer's state income tax bill. Such a program is especially suited to providing relief to homeowners whose current income is low relative to their property wealth, as may happen with retirees. However, circuit breakers have been criticized for providing more relief to those with greater property wealth (holding income constant), and for providing forgiveness of tax liabilities when deferral may be more appropriate (such as in the case of those with temporarily depressed income or retirees).[75]

Circuit breaker programs offer policy-makers flexibility in terms of establishing a standard for excessive property tax burdens and the use of eligibility standards permit programs to be targeted to particular classes of taxpayers, in terms of income, age, ownership status, or particular classes of property, such as residential or agricultural. Finally, since the relief is usually provided through an income tax credit, circuit breaker programs can be, and are often designed to provide benefit to renters as well.[76]

In 1992, thirty-four states and the District of Columbia had some form of circuit breaker program. The specifics of these programs vary considerably across states, but to the extent information is available and comparable, some summary and comparison can be made. Of those states with programs, five limit eligibility to homeowners and twenty-eight make some provision for renters. The renters' eligibility is based on a presumption that some fraction of the rent represents the property tax; the presumed fraction ranges from 8.5 percent (Nevada) to 35 percent (Connecticut).[77] Twenty-nine states provide income limits for eligibility (one state, Maryland, imposes a limit on net worth), twenty-five states have programs limited to elderly and sixteen have programs with other limits, such as disabled or veteran status. In only three states and the District of Columbia is the cost of the relief borne by the local government; in the balance, the states finance the relief, usually in the form of a credit against state income tax liabilities. The average per household benefit for homeowners ranged from $80 (California) to $551 (Wyoming). In states in which benefits were paid to renters, the average benefits were typically lower, ranging from $39 (Arizona) to $385 (Connecticut).[78]

Of twenty-nine states reporting income eligibility criteria, eighteen set the income limit between $10,000 and $25,000.[79] Of the eighteen states for which renter benefits depend on a fraction of the rent paid, five assigned a fraction between 11 and 15 percent. In many states, the proportion of income which is used to define an excessive property tax burden varies with the level of income; those fractions range from 0 to 13 percent, with most in the 3 to 6 percent range. Most states rebate less than 100 percent of the excessive tax burden; some as low as 35 percent.

Circuit Breaker Simulations

We turn now to the results of a number of simulations which were performed in order to answer the following questions about the fiscal impacts of alternative circuit breaker programs in the state of Ohio. What would such a program cost? How many households would benefit? How would the benefits be distributed across income classes and category of tenure (owner or renter)? The hypothetical programs are defined by their eligibility criteria, by the definition of overload in terms of the effective property tax rate, by the portion of the overload rebated, by any limit on the magnitude of the rebate, and by the fraction of rent that is deemed to be property tax. The amount of rebate or relief, CB, is computed by the following formula:

$$CB = t\,(PT - k \cdot I), \text{ or}$$
$$CB = CAP, \text{ whichever is greater}$$

where I represents household income, k represents the proportion of income which defines the excessive burden threshold, PT represents the amount of property tax paid, t represents the fraction of the excessive burden which is rebated by the government, and CAP represents the maximum amount of rebate granted. For renters, the term PT is replaced by where AR represents the annual rent payments and p represents the fraction of rent deemed to be property tax.

These computations may be explained by way of an example. Suppose that *k*, the threshold burden was 3 percent; that *t*, the proportion of the excess burden to be rebated was 100 percent; and that *p*, the fraction rent assumed to be property tax was 12 percent. Then, for a household with income of $35,000 and paying $1,200 in property taxes, the rebate would be computed as

$$150 = 1.00 \cdot (1{,}200 - 0.03 \cdot 35{,}000).$$

Alternatively, consider a household with an income of $18,000 which pays $7,200 per year in rent. In this case, the property tax burden is assumed to be $864 = 0.12 · 7,200 and the rebate would be computed as

$$\$324 = 1.00 \cdot (864 - 0.03 \cdot 18{,}000).$$

Ten different programs, as described in Table 7-16, were simulated. Renters are included in all of the plans; however, the results report total cost, number of beneficiaries, and average benefit separately for homeowners and renters, so the impacts of excluding renters are easily obtained. The particular parameter values for *k, t, CAP*, and *p* were selected to be repre-

TABLE 7-16
Definitions of Hypothetical Circuit Breaker Programs

Plan	Eligibility	Definition Of Overload(R)	Maximum Relief (CAP)
A	Income < 15,000 Age > 60	3%	$1,000
B	All	3%	$1,000
C	Income < 15,000 Age > 60	6%	$1,000
D	All	6%	$1,000
E	All	1%	$1,000
F	Income < 15,000 Age > 60	1%	$1,000
G	Income < 25,000 Age > 60	3%	$1,000
H	All	3%	$1,500
I	Income < 30,000 Age > 60	3%	$1,000
J	All	3%	$1,000

sentative of programs in place in the other states and to provide measures of the effects on program costs and benefits of the various policy decisions which might be made about such a program. In all cases 100 percent of the overload is rebated, i.e., $t = 1$ for all plans.

The simulated plans are quite simple in that the parameter values are the same for all taxpayers; for many existing programs, the value of the k and t vary with income. The Census defines income in a particular way; the actual income definition that might be adopted will likely differ. For example, adjusted gross income is an income measure that is readily available and that makes administration of the circuit breaker easier than other income definitions.

Table 7-17 summarizes the simulation results with respect to the plans' costs and average benefits, in total and distributed across homeowners and renters. The computations are based on data from the 1990 Census which reports household income and property tax payments for 1989, and rent and demographic information as of April, 1990. Since the rebate is based on the difference between taxes paid (or imputed) and some fraction of income, extrapolations of the results to subsequent years are sensitive to differential rates of inflation for property taxes and income. For example, if property taxes rise while income remains stagnant, simply inflating the results would understate the changes in the rebate. Conversely, if average incomes rise faster than average property taxes, fewer households would qualify and inflating the results reported here would overstate the changes in the total cost and average rebate. Further, changes in the distribution of income would affect the rebates under these plans, even if the average property tax and income remained the same. So, the results should be interpreted as representing the consequences of the various plans had they been implemented in 1990 and *indicative* of the consequences of implementing the plans in later years.

Plan **A**, which we use as the baseline, provides benefits to low-income elderly households (household income less than $15,000 and at least one household member 60 years old or older) for which the property tax burden exceeds 3 percent of household income. The rebate is equal to 100 percent of the excessive burden, subject to a maximum of $1,000. Renters participate in the program, with 12 percent of their rent being treated as property taxes paid. Plan **A** would cost just under $100 million per year, which is approximately 47 percent of the residential property taxes paid by low-income elderly households in 1989. About 62 percent of low-income elderly households would receive relief averaging $301 per household.[80] Seventy-seven percent of the relief dollars would go to homeowners, who represent 63 percent of the beneficiaries. As may be seen from Table 7-17, the implied tax burden for renters is smaller, on average, than for homeowners, and the average benefit is correspondingly smaller.[81]

If eligibility is not limited to the low-income elderly, as in Plan **B**, and holding all other parameters of the program constant, the total cost of the relief program rises to almost $360 million. This represents about 13 percent

TABLE 7-17
Summary of Simulation Results

Plan		Total	Homeowners	Renters
A	Total Relief (000s)	$ 98,601	$ 76,304	$ 21,870
	Beneficiaries	327,318	206,422	120,896
	Average Relief	$301	$372	$180
B	Total Relief (000s)	$ 359,182	$ 268,108	$ 91,074
	Beneficiaries	1,192,538	731,295	461,243
	Average Relief	$301	$367	$197
C	Total Relief (000s)	$ 48,477	$ 39,650	$ 8,827
	Beneficiaries	156,029	116,357	39,672
	Average Relief	$310	$341	$222
D	Total Relief (000s)	$ 117,747	$ 79,694	$ 38,054
	Beneficiaries	405,020	221,988	183,032
	Average Relief	$291	$359	$207
E	Total Relief (000s)	$1,327,987	$1,024,150	$ 303,837
	Beneficiaries	3,306,390	2,754,060	1,143,198
	Average Relief	$402	$473	$265
F	Total Relief (000s)	$ 160,571	$ 116,667	$ 43,903
	Beneficiaries	438,510	269,700	168,810
	Average Relief	$366	$433	$260
G	Total Relief (000s)	$ 143,657	$ 118,335	$ 25,323
	Beneficiaries	463,397	328,071	135,326
	Average Relief	$310	$361	$187
H	Total Relief (000s)	$ 377,315	$ 285,659	$ 91,656
	Beneficiaries	1,192,538	731,295	461,243
	Average Relief	$316	$390	$199
I	Total Relief (000s)	$ 155,597	$ 129,806	$ 25,791
	Beneficiaries	497,534	360,494	137,040
	Average Relief	$313	$360	$188
J	Total Relief (000s)	$ 384,110	$ 292,453	$ 91,656
	Beneficiaries	1,192,538	731,295	461,243
	Average Relief	$322	$400	$199

Source: Author's calculations based on *1990 Census of Population and Housing, Public Use Micro Sample.*

of the total residential property tax paid in 1989. Twenty-eight percent of households in the state would receive benefits. The average rebate for those who receive relief is about the same as the baseline plan. Furthermore, under this unrestricted eligibility standard, the distribution of benefits between homeowners and renters changes somewhat. A smaller percentage of all households live in owned homes than do the low-income elderly, so a slightly smaller proportion of the benefits accrue to homeowners (75 percent) than under the baseline plan (77 percent). As in the baseline plan, the average benefit is considerably larger for homeowners than for renters.

Plan **C** maintains the general eligibility requirements of the baseline plan, but raises the threshold property tax burden which is considered excessive from 3 percent of income to 6 percent. Thus, the total property taxes considered excessive falls, the total cost of the rebate program falls to $48 million, and the number of beneficiaries falls to about 48 percent of those receiving benefits under the baseline plan. Most of the households that receive benefits under both plans (Plan **A** and Plan **C**) receive smaller benefits under Plan **C**. However, since most of those who receive benefits under Plan **A** but receive no benefits under Plan **C** had received relatively small benefits, the average benefit under Plan **C** is somewhat higher: $310 versus $301 under Plan **A**.[82]

Plan **D** has no eligibility requirements and, like Plan **C**, sets *k* equal to 6 percent. The differences between Plan **D** and Plan **B** are similar to that found between Plan **A** and Plan **C**.

Plans **E** and **F** are similar to Plans **A** and **B**, except that the definition of overload, i.e., *k*, is reduced to 1 percent. Relative to Plans **A** and **B** the effect of reducing *k* to 1 percent is to increase the cost by 63 percent and 269 percent, respectively. Reducing *k* when there is no income limit greatly expands the cost of the program because it brings into the program those households that pay large property taxes, i.e., those at the upper end of the income scale.

In Plans **H** and **J**, the maximum relief is raised from $1,000 to $1,500 and $2,000, respectively, and there is no income or age limit. Plan **H** results in a 5 percent increase in the total cost over Plan **B**, to just over $377 million and a small increase in the average benefit to $316. Plan **J** has a similar effect. The modest increase is a consequence of the relatively small number of beneficiaries under Plan **B** who receive the maximum relief.

Finally, Plans **G** and **I** increase the income limit to $25,000 and $30,000, respectively. Plan **G** increases the cost of the program relative to plan **A** by 45 percent. This increase is due mainly to an increase in the number of beneficiaries and not to an increase in the average benefit. Plan **I** increases the cost of the program relative to plan **A** by 58 percent, and again the average benefit increases only marginally from $301 to $313.

Distributional Considerations

Table 7-18 shows the distribution of relief under the baseline circuit breaker plan. The baseline plan is progressive; the average dollar of relief going to the lowest income classes is greater than that going to higher income classes and a larger share of lower income households benefit.

Table 7-19 shows the distributional results under Plan **B**. The relative progressivity of the circuit breaker plan is more evident; nearly 60 percent of the relief dollars accrue to households with incomes less than $17,500. About 7 percent of households with incomes greater than $40,000 receive benefits under the circuit breaker.

TABLE 7-18
Circuit Breaker Plan A

Income Class (000s)	Average Benefit (Per Beneficiary)	Percent Of Total Relief	Percent of Eligible Households Benefiting
0	$480.99	4.57	89.8
< 1.0	331.61	1.64	91.3
1 - 2.5	371.44	3.54	82.8
2.5 - 5.0	251.23	11.94	70.4
5.0 - 7.5	272.33	21.44	66.2
7.5 - 10.0	308.21	21.29	62.7
10.0 - 12.5	313.74	19.24	60.0
12.5 - 15.0	318.24	16.33	56.6

Source: Author's calculations based on *1990 Census of Population and Housing, Public Use Micro Sample.*

TABLE 7-19
Circuit Breaker Plan B

Income Class	Average Benefit	Percent Of Total Relief	Percent Of Eligible Households Benefiting
0	$431.35	3.43	90.0
< 1.0	515.43	2.05	92.8
1 2.5	322.15	3.30	85.6
2.5 - 5.0	257.24	8.02	71.5
5.0 - 7.5	262.03	10.49	70.2
7.5 - 10.0	271.75	9.14	64.8
10.0 - 12.5	263.83	8.03	59.3
12.5 - 15.0	273.91	7.01	51.6
15.0 - 17.5	280.90	6.41	41.8
17.5 - 20.0	296.26	5.23	34.0
20.0 - 25.0	310.65	8.76	27.1
25.0 - 30.0	327.17	6.38	20.1
30.0 - 35.0	341.86	4.86	15.3
35.0 - 40.0	327.03	3.60	13.5
40.0 - 50.0	364.45	4.82	10.2
50.0 - 75.0	442.11	4.92	7.0
75.0 -100.0	540.10	1.49	6.4
100.0-150.0	659.01	0.84	6.1
> 150.0	295.49	0.02	0.5

Source: Author's calculations based on *1990 Census of Population and Housing, Public Use Micro Sample.*

LAND VALUE TAXATION

Currently, land and improvements in Ohio are assessed at the same percent of value, i.e., 35 percent. Many individuals have argued that land should be taxed more heavily than improvements; the extreme case of only taxing land was advanced by Henry George (1879), whose writings led to the single tax movement.[83] There are many examples of countries that have in the recent past, or are now taxing land more heavily than improvement, for example, New Zealand, the Netherlands, Australia, South Africa, Denmark, and Taiwan. In the United States, early property taxes were essentially land value taxes; in fact, Ohio had a land value property tax from 1803 until 1825. Hawaii had a land value tax but has since dropped it. Fairhope, Alabama has a revenue system that results in only the value of land being taxed. Pennsylvania allows its cities to tax buildings at a lower rate than land, a system referred to as a graded tax or split rate system, and some 48 cities have done so. Pittsburgh has taxed land more heavily than buildings since 1914, and in 1979 and 1980 restructured the tax so that land is taxed at more than five times the rate on structures.

The basic argument that has been advanced in favor of land value taxation is that land value taxation results in economic neutrality. The supply of land is essentially fixed, and thus a tax on land will not alter the supply of sites. Land taxes should be fully capitalized into the value of the property, and thus the rent to the user will be the same before and after the imposition of the tax. Therefore, a tax on land should be neutral with respect to the intensity and timing of the use of the land.

The property tax on improvements, however, is not neutral. Higher property taxes are a penalty on improvements and thus the tax discourages investment in structures. The literature suggests that shifting to a land value tax will have two effects.[84] First, it will reduce the liquidity of land owners, thus encouraging more rapid development. Second, reducing the tax on improvements increases the return on capital investment, thereby, creating an incentive for new construction. Brueckner (1986) has shown that a shift from a property tax system that taxes land and structures equally to a graded system will increase the intensity of use of land. Mills (1981) has shown that it is also possible for a graded system to have a timing effect on the development of land, hastening economic development.

Netzer (1966) cites a number of studies that investigated the developmental effect of land value taxation in other countries. These studies did not find any significant effect. Most of the more recent empirical studies, for example, Richman (1965), Woodruff and Ecker-Racy (1969), and Clark (1974), of the effect of a switch to land value tax, or a split rate tax, find little effect. Some studies, for example, Archer (1972), Grieson (1974), and Pollack and Shoup (1977) do find a modest effect on real estate investment. A review of the literature on land value taxation is provided by Cuddington (1978).

Several studies have been conducted using Pittsburgh's recent experience with graded rates as a case study. Studies conducted in the early 1980s found no effect on development,[85] but more recent study by Oates and Schwab (1992) finds substantial effects. After the adoption of a more extreme graded tax system at the end of the 1970s, Pittsburgh experienced a strong building boom, far in excess of anything that took place in the other major cities in the region. The building boom was basically a center city phenomenon; it did not extend to the rest of the metropolitan area. It was, moreover, a boom in commercial building activity.

But Oates and Schwab are quick to point out that there are other possible reasons for the building boom, and while they tried to separate out these other causes, it is not possible to isolate the fiscal experiment from all of the possible causes using one case study.[86] They conclude (p. 10), "What the Pittsburgh experience suggests to us is that the movement to a graded tax system can, in the right setting, provide some stimulus to local building activity."

Any developmental effect from a graded tax system results from the reduction in the tax on structures, the increase in the tax on land merely replaces the lost revenue. The development effect should also be found if property taxes are reduced, either in general or through tax abatement programs such as enterprise zones. The evidence suggests that reduced property taxes do not result in large increases in investment in the area. (The effect of tax abatement programs and enterprise zones is explored more fully by Wasylenko (1995) in this volume.)

In the six Ohio counties containing the larger cities, land values comprise from 18 to 27 percent of the total value of industrial property and from 22 to 30 percent of the total value of commercial property. Thus, assume that land is 25 percent of value and that the effective millage rate, i.e., net of the tax reduction factor, is 65 mills on Class 2 property, which is consistent with the actual rates in Cleveland and Cincinnati. This implies that to maintain constant revenue, for every reduction of one mill on improvements, the millage rate on land would have to increase by 2.2 mills. For example, consider a property (land and structure) with a taxable value of $1 million. If the millage rate on the structure was reduced from 65 mills to 50 mills, then to collect the same $65,000 in revenue, the millage rate on the land would have to be 110 mills.

REDUCING RELIANCE ON PROPERTY TAXES

The property tax is not a very popular tax (ACIR 1993). There are several reasons for this opinion. First, payments are frequently made in large installments, unlike the sales tax which is paid "a penny at a time." Second, because of errors in the assessment of property, horizontal inequities exist, i.e., properties of equal fair market value are given different assessed values. Third, although property value is positively associated with income, there is large variation in the value of property owned by individuals with similar income. Thus, the magnitude of the tax that some individuals pay is only loosely related to current income; for example, retirees who continue to live in a large house after retiring pay a much larger property taxes relative to their income then a younger couple with the same income.

These problems can be summed up in the following two quotes:

> If we sum up all these inherent defects, it will be no exaggeration to say that the general property tax in the United States is a dismal failure . . . one of the worst taxes known in the civilized world. . . it's retention can be explained only through ignorance or inertia. (Seligman 1885)

> If any tax could have been eliminated by adverse criticism, the general property tax should have been eliminated long ago. One searches in vain for one of its friends to defend it intelligently. ... Should some prosecuting attorney drag the tax as a culprit before a bar of justice, he would be embarrassed by the abundance of expert evidence against it...Yet the tax persists. (Jensen 1931)

Despite the continued criticism and attempts to restrict its use through tax limitation movements, the property tax persists. In the past, many students of the property tax foresaw a continuing decline in the importance of the property tax (Netzer 1983), while more recently the opposite view has been espoused (Bahl, Sjoquist, and Williams 1990).[87] Beginning in the early 1980s, the relative reliance on property taxes by local governments begin, after decades of decline, to increase. Within the past few years, interest has been created, with Michigan as the catalyst, to reduce school property taxes by increasing state funding of education. Other states are discussing significantly increasing state spending on education as a way of reducing or eliminating property taxes for school purposes. For example, the Wisconsin state government recently voted to do this, but without a plan for implementing the change. Discussions are being held in South Carolina, Pennsylvania, Georgia, New Hampshire, and elsewhere.

The movement to shift education funding to the state is fueled in part by high property taxes. For example, Michigan and Wisconsin have very high property taxes per capita (Table 7-1). Elsewhere, the gradual assumption of education financing by states is the result of court orders and general reform.[88]

Should Ohio consider replacing its property tax, in whole or part, with another revenue source? Ohio's property taxes are not high relative to other states ($540 per capita compared to the United States average of $666 per capita), so the push that exists in states such as Michigan is not as strong. Second, for decades voters have determined directly not just the millage rate, but, through the tax reduction factor, the actual revenue collected. Third, residents in several school districts have had the option of adopting an income tax as a substitute for increases in property taxes.[89] Sobul (1993) reports that between 1989 and 1992, 206 school districts put the income tax on the ballot at least once. Eighty-three of those districts, or 40 percent, adopted the income tax. Less than 20 percent adopted it on the first attempt; in total, the 206 districts held 315 elections. The districts adopting the income tax were generally in areas in which there is no municipal income tax. It is also of interest to note that most of the income tax adoptions were in the northwest part of the state, which is the section of the state in which the residential share of the property tax base has increased the most. So given the opportunity to adopt a substitute for the property tax, voters in many districts have chosen not to.[90]

It is thus difficult to argue that there is a strong need or desire to replace the property tax with some alternative tax. However, the real property tax base has not grown much in inflation adjusted terms and its elasticity is low. Furthermore, the state's share of expenditures on education is low relative to the rest of the United States. As noted above, the state is in litigation over its school funding program, having lost in the lower court. Given all of that, and that almost all of the local funding for education comes from property taxes, the state should consider finding an alternative or additional source of revenue for education.

There are several issues involved in shifting from the property tax to state taxes. If the shift away from property taxes is to be significant, then it will be necessary to rely on increases in either the sales or the income tax, or a combination of the two. While additional revenue could be obtained from revenue sources such as increased taxes on cigarettes, these sources cannot produce sufficient revenue to replace a sizable percent of the property tax revenue.

One approach to reducing property taxes is to adopt a very extensive circuit breaker program. By setting the parameters appropriately, the amount of property tax relief that is granted can be made very large. Relying on a circuit breaker allows the state to target the property tax relief by income level. Assuming the typical design, the circuit breaker will direct relief to owner occupied and renters, but not to business.

With an expansive circuit breaker program, increases in property tax rates will have very small tax consequences for individuals who qualify for the circuit breaker. In other words, the state will pay a large percent of any property tax increase. Thus, voters are likely to support increased property tax rates, letting the state pay for their share of the property tax increase. The result will be higher property tax rates on businesses, and greater spending at the local level.

Another approach is to replace part of the 20 mill qualifying levy for schools with an increase in state aid. For FY95 the state average effective (post reduction factor) millage on residential and agricultural property for schools is 29.06 (Ohio Department of Education 1994). Thus, most of the school property taxes are raised by the qualifying 20 mills. The state could reduce the 20 qualifying mills and replace the lost revenue by increasing its contribution to the foundation grant. Reducing the qualifying millage by 7 mills will cost about what an increase of 1 percentage point on the sales tax will yield.[91]

Reducing the qualifying millage will not produce the same type of incentive as the circuit breaker. If the local school district wants to increase the local contribution beyond the lower qualifying levy, it will cost the local residents one dollar for every dollar it raises, less any rollback credit that is granted. Given that property taxes are now lower, residents may decide to increase the millage rate some, but the incentive to do so is much less than with the circuit breaker program.

Alternatively, the state could increase the foundation grant, mandating a rollback in school property taxes. Providing property tax relief by reducing the qualifying millage rate versus increasing the foundation grant will result in different distributions of the property tax relief. Reducing the qualifying millage will reduce every one's property tax by the same number of mills. Thus, those individuals with high property values will receive more dollars of tax relief than someone with small property value. The property tax relief from an increase in the foundation grant will depend upon the number of students in the district. If every district had the same ratio of students to property owners, then every property owner in the state would receive the same dollar amount of property tax relief.

Some states, e.g., New Mexico and Washington, have put restrictions on the ability of districts to spend large amounts per student relative to the state norm. These restrictions might be imposed to limit inequality in funding or to limit property taxes. If it is desired to restrict local topping up of state spending, then a requirement for a super majority vote on millage levies beyond a certain rate could be imposed either separately or as part of an increase in state spending on education. Alternatively, if local spending, defined either in terms of per student or as a percent of the state grant plus the local contribution from the qualifying millage, exceeds some set amount, then the state might impose a "tax" on the excess. For example, if the local district expenditures exceeded, say, 40 percent of the total of the state grant plus qualifying millage revenue, then a percentage of the excess, say 25 percent, would be paid to the state. The revenue raised this way could be put into a special fund and redistributed to all school districts; this is one version of a pooling program.[92] The two variables, the level that defines the excess and the "tax" or payment rate, can be varied to make it more or less expensive to exceed the desired expenditure level. Such a plan also addresses the equity in school funding raised in the recent court case.

SUMMARY

Ohio's reliance on property taxation, either in total or as a share of total revenue is below that of the nation and its surrounding states. The property tax is used primarily by school districts. Growth in the real property tax base has been slow relative to the growth in income, and there are substantial differences across the state in the rate of growth of the base.

While the property tax appears to be well administered, it is a complicated system. There are several options for reform of the real property tax that might be considered.

- Increase the frequency of re-appraisals and updates so that inter-county and intra-county differences in actual assessment rates are reduced.
- Adopt qualification requirements for assessing officials, both those directly employed by the county auditors and employees of firms hired to conduct re-appraisals and updates.
- Shift from an assessment rate of 35 percent to an assessment rate on real property of 100 percent, and reduce millage rates in order to maintain revenue neutrality.
- Since there is evidence that the current procedures result in current use values for agricultural land that are too low, change those procedures.
- Tax exempt property has increased over time and there is evidence that the concept of tax exempt property has been broadened. Thus, consider conducting a careful study of the state's policy toward exempt property.
- The tax reduction factor is a source of complexity and results in numerous millage elections. Consideration should be given to three options:
    - eliminate the tax reduction factor;
    - allow an adjustment for inflation in the calculation of the tax reduction factor; and
    - change voting on school millage levies to a vote on school expenditures, either total or per student.

- Eliminate the 10 percent and 2.5 percent rollbacks and use those funds to design a grant program to local governments and to expand the homestead credit into a full circuit breaker program.

APPENDIX
GLOSSARY OF PROPERTY TAX TERMS

Annual Revaluation–The county auditor is obligated to make necessary changes in assessed value each year if he finds value has changed from the value at which it is listed on the tax list; but he can only be ordered to do so by the Tax Commissioner in years of sexennial re-appraisal or triennial revaluation.

Assessed Value—The portion of true market value to which the tax rate is applied to obtain the amount from which reductions are made to determine the net taxes due. The percentage of appraised value used in determining assessed value for real property is 35%. For personal property it is: public utility property—88%; electrical production equipment—100%; all other personal property—25%.

Homestead Exemption—Tax relief granted to qualified elderly and disabled homeowners. The tax reduction is equal to the gross millage rate multiplied by a reduction in taxable value determined by the income class of the homeowner.

Inside Mill—A tax levied "inside" the ten-mill limitation; inside mills need only be approved by the taxing authority of the taxing district that levies the tax.

Levy—To impose a tax (verb); the tax imposed (noun). Types of tax levies: (1) debt levy—a tax imposed for the purpose of paying the interest on and retiring bonds issued by a taxing district; (2) general levy for current expenses—a tax imposed for the purpose of paying for all expenditures of a taxing district except debt retirement or certain permanent improvements (proceeds from a general levy are deposited in the general fund of the taxing district); (3) special levies—taxes imposed for one of several specific purposes enumerated by statute. Special levies may not be used for any purpose other than that for which they were voted. A special fund is created for each special levy, and proceeds from each special levy are deposited in the appropriate fund.

Mill—A unit of value equal to 1/10 of one cent ($0.001).

Outside Mill—A tax levied “outside” the ten-mill limitation; outside mills require the approval of the electorate.

Real Property—Land and improvements.

Sexennial Re-appraisal—Once every six years, each county must revalue all real property; re-appraisals are staggered so that in each year they are conducted in some counties.

Tax Commissioner—Chief Officer of the Department of Taxation; the Commissioner administers the assessment of personal and railroad property, supervises the taxation of real property in the state, and is charged with the duty of achieving uniformity in the taxation of real property.

Tax Reduction Factor—(Sometimes referred to as a real property tax credit or by the name of its predecessor, the H.B. 920 credit.) Real property taxes on each of two classes of real property in each taxing district are reduced by a percentage so that the total taxes collected from that class do not exceed the amount of taxes collected from that class in the preceding year, except for the additional revenue generated by new improvements.

Tax Rate—The number of mills by which taxable value is multiplied to determine the amount from which certain reductions are made to determine liability for taxes; prior to those adjustments, each mill generates $1.00 of taxes for every $1,000 of taxable value.

Taxing Authority—The governmental body or agency within a taxing district that approves the levy of a tax on property; e.g., the city council in a city, the board of township trustess in a township, the board of education in a school district.

Ten-Mill Limitation—The sum of the tax rates levied against any given piece of taxable property cannot exceed ten mills unless the excess is approved by a majority of the electors voting on the issue in the taxing district that imposes that excess. It is important to note that the ten-mill limitation does not allow each subdivision to levy ten inside mills; rather, the ten-mill limitation is reached when the sum of all inside mills levied by all subdivisions equals ten mills as applied to property in a given taxing district.

Triennial Revaluation (Update)—In the third year following re-appraisal, the Tax Commissioner orders a county auditor to increase or decrease the assessed value of all real property in the county of certain classes of real property if the Commissioner determines it is not valued as required by law.

True Value or Fair Market Value—The price at which property would be exchanged between a willing seller and a willing buyer, neither being under compulsion to sell or buy and each having knowledge of the pertinent facts.

10% Rollback—Each real property tax bill is reduced by 10%; the state reimburses local taxing districts for the revenue lost from the 10% reduction.

2-1/2% Rollback—In addition to the 10% rollback, owner-occupied residential property qualifies for a further 2-1/2% reduction in property taxes; the state reimburses local taxing districts for the lost revenue.

Uniform Rule—Section 2 of Article XII, Ohio Constitution, requires that land and improvements be taxed uniformly; different classes of real property (e.g., residential, agricultural, commercial, industrial) may not be taxed at different levels of assessed value anywhere in the state, or at different tax rates within the same taxing district, except as expressly authorized by Section 2a of Article XII.

Source: Ohio Department of Taxation.

ENDNOTES

1. The author wishes to thank the following individuals for their assistance in preparing this chapter: W. Loren Williams, Adam Korobow, Chris Geller, Ronald Mucha, Michael Sobul, Ron Hohman, and Matthew Cohen.

2. United States Bureau of Census (1993).

3. For a history of the property tax see Jensen (1931), chapter II.

4. See the Advisory Commission on Intergovernmental Relations (1963) and Aronson and Hilley (1986).

5. See the Advisory Commission on Intergovernmental Relations (1988) and Mullins and Joyce (1994).

6. For a discussion of alternative property tax system across countries, see McCluskey (1991) and Bahl and Linn (1992). Differences across states are described in Clatanoff (1986) and Reeves (1983). For a general discussion of the property tax, see Woolery (1989), Netzer (1966), and Ralphaelson (1987), pp. 201-228.

7. See Raimondo (1992), pp. 156-161.

8. See Shoup (1983) for a comparison of the property tax against sales and income taxation using a multiple of criteria (see also Cline and Shannon (1983)).

9. The data for fiscal year includes data for governments whose fiscal year ended either on June 30, 1991 or within the 12 previous months.

10. See Citizens Research Council of Michigan (1994) and Ohio Public Expenditure Council (1994).

11. It is commonly reported that currently in Ohio about 70 percent of real property tax revenue goes to school districts.

12. The ACIR has long advocated a balance in state and local tax structures; see ACIR (1967). However, as Ladd and Weist (1987) point out, there are other policy objectives, e.g., responding to tax competition, equity concerns, economic distortions, and income elasticity, that may not be served by a strict adherence to a balanced tax structure. See also Dearborn (1995) in this volume.

13. The income elasticity of the property tax is estimated to be 0.78 (see discussion below), while Fox (1995), in this volume, estimates the elasticity for the sales tax to be 0.97, and Wallace (1995), in this volume, estimates the elasticity for the income tax to be 1.27.

14. See the Appendix for a definition of these terms.

15. Data splitting out property taxes by type of local jurisdictions are not available from the Bureau of Census on an annual basis prior to 1975.

16. Ohio low does not specify the assessment rate, only the maximum rate. However, the rate must be uniform across the state.

17. From 1971 until 1973, minerals was included as part of agriculture. Thus, the mineral category was also excluded.

18. The assessment ratio is the ratio of the taxable (or assessed value) to fair market value. In Ohio, the legal assessment ratio is 35 percent, but the actual ratio differs from year-to-year.

19. Note that neither the tax reduction factor nor the property tax rollback need to be taken into consideration in calculating the income elasticity since they do not effect the value of the property tax base. They effect only the actual tax paid.

20. The Ohio Tax Study Commission (1967) reported an elasticity of 1.1.

21. Excluding agriculture and estimating the elasticity over the period 1974 to 1992 yields an estimated elasticity of 0.85, which is greater than when agriculture is included.

22. See Anderson (1992) for a discussion of estimates of the income elasticity of the property tax.

23. We regressed the year-to-year elasticities against a time trend. The coefficient on the time trend was small and not statistically significantly different from zero.

24. See also Bon (1989).

25. A similar, but more pronounced difference was found in Georgia.

26. $426,432 is actually the base per student for the third highest school district. The school districts with the highest two values are considered anomalies.

27. Residential includes housing of four units or less. The data in Table 7-10 do not include agriculture, although agricultural property includes some housing.

28. See Duchi, Hawkins, and McHugh (1995), in this volume, for a discussion of the decline in manufacturing activity in Ohio.

29. There are records that allow the government to determine whether the proper tax was paid. But the taxpayer does calculate his or her taxes; the records are used for the very few taxpayers who are actually audited each year.

30. While fair market or true market value is the most commonly used basis for assessment, there are alternatives in use. For example, Indiana uses "true tax value" which requires assessment be based on a specific cost approach to valuation (LeVan 1994) and California essentially uses acquisition value (O'Sullivan, Sexton and Sheffrin 1995).

31. Officials from a property appraisal firm with whom we spoke said that the per parcel cost of a appraisal was in the $7.00 to $9.00 range in Ohio, but could be as much as $25 dollars in a state like New York.

32. See Woolery (1989) for a discussion.

33. In the Park Investment cases in the early 1970s the Ohio Supreme Court ruled that properties were not being assessed uniformly.

34. A comparison across states in how assessment-sales ratio studies are conducted can be found Dornfest (1993).

35. The coefficient of dispersion is the average percentage deviation from the median assessment ratio, i.e., $(\Sigma|R_i - M|) / N$, where R_i is the sales assessment ratio for the ith parcel, M is the median sales assessment ratio, and N is the total number of parcels.

36. See Aaron (1975).

37. For a list of such studies see, for example, Borland (1990) and Bowman and Mikesell (1990).

38. See Eckert and Malme (1991).

39. Ohio Code Annotated §5715.012 specifies that the Tax Commissioner will conduct a sales-assessment ratio study, but restricts its use for equalization purposes unless the Commissioner finds that there are sufficient like parcels included in the sample of sold properties.

40. This was a recommendation made by the Ohio Joint Committee to Study State Taxes (1982).

41. Annual updates were required from 1972 to 1975.

42. Telephone conversation with an official from an appraisal firm.

43. Many states have established classification schemes under which each identified class of property is assessed at a different rate. For a discussion of property tax clas-

sification and the arguments for and against, see Bowman (1991). He concludes that the case for uniformity is stronger than for classification. See also Roemer (1983).

44. For a discussion of 100 percent assessment, see Aaron (1969) and Shannon (1967).

45. See for example, Minnesota Department of Taxation (1993, p. 35) and Woolery (1989).

46. See Ohio Code Annotated §5713.30 and §5713.31.

47. See for example, Chicoine, Sonka and Doty (1982) and the references they cite and also IAAO (1974).

48. The procedures for determining current use value are specified by the Department of Taxation. Ohio statues do not specify how current use value will be determined.

49. For a complete explanation, see Ohio Department of Taxation (1994).

50. Appraisers are required to determine the fair market value for agricultural land.

51. For more complete discussion of the capitalization issue see Yinger, Bloom, Borsch-Supan, and Ladd (1988). Kendel (1994) in his letter to David L. Sjoquist takes exception to several of the points made in the text.

52. By way of comparison, in Nevada exemptions in 1980-87 amounted to 12.5 percent of gross assessed value, Bowman (1990).

53. For a discussion of early trends in property tax exemptions in the United States see Quigley and Schmenner (1975).

54. For a complete discussion of property tax exemptions for economic development purposes, see Wasylenko (1995), in this volume.

55. Similar arguments are made by Quigley and Schmenner (1975) and McLean (1994).

56. The Joint Committee to Study State Taxes (1982) also called for a review of property tax exemptions, noting that the definition in the state statutes of exempt property was ambiguous and that judicial interpretations enlarged upon the original intent. The Ohio Tax Study Commission (1967) called for more specific guideline or what property should be exempt.

57. For a history of Ohio's limitations on property taxation see Levin (1977).

58. The inside millage is allocated to the local governments in which a parcel is located on the basis of the average of millage rates within each of those jurisdiction between 1929 and 1933. This allocation scheme differs from that used in California where relative tax collections are used (see O'Sullivan, Sexton, and Sheffrin 1995).

59. Some authors put the original date of the rollback provision at 1927. We use the date cited by Levin (1977).

60. See Mueller (1989) for a discussion of these points of views and a survey of the relevant literature.

61. See Cornia (1995), in this volume for a discussion of personal property taxation.

62. Fleeter (1992).

63. Ordeshoulz (1979) obtains survey results that suggest that the more complex the property tax structure, the less likely an individual is to know his or her actual property tax payment. This suggests that more complexity leads to less understanding.

64. See the discussion of property tax incidence, p. 419.

65. The assessment of agricultural land on the basis of current use value results in another class of property.

66. This was proposed by the Joint Committee to Study State Taxes (1982).

67. See Ebel and Ortbal (1989).

68. This calculation ignores other factors such as the deductibility of property taxes for the federal income tax.

69. For a discussion of the principles of business taxation see Oakland (1992).

70. The Joint Committee to Study State Taxes (1982) recommend eliminating the 2.5 percent rollback and converting the 10 percent rollback into a homestead credit.

71. There is a third view of the incidence of the property tax, i.e., that the property tax is a benefits tax. Hamilton (1975), for example, argues that property tax payments equal the value of the public services provided by local governments. At least two recent empirical studies do not find support for the benefit tax view of the property tax (Carroll and Yinger 1994; and Wassamer 1993).

72. Wheaton (1984) finds that gross rents on commercial property do not vary across jurisdiction in response to differences in property tax rates. Thus, it appears that land and property owners bear the burdens of inter-jurisdictional tax differences.

73. Ihlanfeldt (1982), using data from the Annual Housing Survey, found that the property tax on residential property is highly regressive for low-income households, but proportional at higher income levels.

74. This section was originally drafted by W. Loren Williams.

75. See Aaron (1975) and the references therein.

76. Schroeder and Sjoquist (1976), p. 1.

77. It is impossible to establish the "correct" fraction, since it depends on share of the tax burden borne by renters and landlords, the relationship between rent paid and taxable value, which probably varies with value, and assessment practices. A recent and careful study by the Minnesota Department of Revenue (1993, p.33) concluded that 51 percent of the property tax on rental property was paid by tenants and that the property tax burden averaged 16.5 percent of rent paid.

78. ACIR (1993), Table 41, pp. 142-48.

79. ACIR (1993), Table 42 provides the basis for this summary and offers much more detail and precision about the various programs.

80. Average benefits are computed over only those households which receive some positive amount of relief.

81. Average annual rent was $3,868, which implies a tax burden on renters of $464 (= 0.12 3868); whereas the average property tax paid was $718.

82. For example, consider two households. The first pays $400 in property taxes; the second pays $1,500. They both have incomes of $12,000. Under Plan **A**, the first receives a rebate of $40 and the second receives $1,000; the average benefit is $520. Under plan **C**, the first receives no benefit and the second falls to $540. The average is computed only for those who receive benefits, so the average rises to $540.

83 For a general discussion of land value taxation see Netzer (1966).

84. See, for example, Bentlick (1979) and Pollakowski (1982).

85. See Pollakowski (1982) and Pennsylvania Economy League (1985).

86. Bourassa (1990) found that the split rate tax in Pittsburgh encouraged housing development, but found no such effect in two other cities in Pennsylvania.

87. For a discussion of the implication of the changing U. S. industrial structure on the property tax, see Hicks (1983).

88. For a discussion of the effect of court orders and education reforms on state funding of education see Bahl, Sjoquist, and Williams (1990).

89. Wallace (1995), in this volume, considers the use of the local income tax as an alternative to the local property tax.

90. It should be noted that voters rejected substituting the income tax for the property in several states but seem to favor the use of sales tax.

91. One mill will yield about $135 million, and thus, seven mills will cost $945 million. In 1994, the sales tax yielded $4,468 million, or $893 million per each percentage point. Assuming an increase of 5 percent for FY95, one percentage point will yield $938 million.

92. See Fleeter (1993) for a discussion of pooling.

8 Metropolitan Area Revenues

Philip Dearborn

INTRODUCTION

Three out of four Ohio residents live in one of the ten largest metropolitan areas in the state. These ten urban centers are the backbone of the state's economy, and their continued prosperity will be critical to Ohio's future. The core central cities of the metropolitan areas were, for most of Ohio's history, the economic, social, and cultural engines that powered those areas. Today, there is clear evidence that at least some of Ohio's central cities are seriously disadvantaged and have problems that need state attention.

In recent decades, the financial, physical, and social conditions of central cities nationally have been declining rapidly, resulting in wide disparities between cities and their suburbs. As a consequence, central cities are seen increasingly as economically troubled repositories of the poor and disadvantaged populations in metropolitan areas, with resulting severe social, educational, and racial problems. Some observers even have suggested that central cities may no longer be important to the future of urban areas (Garreau 1991).[1] Other researchers have found evidence that the health of metropolitan areas, and even states, may be interrelated to the health of their central cities (Ledebur and Barnes 1993; Rusk 1993; Nathan and Adams 1976).[2]

Because of their importance to the state as a whole, this chapter examines how Ohio's major metropolitan areas, and especially the central city governments and school districts, are affected by the state's tax and aid policies.

The ten largest Ohio metropolitan areas have a combined population of 8.3 million, out of the state's population of 10.8 million. The ten central cities' population is only 2.6 million, however, about 31 percent of the metropolitan areas' total, and less than a quarter of the state's population. In every metropolitan area except Toledo, the central city represents less than half the metropolitan population, and in the Youngstown and Dayton areas, the central city population is less than 20 percent.

Before assessing the revenue structures in central cities and metropolitan areas, the very different economic and demographic characteristics between the central cities and surrounding suburbs will be examined. The state tax and aid policies for all local governments will be reviewed to put the metropolitan structures in the overall state perspective. Finally the tax structures for central cities, central city school districts, and urban counties will each be looked at for strengths and weaknesses.

METROPOLITAN AREA DEMOGRAPHIC AND ECONOMIC CHARACTERISTICS

Because statistics on taxes and grants in Ohio are generally kept by counties, not metropolitan areas, the county in which the central city is located will be used instead of the metropolitan area for most analyses. The ten urban counties average about 72 percent of metropolitan area population, with only two counties, Hamilton and Mahoning, with less than 60 percent (see Table 8-1).

There is a wide range in the central city populations as a percentage of county populations. Hamilton's population equals about 21 percent of Butler County. In contrast, Toledo has about 72 percent of the Lucas County population, and Columbus, about 66 percent of the Franklin County population. The ten cities combined equal about 43 percent of the ten county total population, but six of the ten cities have less than 40 percent of their county's population. In each instance, the central city remains the largest local government in the county. While central city school districts have somewhat different boundaries than the cities, they have the same general economic and demographic characteristics.

The most apparent indicator of the decline of Ohio's central cities is the loss of population. In Ohio, all of the ten central cities, except Columbus, have been losing population in recent decades (see Table 8-2). Columbus has gained population since 1970 by annexing adjoining areas, an alternative

TABLE 8-1
Population of Ohio Metropolitan Areas: 1990

Central City (Urban County)	Metropolitan Area Population	Urban County Population	Percent of Metropolitan Total	Central City Population	Central City as a Percent of County
Hamilton (Butler)	291,479	291,479	100.0	61,368	21.1
Cleveland (Cuyahoga)	1,831,122	1,412,140	77.1	505,616	35.8
Columbus (Franklin)	1,377,419	961,437	69.8	632,910	65.8
Cincinnati (Hamilton)	1,452,645	866,228	59.6	364,040	42.0
Lorain (Lorain)	271,126	271,126	100.0	71,245	26.3
Toledo (Lucas)	614,128	462,361	75.3	332,943	72.0
Youngstown (Mahoning)	492,619	264,806	53.8	95,732	36.2
Dayton (Montgomery)	951,270	573,809	60.3	182,044	31.7
Canton (Stark)	394,106	367,585	93.3	84,161	22.9
Akron (Summit)	657,575	514,990	78.3	223,019	43.3
Total Ten Largest	8,333,489	5,985,961	71.8	2,553,078	42.7
State Population	10,847,000				

Source: U.S. Department of Commerce, Bureau of the Census, 1990 Census of Population, Metropolitan Areas, Section 1 (Washington, D.C.)

not generally available to the other cities, because suburban cities ring their borders and cannot be annexed without their permission. Although the rate of population loss slowed from 12.3 percent between 1970 and 1980 to 4.3 percent between 1980 and 1990, four of the cities (Cleveland, Youngstown, Dayton, and Canton) still experienced a population loss of more than 10 percent in the 1980s. Despite the apparent slowing of population decline in the 1980s, it seems likely that the losses are continuing in the 1990s.

The significance of population losses is determined by how those losses affect the overall composition of the residents that remain. Unfortunately, in Ohio cities, the evidence is that wealthier residents are leaving, a large proportion of poorer residents is remaining, and the numbers of poor are increasing. In 1990, six of the central cities had poverty rates[3] exceeding 20 percent of their population, and two more were at 19 percent (see Table 8-3). Youngstown's poverty rate was 29 percent and Cleveland's was just

TABLE 8-2
Changes in Central City Populations: 1970–1980; 1980–1990

Central City	1970	1980	Percent Change	1990	Percent Change
Hamilton	67,865	63,189	-6.9	61,368	-2.9
Cleveland	750,879	573,822	-23.6	505,616	-11.9
Columbus	540,025	564,871	4.6	632,910	12.0
Cincinnati	453,514	385,457	-15.0	364,040	-5.6
Lorain	78,185	75,416	-3.5	71,245	-5.5
Toledo	383,062	354,635	-7.4	332,943	-6.1
Youngstown	140,909	115,436	-18.1	95,732	-17.1
Dayton	243,023	203,371	-16.3	182,044	-10.5
Canton	110,053	94,730	-13.9	84,161	-11.2
Akron	275,425	237,177	-13.9	223,019	-6.0
Total	3,042,940	2,668,104	-12.3	2,553,078	-4.3

Source: U.S. Department of Commerce, Bureau of the Census, 1990 Census of Population, Metropolitan Areas, Section 1 (Washington, D.C.)

TABLE 8-3
Poverty Rates: 1990

	City				
Central City	1980	1990	Percent Change	Suburbs 1990	Difference Between City and Suburb
Hamilton	13.4	16.8	3.4	7.3	9.5
Cleveland	22.1	28.7	6.6	5.4	23.3
Columbus	16.5	17.2	0.7	6.8	10.4
Cincinnati	19.7	24.3	4.6	7.2	17.1
Lorain	13.4	19.8	6.4	6.4	13.4
Toledo	13.6	19.1	5.5	6.0	13.1
Youngstown	18.2	29.0	10.8	8.8	20.2
Dayton	20.8	26.5	5.7	7.3	19.2
Canton	15.5	21.9	6.4	6.5	15.4
Akron	15.0	20.5	5.5	6.0	14.5
State of Ohio	10.3	11.5	1.2		
United States	13.0	13.1	0.1		
Central Cities Only	15.7	18.1	2.4		

Source: U.S. Department of Commerce, Bureau of the Census, 1980 and 1990 Census of Population and Housing (Washington, D.C.)

slightly less. The poverty rates in all ten cities exceeded the 13 percent national rate, as well as the 16.6 percent rate for cities over 50,000 population, and all but Columbus and Hamilton exceeded the 18 percent national rate for central cities. In contrast to the central cities, the highest suburban poverty rate was 8.8 percent in Youngstown's suburbs, with all the other rates less than 8 percent.

Adding to this grim poverty picture, the central cities' poverty rates all increased between 1980 and 1990, led by Youngstown with a 10.8 percentage point increase, followed by Cleveland with a 6.6 percentage point increase. It seems clear that the out migration from central cities has not been led by poor residents.

Another perspective on the plight of central cities can be gained by examining the incomes of city residents compared to those in the surrounding suburbs. Incomes per capita in all ten Ohio central cities trail suburban incomes by large margins (see Table 8-4). Only Cincinnati and Columbus have incomes that reach even 80 percent of that of their suburbs, and Cleveland's per capita income is barely above 50 percent of suburban levels. In six of the ten central cities, incomes are less than three-quarters of those in the suburbs.

This general pattern of poor central cities surrounded by affluent suburbs is, of course, not unique to Ohio. A look at five cities often compared to Ohio's major cities shows that Detroit is worse than any Ohio city measured by either poverty rates or per capita income (see Table 8-5). Buffalo, Milwaukee, Pittsburgh, and St. Louis are generally comparable to the five largest Ohio cities by both measures.

TABLE 8-4
Per Capita Income in Central Cities Compared to Suburbs: 1990

Central City	Central City	Suburbs	City as a Percent of Suburb
Hamilton	11,108	15,132	73.4
Cleveland	9,258	17,317	53.5
Columbus	12,970	16,171	80.2
Cincinnati	12,547	15,300	82.0
Lorain	10,676	14,055	76.0
Toledo	11,894	16,474	72.2
Youngstown	8,544	13,366	63.9
Dayton	9,946	15,513	64.1
Canton	10,133	14,243	71.1
Akron	12,015	15,798	76.1

Source: U.S. Department of Commerce, Bureau of the Census, 1980 and 1990 Census of Population and Housing (Washington, D.C.)

TABLE 8-5
How Do Ohio Cities Compare?

Central City Personal Income as a Percentage of Suburbs

Detroit	52.8	Cleveland	53.5
Milwaukee	62.2	Toledo	72.2
St. Louis	66.9	Akron	76.1
Buffalo	68.9	Columbus	80.2
Pittsburgh	87.0	Cincinnati	82.0

Detroit	32.4	Cleveland	28.7
Buffalo	25.6	Cincinnati	24.3
St. Louis	24.6	Akron	20.5
Milwaukee	22.2	Toledo	19.1
Pittsburgh	21.4	Columbus	17.2
All Central Cities	18.1		

Source: U.S. Department of Commerce, Bureau of the Census, 1980 and 1990 Census of Population and Housing (Washington, D.C.)

Population losses coupled with increasing proportions of poor residents present two potential problems for the governments of central cities, namely, higher costs of services required to provide for poorer residents and a smaller revenue base from which to finance those services. From a tax perspective, the disparities between the wealth of central city residents and those of the suburbs mean that for most taxes the revenues will show similar disparities in yields.

Ideally, state policies will provide a way of mitigating these disparities. Such policies may include authorizing local taxes designed to overcome the effects of disparities; state grants that equalize for disparities; or some form of regional financing of services heavily used by poorer city residents. The balance of this chapter will focus primarily on how city-suburban disparities affect local revenues, and how state tax and revenue policies relate to those disparities.

STATE TAX AND GRANT STRUCTURE FOR LOCAL GOVERNMENTS

Before looking at taxes and revenues in specific metropolitan areas, it is helpful to review how local governments in Ohio are generally financed. In

1992, major local taxes provided about $10 billion in revenues, split almost equally between school districts and all other local governments (see Table 8-6). By far the largest local tax source was property taxes, consisting of $4.7 billion in real property taxes, $1.2 billion of business tangible property taxes, and almost a billion of public utility personal property taxes—more than two-thirds of total local tax revenues. All school tax revenues, except for a small amount derived from school income taxes, came from property taxes. Municipal income taxes account for about one-fifth of tax revenues, the second largest source of local tax revenues. Though the tax system is dominated by property taxes, it is quite diverse.

State payments to local governments totaled $5.1 billion in 1993, excluding transportation payments, with over $3.5 billion (68 percent) going to local schools as basic school aid (see Table 8-7). Much of this school aid is targeted to poorer school districts, but a recent court decision found that the proportion of state aid targeted for poorer districts is inadequate to offset their revenue disparities.[4] Although the decision was based on the effects of the formula on a poor rural school district, if the decision is not reversed on appeal, it may result in changes in state aid formulas affecting all school districts. How such changes may affect central city school districts cannot be predicted.

General assistance payments to non-school local governments were distributed mainly through what are referred to as "local government funds."

TABLE 8-6
Local Government Tax Revenues: 1992
(In Millions of Dollars)

Taxes	Total	Percent Distribution	Schools	Non-School
Property Taxes, after reductions (1993)	4,676	46.6	3,327	1,349
Tangible Personal Property	1,201	12.0	846	355
Public Utility Personal Property	955	9.5	673	282
Municipal Income	2,105	21.0		2,105
County Sales (1993)	649	6.4		649
Regional Transit Sales (1993)	175	1.7		175
Lodging Tax	52	0.5		52
Real Property Conveyance	48	0.5		48
School District Income Taxes	47	0.5	47	
Local Inheritance Tax	130	1.3		130
Total Taxes	10,038	100.0	4,893	5,145

Source: Ohio Department of Taxation.

TABLE 8-7
State Payments to Local Governments: 1993
(In Millions of Dollars)*

	Total	Schools	Non-School
School Aid (1992)	3,526	3,526	
Local Government Fund:			
Municipal Income Tax	35		35
Undivided	419		419
Revenue Assistance	59		59
Property Tax Reimbursements:			
10% Reduction	532	348	184
2.5% Reduction	75	49	26
Homestead Exemption	52	34	18
Tangible Property, $10,000 reimbursement (1992)	76	54	22
Library and Local Government Fund	285		285
Total	5,059	4,011	1,048

Source: Ohio Department of Taxation and Office of Budget and Management.

*Does not include transportation payments

Each of the state's 88 county governments has a local government fund into which the state makes payments from state-imposed taxes. The county allocations are based on a complex formula that takes into account both population and property values. A portion of the distributed funds is designated to be distributed to municipal governments, with the balance available for distribution by county budget commissions to the county government, and to municipalities, townships, and special districts based on "needs."

For 1992, state payments to local government funds, including those for libraries, were about $800 million. Because the records on distributions within counties are kept by the counties and are not tabulated by the state, the relative distribution of these payments between central cities and suburbs could not be determined. However, because of the special needs of central cities caused by fiscal disparities, it is likely that they fared better than suburban governments.

The balance of state payments, about $730 million, were to reimburse all local governments for state-ordered reductions in local property taxes.[5] The distribution of this aid among local governments is generally in proportion to their property tax collections. Therefore, local governments with large property tax bases and high property tax rates benefit disproportionately. This result raises an issue of whether size of property tax bases and tax rates are the proper criteria for distributing such a large portion of state aid.

From 1983 to 1991, increases in state aid averaged about 8 percent annually for both city governments and school districts in Ohio. However, there were sharp year-to-year differences in the amount of increases and in the treatment of the two types of local government (see Figure 8-1). Compared to all states, Ohio provides a little less in state aid to cities and schools, and a little more to counties (see Figure 8-2).

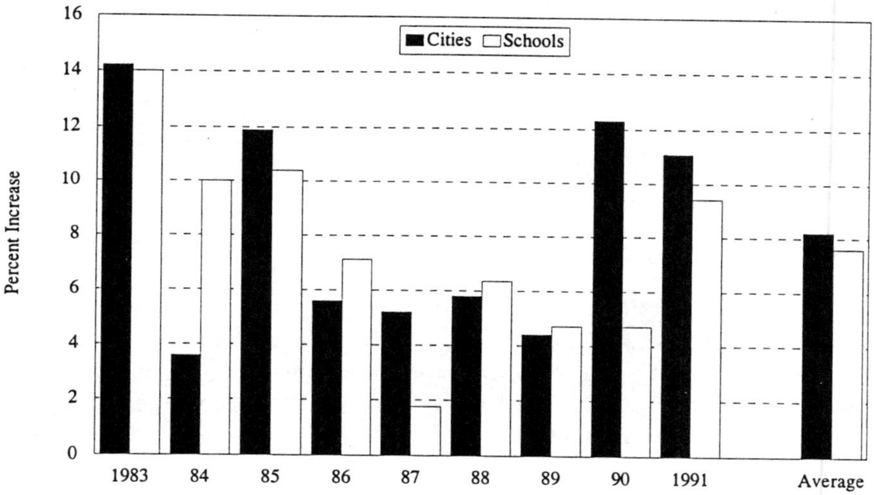

FIGURE 8-1. Annual increases in state aid.

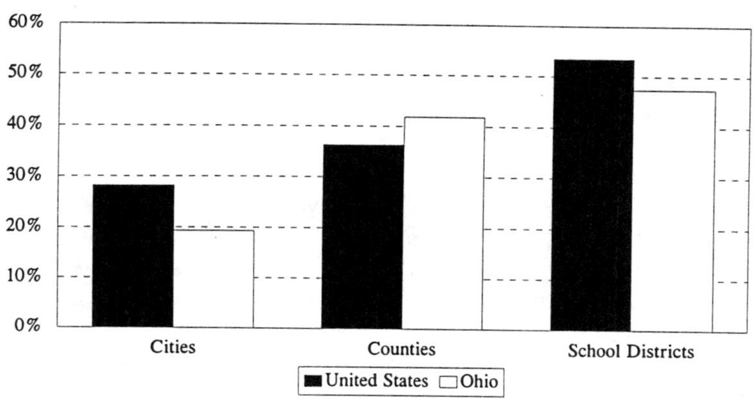

Source: U.S. Department of Commerce, Bureau of the Census, *State Government Finances: 1992*, Washington, D.C.

FIGURE 8-2. Aid as a percent of total general revenue.

REVENUE STRUCTURES OF GOVERNMENTS IN METROPOLITAN AREAS

Within the general allocations to local governments of taxing powers and state payments, there are very different financing patterns among central cities, central city school districts, and urban counties, as well as differences among metropolitan areas. These differences result from variations in tax structures and from different compositions of tax bases. An understanding of these differences is important to evaluate the impact of reform of the state tax system on the finances of the various types of governments. In this section, the revenue structures of central city governments and school districts and of urban county governments will be reviewed, and the strengths and weaknesses of those structures relative to their tax bases will be assessed.

CENTRAL CITIES

The revenue profile of central cities is quite different from that of other local governments. The six central cities for which comparable data are available average 52 percent of their revenues from the municipal income tax, only a little more than 10 percent from property taxes, and about 21 percent from state and federal payments, with the balance from charges and miscellaneous sources (see Figure 8-3). This pattern is relatively consistent across the metropolitan areas, especially the high dependence on the municipal income tax and the low use of property taxes.

This revenue structure generally has performed well in recent years, when judged by annual revenue increases. Between 1983 and 1991, five of the seven cities for which comparable information could be obtained (Youngstown and Canton excepted) averaged annual increases in own-source revenues that were greater than inflation. Four of these cities had revenues increasing at rates exceeding those for all Ohio cities (see Figure 8-4).

The apparent reason why central city revenues growth was so robust is the heavy dependence on the municipal income tax. In Ohio, cities are permitted to tax all wages, salaries, and other compensation earned by residents, and may also tax earnings by non-residents who work in the city. The income tax also applies to business net profits attributable to activities in the municipality. This relatively broad base (including resident businesses and non-resident individuals) offsets the relatively low income base of city residents, and permits the city to share in the general prosperity of the metropolitan area. Moreover, the income tax has given the city a buoyant revenue source. The average annual changes in income tax revenues compared to average annual changes in property tax revenues shows that income tax rev-

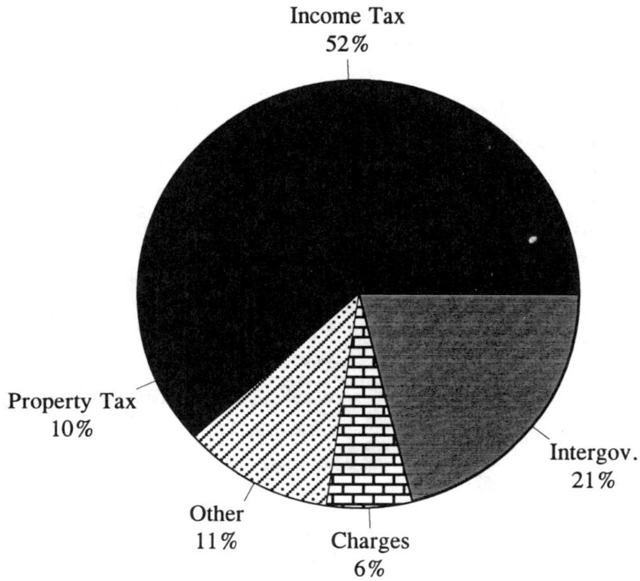

Average of Selected Central Cities

FIGURE 8-3. City revenue sources—all government funds, except capital.

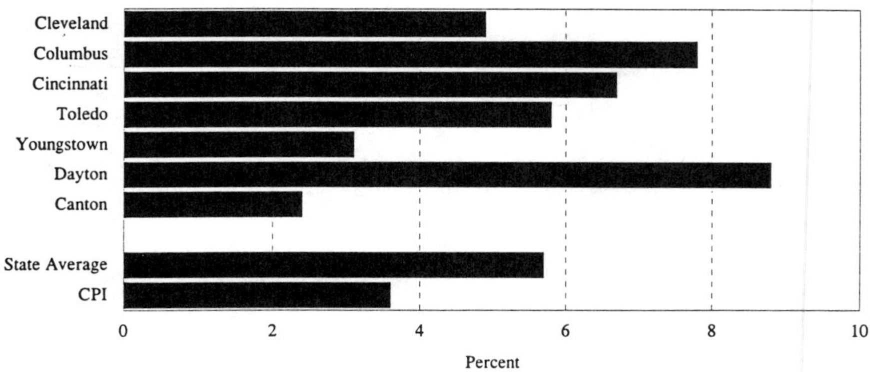

FIGURE 8-4. City owned source general revenues average annual increase, 1983–1992.

enues increased faster in each city (See Figure 8-5). With over half of their revenues from income taxes and only about 10 percent from property taxes, this means the central city tax structures are much better positioned to offset the adverse effects of economic disparities on their tax bases.

While the municipal income tax has performed well for central cities over the long term, it is subject to some instability over the business cycle. In the recession of the early 1990s, both Cleveland and Toledo experienced negative growth rates, and even Columbus had a noticeable dip in revenue increases (see Figure 8-6). Because much of a city's spending is for payrolls

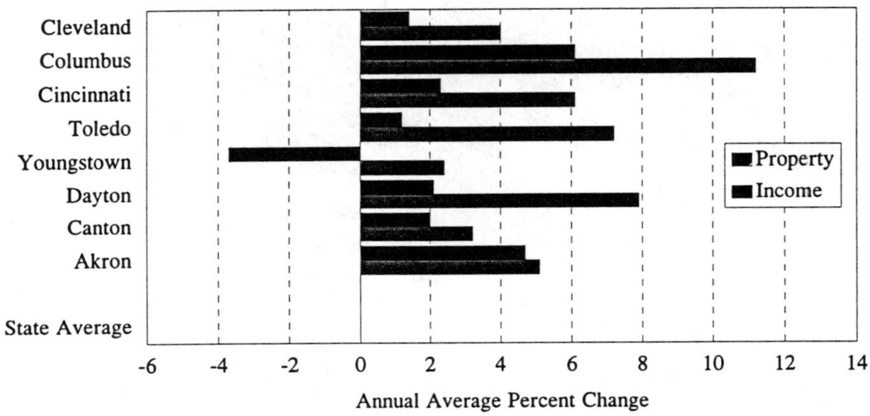

FIGURE 8-5. City property taxes compared to city income taxes—average annual increase, 1993–1991.

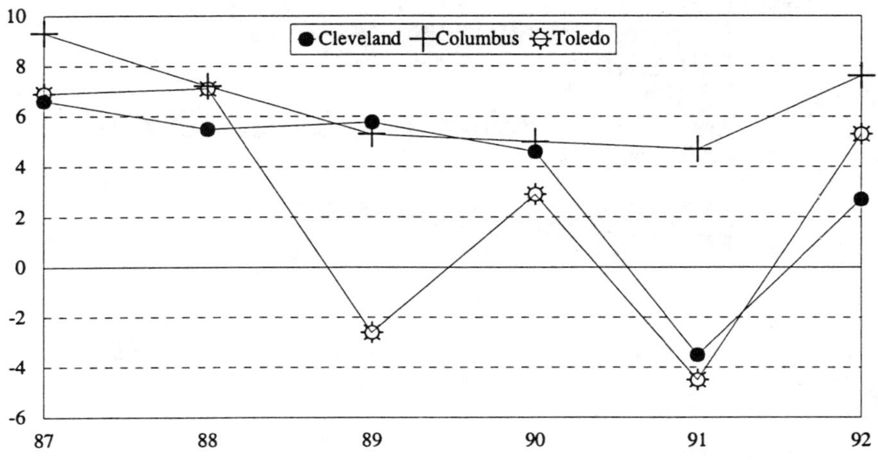

FIGURE 8-6. Annual income tax revenue changes, selected cities.

associated with basic city services, such as police, fire, and sanitation, it is not practical to make sudden sharp cuts in spending in reaction to cyclical declines in revenues. As a result, several cities, including Cleveland, had trouble balancing their budgets and incurred deficits in the recession. Nevertheless, by developing "rainy day funds" or using other financial management practices, cities should be able to weather these periodic dips in income tax revenues in the future.

Nationally, Ohio is one of only eight states that permit city income taxes. Of the 635 cities with income taxes (excluding Pennsylvania), 512 are in Ohio (see Table 8-8). Thus, Ohio has a relatively unusual city tax structure, but one that seems to be serving central cities well.

The revenue structures of Ohio central cities appear to be designed to cope with the underlying economic disparities reviewed earlier, and no alternatives that would improve their tax structures are suggested here. The focus in this study is on reform of the state tax system. If changes are recommended in the state income tax or in the ways local income taxes are imposed, the effects of those changes on central cities should be carefully evaluated.

TABLE 8-8
States with Local Income Taxes: 1992

State	Cities	Counties	School Districts
Alabama	11		
Delaware	1		
Indiana		88	
Iowa			178
Kentucky	86	29	
Maryland	1	23	
Michigan	20		
Missouri	2		
New York	2		
Pennsylvania*			
Ohio	512		76
Total	635	132	254

Source: ACIR, *Significant Features of Fiscal Federalism*, 1994 (Washington DC, 1994).

*2,832 various types of local governments levy local taxes.

Central City School Districts

In contrast to city governments, central city school districts rely almost entirely on property taxes for local support of schools. The ten central city school districts average 46 percent of their revenues from property taxes, with state payments, including property tax rollback payments, providing about 49 percent, and only about 5 percent from other sources, including the school income taxes (see Figure 8-7).

The pattern of revenues, however, varies considerably among the school districts. Youngstown receives over 64 percent of its revenue from state payments, and only 33 percent from property taxes. In contrast, Columbus receives 38 percent from state aid and 58 percent from property taxes. These variations result from differences in the size of property tax bases and the compensating effects of the state aid formula. Columbus ranks 119th in the state in the size of its property tax base, with a value per pupil of $91,443, while Youngstown ranks 537th, with a value of $38,195.

The central city dependence on state grants to offset weak property tax bases can be a problem when state aid falters, as it did in 1992. In that year, state aid for schools from the general revenue fund decreased from $2.94 billion to $2.90 billion (in nominal terms). All the central cities except Hamilton and Lorain suffered a resulting decrease in state aid in that year

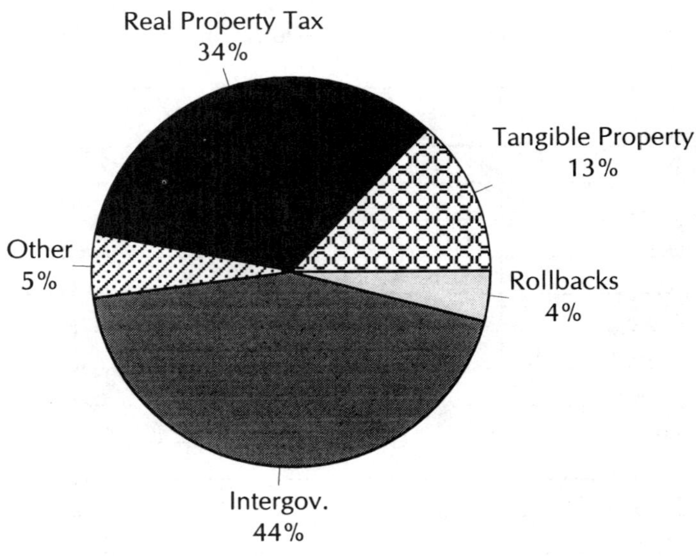

FIGURE 8-7. School district revenue sources—all government funds, except capital.

(see Table 8-9). In 1993, however, all the cities again had increases in state aid as the total state aid increased to $3.14 billion.

The central city school districts have experienced good annual revenue growth from local taxes (principally property taxes). Among the seven cities for which comparable information could be obtained, the average annual increase between 1982 and 1991 ranged from 4.1 percent in Cleveland to 8.8 percent in Cincinnati, with four of the cities exceeding the statewide average of 7.0 percent (see Figure 8-8). Some of these increases were attributable to voter-approved rate increases, but the exact amounts could not be determined.

This good property tax performance continued through 1992 and 1993 (see Table 8-10) However, the increases in property taxes were not sufficient to offset the effects of low state aid in 1992, and six of the ten cities had total revenues decline in that year.

Despite this favorable property tax growth, the central city property tax bases are not good revenue generators relative to those of the suburbs. On a per pupil basis, the central cities average only about 70 percent of the suburban bases, with Cleveland, Toledo, and Youngstown below 60 percent (see Table 8-11). This leaves the cities in a position of (a) imposing higher tax rates than the wealthier suburban systems, (b) dependence on state aid to offset their weak tax bases, or having lower per pupil spending. This condition will prevail as long as local school districts are heavily dependent on property taxes.

TABLE 8-9
Changes in State Aid to City School Districts

School District	Percent Change 1991-1992	Percent Change 1992-1993
Hamilton	3.6	7.1
Cleveland	-2.2	2.1
Columbus	-7.6	0.7
Cincinnati	-0.8	4.8
Lorain	4.5	3.0
Toledo	-5.6	12.5
Youngstown	-5.8	15.0
Dayton	-6.6	9.2
Canton	-3.4	10.1
Akron	-1.3	2.6
Total	-3.4	5.3

Source: Ohio Department of Education, Division of School Finance.

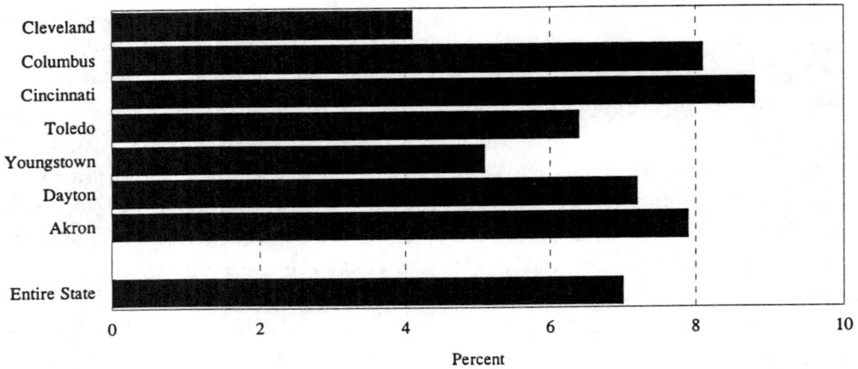

Local taxes are primarily property taxes

FIGURE 8-8. Central city school tax revenues—average annual change, 1982–1991.

TABLE 8-10
Property Tax Changes and Total Net* Revenue Changes Central City School Districts

School District	Property Taxes		Net Revenues	
	Percent Change 1991-1992	Percent Change 1992-1993	Percent Change 1991-1992	Percent Change 1992-1993
Hamilton	3.3	-0.3	-2.8	6.4
Cleveland	-1.3	2.6	-10.5	6.6
Columbus	21.8	12.9	7.5	9.1
Cincinnati	23.1	12.1	11.5	9.0
Lorain	-0.4	6.5	2.9	2.8
Toledo	8.1	10.3	-0.3	10.8
Youngstown	1.8	7.6	-3.4	10.8
Dayton	2.0	10.8	-2.5	8.6
Canton	13.5	-1.6	5.2	3.7
Akron	0.9	0.4	-0.8	1.5
Total	10.3	8.4	0.2	7.6

Source: Ohio Department of Education, Division of School Finance.

*Loan transactions were netted out.

TABLE 8-11
City School District Total Property Tax Base Per Average Daily Membership (ADM) Compared to Balance of County: 1992

School District	City Tax Base Per ADM	Balance of County, Tax Base Per ADM	City Percent of Balance of County
Hamilton	5,674	8,400	67.5
Cleveland	7,153	13,693	52.2
Columbus	9,710	10,095	96.2
Cincinnati	9,731	13,539	71.9
Lorain	4,638	7,144	64.9
Toledo	5,953	11,072	53.8
Youngstown	3,639	6,636	54.8
Dayton	6,291	9,192	68.4
Canton	5,873	7,097	82.8
Akron	6,286	9,927	63.3
Average	7,364	10,461	70.4

Source: Ohio Department of Education, Division of School Finance.

The weaknesses in the central city property tax bases compared to those in the suburbs have to do with both total values and the composition of the bases. A much higher proportion of the central city bases is composed of tangible personal property because of their concentrations of industry and businesses. As a result, although the real property bases of the cities average only 64 percent of those in the suburbs, the tangible personal property tax bases average 95 percent, and the per pupil base is higher than in the suburbs in Columbus, Dayton, and Canton (see Table 8-12).

This means, that to the extent that central cities have a positive feature in their property tax bases relative to the suburbs, it is the tangible personal property component. If the recent reductions in that component of the property tax base continue, or if tangible personal property taxes were recommended for elimination to improve the Ohio business climate, as some have proposed, central city schools would face a much larger problem in replacing lost revenues than would suburban school districts.

One alternative that is available to replace property taxes as a source of local revenues is the school income tax. Currently, no central city system and only a few suburban systems in metropolitan areas use this tax. The school income tax has the potential to raise substantial amounts of revenues—for example, a one percent income tax could replace two-thirds or more of the tangible personal property tax revenue for most central city schools—but it has some clear disadvantages as it is now structured (see Table 8-13).

TABLE 8-12
City School District Tangible Personal Property Tax Base Per Average Daily Membership (ADM) Compared to Balance of County: 1992

School District	City Tax Base Per ADM	Balance of County, Tax Base Per ADM	City Percent of Balance of County
Hamilton	1,238	1,863	66.5
Cleveland	2,057	2,283	90.1
Columbus	2,118	1,802	117.5
Cincinnati	2,429	3,227	75.3
Lorain	1,282	1,746	73.4
Toledo	1,591	2,456	64.8
Youngstown	1,173	1,416	82.8
Dayton	1,897	1,656	114.5
Canton	2,482	1,490	166.6
Akron	1,606	1,844	87.1
Total	1,940	2,043	94.9

Source: Ohio Department of Taxation and Department of Education.

TABLE 8-13
School Tangible Personal Property Taxes Compared to School Income Taxes: 1992 (in 000s)

School District	Personal Property* Tax Receipts	Income Tax 1 Percent	Difference
Hamilton	4,671	6,329	1,658
Cleveland	66,415	32,176	(34,239)
Columbus	64,752	49,225	(15,527)
Cincinnati	58,222	41,403	(16,819)
Lorain	6,918	6,055	(863)
Toledo	34,487	25,937	(8,550)
Youngstown	8,129	5,931	(2,198)
Dayton	28,089	15,776	(12,313)
Canton	10,097	5,568	(4,529)
Akron	21,380	21,678	298
Total	303,160	210,078	(93,082)

Source: Ohio Department of Taxation.

*Includes public utility personal property.

The optional school income tax applies only to resident personal incomes. Therefore, central city school district revenues would substantially trail that of a comparable tax by suburban school districts, and would result in disparities in revenue bases comparable to those in the property tax base (see Table 8-14). As a result, if the suburban systems enacted the school income tax, they would have a substantial revenue advantage. If the suburbs did not enact the tax, the central city school income tax could then encourage more high income residents to move to the suburbs.

A newly enacted alternative state law provides for school systems to share the municipal income tax with city governments. This alternative holds much more promise for central city school districts, but it requires a willingness of cities to share their tax base, plus a favorable vote of city residents. A comparison of the difference between the municipal income taxes imposed on earnings and the school resident income tax shows the very large improvement in revenues that school districts could realize from this alternative (see Table 8-15).

Urban Counties

Urban county governments overlay the metropolitan areas and provide many services to residents of central cities and suburbs. Because of their broad tax bases, counties are able to redistribute revenues from wealthier

TABLE 8-14
Revenue from a 1 Percent School Income Tax: Central City and Balance of County, Per Pupil in Average Daily Membership

School District	City School District	Balance of County	Difference	City as a Percent of County
Hamilton	621	747	126	83.1
Cleveland	441	1,259	818	35.0
Columbus	781	1,000	219	78.1
Cincinnati	852	1,180	328	72.2
Lorain	573	725	152	79.0
Toledo	670	966	296	69.4
Youngstown	425	825	400	51.5
Dayton	520	1,010	490	51.5
Canton	432	737	305	58.6
Akron	651	992	341	65.6

Source: Ohio Department of Taxation.

TABLE 8-15
Comparison of School Resident Income Tax to Municipal Employment Income Tax (in 000s)

School District	Resident Income Tax 1 Percent	Employment Income Tax 1 Percent	Residents as a Percent of Employment
Hamilton	6,329	7,951	79.6
Cleveland	32,176	109,125	29.5
Columbus	49,225	131,731	37.4
Cincinnati	41,403	88,408	46.8
Lorain	6,055	7,293	83.0
Toledo	25,937	49,077	52.8
Youngstown	5,931	12,912	45.9
Dayton	15,776	40,953	38.5
Canton	5,568	14,079	39.5
Akron	21,678	36,090	60.1
Total	210,078	497,616	42.2

Source: Ohio Department of Taxation.

parts of metropolitan areas to provide services to poorer sections, including a variety of social and health service responsibilities. Because many of these programs are mandated by the state, counties receive large amounts of state aid (42 percent of revenues), including pass through federal aid. Locally, they get about 28 percent of their revenues from property taxes, and another 13 percent from sales taxes, with the remaining 17 percent from charges and other sources (see Figure 8-8).

The revenue structure for urban counties is diversified, and has provided good annual average growth of revenues over the period 1983-1991 (see Figure 8-9).

Because of the counties' broader geographic base, property tax revenue growth has far exceeded the growth rates for property tax revenues in the central cities. Overall, property taxes provide a dependable and growing county revenue source (see Figure 8-10).

The county sales tax is much less important, and is not used uniformly by all urban counties. It does, however, provide an important alternative revenue source for counties that want to reduce their dependence on property taxes. Because the sales tax is not relied on heavily by most counties, its sensitivity to downturns in recessions, as illustrated by a sharp decline in 1990 and 1991 in the three largest counties, should not create any undue problems (see Figure 8-11).

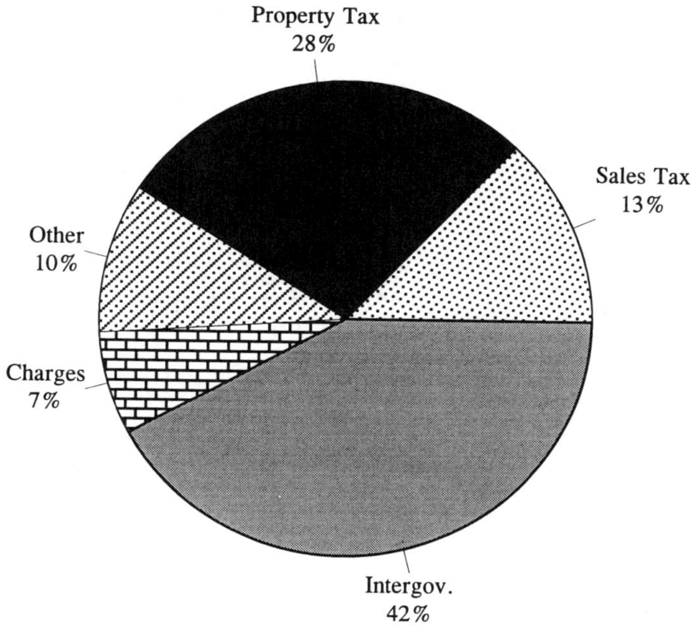

Average of Selected Urban Counties

FIGURE 8-9. County revenue sources—all government funds, except capital.

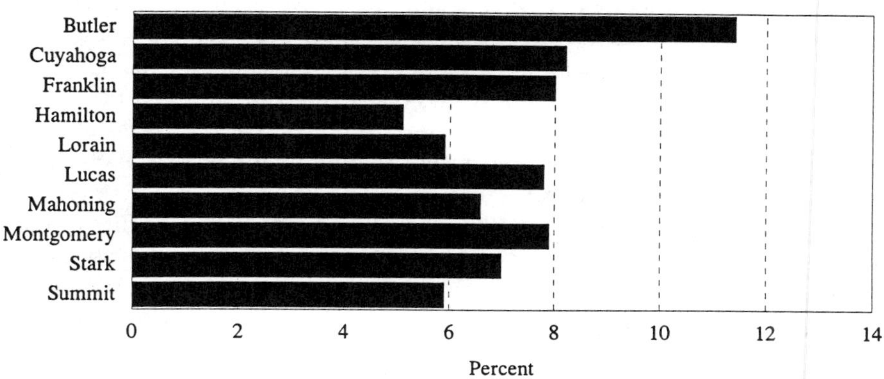

FIGURE 8-10. County own source general revenues average annual increase, 1983–1991.

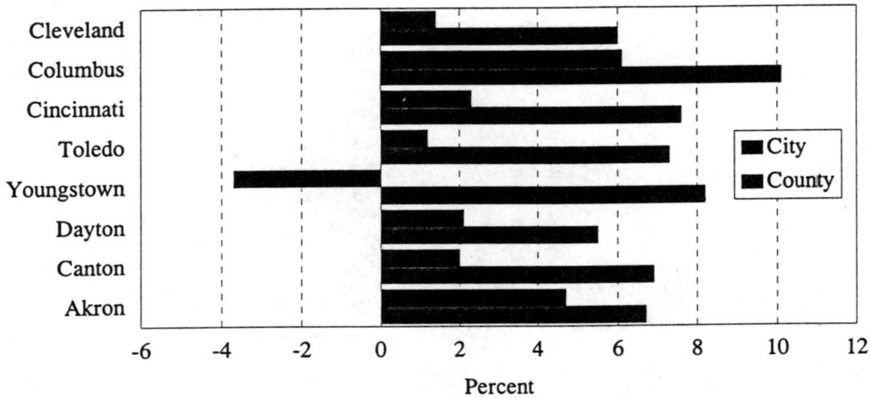

FIGURE 8-11. City property taxes compared to county average annual increase, 1983–1991.

County sales taxes are permitted in 27 states. While there is some risk that shopping center location decisions may be affected by local sales taxes, counties generally cover a broad enough geographical area to minimize this risk, especially at the relatively low county rates in Ohio (Figure 8-12).

Overall, the urban county revenue structure seems designed to provide an adequate and growing stream of revenues.

CONCLUSIONS

The revenue structures in Ohio urban areas have been working reasonably well in recent years. While there are troubling aspects about some features of local revenues, such as the use of tax reduction factors, the need for frequent property tax referendums, the distribution of state aid based on property tax rollbacks, and the sensitivity of municipal income taxes to economic downturns, these problems do not require major structural changes in the existing revenue systems.

Central cities have fared surprisingly well because of their ability to tax business income, and the earnings of non-residents working in the city. As a result, the state should be careful that any efforts to improve the state and local government income tax structure do not adversely affect central cities.

The urban counties have a diversified revenue base that is able to spread the costs of urban services across a wide geographical area. This has resulted in property and sales tax revenues that reflect the overall economic performance of metropolitan areas. Therefore, no changes to the urban county revenue structures are suggested.

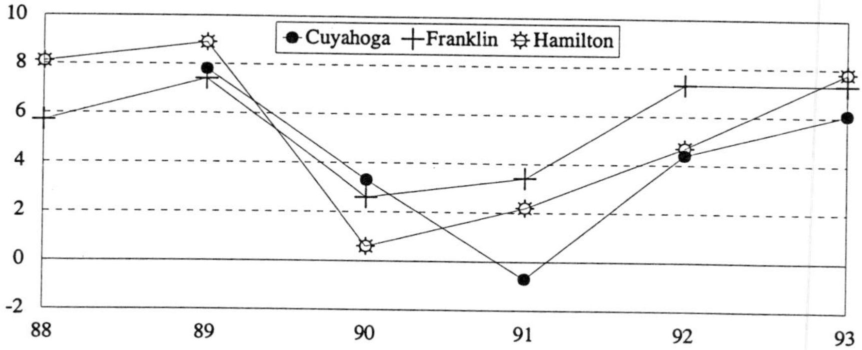

Based on uniform one percent rate

FIGURE 8-12. Annual sales tax revenue changes, selected counties.

Central city school districts have not fared badly, despite their almost complete dependence on property taxes for local revenues. However, the weakness of their property tax bases, coupled with their heavy dependence on tangible personal property taxes and state aid, makes them particularly vulnerable to changes in state tax or aid policies. State school aid must continue to reflect the need to equalize central city school district revenues to offset their weak tax bases, and any changes in the tangible personal property tax must recognize the disproportionate effects that such changes will have on them.

ENDNOTES

1. Garreau, (1991).
2. Ledebur and Barnes, (1993); Rusk, (1993); Nathan and Adams, (1976).
3. The poverty rate is defined as the percent of the population below the poverty line.
4. The case of DeRolph v. State of Ohio.
5. For a discussion of these state-ordered rollbacks, see David L. Sjoquist, chapter 7 in this volume.

9 The Role of Fiscal Incentives in Economic Development: How Ohio Stands Relative to its Competitor States

Michael Wasylenko

INTRODUCTION

The competition among states for jobs has increased the use of fiscal incentives from their already high levels. At the same time, some academics have warned state policy-makers that fiscal incentives do not in the end create more jobs in their states. Nonetheless, academic studies do not all reach the same conclusions, and economic development practitioners increasingly hear from businesses and private organizations that policy on tax and fiscal incentives are central to keeping existing businesses in the state and attracting new businesses to the state. With competition for jobs at an all time high, the size of the awards to businesses has increased. The competition among states has prompted Governor James Edgar of Illinois to call on states to slow the race for businesses and reduce the amounts paid for "new jobs."

This chapter acknowledges that there are conflicting signals in the literature on fiscal incentives. Some researchers find that taxes matter in location decisions, while other researchers do not confirm their results. Social science researchers can not claim absolute certainty about the effects of fiscal incentives, and intelligent policy will take account of theory, empirical evidence and judgment. It is infeasible to make economic development policy based on scientific-style research, where results would be confirmed over and over again before they become accepted into the scientific community.

The main conclusion of this inquiry is that fiscal incentives used prudently can maintain the fiscal competitiveness of the State of Ohio, and create a co-operative state-private sector business climate. For example, tax systems are not perfect and, even in low-tax states, flaws in the tax system can at times adversely affect certain firms and industries. However, Ohio, like most other states, has programs that create many different types of incentives, not all of which policy-makers would endorse.

This paper is organized as follows. The following section discusses relevant economic characteristics of Ohio. For example, the regional economic diversity within the State, the major business taxes in Ohio and the tax system in Ohio compared with major competitor states are reviewed to give adequate background for the analysis and the suggested reforms that follow. A third section reviews what is known about the effects of economic development programs in states and some other areas. The section examines what others have to say about whether fiscal incentives attract jobs. The conclusion is that the smaller the area over which location choice is being made, the more likely it is that fiscal incentives play a role in the location choice. Accepting that states will continue to use fiscal incentives, the section turns to a discussion of whether capital, labor or place subsidies are more effective instruments for economic development. Capital and labor subsidies have different effects and each subsidy can create very different types of jobs. The specific population subgroups who benefit from these programs are also discussed within this section. The section closes with a recommendation that states evaluate economic development programs with an eye toward redesigning the least effective of the programs and perhaps expanding the most effective, given the states objectives.

A fourth section focuses on Ohio's economic development and fiscal incentive programs. Ohio has a considerable number of programs in its portfolio of incentive packages, and relies on Enterprise Zones as its major program. The fifth section compares Ohio's fiscal incentive programs with its major competitor states. It has more incentives than most of its competitors. The conclusion section which follows suggests several different types of reforms that Ohio might follow both to modernize its tax structure and to enhance economic development.

BACKGROUND ON OHIO

Ohio has a highly urbanized population. About 64 percent of the state's 10.8 million residents live in one of the six metropolitan areas (Cleveland, Cincinnati, Columbus, Dayton, Akron and Toledo), and 74 percent of the state's residents live in urban areas.

Three industrial sectors, health and services, manufacturing, and wholesale and retail trade employ 71 percent of the total number of employees, with services and health employing 26 percent, manufacturing employing 21 percent, and wholesale and retail trade employing 24 percent of the total workers in 1993.[1] The fortunes of any economy are linked to the fortunes of the resident industries, and especially to those industries that employ most of its working population. Thus, while Ohio should welcome more businesses in all industries, its fortunes are largely tied to health and services, manufacturing, and wholesale and retail trade. Below, the economic and fiscal aspects of Ohio are summarized.

Regional Economies Within Ohio

Economic prosperity is enjoyed in many of Ohio's counties. A significant share of Ohio's counties, however, have relatively high unemployment rates. For example, counties in the south and eastern portions of the State lie in the hills of Appalachia and suffer the highest unemployment rates in Ohio. The counties along Lake Erie, in North Central Ohio and in Western areas of Ohio also have relatively high unemployment rates. By contrast, counties on a Southwest-Northeast diagonal across Ohio and some counties in the Western part of the State have relatively low unemployment rates.

To elaborate, in May, 1994, the unemployment rate in Ohio was 6.2 percent compared to a rate of 5.9 percent in the United States. However, 36 counties in Ohio had unemployment rates of 5.9 percent or lower, while 31 counties (all except two are in the southern or eastern portion of the State) had unemployment rates above 7.0 percent, and three of the 31 counties had unemployment rates above 11 percent (See Table 9-1).

The uneven nature of economic development across the state, at least as exhibited by the wide variation in unemployment rates, suggests that economic development programs could be targeted spatially as well as targeted toward particular segments of the population. For example, several persons interviewed in Ohio cited creation of low-skilled jobs as a way to target jobs toward people in high unemployment areas. Ohio has several new economic development programs that target lower-skilled workers.

On the other hand, the Greater Columbus Chamber of Commerce has targeted corporate data centers, survey research firms, research and development in medical technologies, research and development in information technologies, and electronic and text retrieval services among others. With OCLC and telecommunications services already in the Columbus area, the Chamber is building on the strengths of the existing industry. Instead of low-skilled jobs, part of the strategy calls for the creation of several chaired faculty positions in Computer Sciences at Ohio State University. The Chamber also calls for lower level technical training, greater parental involvement in

TABLE 9-1
Number of Counties in Ohio by Unemployment Rates, May 1994

	Unemployment Rate 5.9 percent or Lower[a]	Unemployment Rate Between 6.0 and 7.0 Percent[b]	Unemployment Rate Greater than 7.0 Percent
Number of Counties	36	22	31

Source: Ohio Bureau of Employment Services.

[a]In May 1994, the unemployment rate in the United States was 5.9 percent. This column enumerates the Ohio counties with unemployment rates at or below the United States average in May 1994.

[b]In May 1994, the Ohio unemployment rate was 6.2 percent. This column enumerates the Ohio counties with unemployment rates between 6.0 and 7.0 or between just above the United States average and 10 percent above the Ohio state average unemployment rate.

schooling, and upgrading other human and physical support systems that undergird such high-technology industry.[2]

Competitor States

The Ohio Economic Competitiveness Project sponsored by the Ohio Department of Development (ODOD) has identified the five states that border Ohio (Kentucky, Indiana, Michigan, Pennsylvania, and West Virginia) and five other growth states (Illinois, Tennessee, North Carolina, South Carolina and California) as most likely to compete with Ohio for new jobs. ODOD officials noted that Ohio competed most often with Indiana and Kentucky as alternative business locations.[3]

Major Business Taxes in Ohio

Businesses in Ohio pay three major taxes: local property tax, the corporate franchise tax and sales taxes on business purchases. Many of the economic development programs in Ohio involve abatement of the local property or corporate franchise tax. A brief fiscal review of the taxes here will help put the economic development programs in perspective, and set the stage for an evaluation of the development programs.

To begin, note that Ohio is a relatively low-tax state. In state and local taxes as a percentage of personal income, Ohio ranks 30 among the 50 states in 1991. Its two major competitors and neighboring states, Kentucky and Indiana rank 17 and 36, respectively.[4]

Property Tax

Local governments in Ohio rely on three taxes: property tax, income tax and sales tax. Because of the diverse local revenue sources in Ohio, the effective real property tax rate is about 1.75 percent, which is under the average for the United States. The property tax is not a major revenue source for municipalities, as many rely on the local income tax and sales tax as major sources of revenue. The property tax is a major source of revenue for school districts, however. About 70 percent of property tax revenue funds local schools, and property tax reform that reduces property taxes has major implications for funding local schools. About $4.7 billion was collected from the real property tax in 1993.[5]

In addition to real property taxes, personal property taxes are levied on tangible business property including machinery, equipment and inventories. Tangible personal property is assessed by law at 25 percent of true value (cost less state specified deprecation), and the millage rate is 65.31 mills (in 1992). Thus, the effective tax rate is 1.63 percent. About $1.2 billion was collected from the personal business tangible property, of which $500 million came from the tax on business inventories.[6]

There are special assessment rates for public utility properties. Real property is assessed at 35 percent of market value. Personal property is assessed at 88 percent with several exceptions, such as for electrical production equipment and telephones companies with fewer than 15,000 access lines, which are both assessed at 100 percent. Other exceptions include railroads' personal property, which is assessed at 25 percent, and rural electric companies, which are assessed at 50 percent of market value. In conversation with representatives of the electrical utilities companies, they mentioned the 100 percent assessment rate as making it difficult for them to compete on price with alternative fuels sources and perhaps raising the price of electricity in Ohio and, therefore, the cost of doing business.

The property tax on inventories is controversial in Ohio. Persons interviewed in local governments pointed out that the inventory tax is a major impediment to attracting business to Ohio. Business persons note that "the worse my year (the more inventory) the more tax I pay." Among the major competitor states, Indiana, Kentucky and West Virginia tax business inventories. California, Illinois, Michigan, North Carolina, Pennsylvania, South Carolina, and Tennessee do not tax inventories.[7] In fact, local governments in 40 of the 50 states exempt inventories from property taxation.[8]

Ohio exempts certain inventories from local property taxation. For example, all inventories in foreign trade zones that are exempt from taxation under federal law are exempt from local property taxation. Property inventory shipped from outside Ohio and held in Ohio for storage only (not processing) is also exempt from local property taxation (this rule applies in all states under the exemption for interstate commerce). Qualified personal property within an Enterprise Zone is also exempt from all or part of the local property tax.

Another area of discussion about local property taxation centers on taxation of business machinery and equipment. While there are arguments on both sides of this issue concerning what constitutes wealth and property, 39 of the 50 states levy a property tax on business depreciable fixed assets. Two of Ohio's major competitor states, Illinois and Pennsylvania, exempt business fixed assets from the property tax (Mikesell 1992). Moreover, exempting business fixed assets from property taxation in Ohio would mean that between $0.9 and $1.0 billion of local property tax revenues would have to be replaced.

Franchise Tax

The State of Ohio levies a franchise tax; the corporation pays the greater of the tax on its net worth or its net income. The tax on net worth adds to the stability of the tax revenue over time. However, in interviews with persons working in the economic development areas of the State, they mentioned that corporation heads saw the tax on net worth as unfair. The nominal tax rate of 8.9 percent is within the range of the tax rates in the competitor states; Kentucky's tax rate is 8.25 percent and Indiana levies a more complex tax, whose rate is less than 7.9 percent due to the partial deductibility of corporate taxes paid in Indiana. The State of Ohio collects about $0.8 billion from the corporate franchise tax, despite the high tax rate.

The net worth tax is probably obsolete and a candidate for fiscal reform based on economic development considerations alone. While the net worth provision serves to stabilize revenue by insuring that corporations pay at least some tax, the net worth tax discriminates against Ohio-based firms compared to the income tax. Two factors (payroll and property) are used to allocate net worth to Ohio establishments for the net worth tax, whereas three factors (payroll, property and sales) are used to allocate income to Ohio establishments for the income tax. By excluding sales from the allocation of net worth, Ohio-based export firms have a greater share of net worth allocated to them than the share of income allocated under the income tax. In addition, the net worth tax levies burdens on assets that are also subject to the property tax, creating a double-tax situation. For both reasons, the net worth tax appears to harm the economic development potential of Ohio. [9]

Sales Tax

Ohio exempts purchases of capital equipment and of tangible personal property used in production from sales tax. Nonetheless, about 30 percent of Ohio's state sales tax revenue is derived from taxes paid on business purchases. While the 30 percent figure is not uncommon among states, Ohio's manufacturer's sales tax exemption for intermediate goods is based on a list of items that are exempted rather than a blanket exemption for items used in the manufacturing process. Using a list makes the sales tax easier to administer, because without a list the Department of Taxation would have to determine whether some goods were used by manufacturers or by consumers. Moreover, the large amount of revenue from business purchases effectively expands the tax base and reduces the sales tax rate necessary to raise the given amount of revenue.

The sales tax levied on intermediate goods causes tax pyramiding, however, where sales taxes levied on purchases for production get passed on in prices at the retail level and an additional sales tax is levied at the retail level. Thus, the effective sales tax rate varies among final goods, depending on the extent to which each good is made using materials and equipment that are exempt from sales taxation. Ohio might want to adopt a more integrated plant approach, where all materials and equipment at the plant are exempt from sales taxation. That would give Ohio firms a competitive edge.[10]

Summary of Business Fiscal Climate in Ohio and Competitor States

Seven key features of the fiscal climate affecting business in Ohio and in ten of its competitor states are listed in Table 9-2. Overall, Ohio is competitive with the other states in its fiscal climate. Ohio exempts most manufacturing machinery and equipment from the sales tax. Only Kentucky and Michigan among the competitor states do not exempt machinery and equipment. As noted above, Ohio collects 30 percent of its revenue from intermediate goods and, while that is similar to other states, reforming the treatment of taxes on intermediate goods might give Ohio firms a competitive advantage. Similarly, Ohio is competitive with its sales tax rate. As noted above, the franchise tax is somewhat out of date. Ohio's rate for the corporate income tax is somewhat above the average for competitors.

The personal income tax structure has a top rate of 7.5 percent on taxable income above $200,000, which is higher than most of the competitor states, but taxpayers with taxable incomes below $100,000 pay a marginal tax rate of less than 6 percent. More problematic than high marginal rates at the top of the income distribution is that the 0.743 tax rate at the bottom taxes persons with very low-incomes, as there is no standard deduction and a small personal exemption, making minimal the zero tax bracket amount. The small range for the zero bracket taxes the working poor at low rates and creates administrative cost at the bottom of the distribution to generate a small amount of revenue. Reform of the personal income tax rates at the highest levels could also receive some attention.[11]

Despite some problems within certain taxes, Ohio has a considerable advantage in the overall level of taxation in that its state and local revenue as a percentage of personal income is 10.7, and Ohio ranks fifth highest among the 11 states, where the percentage ranges from 9.0 in Tennessee to 12.0 in West Virginia. Nonetheless, in two areas, Ohio appears to have a competitive disadvantage. Its maximum weekly unemployment compensation rate at $319 is second highest to Pennsylvania at $337. Illinois' stands at $311 and the maximum in the other nine states ranges from $185 in Tennessee to $293 in Michigan. The second area is the property taxation of inventories at the local level. Seven of its 10 competitor states exempt inventories from property taxation. Moreover, businesses in Ohio see the personal property tax on inventories as onerous and unfair. Ohio local governments also levy property taxes on business depreciable assets or equipment and machinery. Only,

TABLE 9-2
Tax Features of Selected States

Tax Features	Ohio	Indiana	Kentucky	Michigan	Illinois	West Virginia
1. Exemption of mfg. machinery and equipment from sales tax (Source 1)	X	X			X	X
2. Business Property Tax Exemptions: Inventories Depreciable Fixed Assets (Source 2)				X	X X	
3. State Sales Tax Rate Range of Local Sales Taxes (Source 3)	5.0 0 to 2.0	5.0 0.5 to 2.0	6.0 NA	4.0 NA	6.25 0 to 2.25	6.0 NA
4. State Personal Income Tax Rate Taxable Income for highest tax rate Local Personal Income Tax Rate (Range) (Source 3)	0.743 - 7.5 @$200,000 1.5 to 2.25	3.4 NA	2.0 - 6.0 @$8,000 1.45 to 2.95	4.6 0.075 to 3.0	3.0 NA	3.0 - 6.5 @$60,000 NA
5. State Corporate Income Tax Rate (Highest rate) (Source 3)	8.9	3.4 + 4.5	8.25	2.35	4.8	9.075
6. Unemployment Compensation Maximum Weekly Benefit (Source 4)	$319	$192	$229	$293	$311	$280
7. State and Local Revenues as a Percent of State Income (Source 3)	10.7	10.4	11.6	11.6	10.6	12.0

continued

TABLE 9-2 (continued)
Tax Features of Selected States

Tax Features	Pennsylvania	North Carolina	South Carolina	Tennessee	California
1. Exemption of mfg. machinery and equipment from sales tax (Source 1)	X	X 1%	X	X	X
2. Business Property Tax Exemptions					
Inventories	X	X	X	X	X
Depreciable Fixed Assets (Source 2)	X				
3. State Sales Tax Rate	6.0	4.0	5.0	6.0	6.0
Range of Local Sales Taxes (Source 3)	0.0 to 1.0	2.0	0 to 1.0	1.75 to 2.5	1.25 to 2.25
4. State Personal Income Tax Rate	2.95	6.0 -7.75	2.5 - 7.0	NA	1.0 - 11.0
Taxable Income for highest tax rate		@$60,000	@$10,600		@$207,200
Local Personal Income Tax Rate (Range) (Source 3)	1.0 to 4.96	NA	NA	NA	NA
5. State Corporate Income Tax Rate (Highest Rate) (Source 3)	12.25	7.75	5.0	6.0	9.3
6. Unemployment Compensation Maximum Weekly Benefit (Source 4)	$337	$282	$203	$185	$230
7. State and Local Taxes as a Percent of State Income (Source 3)	10.1	10.3	10.6	9.0	11.3

Sources: 1. Economic Development Reports (Various States), 1994 and Fox (1994).
2. Commerce Clearing House, State Tax Reporter, 1993 and Mikesell (1992).
3. Advisory Commission on Intergovernmental Relations, Significant Features of Fiscal Federalism, Washington, D.C. February 1993.
4. State Policy Reports, Vol. 12 number 4 , July 1994 (second issue of two) State Policy Research Corp. Columbus Ohio.

Illinois and Pennsylvania among the ten competitor states exempt equipment and machinery from property taxation, and that is less of a competitive disadvantage than the property tax on inventories.

ECONOMIC DEVELOPMENT SUBSIDIES: INCENTIVES AND EFFECTS

Economic development programs and subsidies are controversial in virtually all states. Political and economic debates generally center around whether the jobs would have located in the state in the absence of the subsidy or, to put it another way, how many jobs does the subsidy create and are the benefits of the job creation worth the costs. In fact, however, if it is accepted that economic development subsidies will exist and that Illinois Governor James Edgar's pleas for an end to the tax abatement battle will not be heeded, then questions about the cost of the subsidies, although important, should be broadened to consider how well the design of the subsidies match the objectives, and whether the objectives themselves are desirable.

In this section, issues related to the design of efficient subsidies for businesses are addressed. It is not unusual for states to pursue about 20 different initiatives to help attract and retain businesses. For example, Ohio has economic development initiatives that include property tax abatement, wage subsidies, capital and interest rate subsidies, as well as subsidized worker training programs. Policies address both the demand and supply sides of the market. Demand-side policies aim at making the state more attractive to businesses, or engage in activities that increase the demand for state products, or increase the demand for the state as a locational choice. For example, a state program to enhance export demand for products of in-state companies might consist of a Governor and other state officials visiting other countries and, as part of the mission, touting the products that can be exported from their state. States also have programs to reduce the paper work associated with exporting to other countries. Other demand-side subsidies include training programs in community colleges designed to increase the number of entrepreneurs and business start-ups, business-related applied research (scientific, technical and other) done at universities and colleges around the state, and other business support programs. The effectiveness of these programs has not been studied, and there is little to report to guide policy on the demand side of the market. Nonetheless, a number of authors (Eisinger 1988; Fosler 1988; Pomp 1988; and Vaughn 1979) have argued for demand-side over supply-side subsidies .

Supply-side subsidies are programs designed to reduce the cost of capital, labor or taxes in a state. Such subsidies are often characterized as smokestack chasing or the "buffalo-hunt" approach, because the supply-side subsidies are typically negotiated with relatively few firms that a state may want to attract within its borders. While both demand- and supply-side subsidies involve interstate competition for jobs, the demand-side subsidies specifically improve the quality of life in a state by enhancing the training and productivity of the work force, or by improving infrastructure. Supply-side subsidies typically have the character of competing in specific instances directly with other states for firms and establishments by reducing taxes or providing capital subsidies to recruit a few firms. The direct state-to-state competition have made supply-side subsidies expensive and inefficient ways to build industry in a state.

Most subsidy dollars are spent on the supply side of the market through tax incentive (relief) programs and reduced loan rates for firms to acquire capital. The amount of dollars spent on these programs through tax abatement or through capital subsidy warrants careful study. The most hotly debated question about the subsidies is whether they do in fact attract jobs to the state or locality granting the subsidy, and a secondary point is whether the amount paid for the subsidy is worth the number of jobs created. A more pointed set of questions relates to the targeting of the subsidies, or which segments of population and industry should benefit from the subsidy. An alternative way to address targeting is to identify the specific objectives of the subsidy program.

Targets can be distressed regions within the state (place subsidies), or particular populations (people) within the state. Enterprise Zones are examples of place subsidies, where businesses located in areas of a state are eligible for a set of subsidies. People-based subsidies can have very general targets, such as lower taxes in general for job creation, or quite specific targets, such as job creation for lower-skilled or high-tech workers. Both place- and people-based subsidies can be geared to particular industries, such as manufacturing or high-tech within manufacturing. The subsidies can be directed to all firms in a targeted industry, to new firms, or to existing firms that create additional jobs or investment.

A related set of issues are the social implications of job creation, or what persons or groups (the poor, single mothers, or high-skilled workers) benefit from job creation in the State. The wage levels of the new jobs as well as the nature of the jobs created are also of interest. The creation of low-wage, part-time jobs creates fewer benefits than full-time jobs, for example. Despite these concerns, Bartik (1991) has argued that job creation for lower-skill workers, for instance, can itself create a learning environment where workers acquire on-the-job skills that make them more employable in the longer run (hysteresis effects). Jobs for lower-skilled workers can also lead to less dependence on unemployment insurance or welfare. More jobs also create more tax base growth from workers and businesses.

Do Subsidies Attract Jobs?

The evidence on effectiveness of tax incentives for attracting jobs relies on the more general literature about the effect of taxes and expenditures on investment and job growth. Studies exist to buttress almost any case about tax incentives. Some studies (Papke 1987 and 1991a) find significant impacts of taxes on job growth, while others (Carlton 1983) find that taxes have no impact. In a thorough review, Bartik (1991) summarizes the results of the literature. His summary of the literature, reported in Table 9-3, suggests that tax incentives are less effective (lower elasticity) when the industry location choice is being made between states and areas of the country, and are more effective when the industry location is being made among alternative sites within a metropolitan area. The size of the elasticities (the responsiveness of jobs creation or investment to tax rates) are clearly smaller for inter-area location choices than for intra-area location choices. This finding has become almost conventional wisdom among researchers in the economic development area. Put differently, the smaller the area over which a firm is making

TABLE 9-3
Summary of Econometric Results for Tax Effects on Business Location

Business Location	Percentage of Studies with at Least One Statistically Significant Tax Effect [a]	Median Elasticity [b]
Inter-area studies (between states or metro areas)	70 percent (57 studies)	-0.15
Inter-area studies (control for level of public services)	92 percent (12 studies)	-0.35
Inter-area studies (control for fixed-effects[c])	80 percent (30 studies)	-0.27
Intra-area studies (within a metropolitan area)	57 percent (14 studies)	-1.59
Intra-area studies using specific community data	70 percent (14 studies)	-1.95

Source: Bartik (1991), page 40-41.

[a]In 70 percent of the 57 studies, for example, at least one of coefficients on the tax variables was statistically different from zero.
[b]The middle value of the tax elasticities in the 70 studies was -0.15 or a one percentage change in the value of the tax coefficient produced a 0.15 percent reduction in the value of the economics development measure (employment, income, etc.).
[c]Fixed effects estimators require a pooled cross-section and times series for states (or a panel data set) so that dummy variables representing each state can be used to account for unobserved variables that may differ among states. This type of estimation is more reliable econometrically than estimation based only on one year of data for a cross section of states.

a choice, the more likely it is that other things will be the same and that taxes, therefore, could play a more decisive role.

Two other findings are worth mention. First, most studies have examined data from the 1960s and 1970s to find significant effects for the fiscal variables. More recently, Carroll and Wasylenko (1994) have studied the effects of fiscal variables on employment across states and across time. They find that the fiscal variables have much less influence on employment in the 1980s than in the 1970s. There is reason to remain somewhat skeptical about the effectiveness of tax and other subsidies for attracting industry to states. Foreign direct investment in states, on the other hand, appears very responsive to lower corporate income tax rates (Ondrich and Wasylenko 1993; and Hines 1993).

Two conclusions emerge from this series of studies. Aggregate studies that examine the total employment in states or regions do not typically account for the nuances of the tax systems that each of the states might have. Some taxes in every state are no doubt annoying to some industries; however, aggregate data on either taxes or industry location will generally not contain sufficient detail to capture the negative effects of particular tax issues. Thus, using abatements to rid the system of annoying taxes that strike particular industries might have significant effects on the industry's location. An alternative to abatement is to reconsider the tax code and make the marginal effective tax rates more even (or fair) across industries.

Secondly, the results about tax effects are not very stable across time and across studies. Some reviewers have contended that more recent studies that have used more modern techniques tend to uncover the effects of the fiscal variables more regularly. A recent study using modern techniques (Carroll and Wasylenko 1994) casts doubt on that statement. At best, it can be said that the average level of taxes are not a major factor guiding investment and location decisions in most states. Nonetheless, a consensus among researchers suggests that on average taxes do have modest effects on location choices, and the modest effects of taxes for average tax states are accentuated in very high tax states (Wasylenko 1993). For example the degree to which lower taxes can affect location choice depends on the product of the average effect, reported in Table 9-3, and the degree to which any state deviates from the average tax burden. High tax states with their large deviations from the average tax burden will, therefore, lose more business than the average tax states. As if to buttress the consensus among researchers, the highest tax states, such as Minnesota, Wisconsin and New York, have recently acknowledged that high taxes may be responsible for the low job creation in those states(State Policy Reports 1994).

The bottom line in this case is whether or not tax abatement attracts jobs. Critics of abatement contend that the jobs would have come anyway and the abatement is merely a corporate giveaway (Pomp 1985). Others contend that without the abatement the jobs would not come and that the state or locality would not have the revenue in the absence of the abatement; thus, the abatement does not cause a "true" revenue loss. The truth is apparently somewhere in between these extremes, and no one is sure quite where. The Nebraska Department of Revenue assumes, for example, that 30 percent of the total jobs that firms create when they receive the Nebraska subsidy are attributable to the subsidy and the other 70 percent would have come to Nebraska without the subsidy. In the absence of better evidence and larger tax elasticities, that assumption, while not unreasonable, probably attributes more power to incentives to attract industry than is warranted (Philips 1994).

Morse and Farmer (1986) have written one of the few studies that examine the efficacy of tax subsidies. They examined Ohio's Community Reinvestment Area property tax exemption. Surveying 24 companies, four of which were newly locating companies and 20 of which expanded in place, the subsidy was not found to influence the relocating companies, and only one of the company expansions was attributable to the tax exemption. However, the one expansion accounted for 25 percent of the total new investment undertaken by the 24 companies. In assessing whether the tax abatements cost communities more than the tax collected from the one firm contributed to the tax base, Morse and Farmer noted that the State of Ohio replaced some of the forgone revenue lost in the school district, and that obviously made the abatement more worthwhile for the local communities. Without state replacement, revenues forgone would have exceeded the extra revenues due to the firm expansion. Morse and Farmer considered only the fiscal benefits of the investment and not the other economic benefits. However, their survey results suggest that tax abatements have a very limited impact on investment and location. Their results are consistent with the more general literature on taxes and their effect on firm locations.

Other evidence in Bartik et al. (1987) suggests that the Saturn plant location decision was driven more by the lower cost of labor in Tennessee for suppliers to the Saturn plant than by the lower taxes. Fox (1990) suggests that factors associated with the Nissan plant location in Tennessee rather than Georgia are not known for sure, as firms do not make public their specific reasons for particular location decisions.

A related question is the origin location of the firms taking advantage of the subsidy. Some firms may relocate from within the same state to take advantage of the subsidy that accrues to them because they relocate a business to a designated area of the state. In effect, the firm has not created new jobs. However, if the intention is a place-subsidy or to attract jobs to a particular location, the firm's relocation might be looked upon favorably. In Britain, for example, about 86 percent of the jobs created within Enterprise Zones were relocations from outside the zone and in many cases from within the same county. That combined with the slower employment growth in Enterprise Zones than in the rest of the counties and the large cost per job created led to the phaseout of the British Enterprise Zone system (Ladd 1993). In Ohio, the degree to which the "new jobs" are merely relocations within a state or county will determine to some extent the desirability of the job program and the degree to which other social objectives, such as the creation of jobs for lower-income residents, are necessary to justify the program.

Effects of Capital, Labor And Place-oriented Subsidies

Many economic development programs grant abatements for taxes on capital and offer subsidized interest rates on loans, while other programs subsidize wages of employees, grant subsidies per worker hired, or offer employees training. These programs can have very different effects on the relative prices that each firm faces for labor versus capital and for skilled (more highly paid) and unskilled labor. The change in factor prices affects the firm's choice to hire more capital or more labor. The type of worker training offered and paid for can also influence the types of employees that ultimately find jobs at the new firms.

More important to existing firms is whether the subsidies are offered alike to new, expanding, and existing firms. Offering subsidies or abating taxes only for new firms or expansions reduces the revenue losses to states, but that policy also raises considerable inequity between new firms and existing employers who in many cases may compete for sales with the new, subsidized competition.

Capital Versus Labor Subsidies. A state with a desire for economic growth should hope to attract new investment and capital-intensive industries. The United States economy has been shedding labor-intensive industries, and in the 1980s wage growth occurred in already high-paying occupations that used high technology and especially those industries investing in computer equipment (DeLong and Summers 1991). A state looking toward the future will want to encourage investment in modern plant and equipment. The first issue is adopting policies to attract capital equipment. Evidence from the investment literature suggests that low user costs of capital or low taxes on capital induce investment, especially in equipment (Bosworth and Burtless 1992; also Auerbach and Hassett 1992). Note also that policies to foster capital investment are compatible with worker training programs that impart skills necessary to use the capital equipment.

A second issue for states to consider is that capital intensive investment is most compatible with jobs for skilled workers, and capital generally substitutes for low-skilled workers (Kesselman, Williamson and Berndt 1977; Bergstrom and Panas 1992). Moreover, in their simulations, Kesselman et al. find that tax credits for employment increase the number of jobs dramatically compared to investment tax credits (for equal revenue forgone), and that marginal employment tax credits (tax credits for new employees hired) have the largest effects on employment.[12] Furthermore, they point out that employment tax credits need to be targeted at the jobs that you want to create.

The flip side then, is that states will also want to create jobs for lower-skilled workers. Creating low-skilled jobs will require subsidies that reduce wages of low-skilled workers to induce firms to hire such workers. Those subsidies can be paid directly to workers, such as earned income tax credits, and workers might, in turn, accept lower wages. On the other hand, the subsidies could be paid to firms in the form of subsidizing day care of employees, reducing the costs of unemployment and worker's compensation programs for low-pay workers, and subsidies to employers who hire low-skilled workers in special categories or locations. The point here is that one type of program will not simultaneously enhance economic growth and address job creation for lower-skill workers. Both capital and labor subsidies might be pursued simultaneously, if the programs are targeted at different labor subgroups.

Wage versus Employment Subsidies. The above argues for employment subsidies in certain circumstances. A more subtle point relates to the form of the labor subsidy. A subsidy to all new hires (or all labor) in the form of a percentage of the wage bill reduces the wage bill equally for high and low paid workers in the absence of fringe benefits. If fringe benefits are paid to employees, however, and the cost of fringe benefits, such as health care, are the same for high-paid and low-paid employees then a subsidy based on a percentage of the wage lowers the price of high-paid employees relatively more than the price of low-paid employees. Thus, the percentage of wages subsidy in the presence of fringe benefits could favor, at the margin, substitution of skilled (high paid) for unskilled workers, and might attract industries that use high-skilled labor more intensively.

In contrast, a subsidy to labor paid in the form of a fixed amount per worker, say $1,000 per year for each worker hired, will reduce the cost of lower-paid workers compared to higher-paid workers and encourage the substitution of lower-skilled for more highly-skilled, better-paid workers. Economic development plans with intentions of creating jobs for particular types of workers should pay careful attention to the type of subsidy (labor versus capital) and to the design of the labor or capital subsidy program.

Which Workers Benefit From Subsidies?

Migration of workers into and out of areas can reduce or eliminate the effectiveness of targeting certain jobs to residents in specific locations.

Marston (1985, p. 74), for example, has argued that shocks or subsidies in particular labor markets only temporarily reduce the unemployment in the area. In a short period of time, however, in-migration of better workers to the area eliminates the benefits to the original residents of the area. In contrast to that argument, Cross (1988) and Bartik (1991) contend that even temporary employment of previously unemployed persons imparts work skills to persons (hysteresis effects) and leaves them permanently more likely to find jobs. Nonetheless, based on 18 studies cited in Bartik (1993), he concludes that 60 to 90 percent of jobs created by employment programs in the long-run go to in-migrants to the area or unintended beneficiaries. A recent finding by Blanchard and Katz (1992), however, suggests that in the long run new in-migrants to the area take all of the newly created jobs.

There is also disagreement in the literature over which racial, gender and age groups benefit from job growth. Several studies (Frey and Speare 1988; Moore and Laramore 1990; Bound and Holzer 1991; Freeman 1991; and Bartik 1992) find that job creation programs increase employment among blacks more than whites, while other researchers find no differences (Ihlanfeldt 1992) or even less job effects for blacks than whites (Ihlanfeldt and Sjoquist 1991). Similar controversy exists for females versus males (Mooney 1969; Moore and Laramore 1990; and Fleisher and Rhodes 1976), but youths appear to have the edge over other workers when local economic conditions improve (Freeman 1982; Welch 1990; and Bartik 1992). The main point here is that to achieve particular outcomes, subsidies need to be targeted. However, narrowly targeted programs are unpopular with businesses because the programs are difficult for businesses to administer. Moreover, the migration of labor into targeted areas will substantially reduce benefits to the originally targeted residents of the area.

Subsidies to All Firms or New Employers?

When subsidies are offered to new or expanding firms, existing firms that have been in place for years generally find the practice unfair. Subsidies are offered in many cases to newer firms whose products compete with the existing firms. This creates a problem for states and localities offering the subsidies. Extending subsidies more generally to firms levels the playing field, but also becomes much more expensive in terms of forgone tax revenue (or direct subsidy expense), and makes the programs much more expensive per job created. Moreover, lower taxes, rather than general subsidies to firms, are more easily understood and administered.

On the other hand, generous subsidies to a selected firm may also create public relations problems for the firm. For example, Bartik et al. (1987) suggest that General Motors may have feared negative publicity and thus future pressure to increase tax payments as a result of Minnesota's very generous tax abatements offered to counteract its very high taxes.

When the costs of creating new employment become very high, legitimate questions can be asked about whether government might create jobs more efficiently and effectively. Political opinions differ, as some note that the taxes are not the governments money to begin with, while others worry how to finance public services in the absence of a stable tax base. When the business climate of a state becomes so problematic that tax breaks need to be granted routinely to attract businesses, it may be a symptom of problems with the tax code itself and a signal that tax reform might be a more useful approach than ad hoc tax deals and abatement programs that inevitably treat some groups unfairly. In effect, tax reform treats existing and new firms equally, and responsible reform will also replace systematically the tax revenue lost due to reform.

Enterprise Zones

State Enterprise Zones have become commonplace, with 37 states and the District of Columbia having Enterprise Zone programs. State Enterprise Zones generally consist of tax credits (generally against corporate and property taxes) for investment and new employment, and the zones are usually located in economically distressed areas of the state. Most authors writing about Enterprise Zones have criticized them for not attracting jobs or, when there has been job growth in the zones, the job growth has been attributed to factors other than the subsidies and tax incentives. Indeed, it is difficult methodologically to separate the job growth that would have occurred within the zone in the absence of zone designation and subsidies from the job growth that occurred as a result of the zone designation and subsidies.

Papke (1993) and Gravelle (1992) developed theoretical models of the employment and wage gains that are likely to result from Enterprise Zone policies. Papke constructed a simulation model of employment stimulus within the zones that could result from employment and capital subsidies. The effects of the subsidies on wages and jobs in her models depend on the labor supply behavior of zone residents, the increase in demand for zone products when their prices are reduced (as a result of the lower labor and capital costs), and whether the subsidies are targeted specifically at zone residents. The higher the demand elasticity for the product (or the greater the demand for output when the subsidies reduce the prices of goods in the zone) and the lower the labor supply elasticities, the more the employment subsidies targeted at zone residents raise wages of zone residents. She further notes that capital subsidies at low elasticities of product demand and low labor supply elasticities can actually reduce wages in the Enterprise Zone.[13]

Papke suggests that the potential for higher product demand is low in Enterprise Zones (at least in Indiana) because most products are not exported from the zone but sold locally. Thus, she reasons that subsidies of inputs within Enterprise Zones are not likely to have large effects on employment or wages. Moreover, she cautions against the use of capital subsidies in Enterprise Zones as mechanisms to increase employment among low-skilled zone residents, as capital subsidies can in her model reduce the wages of unskilled labor, depending on the strength of the substitution of capital for low-skilled labor.

Gravelle (1992) extends Papke's analysis and considers whether policies within the zone affect wages and employment at locations outside of the zone. That is, increased wages in the zone can affect wages in areas outside the zone. Gravelle notes that the larger the number of areas that become zones (such as in Ohio) the more important the general effects outside the zone become. She finds, for example, that the increase in zone wages and employment become smaller as the number of zones increases and that wages and employment outside of the Enterprise Zone will fall as zone wages and employment rise. Thus, the more areas that are designated Enterprise Zones the more likely it is that employment and wages are raised only slightly in zones and that the primary effect of Enterprise Zones is inefficiency in the location of investment.

Ladd (1993) gives an overview of the evaluation literature on Enterprise Zones. We have already alluded to the experience in Britain with Enterprise Zones and the British Government's decision to phase out the zones. The evaluation literature in the United States suggests that in the zone in Hagerstown, Maryland (General Accounting Office 1987), for example, two employers are responsible for the job growth in the zone. In one case, the employer was unaware of the zone subsidies and the other employer answered that he would have located within the zone area without the Enterprise Zone program. Rubin (1990) reports that only 32 percent of employers in ten New Jersey Enterprise Zones acknowledge that the tax incentives were the primary reason for their expansion or location within the zones.

Indiana has 18 Enterprise Zones located in distressed urban areas. The major tax break in the zones is abatement of the personal property tax on inventories. Papke's (1991b) analysis suggests that investment in machinery and equipment in the zones declined by 9.8 percent, inventories increased by 8.0 percent, and unemployment insurance claims for residents of the zones and of areas outside the zone declined by 25 percent. However, (Papke 1993) reports that between 1980 and 1990 zone areas lost population, and had much lower growth in per capita income than in non-zone areas. Unemployment did fall more in zone areas than in non-zone areas, but the difference was small (0.11 percent). She also concludes that in spite of her evidence on the reduction in unemployment rates within the zones, the income numbers suggest that zone residents are not better off with the Enterprise Zone program.

Erickson (1992) is somewhat more optimistic about the success of Enterprise Zones. While acknowledging that success of the Enterprise Zone is concentrated in a limited set of high-performing zones among the set of all zones, he concludes that most of the jobs created in the zones are not due to firms relocating from outside the zones but to new or expanding firms, that zone residents filled 60 percent of the new jobs, and that low-income and unemployed workers received a significant share of the new jobs. Erickson acknowledges, however, that the job creation can not necessarily be attributed to the tax incentives offered in the zones.

Ladd (1993) concludes from her survey of the studies cited above that place subsidies and even people-based, place-based subsidies have failed to raise employment levels and the well being of zone residents. That conclusion should cause states to reexamine their Enterprise Zone programs. The programs are costly and the benefits elusive. Enterprise Zone programs or spatially-targeted subsidies are by most evidence inefficient mechanisms by themselves for increasing the employment of residents of distressed areas.

The Cost of Jobs

In spite of the evidence that the tax abatement subsidies have limited effects on the locational decisions of most firms, states have raised the ante on paying for jobs, especially when it comes to chasing large manufacturers who might locate there. The danger of the subsidies is that they are becoming more expensive as states fall over themselves outbidding one another for a plant. On the other hand, it should be understood that states must create a hospitable business environment, and this may include some combination of training and meaningful tax breaks and financial incentives. States are gradually becoming more conscious of the costs of these subsidies, however.

The figures reported in Table 9-4 illustrate that the costs of job creation can become very high. The cost estimates per job range from $4,564 in a New Jersey Enterprise Zone to $166,667 at Mercedes Benz in Alabama. The benefits of state job creation lie in the sustainability of the jobs created and the number of other jobs that may be created when the Mercedes plant attracts supplier and other related firms to the state. But still, states and localities should determine how much they want to spend to create each type of job, and be realistic about the so called multiplier effects of the initial investment. The amount of competition for jobs among states has often spun job creation costs out of control.

TABLE 9-4
Estimates of the Cost of Creating a Job for Various Subsidized Projects

JOBS Program Hamermesh (1978)	$10,782 in 1990 dollars
Urban Development Action Grant Program Bentick (1981)	$17,058 in 1990 dollars
Local Public Works EDA Program Bentick (1981)	$88,000 in 1990 dollars
N.J. Enterprise Zone Rubin (1992)	$8,000 to $13,000 in 1992 dollars
Indiana Enterprise Zones J. Papke (1990)	$4,564 per job and $31,113 per job for zone residents (1990 dollars)
Toyota Plant, Kentucky Phillips (1994)	$81,050 (1993 prices)
Fuji-Isuzu Plant (Indiana) Phillips (1994)	$68,275 (1993 prices)
Saturn Plant (Tennessee) Phillips (1994)	$12,168 (1993 prices)
Mercedes Plant (Alabama) Phillips (1994)	$166,667 (1993 prices)
LB775 Nebraska	$28,685 to $95,947 (1993 prices)
Honda Plants Marvel and Shkurti (1993)	$76,768 (1993 prices)
Diamond Star Plan, Illinois Phillips (1994)	$36,630 (1993) prices

Source: Author based on studies cited in Table.

EVALUATION OF PROGRAMS

States do not always evaluate the effectiveness of their economic development programs. This is due in part to the complexity of the task. Moreover, the literature on evaluation has not matured sufficiently to yield readily-implementable and well-understood procedures. Nonetheless, some authors and states have advanced the level of the analysis.

Marvel and Shkurti (1993) have evaluated the benefits and costs of Ohio's subsidy to the Honda plant in Marysville. They conclude that the nominal subsidy costs per job would be recovered in extra state and local revenues in three years or less. But they also recognize several problems with the estimates. It is not clear whether the Honda subsidy later obligated the State of Ohio to give state assistance of $17.8 million to domestic automakers (Ford, General Motors, and Chrysler) as well. Moreover, Marvel and Shkurti's estimates of the costs per job vary between $2,500 and $66,000 depending on whether the time value of money is accounted for. A similar adjustment for the time value of money would have to be made on the tax revenue or benefit side of the analysis as well. They also suggest that the indirect effects of three additional jobs created for each Honda job seem exaggerated, because a much higher multiplier was used (a multiplier of 3.0 rather than a more usual 2.0) than normally associated with investment projects. The use of a smaller and more realistic multiplier effectively increases the cost per job. Moreover, they caution that the benefit calculations hinge on whether the tax abatements were necessary to attract Honda to Ohio. As a final caveat, they note that the Volkswagen plant in New Stanton, Pennsylvania did not provide the sustained economic benefits that were promised. Thus, the positive effects of the Honda plant may not necessarily be generalized to other such investment subsidies.

Ohio and some other states formulate a tax-expenditure budget, which accounts for tax credits firms have taken for economic development efforts. Unfortunately, the cost of direct loans, interest rate subsidies and other economic development programs are not tax-based programs and therefore are not included in the tax-expenditure budget. It is typically difficult to obtain comprehensive information on the cost of economic development programs.

Massachusetts has taken another approach to evaluation. That State uses a three-stage analysis, labeled the Massachusetts Dynamic Analysis Model, to assess the effectiveness of its subsidy programs. In the first stage of the analysis, a microsimulation is performed on households and businesses. In Dildine (1993) the simulation derives first-round changes in income, consumption, capital costs, wages and factor supply.[14] In a second stage, those initial changes are fed into a regional macroeconomic model that accounts for interindustry transactions and the effects of the changes on the migration of labor and capital into and out of Massachusetts, and develops the total changes (direct plus indirect) that result from the policy change. The regional model embodies a state input-output table as well as econometric models. In a third stage, the total changes in income, consumption, earnings and business profits are fed into a tax revenue model to derive the revenue gains (losses) from the policy.

The Massachusetts model emphasizes revenue, which, while a major issue in policy debates, is of course not the singular focus of economic development programs. As indicated earlier, the benefits of the program, such as job creation and sustained economic growth are also important. The Massachusetts model is capable of estimating most of these beneficial effects as well, and the model represents an innovative approach to economic development programs.

Program evaluation must confront a host of issues related to economic development. It must begin with an examination of the objectives of the programs and whether the programs are designed in concert with the objectives.

Evaluators must also be realistic about the effectiveness of tax incentives in attracting industry. For example, place-based subsidies targeted to distressed areas may not overcome the deteriorated infrastructure or the lack of a trained labor force in the areas. Moreover, new firm startups are often not responsive to most corporate income and property tax incentives because profits are low or they rent space and machinery and pay no property taxes directly. Dildine (1993) notes, for example, start-up costs, high risks, and the deductibility of research expenses can make non-refundable income tax incentives very unreliable as incentives for high-tech companies. Sales tax relief (and property tax relief) for purchases of business capital and services may be more effective as a business incentive. Its cash-flow is surer and earlier than other tax incentives. High-tech firms depend on human resources and may be attracted to university areas and nurturing communities with a quality life style. Thus, tax incentives might have to be quite large to lure high-tech firms out of such friendly environments. Moreover, for high-tech firms employment growth may depend on how well the firm copes with competition and product obsolescence rather than on the size of the tax incentive.

Among the other serious drawbacks of industry subsidies are the discrimination against existing businesses, competition among jurisdictions that escalate the cost of subsidies, and the proliferation of (Enterprise) zones and subsidy programs. The discrimination against existing firms is serious enough in some states to create political backlash or the expansion of the tax incentives to existing firms. While expanding incentives to all firms is perceived as more fair, the practice is expensive and calls the question of whether the incentives create jobs and at what cost.

On the increased and often destructive competition among jurisdictions, Wasserman (1994), for example, finds that in the Detroit metropolitan area there has been a six-fold increase in the use of local economic development incentives over a ten to fifteen year time span. The level of intra-metropolitan competition is large and that reduces the likelihood that incentives are generating beneficial employment effects for the region as a whole. For example, Gravelle demonstrates that a proliferation of targeted areas and subsidies is not efficient. The more places that are subsidized the more likely the effects are small and dissipated throughout the system. Put another way, the greater the number of opportunities for subsidies in various places, the less likely the programs will hit their targeted or intended areas. The general conclusion in the literature is that place subsidies have not worked well to lift the level of economic development.

What Should States Do?

The competition for industry among states is unlikely to end, and tax incentives are part of the fiscal climate package states offer. However, states should be realistic about what they are spending, who they are attracting and which population groups are protected or helped. Private-public partnerships are probably no less important than tax incentives. Incentives to new and existing industries are necessary to attract and retain large corporations in the competitive environment that exists among states. But tax incentives are inefficient mechanisms in that they do not attract many jobs that would not otherwise come to the state, and states should exercise caution in spending for "jobs." A thorough cost-benefit analysis done by a third party in the state, such as a legislative analysis group, will give a state a better handle on the likely benefits of attracting a particular firm to the state compared to the costs.

Most important, tax incentives should not be used as a back-door to repair particular deficiencies in a tax system. This type of band-aid approach to tax reform creates more inequities and inefficiencies than it resolves. If taxes bite too hard or too unevenly, the tax reform route should be taken. It is often the case that sound tax and fiscal policy obviates many of the tax incentives that businesses seek.

ECONOMIC DEVELOPMENT PROGRAMS IN OHIO

Ohio has an extensive set of economic development incentives at both the state and local levels of government. Local governments participate actively in property tax abatement through an extensive number of Enterprise Zones throughout the State of Ohio and other abatement programs, while State government abates franchise taxes and provides direct loans, loan guarantees and bond funds. In many respects, the activities of Ohio's local governments in tax abatements are unusual among states. Local government incentives are much more far reaching than what local governments in other states typically offer. The following sections review the major economic development programs of local and the State governments in Ohio.

Ohio Local Government Development Programs

Localities use Enterprise Zones, Community Reinvestment Areas and Tax Increment Financing as tax abatement or subsidy methods to attract businesses. The extent of these programs is described below.

Enterprise Zones

The Ohio Enterprise Zone Program was created in 1982 to complement the then-proposed Federal Enterprise Zones. (The latter were never created, however.) The 1982 Ohio program focused on urban areas and allowed property tax (real and personal) exemptions for new investments and related inventories for up to ten years. State franchise tax incentives were also available. The program had a 5-year life.

In 1987 Ohio re-evaluated its Enterprise Zone program. The program was extended to December 31, 1992 and rural areas were allowed to participate.

Between 1987 and 1992, several amendments to the Enterprise Zone legislation were made that increased the eligibility of rural counties to designate Enterprise Zones, allowed school boards to comment and review the proposed property tax incentive agreements, and permitted local governments to compensate school boards in part for revenues forgone as a result of the Enterprise Zone agreements. Nonetheless, disagreements about the amount of fiscal compensation paid to school districts and the intrastate relocation of establishments into Enterprise Zones represented significant hurdles to the extension the Enterprise Zones beyond 1992. The Zones were extended twice more through July 1, 1994, with the intention of improving the program. Effective July 22, 1994, the Enterprise Zone Program was significantly modified. The program is now scheduled to sunset on December 31, 1997. The new law restructures the Ohio Enterprise Zone Program, Community Reinvestment Area and Tax Increment Financing Programs. Existing Enterprise Zone agreements are grandfathered under the new law (SB 19), but all new agreements within existing Enterprise Zones are subject to the new law.

New Enterprise Zones are created by petitioning to the Ohio Department of Development. Once a zone is created, businesses locating or expanding within the zone may become eligible for zone fiscal benefits. As under the former laws governing Enterprise Zones, business location within the zone, however, does not automatically confer zone benefits or tax exemptions. For example, under no circumstances are zone benefits available to retail businesses; the feeling in Ohio (and other states) is that these jobs follow the population and would locate in the zone without the tax benefits. As well, the magnitude of the new investment in the non-retail business must meet certain criteria. Furthermore, each business enters into a separate agreement with the municipality or township operating the zone. Below the rules governing Enterprise Zones under the new law are described and some of the differences between the new law and the immediate past laws are highlighted.

Pre-Existing Zones. Enterprise Zones established prior to July 1, 1994 continue to have tax exemption authority, but any new agreements between the municipalities and businesses must adhere to the criteria that guide such agreements in newly created Enterprise Zones. The principal difference for the pre-existing zones is that they are now limited zones and thus may not grant new tax abatements to plants relocating to the zone from within the State of Ohio. Any existing agreements between municipalities and businesses in these zones, however, are grandfathered.

Criteria for New Zones. In a rural county with under 300,000 population the proposed Enterprise Zone must have at least 1,000 residents within the proposed zone boundary. In counties with populations of 300,000 or greater, the proposed area must have at least 4,000 residents within the proposed zone boundary. In all cases, the zone must have a contiguous land area. The Ohio Department of Development encourages municipalities and townships to designate zone boundaries according to census tracts or blocks to ease data collection in the event that distress criteria related to poverty or unemployment of residents within the zone would become necessary, as such data are generally available on census tract basis. Moreover, under the new law there are two types of zones, limited and general. Only general zones may grant tax abatement to plants or firms that relocate within the State of Ohio.

Limited Zones. A limited Enterprise Zone can be created subject only to the population criteria stated above. The municipality can grant property tax relief to certain non-retail businesses locating within the zone. The businesses may be a new firm in Ohio, a new plant in Ohio that does not result in a reduction of employment or assets elsewhere in Ohio, an expansion at an existing site, or a relocation from outside of Ohio. Limited Enterprise Zones may not grant tax abatements to plants or firms relocating within the State of Ohio. The investment must meet certain size criteria to qualify for abatements, however (see below).

General Zones. A general Enterprise Zone may grant tax abatement to firms relocating within the state of Ohio as well as any non-retail firm or establishment locating within the zone (subject to the size criteria). To become a general zone, SB 19 requires the zone area to meet certain distress criteria. Proposed general zones within MSA central cities and Appalachian counties must meet only one of the distress criteria. Proposed general zones in all other areas must meet two of the distress criteria. The six distress criteria are as follows: 1) concentrated unemployment (zone unemployment exceeding 125 percent of the state average during the most recent 12 months), 2) prevalence of commercial or industrial structures that are vacant or demolished or vacant and tax delinquent (must exceed 5 percent of all zone commercial and industrial structures), 3) population loss of 10 percent or more between 1970 and 1990, 4) concentrated low- to moderate-income in the zone (at least 51 percent of the population is below 80 percent of the area's median income, 5) specific vacant industrial facilities, 6) the income weighted tax capacity of the school district is below 70 percent of the state-wide average.

Project-Size Criteria. A business is eligible to receive Enterprise Zone benefits under one of the four criteria: 1) it establishes a new facility in an area where the business has not previously operated, 2) expands by at least 10 percent at an existing site by adding land, buildings machinery, equipment or other materials, 3) makes renovations to an operating facility equal to 50 percent of the property value for property tax purposes, 4) makes renovations to a vacant facility equal to at least 20 percent of its market value as determined for local property tax purposes. As already noted, businesses relocating within the state of Ohio are not eligible for Enterprise Zone credits unless they relocate to a distressed-based general Enterprise Zone.

Property Tax Abatements. Local governments certified by Ohio Department of Development as Enterprise Zones can grant real and personal property tax exemptions of up to 75 percent (in municipalities) and up to 60 percent (unincorporated areas) of the value of the new investment. The term of the incentives can be for up to ten years. To build some flexibility into the benefit program the municipality or township can also front load the tax benefits by granting real and personal property tax exemptions in excess of 75 percent (or 60 percent in the case of townships) in any given year. In this case, the average exemption for municipalities can not exceed 60 percent (50 percent for townships) over the term of the exemption. Municipalities and townships may exceed the exemption limits, regardless of the average, if the affected school board specifically approves the proposal. (Otherwise school boards must be informed of the exemption, but the board's approval is not required.)

Additional Property Tax Abatements. In two situations, the tax exemptions in an Enterprise Zone may be extended to include existing real and personal property. First, if a business plans to purchase and operate a manufacturing plant that has employed an average of 1,000 people per year during the past five years and the plant has closed or announced closure proceedings, the local government may grant an exemption of up to 100 percent of the existing real and personal property for up to ten years. The second case is if a business agrees to improve an environmentally contaminated facility expending at least 250 percent of the existing value of the facility on a new investment project, including at least 10 percent of the investment in environmental clean-up activities, the local government can grant exemption of 50 percent of existing real property and 100 percent of new real and personal property in the project.

Employment Incentives Through the State Franchise Tax. State franchise tax incentives are extended to non-retail businesses that have an Enterprise Zone agreement provided that the businesses created jobs, did not close a plant or otherwise reduce employment at any other Ohio location, and at least 25 percent of the new jobs are filled by individuals from disadvantaged categories. Disadvantaged worker categories include any one of the following: 1) unemployed for at least 10 weeks and a resident of the county where the Enterprise Zone firm is located, 2) Job Training Partnership Act (JTPA) eligible and a resident of the county where the Enterprise Zone firm is located for at least six months, 3) recipient of Aid to Dependent Children (ADC), General Relief (GA), disability insurance, or unemployment compensation and resident of the county where the Enterprise Zone firm is located for at least six months, 4) handicapped person and resident of the county where the Enterprise Zone firm is located for at least six months, or 5) resident of the Enterprise Zone in the county where the project is located for at least one year. The non-refundable franchise tax exemptions are as follows: 1) exemption of all real and personal property lying in the local Enterprise Zone from the asset- or income-based calculation of the corporate franchise tax base, 2) reduction of the payroll numerator (in the allocation formula of the corporate franchise tax) by the wages paid to individuals hired who met one of five disadvantaged categories, 3) a credit of up to $300 or actual reimbursement (whichever is less) to the business for day care services provided for new employees who met one of the five disadvantaged categories, and 4) a credit of up to $1,000 or actual costs to the business for training employees who met one of five disadvantaged categories and who subsequently work at least 90 days at the facility.

The franchise tax credits are available for one year and renewable for up to three consecutive years. Renewal certificates, however, must document that at least 10 percent of the supervisory personnel of the facility met one of the five hiring categories.

The franchise tax exemptions have the appearance of subsidizing capital. But all of the subsidies depend on hiring a particular type of labor, and are in fact subsidies to labor. While hiring reduces the state franchise tax, the marginal price of capital has remained the same in the sense that purchasing a new piece of capital will still have the same after-tax price.

Additional Incentives For Distressed Zones

A business with an existing Enterprise Zone agreement and located within an MSA Central City or Appalachian County can also apply for an Employee Tax Credit certificate or Extension of Benefits consideration for each eligible new employee who is a recipient of ADC or GA and who resided for at least one year in the county where the facility is located.

Employee Tax Credit Certification. The certificate entitles the business to a $1,000 non-refundable state franchise tax credit for each eligible employee for each taxable year of the agreement. The credit can be carried forward for three years but is not refundable.

Extension of Benefits Certification. The employer can apply to the Department of Human Services to receive reimbursement for the costs of comprehensive medical insurance provided by the employer up to the amount of the state and local share of the average per person cost of such health care services for up to 21 months for each eligible new employee.

Observations on Enterprise Zones in Ohio

There are 247 known Enterprise Zones in Ohio, and only a few counties in the state do not have Enterprise Zones. The new Enterprise Zone law (SB 19) has created two levels of Enterprise Zones, limited and general, where the latter may grant zone benefits to relocating firms as well as other new investments and firms in general Enterprise Zones may qualify for employment tax credits against the corporate franchise tax. In addition, large firms qualify for property tax abatement on existing as well as new property value.

Property tax abatement and inventory tax abatement in particular are the most used tax advantages in Enterprise Zones. For example, according to Ohio Department of Taxation estimates, only about 10 percent of Enterprise Zone firms utilize the franchise tax credits. According to the Ohio Department of Taxation, the revenue lost from the day care and training provisions is about $0.8 million in 1994, and the exclusions of wages and property due to Enterprise Zones from the apportionment formula of the corporate franchise tax is minimal. There are apparently a limited number of disadvantaged workers with enough skills to be eligible for hire under the criteria set forth in this program. The amount of franchise tax credits taken as a result of job creation, however, is not known, because the program is new this year (State of Ohio Executive Budget, pp. 16, 18, 21, 24).

The new legislation requires localities to file an annual report with the Ohio Department of Development. However, there has been very little monitoring of Enterprise Zones until now, and, as a result, neither the number of companies receiving abatements nor the amount of personal property taxes abated are known. (Below, the abatement value of real property tax abatements is reported, however.)

Finally, as noted in the presentation of the data on the property tax, 70 percent of revenues from property taxation are used to fund schools. The municipalities granting the tax abatement are exempting school district properties from taxation as well. Unless the municipalities or townships want to exceed the Enterprise Zones guidelines for abatement on an individual property, the school districts' approval is not required and generally not sought.[15] At the same time, it is reported that officials in many school districts feel that the municipalities granting tax abatement are making it more difficult to fund local education, while proponents of Enterprise

Zones argue that the firms would not be in the school district at all except for the Enterprise Zone. While no doubt there is some truth on both sides of this argument, the asymmetry of the municipality granting a tax abatement for what is largely school district revenue does not give the appearance of a well-designed fiscal incentive package from the point of view of school districts.

Community Reinvestment Areas

Since 1978, municipalities, counties as well as unincorporated areas have had the power to create Community Reinvestment Areas (CRA). The areas must have some residential housing within them, and the properties within the CRA are eligible for tax exemptions on the increased value of property resulting from improvements. To create a CRA, the local government must demonstrate to ODOD that the areas current condition discourages the repair of existing buildings or new construction. In the case of residential properties within a CRA the exemptions on new improvements are automatic, while commercial and industrial properties within the CRA must negotiate with the local government to receive the CRA tax exemptions. The exemption may be up to 100 percent of the property tax due on the improved real value of the property.[16] (No abatements are granted for personal property under CRAs, but a CRA can exist within an Enterprise Zone and both real and personal property abatements can be had.) In addition, under the new law, commercial and industrial beneficiaries must replace 50 percent of the forgone revenue through direct payments in lieu of taxes or through the direct provision of public services, such as infrastructure, that benefit others in the community besides the particular firm.

The maximum periods of the tax abatements vary by type of property:

- 10 years for dwellings containing no more than 2 family units with remodeling costs of at least $2,500,
- 12 years for dwellings containing more than 2 units and for commercial and industrial properties with remodeling costs of at least $5,00; and
- 15 years for dwellings and commercial and industrial structures that are newly constructed.

Other Local Property Tax Exemptions

There are three additional instances when property taxes or incentives are abated. Inventories brought to Ohio that are not processed and then shipped out-of-state are exempt from property taxes. For example, The Limited, a national clothing retailer, ships clothing and accessories to Ohio for distribution to Limited stores in the Midwest and East. The clothing and accessories are not processed in Ohio, except for repackaging the items to fill orders from each Limited store. In practice, The Limited corporation keeps the inventories in Ohio for under 48 hours in most cases.

The exemption for property taxes on inventory extends to foreign trade zones. Within a foreign trade zone the exemption applies to inventory that is processed or manufactured as long as the product is exported from Ohio. In addition, pollution control facilities and devices are exempt from both property and sales and use taxes.

Tax Increment Financing

Taxes due on the increased value of real property from new investment in improvements may be redirected, at the local governments' option (county, municipality or township), to a special fund to finance certain infrastructure. The law provides that up to 75 percent of the taxes due on the value of the new improved property may be redirected for up to ten years; local governments must obtain the approval of the school board if it wants to redirect revenues for a longer period of time or for more than 75 percent of the new improvements. The infrastructure, however, must have a public purpose, such as publicly-owned road, water access or sewer.

Tax redirection is not the same as tax exemption, and tax increment financing is not used frequently. There are, for example, only 12 agreements on file with the Ohio Department of Development. Nonetheless, other local governments are redirecting what are largely school district property tax revenues to fund infrastructure.

Amount of Property Taxes Abated

While the State of Ohio does not perform a formal analysis of the local abatement programs, the Ohio Department of Taxation does compile the value of the exempt real property from County Auditors Reports. In 1992, for example, the value of real property exempted from local property taxes from Community Reinvestment Areas, Enterprise Zones, and Tax Increment Financing amounts to less than 1 percent of the total assessed value of real property. Of the exempt real property, exemptions due to CRAs account for 80 percent of the exempt property and exemptions due to Tax Increment Financing account for all but a fraction of the remainder. Real property tax exemptions in Enterprise Zones amount to less than 1 percent of the exempt value of real property. As noted above, the value of the abatements for personal property taxes are not compiled, but the number of Enterprise Zones in Ohio suggests that substantial personal property tax abatement on inventories exists.

State Economic Development Programs

At the state level, economic development programs consist of direct loans, loan guarantees, bond funds, technical assistance and some state corporate income tax credits for employment and investment. In addition, machinery and equipment purchased for use in manufacturing, packaging or handling, and transportation is exempt from the state's sales and use tax (Fox 1994). Tax policy experts agree that intermediate goods should be exempt from sales taxation to avoid tax pyramiding, where final goods have different effective tax rates when intermediate goods or capital are taxed and final goods do not all have the same number of stages of production across industries. Thus, while some count the exemption of machinery and equipment as a development incentive, it can also be viewed simply as sound tax policy. Nonetheless, the estimated tax expenditure for the exemption of machinery and equipment from the sales and use tax is $329.9 million in FY94. By that figure, the sales and use exemption for manufacturing machinery and equipment is by far the largest economic development incentive in the State of Ohio. Below the major State programs are described.

Direct Loan Programs. The largest of the loan programs is the 166 Loan Program administered by the Ohio Department of Development. The loans are targeted at ongoing manufacturing businesses for acquiring land and buildings, new construction, renovation or acquiring machinery and equipment. The manufacturer must own and occupy the building, and the guidelines of the program give priority to projects which demonstrate that one job will be created per $15,000 of loan funds. Officially, loans for sums between $200,000 and $1,000,000 are made, but Ohio Department of Development officials noted that a number of loans have been made for $2,000,000 and loans of $5,000,000 have been offered. The state loan is generally about 40 percent of the cost of the project; a bank finances about 50 percent and the owner has 10 percent equity. The terms of the loans are 15 years for real estate and 10 years for machinery and equipment. The interest rate is two-thirds of the prime rate; additional fees include a one-quarter percent annual servicing fee, a one-time processing fee of 2 percent of the loan amount and a $1,500 non-refundable application fee. The source of funds is state bonds. Between 50 and 80 companies per year receive loans from the 166 program. An important point is that when 166 loan funds finance a project, the contractor performing the construction, renovation or installation of machinery must hire workers at the prevailing wage in an area.

There are two loan programs that target funds to minority-owned (51 percent minority-owned) businesses. The minority direct loan program provides funds for the purchase or improvement of fixed assets. The State of Ohio will finance up to 40 percent of the project costs or up to $700,000 whichever is less. Projects that create jobs at Ohio's pre-set wage rate will receive priority, and loan guidelines permit $15,000 in loan money per job created. The terms of the loans were (July 1994) 3.5 percent for up to 10 years. Contractors performing the improvements must hire workers at prevailing wage rates.

A so-called mini-loan program is directed at small businesses with 25 or fewer employees. The program targets 50 percent of the funds to businesses owned by minorities or women. The loan funds projects of $100,000 or less for fixed assets and equipment for small businesses. The program provides up to 45 percent of an eligible bank's loan to the business for up to ten years. The interest rate on the state-guaranteed portion of the loan was 5.5 percent in July, 1994.

ODOD reports that the default rate on the loans is very small. The direct loan program represents the State of Ohio subsidizing capital expansion by offering lower interest rates through tax-exempt state bond funds.

Ohio Enterprise Bond Funds. The Enterprise Fund is designed to provide long-term, fixed-rate financing for larger qualified commercial and industrial businesses. The Enterprise Fund issues both tax-exempt and taxable bonds. The State reserves the tax exempt financing for manufacturing industries. Eligible projects include industrial job creation or retention projects, commercial real estate projects, public improvement projects related to economic development, and other projects as well as minority-owned or female-owned businesses. The Fund may not be used for working capital, refinancing, inventory or receivables, rolling stock, or goodwill.

Loan amounts range from $1 million to $10 million for up to 90 percent of the project costs. Each borrower must provide 10 percent equity and must set aside 10 percent of the loan amount into a reserve fund, which earns interest for the borrower. The terms of the loans are 15 to 20 years for real estate and generally between seven and ten years for equipment and are limited to 120 percent of the average life of the project. The interest rates are market determined. As of July 11, 1994, the interest rate on tax-exempt bonds was 5.75 percent for seven-year loans and 6.85 percent for 20-year loans. Taxable bond interest rates were between 2.0 and 2.33 percentage points higher (depending on the term of the loan) per year.[17] Projects are subject to prevailing wage rules in construction of plants and installation of equipment. Between six and ten loans are made to large companies each year.

Business Development Fund. The business development fund (412) began in 1982 and is a grant to support public infrastructure improvements for manufacturing, research development, high technology and distribution companies. Companies or local governments may apply for the art of the $7.5 million available for this purpose. Grant amounts average about $1,000 per job created by the project. Substantial local government financial support for the infrastructure project is expected, and the state grant is paid only upon completion of the infrastructure project. The Development Fund is intended as an inducement or catalyst and is not intended to finance the entire cost of the infrastructure improvement.

Child Day Care Grant Program. To encourage new childcare relationships among communities, businesses and governments, the state provides up to $50,000 for expansion of daycare centers or new daycare centers. The intention is to enhance the employment and job-training opportunities for employees and employers.

Industrial Training Program. Manufacturing and manufacturing-related businesses are eligible to receive grant funding for up to 50 percent of the costs of training workers. The program began 15 years ago and about 150 companies utilize the program annually. The total amount of grant funds is $8.0 million annually. Businesses apply to the program through one of 12 districts run by a consortium of public schools and business organizations. Most of the grants support the retraining of existing workers in a classroom setting. Training largely consists of work on understanding manufacturing processes, basic statistics for process or quality control and reading blueprints.

Ohio Job Creation Act. The Act became effective in 1993, and had three components. One component is a corporate franchise tax credit related to the wages paid to new employees. A second part awards corporate franchise tax credits for increases in sales outside of Ohio. A third portion awards a sales tax exemption for purchases of machinery and equipment used primarily for research and development.

- *State Job Tax Credit.* As of 1993, certain qualified expanding firms within Ohio and relocating firms from outside of Ohio can qualify for an employment tax credit. Firms should be in manufacturing, high technology, research and development, distribution, computer, telecommunications or other information-based industries. Retail projects and other lower-paid service projects are not eligible. The credit applies to the net increase in full-time positions, and the project must create at least 25 full-time jobs within three years. The jobs must pay wages in excess of 150 percent of the minimum wage, and the company must commit to substantial investment in land, building machinery or equipment, or infrastructure. The corporate franchise tax credit is typically for between 50 and 75 percent of the amount withheld from eligible employees for personal income tax purposes. The higher percentage credits go to projects with more jobs, higher wages, more frequent use of Ohio suppliers, or to firms locating in distressed communities, or hiring a certain percentage of disadvantaged or minority persons. Projects that also receive other assistance from the State will receive a lower credit percentage. Local community support of the project is also crucial to qualify for the tax credit.

The job credit became effective in 1993, and to date there is no estimate of the credit used for FY94. The intention is, of course, to subsidize firms creating better-paying jobs in preferred industries in Ohio. The job credit program is biased toward new and expanding firms and against stable firms. But with State personal income tax rates of about 6 percent of taxable income in Ohio, the credit amounts to no more than about 4 percent of the wage bill. The credit makes higher-paid workers less expensive than lower-paid workers, if the jobs carry fringe benefits, and thus also encourages higher-paid jobs. The jobs credit is refundable and, therefore, is effective for any amount of the corporate franchise tax liability.

This subsidy to labor operates through the corporate franchise tax. However, the subsidy reduces the marginal price of labor and not the marginal price of capital, and is thus a labor subsidy.

- *Export Credit.* The export tax credit is non-refundable and allows a credit on the corporate franchise tax to corporations that increase exports from Ohio and also increase their Ohio property or their Ohio payroll. The credit is computed as 10 percent of the pre-tax profit due to an increment in export sales, multiplied by the average of the Ohio payroll and property apportionment factors multiplied by the greater of the Ohio increase in the payroll factor or the Ohio property increase factor. The credit is of primary benefit to companies that have increased their property or payroll factor substantially as well as their export sales. The Ohio Department of Taxation estimates that the credit will cost between $1 million and $2 million in FY94.

- *Research and Development Sales Tax Exemption.* The Act exempts purchases of machinery and equipment used primarily for research and development from the state and county sales tax. Research and development means designing, creating, or formulating new or enhanced products, equipment or manufacturing processes as well as conducting scientific or technological inquiry or so-called pure research in the physical sciences. The estimated tax expenditure is $15.6 million in FY94.

Investment Tax Credit. Effective January 1, 1995 through June 30, 1996, the State of Ohio has an additional tax credit for manufacturing machinery and equipment. If the manufacturer purchases new machinery and equipment in a fiscal year amounting to more than 20 percent of its United States tangible personal property value, the manufacturer receives an investment tax credit equivalent to 20 percent of the cost of the machinery and equipment. The credit is not refundable if the firms tax liability is less than the credit, but the credit can be carried forward for three years.

In fact, the credit is expected to benefit a few taxpayers each year. However, it has large incentives for big capital investors. As noted above capital subsidies tend to benefit relatively skilled workers, who are complementary with the capital being purchased.

Assessment of State Programs

Subsidies to capital and labor exist side-by-side in Ohio and in many other states. This practice is standard and states typically offer bond funding for business expansions or new businesses, limited employment subsidies for workers from disadvantaged categories, as well as investment subsidies. In effect, Ohio has adopted programs to address employment problems in distressed areas, as well as adopted programs designed to attract high-tech firms for future growth of the State economy.

The State of Ohio does not formally evaluate its loan, tax credit, training or other programs. Which programs attract more businesses would be worth some investigation. Retailoring the programs to meet more current needs and policy concerns would be one beneficial outcome of a careful evaluation. While there is nothing unusual about states having a broad array of programs to meet needs, there are a growing number of programs in Ohio and some attention should be paid to the effectiveness of the different programs with the idea of reallocating funds, where necessary, toward more effective programs.

ECONOMIC DEVELOPMENT PROGRAMS IN COMPETITOR STATES

Comparisons of Ohio's business climate with neighboring states are reported in Laird-Duchi (1994). Ohio finishes fifth of the six neighboring states in a manufacturing study done by Grant Thorton (1990). Ohio's strength, on the other hand, lies in its relatively better ranking on factors within government control, according to that study. The 1994 Development Report Card for States ranks Ohio similarly high on fiscal stability and balanced revenue sources. Another strength in Ohio is the strong human capital embodied in its workforce.

Ohio's weaknesses lie in its high levels of unemployment compensation and worker's compensation payments as well as unionization and work stoppages in the manufacturing sector. Nonetheless, the Ohio Competitiveness Project, sponsored by the State of Ohio Department of Economic Development, ranks Ohio in the middle of its five neighboring states.[18]

In this section, the competitiveness of Ohio's tax and financial incentives, reviewed above, are evaluated. Virtually all states give tax and financial incentives to new and expanding businesses. A comparison of tax incentives offered in Ohio and ten of its competitor states is given in Table 9-5. Compared to most of its competitor states, Ohio has an ambitious set of tax and financial incentives in its portfolio. The Ohio Economic Competitiveness

Project (Ohio Department of Development 1993; Summary, page 31) noted that Ohio ranks either even with or better than each of the ten competitor states on tax and financial incentives, and Ohio ranks worse than only a few of its competitors in the other categories of economic development programs. For example, Ohio ranked lower than six states on business development programs; that, however, was Ohio's lowest ranking in this group.

Most of the competitor states offer direct loans, tax-exempt bond financing, loan guarantees, seed money grants for new initiatives, and job training programs. The three states in this group that levy a property tax on inventories offer warehouse freeport in which inventory shipped to the state, not processed and then shipped out of the state is not subject to the property tax on inventory. Technical assistance to businesses in the form of a one-stop business permit section, international trade assistance, business development assistance, labor-management cooperation and other technical assistance are generally offered. Fewer states offer foreign trade zones; only six of the 11 states offer some form of property or sales tax abatement on pollution control facilities.

Ohio and eight of its competitor states—California, Indiana, Illinois, North Carolina, South Carolina, Tennessee, Pennsylvania and West Virginia—exempt purchases of manufacturing machinery and equipment from the sales tax (or tax it at a significantly reduced rate as in North Carolina). While the sales tax exemption represents quite sound tax policy, the amount of revenues forgone from this exemption is more than any other state economic development program individually and probably more than the subsidy value of all programs combined.

Ohio stands apart from other states in two major areas: state corporate income tax credits for employment and investment, and Enterprise Zones. Only three of Ohio's competitor states follow Ohio in offering state corporate income tax credits for both employment and investment, but nine of the 11 states offer tax credits for either employment or investment. Six of the 11 states have Enterprise Zones.

The two most competitive states with Ohio are Indiana and Kentucky. Indiana offers a set of tax and financial incentives very similar to Ohio, and Indiana levies a property tax on business inventories as does Ohio. Kentucky offers fewer incentives than either Ohio or Indiana; levies a property tax on tax business inventories; and levies a sales tax on purchases of manufacturing machinery and equipment.

The key difference between Ohio and Indiana on economic development incentives is the extent of Enterprise Zones. Ohio has 247 zones and Indiana has 18 zones. The principal tax benefit in the zones in each case is the abatement of the personal property tax on business inventories. Enterprise Zones in Indiana are located in economically distressed areas, whereas, in general, zones in Ohio do not generally satisfy distress criteria. Ohio is much more liberal than Indiana about forgiving personal property taxes on inventories. However, firms in Ohio do not automatically qualify for tax credits when lo-

TABLE 9-5
Business Incentives in Selected States

Business Incentives	Ohio	Indiana	Kentucky	Michigan	Illinois	West Virginia
1. Exemption of mfg. machinery and equipment from sales tax	X	X			X	X
2. Foreign Trade Zone a. Inventory exempt from property taxes b. Goods exempt from duty	X X	X X				
3. Pollution Control Facilities exempt from: a. Property tax b. Sales tax c. Other Abatement	X X	X	X X			
4. Direct Loan Programs	X	X	X	X	X	X
5. Seed Money Grants	X	X		X	X	
6. Grant/Loans for Daycare	X					
7. Bond Funding	X	X	X	X		X
8. Job Training	X	X		X		X
9. Enterprise Zone Tax: a. Property tax abatement b. Other tax abatement	X X	X X	X		X X	
10.Tax Increment Financing	X	X		X	X	
11.Technical Assistance to Business (Export Promotion or Other)	X	X			X	
12.Technology Center	X	X				
13.Foreign Trade Zones	X	X				
14.State Income Tax Credit: a. Investments b. Employment (or training)	X X		X X		X X(Training)	X X
15.Other Local Property Tax Incentives	X CRA	X ERA	X		X	
16.Comprehensive package of credits (sales, property income, workers compensation) for investment and job expansion						X
17.Site Improvement (Infrastructure)						
18.Warehouse Freeport (Inventory not processed exempt from property tax,)	X	X	X	NA	NA	X

continued

cating in the zone, but must enter a specific agreement with the municipality, township or county running the zone.

There are no existing estimates of the added profits that a typical Ohio firm receives due to the exemption of inventories from the personal property tax. Papke and Papke (1992) have estimated that in Indiana total elimination of the property tax on inventories raised after-tax profit rates as much as 1 to 7 percent, depending on the initial property tax rate. With Ohio's relatively low property tax rate and its forgiving 75 percent or less of property taxes on inventories, the benefits probably fall to the lower half of that range, however. The larger issue is that the tax exemption is limited to operations within Enterprise Zones.

TABLE 9-5 (continued)
Business Incentives in Selected States

Business Incentives	Pennsylvania	North Carolina	South Carolina	Tennessee	California
1. Exemption of mfg. machinery and equipment from sales tax	X	X 1% rate	X	X	X
2. Foreign Trade Zone a. Inventory exempt from property taxes b. Goods exempt from duty		X			
3. Pollution Control Facilities exempt from: a. Property tax b. Sales tax c. Other Abatement		X 1% rate X	X	X •X	
4. Direct Loan Programs	X	X	X	X	X
5. Seed Money Grants	X	X	X	X	
6. Grant/Loans for Daycare			X		
7. Bond Funding	X	X	X	X	X
8. Job Training		X	X	X	X
9. Enterprise Zone Tax: a. Property tax abatement b. Other tax abatement	X				X
10.Tax Increment Financing					
11.Technical Assistance to Business (Export Promotion or Other)	X	X		X	X
12.Technology Center					
13.Foreign Trade Zones					
14.State Income Tax Credit: a. Investments b. Employment (or training)	X	X	X X	X	X
15.Other Local Property Tax incentives	X		X Real, Personal		
16.Comprehensive package of credits (sales, property income, workers compensation) for investment and job expansion					
17.Site Improvement (Infrastructure)		X			
18.Warehouse Freeport (Inventory not processed exempt from property tax)	NA	NA	NA	NA	NA

Source: Author.

Note: NA means not applicable. Those states do not tax inventories and there is no need for Warehouse Freeport to exempt goods in transit from property taxes on inventories.

CONCLUSIONS

The chapter questions the efficacy of some economic development programs as they generally apply in states and particularly in Ohio. Nonetheless, the chapter acknowledges that, despite a lack of strong evidence for tax incentives affecting business location decisions among states, judgment suggests that poorly designed tax policy may play a strong negative role in location decisions. States will typically want to attract capital-intensive industries due to their strong link to the creation of high-skilled jobs that pay higher wages. In this case, low marginal tax rates on capital will be important, and training programs for persons accepting the high-skilled jobs may be consistent with attracting capital-intensive industries. At the same time, most states also have lower-skilled workers, and job creation for these workers will also be an important component of economic development policy. Typically, low-skilled jobs are created through some form of wage subsidy.

The first choice for attracting businesses is a well-designed tax system that results in the same marginal after-tax price for capital across industries. Alternatively, taxes that have higher marginal rates for some industries than for others will likely discourage investment in the higher tax industries. In Ohio, for example, the property tax on the value of inventories places a larger tax burden on businesses that hold inventories than on businesses that can implement just-in-time delivery of parts and products, such as the automobile industry. Still, if there are inventories of unsold cars, the property tax might tax automobile inventories at a point when industry profits are low.

Turning to the specifics of tax policy and economic development in Ohio, it ranks about 30 of the 50 states in average tax burdens, and is not considered here as a high-tax state. Nonetheless, several aspects of its tax code are problematic for industries, and appropriate reform can enhance economic development in the State.

The most glaring tax issue in Ohio is the local property tax on business inventories. The tax raises about $500 million of revenue annually and about 70 percent of property tax revenue accrues to school districts. The property tax on inventories itself has probably spawned many of the 247 Enterprise Zones in Ohio, which are largely established to avoid the property tax on inventories. The problem is that only non-retail industries in the zones qualify for the property tax exemption. While that type of industry targeting might be considered economically efficient, there appears to be substantial administrative costs to setting up the zones and reaching agreements with individual firms about the amount of the property tax that will be abated. With 40 of the 50 states not taxing business inventories, a priority for tax reform in Ohio is elimination of the property tax on inventories and with it the necessity to create more Enterprise Zones.

The advantages to inventory property tax reform include more horizontal equity among companies because all companies would have relief from personal property taxation, and not only the companies that have struck a deal within Enterprise Zones. Vertical equity, to the extent that the property tax is a tax on capital and not shifted to other factors, might suffer somewhat, but that depends on how the lost revenue is recouped from other taxes or state aid. Replacement of local revenues is an important issue here, and school districts will be affected more than other local government units.

The corporate franchise tax in Ohio is levied on either a firm's net worth or income, depending on which tax base yields more revenue for a firm in a given year. The net worth aspect of the tax is obsolete for several reasons. First, the formula used to allocate Ohio's share of any multi-state firm's net worth to Ohio is not the same as the formula used to allocate the firm's income to Ohio. The allocation formula used for the net worth tax effectively increases the burden on net exporting firms compared to the income tax allocation formula. In addition, the net worth tax subjects machinery and equipment to a second tax after the personal property tax has already been levied on gross worth. For both of these reasons the net worth component of the corporate franchise tax should be eliminated. Vertical equity would not seem to be harmed as corporate profits would continue to be taxed. Revenue stability may be reduced as the net worth component enforces a minimum tax payment for unprofitable firms, but the tax treatment of these firms is somewhat arbitrary under the net worth/income tax system. Such a system is outdated and that combined with the relatively high tax rate for the corporate franchise tax, as presently structured, can only reduce the attractiveness of business location in Ohio.

A third issue is that although Ohio exempts business purchases from sales taxation, it administers the exemption by listing the items that are exempt. Thus, some items purchased by businesses are taxed, with the result that about 30 percent of sales tax revenue is derived from business purchases. Ohio should adopt a more integrated plant approach where all materials and equipment at the plant are exempt from sales taxation. That would give Ohio firms a more effective competitive edge.

Even with sound tax policy, the reality in any state is not whether it will offer financial and other incentives to businesses, but how many and for what purposes. Ohio takes a very aggressive stance in attracting and retaining jobs for residents of the State. In comparison to competitor states, such as Indiana, Kentucky, North Carolina and South Carolina, the aggressive stance taken by the State of Ohio appears warranted as a defensive strategy. Ohio is not a particularly high-tax state, but neither are the other four states mentioned, and still incentives seem to play a major role in many policymaker's minds in the attraction of businesses to these states. In many respects, however, Ohio's array of programs does not match well with its development problems. The Enterprise Zone program, for example, has only recently developed two different zone designations to target more job credits to distressed zones. Even so, there is considerable debate about whether spatial targeting is effective in alleviating economic distress in areas with high unemployment rates. Evidence suggests that 60 to 100 percent of the benefits of spatial targeting accrue to non-zone residents either through labor force migration into the targeted areas or simply missed targets within the Zone. Still other research finds that the greater the number of Enterprise Zones in a state, the less likely it is that wages or employment increase within the targeted Zones. For Ohio, with its large number of Zones, it is very likely that employment and wage benefits are small and not well-targeted toward the intended groups of workers.

Much of the rationale for Enterprise Zones in Ohio rests on relieving the property tax on inventories. As noted already, there is little rationale for the taxation of inventories, and Ohio is among a small number of states that still tax business inventories under the property tax. Moreover, reducing property taxes on inventories through ad hoc agreements drawn between firms and municipalities, townships and counties is very inefficient administratively. In addition, Ohio's school districts receive over 70 percent of the property tax revenues, and other local governments are empowered to forgive the property tax on inventory, in most cases, without school district approval. Such a practice is disruptive to fiscal federalism: it compromises the flow of school revenues, and either increases disparities in educational finance or places an additional strain on the system that distributes state aid to education.

As noted, economic development policy typically has at least two targets: 1) attracting capital-intensive industries that traditionally create high-paying, high-skilled jobs and 2) providing employment opportunities in other industries for lower-skilled workers. To attract capital-intensive and growth-oriented industries, Ohio and other states need to adopt tax systems with low marginal tax rates (but not necessarily low average tax rates) on investment. Accelerated depreciation or immediate write-off of capital and investment tax credits all reduce the marginal tax price of capital.

Creating incentives to work and jobs for lower-skilled residents will continue to be an important item on policy-makers' agendas, as the nation attempts to reduce dependency among its population and increase the work efforts of low-income persons. The findings in the literature suggest that job creation programs should not be spatially targeted, but that people-based, rather than place-based, wage, health care and daycare subsidies may be important in job creation for low-income workers. Ohio has some of these programs in place, but many are spatially targeted. Spatial targeting should be phased out in Ohio as property tax reform on inventories is adopted. Ohio has a standard array of subsidized loans, loan guarantees, and bond finance that meet the competition in other states. These programs should remain in place for now. However, a general recommendation for Ohio and other states is the evaluation of all economic development programs. For Ohio in particular, little is done at present to evaluate the economic impact of either state or local economic development programs. What evaluation exists consists of determining which programs are administered well and whether the firms receiving the subsidies meet the criteria set out for the programs. An evaluation of the economic effectiveness of the programs is needed to determine which programs are more effective in meeting the economic development goals of creating investment or employment in the State. Such an evaluation will help to determine which programs, if any, should be expanded and which could be contracted or eliminated. Monitoring of the programs and evaluating their contributions to economic development should become a regular part of the State's administration of its economic development programs.

ENDNOTES

1. In contrast to Ohio, about 16 percent of United States' employment is concentrated in manufacturing and 22 percent in services. The United States as a whole has about 24 percent of employment concentrated in wholesale and retail trade. See McHugh (1994a) Table 22B.

2. *Greater Columbus Economic Strategy*, prepared for The Greater Columbus Chamber of Commerce, 114 pages (no date).

3. See Ohio Department of Development (1993). State competitors were selected according to Ohio Department of Economic Development staff views on which states compete with Ohio most frequently for new firms.

4. Advisory Commission on Intergovernmental Relations (1993). McHugh finds similar rankings among the three states when comparisons are made on the basis of their relative tax efforts. See McHugh (1994a) Table 1a.

5. For a discussion of real property taxes in Ohio, see Sjoquist (1994), p. 73

6. Taxation of personal property is discussed in more detail in Cornia (1994).

7. Although local governments in Kentucky do not levy a property tax on business inventories, the state of Kentucky levies a tax rate of one-half mill on business inventories.

8. See Commerce Clearing House (1994b). Chart 20-150. p. 2023.

9. A more detailed account of the corporate franchise tax and the rationale and options for its reform can be found in Martinez and Grace (1994).

10. For more discussion of the sales tax in Ohio, see Fox (1994).

11. For a more extensive discussion of the personal income tax in Ohio, see Wallace and Edwards (1994).

12 Kesselman et al. (1977) estimate that employment levels in the United States would have been 1 percent higher in 1971 if employee tax credits were used in the 1960s and 1970s rather than investment tax credits.

13. Murray (1994) finds that the cost per job created is 15 times higher when investment is subsidized than when employment is subsidized directly.

14. Microsimulation models the economic behavior of households and businesses in relation to one another. For example, the model would determine household consumption and income, and firm production and profits. The parameters of the model would be set according to plausible estimates of behavior from other empirical-based economic models. Using the model and the parameters, the responses of households and firms to changes in economic development programs can be assessed. These changes are then typically fed into other stages of the analysis.

15. This practice varies of course by municipality. For example, Mr. Garber of Delaware County (north of Columbus) reported to me that school districts in Delaware county are consulted during the negotiations over Enterprise Zones.

16. Under the previous law, CRAs gave 100 percent exemptions (no discretion) for property taxation of new improvements. The previous CRA agreements are grandfathered under the new law. The new law, however, introduces local government discretion in that the local government can grant a total or partial exemption for property taxation of new improvements.

17. In addition, there are a $1,500 application fee, closing costs that range between 2.5 and 3.0 percent of the loan, and annual fee of 0.25 percent of the loan balance, and a $20,000 application fee refunded at the closing.

18. For more information on the business climate in Ohio, see Duchi (1994).

10 Corporate Taxation: The General Franchise Tax

Jorge Martinez-Vazquez and Martin Grace[1]

CURRENT STRUCTURE

The franchise tax is actually composed of two alternative taxes, one falling on net income and the other falling on net worth. The net worth statute dates from 1903 and has not been revised since 1936. Corporations in Ohio must compute both the tax on a net worth basis and the tax on a net income basis and pay the higher of the two. In any case the tax paid cannot be less than a minimum tax of $50. Ohio banks and other depository financial institutions pay a modified franchise tax only on a net worth basis, but at a higher tax rate. The franchise tax on financial institutions is discussed in Chapter 11 of this book. Ohio corporations pay an additional "litter tax" in two tiers, although the second tier is paid only by "litter stream" companies.

These are some of the most important features of the corporate franchise tax:

- *Relative importance*. The franchise tax is the third most important source of tax revenue in the state of Ohio. However, this tax represents a relatively small share of total general revenues. As shown in Figure 10-1, 1993 revenues from the corporate franchise tax represented 7.7 percent of total revenues. By comparison, in the same year the personal income tax raised 40.7 percent of total revenues and the sales tax raised 36.3 percent.

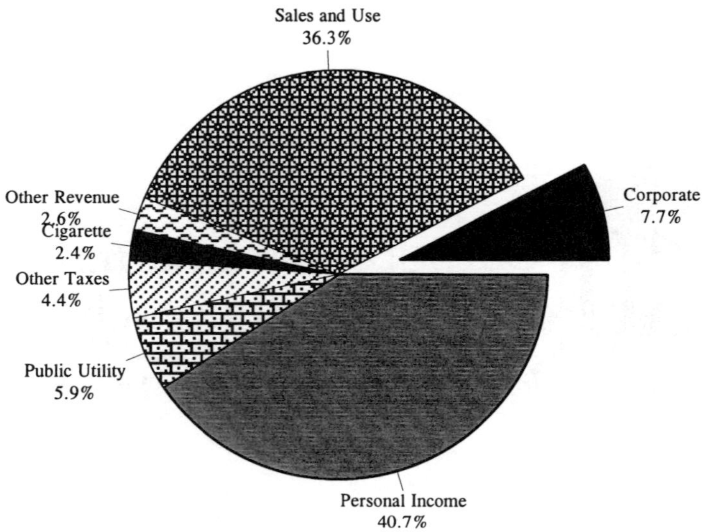

Source: Ohio Department of Taxation

FIGURE 10-1. Ohio 1993 general revenues by type as a percentage of total general revenue.

- *Volatility of tax revenues*. Tax liabilities from the corporate franchise tax for the last ten years are presented in Table 10-1. Several things are noticeable from this time series. First, although over the past ten years the two taxes on net worth (the general net worth franchise tax and the tax on financial institutions) have had some ups and downs, for the most part revenues have increased steadily. Some of the variability of the general net worth tax has been produced by the dual nature of the tax. In years of economic expansion more firms had higher net incomes and therefore paid the net income tax rather than the net worth tax. The time series for the net income tax reflects the volatility of its tax base (profits) over the business cycle. Revenues from the corporate net income tax have moved with the business cycle. Profits are by far the most volatile component of the state's gross income. Consequently, revenues from corporate income taxes are less reliable than those coming from other taxes, including the personal income tax, sales tax, and property tax. The instability of the net income tax has imposed a roller coaster effect on the overall collections from the franchise tax, as illustrated in Figure 10-2. The peaks and valleys in tax collections in Figure 10-2 are quite pronounced, even though they are expressed in real terms (constant 1987 prices).

TABLE 10-1
Total Corporate Franchise Tax Liability, Tax Years 1983–1993

	Liability Before Litter Tax, Surtax and Credits* Non-Financial Institutions				Liability After Litter Tax, Surtax and Credits		
Tax Year	Minimum ($50) Taxpayers	Net Worth Taxpayers	Net Income Taxpayers	Total	Non-financial Institutions	Financial Institutions	Total
1983	$11,404,800	$147,735,230	$332,041,840	$491,181,870	$486,431,925	$37,405,560	$523,837,485
1984	3,962,800	152,794,129	392,943,381	549,700,310	526,520,864	98,853,844	625,374,708
1985	3,480,493	144,100,946	522,502,099	670,083,538	661,568,822	98,650,431	760,219,253
1986	3,418,864	156,793,269	539,368,861	699,580,994	695,018,816	93,705,954	788,724,770
1987	2,783,324	172,179,120	490,115,343	665,077,787	630,587,449	104,670,239	735,257,688
1988	3,003,242	168,554,036	542,200,372	713,757,650	666,389,890	109,640,240	776,030,130
1989	2,835,850	163,646,944	598,482,693	764,965,487	722,042,029	130,125,260	852,167,289
1990	3,031,624	182,506,786	537,005,053	722,543,463	684,708,345	142,896,321	827,604,666
1991	3,614,626	202,190,495	444,733,217	650,538,338	609,690,068	147,271,175	756,961,243
1992	3,719,592	224,748,796	385,027,710	613,496,098	580,451,785	157,912,202	738,363,987
1993	2,501,161	228,158,717	401,836,889	632,496,767	615,784,545	173,074,954	788,859,499

Source: Ohio Department of Taxation.

*Only liability BEFORE litter tax, surtax and credits can be identified by type of tax base (net worth or net income) for non-financial institutions. Liability for financial institutions, which pay tax based on net worth only, can only be identified AFTER credits.

- *Shifting importance of net income and net worth taxes.* The net worth tax component of the franchise tax has played an increasing role in overall revenues since the late 1980s as documented in Figure 10-3.

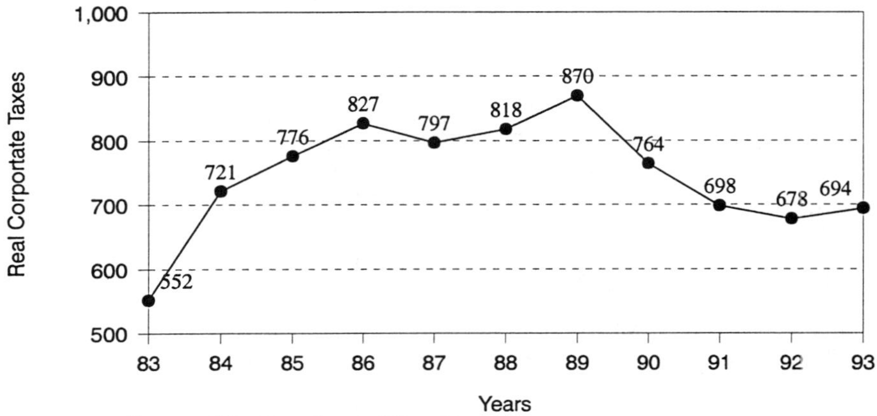

Source: Ohio Department of Taxation.

Note: Deflator from Economic Report of the President except 1993; 1993 deflator estimated using *Survey of Current Business*.

FIGURE 10-2. Real corporate franchise tax collections (1987 dollars: millions).

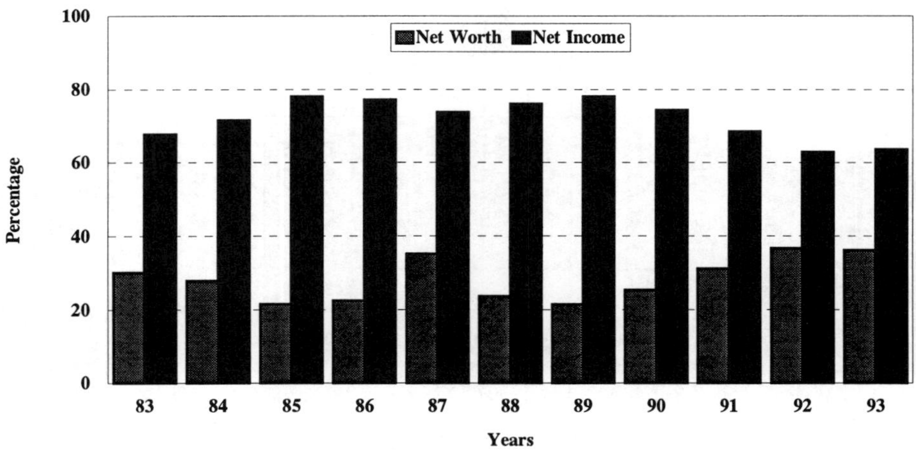

Source: Ohio Department of Taxation.

Note: Totals do not add to 100% due to minimum ($50) taxpayers.

FIGURE 10-3. Liability of N.W. taxpayers vs. N.I. taxpayers as a percentage of total corporate tax liabilities.

• *Tax payments are concentrated from a small group of taxpayers.* Although the concentration of tax payments by a relatively small group of taxpayers is common to other taxes, corporate income taxes have traditionally been more concentrated than other taxes. Ohio's corporate franchise tax is not an exception to this rule. As shown in Figure 10-4, over 80 percent of the net worth tax in 1993 was paid by 10 percent of the taxpayers. The level of concentration was almost as high for the net income tax. The highest decile of taxpayers paid just a little under 80 percent of total net income collections (Figure 10-5).

STRUCTURE OF THE TAX

Nexus. The franchise tax is levied on Ohio and non-Ohio corporations for the privilege of doing business in the state. The presumption of the general obligation to pay franchise tax in Ohio is established by doing business in

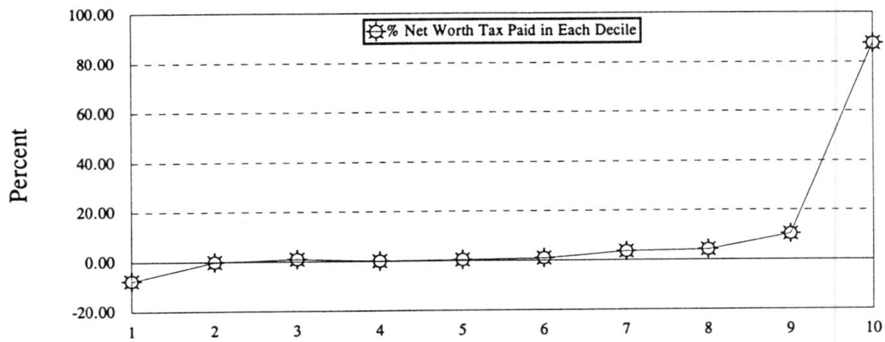

FIGURE 10-4. Net worth tax paid 1993 by net worth deciles.

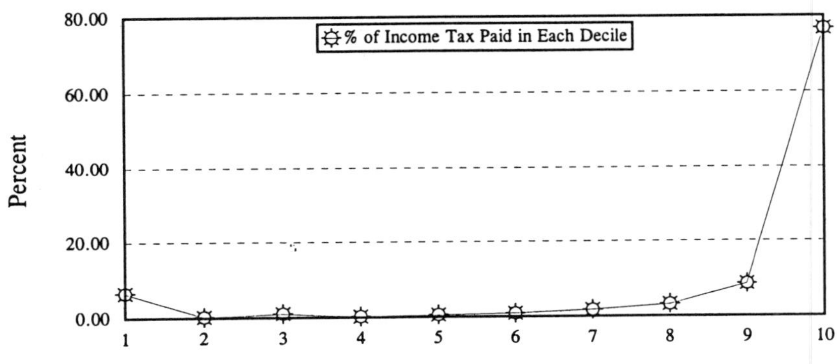

FIGURE 10-5. Net income tax paid 1993 by net worth deciles.

Ohio, owning capital or property in the state, or holding a charter authorizing the corporation to do business in Ohio.[2]

Scope of the general franchise tax. Besides all C corporations, agricultural cooperatives (Chapter 1729 corporations) and business trusts are also required to file the franchise tax. An S corporation is not subject to the franchise tax unless it functioned as a C corporation for part of the tax year. Other corporations not subject to the franchise tax include public utilities[3] (which are required to pay an excise tax on gross receipts under Chapter 5727 of the ORC), insurance companies (which pay a premium tax and are required to file annual reports with the Superintendent of Insurance), and "dealers in intangibles" (which also pay a separate tax).[4]

Holding companies must file the Supplemental Franchise Tax Schedules for holding companies of insurance companies, public utilities, and financial institutions, if the holding company owns at least 25 percent of the issued and outstanding shares of common stock of one or more financial institutions, or if the holding company owns at least 80 percent of the issued and outstanding shares of common stock of one or more public utilities or insurance companies.

Computation of the Tax

The franchise tax must be computed by all corporations obliged to file a return on both bases, net income and net worth. The statutes for the franchise tax in the Ohio Revised Code (ORC) are often the subject of interpretation by the Tax Commissioner's rulings and opinions, the decisions of the Ohio Board of Tax Appeals, and the Ohio Supreme Court. The main steps in the computation of corporate franchise tax liability for 1994 are summarized in Table 10-2.

Computation of the Net Income Tax

1. *Tax base.* The initial base for the net income tax is federal taxable income, before net operating loss deduction and special deductions. Of course, the amounts reported on the federal tax forms and the Ohio adjustments to federal taxable income are subject to verification and audit by the Ohio Department of Taxation.

2. *Adjustments to federal taxable income.* Federal taxable income is adjusted by several additions and deductions. The additions are only for the valuation limitation on losses from capital (or 1231 assets) and losses from the sale of Ohio public obligations. The deductions are more substantial but fairly standard. They include: valuation limitation

TABLE 10-2
Computation of Corporation Franchise Liability for 1994

A. Net Income Basis

1. Federal Taxable Income
plus additions
minus deductions (foreign income, dividends, U.S. interest, other)

2. Base Income
minus allocable income everywhere

3. Apportionable Income
times (income) apportionment ratio (4 factors: property, payroll, double weighted sales)

4. Apportioned Income
plus Ohio allocable Income
minus Ohio NOL
plus Other adjustments (related entity, transfer on corporation)

5. Ohio Taxable Income
times 0.051 for first $50,000 and
0.089 for income over $50,000

6. Ohio Tax on Net Income

B. Net Worth Basis

1. Total Net Worth
Sum of capital stock (less treasury stock)
plus retained earnings and additional paid-in capital
plus reserves and deferred taxes

2. Minus Exempted Assets
(including: goodwill, appreciation, and other)

3. Equals Net Value of Stock
times (net worth) apportionment ratio (2 factors: total assets and receipts)

4. Taxable Net Worth
times 0.00582

5. Tax on Net Worth Basis

C. Final Tax Liability

1. Franchise Tax Due (the largest of)
Net income or net worth basis

2. *plus* Tier One and Tier Two Litter Taxes

3. Total Tax Due
minus non-refundable credits (investment in subsidiaries, export sales, qualifying investment)
minus refundable credits (new jobs, qualifying investment) and advanced payments

4. Balance Due (or Overpayment)

on gains from capital (or 1231 assets), gains from the sale of Ohio public obligations, dividends received, interest from Ohio public obligations, and net interest from United States obligations.[5]

Ohio corporations are allowed to deduct net income from foreign sources. However, this deduction was amended in 1991 to limit it in some cases to a percent of the foreign source income. The rationale was that some of the operating expenses deducted by the corporation are also attributable to foreign income. In particular, ORC section 78, foreign dividend gross-up, and ORC section 951 (subpart F) are deductible in full. However, foreign dividends of affiliated corporations that do not transact or hold assets in the USA can be deducted by 85 percent, and foreign royalties can be deducted by 90 percent. Income from technical services performed in the United States for a foreign firm is not at all deductible.

3. *Allocable income.* The Ohio corporate franchise tax, as in many other states, distinguishes between allocable income and apportionable income. Allocable income is either entirely included or entirely excluded from the tax base of the corporate income tax in the state. In the case of apportionable income, part of the income is included in the base by using an apportionment formula reflecting how much of the corporation's business is transacted in the state.

   Ohio statutes make no distinction between business and nonbusiness income in the designation of allocable income. The issue of what income is allocable versus apportionable has often been the subject of appeals by taxpayers because allocated income, unlike apportioned income, enters the tax base at 100 percent.[6] The following types of income are fully allocable to the state of Ohio: net rents and royalties from real property located in the state and from tangible personal property utilized in the state, capital gains and losses from the sale of property located in the state, and dividends which are not otherwise deducted or excluded from net income.[7] Also, net patent, franchise, and copyright royalties and technical assistance fees are allocable to Ohio to the extent that the activity takes place in Ohio, and that they do not constitute the corporation's principal source of income.[8]

4. *Apportionable income and formula.* A large number of corporations with an obligation to file a corporate franchise tax return in Ohio do business in other states besides Ohio. This raises the necessity of determining what part of the corporation's net income ought to be taxed in the state of Ohio. Except for those income items that are considered directly allocable to Ohio or other states, all other income derived by the corporation is apportioned to the state of Ohio using a conventional three factor formula based on property, payroll, and sales, but

with the sales factor double-weighted. The composition of the formula is illustrated in Table 10-3.

5. *Taxable income.* In order to arrive at Ohio taxable income for the corporation, the sum of the apportioned income and allocable income within Ohio is first adjusted by the income or losses of transferor corporations and "related entity and related member" from combined reports. The second adjustment is for net operating losses.

6. *Net operating losses.* In the calculation of the net income tax, corporations are allowed to take a deduction for net operating losses (NOLS) realized in past periods. NOLS are allocated and apportioned, inside and outside Ohio, for the year in which the NOLS have occurred in the same manner that net income would have been allocated and apportioned. NOLS incurred in or after 1982 can be carried forward for 15 consecutive years, starting the year after the NOL occurred.[9] There is no carry back provision.

TABLE 10-3
Net Income Apportionment Formula

$$\text{Ohio Apportioned Net Income} = \text{Total Net Corporation Apportionable Income} \times \frac{\text{Property} + \text{Payroll} + \text{Sales} + \text{Sales Factors}}{4^{*}}$$

**Reduced by number of factors with a denominator of zero.*

The factors are computed as follows:

$$\text{Property Factor}^{*} = \frac{\text{Average cost of owned or rented real and tangible personal property used in business in Ohio}}{\text{Average cost of such property used everywhere}}$$

$$\text{Payroll Factor}^{**} = \frac{\text{Total compensation paid in Ohio}}{\text{Total compensation paid everywhere}}$$

$$\text{Sales Factor}^{***} = \frac{\text{Sales in Ohio}}{\text{Sales everywhere}}$$

**Excludes cost of pollution control, coal conversion, solid waste energy conversion, thermal efficiency improvement, energy conversion facilities, property that generates rental income, property in a qualified facility in an enterprise zone, and property used exclusively for qualified research in Ohio.*

***Excludes compensation to certain employees at a qualified facility in an enterprise zone, and compensation to employees engaged in qualified research in Ohio.*

****For sales of tangible personal property, sales inside and outside of Ohio are determined by the final destination of the property sold; other sales are sitused according to where the income-producing activity takes place. Sales derived from allocable income are not included in this factor.*

One peculiarity of the dual nature of the Ohio franchise tax is that the carry forward of losses is of no benefit in the computation of the alternative net worth tax that corporations may have to pay even in those years in which they have made positive net income.

COMPUTATION OF THE NET WORTH TAX

1. *Tax base.* The tax base for the net worth tax is computed as the total book value of the corporation's capital, surplus, retained earnings, and reserves. The value of the corporation's issued and outstanding shares of stock for the purposes of the net worth tax is based on the book value kept according to generally accepted accounting principles.[10]
2. *Exempted assets.*. Certain assets are exempt from the base of the net worth, including "goodwill," appreciation, land used in agriculture, research facilities, and pollution-and-energy-saving assets after certification by the Tax Commissioner. Goodwill is the cost in excess of fair value of the net assets acquired.[11] The list of currently exempt assets is in Box 10-1.
3. *Net worth apportionment formula.* Many of the corporations liable for the net worth tax in Ohio are also doing business in other states besides Ohio. The share of the corporation's net worth subject to tax in Ohio is determined through the application of an apportionment formula which is different from the apportionment formula used for net income tax purposes. The apportionment formula for net worth is based on two single weighted factors; property and "business done" in Ohio. This formula is illustrated in Table 10-4.

OTHER TAXES

There are two litter taxes levied with the franchise tax. These taxes were scheduled to expire in 1993 but have been extended through 1995. It is quite possible that the state legislature will prolong their lives beyond 1995.

All corporations except "litter stream corporations", financial institutions, family farm corporations and those paying the minimum tax of $50, pay the "tier one litter tax." The tax has a cap of $5,000[12] and it is computed as the larger of the following two bases:

a. Net income basis: the first $50,000 of Ohio taxable income is taxed at a rate of 0.11 percent and for taxable income above $50,000 the rate is 0.22 percent.

b. Net worth basis: Net worth taxable value at a rate of 0.014 percent.

BOX 10-1
Assets Exempt from The Net Worth Tax

Certain valuation reserves;

Taxes due and payable;

Goodwill, appreciation, and abandoned property;

Specified investments in public utilities, insurance companies, and financial institutions in which the taxpayer has ownership interests as required by statute (investments and business attributed to these companies are also eliminated in determining the property and business fractions for apportioning net worth);

Certified Ohio pollution control facilities;

Certain facilities designed to convert coal into other fuels or to desulphurize coal (assets excluded for 30 years);

Certified Ohio civil defense structures;

Certified Ohio energy conversion, thermal efficiency improvement, and solid waste energy conversion facilities;

Voting stock and participation certificates of production credit associations;

Land in Ohio devoted exclusively to agricultural use;

Property within Ohio used exclusively for qualified research;

Qualified improvements to property located in an enterprise zone.

(ORC 5709.25, 5709.35, 5709.50, 5709.65, 5733.05, and 5915.29)
Reproduced from Department of Taxation Annual Report.

TABLE 10-4
Net Worth Tax Base Formula

$$\textit{Ohio Taxable Value} = \begin{bmatrix} \textit{Total Net Worth} \\ \textit{minus} \\ \textit{Exempted Assets} \end{bmatrix} \times \frac{\textit{Property + Business done factors}}{2}$$

The factors are computed as follows:

$$\textit{Property Factor} = \frac{\textit{Book Depreciated Value of Ohio Assets}^{*}}{\textit{Book Value of Total Assets}}$$

$$\textit{Business Factor} = \frac{\textit{Ohio Business done}^{*}}{\textit{Total Business done}^{**}}$$

**Excludes value of pollution control, coal conversion, solid waste energy conversion, thermal efficiency improvement and energy conversion facilities, goodwill, appreciation, abandoned property, qualified property in an enterprise zone, and property used exclusively for qualified research.*

***Business done for the sale of tangible personal property is determined by the final destination of the goods. For other types of sales business done is determined according to the situs of the sales.*

The "tier two litter tax" applies only to those corporations that manufacture or sell litter stream products. These are defined to include all types of alcoholic beverages, soft drinks, packaging and containers, cigarettes and other tobacco products, matches, candy and gum.

The "tier two litter tax" is also computed on the larger of the two alternative bases of net income and net worth. The rates are double those of the "tier one litter tax". The only exception is for the first $50,000 of net income, to which the rate of 0.11 percent is applied. The "tier two litter tax" is capped at $10,000.

CREDITS

First, there is a credit for investment in qualified subsidiaries.[13] The objective of this credit is to address the double taxation of net worth at the parent and subsidiary levels. The credit is for investment in qualified subsidiaries when the parent company owns more than 50 percent of the capital stock of the subsidiary and when during the fiscal year both parent and subsidiary paid the franchise tax on a net worth basis. The credit equals the lesser of the following:

- The tax charged on the corporation's net worth represented by investments in its subsidiaries.

- The amount by which the corporation's net worth tax exceeds its computed (but not paid) net income tax.
- The amount by which the net worth tax of its subsidiaries exceeds the computed (but not paid) net income tax.
- The credit for investment in qualified subsidiaries is being phased in over a period of six years starting in 1990, according to the following schedule:

Tax Year	Percentage
1990	25
1991	50
1992	50
1993	50
1994	75
1995	100

Second, there is a credit for qualifying new investment, which has the objective of reducing the double taxation of real assets under the franchise and property taxes. Corporations may claim a credit against the franchise tax liability for the difference between the property tax paid on certain qualifying property and the tax that would have been paid had this property been listed at a lower rate set forth in ORC section 5733.061 (B). The credit applies to equipment and machinery for manufacturing or refining acquired after 1978 and not previously owned and credited by other taxpayers. This credit is not refundable, but when the credit exceeds the tax liability it can be carried forward for three years provided that the property has not been sold.[14]

Third, there is an export sales credit. This applies to corporations that increase their export sales at the same rate they increase their Ohio property and/or payroll. The credit can be claimed through the year 2005 and is computed on the basis of a formula incorporating the incremental changes in export sales and property and payroll factors.

Fourth, there is a "new jobs credit" which is refundable and calculated as the amount of Ohio income tax that the employer withheld from its employees times the percentage agreed with the Tax Credit Authority. Rehired or laid-off workers called back to work in a new facility or in the production of new goods or services qualify for the new jobs credit. This new credit is administered by the Tax Credit Authority and the Ohio Department of Development.

Fifth, there is a credit for qualified non-retail corporations locating in "enterprise zones." This credit is equal to the amount reimbursed to specified employees for the cost of day care services (up to a maximum of $300 per child) plus the amount reimbursed to specified employees for training costs (up to a maximum of $1,000 per employee).

Other tax benefits. In addition to the tax credits discussed above, corporations are eligible for several other tax benefits. Corporations that invest and create new jobs in certified enterprise zones can receive several tax benefits from the franchise tax, including an employee training credit, a day care credit, exclusion of qualifying property and payroll factors for the apportionment of the net income tax, and the exemption of qualifying property from the base of the net worth tax. Furthermore, the net book value of property within Ohio used exclusively for qualified research activities is excluded from the numerators of the apportionment factors for the net income and net worth taxes. This property is also treated as exempt in the computation of the net worth tax base.

Combined income reporting. At present, the majority of corporations file a separate entity tax return. However, taxpayer corporations have the option of using a combined report for the apportionment of their incomes to the state.[15] Combined reports apply only to the net income portion of the franchise tax. No similar option exists for the net worth tax.

More specifically, any corporation subject to the franchise tax that directly or indirectly controls over 50 percent of the voting stock of other corporation(s) subject to the franchise tax in Ohio may elect to combine incomes for the purpose of apportioning income taxes.[16] There is no obligation to include all the eligible corporations in the combined report, and related subsidiaries may elect to file a combined report without the inclusion of the parent corporation. If related entities are excluded from the combined report, the Commissioner requires an explanation for the exclusion.[17] Once combined income filing is selected by a group of corporations, they cannot opt out without written permission of the Tax Commissioner.[18]

Finally, the Commissioner may require combined income reporting for a group of interrelated corporations if it is felt that a combined report is necessary to properly reflect income and tax liability. Often such rulings have been appealed.

DISTRIBUTION OF LIABILITIES

The distribution for 1993 of net worth and net income tax payments among corporations grouped by level of net worth and by economic sector is presented in Tables 10-5 and 10-6, respectively. In 1993 there were 107,824 filers, of which 84,391 or 78.3 percent were net worth taxpayers, and 23,433 or 21.7 percent were net income taxpayers. The distribution of taxpayers between the two bases contrasts with the distribution of revenues. The net worth tax yielded $228 million or 36.2 percent of total franchise tax revenues, while the net income component yielded $402 million or 63.8 percent

TABLE 10-5
Reported Tax Liability by Tax Base and Net Worth, 1993

Net Worth	Tax Liability before Litter Tax and Credits					
	Net Worth Payers	Number of Filers	Net Income Payers	Number of Filers	Total Liability	Number of Filers
$< 0	$1,062,274	20,646	$27,576,223	1,799	$28,638,497	22,445
0 - 1	3,457,697	8,885	3,766,570	549	7,224,267	9,434
2 - 200,000	10,877,777	35,275	21,371,425	12,226	32,249,202	47,501
200,001 - 500,000	11,191,797	7,164	14,698,029	3,001	25,889,826	10,165
500,001 - 2,500,000	24,690,981	6,178	37,390,834	2,695	62,081,815	8,873
2,500,001 - 5,000,000	8,623,498	1,409	19,049,265	742	27,672,763	2,151
5,000,001 - 20,000,000	20,714,086	2,189	48,876,795	1,134	69,590,881	3,323
20,000,001 - 100,000,000	36,719,759	1,612	67,416,587	852	104,136,346	2,464
100,000,001 - 250,000,000	22,950,564	534	39,480,517	238	62,431,081	772
250,000,001 - 500,000,000	20,978,333	231	29,403,482	93	50,381,815	324
500,000,001 - 750,000,000	12,415,001	83	14,669,812	39	27,084,813	122
750,000,001 - 1,000,000,000	5,447,423	51	6,142,703	13	11,590,126	64
> 1,000,000,000	48,880,774	134	72,188,481	52	121,069,255	186
TOTAL	$228,009,964	84,391	$402,030,723	23,433	$630,040,687	107,824

Net Worth	Litter Taxes, Credits, and Total Reported Liability				
	Tier 1 * Litter Tax	Tier 2 * Litter Tax	New Investment Credit	Subsidiary & Other Credits	Total Liability
$< 0	$304,121	$24,927	$6,002,070	$144,623	$22,820,852
0 - 1	66,541	748	103,825	11,064	7,176,667
2 - 200,000	601,314	17,452	331,145	93,381	32,443,442
200,001 - 500,000	606,341	16,298	687,464	53,085	25,771,916
500,001 - 2,500,000	1,390,911	34,720	1,623,866	191,556	61,692,024
2,500,001 - 5,000,000	629,889	13,784	1,195,312	131,125	26,989,999
5,000,001 - 20,000,000	1,400,574	50,968	2,135,724	776,761	68,129,938
20,000,001 - 100,000,000	1,676,883	56,917	3,547,254	1,167,769	101,155,123
100,000,001 - 250,000,000	818,486	35,961	3,790,020	698,033	58,797,475
250,000,001 - 500,000,000	487,287	12,599	3,118,471	924,131	46,839,099
500,000,001 - 750,000,000	237,755	16,821	1,096,816	454,446	25,788,127
750,000,001 - 1,000,000,000	138,212	7,205	283,147	219,369	11,233,027
> 1,000,000,000	536,361	35,652	7,017,896	2,487,910	112,135,462
TOTAL	$8,894,675	$324,052	$30,933,010	$7,353,253	$600,973,151

* Tier 1 Litter Tax is paid by all corporations. Tier 2 Litter Tax is paid only by "litter stream" corporations.

of total revenues. Litter taxes raised $9.2 million in 1993. Total credits allowed against the franchise tax in 1993 amounted to $38.3 million, of which $30.9 million corresponded to the new investment tax credit.

The distribution of tax liabilities among different firm sizes and economic groups is better visualized in percentage terms. This is shown in Tables 10-

TABLE 10-6
Reported Tax Liability by Tax Base and Industry, 1993

Industry	Tax Liability before Litter Tax and Credits					
	Net Worth Payers	Number of Filers	Net Income Payers	Number of Filers	Total Liability	Number of Filers
Agriculture, Forestry	$1,216,809	1,146	$1,669,607	380	$2,886,416	1,526
Mining	8,857,777	1,014	3,637,913	173	12,495,690	1,187
Construction	7,271,866	7,483	14,951,878	2,165	22,223,744	9,648
Manufacturing	84,341,330	10,431	204,172,971	4,025	288,514,301	14,456
Utilities	21,912,296	3,369	28,796,966	1,019	50,709,262	4,388
Wholesale	17,754,276	6,446	32,419,816	2,318	50,174,092	8,764
Retail	20,527,571	11,125	46,673,693	3,391	67,201,264	14,516
Finance, Insurance, & Real Estate	31,698,024	9,824	23,424,360	2,470	55,122,384	12,294
Services	22,951,030	23,498	37,946,724	5,787	60,897,754	29,285
Not Classified	11,478,985	10,055	8,336,795	1,705	19,815,780	11,760
TOTAL	$228,009,964	84,391	$402,030,723	23,433	$630,040,687	107,824

Industry	Litter Taxes, Credits, and Total Reported Liability				
	Tier 1 * Litter Tax	Tier 2 * Litter Tax	New Investment Credit	Subsidiary & Other Credits	Total Liability
Agriculture, Forestry	$52,418	$336	$8,021	$1,246	$2,929,903
Mining	183,965	860	643,064	105,441	11,932,010
Construction	464,970	5,864	82,770	50,758	22,561,050
Manufacturing	3,678,054	129,536	27,366,195	3,747,747	261,207,949
Utilities	463,486	267	90,612	679,397	50,403,007
Wholesale	913,495	54,012	621,463	560,919	49,959,215
Retail	943,665	106,152	282,134	177,755	67,791,192
Finance, Insurance, & Real Estate	820,690	7,683	175,027	1,257,108	54,518,623
Services	1,135,244	13,317	131,323	563,403	61,351,590
Not Classified	238,688	6,025	1,532,401	209,479	18,318,612
TOTAL	$8,894,675	$324,052	$30,933,010	$7,353,253	$600,973,151

* Tier 1 Litter Tax is paid by all corporations. Tier 2 Litter Tax is paid only by "litter stream" corporations.

7 and 10-8. Smaller firms with a net worth under $500,000 represented 73.6 percent of all taxpayers, but paid only 10.8 percent of all tax liabilities. Firms with net assets over $1 billion represented only 0.17 percent of the total number of filers, but they accounted for 19.22 percent of all liabilities. Credits also tend to be concentrated at the top. Firms with assets over $1 billion claimed 22.7 percent of new investment tax credits and 33.8 percent of all other tax credits. In terms of economic sectors, the manufacturing sector is the largest taxpayer, being responsible for 45.8 percent of total tax liabilities even though this sector represents only 13.4 percent of the total number of filers.

TABLE 10-7
Reported Tax Liability by Tax Base and Net Worth by Percentage of Total, 1993

Net Worth	Tax Liability before Litter Tax and Credits					
	Net Worth Payers	Number of Filers	Net Income Payers	Number of Filers	Total Liability	Number of Filers
$< 0	0.47%	24.46%	6.86%	7.68%	4.55%	20.82%
0 - 1	1.52	10.53	0.94	2.34	1.15	8.75
2 - 200,000	4.77	41.80	5.32	52.17	5.12	44.05
200,001 - 500,000	4.91	8.49	3.66	12.81	4.11	9.43
500,001 - 2,500,000	10.83	7.32	9.30	11.50	9.85	8.23
2,500,001 - 5,000,000	3.78	1.67	4.74	3.17	4.39	1.99
5,000,001 - 20,000,000	9.08	2.59	12.16	4.84	11.05	3.08
20,000,001 - 100,000,000	16.10	1.91	16.77	3.64	16.53	2.29
100,000,001 - 250,000,000	10.07	0.63	9.82	1.02	9.91	0.72
250,000,001 - 500,000,000	9.20	0.27	7.31	0.40	8.00	0.30
500,000,001 - 750,000,000	5.44	0.10	3.65	0.17	4.30	0.11
750,000,001 - 1,000,000,000	2.39	0.06	1.53	0.06	1.84	0.06
> 1,000,000,000	21.44	0.16	17.96	0.22	19.22	0.17
TOTAL	100.00	100.00	100.00	100.00	100.00	100.00

Net Worth	Litter Taxes, Credits, and Total Reported Liability				
	Tier 1 * Litter Tax	Tier 2 * Litter Tax	New Investment Credit	Subsidiary & Other Credits	Total Liability
$ < 0	3.42%	7.69%	19.40%	1.97%	3.80%
0 - 1	0.75	0.23	0.34	0.15	1.19
2 - 200,000	6.76	5.39	1.07	1.27	5.40
200,001 - 500,000	6.82	5.03	2.22	.72	4.29
500,001 - 2,500,000	15.64	10.71	5.25	2.61	10.27
2,500,001 - 5,000,000	7.08	4.25	3.86	1.78	4.49
5,000,001 - 20,000,000	15.75	15.73	6.90	10.56	11.34
20,000,001 - 100,000,000	18.85	17.56	11.47	15.88	16.83
100,000,001 - 250,000,000	9.20	11.10	12.25	9.49	9.78
250,000,001 - 500,000,000	5.48	3.89	10.08	12.57	7.79
500,000,001 - 750,000,000	2.67	5.19	3.55	6.18	4.29
750,000,001 - 1,000,000,000	1.55	2.22	0.92	2.98	1.87
> 1,000,000,000	6.03	11.00	22.69	33.83	18.66
TOTAL	100.00	100.00	100.00	100.00	100.00

* Tier 1 Litter Tax is paid by all corporations. Tier 2 Litter Tax is paid only by "litter stream" corporations.

TABLE 10-8
Reported Tax Liability by Tax Base and Industry by Percentage of Total, 1993

Industry	Tax Liability before Litter Tax and Credits					
	Net Worth Payers	Number of Filers	Net Income Payers	Number of Filers	Total Liability	Number of Filers
Agriculture, Forestry	0.53%	1.36%	0.42%	1.62%	0.46%	1.42%
Mining	3.88	1.20	0.90	0.74	1.98	10
Construction	3.19	8.87	3.72	9.24	3.53	8.95
Manufacturing	36.99	12.36	50.79	17.18	45.79	13.41
Utilities	9.61	3.99	7.16	4.35	8.05	4.07
Wholesale	7.79	7.64	8.06	9.89	7.96	8.13
Retail	9.00	13.18	11.61	14.47	10.67	13.46
Finance, Insurance, & Real Estate	13.90	11.64	5.83	10.54	8.75	11.40
Services	10.07	27.84	9.44	24.70	9.67	27.16
Not Classified	5.03	11.91	2.07	7.28	3.15	10.91
TOTAL	100.00	100.00	100.00	100.00	100.00	100.00

Industry	Litter Taxes, Credits, and Total Reported Liability				
	Tier 1 * Litter Tax	Tier 2 * Litter Tax	New Investment Credit	Subsidiary & Other Credits	Total Liability
Agriculture, Forestry	0.59%	0.10%	0.03%	0.02%	0.49%
Mining	2.07	0.27	2.08	1.43	1.99
Construction	5.23	1.81	0.27	0.69	3.75
Manufacturing	41.35	39.97	88.47	50.97	43.46
Utilities	5.21	0.08	0.29	9.24	8.39
Wholesale	10.27	16.67	2.01	7.63	8.31
Retail	10.61	32.76	0.91	2.42	11.28
Finance, Insurance, & Real Estate	9.23	2.37	0.57	17.10	9.07
Services	12.76	4.11	0.42	7.66	10.21
Not Classified	2.68	1.86	4.95	2.85	3.05
TOTAL	100.00	100.00	100.00	100.00	100.00

* Tier 1 Litter Tax is paid by all corporations. Tier 2 Litter Tax is paid only by "litter stream" corporations.

COMPARISON WITH OTHER STATES

Revenue Performance

Average reliance on the tax. By comparison to other states, Ohio's use of the corporate income tax is below average. This is shown with data for 1991 in Figure 10-6 where Ohio's corporate tax collections as a percent of total tax revenue are compared to those of the eight top industrial states and to the entire United States' average. The comparison with states in the Midwest Region gives similar results (Figure 10-7). In 1991 Ohio was rely-

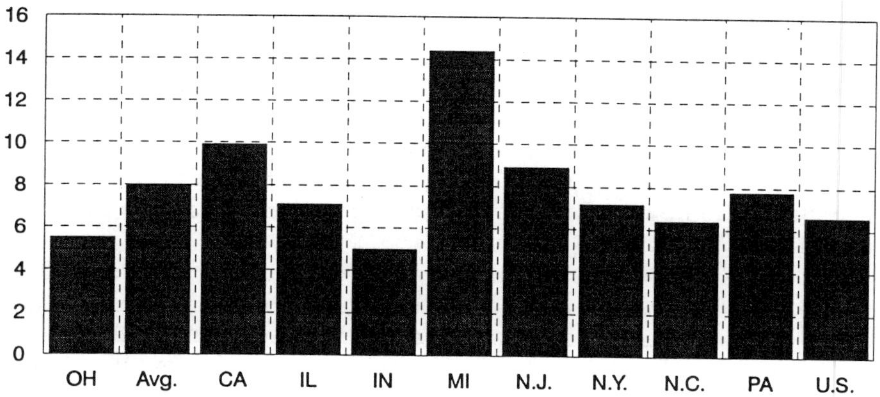

Source: Facts & Figures on Government Finances, 1993
Avg. = Average for the Top Industrial States
U.S. = Average for all States

FIGURE 10-6. 1991 Corporate tax collections as a percentage of total tax revenue: top industrial states.

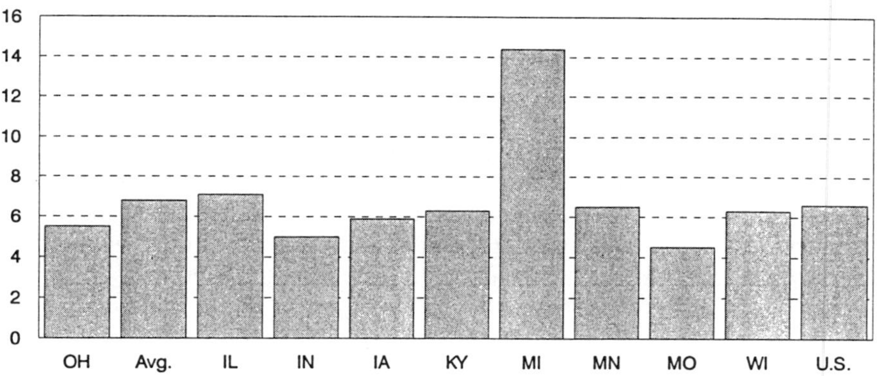

Source: Tax Foundation, (1994).

Avg. = Average for the Top Industrial States
U.S. = Average for all States

FIGURE 10-7. 1991 corporate tax collections as a percentage of total revenue: Midwest region.

ing less on corporate franchise taxes than all other states in the two groups except for Indiana and Missouri.

A different way to compare the performance of Ohio's franchise tax vis-a-vis the average performance for other states is to examine its relative performance or tax effort. The Advisory Commission on Intergovernmental Relations (ACIR) conducts periodic studies of the tax effort of the states.[19]

Tax effort is defined by the ratio of the hypothetical amount of tax revenue that would have been collected had the state used a "representative tax system" to the actual collections in the state.[20] If a state actually collects more under its own tax law than would be collected if the "representative tax system" were in place, then the state has a higher than average tax effort. Similarly, if the state's actual tax collections are less than those raised by the hypothetical representative tax, then the state's tax effort is lower than the average.

Using this approach to examine Ohio's corporate franchise tax performance, we find that Ohio has made a lower tax effort on the corporate income—net worth tax than the average state in the United States in the period 1982-1991. In particular, Ohio has had a lower tax effort than any other of the ten top industrial states with the exception of Indiana (Figure 10-8).

These findings raise a number of intriguing questions for which we have no ready answers. The lower than average performance of the franchise tax in Ohio is unexpected for several reasons. The corporate franchise net income tax in Ohio has, as we see below, a base similar to that in most other states, and the tax rate for nominal net income is among the highest. In addition, the Ohio franchise tax has a net worth alternative base which is substituted for the net income tax when its computation shows a higher liability. Practically no other state has this significant lower floor mechanism to ensure some amount of revenue.

Two explanations are possible for this puzzle. The first is that Ohio is more generous than most other states in granting credits and other tax benefits. Some evidence is presented in this and other chapters of the book that Ohio is more generous than the average state in this respect. The second is that tax avoidance and evasion are considerably worse in Ohio than in other states. However, no data are available to pursue this conjecture.

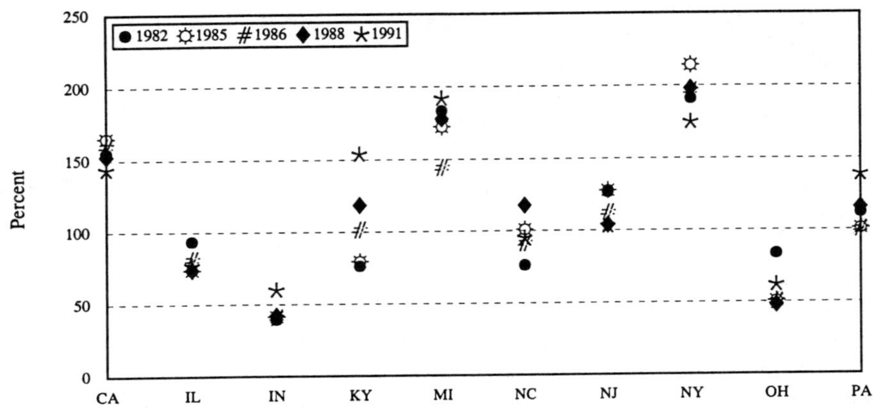

FIGURE 10-8. Relative tax effort for the corporate franchise tax.

The trend toward decreasing importance of the corporate income tax. The ups and downs in the revenues from Ohio's franchise tax from 1983 to 1993 (Table 10-1 and Figure 10-2), and the general decrease in importance of the corporate franchise tax in total tax revenues, mirror the experience of all other states in the same period. This is clearly shown in Figure 10- 9, where the real (at 1987 prices) corporate franchise tax collections for Ohio are compared to the total collections from the corporate income tax for all states.[21]

This pattern of similar behavior in Ohio and the United States is also shown in Figure 10-10 which tracks the percent change from year to year for both series. However, these two figures also suggest a less pronounced profile in the ups and downs of collections for Ohio than for all states. This is most likely due to the dual nature of Ohio's franchise tax, which makes firms pay the highest of the net income tax and the net worth tax components.

The franchise tax has declined in relative importance as a source of revenue over the last ten years. This trend has persisted whether revenues from the net worth tax on financial institutions are included or excluded from the total (Table 10-9). What are the explanations for the declining importance of Ohio's franchise tax in total revenues? To answer this we will need to examine causes for the decline in revenues that have been outside the control of the state, or, differently put, causes for the decline in revenues that are shared with other states. Ohio's experience with a continuing decrease in the importance of the corporate franchise tax does not differ much from that of other states with a corporate income tax, or indeed from the experience of the corporate income tax at the federal level.

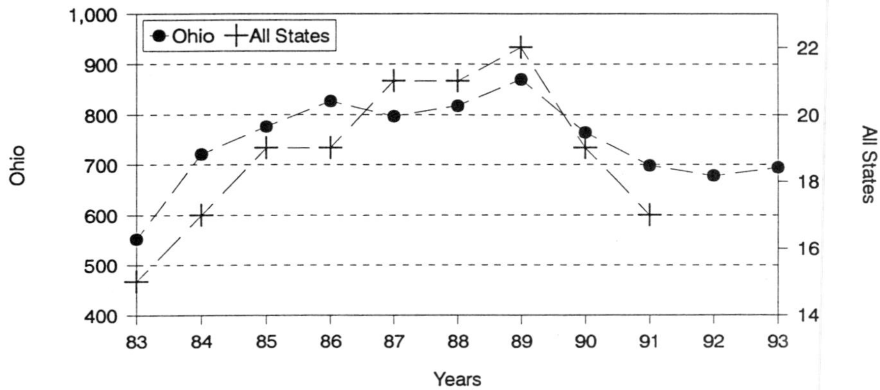

Source: Ohio Department of Taxation.

Note: Deflator from Economic Report of the President.

FIGURE 10-9. Real corporate franchise tax collections for Ohio vs. all states (1987 dollars: Ohio in Millions, Total for all states in billions).

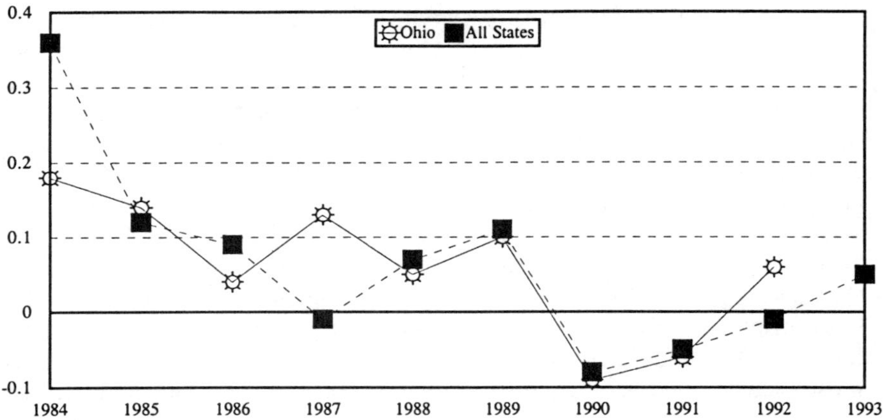

Source: Ohio Department of Taxation Facts and Tax Foundation, (1994)

FIGURE 10-10. Percent change in actual corporate tax revenues (Ohio vs. total for all states).

At the federal level, collections from the corporate income tax have been declining since the 1960s, when the corporate income tax represented as much as one-fifth of total federal tax revenues. Since the mid-1980s and during the 1990s, corporate income tax collections have represented approximately one-tenth of total federal tax revenues. A part of this decline is associated with policy changes granting more favorable tax treatment to corporations, which started with the investment tax credits of the 1960s and culminated with the Accelerated Cost Recovery Act of 1981. The Tax Reform Act (TRA) of 1986 was in part an attempt to turn around the declining revenues from the corporate income tax by taking away many of the tax advantages granted in the past and reducing capital depreciation allowances, and by introducing an alternative minimum tax.

However, there were offsetting changes in the tax environment after 1986. Perhaps the most important was the number of corporations that elected to organize as S corporations after the 1986 TRA. The relative growth in the number of S corporations is commonly identified as a significant source of erosion in corporate tax revenues.

The main reason for electing to organize as S corporations is a favorable tax treatment. Federal law treats S corporations similarly to partnerships. Many states, including Ohio, do the same. The profits (or losses) of S corporations are passed through to shareholders, and taxes are paid only at the personal level. In contrast, profits from C corporations are taxed once at the company level and taxed again as dividend income or as capital gains at the individual level.[22] The growth in importance of S corporations is dramatized

TABLE 10-9
Corporate Franchise Tax Liability as a Percentage of State Tax Revenue

Tax Year	Liability After Litter Tax, Surtax and Credits	
	Excluding Financial Institutions	Total
1983	8.4912	9.1441
1984	7.9320	9.4213
1985	9.0797	10.4366
1986	9.1934	10.4329
1987	7.7637	9.0524
1988	7.7565	9.0327
1989	8.2534	9.7408
1990	7.5291	9.1004
1991	6.6936	8.3104
1992	6.1629	7.8395
1993	6.1454	7.8726

Source: Ohio Department of Taxation.

by the fact that in 1986 they represented 21 percent of all corporations and by 1990 they represented 48 percent. The largest increase happened just after TRA 1986 was enacted. However, these numbers may exaggerate the importance of S corporations. In terms of net income S corporations represented only 9.3 percent of total corporate income in 1990; this was up from 5.9 percent in 1986. In terms of total assets, S corporations are even less important. In 1990 they represented 4. 1 percent of total assets in the corporate sector, up from 1.8 percent in 1986. One reason for this smaller share of income and assets is that S corporations tend to be smaller and in the service sector (32 percent in 1990).[23] However, not all of the decrease in revenues from corporate income taxes can be traced to changes in tax policies. It appears that there has also been a persistent downward trend in the relative importance of the base of the corporate income tax. Auerbach and Poterba,[24] who have studied the decline in federal corporate income tax revenues, find that while the average rate of corporate taxation had fallen by one-third from the mid 1960s to the mid 1980s, in the same period corporate profitability had declined by a factor of two. While it has been relatively easy to disentangle the causes behind lower average corporate tax rates, to date there is no clear understanding of why corporate profitability has decreased by so much. The profit rate has trended downward since the 1960s and dropped most sharply in the 1980s.[25] Many observers associate this sharp decrease with the oil crisis that hit at about the same time. The taxable income of many corporations has also decreased through leverage buy-outs and other means for relying more heavily on debt financing. In more recent years the rate of profitability has turned around, but it has not reached the levels of the 1960s or 1970s.

How Different is Ohio's Franchise Tax?

Nexus. The legal definition and the administrative enforcement of nexus in Ohio are broad by national standards. The state of Ohio is more likely to consider that nexus exists as a result of non-universal business activities, such as the use of a company car for a salesperson or the listing of the company in the phone book in another state. Of the seven non-universal activities used by state tax administrations to determine nexus listed in Table 10-10, Ohio is the only state that uses all of them. In particular, Ohio is one of only four states that considers the presence of a salesperson who only takes orders as evidence of business nexus.[26] Ohio's Department of Taxation maintains several permanent offices in other states which help enforce the state's franchise tax.

Apportionment formulas. Ohio uses a three factor, double-weight sales formula for the apportionment of net income. The more common apportionment formula is a three-factor formula with sales, payroll, and property having the same weights.[27] However, ten other states besides Ohio use the double-weighted sales factor formula. The formulas used in a selected sample of states are surveyed in Table 10-11. The accompanying Table 10-12 summarizes the nature of the modified formulas of all the states not using the straight three factor equally weighted formula. Besides the double weighting of the sales factor, almost every other modification of the formula also involves some other weighting of the sales factor. Three states (Iowa, Texas, and Nebraska) use a single-factor sales formula.

Ohio conforms with the practice of many other states by eliminating a factor if its denominator is zero but leaving the factor in the formula if the numerator is zero (See Table 10-11). Ohio also allows corporations, under some particular circumstances, to use separate accounting rather than the apportionment formula as a method of apportioning income to the state.[28] As seen in the interstate comparisons in Table 10-11 separate accounting as an apportionment method is often completely excluded.

Throwback rule. Ohio does not use a "throwback" rule for the computation of the sales factor of the apportionment formula for the net income tax. Thus, when corporations doing business in Ohio make sales in states without a corporate income tax, those (untaxed) sales enter the denominator of the formula (hence some sales are not apportioned to any state). The problem with this approach is that it opens an avenue for tax avoidance by "transferring" sales to the no-tax state. The use of the "throwback" rule would make

TABLE 10-10
Non-Universal Activities Used to Determine Nexus

State	Licensing Intangible Rights	Licensing of Software	Company Listed in Phonebook	Company Car for Salesperson	Salesperson Sets up Promotional Items	Salesperson Takes Orders Only	Inventory Inspection by Salesperson
Ohio	X	X	X	X	X	X	X
Illinois	X	X	X		X		X
Indiana	X	N/R			X		
Iowa	X				X		X
Kentucky	X	X					X
Michigan		N/R			X		X
Minnesota	X	X			X		X
Missouri	X	N/R	X	X	X		X
Wisconsin							
California	X	N/R			X		X
Colorado							
Florida	X	X	X				
Georgia				X	X	X	X
New Jersey	X	N/R		X	X		X
New York	X	X	X	X			
North Carolina		N/R					
Pennsylvania	X						
Total of All Other States	20	12	4	6	16	2	17
Total of All States Using Activity	32	18	9	11	26	4	27

Source: 1993 Multistate Corporate Tax Guide

X - These items create nexus.
N/R - No report from this state.

such sales part of the numerator of the sales factor for Ohio purposes. Table 10-13 surveys the use of the "throwback" rule in a selected group of states.

Tax base. Ohio couples the state franchise net income tax with federal taxable income before the net operating loss deduction and special deductions.[29] About half of the states choose to couple their corporate income tax bases with federal taxable income, before special deductions; the other half couple with federal taxable income after special deductions. See Table 10-14 for a sample of state practices. Nevertheless, Ohio allows an adjustment deduction from taxable income for dividends received and also allows a reduction for net operating losses in Ohio.

Ohio allows interest from United States Government securities as a deduction from taxable income. However, some states do tax this interest income, as shown in Table 10-15. But in order to tax interest from federal securities these states must also tax interest from their own state securities. This non-discriminatory clause makes the option of taxing federal income

TABLE 10-11
General Formula Apportionment

State	Does State Follow UDITPA?	Generally Used Factors: Sales	Property	Payroll	Are the Factors Weighted Equally?	Does State Allow Separate Accounting?	Does State Eliminate Factor if: Denominator is Zero?	Numerator is Zero?
Ohio	No	X	X	X	No*	Yes*	Yes	No
Illinois	Yes*	X	X	X	No*	Yes*	Yes	No
Indiana	No	X	X	X	Yes	Yes*	Yes	No
Iowa	No	X	---	---	N/A	Yes*	N/A	N/A
Kentucky	Yes*	X	X	X	No*	No	Yes	No
Michigan	Yes*	X	X	X	No*	Yes*	Yes	No
Minnesota	No*	X	X	X	No*	No	Yes	No
Missouri	Yes*	X	X	X	Yes	Yes*	Yes	No
Wisconsin	Yes*	X	X	X	No*	Yes*	Yes	No
California	Yes*	X	X	X	Yes*	Yes*	Yes*	No
Colorado	Yes*	X*	---	X	Yes	Yes*	No	No
Florida	No*	X	X	X	No*	No	Yes	No
Georgia	No*	X	X	X	Yes	Yes*	Yes	No
New Jersey	No	X	X	X	Yes	No	Yes	No
New York	No	X	X	X	No*	No*	Yes	No*
North Carolina	Yes*	X	X	X	No*	No	Yes	No
Pennsylvania	Yes*	X	X	X	Yes	Yes*	Yes	No

Source: 1993 Multistate Corporate Tax Guide.

* More qualifications apply.

less attractive; nevertheless, it is an option that should be considered. The option is especially important if, as discussed in the next chapter, banks and other financial institutions are brought under the general regime of the corporate franchise tax. One of the main problems of doing so is that banks and other financial institutions tend to have abnormally low net incomes when interest from federal securities is exempt.

Tax rates. Only the tax rates for the net income tax are comparable to those used in other states, since Ohio is one of few states with a substantial (uncapped) net worth tax and the only one in which the net worth tax is paid when the liability is larger than under the net income tax. In terms of the net income tax, Ohio's rates are in the upper range of the spectrum. By comparison to a selected group of 16 other states shown in Table 10-16, only four states have higher rates for corporate net incomes than Ohio. The highest rate is charged by Pennsylvania, 12.25 percent. Iowa has a progressive schedule reaching a marginal rate of 12 percent for net incomes above $250,000. Closer to Ohio's rate are Minnesota, with a rate of 9.8 percent, and New York, with a rate of 9 percent.

TABLE 10-12
States with Modified Apportionment Formulas

State	Alternative Formula	Effective Date
Ohio	Double-weighted sales factor formula.	1983
Colorado	By election, a corporation may use either the two-factor formula (sales and property) or the equally weighted three-factor formula.	-
Connecticut	Double-weighted sales factor formula.	1981
Florida	Double-weighted sales factor formula.	1983
Illinois	Double-weighted sales factor formula.	1987
Iowa	Single factor sales formula.	-
Kansas	By election, a corporation may use either the equally weighted three-factor formula or two-factor formula of property and sales (if payroll exceeds average of such factors by 200%).	1988
Kentucky	Double-weighted sales factor formula.	1986
Massachusetts	Double-weighted sales factor formula.	1978
Minnesota	Sales weighted 70% and property and payroll weighted 15%each.	1987
Mississippi	Manufacturing-retailer uses sales, plus average of property-payroll (denominator is two) formula. Manufacturer-wholesaler uses equally weighted three-factor formula. Single-factor sales formula for retailing, renting, servicing and merchandising.	1988
Missouri	By election, a corporation may use either the equally weighted three-factor formula or the single-factor sales formula.[1]	-
Nebraska	Single-factor sales formuala.	1992
New Hampshire	(1.5 sales + 1 property + payroll) ÷ 3	
New York	Double-weighted sales factor formula.	1976
North Carolina	Double-weighted sales factor formula.	1989
Oregon	Double-weighted sales factor formula.	1991
Texas	Single-factor sales formula.	1989
West Virginia	Double-weighted sales factor formula.	1986
Wisconsin	Double-weighted sales factor formula.	1974

Source: Updated from J. Coalson, "State and Local Corporate Tax Roundup," *Corporate Taxation*, Vol. 3, No. 1., May/June, 1992.

[1]Alternative formula is calculated as: $\frac{\text{Missouri sales + all other sales}}{\text{All sales}}$ times Net income

[2]Effective date is 1992, with pre-1992 five year phase-in.

Source: Updated from J. Coalson, "State and Local Corporate Tax Roundup," *Corporate Taxation*, Vol. 3, No. 1., May/June, 1992.

Minimum Tax. Several states use an Alternative Minimum Tax (AMT) together with the regular corporate income tax (Table 10-17). In the selected sample of states only New Jersey uses a fixed amount for a minimum tax. Other states using a fixed amount minimum tax and not shown in Table 10-17 are Massachusetts with a flat tax of $456, Connecticut ($250), Vermont ($150), and Utah ($100). Several states in the selected sample do impose a

TABLE 10-13
Throwback Rules

State	Does State's Throwback Rule Apply to Sales?
Ohio	NO
Illinois	YES. If corporation is not taxable in state where property had its situs or was used.
Indiana	YES
Iowa	NO
Kentucky	NO
Michigan	YES
Minnesota	NO
Missouri	YES
Wisconsin	YES
California	YES
Colorado	YES. State where goods were shipped from.
Florida	NO
Georgia	NO
New Jersey	NO
New York	NO
North Carolina	NO
Pennsylvania	NO

Source: 1993 Multistate Corporate Tax Guide.

minimum tax similar to the federal AMT. This is to ensure that corporations do not take "excessive" deductions based on tax preferences. Corporations need to compute the ordinary corporate income tax and the AMT simultaneously. The latter has a wider base but at a lower rate. Corporations are required to pay the larger of the two. The states of Iowa, New York, California, and Florida all have such a tax. However, none of these states uses the computation of the federal AMT to implement its AMT.

NOL carry forwards and carry backs. As we have seen in the previous section, Ohio allows the carry forward of net operating losses under the net income tax for 15 years and no carry back of losses is allowed. The carry forward provision is almost universal in other states with a corporate income tax, and an allowance of 15 years is the norm. Pennsylvania is the exception, having eliminated the carry forward provision in 1994. About half of the states sampled in Table 10-18 allow the carry back of losses for three years. The use of the carry back provision offers a more favorable treatment to business but at the same time tends to create more instability in state revenue collections.

TABLE 10-14
Conformity to Federal Rules

State	Does State Computation of Taxable Net Income Start with a Figure from Federal Form 1120?
Ohio	Yes. Starts with taxable income BEFORE special deductions.
Illinois	Yes. Starts with taxable income AFTER special deductions.
Indiana	Yes. Starts with taxable income AFTER special deductions.
Iowa	Yes. Starts with taxable income AFTER special deductions and BEFORE NOL.
Kentucky	No.
Michigan	Yes. Starts with taxable income AFTER special deductions.
Minnesota	Yes. Starts with taxable income BEFORE special deductions.
Missouri	Yes. Starts with taxable income AFTER special deductions.
Wisconsin	Yes. Starts with taxable income BEFORE special deductions and NOL.
California	Yes. Starts with taxable income BEFORE special deductions.
Colorado	Yes. Starts with taxable income AFTER special deductions.
Florida	Yes. Starts with taxable income AFTER special deductions.
Georgia	Yes. Starts with taxable income AFTER special deductions.
New Jersey	Yes. Starts with taxable income BEFORE special deductions and NOL on single-entity basis and NOL's.
New York	Yes. Starts with taxable income BEFORE special deductions.
North Carolina	Yes. Starts with taxable income BEFORE special deductions.
Pennsylvania	Yes. Starts with taxable income BEFORE special deductions.

Source: 1993 Multistate Corporate Tax Guide.

Miscellaneous taxes. Ohio is not unique in adding minor miscellaneous taxes to the corporate franchise tax. New Jersey, as Ohio, has litter control taxes. However, most of the miscellaneous taxes in other states are in the nature of small franchise taxes on capital stock or net worth (Table 10-19).

Tax incentives. Ohio offers a number of incentives with the franchise tax, including credits and exemptions, some of which are associated with setting up business in an enterprise zone. Ohio is not out of line with many other states which offer similar incentives. Most offer incentives for enterprise zones. However, Ohio is among the smaller group of states that use the franchise tax rather than sales and income taxes in their incentive programs. Ohio is also the only state that reports using exemptions of assets as a form of tax incentive to business activity.

Combined income reporting for unitary businesses. Ohio allows combined income reporting for a unitary group of corporations as long as the corporations are all Ohio taxpayers and other conditions are met. There is con-

TABLE 10-15
Treatment of Federal Obligations (Dividends and Interest)

State	U.S. Treasury Bills & Notes
Ohio	
Illinois	
Indiana	
Iowa	
Kentucky	
Michigan	(No corporate income tax, single business tax only)
Minnesota	X
Missouri	
Wisconsin	X
California	X (franchise only)
Colorado	
Florida	X
Georgia	
New Jersey	X
New York	X
North Carolina	
Pennsylvania	The deduction for interest income from U.S. obligations is reduced by the interest incurred in carrying the securities and the expenses incurred in the production of such income.

Source: 1993 Multistate Corporate Tax Guide.

X: Interest income from U.S. Government securities is taxable.

siderable diversity among the states on this issue (Table 10-20). While some other states besides Ohio make it optional for the taxpayers to use combined reporting and/or the Department of Taxation to require it, there are many more states that either require combined income reporting or disallow it entirely.

MAIN ISSUES AND PROBLEMS

THE NET WORTH PORTION OF THE TAX

How common is the net worth tax or business assets taxes? An alternative business tax falling on assets or net worth is not all uncommon. In fact,

TABLE 10-16
Tax Rates

State	Tax Rate
Ohio	Greater of ($0 - 50,000 = 5.1%; > $50,000 = 8.9%) or (5.82 Mills multiplied by net worth; a surtax of .11% on the first $50,000 and .22% over $50T of net income or .0014 of net worth).
Illinois	4.0% Corporate Rate + 20.0% Surcharge until 1993 (10% after) + 2.5% Personal Property Tax = 7.3% before 1993
Indiana	3.4% of AGI + 4.5% supplemental net income tax
Iowa	$0-25,000 = 6% 25,001-100,000 = 8% 100,001-250,000 = 10% > 250,000 = 12%
Kentucky	$0-25,000 = 4% 25,001-50,000 = 5% 50,001-100,000 = 6% 100,001-200,000 = 7% > 200,000 = 8%
Michigan	2.35% single business tax
Minnesota	9.8%
Missouri	$0-100,000 = 5.0% 100,001 - 335,000 = 6.0% > 335,000 = 6.5%
Wisconsin	7.9% + 5.0% recycling tax until 4/1/99 (Minimum recycling tax = $25; Maximum = $9,800)
California	9.3%, banks and financial institutions = 10.668%
Colorado	$0-50,000 = 5%; > $ 50,000 = 5.1%
Florida	5.5%
Georgia	6.0%
New Jersey	9.0% + .375% surcharge which is reviewed annually
New York	9.0%; 8.0% graduated rate for small businesses + 10.0% surtax in 1993
North Carolina	7.75% plus surtaxes (1991 = 4%, 1992 = 3%) (1993 = 2%, 1994 = 1%)
Pennsylvania	12.25%

Source: 1993 Multistate Corporate Tax Guide.

Ohio is the only state that requires the tax payer to pay the higher of the two taxes.[30] Several states have a tax on net worth, some of these taxes are capped and work as minimum taxes rather than as alternatives to the net income tax. Others such as Pennsylvania have extremely high net worth tax rates.[31]

TABLE 10-17
Alternative Minimum Tax

State	Does State Impose a Minimum Tax?	Is State-Imposed AMT Similar to Federal AMT?	What is State's AMT Rate?
Ohio	Yes	No	$50
Illinois	No	N/A	N/A
Indiana	No	N/A	N/A
Iowa	Yes	Yes	7.2%
Kentucky	No	N/A	N/A
Michigan	No	N/A	N/A
Minnesota	Yes	Yes, With Modifications	5.8%
Missouri	No	N/A	N/A
Wisconsin	No	N/A	N/A
California	Yes	Yes	7%
Colorado	No	N/A	N/A
Florida	Yes	No	3.3%
Georgia	No	N/A	N/A
New Jersey	Yes, Flat fee: $25 domestic, $50 foreign	No	N/A
New York	Yes	Yes	5%
North Carolina	No	N/A	N/A
Pennsylvania	No	N/A	N/A

Source: 1993 Multistate Corporate Tax Guide.

There are a number of ways to look at the net worth tax and compare across states. First, one could examine the percentage of corporate taxes raised through the net worth tax. By including the financial services tax as part of the net worth tax, Ohio raises almost 50.1 percent of its corporate tax revenues from the net worth tax (Table 10-1). No other state raises as much as a proportion to total corporate tax revenues. However, other states such as Pennsylvania taxes its corporations heavily through a 12.25 percent net worth tax. This is a much higher rate than Ohio's and potentially much more burdensome.

TABLE 10-18
Net Operating Loss Carry Forwards and Carry Backs

State	Carry Backs Allowed?	Carry Forwards Allowed?	No. of Years Carry Backs Allowed	No. of Years Carry Forwards Allowed
Ohio	No	Yes (Ohio loss only)	N/A	15
Illinois	Yes	Yes	3	15
Indiana	Yes	Yes	3	15
Iowa	Yes	Yes	3	15
Kentucky	Yes	Yes	3	15
Michigan	No. NOL is termed "business loss."	Yes. NOL is termed "business loss"	N/A	10
Minnesota	No	Yes	N/A	15
Missouri	Yes	Yes	3	15
Wisconsin	No	Yes	N/A	15
California	No	Yes	N/A	15
Colorado	No	Yes	N/A	15
Florida	No	Yes	N/A	15
Georgia	Yes	Yes	3	15
New Jersey	No	Yes	N/A	7
New York	Yes, limited to first $10T of loss for each year.	Yes, SAF, except limited to first $10T of loss.	3	15
North Carolina	No	Yes, net *economic* loss.	N/A	5
Pennsylvania	None allowed after the 1991 tax year.			

Source: 1993 Multistate Corporate Tax Guide.

Alternative taxes on assets or net worth have become more popular around the world over the last decade, but still are far from common.[32] Some European countries have such a tax. Germany levies a net assets tax with a rate between 0.6 and 0.75 percent, and this tax is not allowed as a deduction or a credit from the regular corporate income tax. Austria has a net asset tax with a rate of 1.35 percent, but this tax is allowed as a deduction from the regular corporate income tax. Norway uses a 0.3 percent tax on net assets, and no deduction is allowed from the corporate income tax.

Business taxes on assets have become particularly popular in Latin America.[33] Mexico implemented an alternative asset tax five years ago and since then many other countries in Latin America such as Argentina and Venezuela, have introduced some form of business asset tax. However, in Latin America this type of tax is actually used as an administrative measure for controlling evasion when the tax administration apparatus cannot make the corporate income tax work properly.[34] For this reason, asset taxes are al-

TABLE 10-19
Miscellaneous Taxes on Business Activities

State	Name of Tax	Tax Base	Tax Rate Schedule
Ohio	Two tier litter tax		
Illinois	Various	N/R	N/R
Indiana	Gross Income Tax	All gross receipts of a taxpayer with special exemptions and/or deductions	Varies
Iowa	N/A		
Kentucky	Corporation License Tax	Capital employed	.21%
Michigan	N/A		
Minnesota	N/A		
Missouri	N/A		
Wisconsin	N/R	N/R	N/R
California	N/A		
Colorado	N/A		
Florida	Intangibles Tax	Stocks, bonds, value of receivables on 1/1	1.5 mills.
Georgia	Net Worth Tax	Net Worth	$10 Minimum to $5,000 on net worth in excess of $22 million
New Jersey	Litter Control Tax	N/R	N/R
	Gross Income Tax Withholding	N/R	N/R
	Spill Compensation Tax	N/R	N/R
New York	Fixed Dollar Minimum	Predetermined dollar amounts, based on gross payroll	Varies
	Capital	Allocated business and investment capital	1.78 mills per $1 of allocated capital; .9 mills per $1 allocated subsidiary capital
	Organization Tax	Authorized and issued capital stock	.05 of 1% of par value; 5 cents per share of no par stock
North Carolina	Franchise Tax	Capital stock, surplus, and undivided profits	$1.50 per $1,000
Pennsylvania	Capital Stock/Franchise Tax	Fixed formula variation of capital stock	13 mills

Source: 1993 Multistate Corporate Tax Guide.

most always used as alternative minimum taxes creditable against the regular corporate income tax and often can be carried forward as a credit for several years.[35]

Advantages of a net worth or business assets tax. The most important advantage of the net worth tax is that it has provided the state with a more stable source of revenues over the years. The data in Table 10-21 show

TABLE 10-20
Unitary Business

State	Treatment of Unitary Business Combinations	Does Unitary Business Include Worldwide Activities?	Is a Water's-Edge Unitary Method Available?
Ohio	Optional only if the unitary members are Ohio taxpayers.	No	Yes, upon arrival.
Alabama	Not Allowed	N/A	N/A
Alaska	Required	Yes, until 1-92 for non-oil cos.	Yes, After 1-92.
Arizona	Required	No	No
Arkansas	Not Allowed	N/A	N/A
California	Required	Yes	Yes
Colorado	Required	No	Yes
Connecticut	Allows taxpayer to petition for an alternative allocation method.	N/A	N/A
Delaware	Not Allowed	N/A	N/A
Florida	Not Allowed	N/A	N/A
Georgia	Optional. State can force Unitary. Taxpayer cannot elect to apply it.	No	No
Hawaii	Required. State's option only.	No	Yes
Idaho	Required	Yes	Yes
Illinois	Required	No (Yes before 1982)	No (Water's-Edge after 1982)
Indiana	Optional for state and taxpayer.	Yes (Taxpayer's option)	Yes
Iowa	Not Allowed	N/A	N/A
Kansas	Required	No	No
Kentucky	Optional for state and taxpayer	No	Yes (All applications of unitary treatment)
Louisiana	Not Allowed	N/A	N/A
Maine	Required	No	No
Maryland	Not Allowed	N/A	N/A
Massachusetts	Not Allowed	No	No
Michigan	Not Allowed (but state can force)	No	No
Minnesota	Required	No	No
Mississippi	Not Allowed (but state can force)	No	No
Missouri	Not Allowed	N/A	N/A
Montana	Required	Yes	Yes (3-year renewable period)
Nebraska	Required	No	No
Nevada	No corporate tax		
New Hampshire	Required	No. (Dividends from foreign unitary affiliates are taxed after a foreign factor relief.)	No. (Water's-Edge is required.)

continued

TABLE 10-20 (continued)
Unitary Business

State	Treatment of Unitary Business Combinations	Does Unitary Business Include Worldwide Activities?	Is a Water's-Edge Unitary Method Available?
New Jersey	Not Allowed	N/A	N/A
New Mexico	Optional for taxpayer. State cannot force.	No	No
New York	Optional for state and taxpayer.	Yes. Alien corporations not included.	No
North Carolina	Not Allowed	N/A	N/A
North Dakota	Required. Commissioner may require or permit unitary treatment.	Yes	Yes
Oklahoma	Optional for state	No	Yes
Oregon	Required	No	No. Required by state.
Pennsylvania	Not Allowed	N/A	N/A
Rhode Island	N/A	N/A	N/A
South Carolina	Not Allowed	N/A	N/A
South Dakota	No corporate tax		
Tennessee	Optional for state	No	Yes
Texas	Not Allowed	N/A	N/A
Utah	Required	If taxpayer elects.	Yes
Vermont	Required. Note that unitary reporting for Vermont is NOT combined reporting.	No	No
Virginia	Not Allowed	N/A	N/A
Washington	No corporate Tax		
West Virginia	Taxpayer may request or state may force.	No	Yes, after formal request by taxpayer.
Wisconsin	Not Allowed. All corporations are taxed as separate entities.	N/A	N/A
Wyoming	No corporate tax		
D.C.	Not Allowed	N/A	N/A

Source: 1993 Multistate Corporate Tax Guide.

liabilities for the corporate franchise tax from 1988 to 1993, together with what the tax liability would have been had there been no net worth tax component in the present franchise tax. Of course, without adjustment of rates, revenues from the franchise tax would have been lower. But what is more important, revenues would have been less stable. The rate of change (positive or negative) from period to period is often twice as much for the franchise tax without the net worth tax as for the franchise tax with the net worth tax. The higher relative instability in the franchise tax without its net worth component is reflected in a coefficient of variation for this series that is double the size of the coefficient of variation for the series including the net

TABLE 10-21
Corporate Franchise Tax Liability With and Without Net Worth Tax Component, 1988–1993

Tax Year	Total with Net Worth	Percent Change over Previous Year	Total without Net Worth: Net Income Basis Only	Percent Change over Previous Year
1988	$719,430,413	---	$586,959,047	---
1989	771,130,137	7.2	645,077,393	9.9
1990	728,156,622	-5.6	585,163,816	-9.3
1991	650,538,338	-10.7	461,164,160	-21.2
1992	613,496,098	-5.7	429,994,616	-6.8
1993	630,040,000	2.7	422,805,000	-1.7
Coefficient of Variation*	0.083	---	0.166	---

Sources: Ohio Department of Taxation, *Annual Report* and our own computation.

*Computed on the ratio of the standard deviation to the mean value in the series.

worth tax. Thus, recent data confirm the intuition that the net worth component of the franchise tax adds stability to overall tax revenue collections.

Are there any other positive side benefits of the net worth tax? The other main advantage of taxes on net worth or assets is, as we have seen, as an administrative measure to control tax evasion and aggressive avoidance. Several other arguments have been used in defense of these taxes, but none is strong or completely convincing.

In the case of a closed economy with little mobility of capital, an asset tax tends to have the same effect as a land tax. It gives an incentive to owners of capital to put capital to its most productive use. One can hardly afford owning capital that is not being used to its full potential. But this argument hardly applies to Ohio or any other state because the economy is fully open and capital is mobile. In an open economy with capital mobility, the tax on net worth will encourage the exit of capital from the state or retard the entry of new capital. To the extent that Ohio taxes capital more heavily than other states (in a combination of property, net worth, and corporate income taxes), then state residents (either as consumers, workers, or owners of land) will tend to pay for the heavier capital taxation. Their payment may take the form of higher prices, lower wages, and lower prices of land or other fixed inputs.

Some economists have supported the idea of a tax on fixed assets because all marginal profits become tax exempt and economic activity is thus encouraged. But this does not apply to the Ohio franchise tax because higher marginal profits will eventually trigger the net income tax. Also important in the long run is the fact that capital assets are not fixed and; consequently, a net worth tax is not free of distortions. On the administrative side, asset taxes reduce the ability of interstate and international companies to do tax planning or transfer pricing schemes to reduce their tax liabilities.

Finally, an additional benefit of a net worth tax is its (potential) simplicity. This is a main reason why the tax has become more popular in developing economies. Tax administration in developing countries tends to be weaker, with limited capabilities to audit, for example, sophisticated tax companies. Taxing net worth is attractive because the tax base is easier to recognize by tax auditors and revenue collectors. As an economy develops, presumably the tax administration, itself, becomes more sophisticated and is better able to administer and audit income taxes, including those of larger multinational corporations.

Disadvantages of a net worth tax. The major problem with Ohio's corporate franchise tax is its net worth component. The unpopularity of the net worth tax among taxpayer corporations, as we will see, is not surprising. The net worth component has caused more litigation problems than any other aspect of the franchise tax. The most important criticisms and shortcomings of the net worth tax are examined in the following paragraphs.

The list of criticisms and shortcomings of the net worth tax is a long one. First, taxpayers feel that the net worth tax is unfair because it puts an additional burden on those companies that have had a bad year, with low income or net losses. The tax comes at a time when enterprises are least able to afford it, and thus it increases their financial risk. This may be particularly damaging to new companies, which often have several years of losses.[35] In 1993, $158 million was paid in net worth taxes (out of a total of $228 million) by corporations with zero or negative net incomes.

Second, the tax is horizontally inequitable because it depends on the structure of the business. Some business sectors may require more (or fewer) capitalization for technological reasons and consequently more (or less) risk and maturation periods for profit-making. In this sense, the net worth tax can be viewed as discriminatory—favoring enterprises that are lightly capitalized, such as those in the service sector, and penalizing enterprises more heavily capitalized, such as those in the manufacturing sector. Both types of companies would pay the net income tax in years of good performance, but in a recession those sectors that are more heavily capitalized may pay a much higher net worth tax.

Third, the net worth tax discriminates against companies with headquarters in Ohio. This arises from the fact that the property factor of the apportionment formula for the net worth tax situses to Ohio intangible assets such as bank deposits, investments in other businesses, and securities that the corporation owns outside Ohio. This penalty is more serious for the parent or holding companies domiciled in Ohio and for those who own most of their assets in intangibles. Discrimination against Ohio companies also arises from the inclusion in the "business done" factor of the net worth formula of receipts from intangible assets which are sitused to Ohio (and only for Ohio companies), regardless of where they may actually be used.

Fourth, the net worth tax is a source of double taxation. This arises first because the net worth tax falls on the same assets as are taxed by the property tax. The issue of double taxation of property has become more acute with the repeal in 1993 of the credit against the franchise tax for property taxes paid. That credit, it has been argued, helped equalize property tax burdens for companies located in different local jurisdictions across Ohio.[37] A second issue of double taxation arises when both parent company and subsidiaries located in Ohio have to pay the net worth tax. However, this form of double taxation is being partially addressed with the new credit for investment in qualified subsidiaries.

Fifth, the net worth tax makes taxpayer compliance much harder and costlier. Both tax bases under the franchise tax, net income and net worth, must be fully computed every year despite the fact that only one will be used. The computation of the net worth tax is especially cumbersome because it requires the situsing of every component in the balance sheet based on complex rules which in some instances go back at least half a century.[38]

Sixth, the net worth tax distorts the method of financing and it encourages thin capitalization. Corporations that add to their real assets by borrowing from a bank or issuing debt will not experience an increase in their net worth tax base. However, those corporations that purchase the same real assets financing them with new equity issues will experience an increase in the tax base by the entire amount of the investment. Thus, the marginal effective rate of taxation on the same asset goes from zero, if financed with debt, to a positive rate of taxation if the asset is not exempt. The effective marginal rate of taxation on any asset also depends on other provisions in the law, ranging from tax credits to depreciation rules.[39]

Seventh, the net worth tax may discourage investment in Ohio if the combination of the net income tax and net worth taxes imposes a tax burden on capital invested in Ohio that exceeds the average tax burden imposed on capital in all other states. A common view of the incidence of the corporate income tax is that the *average* burden imposed by corporate taxes may be paid by all capital owners across the nation. However, taxing capital investment more heavily than the average state will drive or keep investment out of this higher tax state as long as the after tax rate of return to capital is higher in other states. Because of the lower capital investment in the state, the tax burden of higher corporate taxes in reality is shifted to other factors of production in the state that are less mobile, such as labor and land.[40]

This tendency of the net worth tax to drive or keep out corporate investment in Ohio will be more pronounced in the more heavily capitalized sectors, such as manufacturing. Manufacturing has been the backbone of Ohio's economy, although it has suffered a considerable decline in recent times. The question is to what extent the net worth tax has been a significant contributing factor to this decline.

Apportionment Formulas

There are several important differences between the apportionment formulas for net income and net worth. The first and most obvious one is that net income is apportioned according to three factors (payroll, property, and sales, with the latter double-weighted), while net worth is apportioned according to two factors (property and sales). Less obvious but just as important is the fact that the definitions of the property and sales factors differ significantly in the two formulas.

The property factor in the net worth formula includes all types of assets: tangibles and intangibles. In contrast, the property factor in the net income formula includes only real and tangible personal property, including leasehold improvements and the value of rented property. The inclusion of intangibles in the net worth formula has created problems for situsing the property and has given corporations an incentive to establish their legal domiciles outside of Ohio.

The "business done" factor in the net worth formula is also a wider concept than the receipts from sales used in the net income formula. The business done factor includes not only sales of tangible property and revenue from services but also rents and royalties, dividends and interest, patent copyrights, and in some cases the sale of assets.[41] Dividends, interest, royalties, and other intangible income are treated as allocable income under the net income tax and, therefore, do not enter the net income apportionment formula.

The differences in the two formulas highlight some contradictions in the philosophy underlying the two components of Ohio's franchise tax. Under the net income base, a larger part of the tax is shifted to taxpayers outside Ohio by the fact that the sales factor is double weighted. The exclusion of allocable income from the sales factor also has the same effect, since its inclusion would increase the numerator of the factor more than the denominator. The exclusion of intangible property in the property factor of the net income tax also favors Ohio companies, since most of the intangible property would be sitused in Ohio.

Under the net worth tax, the computation of the two factor formula shifts the tax burden more towards Ohio corporations. This is because income from intangible assets is included in the business factor and intangible assets are included in the property factor. As a consequence, Ohio companies experience an increase in both factors vis-a-vis non-Ohio companies, since most intangible property and income have an Ohio situs.

As discussed above, Ohio statutes do not address the issue of what to do with the factors in the net income apportionment formula when part of the corporation's business takes place in a state that has no corporate income tax. By not adjusting the formula to these circumstances corporations actually obtain a lower tax. Some states have adopted adjustments in the formula by following a "throwback" rule, which assigns to the factor numerator of the taxing state the activity carried out in the states without a corporation tax, or a "throw out" rule, which eliminates from both the numerator and the denominator of the factor the activities carried out in the noncorporate tax states.

Reporting: Separate Entity Versus Combined Income Reporting

Most economists would agree that combined income reporting is the only sensible way to go about apportioning income to a state for any corporation that is part of a unitary or related business operating in that state or several states.[42]

The present approach of giving the option to file with combined income reporting when some minimum requirements are met almost certainly guarantees that the only groups of corporations filing combined reports are those that can reduce their tax liability by doing so. Other corporations that use intercorporate transactions within and out of the state for tax planning purposes are not expected, of course, to file combined income reports.

The Tax Commissioner can require combined income reporting for a group of interrelated corporations. In practice this has been a complex and litigious process. In addition, the statutes also limit the initiative of the Commissioner in this respect. For example, since 1992 interest payments between related members, or charges for the use of intangible property, cannot be considered sufficient grounds for requiring combined income reporting.[43]

Thus, the important issue here is how much income tax is avoided in Ohio because the majority of the corporations file as separate entities. Separate entity reporting leaves open many potential loopholes for tax avoidance. These range from the most apparent and well-known, such as the use of out-of-state passive investment companies (better known as Delaware holding companies), to the more sophisticated (and harder to detect) transfer pricing schemes.

Some of these problems have been addressed with recent legislation in Ohio. The reform of the franchise tax law in 1991 ("Budget Bill" Am. Sub. H. 298) had two main objectives. The first was to make Ohio corporations take over certain gains recognized by "non taxpayer" (for Ohio purposes) related entities. The second was to deny Ohio corporations deductions for interest and other intangible expenses (such as charges for the use of intangible property, royalties, patents, copyright fees and licensing fees) paid to "related entities" which for the most part are passive investment companies ("Delaware holding companies 11).[44]

There are other significant forms of intra-unitary transactions that the 1991 reform did not address. These include the use of affiliated non-Ohio companies to hold assets generating investment income, the overstatement of costs and understatement of revenues through transfer pricing, and changes in location to avoid the situsing of assets to Ohio. To be fair, there is no law that can be comprehensive enough to deal with all these issues. But being able to take care of all these issues is the fundamental advantage of combined income reporting.

Minimum Tax

The minimum tax of $50 in Ohio may be too low. It has not been changed for many years despite inflation. In fact, the actual amount of $50 may now be under what it actually costs the Department of Taxation to process a tax return.

Taxing Interest From Federal and Ohio Securities

At present Ohio exempts interest from both federal government and State of Ohio securities. This conforms with the practice of many other states. In order to tax federal interest income it would be necessary to tax Ohio interest income. There are some states that do this. The attraction of this option is that it would facilitate the coverage of financial institutions under the general franchise tax. Banks and other financial institutions earn a good portion of their income from holding federal government securities in their portfolios.

Allocation Versus Apportionment Of Income

Is there a good rationale for keeping the distinction between allocable and apportionable income? Should this distinction be reformed, or even abandoned? Actually there are at least twelve states that do not distinguish between allocable and apportionable income. These are known as "full apportionment states."[45] Many other states, including Ohio, distinguish between allocable and apportionable income. Most often what is apportionable and what is allocable income depends on whether the income is defined as business or non-business income, respectively. Business income is generally defined as that earned during the regular course of business.[46]The presumption for the distinction lies in the fact that some income is not earned by the application of factors of production but simply by the corporate entity itself, and these should be sitused where the corporation is domiciled. For example, dividend income from shares of other companies is considered to be earned by the corporation in a way that is different from the income derived from production and sale of goods and services. Many of the distinctions, such as royalties and technical service fees as passive income, have little economic justification. Ohio is among the few states that make no distinction between business and non-business income but instead allocate certain types of income.

As in other areas of corporate state taxation, the potential for double taxation of certain types of income increases, because the same income may be considered apportionable in one state and allocable in a different state.

The clear incentive for "headquarters" states is to classify income as allocable, because 100 percent of it is taxed in the state. The disadvantage is that a very aggressive position on allocable income may cause some corporations to choose a different state for domicile. States with relatively few or important company headquarters may have revenue advantages with the "full apportionment" approach.

The Use of Corporate Limited Partnerships as a Way to Avoid the Franchise Tax

Partnerships, and in particular corporate partnerships, have been used for some time as a vehicle for tax planning. Multistate corporations may take advantage of different regulations to structure transactions across states boundaries to minimize taxes. One fundamental issue that arises with corporate partners that have no direct business activities in a state is whether or not the corporate partner has tax nexus in the state because of its interest in the partnership doing business in the state. Most states, including Ohio, consider the corporate partner to have nexus in the 46 state.[47] Fewer states treat the partner's distributive share as income from an intangible asset, and they source the income to the situs of the asset, i.e., to the state where the corporate partner has its domicile. The revenue implications of choosing between the two regimes will differ from state to state, depending on the number and importance of out-of-state corporate partners and state domiciled corporations entering partnerships outside the state.

An increasing loophole has appeared in recent times, with non-Ohio corporations taking a limited partnership interest, directly or indirectly through wholly owned non-Ohio subsidiaries in an Ohio partnership. As opposed to the case of a general partnership interest in which the non Ohio corporation or its subsidiaries are declared to have nexus in Ohio, limited partners are treated as individual stockholders and through multi layering of subsidiaries may avoid income taxes entirely.

Ohio has recently adopted legislation recognizing the new business form of "limited liability company. " In practice, this business form is taxed as a partnership that has only limited partners. The important issue here is that this new development could be used for tax avoidance schemes similar to those now being used with limited partnerships.

There are no easy solutions to the problem created by the use of limited partnerships by out-of-state corporations to escape the franchise tax in Ohio. Probably the simplest solution would be to change the law so that corporate limited partners can be ruled to have nexus in Ohio and, therefore, be subject to the corporate franchise tax. However, this approach may face many legal hurdles. A second solution, currently being studied by the Department of Taxation, is to use a withholding system in which the flow-through entity is treated as a taxable entity, and the upstream corporations are credited for taxes already paid. A third solution is for the state of Ohio to adopt mandatory combined income reporting. Relying on discretionary rulings by the Tax Commissioner to require combined income reporting would be very likely too time consuming and, given the past history of similar rulings, ineffective.

Municipal Income Taxes

About 500 local jurisdictions in Ohio levy individual and business income taxes. These taxes represent a significant source of revenue for local governments. One important issue is that this system of local taxation imposes heavy compliance costs on businesses because almost every jurisdiction has a different tax, with variations in the tax base, filing dates, and other administrative procedures. In the extreme case, an Ohio company would have to file close to 500 different taxes with complex administrative and appeal procedures.[48]

Membership in UDITPA

There would be several benefits derived from joining the Multistate Tax Compact (MTC) and subscribing to the Uniform Division of Income for Tax Purposes Act. Many other states do follow UDITPA, although often with some modifications. A selected sample of states that do follow UDITPA is shown in Table 10-11. Among the most important benefits of joining the MTC are easy tax coordination with many other states that have joined the Tax Compact, use of the multistate audits of some corporations undertaken by the Tax Compact, and access to the interpretative rulings for difficult-to-tax economic sectors. On the other hand, Ohio has in its own way adopted many of the rules in UDITPA, and joining would not be cost free. The move might be regarded as anti-business, and the state would have to change important aspects of the franchise tax to adapt to UDITPA.

REFORM OPTIONS AND IMPLICATIONS

REFORMING THE NET WORTH TAX

One major reform option is to *repeal the net worth component* of the franchise tax. The new corporate franchise tax would be based exclusively on the present corporate profit or net income.

The overall impact of this change is shown in columns 2 and 3 of Table 10-22. The overall franchise tax liabilities for 1993 would have decreased from $630 million to $434 million, approximately a 31 percent decline. The elimination of the net worth tax would not affect those corporations that were already paying the net income tax, because this was the higher of either the net worth tax or the net income tax. The corporations that would benefit from the reform are those corporations that were paying the net worth tax. However, some of these corporations that had positive net income would now pay the net income tax. This "residual" net income tax would have amounted to approximately $32 million, and this is included in the total net income tax in column 3 of Table 10-22 of $434 million. The simple repeal of the net worth tax basis produces winners by all asset sizes and in all economic sectors, although winners are concentrated among the largest companies by net worth size.

The repeal of the net worth tax may be accompanied by several additional reforms. A central consideration of the complementary reforms is whether the entire package is to be made revenue-neutral. That is, do the new taxes make up for the losses in revenues represented by the elimination of the net worth tax? Or should no attempt be made to fully recover the lost revenues with the corporate franchise tax, leaving this task perhaps to other elements of the tax structure?

Revenue-neutral reform options. There are, of course, many possibilities that can be devised within the corporate income tax to make up for the revenue losses caused by the repeal of the net worth component. They range from the introduction of a new separate tax on assets to changes in the base and rate of the net income tax. Combinations of several or all of these options could also be used instead of one simple option.

Here we consider three basic options: (i) the introduction of a new net worth tax that differs from the old tax in base, rate, and apportionment formula; (ii) the introduction of a new asset tax, and (iii) an increase in the rate of the net income tax. Changes in the structure of the present net income

TABLE 10-22
Reforming the Franchise Tax: Eliminating Old Net Worth Tax, Revenue Neutral Option 1

Net Worth Tax Using Reduced Base and Income Tax Combined
Revised Tax Rate = 0.138%

Net Worth	Base Corporate Tax	Income Tax	Reduced Base Net Worth Tax	Calculated Corporate Tax	Winners	Losers	Even
Less than 1	$35,862,764	$32,484,779	$1,586,750	$34,071,529	0%	2%	98%
Over 1 - 200,000	32,249,202	22,648,858	78,480	22,727,338	12%	4%	84%
200,001 - 500,000	25,889,826	17,056,832	114,562	17,171,395	71%	26%	3%
500,001 - 2,500,000	62,081,815	41,957,122	991,836	42,948,958	37%	61%	2%
2,500,001 - 5,000,000	27,672,764	20,612,339	1,667,925	22,280,264	24%	76%	0%
5,000,001 - 20,000,000	69,590,881	51,720,568	5,902,115	57,622,683	.20%	80%	0%
20,000,001 - 100,000,000	104,136,346	71,945,004	35,356,683	107,301,687	63%	36%	1%
100,000,001 - 250,000,000	62,431,082	43,731,704	26,183,638	69,915,342	31%	44%	25%
250,000,001 - 500,000,000	50,38,1815	32,558,519	29,098,608	61,657,127	40%	60%	0%
500,000, 001 - 750,000,000	27,084,813	15,493,821	34,332,427	49,826,248	18%	80%	2%
750,000,001 - 1,000,000,000	11,590,126	6,955,357	39,439,230	46,394,587	43%	57%	0%
Over 1 Billion	121,069,256	76,910,625	21,507,447	98,418,072	42%	58%	0%
Grand Total	$630,040,690	$434,075,528	$196,259,702	$630,335,230	17%	19%	0.65

Economic Sectors	Base Corporate Tax	Income Tax	Reduced Base Net Worth Tax	Calculated Corporate Tax	Winners	Losers	Even
Agriculture, Forestry, and Fishing	$2,886,417	$1,822,435	$49,663	$1,872,098	0%	100%	0%
Mining	12,495,690	4,519,910	2,081,746	6,601,656	73%	19%	7%
Construction	22,223,744	16,288,119	1,731,008	18,019,127	52%	42%	5%
Manufacturing	288,514,301	215,100,251	84,620,539	299,720,790	42%	48%	10%
Transportation	50,709,262	30,443,411	5,230,586	35,673,997	66%	24%	11%
Wholesale Trade	50,174,092	36,713,264	13,474,041	50,187,305	30%	32%	38%
Retail Trade	67,201,264	52,503,273	6,217,814	58,721,087	44%	49%	7%
Finance, Insurance, and Real Estate	55,122,385	26,130,085	71,486,014	97,616,100	33%	61%	7%
Services	60,897,755	40,282,818	8,252,912	48,535,730	18%	14%	69%
Unclassified	19,815,780	10,271,961	3,115,379	13,387,340	0%	3%	97%
Grand Total	$630,040,689	$434,075,528	$196,259,702	$630,335,230	17%	19%	65%

tax, such as changes in credits or adjustments to taxable income, would not by themselves make up for the revenue gap produced by the repeal of the net worth tax. More importantly, changes in the structure of the net income tax should be considered in terms of their impact on horizontal equity, economic development, and other objectives rather than in terms of their impact on revenue.

(i) *New net worth tax.* The new net worth tax would be paid by all corporations, including those paying the net income tax. It would be structured in a way that eliminates the main problems now existing with the net worth basis of the franchise tax. The tax base would comprise the corporation's equity account (capital stock net of treasury stock, additional paid-in capital, and retained earnings) and the apportionment ratio would be the three-factor double-weighted sales formula currently used for the net income tax.

The most important change in the tax base of this new net worth tax vis-a-vis the current net worth tax would be the elimination of reserves and deferred taxes. These changes could be justified to the extent that both deferred taxes and reserves are set to offset future liabilities, and in that sense they should not be considered as part of the corporation's net worth. However, this is a debatable point.

In particular, some reserves are set against future contingent liabilities which may never materialize. The level of reserves a corporation sets aside differs by type of business and other characteristics including management style. Even though most businesses have limits on how much they can put into reserves and for how long they will be able to hold idle reserves, it is clear that their exclusion from the net worth tax base is an opportunity for tax avoidance and a source of uneven tax treatment among otherwise similar firms. The data in Table 10-23 show the ratio of reserves and deferred taxes to total net worth by size of firm (measured by net worth) and by economic sector, based on sample data from 1,377 corporation returns for 1993. These sample data show wide variations in the ratio, ranging from close to zero to 10 percent. On the other hand, the inclusion of reserves can lead to the unequal treatment of corporations with equal "long term" net worth.

The inclusion or exclusion of reserves in the tax base will simply translate into a lower or higher tax rate that will need to be applied to attain the revenue target. We used a sample of tax returns to simulate the new net worth as if it had been in effect in 1993.[49] These simulations are presented in the fourth column of Table 10-22. Besides the reduced base for the new net worth tax and the same apportionment formula as for the net income tax, we assume a tax rate of 0.138 percent for the new tax. This rate is dictated by the condition of revenue neutrality for the entire reform option: elimination of the current net worth tax, universal application of the net income tax, and introduction of the new net worth tax with overall revenue neutrality. Table 10-22 is constructed to include the overall or combined tax burden of a universal net income tax and the new net worth tax by asset size and economic sector in the fifth column.

The rate structure of the new net worth tax could be chosen to have different profiles, including other flat rates which will not allow revenue neutrality for the entire package. With revenue neutrality, as simulated in Table 10-22, 19 percent of the corporations would be losers, i.e., would pay a higher combined net income and new net worth tax. The clear net losers are those corporations now paying net income tax which would also have to pay the new net worth tax. Some corporations now paying the net worth tax may also be losers if they have enough positive net income. The simulations show that 17 percent of the corporations would be winners: they would be paying a lower combined tax than under the present franchise tax. The winners would be corporations with low or negative net incomes that are now paying

TABLE 10-23
Ratio of Deferred Taxes and Reserves to Total Net Worth, by Economic Sector and Net Worth Size

Economic Sectors	
Agriculture, Forestry, and Fishing	0.0129
Mining	0.0755
Construction	0.0166
Manufacturing	0.0491
Transportation	0.0981
Wholesale Trade	0.0281
Retail Trade	0.083
Finance, Insurance, and Real Estate	0.0907
Services	0.0122
Unclassified	0.0251

Net Worth ($)	
1	0.0268
200,000	0.0002
500,000	0.1073
2,500,000	0.0255
5,000,000	0.022
20,000,000	0.0397
100,000,000	0.077
250,000,000	0.0477
500,000,000	0.0802
750,000,000	0.0832
1,000,000,000	0.0446
Over 1 billion	0.0825

Source: Based on sample data from 1,377 franchise tax returns.

the net worth tax at a 0.582 percent rate rather than the 0.138 percent rate used in the simulations for the new net worth tax.

Although the majority of corporations, 65 percent, would not be affected by the changes in the net worth tax, the vast majority of these companies are those with net worth between $0 and $200,000.

The winners and losers by size of net worth and by economic sector, as shown in the last three columns of Table 10-22, are quite evenly distributed. Average-size firms in terms of net worth and those in the mining and transport sectors are the more likely winners.

This revenue-neutral simulation allows us to focus on the other important goals of reform. Despite the fact that they produce equal revenues, the universal net income tax combined with a new net worth tax would be generally preferable to the present net worth tax because it would be more horizontally equitable and produce less economic distortion, such as penalization of new enterprises and penalization of corporations domiciled in Ohio. However, the new net worth tax still would discriminate among companies depending on how much of their assets were financed with debt and how much were financed with equity. The next set of revenue-neutral simulations would address this issue.

(ii) *New total assets tax.* An alternative to the new net worth tax is a tax on total (nonexempt) assets. The advantage of the assets tax, vis-a-vis a net worth tax, is that the formula does not discriminate among types of financing; and, therefore, it does not induce thin capitalization. The simulations in Table 10-24 are based again on the premise that the new total assets tax will

TABLE 10-24
Reforming the Franchise Tax: Eliminating Old Net Worth Tax, Revenue Neutral Option 2

Gross Assets Tax and Income Tax Combined
Net Assets Tax Rate = 0.0562%

Net Worth	Base Corporate Tax	Income Tax	Total Asset Tax	Calculated Corporate Tax	Winners	Losers	Even
Less than 1	$35,862,764	$32,484,779	$2,985,589	$35,470,368	0	0.04	0.96
Over 1 - 200,000	35,862,764	22,648,858	107,702	22,756,560	0.14	0.06	0.8
200,001 - 500,000	25,889,826	17,056,832	250,079	17,306,912	0.62	0.18	0.2
500,001 - 2,500,000	62,081,815	41,957,122	818,900	42,776,021	0.42	0.39	0.19
2,500,001 - 5,000,000	27,672,764	20,612,339	1,206,501	21,818,840	0.24	0.59	0.18
5,000,001 - 20,000,000	69,590,881	51,720,568	4,434,451	56,155,019	0.2	0.72	0.08
20,000,001 - 100,000,000	104,136,346	71,945,004	63,873,004	135,818,009	0.59	0.4	0.01
100,000,001 - 250,000,000	62,431,082	43,731,704	24,813,989	68,545,693	0.38	0.38	0.25
250,000,001 - 500,000,000	50,381,815	32,558,519	26,021,706	58,580,225	0.4	0.6	0
500,000, 001 - 750,000,000	27,084,813	15,493,821	26,294,948	41,788,769	0.53	0.46	0.02
750,000,001 - 1,000,000,000	11,590,126	6,955,357	28,661,292	35,616,649	0.43	0.57	0
Over 1 Billion	121,069,256	76,910,625	17,288,963	94,199,588	0.56	0.44	0
Grand Total	$630,040,690	$434,075,528	$196,757,125	$630,832,653	0.18	0.18	0.65

Economic Sectors	Base Corporate Tax	Income Tax	Total Asset Tax	Calculated Corporate Tax	Winners	Losers	Even
Agriculture, Forestry and Fishing	$2,886,417	$1,822,435	$45,102	$1,867,537	0	0.6	0.4
Mining	12,495,690	4,519,910	2,548,231	7,068,141	0.57	0.31	0.12
Construction	22,223,744	16,288,119	1,238,843	17,526,962	0.52	0.28	0.2
Manufacturing	288,514,301	215,100,251	67,156,507	282,256,758	0.45	0.44	0.11
Transportation	50,709,262	3,044,341	4,528,256	34,971,668	0.66	0.27	0.07
Wholesale Trade	50,174,092	36,713,264	18,838,865	55,552,129	0.32	0.46	0.21
Retail Trade	67,201,264	52,503,273	6,744,377	59,247,650	0.44	0.37	0.19
Finance, Insurance, and Real Estate	55,122,385	26,130,085	83,525,498	109,655,583	0.33	0.57	0.11
Services	60,897,755	40,282,818	9,987,571	50,270,389	0.17	0.13	0.69
Unclassified	19,815,780	10,271,961	2,143,876	12,415,837	0.01	0.02	0.97
Grand Total	$630,040,689	$434,075,528	$196,757,125	$630,823,653	0.18	0.18	0.65

have to generate enough revenue to cover the revenue gap produced by the elimination of the present net worth tax. Revenue neutrality would have required a tax rate on total assets of 0.056 percent in 1993. The simulations in Table 10-24 are performed using the apportionment ratio from the net income tax.

The distribution by size of net worth and economic sector of the total assets tax is presented in the fourth column of Table 10-24. The combined burden of the universal net income tax and the new total assets tax is presented in the fifth column. Overall, the distribution of the combined burden by size of net worth and economic sector is quite similar to that in the previous simulation with the "new net worth tax." The percentages of corporations that are winners and losers are almost identical in the aggregate. However, there are more significant differences by net worth size and economic sector of the corporations. These differences between the two sets of simulations highlight the relative arbitrariness of either tax base, as the ratio of net worth to total assets is likely to differ from corporation to corporation for multiple reasons.

Either tax, the new net worth or the total assets tax, still presents the problems of all asset taxes discussed in Section 3 of this chapter. They impose a significant burden on enterprises when they may be least able to afford it, and in particular they penalize new enterprises which tend to go through several years of losses. Either of these taxes may be more acceptable or justifiable at lower levels as a way to charge corporations for the use of public services at the state level.[50] This possibility is further discussed below.

(iii) *Raising the rate of the net income tax.* An alternative way to cover the revenue gap produced by the elimination of the net worth tax is to raise the rate of the net income tax. This simulation is presented in Table 10-25. Based on 1993 tax returns, revenue neutrality would have required an increase in the rate of 3.86 percentage points for net incomes above $50,000. The new tax rate for net incomes over $50,000 would have been 12.76 percent, by comparison to the current rate of 8.9 percent. This would have made Ohio the state with the highest corporate income tax rate. At present, the highest rate is Pennsylvania's 12.25 percent. The simulations assume that the current rate of 5.1 percent for net incomes below $50,000 stays the same. The intended effect in the distribution of tax burdens is a more skewed distribution, since now only those companies with positive net incomes would pay tax. However, companies that now are paying the net worth tax will not necessarily be large winners from this change. There are quite a few corporations paying the net worth tax at the present time that do have positive net incomes, and these companies would have to pay the new net income tax at a considerably higher rate.

Non-revenue-neutral reform options. As we have seen in the second section, some states have along with the corporate net income tax a corporate

TABLE 10-25
Reforming the Franchise Tax: Eliminating Old Net Worth Tax, Revenue Neutral Option 3

Levy Additional Income tax on Net Income over $50,000
New Tax Rate = 3.86%

Net Worth ($)	Base Corporate Tax	Income Tax	Additional Income Tax	Calculated Corporate Tax	Winners	Losers	Even
Less than 1	$35,862,764	$32,484,779	$12,653,125	$45,137,904	0%	1%	99%
Over 1 - 200,000	32,249,202	22,648,858	1,080,760	23,729,619	14%	1%	86%
200,001 - 500,000	25,889,826	17,056,832	993,127	18,049,960	71%	13%	16%
500,001 - 2,500,000	62,081,815	41,957,122	11,892,096	53,849,217	42%	58%	1%
2,500,001 - 5,000,000	27,672,764	20,612,339	11,041,390	31,653,729	24%	76%	0%
5,000,001 - 20,000,000	69,590,881	51,720,568	24,143,682	75,864,250	24%	76%	0%
20,000,001 - 100,000,000	104,136,346	71,945,004	39,450,860	111,395,864	74%	25%	1%
100,000,001 - 250,000,000	62,431,082	43,731,704	22,449,196	66,180,900	44%	31%	25%
250,000,001 - 500,000,000	50,381,815	32,558,519	18,573,129	51,131,647	45%	16%	38%
500,000,001 - 750,000,000	27,084,813	15,493,821	13,282,754	28,776,575	19%	80%	2%
750,000,001 - 1,000,000,000	11,590,126	6,955,357	4,460,811	11,416,168	56%	44%	0%
Over 1 Billion	121,069,256	76,910,625	35,909,783	112,820,407	43%	57%	0%
Grand Total	$630,040,690	$434,075,528	$195,930,712	$630,006,240	20%	13%	67%

Economic Sectors	Base Corporate Tax	Income Tax	Additional Income Tax	Calculated Corporate Tax	Winners	Losers	Even
Agriculture, Forestry, and Fishing	$2,886,417	$1,822,435	$532,426	$2,354,861	0%	60%	40%
Mining	12,495,690	4,519,910	2,079,680	6,599,590	73%	20%	7%
Construction	22,223,744	16,288,119	7,215,950	23,504,070	52%	36%	11%
Manufacturing	288,514,301	215,100,251	111,162,795	326,263,046	51%	40%	9%
Transportation	50,709,262	30,443,411	9,651,634	40,095,046	66%	25%	9%
Wholesale Trade	50,174,092	36,713,264	13,743,347	50,456,611	40%	22%	38%
Retail Trade	67,201,264	52,503,273	21,148,548	73,651,821	44%	51%	5%
Finance, Insurance, and Real Estate	55,122,385	26,130,085	10,205,405	36,335,490	43%	23%	34%
Services	60,897,755	40,282,818	16,672,171	56,954,990	20%	12%	69%
Unclassified	19,815,780	10,271,961	3,518,754	13,790,715	1%	1%	99%
Grand Total	$630,040,689	$434,075,528	$195,930,712	$630,006,240	20%	13%	67%

franchise tax based on net worth or assets, which is capped at some maximum payment. In addition, these taxes may have a flat rate or a graduated rate. This form of taxation has been conventionally justified as a minimum payment for the privilege of doing business in the state or as a minimum contribution for the use of services provided by the state, regardless of the profitability of the corporation. The final form such a tax may take is varied. One such schedule, which has been suggested by the business community, is presented in Table 10-26.[51] It presents a graduated system of tax payments starting at $250 for those corporations with net worth (net capital stock plus additional paid-in capital plus retained earnings) below $10,000; it adds $500 more in payment for net worth between $10,000 and $50,000, and so on; and it is capped with a payment of $25,000 for net worth of over $100 million.[52] Note that this option would change the minimum tax payment of the franchise, currently at $50 to $250.

One important implication of using this form of declining schedule as opposed to a flat tax rate, for example, is that it tends to be regressive. This is clear from inspection of Table 10-26. At the mean value of the first bracket the marginal and average rates represented by the payment for the bracket are 5 percent. The corresponding payment for the next-to-last bracket represents a marginal rate of 0.04 percent and an average rate of 0.14 percent, both evaluated at the mean value of the bracket.

Table 10-27 shows the results of a simulation using the schedule shown in Table 10-26 and assumes the current net worth tax base, apportionment formula. The simulations show that revenue from this tax will decrease slightly from $630 million to $576 million. The losers will be concentrated in the lower net worth categories. In terms of industry classification, all industries have a high proportion of losses if this type of tax is imposed.

A different option is simply to reduce the net worth tax base, by defining the base as made up of net capital stock, paid in capital, and retained earnings. Several rate simulations were run on this base. First we set the net worth tax rate at 0.1 percent. This yielded a loss of tax revenue of approximately $54 million, approximately 6 percent of corporate tax revenue. With a net worth tax rate of 0.075 percent, revenue loss increased to $89 million, or for 14 percent of current tax revenues, with a rate of 0.05 percent, rev-

TABLE 10-26
Tax "Rate" Schedule for the New Net Worth Tax Proposed by the Private Sector

Net Worth ($)	Tax ($)
0 -10,000	250
10,001- 50,000	500
50,001 - 100,000	1,000
100,001 - 250,000	2,500
250,001 - 500,000	5,000
500,001 - 750,000	7,500
750,001 - 1,000,000	10,000
1,000,001 - 10, 000,000	15,000
10,000,001 - 100,000,000	20,000
Over 100,000,000	25,000

TABLE 10-27
Reforming the Franchise Tax: Replacing Net Worth Tax with Capped Net Worth Tax, Non-Revenue Neutral Option 4

Net Worth Tax Using Fixed Tax Liability for Each Level of Net Worth

Net Worth	Base Corporate Tax	Income Tax	Reduced Base Net Worth Tax	Calculated CorporateTax	Winners	Losers	Even
Less than 1	$35,862,764	$32,484,779	$2,369,110	$34,853,889	0%	100%	0%
Over 1 - 200,000	32,249,202	22,648,858	1,984,243	24,633,101	0%	100%	0%
200,001 - 500,000	25,889,826	17,056,832	1,486,114	18,542,946	0%	100%	0%
500,001 - 2,500,000	62,081,815	41,957,122	8,750,593	50,707,715	0%	100%	0%
2,500,001 - 5,000,000	27,672,764	20,612,339	6,484,011	27,096,350	24%	76%	0%
5,000,001 - 20,000,000	69,590,881	51,720,568	12,673,574	64,394,142	15%	85%	0%
20,000,001 - 100,000,000	104,136,346	71,945,004	48,808,100	120,753,104	25%	75%	0%
100,000,001 - 250,000,000	62,431,082	43,731,704	25,239,431	68,971,135	16%	84%	0%
250,000,001 - 500,000,000	50,381,815	32,558,519	15,551,377	48,109,895	40%	60%	0%
500,000,001 - 750,000,000	27,084,813	15,493,821	6,771,767	22,265,588	7%	93%	0%
750,000,001 - 1,000,000,000	11,590,126	6,955,357	5,975,200	12,930,557	44%	56%	0%
Over 1 Billion	121,069,256	76,910,625	6,161,162	83,071,787	30%	70%	0%
Grand Total	$630,040,690	$434,075,528	$142,254,682	$576,330,210	7%	93%	0%

Economic Sectors	Base Corporate Tax	Income Tax	Reduced Base Net Worth Tax	Calculated Corporate Tax	Winners	Losers	Even
Agriculture, Forestry and Fishing	$2,886,417	$1,822,435	$102,685	$1,925,119	0%	100%	0%
Mining	12,495,690	4,519,910	2,205,200	6,725,109	24%	76%	0%
Construction	22,223,744	16,288,119	5,138,173	21,426,293	8%	92%	0%
Manufacturing	288,514,301	215,100,251	68,865,033	283,965,284	23%	77%	0%
Transportation	50,709,262	30,443,411	6,383,597	36,827,008	7%	93%	0%
Wholesale Trade	50,174,092	36,713,264	13,783,118	50,496,382	13%	87%	0%
Retail Trade	67,201,264	52,503,273	7,704,923	60,208,196	11%	89%	0%
Finance, Insurance, and Real Estate	55,122,385	26,130,085	17,188,001	43,318,086	20%	80%	0%
Services	60,897,755	40,282,818	16,547,712	56,830,531	3%	97%	0%
Unclassified	19,815,780	10,271,961	4,336,240	14,608,201	0%	100%	0%
Grand Total	$630,040,689	$434,075,528	$142,254,682	$576,330,209	7%	93%	0%

enue losses increased to approximately $124 million, or about 20 percent of current tax revenues, and with a rate of a 0.01 percent, revenue losses amounted to $182 million, or approximately 28 percent of current revenues. In all these simulations the majority of taxpayers were not affected, and the number of winners and losers were of similar magnitude. Losers were concentrated in mining, construction, manufacturing and transportation, while winners were concentrated in wholesale and retail trade.

OTHER REFORM OPTIONS

Coverage. The corporate franchise tax at present gives special treatment to corporations that are financial depositary institutions and exempts corporations in other sectors, most importantly public utilities, telecommunications companies, and insurance companies, which are subject to special taxation regimes. Although at some point there may have been justification for the special tax regimes, such as the existence of monopoly power, or difficulties in administering and enforcing a franchise tax in these sectors, most of these reasons have now largely or completely disappeared. An important option for reform of the franchise tax is to make its coverage universal to all business corporations. There should not be any major difficulty in doing this, as long as those corporations thrown back into the general regime are subject to the federal corporate income tax. This universal coverage option under the corporate franchise tax does not preclude special taxation regimes, of course, because of the difficulty in applying sales taxes to financial institutions and insurance companies, and the desirability of excise taxation of some utility services.

Apportionment formulas. Several options for reform should be considered in the apportionment formulas of the franchise tax. First we examine the options with respect to the apportionment formula for the net income tax. Next, we discuss options for the apportionment formula for the net worth tax, if this tax is to be kept in some form.

Heavier weight to sales in the net income formula? During the past decade, we have seen many states, including Ohio, that have used modified apportionment formulas. The most common modification has been the switch to a double-weighted sales factor in the traditional three-factor formula. The latter is the apportionment formula used for the net income tax component in Ohio's franchise tax. Several states have adopted formulas that give the sales factor an even larger weight, including the use of the sales ratio as the only factor in the formula.

The fundamental reason for adopting formulas giving more weight to the sales factor is to decrease the tax burden of companies with property and payroll in the state and increase it for out-of-state companies selling (but not producing) commodities within the state. The longer term goal of this policy is to encourage the location of businesses in the state.

The issue is whether the State of Ohio should consider a single-factor sales formula for the net income tax. The answer may be yes if the objective is to let Ohio become more competitive in attracting business locations vis-a-vis other states that already have adopted modified apportionment formulas. This statement does not assume that changes in the apportionment formula and therefore in state franchise taxes are decisive in affecting business location. However, this is an issue on which there is no convincing empirical evidence one way or another.[53] It should also be understood that the competitive margin granted by modifications in the formula would be erased as soon as other states introduced similar modifications in the apportionment formula.

To explore the impact of switching to a single sales factor for the net income tax in Ohio, we ran a simulation isolating this factor from any other changes. The results are presented in Table 10-28. The move would have

TABLE 10-28
Simulation Results of Moving to a Single Sales Factor for the Net Income Tax

Net Worth ($)	Base Corporate Tax	New Corporate Tax	Winners	Losers	Even
Less than 1	$35,862,764	$34,735,433	0.6%	0.4%	99.0%
Over 1 - 200,000	32,249,202	2,222,534	1.4%	0.0%	98.6%
200,001 - 500,000	25,889,826	2,118,991	20.2%	1.5%	78.3%
500,001 - 2,500,000	62,081,815	21,540,353	31.4%	8.0%	60.6%
2,500,001 - 5,000,000	27,672,764	19,932,529	66.1%	6.8%	27.1%
5,000,001 - 20,000,000	69,590,881	45,915,902	57.1%	13.1%	29.8%
20,000,001 - 100,000,000	104,136,346	129,760,020	9.3%	12.1%	78.5%
100,000,001 - 250,000,000	62,431,082	73,473,463	6.0%	18.0%	75.9%
250,000,001 - 500,000,000	50,381,815	60,251,007	4.1%	12.4%	83.4%
500,000, 001 - 750,000,000	27,084,813	44,797,523	2.0%	42.8%	55.2%
750,000,001 - 1,000,000,000	11,590,126	23,341,017	0.0%	31.0%	69.0%
Over 1 Billion	121,069,256	150,329,233	3.7%	54.0%	42.3%
Grand Total	$630,040,690	$608,418,004	6.2%	5.1%	88.7%

Economic Sectors	Base Corporate Tax	New Corporate Tax	Winners	Losers	Even
Agriculture, Forestry, and Fishing	$2,886,417	$1,440,781	40.0%	20.0%	40.0%
Mining	12,495,690	12,511,913	14.7%	6.2%	79.1%
Construction	22,223,744	20,509,373	18.8%	13.5%	67.7%
Manufacturing	288,514,301	335,171,073	18.6%	17.7%	63.8%
Transportation	50,709,262	34,939,703	13.1%	6.4%	80.5%
Wholesale Trade	50,174,092	45,808,991	11.1%	6.3%	82.6%
Retail Trade	67,201,264	52,729,962	30.3%	11.8%	57.9%
Finance, Insurance, and Real Estate	55,122,385	40,172,667	10.4%	3.3%	86.3%
Services	60,897,755	53,749,529	3.9%	6.5%	89.6%
Unclassified	19,815,780	11,384,010	0.2%	0.1%	99.7%
Grand Total	$630,040,689	$608,418,004	6.2%	5.1%	88.7%

produced a decrease in franchise revenues in 1993 of approximately $21.6 million, or a 3.4 percent decrease in revenues. This change is small enough to be associated simply with the sampling error in the simulation. Notice, however, that these results represent static changes for that particular year. That is, the results do not include any potential gains in revenues that may be realized from additional corporations moving production activities to Ohio. The distribution of winners tends to favor middle sized firms (in net worth), which are more likely to have payroll and property used in production in Ohio. The losers tend to be larger-size firms, which have relatively more sales than labor and property used in production in the state. Most of the small firms which tend to be 100 percent Ohio operations, with an apportionment ratio of 100, are not affected by the change. The distribution of winners and losers by economic sector is more even. Every sector has more winners than losers except for the service sector. On the whole, 88.7 percent of the companies are not affected, but that is mostly because of the much larger number of companies that are all Ohio companies.

Are there any significant arguments against the change in the apportionment formula? One consideration is the fact that by adopting a single sales factor Ohio would move state corporate taxation still further from a uniform apportionment system such as the one predicated in UDITPA.[54] The lack of a uniform system creates the possibility of over-apportionment of corporation incomes among those states with a corporate income tax.[55] Those companies more adversely affected by the possible change in the apportionment formula, large corporations with extensive sales in Ohio and relatively small production facilities, will likely put up a strong campaign calling the move unfair.

A priori there is no overwhelming reason to use one formula over another in apportioning income. Justifications of any of the formulas can be made *ex-post,* each one better capturing the underlying causes of the tax base. In reality, the multiplicity of formulas and apportionment schemes used in other states puts Ohio, as any other state, in the position of having to care only about what formula will maximize revenue over the long run. It is important to emphasize again that the revenue perspective must be a long-term perspective, because the tax base in the state may increase or decrease as more companies locate in or outside Ohio in response to the formula adopted. Revenues in the long run will also be affected by the apportionment formulas adopted by other states. Unfortunately, there is no evidence on how important any of these effects may be on a state by state basis.

Reforming the apportionment formula for the net worth tax. If the net worth tax were to be kept either in its current form or as a new modified net worth tax excluding reserves and deferred taxes from the base, there are several possibilities for changing the apportionment formula for either tax. The current two factor formula could be substituted with the three-factor double-weighted formula used in the net income tax. This would have the effect of shifting the burden of the net worth tax toward out of state companies. This would be so because of the double weighting of sales and because of the exclusion of intangible income and assets from the computation of the sales and property factors, respectively. The *a priori* expectations of the impact of this change is that most winners would be concentrated among small and middle-sized companies, which would tend to be Ohio companies, and most losers would be concentrated among larger size companies, which would tend to include more non-Ohio companies.

A second possibility would be to apportion the net worth base with a two-factor formula based on sales and property, as computed now for the net income tax. This change should still lighten the tax burden of Ohio companies compared to out-of-state companies, but quite probably less than by using the double-weighted sales three factor formula of the net income tax. A third possibility would be to use a single-factor formula, with the choice being between the property factor and the sales factor.

Use of the throwback rule. Ohio could join other states in introducing a throwback rule in the computation of the sales factor in the apportionment formula for net income taxes. Of course, this would help increase revenues from the franchise tax, but in minor amounts. What the rule would do is apportion corporate income to the State of Ohio that otherwise might not be apportioned anywhere else. However, given the many differences in apportionment formulas across states under which multistate corporations have to file, the introduction of a throwback rule would tend to destroy the little cushion corporations may have to avoid the over-apportionment and, therefore, double taxation of their incomes.

Raise the minimum payment of the franchise tax. Regardless of what is done in other areas of the franchise tax, there is the option to increase the minimum payment under the franchise tax from its current $50 level. The current $50 may be too low to cover the expense to the Tax Department of processing a tax return. The increase in the minimum payment can be made part of a new net worth tax, as we have seen above. Table 10-29 shows the potential impact on revenues of raising the minimum payment by $50 steps from the current level of $50 to $500. At the present level of $50 the minimum tax raises $2.2 million, representing 0.36 percent of corporate franchise tax revenues. With a minimum tax of $500, revenues raised would have been $22.4 million, or 3.56 percent of corporate franchise tax revenues. These calculations are performed on the basis of the number of corporations that should have paid the minimum tax in 1993.

Tax rates. Ohio already has one of the highest corporate income tax rates, as discussed in Section 2. Still the possibility is there to increase tax rates. An increase of 1 percent in the top rate for net incomes above $50,000 would have generated between $40 million and $50 million in additional tax revenues in 1993.

TABLE 10-29
Effect on Tax Revenue of Increasing the Minimum Corporate Tax

Minimum Tax Amount	Amount of Revenue Generated	Percent of Total Current Tax Revenue
$50	$2,242,750	0.3560
$100	$4,485,500	0.7119
$150	$6,728,250	1.0679
$200	$8,971,000	1.4239
$250	$11,213,750	1.7798
$300	$13,456,500	2.1358
$350	$15,699,250	2.4918
$400	$17,942,000	2.8477
$450	$20,184,750	3.2037
$500	$22,427,500	3.5597

Other possibilities for reform in the rate structure include changing the net income threshold of $50,000 for the current lower rate of 5.1 percent, changing the lower rate itself, and introducing one or more additional brackets. Several states, including Iowa, Kentucky, and Missouri, have graduated progressive rate schedules. The advantage of the present system, with a lower rate for relatively small levels of income, is that it does offer some advantage to small businesses without sacrificing a large sum in revenues and without giving strong incentives for the breakup of larger companies into smaller units. This is a common criticism of progressive rate schedules for corporate income taxes. However, there is little empirical evidence on how important these effects may be in reality.

Credits and other tax benefits. There are, as we saw in Section 1, many tax credits and other tax benefits that undermine the revenue-raising capacity of the franchise tax at the present time. Some of the credits appear to be justified, in order to avoid the double taxation of assets. But most of the credits have been introduced in the spirit of the necessity of special treatment to encourage certain activities. There is no general consensus among economists about the desirability and effectiveness of these incentives; the experience of different tax systems with a variety of tax benefits is that many of these interventions do not seem to produce the desired objectives, and sometimes they may actually be harmful because of the misallocation of resources they induce.

The reform of the corporate franchise tax is clearly an opportunity to review and simplify the system of credits and tax incentives under the franchise tax. If the franchise tax is simplified with the elimination of the net worth component, there will be room to further simplify the system of tax benefits and tax incentives.

Make all allocable income apportionable. As we have seen, Ohio allocates certain types of income, mostly from intangible assets, regardless of whether these incomes have a business or non-business source. Some states also allocate to the state non-business income. Yet some other states make no distinction between business and non-business income and make all types of income apportionable, as opposed to allocable.

One option for reform in Ohio is to make all types of income apportionable. This possibility is simulated in Table 10-30. This change would have been a mild revenue winner in 1993, raising $23.5 million in additional tax revenues. Again in this case, all-Ohio companies (small and middle- size) tend to be relative winners since all their incomes that before were 100 percent allocable are now apportionable at less than 100 percent, if the corporation has business outside Ohio. The relative losers tend to be larger non-Ohio companies which before could exclude allowable income not sitused to Ohio, but now would have to include all those incomes as apportionable. The distribution of winners and losers by economic sector shows

TABLE 10-30
Corporation Tax without Using Schedule C (Allocable Income) in Computing Taxable Income

Net Worth ($)	Base Corporate Tax	New Corporate Tax	Winners	Losers	Even
Less than 1	$35,862,764	$34,427,439	0%	3%	97%
Over 1 - 200,000	32,249,202	2,504,658	5%	1%	94%
200,001 - 500,000	25,889,826	2,268,087	42%	19%	39%
500,001 - 2,500,000	62,081,815	22,980,754	49%	15%	35%
2,500,001 - 5,000,000	27,672,764	22,903,800	34%	5%	61%
500,000,001 - 20,000,000	69,590,881	57,024,704	40%	16%	44%
20,000,001 - 100,000,000	104,136,346	157,289,230	31%	53%	16%
100,000,001 - 250,000,000	62,431,082	78,633,555	26%	37%	37%
250,000,001 - 500,000,000	50,381,815	67,935,855	21%	76%	3%
500,000,001 - 750,000,000	27,084,813	49,018,931	39%	56%	6%
750,000,001 - 1,000,000,000	11,590,126	24,047,070	17%	83%	0%
Over 1 Billion	121,069,256	134,523,081	54%	44%	2%
Grand Total	$630,040,690	$653,557,165	12%	15%	73%

Economic Sectors	Base Corporate Tax	New Corporate Tax	Winners	Losers	Even
Agriculture, Forestry, and Fishing	$2,886,417	$1,249,378	10%	0%	90%
Mining	12,495,690	12,029,018	29%	44%	27%
Construction	22,223,744	18,732,813	47%	20%	34%
Manufacturing	288,514,301	360,418,276	27%	44%	28%
Transportation	50,709,262	38,412,253	50%	14%	35%
Wholesale Trade	50,174,092	46,687,465	22%	23%	55%
Retail Trade	67,201,264	55,493,993	50%	19%	31%
Finance, Insurance, and Real Estate	55,122,385	46,137,737	39%	43%	18%
Services	60,897,755	62,216,255	8%	14%	78%
Unclassified	19,815,780	12,179,976	0%	3%	97%
Grand Total	$630,040,689	$653,557,165	12%	15%	73%

the same result. Those sectors that are more likely to have Ohio companies (e.g., construction and retail trade) tend to be winners.

Should Ohio require combined income reporting for unitary businesses? The advantages of mandating combined income reporting for unitary businesses are many. Fundamentally, combined income reporting eliminates artificial discrepancies in the tax base through accounting and arbitrary allocations of revenues and expenses across state boundaries.

However, combined income reporting is still controversial as an apportionment method. Critics have argued that combined income reporting is contrary to the arm's-length standard and to the formulary apportionment of a single taxpayer's income. The counter answer from proponents of combined income reporting is that the arm's-length standard and single taxpayer formulary apportionment have become fictions in a world where unitary businesses have at their disposal a variety of avenues to artificially reduce their state tax liabilities.

Combined income reporting is not a panacea, either. Mandating it will require a very clear set of regulations in complex areas. Combined reporting should be distinguished from consolidated return filing. The following paragraphs describe some of these distinctions, and briefly review the scope of issues that would have to be decided if mandatory combined income reporting were adopted.

Combined reporting is an approach for determining the income attributable to a state from each of the corporations that are members of an affiliated group of companies conducting a unitary business in several states.[56] When there is more than one corporation in the affiliated group doing business in the state, the unitary income apportioned to the state is in turn apportioned among the different companies with nexus in the state.[57] Depending on the type of combined reporting, not all affiliated corporations in a group may be combined. Combination applies to a "unitary business," and the determination of what this is can vary.

It is important to distinguish between the filing of "combined income reports" and the filing of "consolidated returns." These two terms are at times used interchangeably, but they are quite different things. The objective of combined income reporting is not to tax the income of the affiliated group as a whole or the filing of a consolidated return. Rather, the objective is to determine the portion of the income from the unitary business attributable to the companies with nexus or operations in the state. The combined income report is an information return rather than a tax return. Each corporation in a combined report with nexus in the state still has to file its own corporate tax return. See Box 10-2 for the steps followed in combined income reporting.

By contrast, in a consolidated return the total net income of the corporations in the group is filed in a single return and a single tax is paid (even though each of the corporations is jointly and severally liable for payment). In the case of consolidated returns, net income is not limited to that related to a specific unitary business. Of course, when the consolidated business operates in more than one state, apportionment will be necessary in the consolidated return. See Box 10-2.

Two important decisions would have to be made if the State of Ohio were to require combined income reporting for all unitary businesses. These concern the "basis," or how far and wide the combination should go, and the "standards," or how to determine which corporations should file a combined report.[58]

The choices for basis are essentially three, although some combinations of these three are also possible: worldwide combination, which includes all domestic and foreign income; domestic or water's edge combination, which includes only United States source income; and a nexus combination which includes only companies with nexus in the state, or corporations domiciled in the state, or some combination thereof.

BOX 10-2
State's Apportionment in Combined Income Reports*

Under a combined income approach the share of income of the unitary business that is taxable in the state is determined as follows:

First, define the scope of the unitary business and what corporations should be made part of the combined report.

Second, determine the net income derived by the unitary business inside and outside the state, eliminating all income and expenses attributable to internal transactions within the unitary group itself.

Third, determine the share of the unitary group's income that is allocable to the state and then determine the part of the unitary business income that is apportioned to the state, and apply the statutory formula for apportioning the unitary business income (not directly allocable).

Fourth, divide the total net taxable income of the unitary business attributable to the state among the corporations of the group that have nexus within the state according to the distribution among them of the factors used in the apportionment formula.

*Adapted from John L. Coalson, Jr. and Michael T. Ptrik, "Consolidated or Combined Returns and Alternative Corporate Reporting Methods: A Georgia Perspective," Journal of State Taxation, Vol. 8, No.2, Fall 1989, pp.132-151.

The standards used to determine when a group of affiliated companies actually constitutes a unitary business vary. The most common standard is based on the "three unities" of common ownership, common management, and common operation or use. Common ownership is typically interpreted to exist when 50 percent or more of the stock of a corporation is owned by another corporation. Common management is typically interpreted to exist when there are overlapping boards of directors or common managers in key positions. Common operation is interpreted to exist when there are common functions of management, financing, accounting, advertising, or purchasing.

Other standards used rely on the existence of dependency or contributions between affiliated corporations, similarities in the line of business, or significant intercorporate transactions.

Net operating losses. The state could introduce a carry back provision for NOLS, to be more competitive. However, the present provision of no carry back allowed does not put Ohio at a disadvantage with neighboring states and avoids some of the revenue instability associated with the carry back provision.

Joining the Multistate Tax Compact? Joining the Multistate Tax Compact and subscribing to UDITPA (The Uniform Division of Income for Tax Purposes Act) would require some important changes in the Ohio corporate franchise tax, most importantly in the apportionment formula. There would be the advantage of adding clarity and standardized procedures. The state tax administration also would benefit from the multistate audits and interpretive rulings done by the Tax Compact for specific business sectors. However, joining UDITPA may be unfavorably regarded in the business community.

The reform of local income taxes. There is ample room for standardization and simplification of these taxes. Ideally, at the very least, all local jurisdictions would adopt the same basic tax structure and procedures, although they would be able to vary the rates. Some degree of discretion in the ability to raise revenues is desirable, to increase efficiency and accountability in local governments.[59] Under this approach each business would still have to file a tax return in each of the jurisdictions where it operates. An even more simplified approach would be to rely on centralized filing with the State Department of Taxation and to devise a system for the apportionment of collections among local jurisdictions. This approach would significantly reduce compliance costs for businesses, and in theory it could be structured to allow differentiated rates for local jurisdictions.

Elimination of the Franchise Tax

The last option to consider is the complete elimination of the corporate franchise tax. Four states (Nevada, South Dakota, Washington, and Wyoming) have at present no corporate income tax.[60] The substitution of corporate income tax revenues with existing taxes, such as the personal income tax or the sales tax, is quite feasible. The corporate income tax yielded $630 million in 1993. This revenue could have been collected from the personal income tax by either of two changes: 1) getting rid of the following credits and income exclusions: social security and railroad retirement exclusions, personal exemption credits, senior citizen credits, joint filer credits, and retirement income credits (all major credits and adjustments on the individual income tax); or 2) by a 0.5 percent surcharge on taxable income (effectively increasing all rates by 0.5 percent). The elimination of the corporate income tax would create a more attractive business climate. State corporate income taxes, including the corporate franchise tax in Ohio, represent double taxation of corporate income because of their lack of integration with the personal income tax. This double taxation is imposed on top of the double taxation of corporate income at the federal level where there is no integration of the two taxes either. An additional attraction of completely eliminating the corporate income tax is that the state would not have to continue to rely on an unstable and probably declining source of revenues. The main disadvantage of eliminating the corporate franchise tax is that there would be a shift of tax burdens now borne by nonresidents (as owners of capital and consumers) to state residents. Although a portion of the franchise tax is surely exported, that may not be the case with substitute taxes such as the personal income tax or the sales tax.

APPENDIX

TAX RETURN SAMPLE DATA USED IN THE MICRO-SIMULATIONS

Sampling was performed on the basis of a master file of taxpayers from the Ohio Department of Taxation. This file had information coded from the first page of the corporate return. In total there were approximately 107,000 taxpayers. Most of the information needed to construct the tax calculator was not available from the tax return's first page. This necessitated the drawing of a sample of fully filled-out tax returns. The sample originally designed contained the complete set of the largest 500 companies in terms of tax liability. We added to them a random sample of just over 1 percent of the remaining firms that accounted for an additional 1,000 firms. A small number of firms with no taxable income but "large" net worth tax liability was also included to make sure that firms were represented.

After the coding of entire data, some tax returns were not usable due to taxpayer errors and omissions. In addition, some tax returns were not available because they were in the audit process. The final sample contained 1377 firms representing 44.2 percent of the total franchise tax revenues collected by the state. The results from this sample were "blown-up" to the entire set of taxpayers. Because we used three different samples (a full sample of the largest companies, a full sample of zero or low profit but high net worth firms, and a random sample of the remaining firms), different "blown up" factors were used so that the revenue contribution for each sample matched the population from which it was drawn. The sample returns after being "blown-up" replicated 99 percent of the actual revenue collected in 1993. The tax calculator built replicated the corporate income tax forms. The calculator was used to develop the base core analysis and was modified to develop the simulation results.

ENDNOTES

1. The authors would like to thank the Ohio Department of Taxation for the effort of collecting the sample return data used in the simulation of the corporate franchise tax in this chapter and for general information and guidance. We would also like to thank Wen Tsui and Joe Timmerman for their valuable research assistance. We would also like to thank the Tax Committee of the Ohio Chamber of Commerce for information and insights in the various corporate income tax issues covered in this chapter.

2. "Doing business" in the state is evidenced by a number of activities, such as listing the company in the phone book or the licensing of software. Ohio takes one of the most aggressive stands in determining nexus. Some of these are reviewed below in the comparison of Ohio franchise tax with that in other states.

3. Since 1993 railroad companies no longer pay the public utility excise tax and are instead subject to the regular franchise tax.

4. Other corporations exempted from the franchise tax are nonprofit corporations (except for some consumer and agricultural cooperatives), municipal corporations, credit unions, real estate investment trusts, regulated investment companies, and real estate mortgage investment conduits (ORC 1733.43, 5733.01, 5733.09, and 5733.10).

5. States are not allowed to tax interest from federal obligations if they exempt interest income from state public obligations.

6. See the Department of Taxation's Annual Report 1992, page 21, for recent significant court decisions involving the issue of allocable versus apportionable income.

7. Dividends are allocated to the state according to the "Ohio-to-be-everywhere" ratio for the book value of assets of the payor company. Dividends from Domestic International Sales Corporations and from corporations for which there is no information on the location of assets are apportioned.

8. Trademark royalties are not considered patent or copyright royalties, and they are treated as apportionable income.

9. Prior to 1982 the carry forward period was five consecutive years.

10. The gross profit portion of income received but not yet earned is includable in the value of the stock, as are net deferred tax liabilities. Contingent liabilities are included in the computation of net worth if the corporation cannot reasonably estimate the amount of the liability or if it cannot be established that the liability is to be incurred in the current period.

11. Intangible assets are not part of goodwill if they can be sold and purchased separately with an identifiable value.

12. This tax offers a mild incentive for filing a combined franchise report. The entire group of corporations pay only the two tier litter tax once as a group rather than individually by each corporation.

13. For a more detailed analysis of the effects of credits, or economic development in Ohio, see Michael Wasylenko, "The Role of Fiscal Incentives in Economic Development: How Ohio Stands Relative to its Competitor States," Chapter 9 in this volume.

14. The Amended Substitute Bill 32 extended the credit for qualifying new investments with respect to property acquired before 1989. This Bill also created a refundable credit, while the original new investment credit is a non-refundable credit.

15. The conditions are regulated in Ohio Revised Code Section 5733.052 and Tax Commissioner's Rule 5703-5-06.

16. Each of the corporations combining incomes must have income other than dividend income within Ohio.

17. Corporations without business nexus in Ohio may be included in a combined income report with approval of the Commissioner. However, these corporations must derive income in the same fashion as the taxpayer corporations.

18. In a recent case the Ohio Board of Tax Appeals held that corporations filing combined franchise tax reports for prior years may not add retroactively another corporation to the combined group without consent of the Commissioner. The Commissioner had withheld consent, arguing that the subsidiary which was trying to add to the combined group had no income allocable or apportionable to the state of Ohio (*The Tranzonic Companies and Subsidiaries v. Tracy,* Ohio Board of Tax Appeals, December 4, 1992).

19. ACIR (1993).

20. The representative tax system is defined by the ACIR at the average state corporate income tax rate times the national corporate profits apportioned to the state according to a three factor (sales, property and employment) formula.

21. Note that Figure 1-9 uses two scales, in millions for Ohio and in billions for all states.

22. However, S corporations do face a number of restrictions which do not affect C corporations. S corporations cannot have more than 35 shareholders, they can issue only one type of stock, they must be domestic corporations, and they may not be part of an affiliated group.

23. See Robert Carrol and David Joulfaian (1993).

24. See Alan J. Auerbach and James Poterba (1993).

25. From an average of 10.9 percent in the 1960s the profit rate fell to 7.2 percent during the 1970s and 4.9 percent during the first half of the 1980s.

26. The Supreme Court has ruled that the taking of sales orders by a traveling salesman does not constitute nexus when those orders are filled and delivery is made from a location outside of the state. However, a permanent employee in the state for sales activities may be outside the spirit of the Supreme Court ruling.

27. For the rationale behind different formulas, see Peggy B. Musgrave (1994b).

28. Approval of the Tax Commissioner is required.

29. These deductions are related to the domestic corporation dividends subject to the 70 percent deduction.

30. Of course, the federal government imposes an alternative minimum tax but this falls on income (at 20 percent on the regular net income base grossed up for tax preferences) rather than assets.

31. Besides Pennsylvania, other states with significant net worth taxes are Alabama, Kentucky, Louisiana, Mississippi, North Carolina, Tennessee, and Texas.

32. See A. Estache (1990).

33. See Peter D. Byrne (1994).

34. Business taxes on assets are actually used as a method of presumptive income taxation based on the idea that capital assets will produce some minimum rate of return on average or otherwise the enterprise would get out of the business.

35. Allowing the asset tax to be carried forward as a credit still does not solve the major problem discussed below that the tax imposes a burden when the firm can least afford it. Actually, the credit provides relief when the firm is in a better position and may not need the relief as much.

36. Some countries with taxes on gross or net assets have addressed this problem by exempting newly formed companies for several years. Ohio does not have a similar provision regarding the net worth tax.

37. The credit, it is argued, also may have served as a check on property tax increases at the local level, since increases in property taxes meant decreases in state taxes. However, it may have worked the other way around. With the credit in place local jurisdictions may have had an incentive to increase property taxes, since the credit it was the state and not the companies that actually had to pay the tax (for as long, of course, as the companies were paying the net worth tax component of the franchise tax rather than the net income component).

38. The situsing rules are for the most part those in the statutes of the intangible property tax, which was repealed in 1986. In terms of complexity, business representatives often referred to the instructions for situsing, investment in subsidiaries, which is 25 pages long.

39. The marginal effective rates of taxation are calculated by assuming identical pretax rates of return for different assets and economic sectors and calculating an after-tax rules of return for each type of investment after all aspects of taxation affecting those investments are taken into consideration.

40. See Charles E. McLure, Jr. (1986). Peter Mieszkowski and John Morgan (1984).

41. The only receipts excluded from the business done factor are management fees for services by a parent company for a subsidiary without a profit element, and the proceeds from the sale of some assets.

42. See Charles E. McLure, Jr. (1984); George N. Carlson and Harvey Galper (1984) and Alicia H. Munnell (1992).

43. Section 162 of the 1991 Budget Bill.

44. See Jeffrey P. Sherman (1991).

45. See the *1994 Multistate Corporate Tax Guide*.

46. The UDITPA (Uniform Distribution of Income for Tax Purposes Act) approach is to allocate only non-business income. This latter is defined as originating in assets not in use for daily business activities.

47. The Ohio Board of Tax Appeals has ruled that the "aggregate" or (conduit) principle applies to the computation of the franchise tax. This means that all income and deductions realized by a partnership are transplanted as such to the corporate partner for the calculation of its franchise tax.

48. For example, businesses with distribution services among different local governments in theory need to keep track of how long a truck and driver spends in each jurisdiction in the course of a day.

49. We are grateful to the Department of Taxation for making the data available. The sample of tax returns and the micro-simulation methodology are described in the Appendix.

50. Of course, this principle should not apply only to incorporated businesses but rather to all types of legal forms of enterprises.

51. The proposals from the business community with respect to the repeal of the net worth tax have not been necessarily consistent in the sense that they factor both the proposition of revenue neutrality and a reformed net worth tax with a cap and other features (e.g. lower rates) which may make revenue neutrality impossible.

52. The proposal from the business community also suggests that the maximum cap in the schedule should be used for a combined group. However, the rationale of the tax as a minimum payment for services or the privilege to do business in the state suggests that each corporation in a combined group should pay this type of tax separately.

53. See M. Wasylenko, "The Role of Fiscal Incentives in Economic Development: How Ohio Stands Relative to Its Competitor States," Chapter 9 in this volume.

54. UDITPA adopts the three factors formula with equal weights for sales, payroll and property.

55. However, nationwide there does not appear to be significant over apportionment. See Steven M. Sheffin and Jack Fulcher (1984).

56. See for example, James F. Buresh and Marc S. Weinstein (1982).

57. Often the second-stage apportionment is not done with the entire income apportioned to the state assessed to the "key corporation" of the group in the state.

58. Several administrative issues would also need to be addressed, involving rules for the consolidation of intercompany transactions, the merging of different accounting periods, how to address partnerships in the affiliated group, how to deal with foreign source income, and whether there should be some modification of the apportionment formula to recognize the different nature of some of the corporations, such as financial institutions and insurance companies.

59. By efficiency what is meant is that the residents of some jurisdictions may have higher preferences for public services, and the system of local finances should let these jurisdictions fulfill these preferences on a voluntary basis.

60. Michigan does not have a corporate income tax, but it has a "single business tax," which is a modified value-added tax (VAT).

11 Taxation of the Financial Services Industry

Martin F. Grace and Jorge Martinez-Vazquez

FINANCIAL TAXATION

This chapter addresses the taxation of Ohio's financial institutions under the special corporate franchise tax for banks and other financial institutions. This tax applies to corporations conducting certain banking activities within Ohio, and is a tax on net worth. The dealers in intangibles tax will also be discussed in this chapter, although separately. This also is a net worth tax on stock brokers and dealers, mortgage brokers, bullion dealers, and finance and loan companies.

Composition and relative importance. Approximately 87,000 persons are employed in the banking sector in Ohio. This is approximately the same number as are employed in the insurance industry, the motor vehicle manufacturing industry, or the primary metal manufacturing industry. Banks and savings and loan companies contributed approximately $158 million to the state treasury in 1992, as shown in Table 11-1. The Ohio banking industry, for regulatory and historical reasons, is divided into banks, savings and loans, and other credit corporations. From Table 11-1 we see that the banks outnumber the savings and loans, and that they pay about three times more in taxes. In addition, the largest tax-paying banks and savings and loans (those with liabilities over $1,000,000) contribute approximately 60 percent of the corporate franchise tax on financial institutions.

Table 11-2 shows the relative importance of the financial institutions tax

TABLE 11-1
Distribution of Liability by Size and Type of Taxpayer for 1992

	Number of Corporations			Tax Liability by Type ($)			
Tax Liability	Banks	S&Ls	Other	Banks	S&Ls	Other	Total
0 - 10,000	14	18	22	34,259	18,676	26,332	79,267
10,001 - 50,000	60	65	5	1,774,054	2,147,622	137,753	4,059,429
50,001 - 100,000	65	66	4	4,843,829	4,633,539	312,360	9,789,728
100,001 - 200,000	52	34	2	7,533,448	4,896,960	352,443	12,782,851
200,001 - 500,000	50	32	0	15,439,834	9,425,203	0	24,865,037
500,001 - 1,000,000	13	6	0	7,920,016	4,028,768	0	11,948,784
1,000,001 +	22	7	0	80,913,385	13,473,730	0	94,387,115
Total	276	228	33	118,458,825	38,624,498	828,888	157,912,211

TABLE 11-2
Financial Institutions Tax as a Percent of Corporation Taxes

	Tax Revenues Collected	
	Financial Institutions Tax	Percentage of Total Corporation Taxes*
1989	$130,125,260	10.92%
1990	$142,896,321	12.85
1991	$147,271,175	13.46
1992	$157,912,211	14.83

Source: Department of Revenue Annual Reports (various years).

*Includes general corporation taxes, financial institutions tax, and insurance taxes.

relative to all taxes paid by corporations, banks, and insurance companies for some recent years. Since 1989 the percentage represented by the tax on financial institutions in the total of corporate franchise taxes has increased from approximately 11 percent to almost 15 percent. This reflects the fact that the net worth of these institutions has increased over the time period faster than the alternative bases of net income and net worth for general corporate taxpayers.

Figure 11-1 shows the relative changes in the payment of the financial institutions tax during the last decade. The left axis shows the percentage of taxes paid by banks since 1983. This increased approximately 10 percent, from 76 percent in 1983 to 86 percent in 1986, and has decreased just over 10 percent from the 1986 peak. Correspondingly, savings and loans (repre-

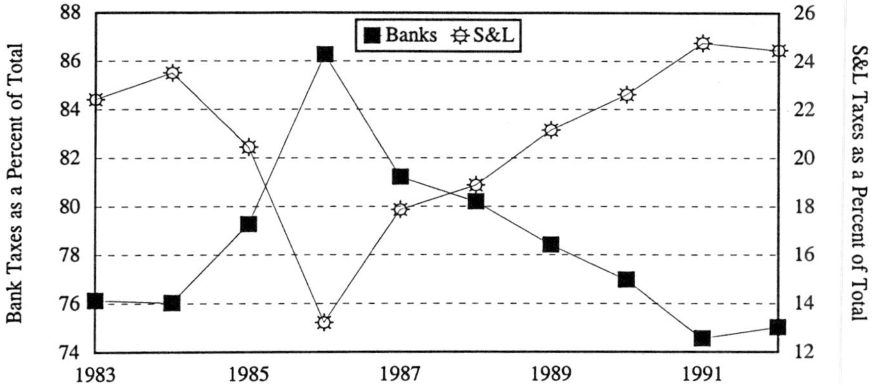

FIGURE 11-1. Percentage of tax receipts by type of financial institution.

sented on the right axis) behaved in an opposite manner during the decade. This change was the result of two forces. First, there was a change in the tax rate. Prior to 1986 savings and loans paid a rate of 21.47 mills on their net worth, while other financial institutions paid a lesser rate of 16.54 mills. As S&Ls recovered from their financial difficulties in the middle 1980s, their contribution to tax revenues also increased.

The income elasticity of the corporate franchise tax on financial institutions is shown in Figure 11-2. The elasticity provides information concerning the tax's relative responsiveness to income in the state. From the figure we see that the income elasticity was relatively constant (but with a tendency to decrease) from 1986 to 1989. However, the elasticity has been very unstable from 1989 to 1991. But during the entire period the elasticity remained over one. This means that the corporate franchise tax on financial institutions has been growing more than proportionally with income in the state.

STRUCTURE OF THE BANK TAX

History of Bank Taxation

State taxation of banks has a long and colorful history, in part, because of Constitutional restrictions on the states' ability to tax federal banks and because of explicit Congressional restrictions on the taxation of federally chartered banks.[1] The Supreme Court in *McCulloch v. Maryland*[2] held that states could not tax national banks using any method save a real property or bank share tax. In the National Bank Act of 1864,[3] Congress specified that states could not tax the real property of a bank at a rate higher than that on other property, and that a bank share tax could not be any higher than the rate on

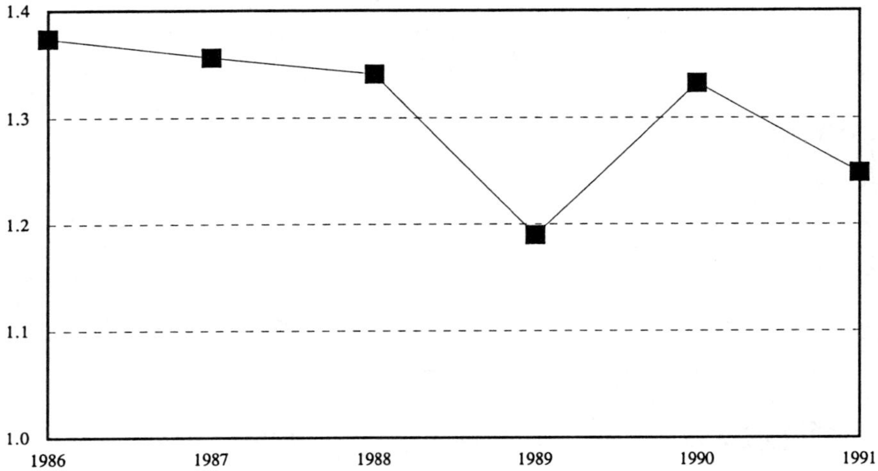

FIGURE 11-2. Financial institutions income tax elasticity.

any other "moneyed capital." Because of these restrictions states limited the tax on state chartered banks, so that the states' banks were not placed at a competitive disadvantage.

The courts interpreted the maximum share tax to be no higher than the rate imposed on other corporations involved in banking or the rate imposed on the intangible personal property of individuals involved in banking. The latter interpretation, according to Fox, required states to impose taxes on a wide range of intangible property.

Over time, as states attempted to raise revenue from the banking industry, the rates increased relative to other forms of intangible personal property. This led to litigation, as the banking industry claimed it was being taxed more heavily than other "moneyed capital." Congress again acted, this time to define taxes that did not discriminate against banks and that could raise revenue from the banking industry. The legislation defined "other moneyed capital" sufficiently narrowly to restrict the potential for bank taxes to be determined as discriminatory. The legislation also allowed for the option of taxing banks based on net income at a rate not to exceed that on other corporations, and a tax on dividends received by shareholders at a rate no higher than that on net income from other monied capital. Because these taxes would generate less revenue than the share tax already being employed in most states, and as income from federal, state, and local securities was exempt from taxation under the law, Congress enacted a third option. This option was an excise tax where net income from all sources was allowed as the tax base.

After this legislation, there were still problems with discrimination. The major issue was the set of taxes that should be used to compare tax liabilities for banks and other corporations. Banks paid only the franchise tax, while all other corporations paid a series of taxes, thus the states gradually increased the tax rate on the banking industry so as to equalize the burden. Congress, in 1969, enacted a law that would become effective in 1976, stating that for the purpose of state or federal tax law, a national bank would be treated as a state bank.

This law brought about two significant changes in federal tax policy regarding banks. First, as long as states do not discriminate against national banks, they can impose any type of tax on banks within their jurisdiction. Second, the comparison, for purposes of determining whether discrimination exists, is to compare taxes on national banks versus taxes on state banks. This contrasts with the previous method of comparing bank taxes to nonbank taxes.

However, there is one remaining limitation on the states' tax power on the banking industry. Securities of the United States government are exempt from taxation by a state, except when it is imposed as part of a nondiscriminatory franchise tax or some other non-income tax imposed on a corporation or as part of a tax imposed on an estate. Thus, the total income of a bank, including interest from federal securities, may be in the tax base as long as the state tax is a franchise tax. The interest cannot be taxed as part of a corporate income tax. This is because a franchise tax is levied on a corporation as a tax on the privilege of doing business in a state, not as a direct assessment on the income earned. In contrast, a corporate income tax is a direct assessment against corporate income.

Ohio's Approach to Bank Taxation

Recent history and present tax. Ohio taxes its financial institutions under the Corporate Franchise Tax, but it uses only the net worth component of the tax. Thus, the problems of the net worth components from the general corporate franchise tax are applicable to the banking industry. Ohio adopted this approach in 1981, after repealing the previous franchise tax exemption for financial institutions. The first rate imposed was 6.5 mills, for tax years 1982 and 1983. In 1983 the rates were increased so that banks were taxed at 15 mills on their net worth, saving and loans were taxed at 21.47, and other financial institutions were taxed at 16.54 percent of their net worth. Currently the tax is 15 mills on net worth for all financial institutions. This tax is similar to the general corporation tax, except for the fact that there is no income tax component, only a net worth component.

Tax base. The tax base for the financial institutions net worth tax is the apportioned net value of the stock of the corporation, defined similarly to the net value of stock for non-financial institutions, i.e., the capital stock (less treasury stock), ownership interest of depositors, retained earnings and additional paid in capital, and deferred taxes and reserves. This is the total net worth. From this amount certain exempted assets, such as goodwill, abandoned property, exempt property, agricultural property, property set aside for R&D, and appreciation, are subtracted to obtain the net taxable value of the stock.

Computation of the tax. To obtain the tax base or value of the financial institution's property, one multiplies the "Ohio ratio" by the tax base. The Ohio ratio is the ratio of the "activity" of the corporation done within Ohio to the "activity" of the company done everywhere. As in the case of the general corporation net worth ratio, the apportionment formula for financial institutions is based upon property and business done in Ohio, and that is compared to the property and business done everywhere. This can be seen in the following allocator:

$$\textit{Ohio Ratio} = \frac{1}{2}\,\frac{\textit{Property within Ohio}}{\textit{Property Everywhere}} + \frac{1}{2}\,\frac{\textit{Business within Ohio}}{\textit{Business Everywhere}}$$

Tax rate. The tax rate is currently 15 mills and it is multiplied by the taxable value to obtain the tax due on the net worth basis. Note that this tax rate is approximately three times the tax rate for the net worth tax on non-financial corporations.

Credits. Savings and loan associations are allowed a credit against their tax due equal to the amount of the annual assessment paid by the S&L to the state division of Savings and Loan Associations, less the amount paid to the Federal Savings and Loan Insurance Corporation (or if not insured by the FSLIC, the amount it would pay if it was insured). In addition to this credit financial institutions (like other corporations) can currently obtain credits for qualifying new investment in property used in manufacturing, export sale credits, enterprise zone day care credits, and enterprise zone training credits.[4] In 1992, the new investment credit amounted to $104,729 and the credit for S&L fees was $930,680. For the financial services industry, credits have little impact on overall final tax liability.

Comparison with Other States

Table 11-3 shows the financial institution tax policies for Ohio, its neighbors, and certain important banking states. Nationwide, some states employ share taxes, and 40 have a franchise tax. Some states use more than one of these taxes, while three states (Louisiana, Nevada, and Wyoming) have no state tax on banking.

As seen from the table, important banking states and Ohio's neighbors are likely to use a franchise tax based on income. This is in contrast to Ohio's net worth franchise tax. There is a mixed treatment of the taxation of federal and state securities; some, like Ohio, exempt all government security in-

TABLE 11-3
State Taxation of Banks by Important Banking States and Ohio's Neighbors

						Interest from Government Securities Taxable		
	Corporate Income Tax Rate	Franchise Tax Rate	Share Tax Rate	Apportion Bank Tax Liability	Franchise Tax based on Income	Federal	Own States'	Other States'
California(1)	0.000	11.107	0.000	y	y	y	y	y
Delaware	0.000	8.700	0.000	n	y	y	y	y
Florida(2)(3)	0.000	5.500	0.150	y	y	y	y	y
Illinois(3)	7.300	0.250	0.000	y	n	n	y	y
Indiana	0.000	8.500	0.250	y	y	n	n	y
Kentucky(2)(4)	0.000	0.001	0.950	y	n	n	n	y
Michigan(5)	0.000	0.000	0.000	y	na	n	n	y
Minnesota	0.000	9.800	0.000	y	y	y	y	y
New Jersey(3)	0.000	9.375	0.000	y	y	y	y	y
New York(3)	0.000	10.350	0.000	y	y	y	y	y
North Carolina	7.905	0.003	0.000	y	n	y	y	y
Ohio(2)(3)	**0.000**	**1.500**	**0.000**	**y**	**n**	**n**	**n**	**n**
Pennsylvania	0.000	0.000	1.250	n	na	n	n	n
South Dakota(3)	0.000	6.000	0.000	y	y	y	y	y

Source: Fox (1993).

Notes:
(1) California levies a $50 franchise tax.
(2) Levies an intangible tax.
(3) Minimum tax is levied if no income is earned.
(4) The tax listed as a franchise tax is an intangible tax on deposits. There is also an intangibles tax of 1.5% on accounts receivables, notes bonds, credits, etc..
(5) Michigan tax is a 2.3% tax on the adjusted tax base.

terest, and some, like New York, tax all income from government securities.

Table 11-4 shows the apportionment factors for financial institutions for a number of selected states. Most states listed in the table allocate net income, and for the most part they use one of the traditional apportionment formulas based on sales, property, and payroll factors. The apportionment formula can be rather complicated in some states, such as New York, which uses the ratio of in-state to total receipts, payroll (with a weight of 80 percent), and includes deposits.

Dealers in Intangibles Tax

Ohio taxes its dealers in intangibles (stock brokers and dealers, bullion

TABLE 11-4
Apportionment Factors for Financial Institutions

State	Financial Institutions	Weighted Equally?
Ohio	Net Worth Only - Business Done and Property	N/A
Illinois	Business Income	N/A
Indiana	Gross Receipts or Sales	N/A
Iowa	Gross Receipts or Sales	N/A
Kentucky	Gross Receipts or Sales; Payroll; Outstanding Loan Balance	N/A
Michigan	Gross Receipts or Sales	N/A
Minnesota	Tangible Property (includes Intangibles); Payroll; Gross Receipts or Sales	N/A
Missouri	Tangible Property; Gross Receipts or Sales; Payroll	Yes
Wisconsin	Gross Receipts or Sales; Payroll	Yes
California	Tangible Property (includes Intangibles); Gross Receigps or Sales; Payroll	N/A
Colorado	Tangible Property; Gross Receipts or Sales; Payroll	N/A
Florida	Tangible Property (includes Intangible; Gross Receipts or Sales; Payroll	N/A
Georgia	Gross Receipts or Sales	N/A
New Jersey	Tangible Property; Gross Receipts of Sales; Payroll	N/A
New York	For Banks Only, Arithmetic Avg. Of Instate to Total Receipts; 80% of Payroll (except General Executive Officers); and Deposits	N/A
North Carolina	Gross Receipts or Sales	N/A
Pennsylvania	Value of Shares	N/R

Source: 1993 *Multistate Corporate Tax Guide.*

dealers, mortgage brokers, and finance and loan companies) based on the value of the firm. This is very much like the net worth tax portion of the corporation franchise tax.

The dealers in intangible tax is a relatively small tax, raising approximately $11 million in 1992. This represents about 1.75 percent of the corporate franchise receipts. In addition, the dealers in intangible tax is a unique tax among the states, as no other state employs this method for taxing dealers in intangibles.

The dealers in intangible tax was first enacted in 1931 at a rate of five mills. This rate did not change until 1971, when the rate was increased to six mills. In 1988 the rate was raised again, by two mills. Thus, the current rate is eight mills, which is assessed against net value. Currently, the receipts of the tax are divided between the general revenue fund (three mills) and the County Undivided Local Government Fund (five mills).

The dealers in intangible tax is, more specifically a tax on the shares of a corporation or partnership dealing in intangibles.[5] Firms are thus assessed on the value of capital, surplus, and undivided profits. Shares owned by financial institutions, domestic insurance companies, other dealers in intangibles, as well as United States Government securities, are excluded from the calculation of net worth. Furthermore, if the dealer is engaged in a multistate operation, the value is apportioned based on the net worth apportionment factor employed in the corporate franchise tax.[6]

The law has some important exemptions which provide loopholes for certain types of firms. Companies covered by O.R.C. § 5725 (dealers in intangibles, domestic insurers and financial institutions) can avoid the intangible tax under *National City Bank of Cleveland v. Porterfield.*[7] In this case the Ohio Supreme Court stated that shares of stock in companies covered under §5725 are not subject to the intangible property tax because the taxes they pay under that statute are *in lieu* of all other taxes. Thus, a large dealer in intangibles can engage in tax planning by rearranging the dealer in intangibles portion of its business as a subsidiary owned by a bank or insurance company. This can be a revenue loser for the state, especially if the dealer in intangibles is large relative to the parent.

One sign of the potential for tax avoidance is shown by the fact that since the rate was increased to 8 mills in 1988, the receipts in each subsequent year have not matched the initial year's total receipts. This is shown in Table 11-5. This is important, because net worth generally increases over time and thus one would expect the revenues to increase or at least be stable. This should translate into increasing or stable tax revenues.

ISSUES AND OPTIONS FOR REFORM IN THE NON-INSURANCE FINANCIAL SERVICE INDUSTRY

Change the Definition of a Financial Institution to Be More Inclusive

Ohio has a problem with its definition of a financial institution subject to taxation under the financial institutions tax. This definition excludes a number of bank competitors from taxation under the law. The definition of a taxable financial institution in Ohio is

> [Every person who keeps an office or other place of business in [Ohio] and engages in the business of receiving deposits, lending money, and buying or selling bullion, bills of exchange, notes, bonds, stocks, or other evidence of indebtedness with a view to profit or is licensed as a small business investment company under the 'Small Business Investment Act of 1958,' . . . or is organized under the Federal Farm Credit Act . . .[8]]

This law is based on an antiquated notion of the banking business. As inter-

TABLE 11-5
Dealers in Intangible Tax Receipts over Time

Year	Receipts in $ Millions
1986	6.9
1987	8.2
1988*	13.4
1989	12.3
1990	8.1
1991	11.6
1992	11.2

Source: Department of Taxation, *Annual Report* (various years).

*Year rate increased to 8 mills from 6 mills.

state banking has grown and as the non-bank financial industry has grown, the distinctions between depository banks and other financial service providers have disappeared. The statute requires that, among other things, a bank must accept deposits in Ohio before the tax can be placed on its activities. Banks can lower their Ohio tax liability by producing financial services outside the state and then selling them back to Ohio residents. They can accept deposits through the mail or by way of interbank electronic transfers. This encourages all non-depository functions to be sent out-of-state and results in revenue loss and potential job loss.[9]

Tax Banks and Other Financial Institutions Like General Corporations with a Franchise Tax

There are two issues here. The first is that different tax treatment leads to different tax burdens. This is a violation of horizontal equity. By taxing all financial corporations and general corporations in a similar manner it is possible to increase the horizontal equity among competitors or potential competitors.

A second issue that has potential ramifications for horizontal equity concerns those banks owned by a holding company. Since the financial institutions tax rate is approximately three times the rate for nonfinancial corporations, a bank owned by a holding company has an incentive to transfer net worth to the parent, thus reducing the yield of the financial institutions franchise tax. Of course, this transfer may be limited by regulatory capital requirements imposed as part of risk based capital rules implemented by federal regulators. This benefits large subsidiary banks which are part of a holding company relative to stand-alone banks.

Since all institutions pay federal tax, one could use the federal tax as a starting point and piggy-back on the federal definition of net income. This is precisely what is done in the non-financial area, and there are strong horizontal equity reasons to treat all corporations as equally as possible. Using income balance sheet information for Ohio banks, from *Sheshunoff Banks of Ohio*, 1993, we simulate the imposition of a net income tax. This simulation applied Ohio's current tax rate and definition of net income and assumed that all profits are apportional to Ohio. This resulted in a tax revenue of \$133 million. This compares to \$173 million in tax revenue collected under the current tax. The difference, 23 percent, may be mitigated if Ohio were to adopt a unitary reporting approach and could be underestimated if the banks apportioned profits to Ohio at a rate significantly less than 100 percent. Further, to the extent that there are taxpayer banks not reported by *Sheshunoff*, the figure could be under representing the actual yield of a net income tax as applied to banks.

Employ an Alternative Minimum Tax to Offset the Lost Revenue from Exempting the Interest of State and Federal Securities

Banks traditionally hold a large percentage of government securities in their portfolios. Because of federal bank tax law, it is not possible to (1) tax these securities under an income tax or (2) tax these securities differentially from state securities under a franchise tax. If Ohio desires to keep its own securities tax-free, then it is possible to employ an alternative minimum tax based on net worth to obtain the revenues lost from the exemption of securities. Thus, a bank corporation would pay an income tax on a base that excludes government security income or an alternative minimum tax. If the bank's income tax liability was less than a certain amount, then the bank would pay an alternative higher amount. Ideally, this amount would be calculated to offset the losses from the exemption of the federal securities.

A quite different approach to this issue of exempt income is to do nothing. Banks and other financial institutions pay no income tax on exempt securities but they also earn lower interest income. Furthermore, all companies including financial institutions, are free to invest in tax exempt securities.

Employ a Higher Rate on the Corporate Franchise Tax

Yet another approach to the issue of banks are being exempt from the taxation of income generated by government securities. Thus, one could exclude these from the tax base, but tax the bank at a higher rate than the general corporation. One could calculate a rate that was consistent with the burden placed on other (nonfinancial) corporations. California does this, as it taxes all non-financial corporations at a flat rate of 9.3 percent and taxes financial corporations differentially at 11.107 percent.[10] However, a tax on a financial institution's capital is not ideal. This is because regulators desire institutions to keep relatively large amounts of capital for solvency purposes. The "safer" a company is the higher its net worth tax liability.

ELIMINATE THE DEALERS IN INTANGIBLES TAX

Because the dealers in intangibles tax is a relatively small revenue-raiser, and because it can be used to avoid a potentially large amount of tax, the obvious option is to repeal the dealers in intangibles tax and tax dealers in intangibles like other corporations. This would increase horizontal equity and place all financial firms on a relatively similar tax basis. The repeal of the tax also would eliminate the need for organizational structural shenanigans to avoid the tax by dealers in intangibles. Changing to an income tax would reduce their ability to avoid paying taxes and would shore up the tax base. An alternative and less drastic structural change that could be used instead of an income tax would be to merely repeal the *in lieu of* provisions of O.R.C. § 5725.26 for dealers in intangibles. This would reduce the incentive to tax plan, but would not really address the horizontal treatment of all financial service firms.

ENDNOTES

1. This section draws from William Fox (1993).

2. 17 United States 316 (1819).

3. 13 Stat. 100-118 (1864).

4. These credits and their rationale are discussed in Chapter 1.

5. O.R.C. § 5725.13.

6. *Ibid.*, § 5725.15.

7. 15 OS2d 3;, 44 OO2d 22, 202; 239 NE2d 61 (1968).

8. ORC § 5725.01 (A).

9. Fox (1990) reports that New York has a similar law, and that the law encouraged Citibank to shift its credit card operation to South Dakota and sell the services back to New York residents.

10. ACIR(1993).

12 Taxation of the Insurance Industry

Martin F. Grace and Jorge Martinez-Vazquez

INSURANCE TAXATION

INTRODUCTION

This chapter examines the insurance industry, its contribution to the Ohio economy, and issues in the taxation of the Ohio insurance industry. Insurance is a very important service provided in the economy, and because of its special nature it is often taxed differently than other types of corporations and even other financial service firms.

Table 12-1 compares the insurance industry with others in the state and shows that the insurance industry pays more in premium and capital and surplus taxes than the banking industry pays in net worth taxes. The insurance tax accounts for approximately 26 percent of corporate franchise taxes (included insurance taxes, corporate net income and net worth tax, and financial institutions taxes). In comparison, the manufacturing sector pays approximately the same amount as the insurance industry, while the service sector pays about 5.5 percent of business taxes. The insurance industry employs slightly more people than the banking sector, while contributing about the same amount to state GDP. Thus, the insurance industry is an important part of Ohio's tax structure as well as the state's economy.

TABLE 12-1
Relative Importance of Insurance Industry Relative to Other Industries in Ohio

Industry	Total Taxes paid to Dept. Of Taxation (1992) (Million $)	Percent of Total Corporation Taxes Paid (1992)[a]	Total Number of Employees	Average Wage	Percent of Ohio GDP (1989)
Insurance[b]	277.1	25.80	90,300	$32,064	1.73
Banking[c]	157.9	15.56	87,200	$24,900	1.85
Services	60.2	5.6	1,490,700	$21,770	16.96
Manufacturing	282.6	26.31	1,278,500	$33,943	27.53
Corporations	630.1	58.65	---	---	---

Sources: Ohio Bureau of Employment Services, U.S. Dept of Labor, Bureau of Labor Statistics, *Employment and Earnings* (1993); Ohio Department of Taxation, and U.S., Dept of Commerce, *Survey of Current Business*.

[a]Includes all corporation net income and net worth taxes, financial institution taxes, and insurance premium taxes,
[b]Premium Taxes only
[c]Financial Institution Taxes Only

PERFORMANCE OF OHIO'S INSURANCE INDUSTRY

In 1993 the state of Ohio was home to 47 life insurance companies and 165 property-liability companies. This number has changed dramatically over time. Over the last 30 years a number of companies have domesticated in Ohio. The increase in the number of property and liability companies occurred after 1979, while the life industry experienced growth until the middle 1970s and then stabilized.[1] The home office of an insurance company contains most of the company's employment base as well as its operations base. Thus, obtaining and retaining home offices would increase employment and economic development in Ohio.[2] Wheaton (1986) found that states' tax policy can penalize the domestic industry in terms of future growth of the industry. Thus, it is important to make sure that there is a full understanding of the effects of all income tax policies and how they interact to effect employment and growth of the state's insurance industry.

INDUSTRY BREAKDOWN

Property and Liability. The Ohio property and liability insurance industry is made up of approximately 800 companies selling insurance for auto, homeowner, commercial, liability, and other coverages. In 1992 approximately 50,000 people were employed in the property-liability insurance industry in Ohio. Of these, 165 were domestic companies, accounting for 57 percent of premiums written in 1992.

Life. The life insurance industry includes 695 companies writing group and individual life insurance. These firms employ approximately 20,000 people in

Ohio. Life insurance is actually two products: one for savings, and one for indemnity in case of death. Since there is a savings component, it is very important that tax policy be structured to be consistent with other savings products. To the extent there is different tax treatment between the savings component of a life insurance product and the savings component of some other financial contract, the state's tax policy could bias or reduce the amount of savings within the state. Of the approximately 695 companies writing business in Ohio, 47 are domestic companies. These companies account for 13 percent of the life business written in Ohio.

Other. In addition to accident and health insurance written by life insurance companies or by traditional property-liability companies, there are a number of other providers of health coverage. There are Blue Cross/Blue Shield providers in Ohio.[3] These companies are now classified as domestic mutual property-liability companies. In 1991 they accounted for $1.885 billion in subscriber premiums, representing 21 percent of the non-life premiums (excluding HMOs) in Ohio. In addition, there are a number of health maintenance organizations (HMOs), with $1.755 billion in premiums in 1991.[4] These companies can elect an exemption from the premium tax in exchange for open enrollment[5] and community rating.[6] However, open enrollment and community rating are potentially very costly and not many HMOs elect this exemption.

There are also a number of fraternal insurance companies. These companies provide coverage to members of certain fraternal organization, such as the Knights of Columbus or the Alliance of Transylvanian Saxons. In Ohio there are 14 domestic fraternals and 63 foreign fraternals. In 1991, these companies accounted for 3.15 percent of total premiums written in the life insurance industry in Ohio.

CURRENT STRUCTURE OF OHIO'S INSURANCE TAX

History of Insurance Taxation

Historically, insurance premiums are taxed, rather than notions of income. This has been done for one major reason: simplicity. The calculation of net income for an insurance company is conceptually quite difficult as premiums are collected now, but losses are not realized until a number of periods henceforth. Thus, there is difficulty in determining net income. Reserves set up for future liabilities appear as income to the tax collector. Even if the tax collector understands the special nature of the insurance contract, the tax collector and the insurer must agree on an appropriate interest rate to discount the reserves to calculate net income for the current year. In addition, even if the reserves are discounted, one may question the appropriateness of taxing reserves. This is because the reserves are the financial capital backing future losses. State solvency regulatory policy requires that the companies keep higher reserves than they might otherwise keep to reduce the risk of insolvency, and thus companies with the required reserves would pay more taxes than those which did not keep the required reserves.

Because of these problems, and the fact that a method of properly discounting the reserves was not available when insurance companies first became taxable, a simple solution of taxing premiums was developed. In fact, this is the predominant method for taxing insurance companies worldwide. However, its use has been strongly criticized, and a responsible state should recognize the implications of the premium tax for the long run viability of the industry.[7]

Structure of the Taxes

Premium tax and franchise tax. Companies writing in Ohio are taxed based on the of 2.5 percent of their gross direct premiums written (premium tax) and 0.6 percent of capital and surplus (franchise tax) if they are an Ohio domesticated (or chartered) company.[8] If the company is a foreign company (or companies chartered outside the state of Ohio) the insurer is taxed 2.5 percent of premiums less return premiums paid for cancellations and considerations received for re-insurance of risks within Ohio.[9] In addition, foreign insurers, if they provide dividends to policyholders can deduct these policyholder dividends if the dividend is in excess of the net cost of insurance.[10] The domestic tax on the minimum basis of 0.6 percent of capital and surplus or two and one-half percent of direct premiums written allows small companies with small capital and surplus (net worth) to be taxed at a relatively low rate. As the company grows and has increasing contributions to capital and surplus, the company pays the premium tax if it is less than the capital and surplus tax.

Box 12-1 shows the schematic for the domestic insurer for determining which tax to pay: the premium tax, which is based on gross premiums, or the capital and surplus tax, which is based on a statutory definition of capital and surplus. Note that this statutory definition includes excess reserves, certain policy holder dividends not paid out, certain reinsurance, and non-admitted assets. From this there is a deduction for ownership of stock in Ohio insurance subsidiaries. For foreign companies, the tax base is direct written premiums net of policy holder dividends.

Based on current law approximately 45 percent of the domestic life industry pays a capital and surplus tax while 65 percent of the property industry pays a capital and surplus tax.

More property-liability companies pay the capital and surplus tax. Further, the property-liability companies paying the capital and surplus tax account for almost 70 percent of domestic premiums. This contrasts sharply

BOX 12-1

Insurer pays the minimum of the two taxes

2.5% Gross Premiums	0.6% of Capital & Surplus
	Capital & Surplus = Excess Reserves + Statutory Reserves + Policy Holder Dividends + Certain Reinsurance + Non-admitted Assets — Common Stock Owned in Ohio Subs

with the experience in the domestic life industry, which accounts for only 6.0 percent of the premiums. Finally, as compared to the industry's median asset size, the property-liability companies are relatively larger than those companies paying capital and surplus taxes in the life industry.

EXEMPTIONS AND OMISSIONS FROM THE TAX BASE

Health premiums by HMOs. Health insurance premiums sold by life and health insurance companies and property-liability companies are treated similarly to other insurance. However, the Blue Cross/Blue Shield companies are subject to different capital and surplus requirements for regulatory solvency purposes than the rest of the industry, and are thus more able to take advantage of the lower tax afforded by the capital and surplus franchise tax.[11]

Some states provide some portion of the health insurance industry with tax advantages.[12] This may reduce the cost of insurance to the consumer as no premium tax is paid. A state may desire to promote the consumption of health insurance by reducing its cost through lower taxation.[13] In Ohio this is partially accomplished through the fact that the Blues can take advantage of their special status and pay the franchise tax rather than the premium tax. However, for horizontal equity purposes state policy should treat all health insurance providers similarly.

As part of Ohio's health care policy, HMOs are potentially exempt from the premium tax. In return, the HMOs agree to have open enrollment and employ community, rather than individual ratings for premium determination. There are a number of issues with regard to this policy. The first concerns horizontal equity. Other types of health insurance providers do pay the premium or franchise tax. This provides an incentive for the potential insured to choose an HMO plan over an insurance plan. A second issue concerns whether HMOs are insurance companies subject to a premium tax. HMOs, if not associated with an insurance company, may actually pay the corporate franchise tax rather than the insurance tax. This may provide the HMOs with a tax benefit.

Table 12-2 shows the size of the HMO population in the state of Ohio. The percentage of individuals in HMOs will likely increase in the future. Thus, the potential exists for a diminishing of the state's premium tax or franchise tax base from traditional health insurance.

In 1991, the loss in premium tax revenue if all HMOs had paid the 2.5 percent premium tax would have been $47.6 million while the loss would have been approximately $2.4 million if all HMO's had paid the franchise tax. The HMO industry would pay if taxed like other insurers, something in between as there are some foreign HMOs operating in Ohio and there are some large Ohio HMOs.

As Figure 12-1 shows, HMO premiums have increased over the last 12 years. As the premiums increase due to individuals and groups leaving traditional insurance policies and switching to HMOs, the loss in terms of tax revenue increases. However, the benefit of having more Ohioans insured may be worth the cost in terms of lost tax revenue and the distortion of the competitive market. If this is true, it makes sense to provide this tax break to all providers of health coverage irrespective of organizational form in exchange for less restrictive underwriting practices.[14]

Annuity Considerations. Annuity considerations are not taxed in Ohio. A number of states, however, do tax these contracts.[15] The majority of states

TABLE 12-2
HMO Enrollment over Time

Year	No. of HMOs	Enrollment	Percent of Ohio Pop
1989	34	1,294,173	11.9
1990	34	1,454,020	13.3
1991	34	1,445,891	13.2
1992	39	1,778,500	16.3

Source: Health Insurance Association of America, *Source Book of Health Insurance Data* (1990-1993).

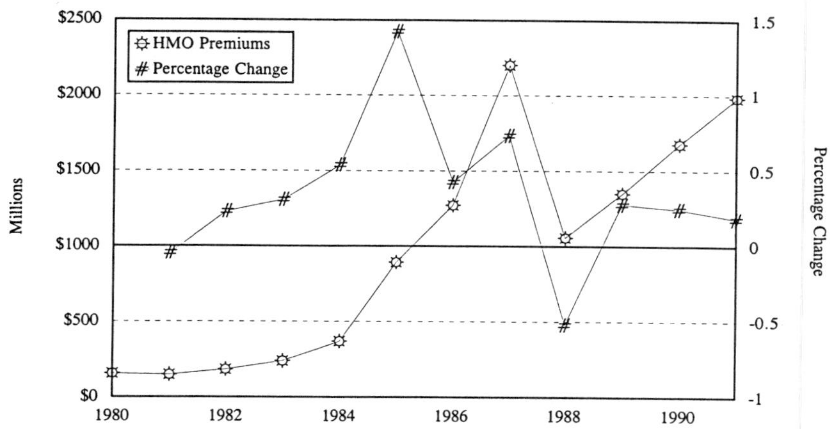

Source: Ohio Department of Revenue, *Annual Report,* (1992).

FIGURE 12-1. HMO premiums over time.

do not tax annuities, and the federal government also treats annuities differently, exempting qualified pension plans from current income taxation. This is because annuities are thought to be savings vehicles for retirement, and the federal policy is to encourage retirement savings. A state that does not tax current annuity considerations is acting consistently with the federal policy, but unlike the federal government, a state that exempts annuity considerations from current taxation is not able to collect taxes when the annuity is paid.

Some states tax annuities, but exempt considerations paid to qualified plans.[16] So, if an annuity is used to fund a retirement savings program, then it is exempt; otherwise it is subject to the premium tax. To gauge the size of the revenues that could be obtained: if Ohio were to tax all annuity considerations it could expect to receive an additional $41,900,000 in premium tax receipts, which would account for almost 15 percent of current premium tax revenues.[17]

A tax on annuities is a tax on savings and, for horizontal equity reasons, a tax must be put on other savings methods if one is placed on annuity consideration. Savings are arguably not the proper subject of taxation as this is the source of the economy's investment and future consumption opportunities. Thus, a tax on savings, especially if out-of-line with other states would reduce savings and potentially impair economic development.

Workers' Compensation. Workers' compensation premiums are also omitted from the Ohio tax base, because workers' compensation insurance is provided by a state-run monopoly. States have different policies on how the workers' compensation market operates. Some states believe that competition will bring about lower rates while others, such as Ohio, believe that a state-run enterprise will serve the better business of Ohio. Because workers' compensation can be a very expensive insurance, the state could decide to provide the insurance free of tax to the business in Ohio. Currently, approximately $2 billion of business is written in workers' compensation insurance premiums and not taxed.

Fire Marshall Tax

Property-liability companies are also subject to a Fire Marshall Tax, which is 0.75 percent and is applied against the proportion of property-liability premiums that cover fire hazards. This percentage differs depending on the line of insurance written. For example, fire insurance is categorized as 100 percent fire coverage, auto insurance is categorized as 10 percent fire coverage, and health insurance is categorized as 0 percent fire coverage.[18]

In 1992 the fire marshall tax collected $6.3 million in revenue, which is used to fund the Office of the State Fire Marshall. The fire marshall tax has been volatile over the decade of the 1980s, and the growth in revenues seems to be trending downwards. The most important item to note, however, that it is combined with the premium tax, and thus the real effective rate of taxation on fire related coverage is potentially greater than 2.5 percent. For example, including the premium tax and the fire marshall tax, the effective rate on large domestics and foreign companies can be as high as 3.25 percent.

Retaliatory Taxes

Insurance taxation among the states is unique because of the interrelationship between the taxation policies of the states. Because Congress granted the states complete authority over the regulation and taxation of the insurance industry, subject to relatively minor constraints, states authorize what has been called "retaliatory taxation."[19] The system of retaliatory taxation seems complex, but in its simplest terms says that if another state taxes Ohio's companies at a higher rate than Ohio does, then companies in those high-tax states must pay to Ohio the premium tax plus a tax based on the amount of the difference in the taxes. For example, Alabama taxes Ohio companies operating in that state at 4.00 percent of premiums if they cover Alabama risks. Thus, an Alabama company writing business in Ohio pays the Ohio premium tax at the rate of 2.5 percent of direct premiums, and an additional tax of 1.5 percent, which is the difference between the rate that an Ohio company would pay in Alabama and the rate applicable in Ohio. Similarly, Ohio companies would pay retaliatory taxes to other states if the

Ohio rate is greater than the state's own rate. For example, Ohio companies writing in Illinois pay the Illinois premium tax of 1 percent plus an additional 1.5 percent in retaliatory taxes to Illinois, because Illinois insurers operating in Ohio would have to pay 2.5 percent to Ohio.

One of the ideas behind the retaliation was to reduce the incentive for states to charge out-of-state companies extremely high rates. Many states discriminate against out-of-state companies in their premium tax rates.[20] This discrimination is legal as long as it passes the equal protection clause's rational basis test.[21]

The retaliatory tax reduces the net effect of this freedom to tax foreign companies. As the rate to foreign companies increases, the rate that the state's own domestics must pay to other states also increases.[22] This has the potential for making a state's own companies less competitive in other states' markets. The higher the state's own rate and the bigger the state's companies are in the national market, the more taxes the state's companies pay to other jurisdictions and the less competitive the company is relative to companies in low-tax states. This, in turn, has effects on the local economy. As the percent of revenues being paid to other states increases due to the home state's tax policy, the less viable is the state's own industry and the lower the employment opportunities there will be in the home state's industry. Thus, a change in the premium tax rate can have a significant effect on the home state's industry even though the home state tax revenues do not change much. More of the fiscal effect of this unique tax interrelationship will be shown in the simulation below.

The retaliatory tax was put in place by the states to keep other states from raising taxes from foreign companies. As a state's rate becomes significantly greater than the average rate among the states, the state's own companies start paying more to other jurisdictions. However, there is another side to this coin that can be employed to Ohio's advantage. Since a relatively large percentage of the Ohio insurance market is served by out-of-state companies, Ohio could reduce its rate below the national average and become a recipient of significant retaliatory tax revenues. In addition, as the rate decreases, the domestics receive a benefit from a lower effective rate versus the foreign companies who now must pay a retaliatory tax to Ohio. Thus, removing the explicit, and perhaps unconstitutional domestic tax, replacing it with a low, but equal tax rate on all companies, Ohio can end up with a constitutional tax preference that can stimulate the insurance industry in the state.

In addition, to the premium tax, other license fees and assessments are also subject to inclusion in the retaliatory tax. This includes assessments for the insolvency funds. The insolvency funds are set up as an *ex-post* insolvency financing mechanism. If a company becomes insolvent, the fund taxes the insurers based on their market share to pay off the Ohio liabilities.

These insolvency assessments are also included in the retaliatory tax calculation in a small number of states.[23]

Foreign Versus Domestic Treatment

Figure 12-2 shows that the ratio of domestic to foreign premiums has increased over time. The domestic industry in 1969 represented about four percent of the total industry's tax contributions. The increase in the early 1980s is the direct result of an increase in the capital surplus franchise tax rate. Since the 1991 increase, the percentage has been relatively stable. By 1993 the domestic industry was paying approximately 20 percent of the premium tax. In contrast, in terms of gross premiums written, the domestic industry wrote approximately 54 percent. This is another indication of the distribution of the tax burden towards out-of-state companies.

A number of states provide some tax breaks solely to domestic companies. These tax breaks are generally of two forms: a rate reduction for investment in certain state assets, or an outright distinction between foreign and domestic companies. Ohio's law, in contrast, is unique. For the first type of preference, a company can reduce its premium tax rate if it invests in state securities or had a relatively high percentage of its assets invested within the state. Alabama, Arkansas, Georgia, and Texas, for example, have laws like this. Although there is no explicit foreign versus domestic distinction in the law, for practical purposes, only small domestics are able to take advantage of the rate reduction, as a large nationwide company could not be expected to invest enough assets in one state to obtain a tax reduction.

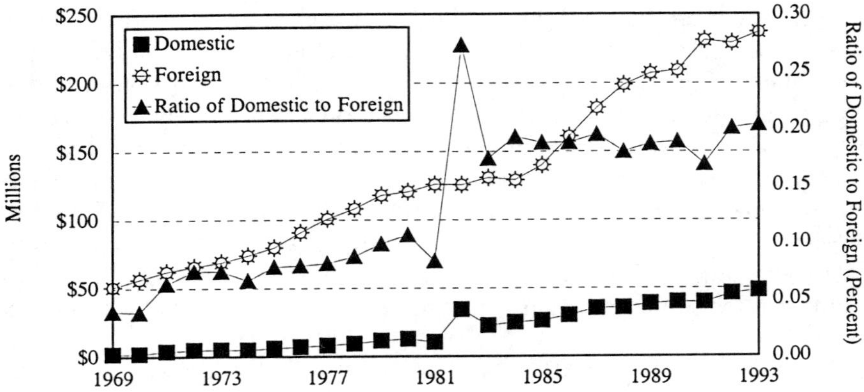

Source: Ohio Department of Revenue, *Annual Report* (1992).

FIGURE 12-2. Premium tax collections (foreign and domestic).

Other states, like Illinois, tax foreign companies differentially higher because the regulators argue that foreign companies are more difficult to regulate for solvency purposes. Other states that employed the discriminatory tax as a method of protecting their domestic industry from interstate competition have either scrapped the differentiation as a result of the Supreme Court's ruling in *Metropolitan v. Ward* or have attempted, like Illinois, to provide a rational basis.

A breakdown of the effective tax rates by foreign and domestic companies in 1992 shows that the domestics do benefit from the lower capital and surplus tax (especially for the domestic property-liability companies). This is shown in Table 12-3. The largest beneficiaries here are in the property-liability industry. Of the domestic industry a large proportion is made up of Blue Cross/Blue Shield premiums. Because of the Blues' ability to use a smaller capital and surplus tax base for regulatory reasons, they tend to reap relatively large benefits from the use of the capital-surplus tax.

A question that needs to be addressed is whether the benefits of this tax break are greater than the costs. One benefit may be that there are more small companies available to provide insurance. However, since there are economies of scale in the provision of insurance, these small companies are not likely to be able to reap the benefits of scale economies that would allow them to compete effectively with larger companies. Thus, the differential taxation may enable potentially inefficient companies to stay in business.

Other Fees

There are a number of important licensing and examination fees paid by

TABLE 12-3
1991 Ohio Insurance Effective Tax Rate for Foreign and Domestic Companies

		Effective Tax Rate (In Percent)
Life and Health	Domestic	1.28
	Foreign	1.80
Property - Liability	Domestic	0.87
	Foreign	2.11

Source: Authors' calculation from Ohio Department of Insurance *Annual Report* (1992) Note: Tax base for comparison purposes is gross premiums written. HMO premiums and retaliatory taxes paid to other states are excluded.

the industry for regulatory purposes. Agents of a company have a $20 license fee, and regulatory examinations are also charged to the firm. In 1992, these fees amounted to over $19 million. The corresponding regulatory expenditures were $12.6 million. Thus, the licenses and fees more than pay for the regulation of the industry.

Guaranty Fund Assessments

Ohio, like all other states except the State of New York, has a post-insolvency assessment due from all companies doing business in Ohio during the year of an insolvency. This assessment is based on the insurer's market share during the year a failed company goes insolvent. Recently, these assessments were minimal, but due to insolvencies outside of the state of Ohio during the mid to late 1980s there were large assessments made against the surviving companies doing business in Ohio. However, these assessments are creditable for the life insurance guaranty fund assessment against the premium tax at a rate of 20 percent a year for five years.[24] There is no corresponding credit for property-liability insolvencies.

Tax Administration

The administration of this tax, unlike most other taxes in Ohio, is under the jurisdiction of the Ohio Department of Insurance. For the domestic companies the Department of Insurance calculates the tax payable based upon the companies' statutory filing of informational returns with the state.[25] For the foreign companies, the companies themselves file a tax return with the Department of Taxation. As the domestic company tax calculation is rather simple, it seems efficient for the Department of Insurance to calculate all domestic company taxes and send out bills.

COMPARISON WITH OTHER STATES

Ohio's Insurance Revenues

Ohio revenues from the premium tax have followed the national trend in premium taxes. Figure 12-3 shows that the national trend is increasing premium tax revenues for the nation. In addition, the percentage change over time is roughly the same for both the state of Ohio and the other states. This implies the Ohio insurance tax revenue stream follows that of the rest of the country. This is to be expected, since the states have very similar tax policies towards insurance.

The growth in Ohio's premium tax revenues seemed to be less responsive to changes in the insurance industry in comparison to the nationwide growth in premium tax revenues from the 1960s until the middle 1980s. From 1986 until the present, the growth rates are very close and likely reflect the increasing efficiency of the insurance market. The cycle in tax revenue growth shown in Figure 12-4 is likely due to the cyclicality of the insurance market.[26] The well-known cycles in the property-liability industry are the subject of tremendous academic and industry debate as to their cause. However, no matter the cause of cycles, they have an impact on revenue growth for the state, making revenue forecasts dependent on the insurance cycle.

The elasticities shown in Figure 12-5 are the percentage changes in premium tax as over the percentage changes in per capita income during the time period. The premium tax income elasticity shows the stability of the tax revenues in changes brought about by recessions and expansions. Taxes are relatively stable if the income elasticity is constant or rising during a recession, and is constant or decreasing in an expansion. One can observe peaks during recessions, and decreases or relatively constant elasticities during expansions. In total, however, the insurance industry's premium taxes provide a relatively stable source of income to the state, even accounting for the insurance profit cycle.

Comparison of Tax Burden with Other States

Most states tax the insurance industry with just a premium tax. Another

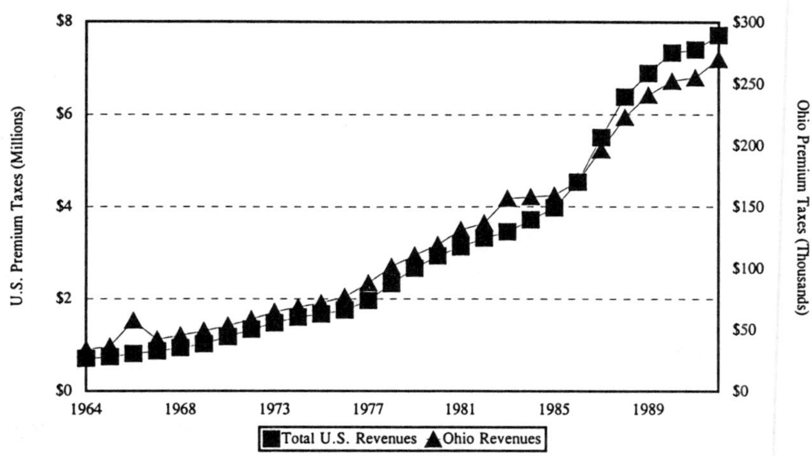

Source: Insurance Information, *Property-Casualty Factbook* (various years).

FIGURE 12-3. United States and Ohio premium taxes.

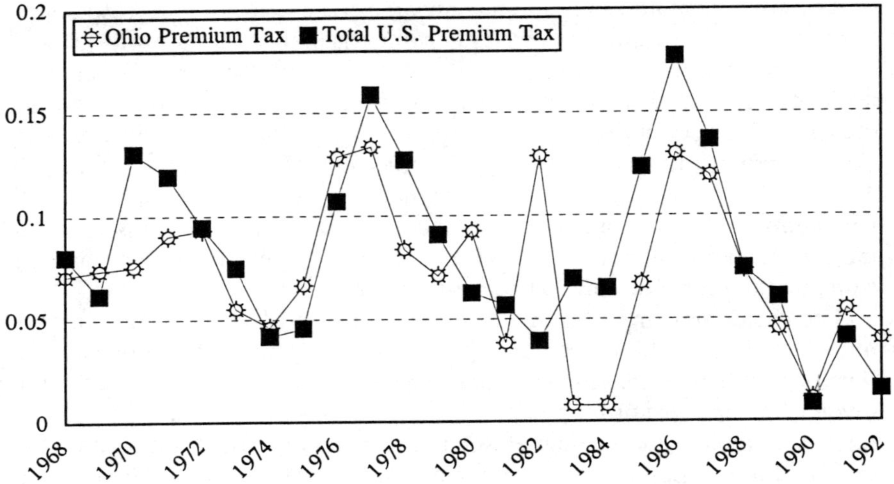

Source: Insurance Information Institute, *Property-Casualty Factbook* (various years.)

FIGURE 12-4. Total United States and Ohio premium tax revenues (% changes).

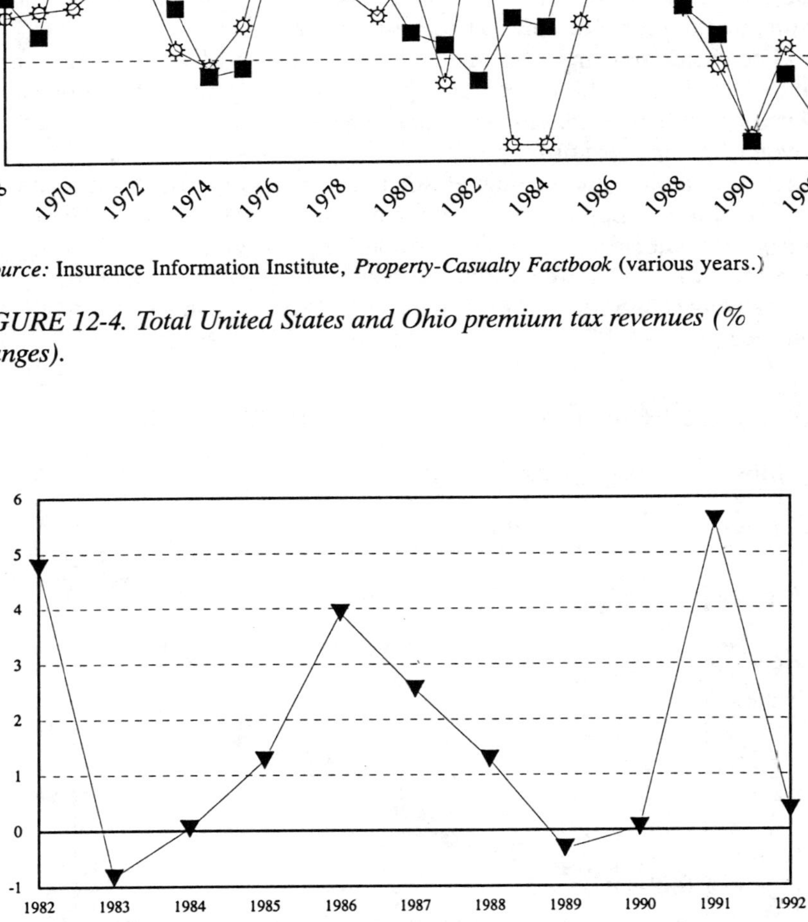

Source: Authors calculations from Ohio Department of Revenue, *Annual Report (1992)*

FIGURE 12-5. Premium tax income elasticity.

group of states uses a combination of a premium tax and an income tax, with a credit for other taxes paid. For example, if a state had both an income tax and a premium tax, it could offer a credit for the income tax paid on the income tax for premium taxes paid. Alternatively, it could offer a credit on the premium tax for income taxes paid. However, as illustrated in Table 12-4, the premium tax is likely to be much greater than the income tax.

There are a number of ways to compare the taxation of the insurance industry between states. First, one could look at the other state's tax rates. This is shown in Appendix Table 12A-1 for the life industry, Table 12A-2 for the property-liability insurance industry, Table 12A-3 for the health insurance industry, and Table 12A-4 for the annuity industry. Ohio's nominal rate is among the higher rates for both the life and health industries and the property-liability industry as Ohio's tax rate for an important part of the industry is 2.5 percent. This is relatively high as there are only a handful of states with higher rates.[27] Examining the tax rate tells only part of the story, especially in a state like Ohio where a significant portion of the industry pays the lesser capital and surplus tax. Thus, examining the effective tax rate provides a different information about the distribution of the tax.

Effective tax rate. There are a number of ways of measuring the tax burden on the Ohio insurance industry. The first is to compare the effective rate for Ohio versus other sates' effective rates. Table 12-5 shows the effective

TABLE 12-4
Effective Net Income Tax Rates for Various Ohio Industries
(In Percent)

Year	Insurance Industry	Retail Trade	Electronics	Banking
1987	21.20	5.80	5.30	6.10
1988	16.90	5.30	5.20	6.00
1989	14.30	5.40	5.10	6.10
1990	16.70	5.10	5.00	6.50
1991	15.60	4.60	6.90	6.10
1992	17.00	6.20	5.00	5.20

Source: Price-Waterhouse and Levin and Driscoll, *Comparative Analysis of the Taxation of the Insurance Industry in Ohio, 1987-1992.* (1994)

rates based on 1991 data for major insurance states and states near Ohio that could conceivably compete with Ohio.

In 1991 the national effective rate was 1.78 percent, while the Ohio effective rate was 1.59.[28] The effective rate for Ohio seems low. This is because the domestic industry has the opportunity of paying the lower of the fran-

TABLE 12-5
Effective Tax Rates for Important Insurance States and Ohio Neighbors

State	Effective Tax Rate (In Percent)	Number of Domestic Companies in 1991
California	2.656	220
Connecticut	1.887	70
Florida	1.142	139
Illinois	0.896	366
Iowa	1.501	228
Indiana	1.160	174
Kentucky	4.046	58
Massachusetts	1.707	68
Michigan	1.193	92
New York	1.336	316
Ohio	**1.588**	**209**
Pennsylvania	1.300	264
Texas	1.931	492
Wisconsin	0.958	222
U.S.	1.728	6002

Source: ACIR (1993). Note the figures do not include the retaliatory tax. In 1991 if the retaliatory tax had been included the effective rate would have been approximately 1.87.

chise tax or the premium tax, and this reduces the effective tax rate of the Ohio insurance industry. If everyone paid the actual tax rate of 2.5 percent then the effective rate would be close to 2.5 percent. Other states in the region, such as Michigan, Wisconsin, Ohio, Pennsylvania, Indiana, and Illinois, have lower effective rates while Kentucky seems to be the only state within the region to have a higher effective tax rate. Illinois, an important insurance state with a very low effective rate, does not tax its domestic industry with a premium tax. Similarly, Michigan's low effective rate is attributed to its low tax rate. However, it should be noted that there is an additional tax not accounted for in these firms. This tax is the retaliatory tax which is discussed further below. This retaliatory tax is paid by the domestic companies to other states. Estimates of the retaliatory tax for the Ohio insurance industry place it at over $50-60 million per year.

Another way is to look at the per capita burden. This is shown in Table 12-6 for a number of years. Table 12-6 contains a great deal of information, but what it shows is that Ohio is under taxing the insurance industry on a per capita basis relative to the national average, but that over time Ohio's per capita tax burden has been increasing. Among its neighbors, Ohio is bettered only by Illinois and Michigan, which is a direct function of these states' tax policies: Illinois does not tax its domestics and Michigan has a low rate. In 1989 Ohio ranked 42nd but, by 1992 Ohio's rank had increased to 39th. At the same time the United States average rank fell from 23 to 27. Thus, Ohio's burden as measured on a per capita basis, while less than the national average, is increasing relative to the nation as a whole. Again, however, the retaliatory tax is not included. In 1991, if the Ohio industry's payments to other states were included, the per capita burden would increase by just over $4. This would increase Ohio's rank by about 10.

Another way to determine a relative tax burden is to look at a standardized tax base across states and a standardized tax rate across states. Using the tax base and the tax rate one can determine a standardized "capacity." By comparing actual revenues received by the state for a particular tax to the capacity determined by the standardized tax base and standardized tax rate, one can then determine whether a state is over- or under-taxing its capacity.

This methodology is what the Advisory Commission on Intergovernmental Relations (ACIR) uses in its study of state tax structures. For the insurance industry the standardized tax base is gross written premiums and the standardized rate is 1.73 percent (representing the United States average tax rate). Figure 12-6 shows that in 1991 Ohio under-utilized its capacity relative to the national average. However, with the exception of California, Connecticut, Kentucky and Texas, the remaining states are also under-utilizing their capacities. In fact, other than Kentucky, Ohio has the highest capacity utilization relative to its neighbors.

The figure should be interpreted with care, however, because like the effective tax rate, the ACIR's methodology does not say anything about the

TABLE 12-6
Insurance Tax and Per Capita Insurance Tax Revenues by State, 1989–1992

State	1989			1990			1991			1992		
	Total (in $000s)	Per Capita	Rank	Total (in $000s)	Per Capita	Rank	Total (in $000s)	Per Capita	Rank	Total (in $000s)	Per Capita	Rank
U.S.	7,340,691	29.57	23	7,369,604	29.63	28	7,721,145	30.69	24	7,875,621	30.88	27
California	1,314,750	45.24	5	1,170,831	39.34	9	1,287,740	42.39	9	1,173,297	38.01	13
Connecticut	175,898	54.31	1	170,163	51.77	2	174,122	52.91	3	160,843	49.02	7
Florida	250,144	19.74	47	322,915	24.87	40	319,567	24.07	41	311,977	23.13	42
Illinois	255,057	21.88	43	166,758	14.59	51	192,876	16.71	51	197,720	17.00	51
Indiana	103,436	18.49	49	107,516	19.39	47	121,809	21.71	44	122,788	21.69	44
Iowa	84,878	29.89	22	86,976	31.32	22	92,288	33.02	18	97,447	34.54	18
Kentucky	151,199	40.57	7	187,573	50.90	3	214,688	57.82	1	206,917	55.10	2
Michigan	76,601	8.26	52	78,647	8.46	52	175,973	18.26	49	178,304	18.89	48
Minnesota	120,639	27.71	29	122,486	28.00	33	129,618	29.25	29	130,617	29.16	33
New York	582,240	32.44	17	699,529	38.88	10	594,889	32.94	19	610,046	33.67	24
Ohio	**252,271**	**23.13**	**42**	**255,149**	**23.52**	**41**	**269,929**	**24.68**	**40**	**281,301**	**25.54**	**39**
Pennsylvania	225,229	27.84	28	352,261	29.65	27	362,473	30.30	25	404,806	33.71	22
Texas	441,550	25.99	35	524,901	30.90	24	595,446	34.32	15	516,081	29.23	22
Wisconsin	76,693	15.76	50	76,882	15.72	50	83,278	16.81	50	68,975	13.78	52

Source: *State Government Finances* (various years); Bureau of the Census Population Projections, 1990-2020, and Insurance Information Institute Factbook (1994). Note that the per capita tax burdens do not include the retaliatory tax. Ohio's burden would be increased by $4.50 per person in 1991 if retaliatory taxes were included.

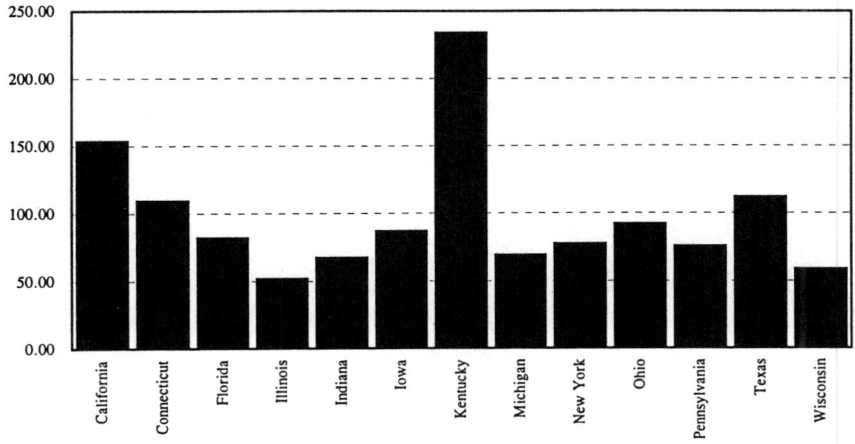

Source: ACIR, (1993).

FIGURE 12-6. Percentage of insurance tax capacity (United States average = 100%).

distribution of the tax burden between foreign and domestic companies and between large and small companies. In addition, it does not include the retaliatory tax. Also, Ohio provides a tax differential for small (and potentially mid-sized) domestics that significantly reduces their tax burden, leaving large domestics and foreign companies with a higher burden.

Figure 12-7 also shows the behavior of important insurance states and neighbors of Ohio taxation of insurance capacity during the last decade. Over time, Ohio's taxation of the insurance industry has remained constant, as the rate appears close to 100 percent during the years studied by the ACIR. Illinois, Indiana, Florida, and Wisconsin also experienced relatively constant tax policies over time. States with a large variation over time, such as Kentucky and Texas, are changing their insurance tax policies and this is reflected in the wide variation of the use of capacity. Of the states shown in Figure 12-7 only Iowa has experienced a declining trend. This is likely due to its desire to encourage the development of the Iowan insurance industry.

MAIN ISSUES AND PROBLEMS

THE PROS AND CONS OF PREMIUM TAXATION

Why use a premium tax? As mentioned above, a premium tax is a relatively simple tax. In general, a company merely adds up its gross written pre-

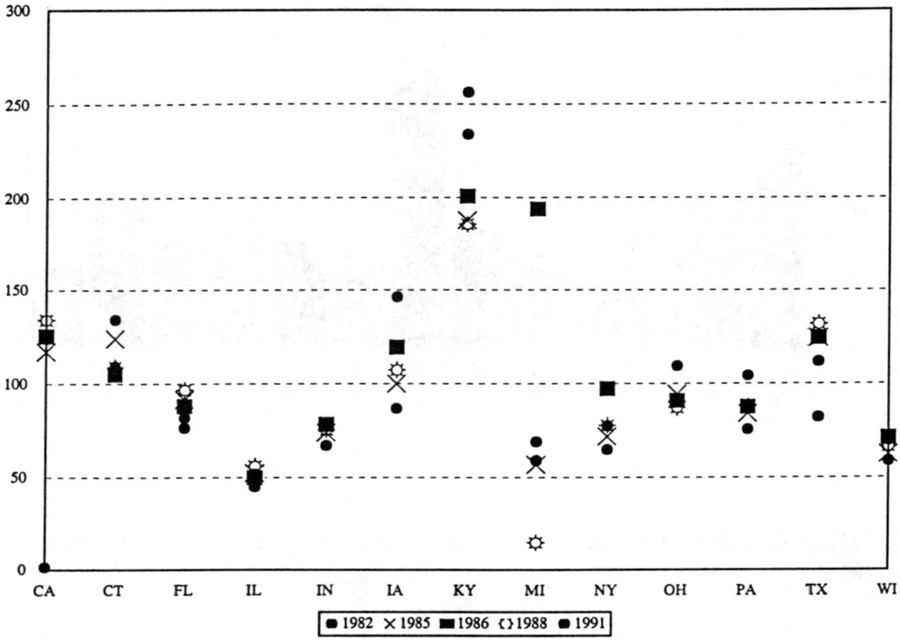

Source: ACIR, *Significant Features* (various years).

FIGURE 12-7. Percentage of tax capacity for insurance premium tax.

miums and applies a tax rate to determine the tax bill. This is a very simple process for the company and a simple tax for the state to administer and audit. In addition, the premium tax generally produces a steadily increasing source of revenue.

Another reason a premium tax is preferable to other taxes is that the states have a long history of using this tax and there have been few complaints. Alternatives such as the income tax are difficult (in theory) to implement. Thus, simplicity, historical inertia, and the difficulty of implementation of alterative taxes are the major reasons to keep and use the premium tax.

Why States should not use a Premium Tax. There are a number of reasons to avoid using a premium tax, as outlined by Skipper.[29] First, the premium tax is regressive, meaning that the lower-income insured pay a higher portion of their income in these taxes than do the higher-income insured.

Second, since cash value life insurance can be a method of savings, a premium tax on cash value life insurance is a tax on savings, which can reduce the incentive to save or provide incentives for the consumer to purchase a savings product from another financial service provider.[30]

Third, the premium tax is regressive against age, health status, risk classification, and occupation. For example, older consumers pay higher premiums for life insurance and non-group health insurance. Thus, older people pay a higher proportion of their income in premium taxes than do the younger insured. The reverse is true for auto policies, as young people are considered higher auto risks and thus pay more premium taxes relative to older drivers. In addition, the insured who are in poor health or in hazardous occupations pay higher health and disability premiums relative to those in better health and lower-risk occupations. Finally, people who live in high-risk areas, such as rural areas without nearby fire departments or those in areas more prone to natural disasters, will pay more in premium taxes as their premiums will be higher than those of people living in low-risk areas.

Fourth, consumers who purchase small policies pay more taxes per unit of insurance than those who purchase larger policies. This is because premiums are set to cover the cost of the risk plus the cost of administering and maintaining the policy. This administration expense is a fixed cost, and for small policies percentage of the premium is relatively high compared to larger policies. This makes the small policy (which contains a higher proportion of expense costs relative to risk costs) bear a larger per insurance unit cost of the premium tax.

Fifth, there are a number of insurance substitutes, most notably self-insurance, which are not taxed. In Ohio, this is more likely to be a problem in the health insurance area. A company could potentially reduce its health care expenses by 2.5 percent by self-insuring. This could be a non-trivial expense for health care coverage.

The availability of tax-free self-insurance may cause the insured to opt out of the market in times of insurance shortages like that experienced in the liability lines during the mid-1980s. As premiums are bid up, consumers will reduce their purchases of insurance and self-insure.

Sixth, the premium tax also has problems when there is differential taxation between foreign and domestic companies. Under Ohio's tax law, companies may be able to benefit from a lower effective tax rate through the capital and surplus franchise tax. Smaller companies are not likely to be as efficient as larger companies because of the tremendous economies of scale in the insurance industry. Thus, the tax preference can protect inefficient domestic firms from competition in the free and open market. In addition, since capital and surplus are not apportioned to all states where an insurer operates, the tax break benefits and encourages single state companies, thus concentrating rather the spreading risk.[31]

Finally, the premium tax must be paid irrespective of whether the insurer earns a profit. This means the tax is regressive against start-up firms those that are losing money. Ohio's tax law provides an alternative tax for small companies through the capital and surplus franchise tax. Since this tax typically benefits smaller companies, a large insurer that is in financial difficulty is hurt by the premium tax and this can affect the risk of insolvency.

The premium tax is regressive against profits, and Table 12-5 shows the effect of this regressivity by comparing effective tax rates based on net income for some industries in Ohio. Neubig (1994) uses a simulation to compute effective tax rates for a number of industries.[32] The tax rate is significantly higher for the insurance industry than for other selected industries in Ohio. However, these other industries (with the exception of banking) are also subject to a sales tax and thus the comparison is not as clean. The best comparison would be between the two financial service industries: banking and insurance. The difference here is 200-300 percent each year. Since banks do compete against insurers and other financial institutions, horizontal equity requires that competitors be treated equally.

Because of the nature of the insurance tax system in Ohio and the other states, there should be two major effects on Ohio companies of changing the premium tax rate. The first is that taxes payable to the state of Ohio change, and the second is that taxes payable to other states by Ohio companies change due to the operation of the retaliatory tax. A tax increase, for example, would increase the premium taxes due to Ohio as well as the premium taxes due by Ohio insurers to states with lower premium tax rates. Similarly, a decrease in tax rates would lower Ohio premium tax collections as well as lowering premium taxes paid to other states for retaliatory purposes, but may cause an increase in retaliatory taxes collected from foreign companies.

SIMULATION OF OHIO'S INSURANCE TAX STRUCTURE

This section is divided into three parts. First, we examine the effect of changing taxes on the insurance industry examining the effects on both the life and non-life industries. Second, we examine the effect of a tax changes on the life and health industry. Finally, we examine the effect of the retaliatory tax on the Ohio domestic industry and the resulting revenue change to the state.

THE PROPERTY-LIABILITY INDUSTRY SIMULATION

Table 12-7 shows the results of a simulation of changing the tax rate on the property-liability industry. The simulation shows that the domestic tax revenue falls as the premium tax is reduced from 2.5 percent to 2.0 percent. As the tax rate falls, premiums are taxed at a lower rate. Those companies that can pay the lower premium tax will do so. However, the franchise tax is

TABLE 12-7
Property-Liability Industry Simulation Results, 1992

A. Property-Liability Simulation of Changing Premium Tax Structure Holding Capital and Surplus Franchise Tax constant (in $ millions).

	Alternative Premium Tax Rates				
	2.00%	2.25%	2.50%	2.75%	3.00%
Domestic Companies					
Premium Tax Revenues	8.56	9.53	10.50	11.37	12.40
Franchise Tax Revenues	25.38	25.49	25.57	25.74	25.74
Total Domestic Tax Payable	33.94	35.02	36.07	37.11	38.14
Number of Companies Paying Franchise Tax	67	68	70	73	73
Foreign Companies					
Premium Tax Revenues	85.26	94.45	104.36	114.57	124.80
Total	119.20	129.47	140.43	151.68	162.94

B. Property-Liability Capital and Surplus Franchise Tax Simulation Holding Premium Tax Rate Constant (in $ millions)

	Alternative Capital and Surplus Franchise Tax Rates								
	0.20%	0.30%	0.40%	0.50%	0.60%	0.70%	0.80%	0.90%	1.00%
Total Domestic Tax Revenues	16.68	22.82	27.42	31.80	36.07	40.33	44.56	48.39	51.48
Franchise Tax Revenues on Capital and Surplus	15.19	14.39	17.64	21.46	25.57	29.62	33.85	27.45	30.54
Number of Firms Paying C&S Tax	86	80	76	73	70	67	67	62	62
Premium Tax Revenues	1.49	8.43	9.78	10.34	10.5	10.71	10.71	20.94	20.94
Number of Firms Paying Premium Tax	21	27	31	34	37	40	40	45	45

Note: Current tax scenario highlighted in grey.

still in effect and there is little change in the number of companies paying the franchise tax over the premium tax as shown in Panel B..

As the tax rate increases the amount of tax payable to Ohio increases, with the increase coming from the increase in the premium tax. For the foreign companies, the change in the premium tax directly affects the premium tax due. As the rate increases, the revenues increase proportionally, while if the rate is decreased the revenue decreases similarly.

Life Insurance Industry Simulation

Table 12-8 shows the life insurance simulation results. The results are similar to those of the property-liability simulation. As the premium tax rate increases, the number of companies paying the franchise tax increases

TABLE 12-8
Life Insurance Simulation Results
Holding Franchise Rate Constant (In Millions)

A. Premium Tax Simulation for the Life Insurance Industry.

	Alternative Premium Tax Rates				
	2.00%	2.25%	2.50%	2.75%	3.00%
Domestic Companies					
Premium Tax Revenues	8.01	8.90	9.55	4.78	2.88
Franchise Tax Revenues	1.87	1.98	2.27	8.19	9.96
Total Domestic Tax Payable	9.88	10.88	11.82	12.97	12.84
Number of Companies Paying Franchise Tax	29	28	27	23	22
Foreign Companies					
Premium Tax Revenues	99.34	111.76	124.18	136.60	149.02
Total	109.22	122.64	136.00	149.57	161.86

B. Franchise Tax Simulation Results for the Life Insurance Industry.

	Alternative Capital and Surplus Franchise Tax Rates								
	0.20%	0.30%	0.40%	0.50%	0.60%	0.70%	0.80%	0.90%	1.00%
Total Domestic Tax Revenues	5.00	7.01	8.80	10.33	11.84	11.19	11.47	11.70	11.93
Franchise Tax Revenues on Capital and Surplus	0.58	1.39	2.12	3.79	2.29	9.03	9.65	9.65	9.65
Number of Firms Paying C&S Tax	32	32	32	30	27	24	21	17	13
Premium Tax Revenues	4.42	5.62	6.68	6.54	9.55	2.16	1.82	2.05	2.28
Number of Firms Paying Premium Tax	17	17	28	25	22	19	17	17	17

Note: Current tax scenario highlighted in grey.

slightly and the total amount of revenue increases slightly. As the rate increases, however, the premium tax becomes the lesser of the capital tax and premium tax revenues decline. Franchise tax revenues increase almost enough to offset the loss of the premium tax revenues when the rate increased to 3.0 percent. For the foreign companies the rate changes directly affect the premium tax bill. As the rate increases the foreign premium tax bill increases and as the rate decreases the foreign tax bill decreases. Premium tax changes have a larger revenue affect in the foreign market them in the domestic market.

Panel B of the Table 12-8 shows the effect of changing the capital and surplus rate on the revenues collected from the domestic industry. The current rate is 0.6 percent. Reductions in the rate cause the number of companies paying the capital and surplus tax to increase and the amount collected by both the premium tax and the capital and surplus franchise tax to decrease. As the franchise tax rate increases, the number of firms paying the franchise tax decreases, but the franchise tax revenues increase dramatically. In contrast, as the tax rate increases the premium tax bill falls as more is collected through the franchise tax. Overall, the total tax bill from domestics increases as the franchise tax rate increases from 0.2 percent to 1.0 percent, but at the cusp of moving from 0.6 percent to 0.7 percent, the total amount of tax decreases slightly. This is due to the fact that the mixture of companies paying the franchise tax changes dramatically. Certain companies with previously large premium tax bills are now paying a slightly lower franchise tax.

Retaliatory Tax Simulation

The retaliatory tax due to Ohio is relatively small, amounting to approximately \$2.5 million in 1993 and representing 0.9 percent of the total franchise and premium tax bill for insurance companies. However, the retaliatory tax paid by Ohio companies to the rest of the states is substantial. Through a simulation of the retaliatory tax provision of Ohio's insurance tax law it was determined that at the current rate, Ohio companies paid approximately \$58 billion to other states. Table 12-9 shows the results of the simulation. As the rate is reduced from the current 2.5 percent, we see an increase in the amount collected by Ohio. The amount collected does not

TABLE 12-9
Retaliatory Tax Simulation (In Millions)

	Collected by Ohio	**Paid to Other States**		
Rate	Total	Life	Property-Liability	Total
2.50	2.54	12.38	46.00	58.38
2.25	3.26	8.20	26.38	34.58
2.00	5.32	4.66	10.85	15.51
1.75	19.79	2.65	5.43	8.08
1.50	34.72	1.33	2.53	3.86
1.35	43.72	0.66	0.77	1.42

Note: Current tax situation is highlighted in grey.

seem to increase dramatically until the rate falls below 2.0 percent. This is to be expected, since the United States average rate is slightly less than 2.0 percent. In addition, as the rate falls the amount paid to other states decreases. This is also expected, as the states' retaliatory provisions require payment only if the home state taxes at a higher amount. Thus, Ohio companies would benefit dramatically as a result of a reduction in the rate.

REFORM OPTIONS AND IMPLICATIONS

OPTIONS FOR REFORM

Equalize foreign and domestic rates. By trading all foreign and domestic companies similarly it would be possible to lower the effective tax rate. This is shown in Table 12-10. Table 12-10 has the total premiums written for the Ohio insurance industry. For the first comparison, by adding up all the life premiums (net of annuities) and including the fraternal life premiums to the sum of property-casualty premiums (net of HMO premiums) and dividing this by the total premium and franchise tax collected, the revenue neutral rate would by 1.83 percent in 1993. This is shown as Ratio 1. Over the last five years Ratio 1 has been relatively stable ranging between 1.77 percent to 1.83 percent. Adding the fire marshall and retaliatory tax collections into the numerator yields Ratio 2. Thus, the revenue neutral level of insurance taxation would be 1.87 percent in 1993. This amount has ranged between 1.85-1.90 percent in the last five years.

Note that Ratio 2 rate is biased upward. This is due to the operation of the retaliatory tax. At a rate of 1.90 percent, the Ohio rate will be lower than the national average and potentially significant retaliatory tax revenues will accrue. These additional revenues could then be employed to lower the effective rate further, which in turn will generate a further collection of retaliatory taxes. Table 12-9 shows that by moving from a rate of 2.50 percent to a rate of say, 1.75 percent will yield almost $20 million in retaliatory collections. Those effected by equalizing the rate would be those in the domestic industry paying the capital and surplus tax. These are predominantly small property-liability companies and the Blues. However, the larger companies operating in interstate markets would benefit tremendously because the retaliatory tax burden would be dramatically reduced. At an effective rate approaching 1.35 percent our simulation predicts a net gain of $43 million—due to foreign company payments of retaliatory taxes due to Ohio.

Equalize tax treatment between HMOs and health insurers. By exempting all health insurers and HMOs from paying the premium or franchise tax, there would be a loss of revenue. If we were to use a rate applicable to all other insurers, the effective rate on gross premiums written net of policyholder dividends would be approximately 1.64 percent (in Ratio 2A). This is

TABLE 12-10
Calculated Effective Rates from Broadening the Tax Base and Taxing All Premiums Equally

	1993	1992	1991	1990	1989
Total Life Premiums and Annuity Considerations	$9,081,722,000	$7,497,835,000	$7,194,570,066	$7,169,898,105	$6,565,924,100
- Domestic annuity considerations	178,219,000	221,949,000	183,739,076	125,871,164	143,772,221
-Foreign annuity considerations	1,440,366,000	1,473,470,000	1,515,980,025	1,625,038,500	1,472,956,281
+all Fraternal Premiums	223,328,000	249,892,000	197,718,328	168,791,724	148,232,527
Net Life Premiums	7,686,465,000	6,052,308,000	5,692,569,293	5,587,780,165	5,097,428,125
Total PC Premiums	12,285,361,000	11,554,705,000	11,069,768,005	10,670,968,663	10,029,780,202
-Domestic HMOs	2,378,568,000	2,183,931,000	1,900,930,864	1,593,099,358	1,317,552,690
-Foreign HMOs	88,315,000	43,787,000	82,547,481	85,341,646	30,687,230
Net PC Prems	9,818,478,000	9,326,987,000	9,086,289,660	8,992,527,659	8,681,540,282
Total Net Premiums (Net Life + Net PC)	17,504,943,000	15,379,295,000	14,778,858,953	14,580,307,824	13,778,968,407
Total Premium & Franchise Tax collected	319,565,254	282,668,411	270,980,387	259,462,913	244,254,539
Total Premium, Franchise, Fire Marshall & Retaliatory Taxes	327,357,383	291,489,583	280,947,009	270,274,666	255,056,067
(1) Ratio of Premium and Franchise Taxes to Total Net	1.83%	1.84%	1.83%	1.78%	1.77%
(2) Ratio of All taxes to Total Premiums	1.87%	1.90%	1.90%	1.85%	1.85%
(1A) Ratio 1 with HMOs Paying Premium Tax	1.60%	1.61%	1.62%	1.60%	1.61%
(2A) Ratio 2 with HMOs Paying Premium Tax	1.64%	1.66%	1.68%	1.66%	1.69%

Source: Ohio Department of Insurance, *Annual Report* and unpublished data. Note: Equalized tax rate does not include potential retaliatory taxes collected by the State of Ohio as a result of lowering the effective rate. Inclusion of such taxes will lower the effective rate.

still less than the current 2.5 percent rate, and is lower than the national average effective tax rate. In addition, the simulation of the retaliatory tax shows that by reducing Ohio's effect rate it is possible to increase Ohio's collections from the retaliatory tax by more than $20 million. This could be used to lower the effective rate further.

Employ an income tax on the insurance industry. Since the premium tax is a tax on gross receipts rather than net income there is a relatively large difference between the burden on a corporation paying a net income tax and the burden on an insurance company paying a premium tax, all other things equal. Table 12-4 above shows that the effective income tax rate on the banking industry is about one-third that on the insurance industry.

The two industries should have approximately the same burden, as they are similar in many respects. In 1992, for example, the effective net income tax rate was 17 percent. By reducing that rate to what a non-financial corporation pays, it would be possible to lessen the burden. However, the effective tax rates shown in Table 12-4 do not include the effect of sales or other property taxes, and thus a strong argument can be made that the effective rate need not be reduced to the 5-6 percent range.

An income tax could be implemented relatively well, as insurers currently pay federal income taxes and, as with the non-financial corporations, Ohio could piggy-back on the federal definition of income. This would increase horizontal equity, especially if other financial institutions were taxed on an income basis. The problems with piggy-backing on the federal definition of net taxable income are three-fold. First, there is still some debate over the proper definition of income for an insurance company, and this debate becomes even more technical depending on the organizational form of the insurer, .i.e. whether it is a stock or mutual company. Second, by tying to the federal definition, Ohio takes all the potential problems of defining income and incorporates them into its tax law. Third, an important issue concerns the appropriate apportionment formula. Since insurers do not have large amounts of property, it may be appropriate to use a single factor formula based on sales or gross premiums written. Most states with corporate income taxes on insurance use this single factor apportionment formula. This formula would benefit domestic insurance companies for exactly the same reasons that single sales apportionment factor in the general corporate income tax would benefit Ohio corporations.

APPENDIX A
PREMIUM TAX RATES FOR VARIOUS LINES OF INSURANCES

TABLE 12A-1
Life Insurance Premium Tax Rates, 1993

State	Domestic Rate %	Foreign Rate %	State	Domestic Rate %	Foreign Rate %
Alabama (1)	1.00	3.00	Nebraska	1.00	1.00
Alaska	2.70	2.70	Nevada (2)	3.50	3.50
Arizona	2.00	2.00	New Hampshire	2.00	2.00
Arkansas1 (1)	2.50	2.50	New Jersey	2.01	2.01
California	2.35	2.35	New Mexico (1)	3.00	3.00
Colorado	2.25	2.25	New York (6)	0.80	0.80
Connecticut	2.00	2.00	North Carolina (7)	1.90	1.90
Delaware	2.00	2.00	North Dakota	2.00	2.00
D.C.	2.25	2.25	Ohio	2.50	2.50
Florida	1.75	1.75	Oklahoma (10)	2.25	2.25
Georgia (1)	0.50	2.25	Oregon	2.25	2.25
Hawaii	2.75	2.75	Pennsylvania	2.00	2.00
Idaho	3.00	3.00	Rhode Island	2.00	2.00
Illinois	0.00	2.00	South Carolina	0.75	0.75
Indiana	2.00	2.00	South Dakota	2.50	2.50
Iowa	2.00	2.00	Tennesse (1)	1.75	2.00
Kansas	1.00	2.00	Texas (1)	2.40	2.40
Kentucky	2.00	2.00	Utah	2.25	2.25
Louisiana	2.25	2.25	Vermont	2.00	2.00
Maine	2.00	2.00	Virginia (2)	2.25	2.25
Maryland	2.00	2.00	Washington	2.00	2.00
Massachusetts	2.00	2.00	West Virginia	3.00	3.00
Michigan	1.33	1.33	Wisconsin (8)	2.00	2.00
Minnesota	2.00	2.00	Wyoming	1.60	1.60
Mississippi	3.00	3.00			
Missouri	2.00	2.00			
Montana (5)	2.75	2.75			

Source: CCH, State Tax Guide, ACLI

(1) Can reduce if investing in assets within the state.
(2) Domestic mutuals pay 1.00%.
(3) Franchise tax on all legal reserve mutuals based domestically.
(4) Franchise tax based upon authorized capital stock.
(5) Plus an additional 7.00% surcharge.
(6) Premium tax and income tax are payable up to 2.6% of premiums.
(7) 7.25% for 1992.
(8) Domestic rate is graduated and increases to foreign.

TABLE 12A-2
State Premium Tax Rates on P&C Companies, 1993

State	Domestic Rate %	Foreign Rate %	Fire Rate*	State	Domestic Rate %	Foreign Rate %	Fire Rate
Alabama	4.00	1.00	+0.08	Nebraska	1.00	1.00	1.08
Alaska	2.70	2.70	+0.08	Nevada	3.50	3.50	
Arizona	2.00	2.00	2.20	New Hampshire	2.00	2.00	
Arkansas (1)	2.50	2.50		New Jersey	2.01	2.01	
California	2.35	2.35		New Mexico (2)	3.00	1.90	
Colorado	2.25	2.25		New York (12)	1.30	1.30	
Connecticut	2.00	2.00		North Carolina (13)	1.99	1.33	3.32
Delaware	1.75	2.00	2.00	North Dakota	1.75	1.75	
D.C.	2.25	2.25		Ohio(9)	2.50	2.50	3.25
Florida	1.75	1.75	1.00	Oklahoma (10)	2.25	2.25	2.63
Georgia (2)	2.25	0.50		Oregon	2.25	2.25	3.25
Hawaii	4.70	4.70		Pennsylvania	2.00	2.00	
Idaho (2)	3.00	1.60		Rhode Island	2.00	2.00	
Illinois(5)	0.00	2.00	2.50	South Carolina	1.25	1.25	2.35
Indiana (2)	2.00	2.00	2.50	South Dakota	2.50	2.50	2.55
Iowa	2.00	2.00		Tennessee	2.50	2.50	3.25
Kansas	2.00	1.00	2.00	Texas (2)	3.50	3.50	
Kentucky	3.50	3.50	4.25	Utah	2.25	2.25	
Louisiana (4)	1.25	1.25	2.00	Vermont	2.00	2.00	
Maine	2.00	2.00	3.00	Virginia	2.25	2.25	
Maryland (2)(6)	2.00	2.00	2.00	Washington	2.00	2.00	
Massachusetts(12)	2.28	2.28		West Virginia	3.00	3.00	4.00
Michigan (11)	1.33	1.33		Wisconsin	2.00	2.00	2.38
Minnesota	2.00	2.00		Wyoming	1.60	1.60	
Mississippi	3.00	3.00	4.00				
Missouri (7)	2.00	2.00					
Montana (8)	2.75	2.75	3.75				

Source: CCH, *Multistate Tax Guide*, NAIC, *Retaliatory Tax Manual (1993)*.

*Fire marshall taxes are added on to fire related lines of insurance. For states with differential rates between foreign and domestics, the rate is shown as an add on, for states with non discrimination between foreign and domestic, the rate shown is the total and final rate.

(1) Retaliatory taxes are 0 for companies with 15% or more of their assets in Arkansan owned companies.
(2) Qualified companies with investment in state can conceivably reduce to rate of domestics.
(3) Also corporate income tax (Indiana Financial Institutions Tax) of 8.5% on AGI.
(4) Including retaliatory taxes.
(5) Domestics pay an income tax.
(6) No premium tax payable for domestic mutual fire companies.
(7) Small mutual taxed lower.
(8) There is an additional 7% surcharge on premiums.
(9) Fire rate is maximum possible fire rate. Fire rate is 0.75 percent times the amount of fire business contained in the line.
(10) Can reduce up to 50% if company has home office in state
(11) Michigan Single Business Tax taxes premiums at 1.33%.
(12) Domestics pay 1 percent on gross investment income.
(14) Domestic fire pays 2.66

TABLE 12A-3
Health Insurance on Annuity Premiums, 1993

State	Domestic Rate %	Foreign Rate %	Blue Cross Exemption*	State	Domestic Rate %	Foreign Rate %	Blue Cross Exemption*
Alabama	1.00	3.00		Nebraska (2)	0.50	0.50	
Alaska	2.70	2.70		Nevada	3.50	3.50	
Arizona	2.00	2.00		New Hampshire	2.00	2.00	Yes
Arkansas	2.50	2.50		New Jersey (3)	1.05	1.05	
California	2.35	2.35		New Mexico	3.00	3.00	
Colorado	2.25	2.25		New York (4)	0.80	0.80	
Connecticut	2.00	2.00		North Carolina	1.90	1.90	
Delaware	2.00	2.00		(8)	1.75	1.75	
D.C.	2.25	2.25		North Dakota	2.50	2.50	
Florida	1.75	1.75		Ohio (9)	2.25	2.25	
Georgia	2.25	2.25		Oklahoma	0.00	2.25	
Hawaii	4.70	4.70		Oregon	2.00	2.00	
Idaho	3.00	3.00	Yes	Pennsylvania	2.00	2.00	Yes
Illinois	0.00	2.00		Rhode Island	1.25	1.25	
Indiana	2.00	2.00		South Carolina	2.50	2.50	
Iowa	2.00	2.00		South Dakota	1.75	2.00	
Kansas	1.00	2.00		Tennessee	2.40	2.40	
Kentucky	0.00	2.00		Texas	2.25	2.25	
Louisiana	2.25	2.25		Utah	2.00	2.00	
Maine	2.00	2.00		Vermont	2.25	2.25	
Maryland	2.00	2.00	Yes	Virginia	2.00	2.00	
Massachusetts	2.00	2.00	Yes	Washington	3.00	3.00	
Michigan	1.33	1.33		West Virginia	0.00	0.00	
Minnesota (7)	2.00	2.00		Wisconsin (5)	1.60	1.60	
Mississippi	3.00	3.00		Wyoming (6)			
Missouri	2.00	2.00					
Montana(1)	2.75	2.75	Yes				

Source: ACLI, Premium Tax Manual.

*Not necessarily a complete list.

(1) Also, surtax of 7% (July 1, 1992 - June 30, 1993).
(2) .5% represents "Group" rate. individual rate is 1 %.
(3) 1.05% represents "Group" rate. Individual rate is 2.1%.
(4) Maximum tax liability is 2.6% of premiums. Additional surcharge based on franchise tax.
(5) Domestic companies pay no premium tax, but pay a 3.5% license fee on apportioned gross income.
(6) Will be 1.2% in 1993, and .75% after 1994.
(7) Rate of 1% on Blues commences in 1996.
(8) Blues taxed at 0.50%.
(9) Domestic companies pay the minimum of 2.5% gross premiums tax or 0.6% Capital and surplus tax.

TABLE 12A-4
State Tax Rates on Annuity Premiums, 1993

State	Tax Rate on Qualified Retirement Plans	Tax Rate %
Alabama	1.00	1.00
California	0.50	2.35
District of Columbia	2.25	2.25
Florida (1)	1.00	1.00
Iowa		2.00
Kansas		2.00
Kentucky	2.00	2.00
Maine		2.00
Mississippi		2.00
Nevada		3.50
North Carolina		1.90
South Dakota		1.25
West Virginia	1.00	1.00
Wyoming		1.00

Sources: CCH, *State Tax Guide*, and ACLI.

Note: All other states do not tax annuity premiums.

(1) Exempt if tax savings is passed to customer.

APPENDIX B
DESCRIPTION OF THE OHIO INSURANCE TAX SIMULATION PROCESS

Description of Simulation

The simulation of the insurance tax used the data compiled by the National Association of Insurance Commissioners (NAIC). These data are statutory filings with the states and contain nearly all the information necessary to calculate a taxpayer's actual tax liability.

Domestic Companies

Using information provided by the Department of Insurance and the Nationwide Insurance Group, we calculated the domestic tax bill for each company in much the same way the Insurance Department would calculate it. A very few assumptions needed to be made in order to obtain the final tax total. First, there is a deduction for ownership of stock in Ohio subsidiaries. These companies are not identified separately in the annual statement, as only the total ownership interest in affiliates is reported. Thus, it was assumed after trial and error that ½ of the affiliate investments were in Ohio companies.

FOREIGN COMPANY SIMULATION

The simulation of foreign company tax returns was derived from the tax returns for both the life and health and property-liability industries. All the necessary data were contained on the NAIC statements.

FIRE MARSHALL TAX

All necessary data were available on the NAIC tapes. Tax bills were then estimated using the tax returns.

RETALIATORY TAX

This is a much more difficult tax to estimate, as it requires using the rates and tax base of every state with a lower tax bill. We assumed, to make the project treatable, that each states rate was that reported in Tables A-1 to A-4, and that the tax base in each state was premiums written net of policyholder dividends. This seems to be a very representative tax base, as most states allow for the deduction of policyholder dividends.

The retaliatory tax calculation also includes assessments for insolvency funds and license fees. These were assumed to be fixed and not to change according to changes in rates. This is not necessarily a poor assumption, as the license fees are relatively low and insolvency assessments change every year anyway, depending on the number and size of companies. Recent insolvencies have been relatively small, and do not add or detract from the simulation's general results.

ENDNOTES

1. Data regarding the number of companies in each industry were obtained from the ACLI's *Life Insurance Factbook* for years 1964 to the present and from the III's *Property Casualty Factbook* for years 1964 to 1994.

2. Not all of the 200 or so Ohio companies are true home offices. There are a number of companies that write a very small amount of business and thus do not contribute dramatically to employment opportunities in Ohio. In addition, there are shell companies that may not write any business at all in a given year, but when the parent company deems it necessary, may write business as needed. In addition, there is another set of companies that may operate as captives of a traditional corporation. These captive insurers may write insurance predominantly for the parent company.

3. These companies are Blue Cross-Blue Shield Mutual of Ohio, Central Benefits Mutual Insurance Company, and Community Mutual Insurance company. Central Benefits Mutual is no longer associated with the Blue Cross organization. Data are from Ohio Department of Insurance, *Annual Report* (1992).

4. Ohio Department of Insurance, *Annual Report* (1992).

5. Open enrollment means that enrollment in an HMO is open to any consumer, whether as part of a group or as an individual.

6. Community rating is the practice of rating for determination of premiums a group based on the characteristics of a "community" rather than on the characteristics of an individual.

7. See H.D. Skipper, (1987).

8. Ohio. Rev. Stats. §§5725.18-.26

9. Ohio. Rev. Stats. §§5729.02

10. Ohio. Rev. Stats. §§5729.04. This is more likely relevant for mutuals as stock companies generally do not have participatory policies.

11. This is not necessarily a bad policy, as a health insurance company would not need as much surplus as one that specialized in riskier and longer lines of business.

12. A number of states exempt the Blues, while others provide lower rates to health insurers. Further, studies have shown that states with preferences for the Blues have higher Blue market shares (see, e.g., Frech and Ginsberg (1978)) whether more people are insured because of this preference has not been shown.

13. In addition to some state tax breaks health insurance enjoys a benevolent federal tax policy. For employer sponsored health plans, the employer can deduct the entire cost of the health plan from taxable income. Small business too can take advantage of this deduction. On the individual basis, there is also a deduction if health expenses including insurance are greater than 7.5 percent of adjusted gross income. As there are a number of federal tax preferences for health insurance consumption, a state should as part of its health care policy decide whether the additional benefits of coverage are worth the fiscal costs of differential treatment.

14. There is an important cost to society from trading off open enrollment and community underwriting for a tax break. This cost is one that is generally not discussed outside of the insurance industry; it is the cost of adverse selection. High-risk individuals (i.e., those having a higher than average probability of being sick in the next year) can and will enroll (assuming they can otherwise pay for the coverage) in an HMO, since the community rate is based on average characteristics of the community. By allowing unlimited entry of high risk insured and charging them a price not reflecting their actual risk, the HMO's losses increase. These losses are then (at least) partially spread to the other members of the HMO. For insured who are on the margin whether to purchase health insurance through an HMO or to go without insurance, the open enrollment and community rating make the HMO coverage more expensive and may cause individuals to go without coverage.

15. The states are AL, CA, DC, FL, ID, KS, ME, MS, NV, NC, SD, WV, and WY.

16. The states are ID, KS, ME, NV, NC, ND, and WY.

17. This number assumes all annuities are subject to the premium tax.

18. This determination of percentage of fire coverage was done by the Insurance Services Office.

19. For a description of the state's authority over insurance companies see Kenneth Meyer, "The Political Economy of Insurance Regulation," (Albany: SUNY Press, 1987).

20. The number of states that have blatantly discriminated between foreign and domestic companies has diminished since *Metropolitan Life v. Ward*, 470 United States 869 (1985) where the Supreme Court stated that it was permissible to discriminate between foreign and domestic insurers under the equal protection clause of the XIVth Amendment only if the state had a rational basis for doing so. Some states, like Ohio and Georgia, still provide some domestics with a tax advantage. This will be discussed further below.

21. See *Metropolitan Life Insurance Company v. Ward,* 470 United States 869 (1985).

22. Massachusetts recognized this fact and decided to tax its domestic industry at a higher rate that the foreign companies so the domestic industry would not have to pay increased retaliatory taxes to other jurisdictions.

23. This could lead to a bizarre result if the right fact pattern exists. For example, suppose there is a Kansas company (with a majority of its writings in Ohio) that fails. Kansas' premium tax rate is less than Ohio's; thus a retaliatory tax must be paid to Kansas by Ohio companies writing in Kansas. The tax paid by Ohio companies is increased because of the failure of a Kansas company. Thus, the Kansan treasury benefits from the insolvency of a Kansas firm due to the retaliatory tax paid by foreign companies

24. O.R.C. §3956.20.

25. These informational returns are used to monitor the firm's solvency and contains information concerning premiums, losses, and expenses for the company.

26. See Martin Grace and Julie Hotchkiss, (1994), and Stewart, (1984).

27. The states with statutory rates higher than Ohio are AL, AK, HI, MT, and NV for life insurance and AL, AK, HI, KY, NY, TX, and WV for property-liability insurance. Note that with the exception of Texas, the state markets are relatively small. Thus, Ohio is among the largest markets with a high tax rate.

28. The national effective rate is the sum of all premium taxes collected as a percentage of total direct premiums written. Ohio's effective rate is similarly calculated. Data employed in these calculations and in Table 12-4 are from ACIR (1993). Note that retaliatory taxes paid to other states are not included.

29. H. D. Skipper, (1987).

30. *Ibid.*

31. If these small companies engage in reinsurance to spread the risk, they are still inefficient if a larger company would not have to engage in similar activities.

32. Price Waterhouse and Levin and Driscoll, (1994).

13 Public Utility Taxation

Gary Cornia

INTRODUCTION

In Ohio, three distinct classes of property are subject to the property tax:[1] real property and improvements to real property,[2] tangible personal property owned by businesses, and tangible personal property owned by regulated utilities. The focus of the analysis in this study is on the last of these, the property tax imposed on the tangible personal property owned by electric utilities, gas utilities, and railroads in Ohio.[3] The study targets the administrative and policy issues concerning the personal property tax bases of Ohio-regulated public utilities. The study does not analyze the other major tax paid by utilities in Ohio: the Gross Receipts Tax. This tax is evaluated for the Tax Study Commission in McHugh (Chapter 16, in this volume). The study also does not cover the taxation of the telecommunications industry which operates in Ohio. The taxation of telecommunications industry is analyzed in McHugh (Chapter 15, in this volume). The tangible personal property tax on regulated utilities is administered by state tax officials.[4] In the case of railroads, the real and personal property portions of the property tax base are handled entirely by the Ohio Department of Taxation. For electric and gas utilities, the responsibility for the appraisal of real and personal property is shared between local tax officials and state tax officials. The real property portion of the public utility property tax, which in Ohio has historically represented much less than 10 percent of the total appraised value of a utility, is administered by the county auditor.[5] The auditor functions in this role with limited supervision by the Ohio Department of Taxation.[6]

The Property Tax Division of the Ohio Department of Taxation has the legal responsibility to administer the remaining property tax on utilities (over 90 percent of the total taxable value).[7] This base comprises the tangible personal property owned by public utilities.[8] Figure 13-1 illustrates the administrative and appraisal responsibilities for the classes of property taxes in Ohio.

The legal authority for the determination of the taxable value of public utility personal property, and railroad real and personal property, rests with the Ohio State Tax Commissioner. Utilities are singled out for distinct property tax treatment in Chapter 5727 of the *Ohio Revised Code*. The policy of taxing regulated utilities as a distinct class of property began in 1931.[9] The actual appraisal of the tangible property of a utility is conducted by the Public Utility Tax Section, which is part of the Property Tax Division of the Ohio Department of Taxation. The Property Tax Division employs 66 staff members; the Public Utility Tax Section employs 6 full-time staff.[10] Staff members in the Public Utility Section have experience in finance, economics, accounting, and appraisal.

The Public Utility Tax Section currently appraises the tangible personal property of over 400 public utilities representing 11 regulated industries (Table 13-1). The utilities valued by the Public Utilities Section range in assessed values from several hundred dollars to more than one billion dollars. Excluding telecommunications, over 95 percent of the total assessed value of public utility tangible personal property is represented by the electric utilities, gas utilities, and railroads (Figure 13-2). The relative assessed value of the utilities did not shift dramatically from 1978 to 1993. Within each major utility group, one or two utilities generally dominate in terms of assessed valuation.

TABLE 13-1
Public Utilities Assessed for Personal Property Tax by Type of Utility

CLASS OF UTILITY		NUMBER OF TAXPAYERS
	Electric	13
	Telephone	238
	Natural Gas	32
	Railroad	29
	Pipeline	24
	Rural Electric	30
	Waterworks	29
OTHER:	Water Transportation, Heating, Telegraph	8

Source: Ohio State Department of Taxation

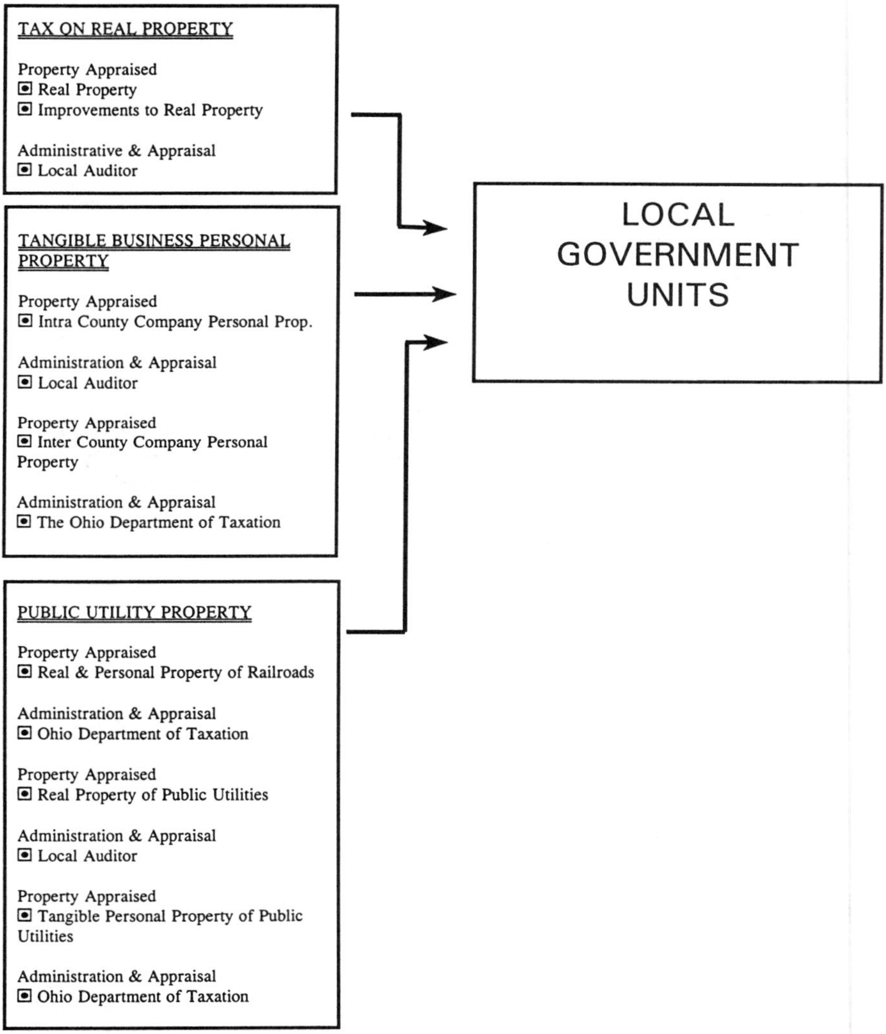

FIGURE 13-1. Administrative and appraisal responsibilities for classes of property tax in Ohio.

This study proceeds in the following manner. First, it offers a limited comparison of the property tax on utilities in Ohio with that in selected surrounding states. Second, it discusses the taxable value and the revenue significance of the property tax between the three classes of property in Ohio. Third, it discusses the economic structure of regulated utilities in Ohio, and the evolving nature of regulatory practice—this section also reviews the economic conditions of regulated utilities in Ohio. The fourth section discusses

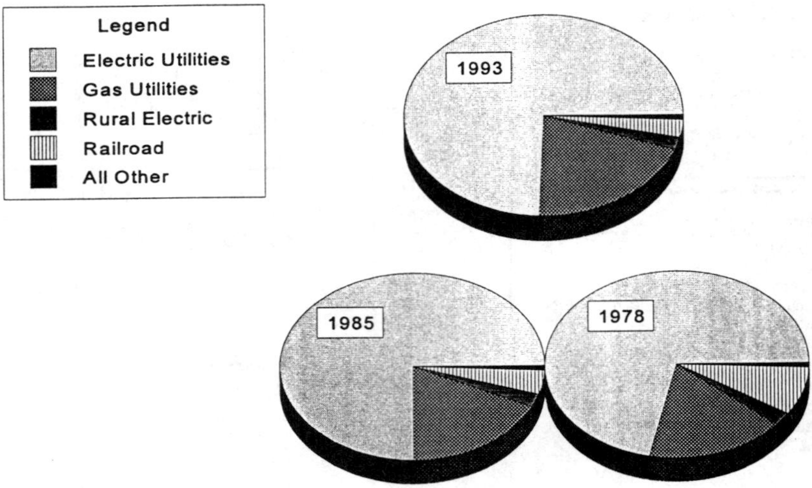

Source: Ohio Department of Taxation data.

FIGURE 13-2. Public utility personal property assessed valuation by type of property: 1978, 1985, & 1993.

the current status of the administration of the property tax on regulated utilities in Ohio. The fifth section discusses the policy issues associated with the imposition of a personal property tax on utilities. The sixth and final section of the paper discusses a series of alternatives for taxing utilities.

INTERSTATE COMPARISONS OF PROPERTY TAXES ON UTILITIES AND RAILROADS

The property tax on Ohio electric and gas utilities is higher than the property tax on similar utilities in surrounding states. Data which compare both the real and personal property tax collected from Ohio utilities, to the total property tax collected from utilities in neighboring states, appears in Table 13-2. The comparisons in Table 13-2 control for the burden of the property tax by standardizing the tax payments in terms of physical output (electric and gas), e.g., tax paid per KWH delivered, or physical investment (railroad).

The property tax burden, including real and personal property taxes, which Ohio electric and gas utilities face is higher than the property tax burden on similar utilities in selected neighboring states. The ratio of the property tax per KWH, when compared to the property tax per KWH in surrounding states, is greater than 20 in some situations. But even within the

TABLE 13-2
Property Tax Burden Comparisons

Electric: Property Tax Per Retail KWH (Cents)		Gas: Property Tax Per McF (Cents)		Railroads: Property Tax Per Road Mile (Dollars)
Ohio				
Cleveland Electric	.66	Columbia Gas	11.5	$ 4,943
Toledo Edison	.59	East Ohio Gas	11.0	
Ohio Edison	.50	Cincinnati Gas	19.8	
Cincinnati Gas & Elec	.47	West Ohio	13.0	
Columbus Southern	.40			
Dayton P & L	.37			
Ohio Power	.24			
Michigan				
Detroit Edison	.44			
Consumers Power	.33			
Indiana				
Indiana Power	.14	Indiana Gas	5.7	$ 3,313
Pennsylvania				
Philadelphia Electric	.19			$ 17
Pennsylvania Power	.17			
West Virginia				
Appalachian Power	.10	Hope Natural Gas	4.0	$ 7,514
Wheeling Power	.03			
Kentucky				
Kentucky Power	.09	Columbia Gas	2.0	$ 3,478
Kentucky Utilities	.05	Louisville Gas & Elec	3.8	

Source: Data provided by Ohio Electric Utilities Institute, Ohio Gas Association, Selected Class 1 Interstate Railroad.

state of Ohio there are differences in tax burdens. Ratios of the property tax per KWH within the state of Ohio differ by factors approaching three. Ratios of similar magnitude are observed between natural gas companies. The story is different when the comparison shifts away from energy utilities to railroads. The Ohio property tax on railroads, compared to the property tax on railroads in selected surrounding states, suggests that Ohio's burden is roughly in the middle.

The data reported in Table 13-2 represent total property taxes imposed on all consumers of electricity, natural gas, and rail services. The data do not allow for a comparison of the relative tax burden between classes of consumers. However, economic analysis suggests that residential consumers will carry a larger share of the tax burden. Residential consumers, in contrast to commercial and industrial users, have few options for alternative energy consumption. Residential consumers either absorb price increases or reduce consumption of the energy source. Using electricity as an example, empirical work confirms that industrial and commercial users of electricity respond to price increases by consuming less electricity. Industrial users can substitute other sources of energy. Commercial consumers can also substitute, but not as easily as industrial users (Chapman et al. 1982). Thus a high property tax imposed on electric utilities may not be an obvious concern for economic development. A large portion of the property tax burden is probably borne by residential consumers, and electric companies that realize lower returns on their investment.

It is important to note that the data in Table 13-2 compare only property tax burdens. When all taxes are considered, the relative burden of Ohio taxes on utilities and railroads may not be as different as Table 13-2 implies. States have discovered a number of utility tax bases on which to impose a tax. Examples of these bases include gross receipts, net income, franchise tax on net income, gross earnings, KWH unit tax, and energy license taxes.[11] Data supplied to the Tax Study Commission by the electric utilities suggest that the overall burden of Ohio taxes is higher than the tax burden in surrounding states (Table 13-3).

TAXABLE VALUE AND REVENUE SIGNIFICANCE OF THE PROPERTY TAX FROM UTILITIES AND RAILROADS

In Ohio, there are two steps in the property tax valuation process. Understanding the two steps helps explain the reason for differences in the taxable value and revenue significance of the Ohio property tax.[12] The initial step in the process, which every taxed parcel must undergo, results in an *appraised* value. The intent of the appraised value is to represent what a professional assessor estimates a property would sell for in a market transaction.[13] The appraised value of a public utility in Ohio is determined by the Public Utility Tax Section. The second valuation step is determining the *assessed* value for property tax purposes. This second step is also performed by the Public Utility Tax Section. The assessed value is the appraised value multiplied by an assessment level. The assessed value is the value that is actually taxed.[14] As discussed, Ohio has three broad classes of property subject to the property tax, real property, tangible personal business property, and tangible personal property owned by regulated utilities. All three classes of property have significantly different assessment levels, established by state law. Locally appraised real property—property appraised by the local auditor—

TABLE 13-3
Total Taxes Per KWH Comparisons

Electric Utility	Total State and Local Taxes Per KWH
Ohio	
Cleveland Electric	1.15
Toledo Edison	1.11
Ohio Edison	0.96
Cincinnati Gas & Electric	0.77
Columbus Southern	0.69
Dayton P & L	0.68
Ohio Power	0.52
Michigan	
Detroit Edison	0.44
Consumers Power	0.34
Indiana	
Indiana Power	0.27
Pennsylvania	
Philadelphia Electric	0.97
Pennsylvania Power	0.87
West Virginia	
Appalachian Power	0.41
Wheeling Power	0.26
Kentucky	
Kentucky Power	0.11
Kentucky Utilities	0.13

Source: Data provided by Ohio Electric Utilities Institute.

has an assessment level of 35 percent. Business tangible personal property has an assessment level of 25 percent. Most utilities in Ohio are assessed at 88 percent of their appraised values. Railroads are assessed at 25 percent of their appraised value. The differences in assessment levels are long-standing tax policies.

Appraised and Assessed Values

Excluding telecommunications, the appraised value of Ohio public utility tangible personal property and railroad property was $10.6 billion in 1990 and $12.4 billion in 1992. On a per capita basis, the appraised values of public utilities represented approximately $974 in 1990 and $1,166 in 1992. These values compare to a per capita appraised value of $37,218 in real property and $6,672 in tangible personal property in 1992. In terms of relative share, utility tangible personal property represents about 2.6 percent of the total appraised property tax base.

Because utility property is taxed at a higher assessment level than other property, the relative proportion of the taxable value of utility property increases. The relative share of total assessed value coming from public utility tangible personal property is close to eight percent of the total assessed value. The per capita assessed value of public utility tangible personal property is compared to the per capita assessed value of the other two classes of property (Table 13-4). Over the short time period compared, the per capita assessed value of real property and public utility tangible personal property has been growing about three times as fast as the assessed value of tangible personal properties. An important reason for the decline in the assessed value of tangible personal property has been the gradual decline in its assessment level (Cornia, in this volume). The assessed value of public utility tangible personal property has increased in per capita terms since 1988 (Table 13-5). However, when changes in the price level are controlled for, the real value of the per capita assessed value of tangible public utility personal property has been constant.

The appraised values of selected utilities and the railroads, covering a 15-year period (Table 13-6), also reveals that in real terms there has been little growth in per capita appraised values except for railroads. The data in Table 13-6 suggest that the appraised value of utilities has kept pace with inflation over the past 15 years.[15] Even in a slow-growth state like Ohio, it is reasonable to expect some real increase in the taxable values of regulated utilities. However, it is important to remember that the data reported in Tables 13-5 and 13-6 are estimated values. As will be discussed, the process to establish the taxable value of gas and electric utilities is based on historical cost less adjustments for depreciation.

TABLE 13-4
Per Capita Assessed Values Public Utility Tangible Personal Property (PUTP), Tangible Personal Property (TPP), Real Property (RP) Selected Years

Class of Property	Year		
	1988	1990	1992
PUTP	$ 1,131	$ 1,192	$ 1,342
TPP	1,570	1,703	1,669
RP	7,758	8,636	9,304

Source: Calculated by author from Ohio Department of Taxation data

TABLE 13-5
Assessed Value of Public Utility Personal Property

Year	Total Assessed Value (Billions)	Per Capita Assessed Value	Real Per Capita Assessed Value[a]
1988	$ 12,217	$ 1,131	$ 1,131
1989	12,466	1,151	1,117
1990	13,016	1,192	1,146
1991	13,896	1,270	1,245
1992	14,789	1,342	1,137

[a]1988 Base Year

TABLE 13-6
Appraised Values of Selected Utility Industries

Investor	Appraised Value (Billions)	Per Capita	Real Per Capita
Electric			
1978	$3,962	$370	$370[a]
1980	4,444	412	322
1985	5,172	452	266
1990	7,338	676	346
1992	8,554	776	370
Rural Electric			
1978	.271	25	25[a]
1980	.300	28	22
1985	.299	28	15
1990	.351	32	17
1992	.390	33	16
Gas Pipelines			
1978	.938	88	88[b]
1980	.999	93	72
1985	1.236	115	70
1990	1.910	176	88
1992	2.107	191	89
Railroad			
1978	723	67	67[b]
1980	1035	93	74
1985	829	78	42
1990	994	97	42
1992	1019	100	42

[a]Base Year - Electric power Price Index
[b]1978 Base Year - Consumer Price Index

REVENUE SIGNIFICANCE

The relative significance of the revenue from the three classes of taxable property is shown in Table 13-7. Real property taxes generated about $4.6 billion in revenue in 1992 for local governments in Ohio. Tangible business property taxes generated $1.2 billion; tangible personal property of public utilities generated $0.95 billion. The significance of the real property portion of the property tax is further illustrated by comparing the per capita revenue contributions of each of the three classes of property. The per capita real property tax portion of the total tax is almost five times as large as the per capita contribution of the tangible personal property tax coming from public utilities. The per capita contribution of the tangible business personal property is slightly more than the share coming from the tax on tangible personal property. The revenue from all personal property taxes in Ohio is about 11 percent of all sources of revenue for local governments. Excluding

TABLE 13-7
Property Taxes Charged on Real Property

Year	Total Taxes (Millions)	Per Capita Taxes	Real Per Capita Taxes
1988	$ 3,482[a]	$ 323	$ 323
1990	4,016[a]	370	336
1992	4,677[a]	424	356
Property Taxes Charged on Tangible Personal Property			
1988	$ 1,005[b]	93	93
1990	1,148[b]	106	96
1992	1,201[b]	108	92
Property Taxes Charged on Public Utility Tangible Personal Property			
1988	$ 709.4[b]	$ 66	66
1990	799.4[b]	74	70
1992	954.8[b]	87	73

Source: Calculated by author with data from *The Economic Report of the President* and *Annual Report*, Ohio Department of Taxation, selected years

[a]Net Total Taxes Charged
[b]1988 Base Year

the personal property tax on tangible business property, the personal property tax on utilities is about 5 percent of the total revenue for local governments in Ohio.[16]

An important consideration for any proposed change in how classes of property are taxed in Ohio is highlighted using property tax revenue data from the ten most populous counties in Ohio. The 1988 and 1992 per capita amounts of property taxes being paid in each of these counties by the three classes of property are given in Table 13-8. Public utility tangible personal property taxes represent approximately ten percent of the total property tax revenue in these larger counties. The total revenue from all property tax sources averaged just over 28 percent of the total revenue for the ten counties. Reducing the amount of personal property tax coming from public utility property would be a serious financial blow to the functioning of the ten

TABLE 13-8
Per Capita Taxes Charged on Public Utility Tangible Personal Property (PUTP), Tangible Personal Property (TPP), and Real Property (RP)—Ten Largest (Population) Counties in Ohio

	1988			1992		
County	**PUTP**	**TPP**	**RP[a]**	**PUTP**	**TPP**	**RP[a]**
Cuyahoga	$69	$126	$453	$88	$138	$606
Franklin	48	100	410	69	133	590
Hamilton	61	127	374	92	155	548
Montgomery	52	107	345	65	111	458
Summit	54	89	367	65	108	466
Lucas	67	116	346	92	122	456
Stark	48	91	245	64	106	337
Butler	41	77	278	58	86	365
Lorain	82	83	306	98	102	383
Mahoning	53	49	273	65	70	328

Source: Calculated by author using Ohio State Department of Taxation data

[a]Net Taxes Collectable

counties listed in Table 13-8. Few local governments could have their property taxes reduced by this percentage and not respond by either lowering their levels of service or increasing revenue from other sources. While no examples are used in the paper, the issue of the importance of the tangible personal public utility property tax is especially important to education in Ohio. Ohio school districts receive over 70 of the personal property tax revenue produced in the state.[17]

PUBLIC UTILITY: ECONOMIC STRUCTURE AND REGULATION

This section is an overview of the structure of the larger—measured in assessed value— regulated industries in Ohio.[18] It discusses the general economic conditions found in those industries in terms of several selected market indicators of economic performance. The section starts with a general discussion of the role played by regulatory bodies in controlling the rate of return earned by utilities. The chapter describes the current state of regulatory policy for the major regulated industries in Ohio.[19]

Regulated utilities in Ohio are subject to oversight by both state and federal independent regulatory agencies. Understanding how regulatory bodies function helps in making informed judgments about the incidence of utility taxes, and the economic consequences of utility taxes on utility operation.[20] Utilities in Ohio are regulated by the Public Utilities Commission of Ohio (PUCO). Larger Ohio utilities are also regulated in certain aspects of their operation by federal regulatory bodies, such as the Federal Communication Commission (FCC), or the Federal Energy Regulatory Commission (FERC).

Independent regulatory bodies are concerned primarily with determining an acceptable rate of return for investors in public utilities and at the same time protecting the amount paid by users or "ratepayers" of utility services. These issues are decided in rate hearings, which are conducted before a regulatory body. When deciding rate issues, state and federal regulators assign values to the variables found in the following model:

$$R = (C - D)r + O + M + T \qquad [1]$$

Where:

R = Allowed return for utility

C – D = Allowed rate base[21]

C = Allowed historical cost of the utility

D = Allowed depreciation
r = Allowed cost of capital
O = Allowed operating expenses
M = Allowed maintenance expenses
T = Allowed federal, state, and local taxes

A regulatory commission must make four distinct decisions when deciding a rate case. The first decision in the process is determining the dollar value of the rate base (C – D), a value found by examining the amount of money invested by the utility over the years of operation. It is usually the reported book cost of the utility (C). The regulatory body then determines the reduction in (C) due to economic depreciation (D). Holding all other variables constant, the larger the allowed rate base (C – D) the larger the allowed return (R).[22]

The second decision is determining the allowed cost of capital (r). The allowed cost of capital (r) is determined by the regulatory body after consideration of the return required by equity and debt holders in nonregulated firms, following an adjustment for differences in risk.[23]

The third decision concerns making allowances for expenses. Allowed operating (O), maintenance (M) and tax (T) expenses are determined by the commissions, based on uniform reporting processes which are required under regulatory accounting procedures.[24] Utilities request to have rates set so that they can recover federal, state, and local taxes from ratepayers.

It is common for regulatory commissions to adjust utility rates for state and local taxes without much disagreement with the utility.[25] Adjustments for federal taxes have been subject to more disagreement between utilities and regulatory bodies. The disagreement usually concerns the timing of the actual payment of federal tax. It is routinely assumed that increases in rates due to taxes were passed on to customers in the form of higher utility bills (Phillips 1993; Case 1993). This assumption about taxes (and other utility expenses) was made because regulated firms were granted an exclusive franchise and faced no direct competition. As Phillips notes, "Given relatively inelastic demand curves for some of their services, higher prices are unlikely to lead to significant decreases in consumer demand" (p. 280). Thus any increase in rates could be passed on to consumers without fear that there existed legitimate consumption options which a ratepayer could use to avoid the tax. Such assumptions need careful analysis in light of the changing economic conditions that face regulated industries. For example, the work of Chapman et al. (1982), cited earlier, reports differences in the response to electric rate changes based on class of consumer.

The fourth decision in the regulatory process is rate design, which determines how the allowed return (R) will be divided between the three main customer groups. Rate design has many implications with respect to the cost of utility services for residential and business uses. Regulatory policy generally grants rates that reflect the costs associated with the provision of the service. For example, residential users place greater demands on utilities during peak energy periods and cause utilities to build larger operating systems. Because of these consumption patterns, residential users are normally expected to pay a disproportionate share of the needed return. Of course, granting lower rates to commercial and industrial users presents regulatory commissions with a number of difficult political issues.

One point is important to note at this juncture: a granted or allowed rate of return does not mean a utility will satisfy the needs of its investors. An allowed rate of return (R) is considered a maximum rate of return, and a utility is not guaranteed that it will earn (R). Not earning the allowed rate of return can occur for a number of reasons. Inflation may eat away at the real value of the allowed return, or the anticipated demand for the service may not materialize. Work by Adolphson et al. (1990) reports that over a five-year period, 76 percent of the electric utilities did not earn their allowed rate of return.

The formal process of having a rate change approved usually takes months of work by both the regulatory body and the utility asking for a rate change (American Gas Association 1986). The initial step in the process in Ohio is for the utility to request a rate adjustment by filing a formal request for rate relief. The request is based on a test year in which the expenses of the utility are documented for the regulatory body. The formal request is reviewed by the regulatory commission staff, who then write a response to the request from the utility. After the request and the response to the request have been submitted, the regulatory commission, or a hearing officer, conducts formal hearings. The hearings may take several weeks or even several months to conduct. Following the hearings a significant period of time may lapse before the regulatory commission responds with a formal decision. During the rate adjustment request period, a growing number of groups representing residential and business users of the regulated service are allowed to give testimony to the regulatory commission. There is a trend in the regulatory processes to have the utility and the regulatory commission avoid lengthy hearing processes.[26] Many utilities and commissions enter into an agreement in which the commission allows firms the opportunity to have quick adjustments made for increased costs, such as fuel. The firms in turn agree not to request a full-blown rate adjustment proceeding.[27]

Independent Regulatory Commissions: State and Federal

In Ohio, public utilities are regulated by the Public Utilities Commission of Ohio (PUCO). The PUCO is administered by a five-person board and each member is appointed by the governor. The PUCO is an independent regulatory body funded by fees imposed by the PUCO on the companies it regulates. Members of the PUCO board must meet certain professional requirements before they can be appointed to serve. The primary requirement is three years of experience in at least one area relating to finance, economics, law, engineering, etc. One member of the board must also be licensed to practice law. The PUCO employs a professional staff of over five hundred. Staff members are trained, or have experience, in such disciplines as law, engineering, economics, and accounting.

The board is given the responsibility to monitor the rates charged to customers of specific services, as well as the quality of services provided by the utilities. Rate determinations assign values to the variables found in equation [1] of this paper. The PUCO also monitors entry into an industry and controls service and quality of service provided in specific markets, such as truck routes.[28]

The primary federal regulatory agency affecting Ohio utilities is the Federal Energy Regulatory Commission (FERC), established in 1977. It evolved from the former Federal Power Commission. The five FERC commissioners are appointed by the president for a five-year term. Each FERC commissioner must have Senate approval, but the appointment is considered nonpartisan. The FERC employs over 1500 professionals and is organized along both industry and functional responsibilities. It is funded by appropriations from Congress and must also seek congressional approval for salary and staffing levels. The FERC, like most independent review bodies, has both legislative or rule-making responsibilities and judicial responsibilities.[29]

ELECTRIC: ECONOMIC CONDITIONS[30]

The production process of the electric industry proceeds in three distinct steps: production, transmission, and distribution of electricity. Production is the generation of electricity in which some form of energy is used to power a generator and produce electricity. Transmission is the movement of electricity between the generation plant and a distribution center. Distribution is the actual delivery of electricity to the final consumer. The electric industry is vertically integrated: the production, transmission, and distribution functions are performed by a single company that serves a specific area. There is a common belief that the vertical integration found in this industry results from the economies of scale associated with the production of electricity (Kahn 1971).

There are four major types of electric operators in the United States: investor-owned utilities, rural electric utilities, government utilities, and specialized generation utilities (Edison Electric Institute 1993). Investor-owned utilities dominate the electric utility industry in the United States. Government utilities include municipal systems, federal agencies, and state power projects. When compared to investor-owned utilities, government utilities usually play a small role in the overall provision of electricity.

The Ohio electrical industry reflects the general pattern of industry organization found in the United States. Ohio has investor-owned utilities, rural electric utilities, and government utilities. The structural makeup of each of the different types of utilities operating in Ohio is briefly outlined in Figure 13-3. Ohio's primary source of electricity is from eight major investor-owned electric utilities. Two large holding companies dominate the market of the investor-owned electric companies in Ohio. The first of these is American Electric Power (AEP), a major player in the electric utility arena. It produces and distributes electricity in seven midwestern states. In addition to being fully integrated in terms of production, transmission, and distribution, AEP owns supplies of fuel (coal). The second holding company is Centerior, formed in 1986 (Moody's Public Utility Manual 1993). (All investor-owned utilities in Ohio are vertically integrated and produce, transport, and distribute electricity.) The eight major investor-owned electric utilities are regulated by both the PUCO and by the FERC. The general geographic area served by the eight investor-owned utilities is as follows:

- Cincinnati Gas & Electric – Southwestern Ohio
- Cleveland Electric – Northeastern Ohio

Production Function	Type of Utility		
	Investor-Owned Electrics	Rural Electrics	Municipal Electrics
PRODUCTION CAPABILITY	YES Substantial	MODEST Produce all of their power in a plant operated with investor-owned utility	MODEST Capacity but infrequently used
TRANSMISSION CAPABILITY	YES Substantial	ALMOST NONE	LIMITED Will build to gain access to power
DISTRIBUTION CAPABILITY	YES Substantial	YES	YES Significant role in 3 large Ohio cities
INDUSTRY CHARACTERISTICS	8 major fully integrated companies	27 RE Co-ops major role in distribution of electricity	Dominated by 3 major municipal firms. Numerous small municipal electrics (83)

FIGURE 13-3. Characteristics of the electric utility industry in Ohio.

- Columbus Southern Power – Central and Southern Ohio
- Dayton Power and Light – Southwestern Ohio
- Monongahela Power – Southeastern Ohio
- Ohio Power – Southern, Central, and Northern Ohio
- Ohio Edison – Northeastern Ohio
- Toledo Edison – Northwestern Ohio

Twenty-seven Rural Electric Cooperatives also provide electric power to customers in Ohio. The major function of rural electric utilities is the distribution of electricity. However, the Rural Electrics generate some of their own power. Their generation plant is operated in cooperation with an investor-owned utility. They transmit the power they generate over the transmission lines owned by the investor-owned utilities. As would be expected, the Rural Electrics distribute power to rural regions in most of Ohio. The Rural Electric companies are essentially unregulated. Independent municipal utilities operate in a number of small and medium-size Ohio cities, and are important distributors of electric power in the larger Ohio cities of Cleveland, Columbus, and Hamilton.[31] There are a total of 84 municipal power systems in Ohio. Municipal electric utilities have limited generation capacity and limited transmission facilities;[32] their major role is the distribution of purchased retail electricity. Their purchased power comes from a number of sources both inside and outside of Ohio. However, most of the power purchased by Ohio Municipal Utilities comes from Ohio generation facilities. Ohio municipal utilities routinely purchase electricity from seven of the investor-owned utilities operating in Ohio. Unlike investor-owned utilities, municipal utilities are not regulated.

In 1993, Ohio investor-owned utilities distributed electricity to 3.8 million residential households; Ohio rural electric companies provided power to 0.285 million residential households (PUCO 1994). Ohio municipal electric companies provided electricity to 0.265 million residential households (Edison Electric Institute 1993). A further breakdown of the percentage sales of electricity by class of user in the United States, the East North Central Region of the United States, and Ohio is given in Table 13-9. Kilowatt sales for both investor-owned utilities and municipal utilities in Ohio are dominated by sales to industrial users, Ohio rural electric utilities retail most of their power to residential users.

The Ohio electric industry is dominated by power generated by coal-fired plants. On average 56 percent of electrical energy in the United States is generated by coal-fired plants, compared to 88 percent in Ohio. Nuclear power generates only about 11 percent of total power produced in Ohio whereas nationally, nuclear energy generates 22 percent of the electric

TABLE 13-9
Kilowatthours Sales by Class of Service:
United States, East North Central Regions, and Ohio (1992)

	U.S.	East North Central	Ohio (Investor Owner)	Ohio (Municipal)	Ohio (Rural Electrics)
Residential	34%	29%	27%	33%	67%
Commercial	26%	25%	22%	24%	11%
Industrial	35%	43%	48%	37%	21%
Other	5%	3%	3%	5%	—

Source: Edison Electric Institute, Statistical Year Book, 1992; Edison Electric Institute, 1992, Statistic Non-investor Owned Electric Utilities, 1993.

power produced in the United States (Edison Electric Institute 1992). However, nuclear generation is concentrated in three of the large investor-owned utilities in Ohio, accounting for over 50 percent of the power produced by these utilities, which charge substantially higher rates than those of other electric utilities in Ohio. In fact, two of the utilities in Ohio with nuclear plants, located in northern Ohio, are among the fifteen utilities with the highest rates in the United States (NARUC 1993).

The issue of the fuel source used by an electric utility to generate electricity is significant. As a general rule, the cost of building a nuclear plant to generate electricity is high, and the operating costs of a nuclear plant are comparatively low, but only when it can cover fixed costs by operating at close to full capacity, with little variation in power demanded (Hyman 1992). Thus it is in the economic interest of an electric utility to generate as much power as possible by using nuclear plants to power the base load of a utility. Base loads represent the constant unwavering demand for electricity. Except for coal-fired generation, plants powered by other fuels were built for peak demand. However, efforts by electric utilities to manage the demand for electricity between nuclear and other plants can be thwarted by conditions over which the utility has little control. For example, consumer behavior appears to be changing with respect to the pattern of the consumption of electricity. Paradoxically, the more reliant homes and businesses become on electric power, the more difficult it is for utilities to manage the load. As Hyman notes (1992), increased use of electrical devices has made peak demands higher and the base loads less important. In Ohio, this means that utilities with substantial nuclear-generating capacity operate at a potential disadvantage.[33]

Average Revenue per KWH for electric utilities in twelve selected states, including Ohio, is listed by class of customer in Table 13-10.[34] When compared to average revenue per KWH in other states, residential average revenue per KWH, commercial average revenue per KWH, and industrial

TABLE 13-10
Average Revenue Per KWH for
Electric Utilities Residential, Commercial & Industrial
Total Customer Averages—Averages for Selected States (1992)

Utility	Class of Customer			
	Residential	**Commercial**	**Industrial**	**Total**
California	9.77	9.52	6.60	8.79
Florida	7.58	6.52	4.62	6.26
Kentucky	5.09	4.95	3.49	4.45
Illinois	10.27	8.06	5.39	7.57
Indiana	6.67	5.89	4.18	5.31
Michigan	8.18	7.39	5.39	7.70
New Jersey	11.10	9.54	7.88	9.78
New York	13.25	11.66	7.67	10.95
Pennsylvania	11.47	8.54	6.15	9.54
Ohio	8.46	7.63	4.78	6.51
Texas	7.80	6.79	4.35	6.19
West Virginia	6.20	5.68	3.88	5.08
Average	8.82	7.68	5.36	7.34

Source: Edison Electric Institute, Typical Residential, Commerical, and Industrial Bills; Investor-Owned Utilities: 1993.

average revenue per KWH in Ohio are generally ranked in the middle of the reported average revenue per KWH. The average revenue per KWH in Ohio is below the average of the twelve states reported in Table 13-10 for all classes of customers.

Average revenue per KWH for the eight Ohio investor-owned electric utilities is listed in Table 13-11, controlling for the three major classes of customers. The average revenue per KWH can be divided into two distinct groups: low revenue per KWH utilities and high revenue per KWH utilities. The ratio between the high KWH revenue utility and the low KWH revenue utility in Ohio is about two. This ratio demonstrates the substantial disparity in the cost of supplying electricity within the state of Ohio.

The average revenue per KWH for municipal and rural electric utilities is found in Table 13-12. A comparison of average revenue per KWH of the investor-owned utilities (Table 13-11) and the municipal and rural electric utilities average revenue per KWH (Table 13-12) reveals a rate similarity between the three systems. However, municipal power on average is lower than investor-owned electric power. These comparisons are important, because they bear directly on the discussion of the degree of competition among the three classes of Ohio electric utilities.[35]

TABLE 13-11
Average Revenue Per KWH for Electric Utilities: Residential, Commercial & Industrial Customer Averages: Ohio Utilities

	Class of Customer			
Utility	Residential (7/92-6/93)	Commercial (7/92-6/93)	Industrial (7/92-6/93)	Total (7/92-6/93)
Cincinnati Gas & Electric	6.78	6.31	4.42	5.51
Cleveland Electric	10.96	9.73	6.60	8.68
Columbus Southern Power	7.02	5.91	4.55	5.98
Dayton Power & Light	7.90	6.43	4.90	6.13
Monongahela Power	5.89	5.54	3.44	4.46
Ohio Edison	10.69	9.62	6.33	8.65
Ohio Power	6.63	5.47	3.15	4.14
Toledo Edison	11.20	10.85	6.61	8.82

Source: Edison Electric Institute, Typical Residential, Commerical, and Industrial Bills: Investor-Owned Utilities: 1993.

TABLE 13-12
Average Revenue Per KWH for Electric Utilities: Residential, Commercial & Industrial Customers' Averages: (1992)

Utility	Residential	Commercial	Industrial	Total
Muncipal	5.56	6.04	4.80	5.17
Rural Electric	7.22	7.23	4.27	6.59

Source: Edison Electric Institute, 1992 Statistics Non-Investor-Owned Electric Utilities, 1993

How investors might view electric utilities in Ohio is given in Tables 13-13 and 13-14. In terms of return on investment for utilities in 1991 and 1992, most Ohio investor-owned utilities earned a return on investment that was above the national average. Ohio utilities that earned a return on investment noticeably below the national averages are the utilities that have nuclear exposure. The problems with nuclear exposure are further illustrated by the data in Table 13-14. This table reports the relationship between the market value of each utility or holding company, and the book value of the utility.[36] Again the data show that for utilities in Ohio without significant nuclear investment, investors are willing to pay a price higher than book value. It is also apparent from this analysis that high revenue per KWH does not result

TABLE 13-13
Return on Investment: United States Average Compared to Ohio Utilities

Utility	1991	1992
U.S. Average	3.50	3.63
Cincinnati Gas & Electric	4.67	4.39
Cleveland Electric	2.86	2.41
Columbus Southern Power	2.89	3.19
Dayton Power & Light	4.44	4.94
Ohio Edison	3.59	3.75
Ohio Power	4.84	4.60
Toledo Edison	1.16	1.65

Source: U.S. Department of Energy; Financial Statistics of Manor Investor-Owed Electric Utilities, Washington, D.C. Selected Years

TABLE 13-14
Market to Book Ratios—Electric Utilities Companies

	Year		
Company	1988	1990	1992
APS	1.27	1.20	1.49
AEP[a]	1.24	1.24	1.44
Atl. Eng	1.20	1.18	1.52
Black Hills	1.91	2.04	2.52
Boston Edison	.76	1.03	1.46
Carolina Power	1.67	1.66	1.76
Centerior[a]	.68	.88	.98
Central Maine	1.20	1.13	1.41
Commonwealth Edison	1.00	1.16	.86
DQE	1.01	1.24	1.45
Detroit Ed	1.15	1.61	1.55
Duke	1.36	1.62	1.78
El Paso	.96	.36	-.38
Florida Progress	1.35	1.38	1.64
Gulf States	.40	.61	.94
Houston Industries	.97	1.29	1.81
KU Energy	1.41	1.43	1.82
Maine Public Service	.92	.91	.97
New England Electric	1.31	1.16	1.68
Ohio Edison[a]	1.13	1.02	1.46
Penn Power	1.32	1.49	1.75
Southern Western Elec	1.02	.95	1.02
TNP	.96	.94	.92
Union Illuminating	.78	1.13	1.37

Source: Calculated by author using Standard & Poor's, Computstat I:.dustrial Files, 1993.

[a]Ohio Service

in a good return on investment or a favorable ratio between market value of equity and book value.

Electric: Regulatory Conditions

Unlike other public utilities, investor-owned electric utilities in the United States and Ohio have not faced substantial deregulatory legislation or deregulatory administrative behavior during the past two decades. Investor-owned utilities continue to operate in markets regulated by state and federal agencies. Utilities are granted geographical franchises and most operate with little direct competition (Porter and Burton 1989). In return for their franchise, utilities provide service to all, provide reliable service, and do not practice price-discrimination (Phillips 1993). The FERC takes the lead in determining the rates charged on interstate sales of electricity, and the state commissions focus on the rates paid by the final consumers. The FERC also plays a key role in the approval of the construction of new electric-generation plants and transmission lines. The major regulatory practices facing electric utilities are described in Figure 13-4. The current regulation scheme, however, does not suggest that electric utilities do not face economic challenges.

The most fundamental challenge for the electric industry will come when customers are able to purchase their electric power from a source other than their local utility. Competition will develop quickly when state regulatory bodies allow the sale of electricity between utilities to go beyond the current practice of wholesale transactions or wholesale wheeling.[37] Retail wheeling would allow customers to contract directly with low-cost providers of electricity. The retail buyers would use the transmission and distribution networks of the local utility to obtain the lower cost electricity. Retail wheeling would leave high-cost utilities with unused capacity and even greater difficulty meeting their current financial commitments to debt and equity holders. Retail customers would of course gain from the adoption of retail wheeling. They could "shop" for the lowest cost source of electricity.

There are several reasons to suspect retail wheeling will emerge in the

- FERC Regulates in the Absence State Regulatory Oversight
- FERC Imposes Uniform System of Financial Accounts
- FERC Has Jurisdiction over Some Wholesale Electric Rates
- Retail Power Rates Established by State Regulatory Commission

Source: Rosenthal, Beth. *Structure and Regulation of the Electric Utility Industry: An Historical Perspective*, Edison Electric Institute, Washington, D.C., 1992.

FIGURE 13-4. Significant regulatory issues/electric utilities.

near future. First, limited retail wheeling is currently being practiced in several states; it has been adopted by legislation in Nevada as a tool to be used in economic-development battles. Wheeling will also be allowed on an experimental basis in selected areas of California and Michigan. Ten other states have recently reviewed retail wheeling. The reviews have been conducted by both legislative bodies and regulatory commissions. Two of the ten states which have examined retail wheeling have been in the Midwest, Illinois and Pennsylvania. Ohio also has a retail-wheeling bill, H.B. 676, introduced in the last general assembly.[38]

Second, a growing inability exists for those electric power companies that need more generation capacity to build new generation plants. They are prohibited from doing so by both financial and political constraints. The inability to add capacity results in demands for purchased wholesale power from other regions, or nontraditional generation systems (Scotto 1992). Third, the wide variability of retail rates between regions is large enough to cause customers in expensive regions to seek less expensive alternatives. In 1994, the differences in retail rates ranged from 5.2 cents per KWH in the Midwest to 10.3 in the northeast (Knutson and McMahan 1994). Fourth, the mere size of the wholesale wheeling now taking place between utilities suggests that electricity can be moved between regions with ease. Finally, while there is some disagreement, it does appear that states do have the right to allow retail wheeling under current federal legislation (Costello et al. 1994).

Some analysts do not expect that retail wheeling will happen in the near future. They note that the politics of the issue of retail wheeling are very complex—an important strike against retail wheeling (Costello et al. 1994).[39] The economic challenge of retail wheeling for high-cost utilities could be disruptive enough to force a fundamental realignment in the industry. One of the major emerging issues facing regulatory bodies is how to deal with the investments that would be "stranded"—left idle by a move to retail wheeling. There are also important technological differences between the gas utility industry—in which retail wheeling is the current practice—and the electric utility industry. For example, natural gas may be stored until needed and also benefits from a very active spot market. Conversely, electric power must be used as it is generated. The technological differences may be subject to question if retail wheeling could ever take place (Costello et al. 1994).

Even if retail wheeling is not adopted as official policy, it is reasonable to assume that price competition will affect utilities. Utility analysts on Wall Street already speculate that high-cost producers will be forced by the market to lower electric prices to reflect regional averages in rates. They feel the process will evolve through a series of price discounts, beginning with industrial and commercial customers. Limited evidence exists that some price competition is already occurring in Ohio among large industrial customers and municipal utilities. Rate discounts occur when industrial users are able to threaten the investor-owned utility with a switch to a municipal supplier or the use of cogenerated electric power. Testimony and written statements to the Tax Study Commission by representatives of investor-owned utilities emphasized the problems of competing with municipal power in Ohio. However, in the long term, significant competition will be strong between the eight investor-owned utilities in Ohio. The cost differential in Ohio between northern utilities (nuclear) and southern utilities (coal) is large enough (Table 13-11) to expect price-equalization within the state.[40]

Gas Utility: Economic Structure

The gas utility industry has four distinct production steps in moving the gas from the well to the final customer. The first step is the process of supplying gas, referred to as field services. The supply of gas is accomplished by removing it from the well and moving it through a series of gathering pipelines to a "sweeting" plant. The supply of gas is concentrated in several geographical areas of the United States. Ohio enjoys a modest supply of natural gas produced within the state, but is a net importer of natural gas. The next step is the transmission of the gas; because of the concentration of natural gas in a few regions, interstate transmission of gas is essential, and the United States has a substantial capital investment in gas-transmission lines running both east-west and north-south. A third step is the storage of gas. Storage may take place prior to the cross-county shipment of gas, or after gas has been moved close to the final market. The last step is the distribution of gas to the final retail, commercial, and industrial customer.

Historically, two distinct types of companies have transmitted and distributed gas in the United States. The first of these was the fully integrated pipeline company. Such a company owned wells, transmitted gas interstate, and distributed gas to local consumers. The second type was the gas company that specialized in one aspect of the gas production process. As will be explained later, the first of these types of organizations, the fully integrated pipeline, will no longer exist in its current form. The specialized gas transmission pipeline is now the typical type of gas-transmission company; the specialized gas-distribution company is now the common method to distribute gas to the final consumer.

The makeup of the Ohio natural gas industry is described in Figure 13-5. Seven large gas-transmission utilities primarily function as gas-transmission operations. Several of the seven are part of diversified holding companies. Several are also part of holding companies that own multiple gas-transmission operations. The largest of the transmission lines operating in Ohio is the tenth largest gas-transmission firm in the United States (Watts 1993).

In Ohio, 11 firms function as both Local Distribution Companies (LDC) and transporters of gas. These firms tend to have relatively large customer bases and systems of distribution; for example, one such firm has over 16,000

	Function
Supply	Gas purchased from offshore, Canada, Southwest United States and Ohio
Transmission	Seven companies: Companies are typical major interstate gas transporters
Transmission and Distribution	Eleven transmission and distribution utilities. One electric utility also transmits and distributes gas.
Distribution	Twelve distribution companies. One electric utility also distributes gas.

Source: The Ohio Gas Association.

FIGURE 13-5. The Ohio natural gas industry.

miles of distribution mainlines in Ohio. It also serves a sizable geographical area; some LDC firms are able to purchase natural gas from Ohio wells. The largest LDC in Ohio purchases one-fourth of its natural gas from the over 20,000 wells operating in Ohio. The largest LDC firms are either linked to electric utilities or are subsidiaries of larger gas transmission firms (Ohio Gas Association 1993). Twelve local gas distribution (LDC) firms deliver gas only to the final consumer; generally these LDC firms are relatively small and serve a limited geographical area.

Gas rates paid in Ohio by residential users are compared to residential gas rates paid in selected other states (Table 13-15). Ohio residential gas rates are quite similar to the residential gas rates paid to each of the 22 utilities in the other 11 states identified in Table 13-15. In terms of the relative ranking of 200 distribution utilities, column two of Table 13-15, Ohio utilities tend to be below the median point. Average commercial and industrial rates in the comparison states reflect a much higher degree of variance, however, and Ohio comes out in the middle of average rates for commercial users and in the upper third of industrial users (Table 13-16).

The ratios of market to book values for selected types of gas transmission and distribution utilities are given in Tables 13-17 and 13-18. Table 13-18 includes utilities that sell both electricity and natural gas. (Gas utilities with service in Ohio are noted in both tables.) These ratios again reflect that investors view gas-related utilities in a favorable manner; i.e., the ratio of market value is greater than book value for most utilities. This is true for both transmission utilities, transmission and distribution utilities, and gas utilities operated by companies with combined electric and gas operations.

TABLE 13-15
Residential Gas Bills Winter: 1992–93

State / Utility	Average Cost Per Therm[a]	Rank
California		
San Diego Gas and Electric	.69	40
Southern California Gas	.63	6
Florida		
City Gas Company of Florida	.70	39
Peoples Gas Company of Florida	.72	22
Illinois		
Peoples Gas, Light & Coke Company	.73	35
Illinois Power Company	.49	145
Indiana		
Citizens Gas & Coke	.56	105
Interstate Power Co	.46	175
Kentucky		
Columbia Gas	.63	63
Louisville Gas	.47	168
Michigan		
Consumers Power	.46	176
Michigan Consolidated	.51	133
New Jersey		
Public Service Electric & Gas	.54	117
South Jersey Gas	.57	104
New York		
Consolidate Ed	.80	18
National Fuel	.71	38
Ohio		
Cincinnati Gas & Electric	.61	79
Columbia Gas	.62	72
Dayton Power & Light	.45	182
East Ohio Gas	.48	152
Ohio Gas Company	.58	96
River Gas Company	.61	77
West Ohio Gas	.54	118
Pennsylvania		
Columbia Gas	.59	89
Pennsylvania Gas & Water	.59	92
Texas		
Entex, Inc	.47	161
Lone Star Gas	.57	102

[a] 1 THERM = 1 CC[F] =100, BTU's

Gas Utility: Economic Regulation

Gas-transmission and gas-distribution processes have undergone significant regulatory changes during the past 20 years. The changes are as widesweeping as the more visible changes in the airline and telecommunication

TABLE 13-16
Gas Utility Industry Average Price of Gas Transported to Commercial & Industrial Users (1992)

State	Class of User	
	Commercial ($/MMBTU)	Industrial ($/MMBTU)
FLORIDA	.15	.39
ILLINOIS	1.17	.60
INDIANA	1.23	.29
KENTUCKY	.72	.39
MICHIGAN	.61	.42
NEW JERSEY	1.28	.78
NEW YORK	.82	.68
OHIO	.75	.44
PENNSYLVANIA	1.46	.6
WEST VIRGINIA	1.75	.25

Source: The American Gas Association, Gas Facts: 1992.

industries. In fact, the regulatory changes in the natural gas industry may have been more disruptive to the organization of this industry than the changes in either airline, transportation, or telecommunication (Phillips 1992). The changes in the gas industry resulted from economic and international political issues which threatened the stability of the regulated gas industry. During the 1970s and 1980s, the natural gas industry suffered from a series of price shocks and supply shortages. At the state level, Ohio was the first to attempt to rectify these problems when PUCO adopted a "self-help guideline." Self-help allowed retail customers to locate gas, enter into a contract for the delivery of the gas, and use intra- and interstate pipelines to transport the purchased gas. The goal of the Ohio policy was to insure stable supplies and prices for end users.

Congress also responded to the shortages of natural gas by the passage of the Natural Gas Policy Act (NGPA) in 1978. The intent of NGPA was to decontrol the price of wellhead gas, and consequently encourage additional supply of gas through exploration. The outcome of NGPA was, as hoped, an increase in the supply of gas. However, a number of areas continued to either suffer unexpected shortages, or oversupplies in natural gas supply (Broadman 1986). The problem was quite simple: gas was deregulated at the wellhead, but

TABLE 13-17
Market to Book Ratios—Gas Transmission & Gas Distribution Companies

Company	Year		
	1988	**1990**	**1992**
Coastal Corp (T)	1.60	1.68	1.23
Eastex Energy (T)	.77	.25	1.33
Panhandle Eastern (T)[a]	1.82	.99	1.32
SONAT (T)	1.08	1.72	1.76
TRANSCO Energy (T)	2.00	1.63	1.33
ARKLA (TD)	2.39	1.99	1.78
Columbia Gas [a](TD)	1.01	1.34	.90
ENSERCH (TD)	1.24	2.07	2.32
National Gas (TD)	1.17	1.42	1.67
Southwestern Eng (TD)	1.59	2.21	2.17
Allegheny & Western (D)	.69	.67	.44
National Fuel (D)	1.13	1.40	1.40
Orbit Gas (D)	.49	.62	NA
Peoples Gas (D)	1.23	1.38	1.76
SE Michigan (D)	1.87	1.61	2.19
Brooklyn Union Gas (D)	1.29	1.37	1.53
Indiana Energy (D)	1.26	1.43	1.92

Source: Calculated by author from Standard & Poor's, Computstat Industrial Files, 1993.

[a]Ohio Service

continued to be regulated during transmission and distribution. These differences in pricing practices continued to cause economic problems.

In response to the continued problems of reliable supplies and prices, the FERC initiated a series of steps to deregulate the transmission and distribution of natural gas. The FERC deregulation approach culminated in FERC Order 636 (Duann 1993). Order 636 has forced the "unbundling" of the gas-transmission system from the gas-distribution system. *Unbundling* refers to

TABLE 13-18
Market to Book Ratios
Selected Combined Gas & Electric Utilities

	Year		
Company	**1988**	**1990**	**1992**
Baltimore G & E	1.31	1.12	1.32
Cincinnati G & E[a]	1.14	1.11	1.29
Cons Ed NY	1.26	1.19	1.56
Dayton P & L[a]	1.23	1.24	2.04
Florida Pub. Utl	1.75	1.19	1.29
Illinois Power	.77	.86	1.17
Minnesota Power	1.40	1.60	2.06
Pacific G & E	1.04	1.40	1.70
S. Indiana G & E	1.50	1.60	1.98

Source: Calculated by author using Standard & Poor's, Compustat Industrial Files, 1993.

[a]Ohio Service

the breakup of vertically integrated firms. In the gas industry it has resulted in three distinct production functions: field services (supply), transmission, and distribution.

A basic change resulting from 636 is that interstate gas transmission companies are required to allow access to their pipeline transportation facilities to firms requesting to use them. Order 636 has changed gas transmission companies from regulated public utilities to "common carriers." That is, gas transmission companies no longer have an exclusive geographical franchise and must accept requests for use of their transmission facilities from any enduser. Under 636, gas transmission pipelines are allowed to recover the fixed and variable costs associated with transmission; however, the rates must be approved by the regulatory bodies. A clear indication of the profound influence of 636 can be found in the comparison of the quantities of gas shipped over interstate transmission lines in 1990 and 1993. In 1990, 96 percent of the gas shipped over interstate transmission lines was owned by the transportation company. By 1993, 87 percent of the gas moved over interstate transmission lines was not owned by the interstate company (Smith 1994). The basic issues of Order 636 are listed in Figure 13-6.

Order 636 has also changed the role of the Local Distribution Companies (LDC). LDCs are now able to contract directly with any supplier of gas, and

- Promulgation of FERC Order 636–Restructuring Rule
- 636 Mandates the "Unbundling" of Pipe Line Transportation
- 636 Mandates the Equitable Provision of all Transportation Services
- 636 Mandates Full Disclosure of Capacity
- 636 Allows End Users to Select Many Suppliers and Use Interstate Lines to Transport the Gas
- 636 Causes Interstate Pipelines to Become "Common Carriers"
- 636 Pipelines Assign Fixed Charges to Customers

FIGURE 13-6. Significant regulatory issues—pipelines.

have the gas transported over a common-carrier gas transmission pipeline (Gregg 1992). This change allows LDCs considerable discretion in terms of where they purchase their gas and, because of a robust spot-market in natural gas, how much they pay for it. LDCs are now entering a competitive environment (Boswell 1992). Gas distribution companies, unlike electric utilities, do not have an exclusive franchise right. For example, if an LDC does not offer gas at a rate close to the lowest market price, noncore users (commercial and industrial) may contract directly with gas suppliers and have the gas transported over a common carrier and LDC pipelines to the plant using the gas.[41] Core-users of gas, such as residential homes, do not use sufficient amounts of natural gas to exercise the option of individually shopping for a different supply of natural gas. Nevertheless, Hatcher and Tussing (1993) assert that core-users can monitor noncore prices and expect the competitive prices of noncore users to be reflected in their rate schedules. Hatcher and Tussing (1993) believe that state public utility commissions, like the PUCO, will monitor the prices being charged noncore customers and influence the prices charged core customers. Readers are reminded that regulatory commissions continue to set rates for natural gas customers. However, the allowed rates are not guaranteed and can be competed away. A tax on natural gas is likely to be passed forward to residential consumers, so that portion of allowed rate is probably made. However, like electricity, a tax on natural gas is less likely to be passed forward to industrial and commercial users. Switching to other fuel sources is possible. Switching is most likely when industrial and commercial consumers can purchase gas from nonregulated brokers who sell out-of-state gas.

Railroads: Economic Structure

Three economic classes of railroads operate in Ohio. The class a railroad is placed in is a function of the level of its operating revenue; its classification is determined by the Interstate Commerce Commission (ICC). A second helpful distinction is to describe railroads in terms of their primary service: 12 Ohio railroads provide switching and terminal service, 14 are considered regional and local in nature, and 4 are major interstate carriers of goods. Figure 13-7 identifies Ohio railroads in terms of class of railroad and type of service provided.

Ohio's 30 railroads rank it fifth in the United States in terms of the number of railroads operating in a state.[42] The most important commodity, in terms of tonnage, carried by Ohio railroads is coal, the majority of which is shipped into the state. The frequency in which Ohio is ranked in the top ten in terms of specific goods shipped reveals the economic importance of Ohio in the Midwest and the United States. In 1992, Ohio was second among all

Class 1	TYPE OF SERVICE
▸Consolidated Rail Corporation	Interstate Transportation
▸CSX Corporation	Interstate Transportation
▸Grand Trunk Western	Interstate Transportation
▸Norfolk Southern	Interstate Transportation
Local/Regional	
▸Ann Arbor Rail	Local and Regional
▸Ashland Rail	Local and Regional
▸Bessemer & Lake Erie	Local and Regional
▸Central Railroad of Indiana	Local and Regional
▸Indiana and Ohio Central	Local and Regional
▸Indiana and Ohio Eastern	Local and Regional
▸Indiana and Ohio Railroad	Local and Regional
▸Indiana & Ohio Railway	Local and Regional
▸Indiana Northeastern	Local and Regional
▸Ohio Central Railroad	Local and Regional
▸R.J. Corman Railroad	Local and Regional
▸Wheeling and Lake Erie	Local and Regional
▸Youngtown & Southern	Local and Regional
Switching and Terminal	
▸Akron & Barberton Belt	Support of Terminal Operations
▸Ashtabula, Carson & Jefferson	Support of Terminal Operations
▸Cuyahoga Valley	Support of Terminal Operations
▸Lake Terminal Railroad	Support of Terminal Operations
▸Mahoning Valley Railway	Support of Terminal Operations
▸Newburgh and South Shore	Support of Terminal Operations
▸Nimishillen and Tuscarawas	Support of Terminal Operations
▸Ohi-Rail	Support of Terminal Operations
▸Ohio Southern	Support of Terminal Operations
▸River Terminal	Support of Terminal Operations
▸Sterling Belt Line	Support of Terminal Operations
▸Youngstong & Southern Railway	Support of Terminal Operations

Source: Association of American Railroads, *Railroads and States*, Washington, DC, 1994

FIGURE 13-7. The Ohio railroad industry.

states in terms of rail carloads handled,[43] fifth in the number of railroads, sixth in total rail miles, and sixth in total employment (Association of American Railroads 1994).

Comparison of economic conditions for railroads is of limited use in this analysis. The large Class 1 systems are part of nationally integrated operations covering many states. For example, one Class 1 railroad operating in Ohio has operations in 20 other states and Canada. Reported data on economic returns of such a railroad would not portray a useful picture for economic analysis within Ohio. In addition, two of the Class 1 railroads in Ohio report their financial data as part of large diversified holding companies.

Railroads: Economic Regulation

The railroad industry, like the gas pipeline industry, has undergone a substantial reduction in the degree of regulatory oversight. During the 1970s, railroads faced uncertain economic conditions, and a number of railroads suffered serious economic setbacks. The Penn Central Railroad, for example, filed for bankruptcy in 1970, and by the mid-1970s, four additional major railroads had also sought bankruptcy protection. The railroads were losing market share as new modes of transportation were emerging for both passenger service and freight service. In the 30 years before 1980, rail-freight ton miles increased 36 percent, while motor-carrier ton miles increased almost 200 percent. There was also a shift of the more profitable freight to motor carriers. Railroads were shipping less, and the goods they shipped were less profitable (Babcock 1984). Many of the freight services competing with railroads were not regulated. The new competition, particularly the truck carriers, benefitted from public subsidies in the form of the construction of the interstate freeway system (Wilson 1981). There was also statistical evidence that the railroads no longer benefitted from economies of scale in their operations and, because of regulation, operated a number of inefficient routes (Keeler 1974). In response to these challenges, the railroad industry sought deregulation.

The first step in this process was the passage of the Railroad Revitalization and Regulatory Reform Act (4-R) passed in 1976. The 4-R act removed some regulatory barriers, but dealt only partially with the challenges facing the rail industry. The next step in the legislative movement to improve railroad performance was the adoption of the Staggers Rail Act in 1980. The Staggers Act requires that the ICC acknowledge the competitive nature of the transportation industry in the United States when making rate decisions. It removes the jurisdiction of the ICC over minimum rates, and allows quarterly adjustments in regulated rates. The main features of the Staggers Act are outlined in Figure 13-8. Boyer (1987) suggests that the deregulation of the rail industry, including both legislative and administra-

- Regulated by the Interstate Commerce Commission
- Deregulation Started With 1976 Passage of Railroad Revitalization and Regulatory Reform Act (4-R)
- Substantial Deregulation Resulting From Staggers Rail Act Passed in 1980
- ICC Still Regulates Where Railroads Have Market Dominance
- Railroads Can Adjust Rates to Changing Market Conditions
- Railroads Can Abandon Money-Losing Service Areas
- Confidential Contracts Allowed
- Revenue Adequacy Must Be Considered by ICC Where Rate Making Jurisdiction is Retained
- Demand and Supply Used to Establish Rates Where Rate Making is Retained

Source: Wilner, Frank N. *Railroads and The Market Place*, Association of American Railroads, Washington, D.C., 1987

FIGURE 13-8. Significant regulatory issues—railroads.

tive changes, has given railroads virtually complete authority over rates. And in situations in which the railroads have market dominance, the pattern of the ICC has been to encourage shippers and the railroads to negotiate a contract solution. Deregulation appears to be helping railroads. Since the adoption of the Staggers Act, a number of indicators suggest that United States railroads are preforming better. For example, intermodal traffic has more than doubled, revenue ton miles has increased 16 percent, and ordinary income has doubled. These changes are accompanied by reduced rates and lower operating costs (American Railroad Association 1993).

Summary: An Evaluation of Regulated Utilities in Ohio

The economic conditions of the three major regulated industries in Ohio resemble the economic conditions of similar industries in other states and regions. There is evidence that some Ohio electric utilities face a disadvantage in terms of rates they charge. These disadvantages appear to be the result of the operation of nuclear power plants. In these situations, consumers are hurt by higher rates and shareholders by lower net returns on investment. There is less reason to expect industrial and industrial commercial users to be hurt. Other Ohio electric utilities compare favorably to most electric utilities in the United States.[44] Ohio electric utilities do not yet face strong economic competition, especially for residential users; however, it would be unwise to continue treating electric utilities as if they will never face economic competition. The competitive nature of the emerging market for electricity will grow more intense.

The natural gas and rail industries face competition. The natural gas transmission and distribution system faces competition between suppliers of the gas and the distributors of gas. The market is characterized by numerous buyers and sellers of gas. Marketing agents have emerged with the purpose of supplying industrial and commercial consumers with the lowest possible price. Tax agents with the Public Utilities Tax Section estimate that one major LDC in Ohio deals with over 150 independent gas brokers. Regulatory bodies still set rates, but the ability to actually earn allowed rates is limited where customers have options. The rail industry is deregulated. Rates are set by negotiation between the rail and the supplier. Railroads have benefitted from this new form of economic regulation. They have used the incentives that accompany competition to reduce rates and improve service.

PUBLIC UTILITY PROPERTY TAX ADMINISTRATION IN OHIO

The administration of a property tax system requires the completion of a number of administrative and technical functions. The administrative functions are similar to running any large complex organization; issues include budgeting, human resource planning, information management, and strategic management. However, the focus of this section will be on the technical and policy issues associated with the valuation of property. The major steps that must be accomplished in the valuation of a property are identified in Figure 13-9.

TIME FRAME FOR ASSESSMENT

The lien date for determining the ownership and the valuation of public-utility personal property is December 31 (Figure 13-10). The actual date for the filing of the personal property tax return is March 1. On the filing date, the public-utility taxpayer must submit an Annual Report, which is prescribed by the Public Utility Section of the Ohio Department of Taxation. The taxpayer is also required to file with the Public Utility Section the annual reports required by both state and federal regulatory agencies.

During the period of March 1 to September 30, the Property Tax Division verifies the accuracy of the filed tax return and determines the appraised and the assessed values of the personal property of the utility. The utility is also notified of the assessed value and is given the opportunity for an informal hearing before the Property Tax Division staff.[45]

After the assessed value of the personal property of the Utility has been determined by the Tax Commissioner, it is apportioned among the various taxing districts in which the utility operates.[46] Following apportionment, the

STEPS	TASKS
DISCOVERY	■ Identify legal owners ■ Identify all taxable property ■ Classify property in terms of use ■ Develop reporting process
VALUATION	■ Develop consistent process for determining appraised value ■ Apply process to discovered property
ASSESSMENT OF TAX	■ Appraised value is multiplied by assessment level to establish taxable value ■ Appraised value is apportioned to specific taxing jurisdictions ■ Property owners are informed of taxable value
BILL AND COLLECT TAX	■ Set tax rates ■ Bill taxpayer ■ Collect from taxpayer
AUDIT	■ Determine if all taxable property is identified ■ Determine if correct value is being applied against property
APPEAL	■ Informal process to "question" appraisal ■ Formal process to "challenge" appraisal

FIGURE 13-9. Steps in property tax appraisal administration.

local taxing districts set the levy and bill the utility for the taxes due. Taxes are paid in two installments, due on December 31 and June 20 of the following year.

Discovery of Property

The discovery of taxable properties is a serious challenge for all property appraisal systems. There is no incentive for taxpayers to report to a revenue

December 31	Lien date for determining ownership and valuation
March 1	Due date for utilities to file their personal property tax return with the tax commissioner. An extension of time, not to exceed sixty days, may be obtained
March Through September	The tax commissioner performs the following functions with respect to each utility: ▸ verifies the accuracy of the tax return and related documents ▸ determines the true value and taxable value of personal property ▸ notifies the utility of the determination ▸ conducts hearings with utility ▸ apportions taxable value among taxing districts ▸ prepares assessments
First Monday of October	Tax commissioner certifies assessment to county auditors and utilities
October	County auditor places taxable values on the Real and Public Utility Tax List
November Election	Voters determine tax rates
December	County auditor calculates the taxes and instructs the county treasurer to collect them
December 31	Final date for paying first-half tax bills, unless extended.
February 15	▸ County auditor and treasurer settle ▸ County auditor distributes first-half taxes to the taxing authorities
June 20	Final date for paying second-half tax bills, unless extended.
August 10	▸ County Auditor and Treasurer settle ▸ County Auditor distributes first-half taxes to the taxing authorities

Source: Ohio State Department of Taxation

FIGURE 13-10. Utility personal property tax calendar.

or tax department either the ownership or accurate value of property. With respect to real property, the discovery of property parcels and the discovery of improvements to real property require considerable effort on the part of the assessor. In cooperation with other government offices, which grant building permits or record the title of properties when an exchange is made, assessors are able to track ownership and value of real property. Many taxing authorities assist in the discovery of real property by employing aerial mapping. There is also a strong movement toward computer-assisted cadastral information systems to help identify and even value real property and improvements to real property (IAAO 1990).

The discovery of personal property for property tax purposes is even more daunting than it is for real property. Personal property neither requires a recording of a deed nor is discovery by computer-enhanced aerial mapping possible. Personal property is mobile and has the potential to be shifted on the lien date to avoid taxation. The difficulty with respect to the discovery of personal property has caused some analysts to question retaining personal property in a modern property tax system (Bland 1989; Netzer 1963). The discovery of tangible personal property requires either an on-site inspection of each facility, or self-reporting by owners of each establishment or firm. The cost of an annual inspection, or even relatively frequent inspections, is so high that it is not a practical approach for discovery. The model followed by most taxing authorities is to require the owner of the personal property to file an annual tax report that describes the nature of the personal property (IAAO 1990).

Filing an annual report is the model used to discover the tangible personal property of public utilities in Ohio. The Public Utilities Tax Section has prepared a specific Annual Report for each class of utility required to be taxed under Chapter 5727 of the *Ohio Revised Code*. In addition to the Annual Report, companies are required to file copies of the annual reports submitted to both PUCO and federal regulatory agencies. These include FERC reports and, in the case of Rural Electrics, reports filed with the United States Department of Agriculture. The Annual Reports filed with the Public Utility Section require the utility company to supply a prescribed balance sheet and a variety of schedules which list tangible property. All reported property is listed in terms of historical cost. Utilities are required to identify their property by the role the property plays in the production and distribution of the products produced. For example, an electric utility must categorize plant in terms of transmission, distribution, production, and general plant. The utility must also report property by age or vintage. Once vintage is reported, and adjustments are made for financing and allowable exemptions, the tax return is ready for submission to the Public Utilities Section.

Because the Utility must provide information to the Public Utility Section which has also been supplied to the regulatory bodies, the difficulty of discovering tangible personal property is reduced in Ohio. There may be little incentive to provide tax authorities with information about tangible personal property, but there is a significant incentive to report the value of all property to the regulatory bodies. The utility is allowed to earn a return only on the value of reported property. The Annual Report filed with the Public Utilities Section, when checked against the data provided to the regulatory body, provides a unique method of discovering tangible personal property.[47]

Discovery is also facilitated by the relatively few firms that are easily identified by coordination with the PUCO.

The Determination of Ad Valorem Value of Public Utility Properties

Two fundamental policy issues must be answered before public utilities can have a property tax imposed on them. The first is "who" will conduct the valuation; the second is "what" valuation method will the appraiser use. The "who" question concerns whether local or state government will do the appraisal. In some states, like Florida and Massachusetts, local tax officials have the legal responsibility to value public utilities. In most states, central tax departments appraise public utilities. A recent study by the State of New York Board of Equalization (1993) reports that 38 states value utility and railroad property at the state level. There are several reasons why central appraisal is better. If local officials value public utility property, local governments must develop expertise, or pay for expertise, for the appraisal of a single large taxpayer. Such a policy results in redundant efforts by government officials. The appraisal of public utility property is complex and the required expertise is expensive to maintain or hire. There is also the concern for the compliance costs of the taxpayer. Forcing a company to deal with multiple county or special government districts is unfair to the company tax officials (ACIR 1963).

The second question of "what" valuation method is used has policy and administrative implications. Three standard methods are used to value property. The taxable value of real property can be determined by capitalizing net income from a property (income approach), comparing the sales price of a similar property (market approach), or estimating the cost of replacing existing structures (cost approach) (IAAO 1990). The method of valuation is determined to some extent by who is given the responsibility for the appraisal. If local officials are given the appraisal responsibility for a multiple jurisdiction utility, they are almost forced to use a cost approach for each type of property they appraise. When used in this manner, the appraisal is referred to as a *summation appraisal*. The individual values of each factor contributing to value are summed to arrive at a final value.[48]

In two-thirds of the states, at least two appraisal methods are used to value property (State of New York Board of Equalization 1993). Generally, the process is to use both an income approach and a cost approach to estimate a unit value. After both values have been determined, the assessor then weights both values and calculates a single unit value (Western State Association of Tax Administrators 1989). The unit value resulting from this approach is called a *unitary* or *unit value*. The unit label is applied because it values the entire firm. The two models of "who" values public utility property and "what" processes are used are described in Figure 13-11.

Descriptions of the methods states use to value utility and railroad properties are reported in Table 13-19. A unit process is used to value railroads operating in Ohio. Ohio railroads file an Annual Report with the Public Utilities Section by March. The Annual Report gives the Public Utility Section data to value railroads using both the income and the cost approaches. The income approach is driven by the amount of income earned by a company. The Annual Report requires each railroad company to report a five-year history of systemwide Net Operating Railroad Income (NORI). NORI is based on the definition used by the Interstate Commerce Commission.[49] NORI is capitalized to estimate the value of the operating railroad system. The capitalization is based on a weighted cost of capital that considers the cost of debt and the required rate of return for equity holders.[50] A basic outline of the process to value a railroad using the income approach is outlined in step one of Figure 13-12. The income approach is used on all four of the Class one railroads in Ohio and 13 of the remaining 32 Class two and Class three railroads in Ohio.

The cost approach starts with original cost as defined in the reports filed by the railroad with the ICC. Accrued depreciation, based on ICC accounting guidelines, is deducted from the original cost. The resulting net book is adjusted for economic and functional obsolescence.[51] The cost method is briefly outlined in Figure 13-12. All 36 railroads in Ohio are appraised by use of the cost approach. In those situations in which both the income and

Summation Method	**Unit Method**
Real properties, improvements, and personality are individually appraised. The values of each property are summed to form a value for the entire firm.	The firm is valued as a whole.
Appraisal Approaches	**Appraisal Approaches**
• Cost approach (on individual items)	• Capitalized Income
• Limited use of sales approach (on individual items)	• Sales Comparison
	• Cost Approach

FIGURE 13-11. Approaches for assessing multi-jurisdictional property.

TABLE 13-19
Property Taxation of Utility and Railroad Property

			Primary Valuation Methods	
State	Level of Administration	Unitary Valuation	Utility[a]	Railroad[a]
California	State	Yes	I, M, C	I, M, C
Illinois	State (Railroads) Locals (Utility)	Yes	I, M, C	I, M, C
Indiana	State	No	C	C
Kentucky	State	Yes	I	I
Michigan	State	Yes	C	C
New York	Local	No	C	C
Ohio	State	No	C	I,C
Pennsylvania	State	No	C	C
West Virginia	State	Yes	I, M, C	I, M, C

Source: State Board of Equalization, Survey of Railroad and Utility Taxation Practices Among the States, Albany, New York, 1993.

[a]I = Income, M = Market, C = Cost

cost methods are relied on, the appraiser must complete the third step illustrated in Figure 13-12. In this final step, the appraiser "correlates" or reconciles the two values by applying his professional judgement to determine a final single value. In making this final estimation, the appraiser must subjectively weight the relative strength of the two indicators of value. The indicator that represents the best estimate of the value of the railroad is given the most weight.

The method used to value railroads is different from the method used to value the other utilities in Ohio. The difference appears to be a direct result of the 4-R Act, which has allowed railroads to argue property valuation and property equalization issues in the federal courts without exhausting administrative and legal avenues of appeal in a state system.[52] This act also established that railroads could not be assessed at assessment levels that exceed the assessment levels of other commercial and industrial property in a state.[53]

The appraisal for property tax purposes of the other regulated utilities in Ohio follows the cost or summation approach. Each individual parcel or item of tangible personal property is valued and then summed to form the total appraisal of the utility. However, unlike other states which use a cost and summation approach, the responsibility for the appraisal of property for utilities in Ohio remains with the Ohio Department of Taxation.

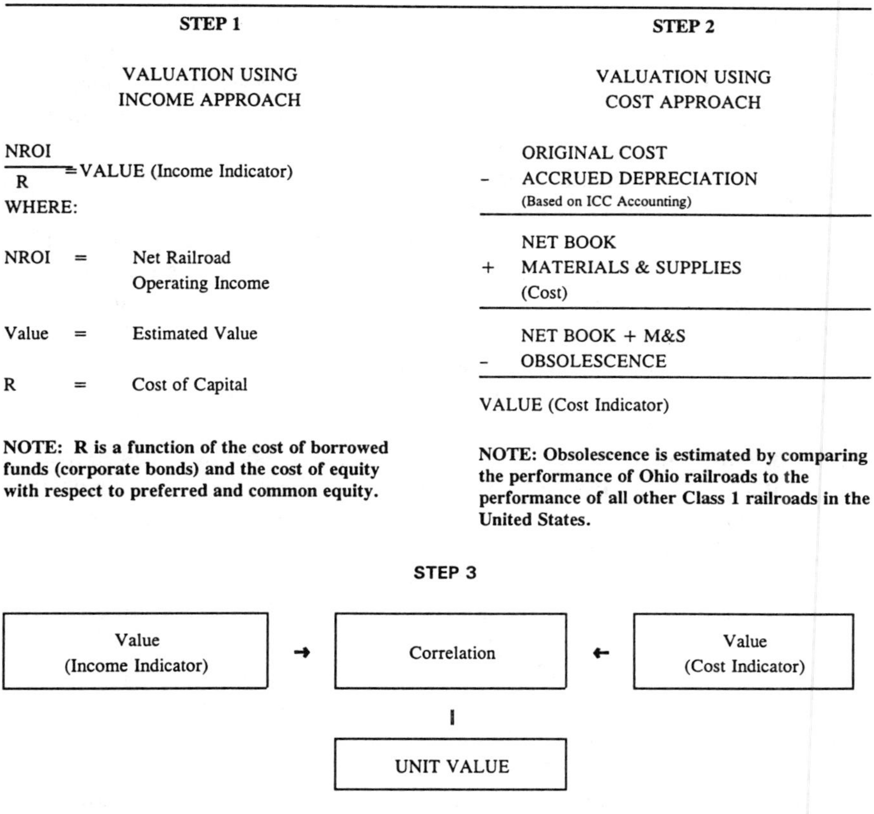

FIGURE 13-12. Unit value of railroad based on income and cost approach.

As noted in the fifth section, which discussed the issue of property discovery, the Public Utility Tax Section requires each public utility to file an Annual Report. The Annual Report has the utility identify personal property in terms of use, vintage, and historical cost. Once the data have been reported, the tangible personal property is appraised using a depreciation schedule. The depreciation schedule declines by an equal percentage amount for each year of ownership and use. The declining value eventually reaches a minimum value. The time to reach the minimum value varies in length, depending on the type of tangible personal property. The schedules for depreciation were developed during the late 1980s by the Public Utilities Section in cooperation with industry officials.[54]

Several concerns are associated with the use of standard depreciation schedules. The first one is why use such schedules at all? According to appraisal theory, tangible personal property depreciation has three causes:

physical deterioration, functional obsolescence, and economic obsolescence (IAAO 1990). Appraisals should account for each of these individual causes of depreciation. For the layman, it is more useful to ask if the appraiser is able to account for the age, intensity of use, frequency of use, and maintenance of tangible personal property. The ability of an appraiser to measure accurately the depreciation caused by each of these forces is limited. Usually, however, an accurate appraisal requires an actual physical examination to determine the extent of depreciation. Unfortunately, a physical inspection of each piece of tangible equipment owned by all the utilities would be impossible. Appraisers must use shortcut methods to value such property.

Shortcut methods present appraisers with two options. First, they can use existing "canned schedules." Appraisers could, for example, choose to base depreciation on standard accounting schedules or IRS schedules. However, these schedules are generally financial or political artifacts, do not have much in common with valuation reality, and are generally referenced as book values in the literature (Alico 1989). There are also commercially prepared depreciation schedules. A common example is the service provided by Marshall Valuation Service. Such schedules may work, but they are generally prepared for generic properties. The second approach is to develop custom depreciation schedules, the approach used by Ohio. The Public Utilities Section has developed its own specific schedule for estimating the depreciation of the tangible personal property owned by regulated utilities.

The second concern is whether the schedule developed by the Public Utilities Section is constructed in a manner similar to the process used for the tangible personal property depreciation schedule. The evidence is that both methods are similarly designed and implemented. The only noticeable difference is the shorter depreciation schedule for tangible personal property and the fewer categories in which to place tangible personal business property.

The development of the depreciation schedules was part of a restructuring of the processes of utility appraisal. The schedules were developed on the basis of data provided to Ohio tax administrators by the larger utilities. During the development of the schedules, the Public Utilities Section also sought input from the PUCO and the FERC on their estimates of useful service lives of utility personal property. The Public Utilities Section annually reviews the depreciation schedules developed by PUCO to see if any major adjustments should be made in the assumptions about the economic life of a facility.

The use of depreciation schedules leads to two related disputes between a utility and a property tax administrator. First, the utility will want to have property placed in the schedule with the shortest expected useful life; and second, the utility will challenge the validity of the length of time used on the schedule. Both issues are raised by utilities in Ohio during property appraisals. The schedules used in depreciating property are listed in Table 13-19.

The actual appraisal process starts when the utility files the Annual Report with the Public Utilities Section. Each report must be accompanied by the regulatory reports required by federal regulatory agencies and the PUCO. A general outline of the process to appraise a nonrailroad utility is given in Figure 13-13, which uses an example from the appraisal of a Local Gas Distribution Company (LDC).

The appraisal of the property flows in a logical progression. The utility files the Annual Report which contains information on the historical cost of its tangible personal property. The next step is to make allowance for property that is not subject to the property tax. In the case of LDCs, this includes pollution control facilities, licensed tangible property, and real property.[55] The value of capitalized interest is also eliminated from the tax base. The fourth and fifth steps are combined on the same schedule on the annual report. On this report, tangible personal property is assigned to a specific classification and controlled for vintage; then appraised value is determined.[56]

Assessment of the Property Tax

In order to actually assess a property tax in Ohio, two additional tasks must be completed by the Public Utilities Section. First, the Division applies a legislatively established assessment level to the appraised value of a property. For personal property assessed by a county auditor in Ohio, the assessment level is set at 25 percent of the appraised value. The assessment level of real property is 35 percent. The value of the assessment level for such property is established by the state legislature. For property assessed by the Property Tax Division, the assessment levels, which are also established by the state legislature, are much higher. The established assessment ratios used on Property Tax Division assessed properties are listed in Table 13-20.

The changes in the assessment levels reported in Table 13-20 occurred over a period of years. The rural electrics were assessed at the same level as other electrics before 1941. In 1941 their assessment level was reduced to 50 percent. The reduction in the railroad assessment level was a response to the 4-R Act. Railroads, according to the 4-R Act, are required to be assessed at the same level as other commercial and industrial property within a state. The reduction in the assessment level of railroads began in the early 1980s. Electric nonproduction equipment was granted a new depreciation schedule during the late 1980s. The higher assessment levels cause utilities to pay higher taxes relative to other taxpayers. The higher burden is especially acute for personal property owned by utilities relative to tangible personal property owned by industrial and commercial firms. A comparison of the relative assessment level of gas utilities in Ohio and the gas utilities in selected states is given in Table 13-21. In terms of property tax assessment levels, Ohio treats utilities differently than other selected states treat utilities.

STEP 1	Reporting of Book Cost of All Tangible Personal Property
STEP 2	Classifying Remaining Tangible Property Into: 1. Production 2. Storage 3. Transmission 4. Distribution 5. General 6. Material and Supplies 7. Property Held for Future Use 8. Current Gas 9. Noncurrent and Nonrecoverable Gas
STEP 3	Removing Exemptions: 1. Certified Pollution Control Facilities 2. Real Property 3. Licensed Motor Vehicles
STEP 4	Removing Eliminations: 1. Capitalized Interest
STEP 5	Reducing Historical Cost by Composite Depreciation 1. Production: 98% to 15% - 25 years 2. Storage: 98.3% to 15% - 30 years 3. Distribution: 98.3% to 15% - 30 years 4. Transmission: 98.3% to 15% - 30 years 5. General Plant: 96.7 % to 15% - 15 years 6. Material and Supplies: 100% Valuation - 8. Current Gas: 120% Valuation - 9. Noncurrent and Nonrecoverable Gas: 100% Valuation -
STEP 6	Sum Values From Step 5 Result Is True Value

FIGURE 13-13. Tangible personal appraisal process of local gas distribution by property tax division.

The second step in assessment requires the Property Tax Division to determine what proportion of a utilities property is taxable by a specific government entity. This process, labeled *apportionment*, is practiced in most states in which the centralized assessment of certain properties is followed. The apportionment of property in Ohio is accomplished by first dividing the total taxable value of a firm by the distribution base—the distribution base varies by the class of utility. The distribution base for railroads is miles of track; for gas it is the cost of taxable properties. The resulting factor from the first operation is then multiplied by the distribution base in a specific taxing jurisdiction. The resulting value is the taxable value for the specific

TABLE 13-20
Assessment Level Percentages for Property Classes in Ohio: 1980, 1990, 1993

Class of Property	Year		
	1988	1990	1992
Electric - Production	100%	100%	100%
Electric	100	88	88
Rural Electric	50	50	50
Gas	100	88	88
Railroads	30	28	26
Others	100	88	88
Real Property	35	35	35

Source: Ohio Department of Taxation

TABLE 13-21
Ratio of Assessment Levels of Gas Utilities to Other Commercial & Industrial Props: Selected States

State	Ratio
Illinois	1.00
Indiana	1.00
Kentucky	1.00
Michigan	1.60
New Jersey	1.00
New York	1.00
Ohio	3.52
Pennsylvania	1.00
West Virginia	1.12

Source: Commerce Clearing House.

taxing jurisdiction. The formula for apportionment in each industry is described in Figure 13-14.

As noted in Figure 13-14, 70 percent of the value of personal property associated with the production of electricity remains in the taxing district where it is physically located on the lien date. The remaining 30 percent is apportioned on the basis of the cost of transmission and distribution facilities.[57] The methods used to apportion cost within Ohio have some foundation in the appraisal literature (Brewer 1972).

Basic Apportionment Process			
Step 1	Statewide Taxable Value / Statewide Distribution Base		= Factor
Step 2	Factor x	Distribution Base In Taxing District =	Apportioned Value For Taxing District

Distribution Bases by Industry	
Industry	Distribution Base
Railroad (Personal Property)	Miles of track and trackage rights
Electric (Personal Property)	
70% of Production Property	Sitused
(30%) of production value	Cost of transmission & distribution property
General Plant and M&C	Cost of transmission & distribution property
Transmission and distribution	
Natural Gas, Heating, and Waterworks (Personal Property)	Cost of Taxable Property

Source: Property Tax Division, Ohio Department of Taxation.

FIGURE 13-14. Apportionment of taxable value of public utilities and railroads.

There are several problems with the current system. First, the current process of apportioning assessed value places a heavy compliance cost on the taxpaying utility and railroad. Each utility must report to the Property Tax Division the location and cost of the distribution base by taxing jurisdiction. There are 4,000 such jurisdictions in Ohio. This process requires that each company maintain an extensive set of records on the physical location of tangible personal property. Unfortunately, the compliance issues associated with reporting data for apportionment purposes cannot easily be passed forward to the Property Tax Division or the Public Utilities Section.

Next, the current apportionment processes in Ohio may also have results which appear somewhat arbitrary. For example, there is no evidence that value is apportioned on the basis of either the revenue needs of local governments or on the burdens the utility property places on local governments. Finally, many local governments may feel they are not getting their "fair" share of a utilities value. An illustration would be a unit of government with a large gas pumping station located within its boundary, but only a small portion of taxable value would be assigned to it for taxation. Unfortunately, there are no obvious alternatives to the current apportionment processes. One suggestion might be to apportion value on a per capita basis. A per capita allocation of taxable value would turn the process into a grant system, which might also be viewed as arbitrary. Revenue would be allocated without regard for the burden imposed on governments by the utility property or the needs of citizens. Perhaps the best solution is to choose the method that results in consistency and ease (ACIR 1963).[58]

Billing and Collection

After the assessed value of the public utility personal property has been assigned by the Public Utilities Section to a taxing jurisdiction, the county auditor is notified. The assessed values are reported by the auditor to each taxing jurisdiction. Upon receipt of the assessed values, the various tax districts establish their tax rate within the context of Ohio law. The resulting tax notice and bill is then sent to the owner of the property. Taxes on public utility properties can be paid in two installments to each taxing jurisdiction as described in the property tax calendar outlined in Figure 13-10 of this chapter.[59]

Audit

The importance of the property discovery process with respect to personal property was discussed earlier in this chapter. The auditing of personal property accounts is also an important step in insuring the integrity of the property tax system. In Ohio, a limited number of post tax audits are conducted on utility personal property accounts. However, as described earlier, because public utility companies must supplement their Annual Reports to the Property Tax Division with reports filed with the PUCO and the FERC, there is less need for a substantial auditing effort on the part of the Division. In reality, when the annual valuation is complete and the appraiser has compared the information received in the Annual Report to the reports filed with PUCO and FERC, he has conducted a through audit of the public utility account.

The current system does have two major shortcomings. It does not allow the Public Utilities Section to check if tangible personal property is being apportioned to the appropriate unit of local government, nor to verify that the utilities are placing their tangible personal property in the proper valuation schedule found in the Annual Report. A firm has the incentive to report property in the most favorable valuation schedule. It is impossible to test how serious these problems are for property tax system.

Valuation Appeals

The "flow" of the valuation appeals process is described in Figure 13-15.

STEPS	ISSUES
Notify public utility of true value and taxable value	*Property Tax Division sends transmittal letter and valuation notice to each taxpayer
Taxpayer has 14 days to request a preassessment hearing with Property Tax Division Staff	*Limited number of taxpayers request hearing
Informal hearing with Property Tax Division Staff	*Issues: Correct obvious mistakes real vs. personal exemptions and exclusions valuation
True value and taxable value corrected if required; taxable value apportioned	
Tax Commissioner certifies taxable values to taxpayer and County Auditors on 1st Monday of October	
Taxpayer has 30 days to request an administrative review with Tax Commissioner	
Hearing with Department's attorney: no formal procedures followed or record made	*May take up to one year to schedule hearing *Legal counsel not required
Tax Commissioner issues Final Determination; copies sent to taxpayer and County Auditor	*Final determination is called a "Journal Entry" *Decision and justification are usually brief

continued

FIGURE 13-15. Appeals process—public utilities.

STEPS	ISSUES
Taxpayer or County Auditor has 30 days to appeal to Board of Tax Appeals	
Formal appeal; court procedures apply; record made; legal counsel required; attorney general represents tax commissioner	*DeNovo proceeding *Board cannot decide constitutional issues *Issues: real vs. personal taxable vs. exempt constitutional issues (record only) *Approximately 20 appeals per year
Board of Tax Appeals issues decision to all parties	
Each party has 45 days to appeal; appeal can be to a court of or directly to Ohio Supreme Court	*Most appeals are directly to Supreme Court
Court appeals	
Ohio Supreme Court	*Hearing on the record *Supreme Court is now using master commissioners *Appeal from court of appeals is by petition

FIGURE 13-15. Appeals process—public utilities (continued)

The appeals process for the tangible personal property of public utilities and the appraised value of railroads initially starts on a informal basis. Taxpayers are given a preliminary notice of their likely appraised value by the Public Utilities Section. This value is reported to the taxpayers before the certified assessed value is given to the local taxing authorities. Taxpayers are then allowed to visit with the Public Utilities Section and request a change in the assessed value. This process is informal and allows the Section to correct any obvious mistakes before the assessed value is given to the local officials. An informal process like the method in Ohio is beneficial to both taxpayer and tax authorities.

The next steps are more "legal"—formality increases as the appeals process moves toward the court system. Appeals beyond the informal appeal process probably require the involvement of legal counsel and possibly outside valuation experts. The appeal process conducted by the Board of Tax Appeals in Ohio usually requires the presence of an attorney and, in the case of utilities, expert witnesses. The decision from the Board of Tax Appeals can be appealed directly to a District Court or to the Ohio Supreme Court.

EVALUATION OF THE CURRENT SYSTEM OF PROPERTY: TAXATION OF UTILITIES AND RAILROADS

This section evaluates the current Ohio system of taxing electric and gas utilities and railroads in terms of several important tax policy criteria. Issues considered are the stability of the tax and concerns about the incidence of each tax. The taxes on electric and gas utilities will be evaluated first.

Electric and Gas Utilities

When compared to other industrial and commercial firms in the state, electric and gas utilities in Ohio have received a higher tax burden on their property. Currently, the assessment levels imposed on electric and gas utilities are just over three times higher than the rates applied against the personal property of commercial and industrial firms in Ohio and over double the assessment level of the real property of such firms. Ohio has not been alone in taxing utilities at rates higher than other firms. There is a tradition in the United States of taxing utilities at high rates. Phillips (1992) identifies several reasons why states tax utilities more heavily than nonregulated firms:

- The large size of utilities simplifies the collection of taxes.
- Utilities have large physical investments and thus are attractive targets for property tax collection.
- Utility taxes produce substantial amounts of revenue.
- Utilities lack strong political support.

Most of Phillips' assertions are valid for Ohio. Utilities in Ohio are few in number, and this simplifies the administration of the tax. The need to deal with just over 400 utilities does simplify the efforts associated with tax administration. Utilities continue to have large physical plants. Unless there is a radical change in Ohio tax policy, utilities can expect to face substantial property tax burdens. Utilities also produce substantial revenue for local governments in Ohio. It is difficult to respond to Phillips' last suggestion. There is no easy way to determine if Ohio utilities suffer from inadequate political clout.

The above does not suggest that problems do not exist with the current system of electric and gas utility and railroad taxation in Ohio; the current system is cumbersome to administer for the State of Ohio. However, the current system is not radically more difficult to administer than the processes found in other states. There is no easy process to value the physical assets of a multimillion dollar company. In fact, the process in Ohio may minimize the state's administrative burden compared to other states, because so much of the burden has been shifted to the utilities when they comply with the property tax. In most states (38), the valuation of a utility is generally based on financial data reported by a company through federal regulatory reports or company data commonly found in the financial press.

The compliance costs associated with this tax scheme are not insignificant. It is almost impossible to compare the compliance costs to those of other states because most utilities valued in Ohio operate only in Ohio; there is no frame of reference. However, tax officials of American Electric Power, which operates in six other midwestern states, feel that the compliance cost in Ohio is greater than in almost all other states in which AEP produces electricity. A serious compliance problem associated with the method in Ohio requires companies to provide data to guide the apportionment of the companies' property values within the state's taxing jurisdictions. Unfortunately, a change to almost any other property-taxing scheme would not reduce the need for companies to report the location of taxable property.

As noted, the system could benefit from a stronger audit system. Almost no auditing is being performed by the Public Utilities Section. The audits would be most beneficial in ensuring that the current apportionment system accurately assigns taxable value to taxing jurisdictions.

There are several advantages to the current valuation system: it is relatively simple, it is understood by both taxpayers and tax administrators, there are few areas of disagreement about valuation responsibilities or the valuation process, and the system also provides for a good informal method to respond to problems about valuation raised by the utilities before the final valuation is certified by the Tax Commissioner. Such a system is especially important to the local governments that receive the tax. It allows the local government to set its budget with some confidence that the value will not be challenged in the formal appeal process with a subsequent loss of taxable value.

The current system is also stable in terms of revenue and valuation. Because the valuation is based on the historical cost of the personal property of the utilities, the taxable value of utilities hardly changes as price levels or income levels change in Ohio. The elasticity of the current property-tax system in relation to income is much less than one. This means that if income in Ohio increases by one percent, the increase in the revenue from the personal property tax would be less than one. Even the general property tax, which is based on current market values, is usually estimated to have elasticities of less than one. The current valuation method is simply not tied in any direct way to the level of personal income in Ohio. Price changes may eventually be reflected in the valuation of the public utilities, but only as the utilities purchase new equipment at higher prices.

Such stability means that increases in prices or income levels, which may force local governments to spend more for services or pay more for employees, can be met only if the rates of taxation on utilities are increased. There is no automatic inflation increase with this tax base. Conversely, when there is a general slowdown in the economy, the amount of revenue coming from the tax remains stable. Revenue stability during an economic downturn is a distinct advantage of this tax.

The evaluation of the equity of the personal property tax on utilities begins with a discussion of how the tax treats utilities. The current tax, like most property taxes, is not sensitive to the economic conditions of the firms being taxed. Firms with substantial physical investment, but low earnings, will pay more property tax than firms with lower levels of investment but enjoy better earnings. Because the tax is not responsive to levels of income, it may not treat firms with a substantial difference in income in a different manner. Examples of this problem are easy to find in the Ohio utility industry. At first blush this problem appears to violate the principle of horizontal equity. This criterion argues that similar taxpayers should be burdened or taxed to a similar degree.

There is also the criterion of vertical equity. An initial discussion on vertical equity concerns the burden of a tax relative to how firms with different income levels are taxed. The personal property tax on utilities is not responsive to the income levels or profits of utilities in Ohio. The tax is based on investment; a heavily invested firm with low profits would be taxed the same as a heavily invested firm with high profits. There are examples of such firms in Ohio. As with the issue of horizontal equity, at first blush the tangible personal property tax imposed in Ohio on utilities seems to violate this criterion.

However, the real question with respect to a utility property tax is who bears the tax in terms of the final incidence. Unfortunately, there is little empirical evidence on the incidence of any tax imposed on a utility. The standard assumption is that a tax imposed on a utility is passed forward to customers (Phillips 1992). Before the deregulation of the natural gas utility, such an assumption for natural gas consumers would have seemed sound.

The assumption that residential consumers bear the property tax on a natural gas utility probably remains intact. The assumption that residential consumers of electricity bear the burden of the tax also seems safe. Regulatory bodies continue to treat taxes as an operating expense and allow them to be reflected in the rate paid by consumers. If these assumptions are correct, then the issues of horizontal equity and vertical equity must be determined by evaluating the electric and gas consumptions patterns of Ohio residential consumers. National data suggest that the consumption of electricity is related to income, and it declines as a percent of income as income increases (Casler and Rafiqui 1993). If these data reflect the consumption patterns of Ohio residences, then we should assume that the portion of the tax borne by consumers is regressive in its effect. If true, if could easily violate the concept of vertical equity.

Issues about who bears the burden of a utility tax when the consumer is an industrial firm or a commercial firm are more difficult to answer. Several plausible assumptions can be made. First, it can be assumed that the utilities try to have residential consumers pay the tax because they are less price sensitive than industrial or commercial consumers. Earlier evidence clearly indicates that the rates for industrial and commercial users of both gas and electricity are lower than they are for residential consumers. However, it seems unlikely that a regulatory body would allow the entire burden of a tax to be imposed on residential consumers. Thus the second assumption is that utility taxes are imposed on commercial and industrial consumers of energy. Once this assumption is made, the analysis of who bears the tax must distinguish between a tax on natural gas and a tax on electricity. It is unlikely that a tax on natural gas can be passed on to industrial and commercial consumers in Ohio. Such firms have options to purchase untaxed gas from nonregulated suppliers. In the long run, much of the personal property tax on the regulated natural gas industry will remain with the gas industry to be borne by either owners of the firm or employees. The portion that remains with the natural gas industry will be any amount in excess of the national average tax burden for such utilities. Owners will bear the burden in terms of lower profits and workers in terms of lower wages. How this spilt is made is open to obvious speculation.

The incidence of the tax on electricity sold to industrial and commercial users is more difficult to determine. In a regulated world, the portion of the total tax that is included in the rates is likely passed on to industrial consumers. One limiting factor would be the price sensitivity of industrial and commercial firms. As noted (Chapman et al. 1982) industrial and commercial firms respond to price increases by consuming less electrical energy. In Ohio the personal property tax on electric utilities is likely passed forward to industrial and commercial consumers. However, the analysis cannot end here. A complete answer requires determining if the taxes can be passed on to the consumers of the goods and services produced and sold by Ohio industrial and commercial firms. In situations in which the tax is passed on to consumers, it is likely regressive in nature. In situations in which the tax cannot be passed on to consumers, it is borne by either the investors in electrical firms or the employees of such firms. No attempt is made to estimate the ultimate burden of the personal property tax imposed on electrical utilities and initially passed on to industrial and commercial users.

It is important to recognize that when retail wheeling is allowed in Ohio, the incidence of personal property tax on industrial and commercial users will shift. The analysis will reflect the outcome developed for the natural gas industry; much of the burden will remain with the electrical industry.

RAILROADS

The administration of the property tax on railroads in Ohio corresponds to the administration of this tax in other states. The similarity is likely a result of the federal legislation discussed above. States have found it easier, or have been compelled, to assess railroads at the same rates they apply to other business property. The valuation method used on railroads in Ohio is virtually identical to the valuation process used in other states. Discussions with several tax representatives associated with railroads found little disagreement with the valuation methods used in Ohio.

In terms of stability, the valuation methods used on Ohio railroads will reflect changes in both price levels and income levels. As a consequence, railroad valuation and the revenue from the property tax on railroads is going to be less stable than the valuations and revenue from other regulated utilities. However, the revenue from this source is still likely to be less responsive than changes in income, because a portion of the valuation continues to be tied to the historical cost of the railroad.

The incidence of this tax on the large interstate railroads can only be guessed. Given the competitive nature of the current transportation system, it seems safe to assume that for many goods the railroads would be unable to pass the tax on to consumers. Attempts to set rates above those charge by inter/intrastate trucks would result in a shift to other modes of transportation. Other situations in which the railroad is the only viable shipper of a good may allow the railroad to pass the tax on to users of the rail service. Coal is an example of such a product; and the ability of the owner of the coal to then pass the tax to consumers is also subject to debate.

DISPARITY IN THE DISTRIBUTION OF THE PERSONAL PROPERTY TAX BASE

Because of the substantial physical investment associated with regulated utilities, the possibility of a disproportionate distribution of the tax base is quite high. An analysis of the per capita distribution of the public utility property tax in each of the 88 counties in Ohio confirms this possibility. The county receiving the highest amount of per capita revenue from this tax collected just under $400, while the county receiving the least amount collected just under $30 per capita. The coefficient of variation, which measures relative dispersion, was 75 percent. This statistic means that on average there is a 75 percent difference from the mean per capita revenue received in the 88 counties. The comparable figure for the real property tax was 52 percent.

When the analysis shifts to the tax base, the dispersion is even greater. The maximum assessed value per capita is over $11,000, and the minimum is just below $600. The coefficient of variation is over 100 percent. The coefficient of variation for the real property tax base is 23 percent.

These reported differences and measured disparities suggest that the property tax on utilities creates equity issues with respect to the provision of goods and services for local governments. Taxing jurisdictions with substantial assessed value per citizen can provide a much greater level of goods and services with minimal tax rates. Jurisdictions with lower assessed values can only provide comparable levels of service by charging higher tax rates.[60]

THE ALTERNATIVES

The alternatives are discussed, to the extent possible, under the assumption that the outcome for Ohio state government and Ohio local governments will be revenue-neutral. Except for leaving the current valuation system intact, all the alternatives discussed reduce the property tax burden on public utilities. However, these alternatives must be considered in the context of the entire Tax Commission study. Other portions of the study offer alternatives and suggestions to replace the revenue reductions that accompany the alternatives discussed below. Although tax on public utilities in Ohio has been studied by previous tax reviews conducted in Ohio, little has been done to respond to the recommendations associated with earlier tax studies. The economics of public utilities have changed.[61] The railroads are now deregulated and also protected by federal legislation that prohibits property tax discrimination. The natural gas industry is also deregulated and restructured. Natural gas pipelines are common carriers, and LDCs wheel gas from brokers to commercial and industrial users. Electric utilities remain regulated but will be confronted with retail wheeling in the future. The following alternatives should be given careful consideration in light of these changing economic conditions. Without change, the current system will start to lose tax revenue. With competition already in place in rail and gas taxpayers already have an opportunity to avoid the heavier taxes associated with a public utility. If the assertion is correct that retail wheeling will occur in the electric utility industry, the loss of tax revenue in that industry cannot be far behind. If there is no change in the current system, a gradual erosion of the tax revenue will occur. The erosion will develop as electrical energy is wheeled to avoid high cost producers. To avoid this erosion, several alternatives are offered for consideration:

- Impose an ad valorem-based excise tax on consumers to replace the property tax.
- Impose a tax on consumers based on units of energy consumed to replace the property tax.
- Retain the property tax but use the unit method to value property.
- Retain the current property-tax valuation method.
- Reduce the assessment level on electric and gas utilities.

Alternative # 1 — Ad Valorem Excise Tax on Consumers

Several Ohio utilities and utility organizations offered testimony to the Tax Study Commission on revenue sources that could be used to replace the reduced or lost revenue that would result from tax reform. A frequent suggestion was to replace the revenue lost from a reduction in the assessment level on the personal property tax and the removal of the gross receipts tax with revenue from an excise tax on consumers of natural gas and electricity. The common term used to describe this tax was an *energy service tax*. Two types of excise taxes were suggested. The first, discussed in this section, was an excise tax on the value of the energy consumed. The second, discussed in the next section, was a tax on the units of the energy consumed, e.g., units of KWH.

The excise tax based on the value of the energy consumed would impose a tax on the bill of the consumer of the energy. Thus the base of the tax would be the dollar value of the energy purchased by consumers of electricity or gas. The excise tax rates proposed with this suggestion ranged up to five percent. One suggestion was to make the rate the same as the state sales tax rate.

This approach, which imposes a tax on the dollar value of the consumers bill, seems to have the most support within the industry. The ad valorem excise tax is responsive to changes in the prices paid for energy. These changes would eventually be reflected in the utility bills paid by energy users. The tax base would become more elastic or responsive to economic changes. The tax would also be regressive if the normal consumption patterns for electricity and gas continue (Casler and Rafiqui 1993).

An important policy consideration associated with this approach would be that all suppliers of an energy-based product would be expected to collect the tax from their customers. The tax would no longer be triggered by designation as a public utility.

ALTERNATIVE # 2 — UNIT EXCISE TAX IMPOSED ON CONSUMERS

As noted, the second suggestion for an excise tax on energy or the energy service tax is to impose the tax on the volume of energy consumed, e.g., KWH of electricity. This proposal has been promoted by Centerior Corporation (1994) and presented to the Tax Study Commission. The Centerior proposal recommends the complete removal of the property tax except for the tax on real property.[62] Like the ad valorem-based excise tax, this tax would be imposed on the consumer and collected by the utility; it would be listed on the bill received by the energy user. Under this scheme, all providers of energy would face a flat fee on each unit of energy sold. For electricity, Centerior (1994) estimates this cost to be about 0.62 cents per KWH. The modeling by Centerior assumes that the energy service tax would be used to replace the Gross Receipts Tax and to effect a complete removal of the property tax. If the Gross Receipts tax is replaced by another tax, or left in place, the energy tax to replace the change in the assessment level of the property tax would fall below 0.40 cents per KWH.

This tax would cause a shift in the tax burden. When the 0.40 cents per KWH is compared to the data in column one of Table 13-2, the shift among utilities is apparent. If we assume that the electric utility tax is passed forward to consumers, then the real shift in burden will be among regions of Ohio.

The service tax based on unit consumptions would be relatively stable. However, like the ad valorem energy service tax, it would be less stable than the current system. Reductions in energy consumption would be reflected in lower tax collections. Conversely, higher patterns of energy consumption would result in more revenue. The swings would be driven by weather patterns much more than by economic activity. Collection of the tax would be triggered by consumption, regardless of the status of the supplier.

ALTERNATIVE # 3 — UNIT APPROACH FOR ALL UTILITIES

The third alternative for reform is to retain the property tax but use a unit method to value electric and gas utilities. Irrespective of the widespread acceptance of the current method used to value utilities in Ohio, a lingering doubt exists about the accuracy of the method. The doubt comes by simply asking if a potential buyer would use the Ohio personal property method to set the price for the purchase of a utility company. There is little evidence in the literature that the cost-based estimates of value, used by Ohio, have credibility in the valuation of a operating firm (Cornell 1992). The cost approach used in Ohio suffers from the following problems:

- Historical cost may not reflect the actual market value of personal property.
- Estimating the economic depreciation associated with machinery or equipment is difficult.
- Estimating economic obsolescence is difficult.

A solution to these problems would be to change utility valuation to a unit approach. Using a unit approach would bring Ohio into line with current tax appraisal practices.[63] The capitalized income developed using the income approach, or a variation of the income approach, would be closer to the way firms are valued by financial analysts and closer to the value sought by informed, willing buyers and sellers (Woolery 1992). Several questions would need to be answered if this process were adopted.

A serious concern is whether the Public Utilities Tax Section is prepared to handle a change to the income valuation process. The staff in the public utilities section are trained, competent professionals, who demonstrate a solid understanding of the regulated industries and firms they have the responsibility to appraise. An income approach could easily require a tripling of the current public utilities staff. No change in the valuation process can be made without an increase in staffing. Because the staff is already using the unit approach to value railroads, the transition would be less difficult. However, a major roadblock to adoption would be that less of the actual process would be self-reporting and self-appraising.

The second concern is how this approach would be accepted by industry. A best guess is that it would result in more disagreement and litigation. Other states using this process have their valuations challenged over such issues as:

- The method to measure economic obsolescence
- The amount of obsolescence granted
- The method to calculate the cost of capital
- The actual cost of capital

- The contribution of deferred federal income taxes
- The level of income to capitalize
- The treatment of intangible value

Litigation typically requires the hiring of outside expert witnesses and legal counsel by both the state and the utility. The cases are time consuming and they increase the uncertainty associated with the property tax system. Increased staffing and litigation are serious concerns. Nevertheless, the use of an income approach would be a change that would result in appraised values being a better representation of the decision base for willing buyers and sellers.

On the basis of interviews with utility tax representatives, it is anticipated that a change to a unit approach for valuation could result in a modest reduction in the appraised value of the regulated firms.

Alternative # 4 — Status Quo for Valuation

The fourth alternative the Commission should consider is leaving the present system of valuation operating as it currently does for regulated utilities. The current system has many positive aspects: the valuation process is understood and accepted by both administrators and taxpayers. While valuation disagreements occur between the State and taxpayers, they infrequently end up in prolonged litigation.[64] Compared to many states, the absence of ongoing litigation in the area of utility and railroad appraisal is a positive aspect of the Ohio system. In a series of interviews with taxpayers, few complaints were raised about the appraisals associated with the current system. However, the compliance costs associated with the current system is an issue. One troublesome area for utilities is keeping informed with respect to the location of property for the apportionment of value to the various taxing districts. However, without a substantial investment on the part of the State of Ohio Department, the current system is the only reasonable method to complete the assignment of property for allocation purposes.

A second concern is how the depreciation schedule is applied. Utilities feel the depreciation schedule is employed without sufficient concern for the changing economic lives of the tangible personal property. The introduction of new technology causes a rapid reduction in the value of current capital investment. This concern is less important in the nontelecommunication utilities. A concern also exists that the current depreciation schedules force properties into unrealistic assumptions with respect to the economic life of a specific piece of property or the rate of depreciation. The depreciation schedules are the result of an appraisal system that, by all appearances, is largely self-assessing. A consequence of this approach is that certain simplifying assumptions must be made to lower the cost of compliance for the utility. As a result, tangible properties are forced into similar, but not precise, classifications with respect to expected economic lives. As Figure 13-14 shows, there is an opportunity to question the depreciation schedules prior to the assignment of the final value determination of the Tax Commissioner. No evidence was found that the Public Utilities Section does not respond to actual data on reduced economic lives.

The unit method used by the Public Utilities Section to value railroads is similar to the processes employed in a number of states to appraise railroads. As part of the unit approach, the income method reflects the valuation approaches found in appraisal books and finance texts, e.g., Woolery (1992) and Cornell (1993). General criticisms of the income method would be difficult to sustain. The cost approach is less common in the finance field, but has the currency of common use among states. As railroads drift farther away from the notion of a cost-regulated utility, the idea of sticking to a cost system based on historical cost is less defensible. However, there is substantial wisdom in retaining a system that is understood by both administrators and taxpayers.

ALTERNATIVE # 5 — REDUCTION IN THE ASSESSMENT LEVEL

A request for reduction of the assessment level was a common theme repeated by every regulated industry official interviewed. These arguments were made in formal meetings, letters, telephone conversations, analysis conducted by outside consultants, and testimony before the Tax Study Commission. The logic of their argument is that most Ohio utilities no longer face the favorable economic climate associated with regulation and exclusive franchise rights. Several industries made the case that excessive property taxes placed them at a disadvantage relative to similar firms operating outside Ohio, or to firms that supply essentially the same service without the burden of heavy taxation because they did not meet the criterion of a regulated utility. The opportunity to avoid the public utilities tangible property tax was obvious for firms marketing gas to industrial and commercial users. Such firms can purchase gas and transport it over distribution lines to endusers without any regulatory oversight. Consequently these "marketing" firms can almost completely avoid the property tax.

Uneasiness about the use of a differential assessment level goes beyond the concerns raised by industry tax and management officials. Property tax policy advocates the uniform treatment of property, regardless of ownership. Nonuniformity in assessment levels creates problems for tax administrators. There are problems of definition. Administrators must determine which classification a firm should be placed in. Even after an initial determination is made, there is no reason to believe that firms will be happy with the consequences.

This is not a riskless change. The revenue loss to local governments would be substantial and would need to be replaced by increases in existing taxes or the introduction of additional taxes on the citizens of Ohio. Alternatives 1 and 2 are examples of replacement taxes. The total revenue loss would be about $0.580 billion if utilities were assessed at the same level as real property, and $0.680 billion if they were assessed at the same level as tangible personal property.

If new revenue sources were not in place, the revenue loss from a reduction in the assessment ratio would need to be phased in over an extended period of time. A phase-in would be necessary to mitigate the revenue shock that would confront local governments. On average, local governments would lose less than five percent of their total revenue if no aid were given to replace the lost revenue. However, for some governments the loss of revenue could be substantial. These governments would need help in the transition. A phase-in would allow time to develop and implement a revenue-sharing system to protect local governments.

If replacement revenues are not adopted, policy makers should consider increasing the assessment level of real properties while reducing the assessment level on public utility properties. Increasing the assessment level of real properties from 35 to 38 percent would add enough assessed value in real property to offset the loss associated with moving utility property to the same assessment level as real property. Real property would need to be assessed at 40 percent if public utility property were assessed at 25 percent. Of course, the revenue shift associated with this change would be obvious, perhaps painfully so, to many taxpayers.

EVALUATION

In this concluding section the current system and the alternatives are evaluated in terms of the criteria used by the Ohio Tax Study Commission. First, each criterion is explained in a context of the public utility industry; then a brief summary of how the alternatives compare to the criterion is offered in a summary table.

Stability

Stability is concerned with the dependability of a revenue source over time. In this analysis, stability is measured in terms of how the value of the tax base changes over time. Stability can be influenced by income growth and price level changes. As discussed in sections 2 and 6, the personal property tax on utilities is a relatively stable source of revenue. The current valuation system does not change the value of the base as the Ohio economy (measured in growth of income) increases or decreases. Because the assessed value is based on historical cost, income-level changes will only matter in the long run. Price-level changes will have a similar effect on the public utility tax base. Price changes only alter the base slowly and over a lengthy period of time. The current public utility property tax has a relatively stable base. The stability of the current base is one of its strongest attributes.

The stability of the base will decline if a decision is made to move to any of the other three bases discussed as alternatives. The most unstable base would be to change to an ad valorem-based excise tax. The base would be influenced by both income and price changes. The elasticity of the base would move in the direction of the elasticity of the sales-tax base. Of course it would never be as elastic as the sales tax, because the regulatory bodies continue to set an upper boundary on rate increases. It would also be influenced by changes in income that might have an impact on the demand for energy. The unit valuation approach is also subject to price income changes. Both types of changes will influence any valuation based on capitalized income. The three alternatives would also be influenced by unexpected weather patterns; e.g., a cool summer would reduce consumption of electricity. The stability issues are summarized in Table 13-22.

Economic Development

Economic development within a region or a state can be influenced by the rates charged for energy. The current property tax system in Ohio contributes to higher energy rates for both gas and electric utilities. However, the gas and electric rates for most Ohio utilities are not substantially different from utility rates found in surrounding states. Electric utilities in Ohio that operate nuclear generation plants face rates disadvantages. Two economic development concerns are associated with the property tax on public utilities. The first is whether the property tax reduces the level of investment by public utilities like electric and gas. The second is whether public utility firms' rates are too high and cause other firms to locate in states other than Ohio. The answer to both questions depends on who actually pays a property tax imposed on utilities. As discussed in the sixth section of this study, the property tax is probably passed on to the residential consumers of both electricity and natural gas. If this assertion is true, the tax probably makes little difference for the level of investment by either electric or gas utilities.

The situation is more complex with respect to the incidence of the tax on industrial and commercial consumers. In the case of gas utilities, the wheeling of gas likely results in a large portion of the tax being borne by the gas utility. The gas utility keeps prices low to compete with less expensive sources of gas. Because of lower prices, the tax may deter additional invest-

TABLE 13-22
Revenue Stability

Tax Evaluation Criterion	Tax Base			
			Excise Base	
Stability	Current Approach	Unit Approach	Volume Determined Base	Ad Valorem Determined Base
Gas & Electric				
C Revenue Stability	Stable; revenue based on historical cost of base	Less Stable; income driven valuation	Less Stable; revenue based on use of energy	Less Stable; revenue based on use of energy and price of energy
C Income Changes	Slow response to changes in income	Responds to changes in income	Base responds to changes in economic activity	Base responds to changes in economic activity
C Price Changes	Slow base response to changes in price	Base responds to changes in price of energy	Base does not respond to price level changes	Base responds to price level changes
Railroad				
C Revenue Stability	NA	Unit method is current process. Stable revenue	NA	NA
C Economic Changes (Income)		Base responds to changes in income		
C Economic Changes (Price)		Base responsive to changes in price of transportation		

ment by gas utilities, but industrial and commercial users should not be hurt by the higher taxes. Electric utility companies are a different story. The incidence of the tax is currently passed on to industrial and commercial users. Some portion of the tax is passed forward to the customers of industrial and commercial firms.

Of course, the current system should be viewed as fluid. The evolution of retail wheeling of electricity will result in electric utilities treating industrial and commercial utilities as gas utilities do. In order to compete, the electric utilities will absorb portions of the property tax. The absorption will cause lower rates of return and will reduce investment by electric utilities. However, industrial and commercial users will benefit from lower rates.

The proposed excise tax, regardless of the base, will benefit gas and electric utilities. The opportunity to avoid the tax by buying energy from untaxed sources will no longer exist. All firms selling energy would pay an energy service tax. The tax would shift to industrial and commercial consumers, and to some of their customers. These issues are summarized in Table 13-23.

TABLE 13-23
Economic Development

Tax Base				
Tax Evaluation Criterion	**Current Approach**	**Unit Approach**	**Excise Base**	
			Volume Determined Base	**Ad Valorem Determined Base**
Economic Development				
Electric Commercial & Industrial	C If tax base absorbed by utilities, may discourage additional investment C Trying to pass tax forward may put some firms at a disadvantage C The problems are highest for users that rely heavily on electricity from high cost producers	Same as Current System	C The proposal would increase the tax for some consumers currently not paying the tax and lower the tax for others. C Lower tax for industrial users could be beneficial C The change would lower the tax for some high cost utilities	OUTCOMES C Essentially the same as volume based excise tax. C This change would not be as beneficial for high cost producers
Gas Commercial & Industrial	Able to avoid tax by using non-regulated seller of gas. Disadvantage to regulated gas industry owners	Same as Current System	C The proposal would increase the tax for some suppliers and lower it for others. C Commercial and industrial users could see increase in gas rates.	C Outcomes essentially the same as volume based tax

HORIZONTAL EQUITY

As discussed, the current system of public utility property taxation treats some gas and electric utilities differently. Municipal electric utilities and rural electric utilities face different tax levels than do investor-owned utilities. Investor-owned electric utilities and gas utilities with newer physical plants also face higher property taxes than older plants, without regard to income. Because of the FERC Order 636, gas utilities also compete against firms with lower tax burdens.

Regulated utilities are also treated differently than other commercial and industrial firms in Ohio. Nonregulated firms are assessed at 35 percent for real property and 25 percent for personal property. The proposed alternatives would reduce the horizontal inequities within the two industries. All firms in both the electric and gas industries would place an excise tax on the bills of customers. These issues are summarized in Table 13-24.

POOR PEOPLE

The current system of taxing the property of electric and gas utilities probably results in a regressive tax. Empirical work reported earlier shows

TABLE 13-24
Horizontal Equity

Tax Base				
Tax Evaluation Criterion	**Current Approach**	**Unit Approach**	**Excise Base**	
Horizontal Equity			**Volume Determined Base**	**Ad Valorem Determined Base**
Electric	C Electric utilities treated the same except for municipal electric and rural electric	C Essentially same as Current System	C All providers treated in similar manner	C All providers treated in similar manner
Gas	C Substantial inequity between regulated & nonregulated suppliers	C Essentially the same as Current System	C All providers treated in similar manner	C All providers treated in similar manner
Railroads	NA	Equal treatment	NA	NA

that the percent of income spent on energy-related purchases decreases as income levels increase. The proposed alternatives will likely do little to remove the regressive sting associated with the taxation of utilities. In fact, the suggestion to impose an excise tax based on consumption would increase the regressive nature of utility taxation. Concerns about the regressive nature of the public utility property tax are described in Table 13-25.

SIMPLIFICATION

The administrative and compliance costs associated with the current system could be reduced if an excise tax alternative were selected. For example, the need for extensive record keeping would be decreased for the utility companies. The problems associated with physical discovery, and especially physical audits, would also decrease. The true market value of the current system could be improved if a unit approach were adopted. However, compliance and litigation costs would increase. Overall, the current system is easy to understand by both the taxpayer and the tax administrator. A brief description of the simplification issues associated with each alternative is given in Table 13-26.

TABLE 13-25
Poor People

Tax Base				
Tax Evaluation Criterion	**Current Approach**	**Unit Approach**	**Excise Base**	
Poor People			**Volume Determined Base**	**Ad Valorem Determined Base**
Electric & Gas	C If tax can be passed forward to residential users, it is likely regressive. C If tax on commercial and industrial users can be passed forward to consumers, it is likely progressive C Tax on gas utilities less likely to be passed forward	C Similar to Current System	C Likely regressive C If tax only imposed on residential & commercial customers, tax is likely to increase in regressiveness	C Likely regressive C If tax only imposed on residential & customers, tax is likely to increase in regressiveness

TABLE 13-26
Simplification

Tax Base				
Tax Evaluation Criterion	**Current Approach**	**Unit Approach**	**Excise Base**	
Simplification			**Volume Determined Base**	**Ad Valorem Determined Base**
	C Current System is simple to understand; compliance and administration costs are high.	C More complicated process; litigation may increase	C Simplification of current system; no need for appraisal; litigation should be reduced	C Simplification of current system; no need for appraisal; litigation should be reduced

ENDNOTES

1. The distinction between the classes of property in Ohio is a consequence of how the property is appraised, the frequency of appraisal, and the level of taxation. These distinctions are discussed throughout the body of this study.

2. The property tax on real property, and improvements to real property in Ohio, is administered by local officials. The primary local tax official in terms of tax administration and appraisal is the county auditor.

3. The property tax on real property will be discussed in Sjoquist (1994); the property tax on tangible personal property is discussed in Cornia (forthcoming).

4. A brief history of how Ohio has taxed public utilities can be found in Battelle, (1982).

5. Real property in Ohio is defined as land and improvements affixed to the land. For utilities in Ohio, most of the taxable value is represented by personal property.

6. The real property of utilities is appraised in the same manner as other commercial and industrial property falling under the responsibility of the county auditor. The method commonly used to appraise commercial and industrial improvements is the cost method. The value used to appraise land is generally based on studies of land sales within a county. Appraisals in Ohio are frequently conducted by a private appraisal firm under contract to the county auditor (Sjoquist 1994).

7. Having local officials value one portion of a utility and state officials value another portion of a utility is unique to Ohio.

8. The term "personal" is a misnomer. In realty, the tax is a tax on machinery and equipment.

9. For a historical discussion of the unique treatment of electric utilities, see Columbus Southern Power Company and Ohio Power Company (1994).

10. The number of FTE used to appraise public utilities and railroads in Ohio is similar to the number employed in surrounding states. See New York State, (1993).

11. Evidence from the mid 1980s suggests that the total state and local tax burden of electric utilities in Ohio, compared to the same burden in other states, puts Ohio above the national average, but substantially lower than the highest state. However, when compared to its immediate neighbors, Ohio was higher than each state except New York and Illinois. See Howe, Edward T., and Donald Reeb, (1987).

12. Section five of this chapter describes in detail the valuation processes followed by the Ohio Department of Taxation for public utilities and railroads in Ohio.

13. Since properties sell infrequently, appraisers must estimate what a property would sell for in the open market.

14. For example if a parcel of property has an appraised value of $10,000 and the assessment level is 50 percent the assessed value is $5,000 ($10,000 * .5 = $5,000).

15. The electric utilities in Table 13-6 are deflated using the price index for the cost of electric power. Railroads and gas utilities are deflated using the Consumer Price Index.

16. For an analysis of the relative contributions of various revenue sources to Ohio local governments, see Dearborn (1994).

17. The importance of the three types of property taxes in the financing of education is illustrated in a recent study completed for the Ohio Governor's Education Management Council. See Fleeter, (1992). The issues associated with intergovernmental fiscal relations in Ohio is are treated in Dearborn (forthcoming) and Sjoquist (1994).

18. The analysis of the paper will not focus on the smaller regulated utilities such as water systems or municipal heating systems. However, those utilities are not unimportant, nor are the taxes paid by those utilities unimportant to the owners and ratepayers. They are not discussed because of data limitations and their relative contribution to the overall taxes paid by utilities.

19. While the regulation of public utilities has a long history in the United States, the deregulation of public utilities has been a constant policy theme of the past two decades. Airlines and trucking are examples of industries which, after years of regulation, have undergone extensive deregulation during this period. Deregulation has dramatically changed the operation of firms in many industries.

20. A complete description of how public utilities are regulated is beyond the scope of this study. For a good review of regulatory behavior see, Phillips, (1993).

21. This is a simplified version of the rate base.

22. It is obvious that the larger the rate base, the greater the return that can be earned by the regulated utility. Because of this, some analysts suggest that the relationship between rate base and amount earned causes excessive investment in capital by utilities. For a discussion of this argument, see Averch and Johnson, (1962). Empirical examinations of this assertion have not been conclusive. See, for example, Callen, Mathewson, and Mohring, (1967).

23. In 1923 the United States Supreme Court established in the *Bluefield* case the ground rules for determining the cost of capital in rate cases. The Court wrote, "The return should be reasonably sufficient to assure confidence in the financial soundness of the utility." See *Bluefield Waterworks & Improvement Company v. Public Service Commission of W. Va*. 262 United States 679 (1923).

24. There is also an area of research that has argued that rate regulation will lead to "expense expansion," in which regulated firms overstate expenses in order to earn a larger return for utility operators. See, for example, Williamson, (1963).

25. The United States Supreme Court ruled in 1922 that taxes levied by all levels of government were recoverable operating expenses for regulated utilities. See *Galveston Electric Company v. Galveston,* 258 United States 388 (1922).

26. The time to complete a regulatory hearing process in Ohio is a function of the size of the requested rate adjustment and the complexity of the issues involved.

27. One concern for utility tax managers is that because of infrequent regulatory hearings, any rate adjustments motivated by increased taxes may not materialize.

28. Several organizations rate state and federal regulatory bodies in terms of how the interests of investors are treated by regulatory decisions. These ratings are listed below. The higher the number in both columns, the more favorably the regulatory body is viewed by the investment community. When compared to selected states, it appears that Ohio is in the middle of the pack in how regulatory decisions affect returns on investment in regulated companies.

Investor Group's Evaluation Of Regulatory Behavior:
Selected State and Federal Agencies

	Merrill Lynch	***Regulatory Research Associates,Inc.***
FCC	5*	—
FERC	3*+	—
ILLINOIS	1*	2
INDIANA	4*	2
KENTUCKY	3*+	1
MICHIGAN	2*	3
NEW YORK	3*–	1
OHIO	2*	1
PENNSYLVANIA	2*+	1
WEST VIRGINIA	2*–	3

29. Other federal regulatory agencies will not be discussed in the chapter because they have little to do with the energy industries. The Federal Communication Commission will be discussed in the chapter on telecommunications (McHugh, 1994b).

30. The section on the electric utility industry will be more detailed than the sections on either the gas utility industry or the railroads. The gas and rail industries have already undergone a number of regulatory changes, which will be reported. However, the regulatory changes facing the electric industry are just beginning to emerge. Thus a fuller discussion of the electric industry is undertaken.

31.The number of customers served by the three largest municipal power companies is modest relative to the large investor-owned utilities. For example, in 1990 Cleveland Municipal power reported 52,000 customers, Columbus Municipal Power reported 10,000 customers, and Hamilton Municipal Power reported 26,000 customers. By contrast, the eight investor-

owned utilities distribute electricity to 3.8 million residential customers. For a complete report on the number of municipal customers see, Energy Information Administration, (1992).

32. The generation of electricity by municipal electric companies is primarily done to generate power for peak demand periods.

33. Recent work by Thompson and Wolf demonstrates that nuclear utilities may suffer from diseconomies of scale. See, Thompson and Wolf, (1993).

34. Average revenue per KWH is the cost of per unit electricity or electric revenue divided by KWH sold. The revenue is the operating revenue reported by the utility.

35. A number of empirical studies have examined the cost differences between publicly operated and investor-operated electric utilities. Some studies have found no differences between the two utilities, some have found public utilities to be more efficient, and others have found investor-owned utilities to be more efficient. For a brief review of this literature, see Bhattacharyya, Parker, and Raffiee, (1994); Atkinson, and Halvorsen, (1986).

36. Usually the comparison between market value and book value of stock is not considered a useful financial ratio. However, when the analysis is focused on a cost regulated industry in which the book value of the utility is closely related to the rate base this comparison does demonstrate the view of investors about the economic viability of a company. See for example, Hyman, Leonard S., (1992).

37. *Wheeling* is a term of art describing the transmission of electricity or natural gas over facilities owned by another company. The utility that transmits the energy is neither the seller nor the buyer of the power. See, for example, Costello, Burns, and Hegazy, (1994).

38. Ohio H.B. 676 was introduced but never got out of Committee in the Ohio House. For a good summary of the current status of retail wheeling around the United States, see Edison Electric Institute, (1994).

39. Others see the process of developing retail wheeling as so far along that they have developed organizational and political models to measure how it is evolving. See Maize, (1994).

40. It would be unfair to criticize the investor-owned utilities that built nuclear facilities in the 1970s and early 1980s. At that time a nuclear plant was economically justified. In fact, according to Alfred Kahn many public utilities were actively trying to become partners in nuclear projects. See Kahn, (1985).

41. A noncore user is a gas user who can switch fuels or uses sufficient volumes of gas to enter into a viable agreement independent of the LDC. Examples are large industrial or commercial users. See Hatcher and Tussing, (1992).

42. As railroads have abandoned lines, there has been a reemergence of small rail companies. See Due, (1984).

43. Rail carloads represents the number of load rail cars that originated, passed through, or terminated in a given state.

44. For example, Dayton Power and Light was recently identified by *Merrill Lynch* as among the best investor-owned utilities in America.

45. A complete description of the appeal process for public utility property will be given in section 6 of this chapter.

46. A description of the apportionment processes will be given in section 6 of this chapter.

47. The discovery of the real property of the utility is handled by the local county auditor's office. The process of discovery of real property is discussed in the chapter dealing with the local property tax (Sjoquist, forthcoming).

48. In Florida, local county officials value public utilities and several of the larger counties use the income approach to value such property.

49. NORI is defined as operating revenues less operating expenses, including current and deferred taxes.

50. For a discussion of estimating the cost of capital, see Brealey, Richard, and Stewart Myers, (1981). The estimation of the cost of capital for railroads has been controversial over the past decade. At issue has been the method of estimating the cost of equity. For examples of the legal cases surrounding this issue see, Fletcher, (1994).

51. Obsolescence is defined as the reduction in value due to changing economic conditions and design limitations. Standard practice for measuring obsolescence requires the appraiser to estimate the reduction in property values caused by factors over which the owner has no control. In the case of railroads this process has been completed by using the "Wisconsin Approach." This approach compares the subject railroad to other operating railroads and adjusts for earning or operating shortfalls. For discussion of the Wisconsin approach and a criticism of the current use by state appraisal authorities, see Adolphson, Cornia, and Walters, (1989).

52. Railroad tax officials have argued for a number of years that they were discriminated against in terms of the property tax. Reeves, a more neutral observer, concurred, writing that "fairly general discrimination" did exist in terms of the property tax. See Reeves, Clyde, (1982).

53. An interesting discussion of the 4-R Act and its effect on property tax policies can be found in Netzer, (1986).

54. The depreciation schedules are on Property Tax Division Form 302; problems or concerns with appraisal are often referenced as "302" issues.

55. Similar adjustments to the tax base are made for all Public Utility Property.

56. One important issue for the natural gas industry is how inventories of gas are appraised. The pipeline industry would prefer a process that values inventory using a 12-month average of stored gas and oil rather than the value of gas and oil on the lien date. The industry argues that a 12-month average would reflect the procedures used in the appraisal of other inventories in Ohio.

57. If a distribution facility has an appraised value greater than one billion dollars, then a limited portion of the plant remains in the tax base of the host taxing jurisdiction. The remaining value is apportioned over the entire system.

58. Changing the apportionment process is almost certain to create substantial shifts in distribution of the property tax. The apportionment system in Idaho was changed, and the result was disruptive for a number of Idaho local governments. See, Hoffman and Wells, (1980).

59. A complete discussion of the billing and collection of the property tax is given in Chapter 14 in this volume.

60. A discussion on the disparity issue is given in Cornia (1994a).

61. See the section on economic structure and regulation in this Chapter.

62. Four states currently use a form of this tax. A proposal for an energy unit tax was also made to the Commonwealth of Pennsylvania during a tax study conducted during the 1980s.

63. A description of the unit method can be found in Figure 13-8, which illustrates the unit approach used on railroads.

64. Litigation in some states can overwhelm the system. In some states, for example, virtually every utility and railroad is in court over valuation issues covering multiple years. Annual Reports from the California Franchise Board indicate that numerous utilities are now litigating substantial issues with respect to property tax matters.

14 Tangible Business Personal Property Taxation

Gary Cornia

INTRODUCTION

The property tax imposed on the tangible personal property of commercial and industrial firms operating in Ohio is the subject of this chapter. The personal property tax on tangible business property is a tax that, with the exception of small firms, virtually every business in Ohio faces. The chapter examines both the policy and administrative issues associated with this tax, including the question whether tangible personal business property should be included in the Ohio property tax base. Four important points need to be understood about the tangible personal business property tax:

- The personal property tax is an important source of revenue in Ohio. In 1994, it produced $1.2 billion, about six percent of total local government revenues.
- The revenue from this tax helps fund local governments in Ohio. Local governments in Ohio which receive revenue from this tax include school districts, cities, villages, special districts, and counties. Seventy percent of the revenue from this tax is used by Ohio school districts (K-12)
- Even though the tax is used exclusively by local governments, the major administrative burden for the tax rests with the Ohio

Department of Taxation. Local governments also establish the tax rates imposed on personal property.

- The tangible personal business property tax is self-reported and self-assessed and is a difficult tax to both administer and comply with.

This chapter proceeds in the following manner. The initial section describes the tangible personal property tax base in the context of the overall Ohio property tax system.[1] The next section reports on the revenue significance of the tax, and also describes in relative terms the personal tax base by industry and by type of equipment taxed. The study then turns to the administration of the tax in Ohio. The fifth section considers the property tax with respect to overall tax policy, and the policy justifications for the inclusion of the tangible business property in the tax base. The final section gives a series of policy alternatives for the consideration of the Ohio Tax Study Commission.

THE REAL AND PERSONAL PROPERTY TAX BASES

When operating managers of firms think of taxes on business, they often ignore property taxes and focus on the more visible taxes, such as the federal corporate income tax (Schmidt 1982). When the general public think of the property tax, they likely think of it only in terms of a tax imposed on land and buildings. Both perceptions are wrong—the property tax is often the largest tax paid by a firm, and the property tax base consists of a number of different components (Rabe and Riley 1994). In addition to the tax on realty (land and buildings), the tax base includes personalty, i.e., property that is not affixed to land or improvements. We differentiate personalty in terms of tangibility. Intangible personal property represents ownership of property that has no independent intrinsic value, e.g., stocks, bonds, bank deposits and saving accounts. Realty and personalty may also be divided between items that depreciate in the normal course of use and items that do not depreciate.[2] For example, in Ohio, commercial inventory is considered tangible personal property, but it generally does not receive any adjustment for depreciation. Most other types of tangible personal property are granted an adjustment for depreciation in Ohio. The four basic types of property that may be included in a property tax base, and examples of each type of property, are given in Figure 14-1. Ohio, at one time, has taxed both types of realty and both types of personalty. Ohio currently includes real property, improvements to real property, and tangible personal business property in the property tax base. Over the past several decades, Ohio has both reduced and narrowed the property tax base. The reduction has been threefold: removing items from the base, lowering the taxable value of the remaining factors in the base, or eliminating the rate applied against a tax base.[3]

Realty	**Personal**
Land ▸ Residential ▸ Commercial ▸ Farm ▸ Mineral	Tangible ▸ Machinery ▸ Vehicles ▸ Furniture ▸ Computers
Improvements ▸ Housing ▸ Commercial buildings ▸ Farm buildings ▸ Industrial buildings	Intangible ▸ Stocks ▸ Bonds ▸ Bank deposits ▸ Copyrights

Source: Herber (1983).

FIGURE 14-1. Classification of property.

Nationwide, the property tax trend has been similar to Ohio's. Nationally, we have narrowed the property tax base by removing personalty and lowered the level of taxes applied against the property tax base (Bowman 1987). The narrowing of the tax base by removing the property tax from personalty is reflected in the reduction in the amount of property tax revenue being generated from this source. Since the mid-1950s, the percent of total property tax assessed value coming from personalty has declined from an average of 20 percent to around 10 percent. Data on the percent of assessed value represented by personal property are reported in Table 14-1. As can be seen in the data reported in Table 14-1, Ohio falls in the bottom quarter of those states imposing a personal property tax. Many of the states listed in the North Central Region have had much greater reliance on the personal property tax than does Ohio.

Legal and Appraisal Practice Definitions of Realty and Personalty

For property tax purposes, the definitions of real and personal property are found in Sections 5701.02 and 5701.03 of the *Ohio Revised Code.* Real property is defined as "land" and "all things contained therein." Improvements are defined as "a permanent fabrication or construction, attached or affixed to land". Personalty is defined as "every tangible thing that is the subject of ownership . . . that does not constitute real property." The definitions of real and personal property were revised in 1992. Intangible personal property was effectively removed from the Ohio tax base in 1986 by reduction of its tax rate to zero. The definitions used by Ohio for real and

TABLE 14-1
Percent of Locally Assessed Personal Property in Locally Taxable Assessed Value

	1956	1966	1976	1986
Northeast	12.86	10.41	7.63	6.43
Connecticut	26.1	22.4	19.4	16.7
Rhode Island	21.9	22.8	21.5	16.7
Maine	20.1	16.8	11.3	12.6
Vermont	16.3	12.3	8.5	7.7
Massachusetts	8.9	6.6	5.8	3
New Jersey	12.9	5.5	2	1.2
New York	0	0	0	0
Pennsylvania	0	0	0	0
New Hampshire	9.6	7.3	0.2	0
North Central	23.38	19	14.75	9.35
Kansas	27	23.6	31.8	29.6
Indiana	32.5	28.4	26	26.1
Missouri	22.2	21.4	20	19.3
Nebraska	23.7	24.9	23.7	13.8
Michigan	30.5	23.3	13.6	12.7
Ohio	23.2	1.6	6.6	5.8
Wisconsin	17.4	15.9	15.1	4.7
Minnesota	20	12.2	0.4	0.2
Illinois	19.1	19	12.7	0
Iowa	14.9	13.4	6.1	0
North Dakota	22.3	20.2	0	0
South Dakota	27.8	24.1	21.1	0
West	18.79	14.43	11.8	7.9
Montana	32.3	28.9	31.3	15
Utah	16.6	16.7	14.5	14.8
Idaho	17.6	15.7	12.3	10.6
Arizona	21.7	13.4	8.6	9.5
Colorado	19.4	13.7	10	9.2
Wyoming	17.6	16.9	11.6	8.4
Nevada	17.9	10.2	13.2	7.3
California	15.9	11.9	10	6.3
Washington	20.9	17.6	15.3	6.2
Oregon	19.6	12.6	7.9	5.9
Alaska	n.a.	18.1	12.7	5.3
New Mexico	7.2	11.9	6	4.2
Hawaii	n.a.	0	0	0
South	23.09	19.67	19.34	18.88
West Virginia	36.4	31	39.6	41.7
North Carolina	33.3	28.1	29.2	29.9
South Carolina	42.4	15.1	15	27.2
Mississippi	33.4	33.1	34.8	26.9
Arkansas	27.5	23.1	24.3	26.9
Louisiana	28.4	38.9	41.1	26.4
Alabama	26.4	24.4	32.2	24.5
Georgia	36.6	30.8	23.1	24.2
Kentucky	12.1	11.6	18.4	24.2
Oklahoma	21.4	19.5	20.3	16.9
Texas	25.8	23.8	5.7	16
Florida	20	15.7	15.6	10.9
Tennessee	9.1	8.2	9.4	9.8
Virginia	20.2	15.4	14.3	9.2
D.C.	16.5	14.4	5.4	5.5
Maryland	3.1	1.4	0.5	0.8
Delaware	0	0	0	0
U.S. Total	17.3	13.1	12.2	10.1
State mean	20.3	16.55	14.28	11.64
State mean (taxing only)	21.7	17.95	15.83	14.14

Source: Mikesell (1992).

personal property are similar to realty and personalty definitions used by commercial appraisers.[4] However, it would be inappropriate to suggest in this study that there is absolute clarity in the current definitions between realty and personalty. Nationwide, courts are frequently called on to determine if property is realty or personalty.[5]

REVENUE SIGNIFICANCE OF THE TANGIBLE BUSINESS PERSONAL PROPERTY TAX

In 1994, the total amount of property taxes charged in Ohio to owners of real and personal property was $7.4 billion.[6] Over 70 percent of property tax revenue comes from real estate and improvements to real estate. The remaining property tax revenue is divided between public utility personal property and tangible business personal property.[7] Public Utilities paid $0.95 billion in personal property taxes; business paid $1.2 billion in tangible business personal property. As noted, revenue from the property tax on tangible personal business property is used to support local governments in Ohio. The percentage distribution of the tangible personal business property tax within Ohio local governments is shown in Table 14-2. Over 70 percent of the revenue from this tax supports Ohio schools. Ohio counties also receive a significant share of the revenue from this tax.

The revenue from the personal property tax, including the personal property tax on public utilities, represents about 11 percent of the total revenue received by local governments. Excluding the personal property tax received

TABLE 14-2
Percentage Distribution of Revenue‡ From Tangible Personal Business Property Tax: Selected Years

	Type of Government			
Year	City and Village	School District	Township	County
1980	10	71	2	17
1985	8	71	4	17
1990	9	71	---	17
1991	9	71	---	20
1991	9	70	1	19

Source: Ohio Department of Taxation; *Annual Reports*, selected years

†Revenue from firms appraised by the Ohio Department of Taxation

from utilities, the revenue from the tangible personal property from commercial and industrial concerns contributes about 6 percent of the total revenue for Ohio local governments. Comparative data from the ten largest (population) counties in Ohio illustrate the relative importance of the revenue from personal property for local governments. The per capita revenue received from the real property tax (RP), the public utility property tax (PUP), and the tangible personal property tax (TPP) are listed in Table 14-3 for 1988 and 1992 for each of the selected ten counties. In these counties, all three sources of revenue from the property tax have been growing. The largest source of revenue is the real property portion of the property tax. While it varies among counties, the property tax on tangible personal business property represented about 23 percent of the total property tax revenue in 1988 and 17 percent in 1992, a substantial decline. On average, the revenue from the tangible personal property tax is slightly over 25 percent of just the revenue from the real property tax. The per capita numbers for the ten largest counties are similar when data from all eighty-eight Ohio counties are examined. In 1990, the median per capita tax charged for the three types of property in all counties in Ohio was \$349 for real property, \$59 for public utility property, and \$81 for tangible personal property.

Stability of Tangible Personal Business Property over Time

The total amount of revenue coming from the tangible business personal property tax has been increasing at a cumulative rate of growth of about 4 percent a year, but has been decreasing in real terms. The total and real revenue from this source for the period 1977 to 1990 is shown in Table 14-4. Part of the loss in real revenue results from a reduction in the percent of the tangible personal business property which can be taxed, and part is a result of the slow growth in the economy, particularly of the heavy industry sector. The revenue flow from the tangible personal property tax scores well on the criterion of stability. Table 14-5 compares the annual rate of growth of the tangible personal property tax to the percent changes in Ohio income and Ohio population (Columns 1, 2, and 3). The revenue from the tangible personal property tax has, over time, increased at rates lower than the growth in Ohio income. The elasticity of the tangible personal property tax was estimated for this study.[8] The estimated results over a 14-year period estimate an elasticity of 0.6. An elasticity of this magnitude confirms that revenue from the tangible personal property tax is very unresponsive to the changes in the Ohio economy. On a comparative basis, the tangible personal property tax is one of the least elastic taxes in the Ohio revenue system. The advantages of such a system are that it is very stable during periods of slow economic growth.

TABLE 14-3
Per Capita Taxes Charged on Public Utility Tangible Personal Property (PUP), Tangible Personal Property (TPP), and Real Property (RP)— Ten Largest (Population) Counties in Ohio

	1988					1992				
County	PUP	%	TPP	%	RP*	PUP	%	TPP	%	RP*
Cuyahoga	$69	10	$126	19	$453	$88	11	$138	16	$606
Franklin	48	9	100	17	410	69	9	133	17	590
Hamilton	61	11	127	23	374	92	11	155	19	548
Montgomery	52	10	107	21	345	65	10	111	17	568
Summit	54	10	89	17	367	65	10	108	17	466
Lucas	67	12	116	22	346	92	14	122	18	456
Stark	48	12	91	24	245	64	13	106	20	337
Butler	41	10	77	19	278	58	11	86	17	365
Lorain	82	17	83	17	306	98	17	102	17	383
Mahoning	53	14	49	13	273	65	11	70	12	328
Average	57	11	96	19	337	75	12	113	18	454

Source: Calculated by author using Ohio State Department of Taxation data

*Net Taxes Collectable

Uniformity of the Tangible Personal Business Property Tax Revenue between Ohio Counties

Within Ohio, the revenue received by local governments from the tangible personal property tax, as well as the revenue from all property taxes, is unevenly distributed. Table 14-6 lists the mean, median, maximum, minimum, standard deviation and coefficient of variation of the per capita revenue received by the 88 counties from real, public utility, and public tangible personal property taxes in 1990. The amount of tangible personal property tax base assigned to a taxing jurisdiction is based on a direct apportionment of the taxable value located in each taxing jurisdiction.

In absolute terms, the difference in the amount of revenue received by a county is greatest for the revenue from the real property tax. There is a difference in per capita revenue from the real property tax of just over $800 be-

TABLE 14-4
Tangible Personal Property Tax Revenue: 1977–1990

Year	Total Revenue (Billion)	Real Total Revenue (Billion)
1977	$ .628	$ .628
1978	.634	.590
1979	.674	.563
1980	.727	.535
1981	.765	.510
1982	.819	.515
1983	.879	.535
1984	.885	.516
1985	.831	.468
1986	.868	.480
1987	.936	.499
1988	.964	.494
1989	1.005	.491
1990	1.079	.500

Source: *Annual Reports*, Ohio Department of Taxation. Economic Report of the President.

tween the highest and the lowest county. The absolute per capita difference is smaller but still substantial for revenue from the public utility and tangible personal property taxes. However, relative to the means, the real property tax base is more uniform, as illustrated by the coefficient of variation reported in Table 14-6.[9] The largest variation is for the public utility property tax.

All three sources of property tax revenue fall short of providing a universally uniform source of local revenue for Ohio counties, i.e., there are wide per capita variations. This may result in inequity in the level of services and goods provided by the tax. Rich units of government, measured in terms of per capita tax base, are able to either provide more services or provide equal services with lower tax rates. This has especially important implications for educational finance.

Appraised and Assessed Values

In Ohio, two steps are followed to arrive at the taxable or assessed value for realty and personalty. The first step is completed when the auditor (assessor) estimates what a particular property would sell for in an open market. In Ohio, the initial estimated value is called the *appraised* value.[10] For example, if a residential property were being valued, the appraised value

TABLE 14-5
Annual Percent Changes in Revenue: Tangible Personal Property Tax, Sales Tax, and Real Property Tax

	Percent Change In		
Year	Tangible Personal Property Tax Revenue	Income Ohio Residents	Ohio Population
1978	1	11	.16
1979	6	11	.62
1980	8	9	.00
1981	5	9	-.09
1982	7	4	-.29
1983	7	5	-.18
1984	1	9	.00
1985	-6	6	-.03
1986	4	5	-.05
1987	8	5	.28
1988	3	7	.36
1989	4	6	.28
1990	7	6	.17
1991	7	4	.85
1992	2	N/A	.73

TABLE 14-6
Variability of Property Tax Revenue Sources in Ohio Counties: 1990

	Per Capita Measures					
	Maximum	Minimum	Mean	Median	Standard Deviation	Coefficient Of Variation
Real Property	$ 1002	$ 175	$ 390	$ 349	$ 152	39%
Public Utility Property	391	27	77	59	58	75%
Tangible Personal Property	229	18	81	77	40	52%

Source: Calculated by author from Ohio Department of Taxation *Annual Reports*.

should reflect what the home would sell for if it were offered for sale in an open market.[11] The Property Tax Division of the Ohio Department of Taxation and local county auditors determine the appraised value of tangible business personal property.[12] Local auditors use valuation guidelines established and published by the Ohio Department of Taxation.[13]

Auditors complete the second step. They reduce the appraised value to an *assessed* value, the product of the appraised value multiplied by an assessment level.[14] The assessment level is the portion of the true value which policy-makers have determined is taxable. The assessment level in Ohio for tangible personal business property is currently 25 percent.[15] An assessment level of 25 means that an item of tangible personalty appraised at $2000 is actually assessed and taxed at $500.

The relationship between the appraised value of tangible personal property and the assessed value of tangible personal property has been changing. The data in Table 14-7 report the decline in the assessment level for personal property since 1978. In 1978, personal property was assessed, depending on type, at 46 or 41 percent of appraised value. The assessment level of personal property has been declining at a steady pace to its present level of 25 percent.

The changing relationship between appraised and assessed values for personal property taxes is illustrated in Table 14-8. The compounded rates of growth in the appraised (column 2) and the assessed values (column 6) have been 6 percent and 1 percent respectively. The annual percentage rates of growth (columns 3 and 7) have ranged from double-digit positive rates to near double-digit negative rates. The negative changes have generally followed reductions in the assessment levels.

TABLE 14-7
Assessment Level of Tangible Business Personal Property: Selected Years

Year	Manufacturing Machinery & Equipment	Manufacturing Inventory	Merchants Inventory	All Other
1978	46	41	41	46
1980	42	37	37	42
1985	33	33	33	33
1990	28	28	28	28
1993	25	25	25	25

Source: Ohio Department of Taxation, *Annual Report*.

TABLE 14-8
Appraised Value, Assessed Value, and Taxes Levied in Millions: 1977–1992

(1) Year	(2) Nominal Appraised Value	(3) Percent Change	(4) Real Appraised Value (CPI)	(5) Real Appraised Value (M&E)	(6) Nominal Assessed Value	(7) Percent Change	(8) Real Assessed Value (CPI)	(9) Real Assessed Value (M&E)	(10) Percent Change (M&E)
1977	30,300		30,300	30,300	13,709		13,709	13,709	
1978	33,023	9	30,693	30,627	14,274	4	13,267	13,238	-3
1979	36,416	10	30,397	30,956	15,020	5	12,537	12,768	-4
1980	39,928	10	29,364	39,271	15,649	4	11,509	11,864	-7
1981	44,043	10	29,362	30,420	16,382	5	10,921	11,315	-5
1982	47,211	7	29,647	30,781	17,165	5	10,779	11,192	-1
1983	48,102	2	29,267	30,538	17,063	-1	10,382	10,833	-3
1984	45,918	-5	26,782	28,486	15,612	-9	9,106	9,685	-11
1985	48,739	6	27,450	29,644	16,084	3	9,058	9,782	1
1986	52,409	8	28,978	31,407	16,771	4	9,273	10,050	3
1987	54,381	4	29,009	32,116	16,858	1	8,993	9,956	-1
1988	56,533	4	28,960	32,562	16,960	1	8,688	9,768	-2
1989	61,193	8	29,906	33,985	17,746	5	8,673	9,856	1
1990	65,975	8	30,590	35,639	18,473	4	8,565	9,979	1
1991	68,845	5	30,631	36,493	18,588	1	8,270	9,853	1
1992	70,773	3	30,569	37,394	18,402	-1	7,979	9,723	1

Source: Calculated by author from Ohio Department of Taxation data.

Adjusting for changes in the price level, the consumer price index (CPI), shows that the real value of the appraised value of tangible personal business property (column 4) has just kept even with inflation over the period reported in Table 14-8. Using the price index for machinery and equipment (M&I) to adjust for inflation, the real value of the appraised property has increased (column 5). However, deflating the CPI or the MEI, the assessed value of tangible personal property has declined. The decline in real terms of the assessed level of tangible personal property largely reflects the reduction in the assessment level for tangible personal business property which has been occurring over the past twenty years. The data in Table 14-8 offer an interesting comparison between the annual rates of growth for the appraised value of tangible personal business property (column 3), the assessed value of tangible personal business property (column 7), and the percent change in real assessed value (column 10). (The data in 1984 reflect policy changes in the tangible personal property tax base, e.g., a reduction in the assessment level of tangible personal property.)

The data in Table 14-9 continue the comparison of the appraised value and the assessed value of tangible personal business property. The comparison is made in per capita terms and covers the same period of time as the previous table. Again, the results are increases in nominal per capita appraised and assessed values and a general decline in the real value (CPI) of the per capita tax base. Different rates of decline are reported when the appraised and assessed per capita values are deflated by MEI. In fact, the per capita appraised value increases in real terms when MEI is used to deflate the series.

Uniformity of Property Tax Bases Among Ohio Counties

The previous section of this study examined the issue of *revenue uniformity* among local governments. The issue of *tax base* uniformity is possibly even more important to local governments. The ability of units of government to provide uniform, or even minimum levels of service is a function of the distribution of the tax base. Richer units of government, measured in terms of per capita taxable value, will be able to provide more services with less tax effort or a minimum level of services with a low tax effort.[16]

As with the sources of revenue from the three property taxes, the per capita bases of the Ohio property tax also reflect differences when measured across the state's 88 counties. Table 14-10 reports the maximum, minimum, mean, median, standard deviation and coefficient of variation (CV) in per capita values for the real property tax base, the public utility property tax base, and the tangible personal property tax base for 1990. The values are reported for the 88 counties in Ohio for tax year 1990.

TABLE 14-9
Real and Nominal Per Capita Appraised Value and Assessed Value, by Per Capita: 1977–1992

	Appraised			Assessed		
Year	Value Per Capita	In Real Terms (CPI)	In Real Terms (M&E)	Value Per Capita	In Real Terms (CPI)	In Real Terms (M&E)
1977	2,828	2,828	2,828	1,279	1,279	1,279
1978	3,077	2,860	2,854	1,330	1,236	1,234
1979	3,372	2,815	2,867	1,391	1,161	1,182
1980	3,698	2,719	2,803	1,449	1,066	1,099
1981	4,083	2,722	2,820	1,519	1,012	1,049
1982	4,389	2,756	2,862	1,596	1,002	1,040
1983	4,480	2,726	2,844	1,589	967	1,009
1984	4,276	2,494	2,653	1,454	848	902
1985	4,540	2,557	2,761	1,498	844	911
1986	4,884	2,701	2,927	1,563	864	937
1987	5,054	2,696	2,985	1,567	836	925
1988	5,235	2,682	3,015	1,571	805	905
1989	5,651	2,762	3,138	1,639	801	910
1990	6,082	2,820	3,286	1,703	790	920
1991	6,293	2,800	3,336	1,699	756	901
1992	6,422	2,774	3,393	1,670	721	882

Source: Calculated by author using Ohio Department of Revenue and U.S. Bureau of Census data.

In terms of variance, the per capita tax revenue and per capita tax base coefficients of variation for tangible personal property are practically identical. The CV for the per capita real property tax base declines by almost half when compared to the CV for per capita revenue. The coefficient of variation for per capita public utility property increases to over 100 percent. The per capita differences show that some counties have a greater ability to provide services based on revenue from the property tax.[17] Part of the differences in low tax bases can be offset by imposing higher tax rates. This practice may be happening in Ohio. The CV is smaller for per capita revenue than it is for the per capita tax base. It appears that Ohio counties overcome low per capita tax bases by increasing rates in some counties, and that in other counties the higher assessed value allows them to impose lower rates. Correlation analysis shows that high levels of poverty are positively

TABLE 14-10
Variability of Property Tax Bases in Ohio Counties: 1990

	Per Capita Measures					
Property Tax Base	**Maximum**	**Minimum**	**Mean**	**Median**	**Standard Deviation**	**Coefficient Of Variation**
Real Property	$ 13,773	$ 4,139	$ 6,946	$ 6,637	$ 1,629	23%
Public Utility Property	11,127	598	1,561	1,882	1,628	104%
Tangible Personal Property	5,272	393	1,559	1,475	856	55%

correlated with public utility property and negatively correlated with assessed values for real property and tangible business personal property. However, on balance, low-income counties have lower assessed values.

Composition of the Tangible Personal Property Tax Base

The distribution of the tangible personal property base has changed between industry groups. Table 14-11 lists the relative assessed values of the tangible personal business property tax base in ten different Ohio industries.

In 1975, the greater part of the tangible business personal property tax base was reported under the general SIC classification of manufacturing, over 80 percent of the tangible personal business property tax base was in manufacturing. The importance of manufacturing in Ohio has declined during the period 1975 to 1992. Manufacturing now represents just over 60 percent of the Ohio tangible personal business property tax base. These changes seem consistent with the shifts in the Ohio economy as well as the national economy, as suggested in other reports presented to the Ohio Tax Study Commission.[18] The growth in the tangible personal property tax base has been in industries related to the service sectors. Growth has been strong in financial firms, service firms, and wholesale firms. It has also been increased in the retail trade sector. The only other industry that has declined in its importance to the tangible business personal property tax base has been construction.

Four classes of personalty are taxed in Ohio: manufacturing equipment, commercial inventories, industrial inventories, and furniture and fixtures. The composition of the tangible business property tax base is changing

TABLE 14-11
Percentage Distribution of Tangible Personal Property Tax Base: Intercounty Corporations

	Year				
Industry	**1975**	**1980**	**1985**	**1990**	**1992**
Manufacturing	81.0	77.2	72.6	65	61.7
Retail	9.3	9.0	9.7	9.4	11.5
Mining	1.8	2.7	2.2	2.2	2.4
Wholesale	3.4	4.9	5.6	5.7	6.0
Services	2.2	2.8	3.6	5.1	5.7
Transportation & Communication	1.0	1.0	1.2	1.4	1.5
Construction	.8	.7	.4	.5	.6
Agriculture	.07	.1	.1	.1	.1
Finance	.8	1.2	2.8	3.8	4.7
Unclassified	—	.3	1.8	5.8	5.8

within these types of personal property. In 1977, 52 percent of the tangible business property tax base was composed of the inventories of the manufacturing and commercial sectors. In 1990, the proportion of the tax base composed of inventories had dropped to 45 percent, and by 1994 it had dropped to 41 percent.[19] During this same period, manufacturing equipment has remained at roughly 35 percent of the total tangible personal property tax base. The growth in the tangible business personal property tax base has been in furniture and fixtures. This portion of the tax base has increased from about 12 percent to over 20 percent. The changing nature of the mix of the property tax base coming from inventories and furniture and fixtures is readily explained. The relative increase in fixtures likely reflects the growing service sector, that is, more office furniture and office equipment, e.g., photocopy and fax machines, and computers.[20]

Table 14-12 gives the percentage distribution of the taxable value of manufacturing equipment, industrial inventories, commercial inventories, and furniture and fixtures for each of the major industries in Ohio. The year reported in Table 14-12 is 1994. Table 14-12 also lists the percent of the taxable value that is exempt from the tangible business property tax.[21] The distribution of the types of tangible personal business property within each industry in Ohio follows expected patterns, i.e., concentration of inventories in retail and wholesale firms, concentration of equipment in manufacturing firms, and furniture and fixtures in finance.

TABLE 14-12
Percent Distribution of Tangible Personal Property for Intercounty Firms by Type of Property by Industry: 1994

	Manufacturing Equipment	Manufacturing Inventory	Retail Inventory	Furniture and Fixtures	10,000 Exemption
Manufacturing	48	35	5	11	—
Retail	1	4	66	29	1
Mining	49	20	7	22	1
Wholesale	11	15	59	16	—
Services	18	3	12	69	2
Transportation/ Communication	37	2	8	53	1
Construction	38	7	13	42	2
Agriculture	30	32	18	16	2
Finance	15	5	16	64	—

Source: The Ohio Department of Taxation, Personal Property Tax Section.

ADMINISTRATIVE RESPONSIBILITIES FOR TANGIBLE PERSONAL BUSINESS PROPERTY TAX

The administration of the tangible personal business property tax is divided between the Ohio Department of Taxation and the 88 elected county auditors in Ohio. The general administrative and appraisal responsibilities for all types of the property in Ohio are illustrated in Figure 14-2. In general, the Ohio Department of Taxation has the lead role for the administration of the tangible personal business property tax. The Department of Taxation designs the forms used by business firms and the county auditors to report tangible property. The Department of Taxation has also developed the depreciation schedules used to value tangible property at the state and local level. The Ohio Department of Taxation is specifically responsible for incorporated firms and for firms that operate facilities in more than one county in Ohio. Such intercounty firms represent about 70 percent of the assessed value of the tangible personal business property in Ohio. Local county auditors have the administrative and assessment responsibility for unincorporated firms and firms that operate in a single Ohio county. The major distinction between county and state filing is whether a firm operates in more than one Ohio county. Local auditors are under the direction of the

Major Function	Date	Issues
Lien Date	January 1	✦ The property value is based on the company's fiscal year.
Forms Filed	February 15 to April 30	✦ Single county taxpayers owe one-half of tax within ten days of filing. ✦ Extension of 45 days can be requested.
Extension Due	June 14	
Assessment Certified	2nd Monday of August	✦ Certification sent to county auditor. ✦ Certification sent to taxpayer.
Payment	September 20	✦ All inter-county taxpayers taxes due to county treasurer. ✦ Single county taxpayers owe second-half of tax to county treasurer. ✦ Payment can be extended 30 days by consent of county auditor and county treasurer.

FIGURE 14-2. Tangible personal business property tax calendar.

Ohio Department of Taxation, and their assessment practices are based on state valuation guidelines.

The number of personal tangible business property accounts that were filed with the Department of Taxation or with county auditors for three selected years are given in Table 14-13. The number of *known* personal tangible business personal property accounts has increased during the period reported in Table 14-13. Since 1985 the number of accounts has increased by about one-third, or over 100,000 new accounts. The accounts are listed in Table 14-13 by three categories: corporate firms that file with the Ohio Department of Taxation, corporate firms that file with the county auditor, and unincorporated firms that file with county auditors.

As indicated, the Property Tax Division is one of eleven divisions in the Ohio Department of Taxation. The Division currently employs more than sixty-six employees. The division has other administrative and valuation responsibilities, including the tangible personal property taxes imposed on public utilities, and dealers in intangibles. Most employees working for the Property Tax Division are assigned to the tangible personal business property tax. The number of employees in the Property Tax Division assigned to

TABLE 14-13
Tangible Personal Business Property Tax, Accounts for Incorporated and Unincorporated Ohio Firms: 1985, 1990 and 1993

	Corporate Firms	Unincorporated Firms	
		Single County	
Year	Ohio Department Of Taxation (Intercounty Returns)	County Auditor	County Auditor
1985	6,892	78,686	74,898
1990	9,487	140,604	100,754
1993	9,851	173,091	123,883

Source: Ohio Department of Taxation.

the tangible personal business property tax are listed in Table 14-14. The number of employees assigned to the tangible property tax in the eight regional tax offices operated by the Department of Taxation are also listed in Table 14. The period of time covered in Table 14-14 is 1980 to 1993.

The number of employees involved in the administration of the tangible personal business property tax has decreased since the mid-1980s. The reductions in some of the regional offices and for some administrative functions in the central office are substantial. The decrease in FTE assigned to this function is difficult to understand in light of the growing number of tangible personal property accounts and the increase in the nominal value of the tangible personal business property tax. More staff may not increase revenue, but would likely improve the administration of the tax. Within counties, the number of employees in the auditor's office assigned to personal property tax administration depends on the size and nature of the county. In the small rural countries, usually fewer than one-half FTE are assigned to the personal property tax. In the mid-size counties about one and one-half to two employees have major responsibility for the personal property tax. In the large urban counties the number of employees with tangible personal property tax responsibilities ranges between 10 and 15 FTEs. These numbers (FTE) are well below the number reported for real property administration.[22]

Time Frame for Appraisal and Collection of Tangible Personal Business Property Tax

Figure 14-2 lists the major calendar deadlines for the tangible personal business property tax. The *Ohio Revised Code* requires that tangible personal property tax taxpayers report all property owned on January 1 and file

TABLE 14-14
Tax Agents Assigned to Tangible Personal Business Property Accounts

	District Office								Department of Taxation			
									Intercounty			
Year	ARK[1]	CIN	CLE	COL	DAY	TOL	YOU	ZAN	CIT*	ICA*	SUP	Total
1980	6	8	9	5	5	7	7	3	5	13	4	72
1981	6	7	9	5	5	7	5	3	5	13	4	69
1982	6	7	8	5	5	9	5	3	5	12	4	69
1983	6	7	8	5	5	7	6	3	5	18	4	74
1984	7	7	9	4	5	8	6	4	9	20	6	85
1985	7	7	9	5	4	9	6	4	7	21	5	84
1986	8	5	9	5	5	8	5	4	19	21	5	87
1987	8	5	9	5	5	8	5	4	10	21	5	85
1988	8	5	10	4	5	7	4	4	9	19	6	81
1989	8	5	9	4	5	5	4	5	9	21	6	81
1990	8	6	9	5	5	5	3	5	6	19	6	77
1991	8	6	7	5	5	5	3	5	10	16	6	76
1992	8	5	7	5	5	4	3	5	5	13	5	65
1993	7	4	7	0	5	4	3	5	5	16	5	61
1994	7	3	7	0	5	3	3	5	5	16	5	59
Highest Staff Level	8	8	10	5	5	9	7	5	10	23	6	96
Percent of Reduction from Highest Year												
	12	62	30	100	0.00	66	57	O	50	30	17	38

Source: Ohio Department of Taxation.

[1]The number of agents in each district office contains one supervisor, except for Akron, which has had two supervisors since 1990.

*CIT: Citation
*ICA: Intercounty Audit

returns between February 15 and April 30.[23] Taxpayers can ask for an extension of 45 days, but taxes from firms administered by the Department of Taxation are due to county treasurers on September 20th of each year. The taxes from the firms valued by the county auditor are due in two payments.

ADMINISTRATIVE ISSUES

On the surface, the administrative issues facing a property tax administrator are similar for both real property and tangible personal property.[24]

Administrators of real and personal property taxes must do the following: discover property, value property, assess tax, bill and collect, provide an appeal system, and audit accounts. These steps and their general sequence in the process of administration are outlined in Figure 14-3.

There are some differences between the administration of a property tax on real property and a property tax on tangible property. While both taxes require the active involvement of tax administrators, the personal property tax also requires a significant role for taxpayers. The personal property tax could not function without the cooperation of taxpayers. The compliance role in real property taxation is passive, unless the taxpayers decide to appeal the valuation of real property.

Discovery of Tangible Personal Business Property

Discovering property is necessary for a property tax system to succeed. Because tangible personalty does not require a building permit to build or

STEP	TASKS
DISCOVERY	■ Identify legal owners ■ Identify all taxable property ■ Classify property in terms of use ■ Develop reporting process
VALUATION	■ Develop consistent process for determining appraised value ■ Apply process to discovered property
ASSESSMENT OF TAX	■ Assessed (true value) is multiplied by assessment rate to establish taxable value ■ Assessed (true value) is listed to specific taxing jurisdictions ■ Property owners are informed of assessed true value
BILL AND COLLECT TAX	■ Set tax rates ■ Bill taxpayer ■ Collect from taxpayer
AUDIT	■ Determine if all taxable property is identified ■ Determine if correct value is being applied against property
APPEAL	■ Informal process to "question" appraisal ■ Formal process to "challenge" appraisal

FIGURE 14-3. Steps in property tax administration.

install, there is no required recording of deeds, and because personalty is usually smaller physically, it is more difficult to discover than real property. Tangible personalty is also mobile and may easily be shifted between taxing jurisdictions on lien dates. Simply put, administrators must work to discover tangible personal property. Even when extraordinary means are not employed to "hide" personal property the discovery of tangible personal property is unlikely to succeed without active programs to find personalty.[25]

The first step in the discovery of tangible personal property is to find firms that may own personalty. Before a taxing authority makes any appraisal, it must be aware that a firm exists. The second step is to find the actual personalty. This step requires either on-site visits by appraisers or self-reporting by individual firms. Self-reporting is the model followed in Ohio, as well as most other states.

The process of finding firms in Ohio concentrates on locating new commercial and industrial operations. The discovery of firms in Ohio is based on formal processes and ad hoc processes conducted by the Property Tax Division, local auditors, and other public officials. The first formal method of discovery, and the most successful method, is conducted by the Property Tax Division in cooperation with the Ohio Secretary of State. It proceeds as follows.

When businesses seek incorporation in Ohio, they must file with the Ohio Secretary of State. The Secretary of State then informs the Ohio Department of Taxation of the incorporation of a business. The Property Tax Division notifies, by letter, newly incorporated firms that they likely have a tangible personal business property tax liability in Ohio. The letter explains the obligation under the Ohio law for personal property taxes. It also explains the penalties associated with noncompliance to the personal property tax statutes. Along with the letter, the newly incorporated firms receive a tangible personal property tax form (Form 920-NT) designed specifically for firms in the start-up phase of operation. About 50 percent of the firms receiving the letter respond by filing the Personal Property Tax form. Firms receiving the letter that was triggered by their incorporation are placed in a Master File maintained by the Property Tax Division.

Firms not responding to the first letter are sent a second letter informing them again that a personal property tax is likely due. If no return is filed following the second letter the Department of Taxation sends them a letter and a delinquency notice. This notice requests information which can be used to determine if the tangible personal property tax is due. The process of sending letters is repeated each year. Firms which have not complied with the letters, and which, in the judgment of the Department of Taxation, should be paying taxes, are contacted and eventually visited by agents from the Property Tax Division.[26]

The second step for discovering new firms is triggered by requests for a firm to begin collecting state sales taxes. All firms selling products in Ohio are required to have a sales tax vendor license in order to collect the sales tax. New firms are required to obtain this license prior to starting operations. License applications are filed with the county auditor. When a firm requests a sales tax vendor license from the auditor, it receives a pamphlet from the auditor which informs the owners that a tangible personal business property tax liability may exist for the firm. This step is not as effective as the notification triggered by incorporation, because firms are not directly contacted by the Property Tax Division and their addresses are not entered into Property Tax Division Master File. The addresses from this process are entered in a second file maintained by the Division of Property Taxation. Property Tax Division employees feel that this second address file is less accurate than the Master File. Property Tax Division employees believe that this second list contains numerous firms no longer doing business or firms operating under multiple names.

Informal systems of identifying businesses also operate in Ohio.[27] County auditors are encouraged to monitor information about known existing firms from the names and addresses provided by the Property Tax Division and to inform the Division of omissions on the Master File. Likewise, local school district officials examine information from the county General Tax Duplicates. The county Duplicates contain information on name of taxpayer, address of taxpayer, and if the taxpayer has paid taxes. Known or suspected firms not listed on the Duplicate are reported. However, much of the effort of school district officials is spent insuring that known taxpayers pay taxes to the correct taxing jurisdictions. Both the local auditor and the school district have strong incentives to identify local taxpayers who are not paying personal property taxes or paying them to the wrong school district.[28] Taxpayers and citizens may also identify and inform a county auditor or the Property Tax Division about firms suspected of not paying personal property taxes.

As noted, the Ohio Department of Taxation also maintains a series of regional tax offices. Staff from these offices occasionally conduct informal programs to identify firms that are not complying with the tangible personal property tax law. Regional auditors compare listings on the Master File to local information, such as business listings in local telephone books. They are also able to find noncompliance firms when they conduct audits and identify the names of firms doing business with existing firms but not found on the Master File. The current systems to discover personal property in Ohio are outlined in Figure 14-4. There is little reason to believe that the Ohio system of discovery successfully identifies all new or even existing firms. The problem of discovery is most serious for firms that do not incorporate, or firms that are currently operating but remain out of the personal property tax cycle. Ohio is not alone among states that have trouble discovering tangible personal property. Criticisms of discovery processes for tangi-

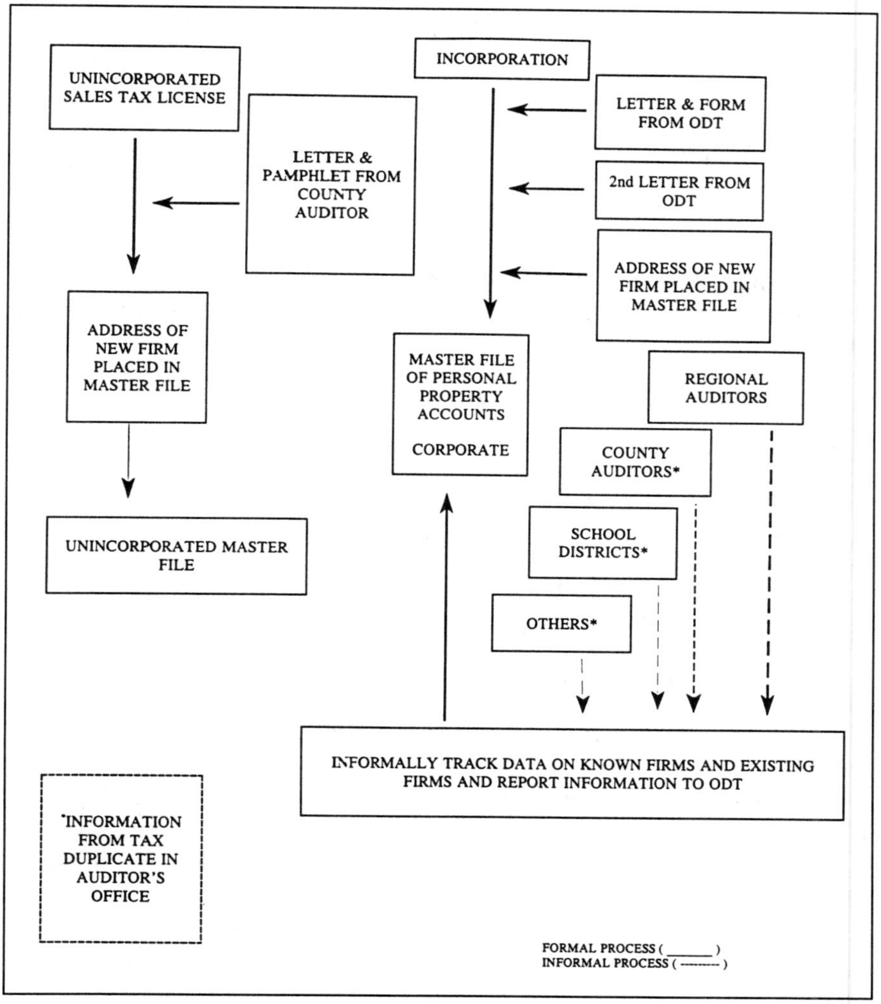

FIGURE 14-4. Discovery of new firms: formal and informal steps.

ble personal property are common for most state property tax systems (Mikesell forthcoming).

Evaluation of Tangible Property Tax Discovery Process

The Property Tax Division is understaffed for the discovery of property. Division staff levels are not adequate to conduct successful discovery efforts. Division administrators concur that more staff and better processes should be implemented. Phone and direct interviews with county auditor personnel found similar concerns about the ability of the "system" to find personalty. Efforts to improve discovery should focus on at least the following three suggestions.

First, there should be a systematic program developed and implemented which the Division follows to identify firms owning tangible personal business property. The International Association of Assessing Officers (IAAO) (1985) has developed a standard to guide personal property appraisal and administration. These standards contain a series of processes that can be used to identify firms.[29] These IAAO processes are relatively simple but do require a commitment of staff and resources. Procedures suggested by the IAAO include the following:

- Examining Chamber of Commerce Membership
- Examining new Business Listings from News Media
- Examining Public Records, e.g., partnership articles, assumed named notices, chattel mortgage records, etc.
- Examining Property Transfer Documents
- Examining Classified Advertisements
- Examining City Directories
- Examining State and Federal Income Tax Records

The IAAO standard does not detail how to implement these processes. However, it seems obvious in Ohio that searches of the listed data sets be compared to known firms listed on the Corporate Master File for the tangible personal property tax and on the second file driven by sales tax accounts. A complete examination of all data on all data sets would be too expensive. However, a series of procedures driven by random comparisons and selected searches for existing firms would be cost effective in identifying firms owning tangible personal property.

Second, improved discovery also requires cooperation between divisions within the Ohio Department of Taxation and other agencies of the State of Ohio. State divisions which license professionals, such as dentists, barbers, and accountants, could share information with the Property Tax Division. The information could be used by the Property Tax Division for comparative purposes. The Property Tax Division should also share information with other Divisions within the Ohio Department of Taxation. The Property Tax Division should purchase data sets from organizations, such as telephone companies, which could be used for computer driven matches with the Master File.

Finally, Farley (1991) observes that personal property discovery is strengthened when local tax officials are actively involved. He suggests that discovery benefits from local officials monitoring construction sites, examining mortgage records, and "driving around." In fact, he describes the results from such activities as "spectacular." He also suggests that the "yellow pages" should be considered a "who's who of personal property." His suggestions for improving discovery are very straightforward—get local officials involved and on the "streets." For example, in Ohio, county auditors could develop relationships with local public agencies that would provide them with information on the status of firms:

- Building Inspection Departments
- Zoning Departments
- Public Safety Departments

Local agencies like the above have a "street-level" understanding of the economic changes that are occurring within a community. If employees of such agencies would monitor the changes occurring and report them to county officials or state officials, they could help keep tangible personal property tax files updated. The information they provide could be completed in a cost effective manner. With more resources and better cooperation, Ohio could improve the discovery of personalty. The importance of using resources to discover new firms is confirmed by Wheeler and Cornia (1989), who report on an audit which found a remarkable level of taxpayer compliance on known personal property accounts. They conclude that if companies are on the tax roll, they will comply with the law.

Valuation of Tangible Personal Business Property for Property Tax Purposes

There are numerous reasons for appraising real and personal property; bank loans, insurance claims, and property taxes are just a few examples (Graham 1989). The goal of realty property tax valuation is to determine what a willing buyer and willing seller would exchange the property for. In Mikesell's (forthcoming) terms, real property is valued using "a current market standard" (p. 214). Because there is often no actual market transaction or sale, the determination of value is based on an estimate of what a property would sell for. Three methods are used by public assessors to estimate what real property would sell for in an open market: income method, cost method, and market comparison method (IAAO 1990). The income method capitalizes net income using a discount rate which an appraiser feels reflects the risk and required rate of return of the potential owner. The cost method is used to determine what it would cost to replace or even reproduce a similar facility using current cost of construction data. The market method examines what similar properties have sold for in recent market transactions.

Tangible personal property can also be valued using all three methods of appraisal. However, tangible personal property is generally valued using a cost method (Mikesell 1992). At first glance, personalty appraisal may appear similar to realty valuation, except the cost method used on personal property differs from the cost method used for the appraisal of real improvements. As noted, cost appraisals of real property improvements estimate how much it would cost to reproduce or replace an improvement at the *current* market cost of land and *current* construction cost of materials (IAAO 1990). The cost standard used to value tangible personal property valuation for property tax purposes is usually based on *historical* or *original* cost less an adjustment for economic depreciation. Historical cost is unlikely to equal the current replacement or purchase price of either real property or improvements. The historical cost approach is used because of the complexity and expense that would accompany the use of income or market approaches to value property.[30]

Ohio, like the other states that impose a property tax on the tangible personal property of businesses, uses the cost approach to value tangible property. The valuation of tangible personal business property in Ohio proceeds as follows. Historical cost for machinery and equipment is recorded by all firms on Ohio Department of Taxation Form 937. This form requires the taxpayer to list tangible property by vintage and historical cost. Adjustments to historical cost are then made on Form 937 based on the type of firm and the age of equipment. Adjustments are based on standardized schedules developed for six major classes of life expectancy. For example, a meat packing firm is classified as a Type III life range, and all of its ten year old meat packing equipment is appraised at 18.8 percent of its historical cost. Conversely, a firm that manufactures aircraft parts is a Type V life range, and all of its ten-year old equipment is appraised at 38.2 percent of its historical cost. The classes of firms found on Form 937 are based on standard SIC classifications. The adjustments are made to historical cost to account for the economic and functional obsolescence associated with the normal operation of the equipment.[31]

If the firm is a corporation and operates in multiple Ohio counties, it is required to file an *Intercounty Return of Taxable Business Property* form. The form (Form 945) is filed with the Property Tax Division of the Department of Taxation. The form requires the firm to list and value all forms of tangible personal property. The firm is also required to list tangible property in terms of its location within a specific taxing jurisdiction. Listing by tax jurisdiction allows the Department of Taxation to inform each government unit of the taxable value of the tangible personal property located within its boundary. Because there are over 4000 taxing jurisdictions in Ohio, listing property in the correct jurisdiction can be difficult for the taxpayer. The values filed on the Form 945 are taken from the depreciation schedule (Form 937) described above. Inventory, both retail and manufacturing, is appraised at cost, with no adjustment for economic depreciation. The form also requires the firm to complete a prescribed balance sheet. The filing of this form is facilitated by the firm receiving from the Property Tax Division Form 945-REC, a computer generated "hard copy" of the personalty filed the previous year. Form 945-REC facilitates the annual filing of the tangible personal business property tax by giving firms a foundation of information from previous filings. However, the major function of Form 945-REC is to assist in the assignment of personalty in the correct taxing jurisdiction.

If the firm operates in a single county, it files directly with the county auditor, using the *County Return of Taxable Business Property* form supplied by the Department of Taxation (Form 920). The valuation process using Form 920 is the same for inter or multi-county firms. The appraisal of machinery and equipment is based on historical cost after adjustments based on age and type of firm from Form 937. Again, the appraisal of inventory is based on cost with no adjustments. Single-county firms are also required to report tangible personalty based on the physical location of the property by taxing jurisdiction. Single-county firms must also complete a balance sheet contained in the form submitted to the county auditor.

The depreciation adjustments to historical cost are driven by the information found in the composite annual allowance procedures found in the *Ohio Administrative Code,* Rule 5703-3-10. The application of the depreciation adjustment results, according to the Ohio code, in a "true value computation" or market value. However, if a firm does not believe that the prescribed depreciation allowance accurately reflects the actual depreciation of its equipment, it may file its estimate of the rate of depreciation it feels it should be granted. If its requested valuation is below book value, it must file Form 902. An intercounty firm is also required to file a form (Form 945-S) if its assessed value increased or decreased by more than $500,000 from the previous tax year. The process of self-assessment for the tangible personal business property tax is outlined in Figure 14-5.

Evaluation of the Valuation of Tangible Personal Property

The current system of tangible business property valuation in Ohio is based on self-reporting and self-assessment. Taxpayers identify tangible

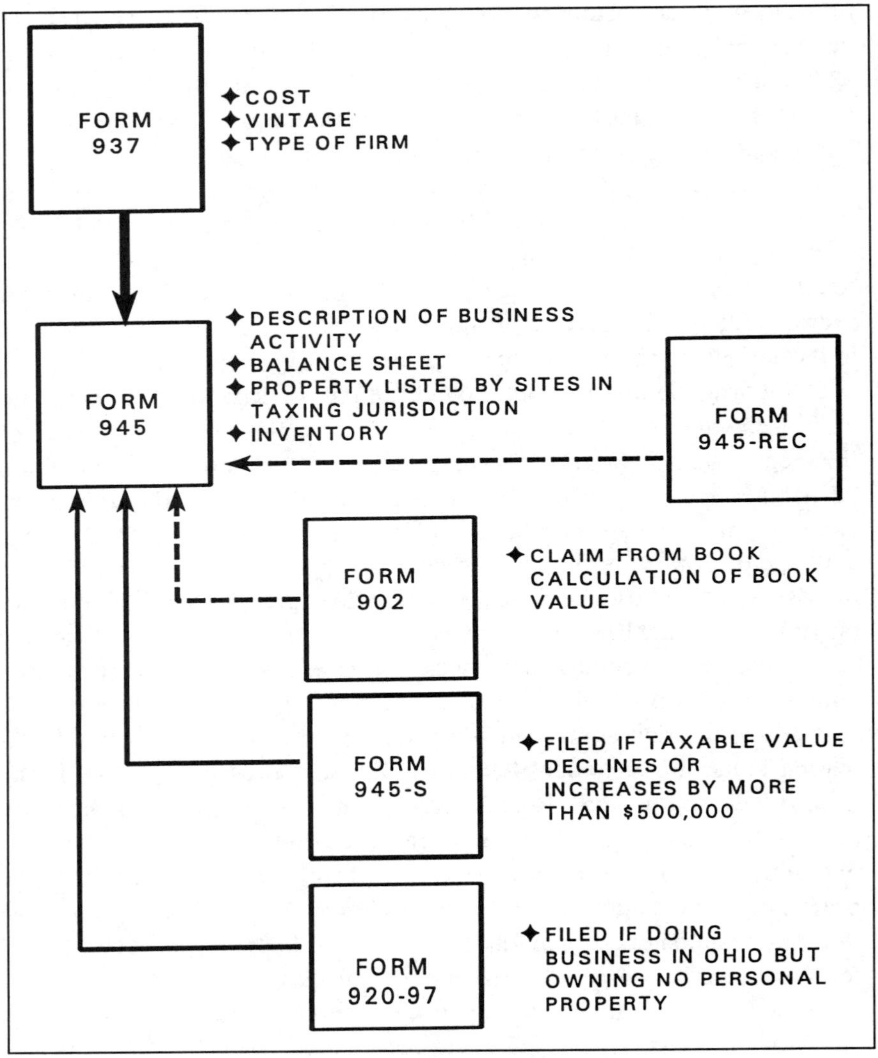

FIGURE 14-5. Process of self-assessment for tangible personal property tax.

property and list the property by age, apply depreciation schedules to the property, and assign the property to specific tax jurisdictions. There are three potential concerns associated with a self-assessment and self-reporting system (ACIR 1963). First, previous sections raised issues about the effectiveness of the discovery of firms in Ohio. (A later section in this study on auditing highlights related discovery problems.) A second concern is whether the process used to report values results in an accurate appraisal. Ohio property tax law requires taxation based on market value. At issue is whether the current system approaches market value. The third issue is that the current system imposes a high compliance cost on the taxpayer.

All these issues are related. Appraisals accuracy can be improved, but only by increasing the compliance and administrative burdens of taxpayers and administrators.[32] Ohio could choose, for example, to have state or county appraisers visit every firm and conduct on-site appraisals. Using this approach the accuracy of personalty appraisals would increase, but the resources required would be substantial. There is an obvious tradeoff between accuracy and the costs of complying with the personal property tax. The Department of Taxation has opted to employ a relatively simple valuation system. Accuracy is reduced, but so is the cost of compliance and administration.

The prime concession by Ohio to reduce compliance costs has been the use of standard depreciation schedules to estimate the value of personalty. Standard depreciation schedules take away the ability of the appraiser to account for unique characteristics of each type of property and firm.[33] Standard schedules force all tangible personalty with the same vintage to be discounted at the same rate.[34] Of course it is unreasonable to assume that all personal property depreciates at the same rate. Nevertheless, given current FTE and financial resources, the Ohio Department of Taxation has limited choice in this matter. Ohio uses a depreciation schedule based on "straight line depreciation." The depreciation curves have a floor for each class of property. There have been infrequent updates of the schedules, and regional modifiers have not been developed for Ohio. The data also do not come to the Ohio Department of Taxation in a computer-readable format. The rate of depreciation used in Ohio for each of the major types of industry is listed is Table 14-15. Six classes of firms have been identified in Ohio, and each class faces a different depreciation schedule. All classes of property are reduced in value; however, the rate of reduction and the minimum value that can be achieved differ by industry class. At issue is whether this simplified model is sufficient?

Developing more accurate appraisal schedules would increase compliance costs, perhaps making them too high for some firms. Firms would end up complying with numerous depreciation schedules. However, without too much additional burden on the Department of Taxation and firms, the process can be improved.

Ohio needs to update the depreciation schedule it uses on personal property. The issue is how? Depreciation schedules can either be developed by the public appraisal agency, purchased from a commercial firm that develops and markets schedules, or based on IRS depreciation schedules. Another approach is to develop hybrid depreciation schedules by examining the depreciation schedules developed in other states or other public agencies. A recent survey of 49 states by the Texas Comptroller found that most

TABLE 14-15
Depreciation Schedules (Expressed as Percents)

Age	Class I	Class II	Class III	Class IV	Class V	Class VI
1	90.0	92.0	93.2	93.9	94.3	94.4
2	63.3	76.3	82.8	86.3	88.1	88.9
3	44.0	60.6	72.4	78.7	81.8	83.3
4	32.0	46.1	62.0	71.1	75.6	77.8
5	20.0	37.9	51.5	63.5	69.3	72.2
6	20.0	29.8	42.2	55.8	63.1	66.7
7	20.0	21.6	36.3	48.2	56.9	61.1
8		20.0	30.5	40.6	50.6	55.6
9		20.0	24.6	35.4	44.4	50.0
10		20.0	18.8	31.1	38.2	44.4
11			18.8	26.8	32.8	38.9
12			18.8	22.5	29.5	33.3
13				18.3	26.2	28.9
14				17.4	22.9	26.2
15				17.4	19.6	23.5
16				17.4	16.3	20.8
17					16.3	18.1
18					16.3	15.4
19						15.4
20						15.4

Source: Ohio Department of Taxation.

COMPOSITE GROUP - LIFE RANGES:
I -Less than 6.0 yrs.
II - 6.0 yrs. to 8.4 yrs.
III - 8.4 yrs. to 11.6 yrs.
IV - 11.6 yrs to 14.8 yrs.
V - 14.8 yrs. to 17.2 yrs.
VI - at least 17.2 yrs.

of the states have opted to purchase commercially prepared depreciation schedules (McMillian 1993). The Texas report suggests a series of advantages associated with a commercially prepared schedule:

- It eliminates the gathering of market data by the public agency.

- Updates of schedules can be routinely provided
- Schedules can be used with a computer.
- Regional modifiers can be provided by the vendor.

As noted, the depreciation schedules used in Ohio are updated infrequently. The Department of Taxation needs to consider purchasing a depreciation schedule from a commercial appraisal firm, or at least modify the current schedule based on internal surveys and reviews.[35] According to the Texas Survey, internal reviews and updates of existing schedules are practiced in several states. However, more frequent updating of schedules requires more staff for the Division of Property Tax and increases the cost of keeping tax forms up to date.[36] At least one, perhaps more, additional employees would be needed in the Property Tax Division of the Ohio Department of Taxation.

Another appraisal issue which policy-makers should consider is trending the historical cost of personalty to account for increases in price.[37] Several states trend the historical costs of personal property during appraisals. Trending is done to reflect a taxable value that approximates what it would currently cost to replace the equipment, or other tangible personalty, less an adjustment for depreciation. A policy of trending tangible personal in property should increase equity between the appraised value of real property and tangible personal property.[38] Equity would be increased even further if trending were adjusted to account for regional differences in personalty costs within Ohio. If a policy of trending were adopted, it would require at least one additional employee for the Property Tax Division. The employee would need to develop trending data schedules for different industries, and design and implement forms. Table 14-16 lists the appraisal processes followed in selected states which place a tax on tangible personal business property. In terms of appraisal practice, Ohio is similar to the states reported in the Texas study. The most significant difference is that some states do trend historical costs, and many states use a commercial (Marshall Swift) depreciation guideline.

In terms of compliance, the current system of self-reporting and self-assessment personal property places a heavy compliance burden on taxpayers in Ohio. Taxpayers must, according to Young (1993), complete the following processes in order to self-assess tangible business personalty:

- Maintain a separate set of physical asset books
- Identify all leased personalty
- Monitor Depreciation Schedules and compare them to State Depreciation Allowances

TABLE 14-16
Tangible Personal Business Property Valuation Procedures: Selected States

State	Procedure		
	Trending	**Cost Basis**	**Depreciation Schedule**
Kansas	No	Original Cost	7 year life - 20% floor
Indiana	No	Original	IRS Schedule
Kentucky	Yes	Marshall Swift	State-Provided Schedules
Michigan	No	Original	Present Value
Missouri	No	Cost Guides	—
Ohio	No	Original Cost	State-Provided Schedules
Tennessee	No	Original	Set by Legislature

Source: McMillian (1993)

- Identify Equipment by Location
- Identity Equipment by Vintage
- Prepare a Difficult Tax Form

These requirements impose two costs on taxpayers: first is the tax paid to the county treasurer, and second is the cost of compliance.[39] The cost of complying with the tax may even be more difficult for small taxpayers. Pearson (1994), a county assessor in Idaho asserts, for example, that small firms face an onerous task of complying with the tangible personal property tax. Interviews with county auditors in Ohio confirm that the compliance problem is serious for smaller firms. County auditors in rural and urban Ohio counties use up to one FTE, helping taxpayers comply with personal property tax requirements.[40]

Assessment of Tax and Billing for Tax

The county auditor combines the assessed values from each of the three sources of the property tax for each taxing jurisdiction in the county.[41] After the tax base for each tax jurisdiction has been calculated, the auditor sends the data on taxable value to the county treasurer. The total assessed value is multiplied by the adopted tax rate; and the total amount of property tax is calculated for each taxing jurisdiction. The tax rate is also applied against the realty and personalty of each taxpayer to determine what that taxpayer owes in property tax. The final step is the preparation and mailing of a tax bill for individual taxpayers.[42]

Auditing

A self-reporting tax system requires an audit process. A reliable audit system identifies individuals or firms that are not complying with the tax law. To be effective, a reliable audit system does not need to actually catch a noncompiler. Concern about being "discovered" and paying significant financial penalties "encourages" taxpayers to comply with the self-reporting requirement. An audit process also educates current taxpayers. Thus an audit system may discover taxpayers who may be paying too much or filing forms incorrectly. Of course, an audit system will likely produce revenue for the taxing unit. Without a functioning audit system, self-reported tax bases will eventually erode, and inequities between taxpayers will increase.[43]

The Property Tax Division has established an integrated audit process. The audit system is directed and driven by the *Ohio Personal Property Audit Handbook,* compiled and maintained by the Property Tax Division. The first step in the audit system, checking the accuracy of the return, begins with the initial screening of the annually filed documents. The screening verifies that the forms have been used properly and that the name and address of the firm have been reported. Failure to meet these requirements will result in the form being returned to the taxpayer for correction. If the forms are correct and are used appropriately, the prescreening proceeds, and the following issues are examined:

- Is the math correct?
- Does the taxpayer use a depreciation schedule different from the state's depreciation schedule?
- Does the taxpayer request a substantial reduction in the appraised value of assets? (If the reduction is greater than $500,000, a special form (945-S) must be filed with the tax return and the county auditor.)
- Was inventory reported by the firm?
- How was inventory value determined?
- Was property listed on balance sheet?
- Is there more than one county location?

The appearance of any of these issues likely triggers an audit of the firm by the Property Tax Division. Audits driven by math mistakes are obviously essential if the tax system is to remain reliable. Other issues that trigger audits, such as reductions in appraised value greater than $500,000, are less obvious.[44]

Audits may also result if a firm not filing an annual return is listed on the personal property tax Master File. If a firm does not file, it is notified by letter that it must either file or submit Department of Taxation Form 920-97. Form 920-97 requests the firm to verify that it has no personal property located in Ohio and does not operate a "business location" in Ohio. The form also requires the firm to complete a prescribed balance sheet. When this form is received by the Division of Property Taxation, it is reviewed by a state auditor. The Property Tax Division may either accept the assertion that no personalty tax is due, or the Division may cause a redetermination of taxes due, or an on-site visit by an auditor.

Audits are also driven by the firm size. Large firms operating in Ohio are the most likely to be "randomly" audited. Auditing decisions driven by the size of the company are common in tax administration. The reason the Property Tax Division audits large firms is simple: audits of large firms have the highest return per audit. Audits are also driven by SIC code. The reason for these audits is similar to the reasons for auditing large firms. Some industries have more problems and generate more revenue during an audit than other industries. Problems typically found during "size" or "SIC" audits do not reflect fraud on the part of firms. Issues discovered during these audits include such things as firms using the wrong depreciation schedule or the wrong class life for specific types of personal property. Disagreement often arises about the value that must be reported as historical cost, but evidence of systematic deception on the part of firms has not surfaced. Audits can also be driven by the discovery of nonfiling firms. The process of discovering nonfiling firms was discussed in the section dealing with the discovery of property. As noted in that section, Ohio would benefit from the commitment of additional resources to discover property.

Audits can be conducted either by auditors located in Columbus or auditors stationed in one of six regional tax offices. Audits are either "desk" audits or "field" audits. A desk audit is conducted by the auditor using the data supplied by the taxpayer. It is driven by previous filings of the taxpayer and is generally concerned with the internal consistency of the data provided. Desk audits correct problems such as depreciation mistakes and the improper listing of equipment. A desk audit is also driven by an "Examination Report," a four-page document consisting of a series of questions for the auditor to answer. The questions focus on determining the internal accuracy and the reasonableness of the data provided by the firm. The completed Examination Report can result in a redetermination of assessed value and taxes due. The appearance of substantial problems may result in a field or physical audit of a firm's personal property. A field audit is, as the name implies, an audit conducted in the field, or the physical location of the firm, and compares company books to the actual personalty. The *Audit Handbook* prescribes the steps that an auditor is expected to follow during a field audit. The steps include policies on:

- The notification of taxpayers about the audit
- The types of questions asked during the audit
- The legal guidelines of the audit
- The reporting of the audit findings
- The review of proposed audit settlements

Data on the per capita amount of tax revenue generated annually by Property Tax Division audits are collected by the Department of Taxation. The total amount of revenue recovered by Property Tax Division auditors over selected years is reported in Table 14-17, which identifies the collections resulting from both field audits and desk audits. The total net per capita revenue from the audits is also reported in Table 14-17. These num-

TABLE 14-17
Ohio State Property Tax—Audit Production Per Employee

Audit Production: Intercounty Central Audit			
Year	Field	Office	Total
1992	$333,341	$355,659	$1,089,614
1990	265,370	118,522	866,957
1989	632,044	87,244	1,310,489
1987	327,694	88,245	861,347
1986	258,420	221,160	763,440
1984	439,780	154,100	754,700
Audit Production: District			
Year	Field	Office	Total
1992	$145,415	$111,569	$328,831
1990	103,961	67,662	243,948
1989	139,382	92,172	283,099
1987	127,494	99,670	256,329
1986	86,632	119,919	249,897
1984	63,164	61,024	326,082

Source: Ohio Department of Taxation, unpublished data.

bers are reported for both the district office auditors and the auditors from the central staff.

On a year-by-year comparison, the amount of revenue recovered by audits conducted by the Property Tax Division varies. Explaining such variation is difficult. However, it would be unrealistic to expect audit production to remain constant or increase at an even pace every year. A successful audit is an audit that certifies that the tax law was followed correctly. Thus many audits lower tax liability, not increase it. There is also a natural unevenness to an audit process. Some years, auditors will simply find firms with substantial problems. Other years, auditors will find fewer firms with fewer problems. Certain aspects of the data in Table 14-17 are important to note. The revenue collected by a field audit is greater than the revenue generated from the desk audits. Of course, field audits are more time-consuming, and on an hourly basis the return may be lower than appears. The amount of revenue per auditor is increasing at both the district and central office levels.

Evaluation of Auditing

The current Ohio system of auditing personal business property tax accounts compares favorably to the processes generally recommended in the public appraisal literature on personal property tax audits. The literature is prepared by the International Association of Assessing Officers (IAAO). The IAAO identifies four types of audits that should be given priority during the audit selection:

- Audits of Large Accounts
- Audits of firms with substantial value changes
- Audits of firms with suspected filing mistakes
- Audits of new accounts

As noted, the Property Tax Division uses audit selection policies based on the first of these three selection criteria. However, the Division needs to consider a program to audit new accounts.

The audit procedures described in the Property Tax Division's *Audit Handbook* also compare favorably to a series of suggested audit procedures developed by Mayes (1989); in turn, they are similar to the audits performed by a public accounting firm during audits of the physical assets of a firm (Wallace 1986).

However, there are still problems with the Ohio audit system. The current personal property tax auditing system could benefit from two changes. These changes are:

- more personnel,
- the selection of audit candidates by statistical inferences.

Both changes are related. The current auditing system audits only a small percentage of all of the personal property accounts in Ohio. In order to audit more accounts, the number of auditors must be increased. Given current revenue production, it seems that additional auditors would be cost-effective. However, the addition of auditors should not be judged only on the basis of financial return. An audit program also educates taxpayers and ensures that firms are treated correctly. A good audit system is not driven solely by finding revenue. More auditors will improve the accuracy of compliance for Ohio taxpayers. Additional auditors will also increase coverage or the probability that a firm will be audited. In Ohio, the possibility of an on-site audit is close to zero for most firms. The low probability of an audit makes it difficult to assert that taxpayers are complying with the tangible personal business property tax law.

As reported in an earlier section of this study, the number of auditing personnel has been declining in number. The reductions have been experienced in both the central office and the district tax offices. The reasons for the reductions probably reflect different assumptions about the importance of tangible personal property in the overall revenue scheme of Ohio. The reductions have been unfortunate. If the reductions are not reversed, or worse, if they continue, the issue of noncompliance may increase.

APPEALS

The appeal of the tangible personal property tax can be triggered by three events. The first occurs if the owner of the personalty fails to file a tax return. Once this is discovered, the tax is imposed, and a penalty of up to 50 percent is added to the tax bill. The taxpayer can appeal the penalty to the state tax commissioner. If the taxpayer is unhappy with the decision from the tax commissioner, the appeal can be pursued through the Board of Tax Appeals and eventually to the Ohio Supreme Court.

The second appeal occurs if a taxpayer files, but fails to pay the tax due. In this situation a late penalty is imposed on the taxpayer. The taxpayer can appeal to the county auditor and to the county treasurer for the removal or reduction of the penalty. Penalties can only be reduced when there is:

- auditor error
- mail delay
- death or serious illness
- incorrect billing

The taxpayer can appeal beyond the county officials to the state tax commissioner. Appeals beyond the tax commissioner are sent to the Board of Tax Appeals and may be appealed to the Ohio Supreme Court. Few appeals go beyond the county officials or the state tax commissioner.

The third appeal event is a result of an assessment action by the Department of Taxation. Upon receipt of Form 945, the Property Tax Division has three options:

- Lower the self-assessment
- Accept the self-assessment
- Process the self-assessment but place assessment in audit file

The first option results when the Property Tax Division believes that the taxpayer has over assessed the value of the tangible business personalty owned by the firm. It is unlikely that an audit is triggered when the Property Tax Division lowers an assessment. There is also no audit when the Property Tax Division accepts the assessed value filed by the firm. The assessed values from both options one and two are certified by the State tax commissioner and sent to the county auditor; they are then placed on the tax duplicate of the county.

An audit is triggered only when the Property Tax Division believes that a firm has filed incorrectly or made a request for a reduction that is not justified. However, the audit does not take place until after the tax year is completed. The value placed on the county tax duplicate is the potentially "incorrect" assessed value. Once a file has been placed in the audit file, it may take up to two years for the audit to be completed. Thus a firm will not know for up to two years if its requested reduction in taxes has been accepted.

The audit process results in an Amended Preliminary Assessment, which is returned to the taxpayer and the county officials where the firm operates. The firm can now either accept the decision made by the audit division, or it can appeal. If it appeals, it must first file with the tax commissioner, who makes a second "amended" assessment. Unhappiness with the tax commissioner's decision can lead to an appeal to the State Board of Tax Appeals. The Board of Tax Appeals' decision can be appealed to the Ohio court system. The process of appeals is outlined in Figure 14-6. Generally, the appeal process is a function of a taxpayer asking for a hearing because of dissatisfaction with the taxable value of property. In Ohio, concerns about the assessed level of tangible personalty are only triggered by the taxpayer seeking a change. These requests will only lead to appeals if the Property Tax Division feels the requests are not warranted. Taxpayers can trigger an audit by a filing that requests a different depreciation schedule than the schedule on Form 937. Taxpayers can also trigger an audit by filing Form 945-S when the value of their assessed property changes more than $500,000. The major shortcoming of the Ohio appeal system is that it is only triggered when the firm requests a change. If the Property Tax Division grants the change, there is no "public" appeal process.

THE PERSONAL TANGIBLE BUSINESS PROPERTY TAX BASE

The evaluation of what constitutes appropriate state tax policy is driven by a series of criteria.[45] This section of the chapter examines and evaluates the tangible business personal property tax base from the perspective of various tax criteria, some of which, such as revenue and base stability, were evaluated in earlier sections of this study.

Comparisons With Other State Tax Bases

An important issue for a state tax system, including the property tax system, is what economic items neighboring states include in their tax base.[46] States that impose a tax on the tax base, or certain elements of a tax base,

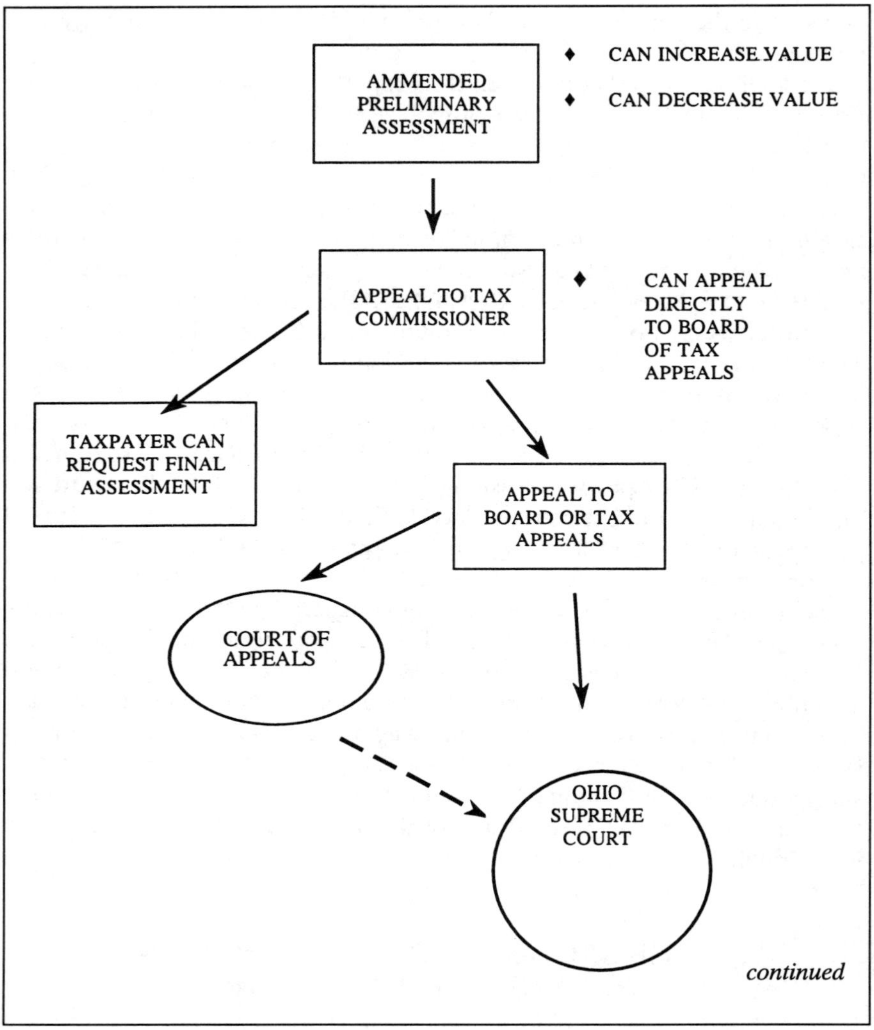

FIGURE 14-6. Appeals process.

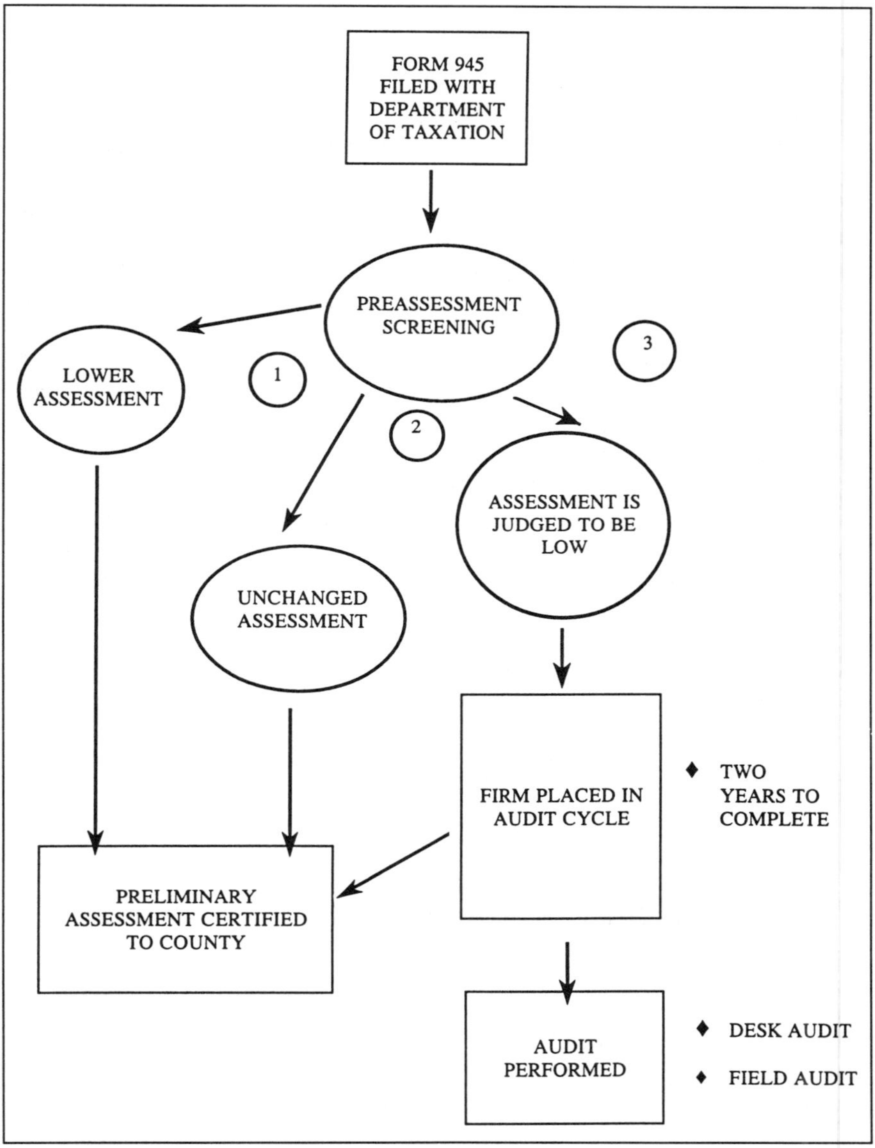

FIGURE 14-6. Appeals process (continued).

may be at a disadvantage if surrounding states exempt the base from the tax system. In terms of the general property tax, all of Ohio's neighbors include real property and improvements to real property in their tax bases. The same cannot be said for tangible personal property. The treatment of tangible personal property by neighboring states, and states that compete with Ohio for capital is listed in Table 14-18. Almost all the states, including those listed on Table 14-18, exempt intangible personal property from the personal property tax base. Three neighboring states, Kentucky, Pennsylvania, and West Virginia, continue to impose a tax on intangible personal property. Nationally, only nine states continue to impose an intangible personal property tax. There is a regional pattern in the use of the intangible personal property tax. Seven of the nine states which use this tax are located in the South.[47] None of the states, with two exceptions, and none of the comparison states, tax household goods.[48] Taxation of business inventory is no longer a common practice in states. Only sixteen states currently tax business inventory. Three of the states which tax business inventory are adjacent to Ohio: Indiana, Kentucky, and West Virginia. Again, the states that tax business inventory are concentrated in the South.

The taxation of depreciable fixed business assets is standard tax practice in the United States. Thirty-nine states which include tangible business personal property in their tax bases. Of the eleven states which exempt tangible personal business assets from the tax base, two are neighbors of Ohio: Pennsylvania and West Virginia; three are in the same general economic region: Illinois, Minnesota, and New York. Conversely, the tax is imposed by the neighboring states of Indiana and Kentucky. However, compared to national averages, Ohio's relative share of revenue from the personal property tax is only about one-half of the share collected in other states (Table 14-1).

TABLE 14-18
General Tax Treatment of Selected Types of Personal Property: Selected States

State	Intangible Personal Property	Household	Business Inventory	Business Depreciable Fixed Assets
California	Excluded	Excluded	Excluded	Tax
Florida	Excluded	Excluded	Excluded	Tax
Illinois	No Tax	No Tax	No Tax	No Tax
Indiana	Excluded	Excluded	Tax	Tax
Kentucky	Tax	Excluded	Tax	Tax
Michigan	Excluded	Excluded	Excluded	Tax
Minnesota	No Tax	No Tax	No Tax	No Tax
New Jersey	No Tax	No Tax	No Tax	No Tax
New York	No Tax	No Tax	No Tax	No Tax
Ohio	Excluded	Excluded	Tax	Tax
Pennsylvania	No Tax	No Tax	No Tax	No Tax
Texas	Excluded	Excluded	Tax	Tax
West Virginia	Excluded	Excluded	Tax	Tax

Source: Mikesell (1992)

WEALTH

Of course, maintaining an economic factor in the property tax base should be based on criteria other than tax policy decisions made by the surrounding states. Other criteria are important to any evaluation. One important issue, especially with respect to the property tax, is whether tangible personal business property represents wealth and ability-to-pay? Mikesell (forthcoming) suggests that tangible personal business property, even though it is a depreciating asset, equates to economic wealth. Other commentators agree with Mikesell. The Advisory Commission on Intergovernmental Relations wrote, "Personal property, no less than real property, is part of the wealth . . . An owner of personal property is as much an owner of property as the owner of land and improvements" (1963, p. 32). On an open market, business personalty can be exchanged for money or other goods. Tangible personalty is also used to produce goods and services that can be exchanged for money or other goods. In terms of measurable wealth and income production, tangible personalty belongs in the tax base.

HORIZONTAL EQUITY

However, the inclusion of tangible personal property may create problems with respect to horizontal equity. Firms with similar net incomes may have significantly different tax levels if one has a high percentage of taxable tangible business assets and the other has few such assets. They may pay roughly similar amounts in income taxes, but the firm with more assets will face a larger share of the property tax.[49]

The tangible personal business tax on commercial and industrial inventories also has a relationship to wealth. Inventories are used to create wealth and are exchanged in a market transaction. However, as Mikesell notes (forthcoming), a growing inventory does not reflect "economic success." A growing inventory suggests that the firm or industry is unable to sell the goods that it is producing, wholesaling, or retailing. Increased levels of inventory are more closely linked with negative cash flows and reduced profits. Taxes based on inventory are not good measures of ability-to-pay. Taxes based on inventory also can contribute to problems of horizontal equity. In terms of horizontal equity, the tangible personal property tax does not score well.

VERTICAL EQUITY

A related concern is the issue of vertical equity. Adjusting the property tax, real or personal, to account for differences in the ability-to-pay has not been easy. Many states have adopted numerous special programs to protect taxpayers from heavy burdens of the real property tax. Some programs to protect against high taxes have been industry-specific. For example, most states have adopted programs to protect agriculture from the real property tax. Most states also have programs to protect certain classes of homeowners from the property tax. Ohio has provided some adjustment to protect small firms from the current personal property tax. All firms are allowed to deduct from their assessed value of tangible personal business property $10,000, and firms with assessed value less than $10,000 are not required to pay any personal property taxes to the local government where they are located. The state in turn protects the local government by granting it a sum equal to the lost revenue. Table 14-19 lists the amount of revenue paid by the state to local governments over the years from 1987 to 1990. The state has also adopted a series of enterprise zones that limit the amount of property tax.[50] On balance, the tangible personal property tax does not allow for easy adjustments to account for ability to pay.

ADMINISTRATION AND COMPLIANCE

Another important criterion is whether the tax is easy to administer and comply with. The property tax in general is a difficult tax to administer. Compliance responsibilities associated with the property tax on realty are relatively modest. Conversely, the tangible personal property tax is difficult to administer and also difficult to comply with. Tax administrators must be creative in their efforts to discover tangible personal property; and heavy compliance burdens are placed on the taxpayer, e.g., reporting and self-evaluation. The costs of both administration and the compliance argue against the inclusion of depreciable assets and commercial and industrial inventory in the tax base.

TABLE 14-19
Tangible Personal Property Tax—Reduction in Value and Amount Reimbursed by State: 1987–1990

Year	Reduction of Taxable Value	Amount Reimbursed By State
1987	934,897,269	56,000,588
1988	961,038,859	59,967,303
1989	999,131,809	64,729,658
1990	1,024,179,877	68,872,182

Source: Ohio Department of Taxation, *Annual Reports*.

VALUATION

A related issue is the problem of valuing depreciable assets and inventory for ad valorem property tax purposes. Valuation of these assets must be based on a formula-driven process that can only approximate true market value. Such a process results in inequities. Some depreciable assets will be overvalued, and some will be undervalued when a formula driven appraisal method is used.[51] On average, the valuation may be roughly equal, with some firms too high and some too low. The valuation of inventories will be less problematic. If an acceptable method of valuing inventory is adopted, it can be applied uniformly to all firms.

ECONOMIC DEVELOPMENT

The final criterion is economic development. What does the tax do to hinder the economic development of the state? Does the tax interfere with the location of businesses within a state, and can it cause existing business to leave the state or pursue growth outside the state? The tax on tangible personal business property may or may not directly hurt the ability of Ohio to attract and retain capital. Two fundamental positions can be taken with respect to tangible property taxation and economic development. First, because so many states have retained tangible personal property in their property tax base, there is little reason to assume that the current system of taxation is harmful to the economic well-being of Ohio. Conversely, others could argue that because important states that compete with Ohio for capital and jobs have removed the tangible property tax from their base, Ohio must follow.[52] However, comparisons must be made carefully. Those states which exclude tangible personal property tax from the tax base frequently define real property more broadly than Ohio does. The result is that property that is taxed as personal property in Ohio is taxed as real property in states like Pennsylvania and New Jersey.[53] A comparison of how states treat tangible personal property is difficult to conduct. Every state is different. The analysis would need to understand how tax bases are defined and how bases are depreciated.

The retention of commercial and industrial inventory in the tax base probably does have economic consequences. The problem of taxing inventory and the negative incentive caused by this practice was noted by Due (1961) over 30 years ago. Few states continue to tax inventory. Taxing commercial and industrial inventory does limit the potential growth of firms that would consider using Ohio as a warehousing or distribution state.

As noted, Ohio has attempted to reduce part of the economic development concerns by the adoption of Enterprise Zones. These zones have been created to encourage economic development in blighted areas of the state.

The role of Enterprise Zones is discussed in *Studies on Economic Development for the Commission* (Wasylenko forthcoming).

ISSUES IN THE TAXATION OF TANGIBLE PERSONAL PROPERTY

The tangible personal business property tax is not a popular tax with business. Perhaps it is even more unpopular than the real property tax. Some of the unpopularity of the personal property tax is deserved: it is a difficult tax to comply with, tax obligations can be very large, tax payments are due in lump sums, and the tax payments may bear little resemblance to the economic health of a firm. In spite of the problems associated with this tax, it does have a number of important attributes:

- A tangible personal business property tax does represent wealth, i.e., the physical asset holdings of a firm.
- A tangible personal business property tax may be effectively administered with taxpayer cooperation.
- A tangible personal business property tax may reach the service-centered economy that is now emerging.
- A tangible personal business property tax can produce substantial revenue.
- A tangible personal business property tax can compensate for services received from local government.

There are of course serious drawbacks with this tax. A partial list of the problems include the following:

- The discovery process may never be sufficient to find new and escaped firms.
- Accurate depreciation schedules are difficult to develop.
- Audit functions may not be adequate.
- Compliance can be expensive.
- The tax base is often unevenly distributed.
- The tax may create economic disincentives for location decisions and economic development.

A resolution for most of the problems requires additional funds and additional employees for administration. In Ohio, resolution may also require some reorganization of the current Division of Property Tax. Changes may also have substantial revenue implications for local governments in Ohio.

Summary of Issues

The issues surrounding the taxation of tangible personal business property are summarized below. Options to resolve the issues are also offered in each issue statement.

Issue #1: Centralization of Administration

The issue of proper administration of this tax is critical if it is retained in the base. A complete centralization of the filing and reporting function for the personal property tax should be considered. If adopted, local auditors would no longer be responsible for the receipt and recording of the data on Form 920; all of the appraisal data would be reported to the Property Tax Division at the Department of Taxation. This change would relieve the local auditor of the responsibility of processing hundreds of forms. The local auditor would be given expanded responsibility to discover and report new and escaped firms. This suggestion would take advantage of the auditing and computer and data entry functions of the Property Tax Division, and also of the ability of local auditors to use their understanding of local economic activity to find firms. Local auditors would help with both the identification of new firms and the assignment of the taxable value of known existing firms to the correct tax jurisdiction. Interviews with local auditors also discovered a feeling on their part that more contact with taxpayers would improve the accuracy of the personal property tax return.

Issue #2: Removal of the Inventory Tax

This option has revenue-significant implications for the state. In spite of the sizable revenue loss for Ohio, it is in the economic interest of the state to consider dropping commercial and industrial inventory from the personal property tax base. Only nine states continue to tax inventory. Ohio is out of line with most states. Commercial and industrial inventories are by their very nature very mobile. A state that places a tax on such factors will always be at some degree of competitive disadvantage when compared to surrounding states. Keeping the tax provides a strong incentive for existing firms that maintain a high level of inventory to expand to other states where inventory is not taxed, and for new firms to select other states when considering location.

Tax administrators and tax policy-makers must move cautiously on this recommendation. The removal of an economic factor from the tax base does not reduce the need for public services or goods. Not only do demands remain, they are usually increasing. If the demand for services remains the same, the removal of the tax means that other taxpayers will have their taxes increased. This proposal may shift the tax from commercial and industrial taxpayers to other commercial and industrial taxpayers, or perhaps to other sectors, like agricultural. The removal of inventory from the personal tax would reduce the tax base by just over 40 percent. A percentage reduction of this amount would reduce the revenue from the tangible personal property by about $0.500 billion. Sectors liable to gain the most from this change would be the retail sector, the wholesale sector, and the manufacturing sector. The biggest reduction in tax would go to manufacturing. As would be expected, two sectors, retail and wholesale, would have their personal property taxes slashed dramatically.

However, the removal of the tax on inventory would make the tangible personal property tax even more stable. A large portion of the tax that is influenced by price-level changes would be removed from the tax base. The remaining tax base, valued on historical cost, would be inelastic.

In order to lessen the burden of the shift, the reduction should come slowly. Perhaps the reduction could come by a lower assessment level being introduced on inventories over an extended time. Reducing the inventory assessment level by 20 percent a year for the next five years would send a positive signal to current and potential firms. It would also lessen the magnitude of the burden associated with the removable of the inventory tax.

Issue #3: Removal of the Tangible Personal Property Tax from the Tax Base

The final issue is whether Ohio should remove the tangible personal property tax from the tax base. There are several reasons why this issue should be reviewed. There is little assurance that this tax contributes to either vertical or horizontal equity. Concerns also exist over the influence of this tax on economic development. Given the slow rate of economic growth in Ohio, taxes that potentially hurt development should be carefully evaluated. Other problems should, of course, be considered before the tax is dropped. The revenue loss would be substantial. Other sources of revenue would need to be found. The shift in the burden is not insignificant. Given the inelastic nature of the tax, there would also likely be a loss in revenue stability.

ENDNOTES

1. Revenue from a tax is a product of the defined tax base multiplied by the tax rate. This study focuses on issues concerning the base of this tax. Property tax rate policy is explained and evaluated in the study prepared for the Ohio Tax Study Commission on real property. See Chapter 7 in this volume.

2. Depreciation in this chapter refers to economic depreciation and not accounting depreciation. Economic depreciation reflects a decline in economic value. Accounting depreciation is the allocation of the cost of a tangible asset's value or cost across time.

3. For a discussion of how states treat intangible personal property, see Bowman, Hoffer and Pratt (1990).

4. See Roberts (1988).

5. The courts have looked beyond the definitions found in state statutes and considered issues such as the intention of the owner with respect to the property. For example, if an owner intends to make property a permanent fixture, it is often ruled to be real property. There are also frequent concerns about how to value property used in both business and personal activities. In such cases the courts have examined concepts like *principal utilization* and *essentially.* See Cypress (1989).

6. Taxes charged do not represent taxes collected. Annually a percent of property taxes is collected late and in some situations never collected. In Ohio, the property tax on tangible personal business property has a delinquency rate of about five percent.

7. The taxation of the tangible personal property owned by utilities is discussed in Chapter 13 of this volume.

8. Elasticity was measured using the standard approach of regressing the log of the change in revenue against the log of the change in income.

9. The coefficient of variation is equal to the standard deviation divided by the mean of the data set. The coefficient of variation expresses the standard deviation as a percentage of the mean.

10. In Ohio, the standard term for appraised value is *true* value. In this chapter, appraised value will be used.

11. The practice of the appraised value being equal to an estimated market value is consistent in both the appraisal literature and Ohio statutes.

12. The appraisal value of tangible personal property is essentially historical cost less an adjustment for depreciation.

13. The administrative relationship between the Ohio Department of Taxation and local county auditors is described in the next section of this study. The role of the taxpayer in appraising personalty is also described in the next section of this study. The next section of this study also describes the significant role played by taxpayers in determining the taxable value of tangible personal property.

14. The economics literature traditionally refers to the assessment level as an assessment ratio. See Rosen (1995).

15. Real Property in Ohio is assessed at 35 percent of appraised value. Public utility property is assessed at 88 percent of appraised value, or in some cases at 100 percent of appraised value.

16. For a discussion of the issues around the per capita distribution and uniformity of a tax base, see Musgrave and Musgrave (1989).

17. The issues around fiscal inequality are discussed in the study on intergovernmental fiscal relations prepared for the Ohio Tax Study Commission. See Chapter 8 in this volume.

18. See Chapter 2 in this volume.

19. The Ohio Department of Taxation, Personal Property Tax Section.

20. The changing nature of the tangible personal business property tax base raises policy questions about who actually pays the property tax. Is the tax paid by the consumer, worker, or owner of capital? These questions cannot be answered easily. However, policy makers must recognize that the ability to pass a tax on to a customer and possibly to a customer living outside Ohio is directly related to the nature of the type of industry and the competitive nature of the firm within the industry.

21. The first $10,000 of each firm's tangible business personalty is exempt from the personal property tax base. However, the firm must file in a timely manner to receive this exemption.

22. FTE numbers reported during interviews with selected county auditors in Ohio.

23. The lien date is January 1 in Ohio. However, Ohio firms are allowed to list the value of their property at the close of their fiscal year, e.g., October 1 or December 31.

24. These issues are also described in the chapter on the property taxation of the tangible personal property of utilities.

25. The problems associated with the discovery of personal property have prompted the recommendation that it be removed from the property tax base. See Aaron (1975).

26. All new firms owning business personalty, and liable for taxes, owe taxes from the time the business starts to function. They must file the personal property tax form (Form 945-NT) within 90 days of incorporation. The taxes for firms operating less than a full tax year are prorated for the period of time they have been in operation.

27. The Audit Function can also be used to identify firms. This portion of the audit function will be discussed in the section dealing with property tax audits.

28. Even in situations in which the firm is exempt from the tangible personal property tax because of size, there is still an incentive to identify all taxpayers. The next section discusses the provision of the Ohio Law to reimburse taxing jurisdictions for exemptions given for smaller firms.

29. The IAAO is a policy organization that focuses on the training and development of public appraisal officials. The IAAO certifies public appraisers and also develops appraisal standards to guide appraiser practices.

30. When private fee appraisers use the cost method they usually value personal property on the basis of reproduction or replacement cost and not historical cost. The difference is that fee appraisers are not doing mass appraisals and have more time and resources for each appraisal. See Watts (1989).

31. *Economic* and *functional obsolescence* are terms used in the appraisal profession. "Economic obsolescence" refers to obsolescence that occurs regardless of use. An example would be a computer rendered obsolete because of technological advances. "Functional obsolescence" refers to the actual wear associated with the use of machinery and equipment. See International Association of Assessing Officers (1990c).

32. Ohio could also increase the penalties for noncompliance.

33. Accurate appraisals for equipment should account for intensity of use, frequency of use and the maintenance performed on equipment.

34. The use of generalized appraisal techniques by which the personalty of an entire firm is valued is also practiced in private or fee appraisals. See Innacito (1989).

35. Numerous sources of data are available that calibrate the accuracy of the depreciation schedules. See Rice (1989).

36. Reports in the literature to update depreciation schedules for specific industries illustrate the difficulty and costs associated with personalty appraisal. See for example, Hobart and Platte (1994).

37. Trending by commercial fee appraisers is commonly used. See Watts (1989).

38. Real property is reappraised in Ohio on a six year cycle. Realty may also be factored every three years between reappraisal. Personalty is appraised every year but on a historical cost less adjustment for depreciation. The more frequent appraisal of personalty is based on a lower value base.

39. The cost of complying with a tax is labeled excess burden or dead-weight loss. See Buchanan and Flowers (1987).

40. Interviews with county auditors in Ohio.

41. As noted, placing personal property in the proper taxing jurisdiction is a major challenge. There are over 4000 districts in Ohio.

42. The determination of tax rates and the process of billing and collecting taxes is also discussed in Chapter 7 of this volume.

43. The serious compliance problems that can develop in a personal property tax system are illustrated in a case study of Harris County, Texas. Harris County Officials found a pattern of non compliance with the personal property tax, fostered by tax professionals. At the conclusion of a lengthy investigation, including the FBI, several appraisal firms and tax preparation firms were prohibited from further tax practice in Texas. The state and county also recovered over $20 million in under reported taxes. County officials concede that the problem was partially a result of administrative inattention to the tangible personal property tax. See Robinson (1992).

44. The Department of Taxation and the Division of Property Taxation have interpreted state law to require that all personal property valuation changes in excess of $500,000 file a special form. The reason for this form appears to be to inform local taxing jurisdictions of substantial reductions in assessed value. The legal requirements for the form are found in sections 5703.14 and 5711.131 of the *Ohio Revised Code.*

45. One criterion that will not be reviewed is political acceptability. The tangible personal property tax has not "enjoyed" strong political support from the business community. An interesting history of attempts to impose a tangible personal property tax in several cities in Canada is found in Levine (1990). The political unpopularity of the tangible personal business property tax is also demonstrated in the trade press in Ohio. See Hirschman (1994).

46. Comparing how a state treats a tax base relative to neighboring states is common in tax analysis. See DeBoer (1992).

47. Ohio imposed a tax on intangibles until the mid-1980s, when the tax rate was repealed.

48. Ohio exempted household furniture in 1931. See Advisory Commission on Intergovernmental Relations (1963).

49. The concern about cash flow and the personal property tax is also an issue with the real property tax.

50. See Chapter 9 in this volume for a discussion of enterprise zones.

51. Some tax consultants now advise clients to appeal personal property valuations because of the fundamental valuation problems associated with a mass appraisal system, such as the one used in Ohio. See Remsha (1992).

52. It has been argued, with no evidence, that the removal of tangible property from the tax base has helped the economic development of Pennsylvania and New Jersey. See Garippa and Davenport (1991).

53. The assertion that states without personal property taxes classify some personal property tax was made in a study conducted for The Ohio Council of Retail Merchants and the Ohio Automobile Dealers Association. See Levin and Driscoll (1993).

15 The Taxation of Telecommunications

Richard McHugh

INTRODUCTION

The field of telecommunications in this country has undergone a technological and legal transformation on a scale, and of a rapidity with which it would be difficult to find parallel. In the past ten years, telecommunications has evolved from an industry comprised of a few very large and regulated "monopolies" to one with many participants furiously competing with each other.

What makes this transformation of an industry interesting for tax policy has been the unique treatment of telecommunications (and other public utilities) in the United States tax system. Unlike other industries which may have experienced fundamental transformations, the telecommunications industry has traditionally been subject to separate forms of taxation, taxed "in lieu" of traditional taxes and often taxed at rates which are differentially high relative to normal industry. As a member of the species of industries classified as a "public utility", the rules of taxation for the telecommunications industry differed from other industries. Now, the changing character of the telecommunications industry calls into question the classification of the telecommunications industry as a traditional public utility and, consequently, its treatment of the industry as a part of this breed.

Not surprisingly, the systems of taxation imposed on this industry have been slow to respond to these changes, largely because of its hallowed place as a reliable source of revenue. However, the transition is underway in many states.

As the character of the industry begins to resemble that of a normal industry, the implications of public policy, including tax policy, for the industry have begun to be considered in this industry as in any other. The effects of the differential treatment of telecommunications were quite benign in the past. The tax liabilities of these regulated monopolies may have been high but they did not have substantive impacts on the returns to investment in, or operations of, these monopolies. Tax rate increases were easily and routinely passed forward to consumers—and in fact were effectively guaranteed to be passed forward to consumers through the rate of return regulation imposed on the industry. Changes in the tax system once barely budged the behavior of telecommunications providers.

Now, the terrain which underlies this system is changing . . . quaking. The problem is: the telecommunications industry doesn't mean just the "phone company" anymore. Now, there are other providers of telephone and telephone-type services. In short, there are alternatives to which the consumer can look. Consequently, tax increases cannot so cavalierly be passed forward to customers, and differential treatment of this sector can cause telecommunications firms to alter their behavior as they consider how their activities will affect the behavior of customers and "competitors."

The implications of these changes in market structure are, by themselves, cause for a re-thinking of the system of taxation. What makes the case for a serious consideration of the system of taxation more compelling and more urgent is the pace of technological change and the growing role of the telecommunications industry in economic growth and regional economic development. Many of the special provisions which apply to this industry under the existing system of taxation, particularly in a state like Ohio, can be deterrents to new investment. With the galloping pace of technological change and the induced obsolescence of existing telecommunications infrastructure, the need for new investment to maintain an adequate and "business-friendly" telecommunications system requires a tax system which is not a hindrance to expansion and the adoption of these new technologies.

All states have confronted, or will confront this public policy challenge. The state of Ohio finds itself, like other states, searching for a rational, internally consistent system to treat this sector. Unfortunately, the current system of taxation in the state of Ohio has become increasingly troublesome to the government and industry. The implementation of the current system of taxation carries with it a host of legal and administrative problems, and the incentives in the existing systems may not be conducive to growth in this increasingly important, key industry. The states across the country have begun to move forward on this issue. In the past few years, many states have substantively altered their method of taxing telecommunications firms.[1] There has been an explosion of changes in these methods of taxation of telecommunications. And, much like any other explosion, there are pieces flying in every direction. There are some consistencies in the changes, but there still does not appear to be any generally accepted or emerging paradigm on the appropriate method of taxation and no standard upon which we might perch to evaluate the "correct" manner to treat these firms.

Among the issues which should be addressed are: What is a telecommunications firm? Do the justifications for the special treatment of this industry still exist? How is telecommunications different from other traditional public utilities or franchise monopolies? How should a separate telecommunications tax treat firms which provide competitive services? How do we treat firms which provide their own telecommunications services as a part of their normal business? How should the tax system treat the alterative forms of telecommunications? How do you ensure equal protection of all providers of that service at a reasonable level of administrative and compliance costs? How does a state replace such a stable and reliable revenue source were the taxation of the telecommunications firms to be altered? What are the implications of this taxation for the equity of the tax system?

In the next section of this chapter, an overview of the history and current structure of taxation in the telecommunications market in the state will be provided. As a part of this discussion, the kinds of businesses and activities of those operating in this market will be described to help understand critical differences in the tax and regulatory treatment of these "actors" in the market. As a part of this section, the current tax structure and trends in the taxation of telecommunications in the state will be compared to that in other states.

In the third section, a discussion of the principles of taxation and an evaluation of the current Ohio structure will be presented. Following that, a more detailed analysis of the economic development implications of telecommunications taxation is provided, assessing past trends in the industry and the growing importance of the telecommunications infrastructure to the state's economy. In the fifth section, the revenue implications of alternative changes in the taxation of telecommunications will be provided. The sixth section overviews some of the other, smaller issues in the design of a telecommunications taxation structure, and the sales taxation of telecommunications in particular. The study concludes with a summary of important issues which have emerged in the taxation of this industry and the options available for reform.

THE CURRENT STATE TAX STRUCTURE

WHO ARE THE ACTORS?

To fully understand the system of taxation in Ohio, its strengths, weaknesses and potential for unequal and inefficient taxation of firms in this market, it is important to first understand who are the "actors" in the market.

As recently as fifteen years ago, the market consisted of the Bell System: AT&T and its affiliated local exchange companies. In 1983, Judge Harold Green, in his Modified Final Judgement, ordered the divestiture of the local exchange companies from AT&T. These local exchanges, the Regional Bell Operating Companies (RBOCs) provided the bulk of local services in the country, while AT&T provided long distance, or inter-exchange services.

Over the intervening years, there have been a variety of technological and market innovations which have permitted new types of businesses to encroach on this service-delivery structure. These new companies provide services which either directly compete with, or provide alternatives to the traditional telephone network.

Below, we provide a discussion of the types of businesses now operating in this market:

- *Local Exchange Companies (LECs).* The local exchange companies are those companies formally established after the divestiture of AT&T in 1983. Under the Modified Final Judgement, the national phone network was broken up into 22 Regional Bell Operating Companies, (RBOCs) and a number of other LECs which provide service to generally smaller rural areas (although there are other LECs which have grown and now serve larger markets, such as GTE and United Telecom.) The LECs primarily provide local or "intra-LATA"2 service through its switched network. The LECs can also provide intra-LATA toll calls. Finally, the LECs provide access to the local switching network for the long distance carriers (the interexchange carriers, or IXCs). There are currently 44 LECs operating in the State of Ohio.

- *Interexchange Carriers (IXCs).* IXCs are the long distance carriers, providing inter-LATA long-distance toll service. In addition, the IXCs can provide intra-LATA toll service, and thus compete with the LECs in this market. The largest of the IXCs is AT&T, which since the elimination of its monopoly on the service, has had its market share of long distance calls drop to 60 percent nationally. Other IXCs operating in the State of Ohio include Sprint/United, MCI and LCI. Currently, there are 68 IXCs operating within Ohio.

  The LECs and the IXCs provide the framework for the bulk of telecommunications services in the nation. However, there are a number of other providers of telecommunications operating in the market or which provide services which compete, or will soon compete, with the LECs and the IXCs.

One such operator is the "Reseller". The resellers are essentially wholesalers of long distance access. A reseller will purchase access to lines, from an IXC, and will re-sell this access to consumers, typically at lower rates. The resellers are often referred to as non-facilities based carriers, and can sell at lower rates since they do not need to maintain the types and quantities of facilities which an IXC or a LEC would.

- *Competitive Access Providers (CAPS).* Most household and businesses gain access to their long distance carrier from their homes or businesses through the LEC in their area. However, there is a growing number of providers of access to the long-distance carriers which "by-pass" the LEC. These firms provide their own telephonic infrastructure (lay their own lines) and link users through their own switching equipment and connect to an IXC. A CAP allows users to access an IXC while avoiding the "access charges" which IXCs must pay the LECs. These CAPS typically target high-volume users (central cities or individual communications-intensive firms).
- *Cellular companies.* Cellular companies also provide telecommunications services, partially or totally by-passing the local switched network through the use of microwave transmission. This technology allows the user the benefits of mobility, but at a higher cost for the service. Cellular companies can carry messages locally and can also provide long distance services by connecting directly to the long distance carriers (IXCs).
- *Paging systems.* The paging systems traditionally provided one-way message delivery between individuals. More recently, the technology has been developed which would allow the recipient of a message to send a response to the page. With this capacity, the paging systems become more akin to a telecommunications service, although not providing voice communication.

In addition, there are a number of potential players in the telecommunications market which have not yet strictly entered the market for telecommunications services but who may soon enter and for whom the current system of taxation is of relevance.

- *Cable companies.* Cable companies traditionally provided one-way delivery of TV signals. However, the cable which carries one-way signals, voice and video signals also now has the capacity to provide two-way, interactive signals—voice, picture and message. They will have the capability of providing telecommunications services identical to that provided in the existing phone system. The limiting factor, at this point, between the provision of one-way and two-way communications is the customer on-premise equipment to transmit the voice messages. These cable companies already have expressed their intent to provide these services in the near future, through a filing with the Public Utilities Commission of Ohio (PUCO). PUCO recently gave permission to a major cable company to wire a large portion of the state for telecommunications services.

- *Personal Communications Services (PCS).* This emerging alternative to traditional local-service provides microwave-based telecommunications services in local areas. PCS offers dial tone service to lightweight pocket phones with individual telephone numbers which can be used without the need to access of the local switched network. Although not in use at this time, the potential is great for penetration into the local telecommunications market in the next year or two.

A Brief History of Telecommunication Taxation in Ohio

The current system of telecommunications taxation in Ohio evolved along the same lines as the taxation of other public utilities, such as electric and natural gas.

Since telecommunications has traditionally been considered a public utility, this sector had been subject to the same taxes as any other public utility. The principal state tax on these public utilities, including all telecommunications firms, is the public utility excise tax, which is a percentage levy on the gross receipts of public utilities.[3]

At the local level, public utilities pay the real and personal property tax. The base of the tax is the assessed value of property, equal to the market value times the appropriate "listing rate". In Ohio, the listing rate is 35 percent for real property and 25 percent for personal property of other private companies. However, public utilities are subject to a higher 88 percent listing rate for personal property. The justifications for the differential treatment of public utilities has been that the utilities have been granted a franchise monopoly and are also given access to public right-of-way to lay their lines.

With the divestiture of the Regional Bell Operating Companies and the advent of new telecommunications technologies, the market changed, particularly for long distance services. The long distance market has become quite competitive. Given the increasingly competitive nature of this market and in recognition of the fact that the long distance market no longer represented a traditional franchise monopoly, in 1987 the State of Ohio passed a law (HB 171) exempting interexchange carriers from the Public Utilities Excise Tax (the gross receipts tax). The State began treating the IXCs as a regular business and subjected them to the Corporate Franchise Tax. With that legislation, the long distance phone charges also were subject to the state and local sales and use tax.

Although the motivation for the change in the treatment of the IXCs was to treat them like a general business, the law did not *fully* change its tax treatment. These firms continued to be treated as a public utility under the personal property tax, subjected them to the public utilities 88 percent listing rate largely because of the concerns for the revenues.[4]

The public utility excise tax has also changed since 1987. In 1991, the access charges received by the LECs from the IXCs were exempted from taxation. Also, two credits were created for the public utility excise tax. First, in 1985, a provision was created allowing for a credit equal to the startup costs of an emergency service telephone system (a "911" system). Finally, effective January 1991, local telephone companies were required to set up a lifeline program for low-income elderly, and the hard of hearing, the expenses of which can be taken as a credit against gross receipts taxes by the local exchange companies.

A significant and ongoing issue in the taxation of telecommunications in Ohio surrounds a suit filed by MCI in 1989. MCI claimed that it had been denied equal protection under the personal property tax law since its personal property was taxed at the higher 88 percent of market value, while its competitors, for example resellers in the long distance market, were taxed at 31 percent of value. In February 1994, the Ohio State Supreme Court issued its decision in the case, stating that MCI should have filed as a general business and, hence, its listing rate should have been that applicable to general business at the time.

The Current Structure Telecommunications Taxation by Type of Company

The current tax structure as it exists in Ohio and the way that it treats different actors in the telecommunications market is presented in Table 15-1. Here, we list each of the taxes to which these firms may be subject and each of the types of firms we have identified. In the first row, we show the tax treatment of the LECs, while in the second row we show the tax treatment of a private business. The remaining rows show the variations in the tax treatment of alternative telecommunications service providers.

Clearly, there is much diversity in how these firms are treated. However, there are a few general principles which help guide in understanding the structure of this table. The first is the distinction between the treatment of public utilities and private businesses, found in the first two rows. As a public utility, the LECs are subject to the gross receipts tax, but not the corpo-

TABLE 15-1
Tax Treatment of Telecommunications Services

	Sales Tax on Services Provided	Corporate Franchise Tax	Gross Receipts Tax	Property Tax Assessed at 88 Percent	Municipal Income Tax
Local Telephone	NO	NO	YES	YES	NO
Private Business	?	YES	NO	NO	YES
Interexchange Companies	YES	YES	NO	YES	YES
Cellular	YES	YES	NO	YES	YES
Private Communication (CAPS Paging)	NO	YES	NO	YES?	YES
Cable TV	NO	YES	NO	NO	YES
Resellers	?	YES	NO	YES?	YES

Source: Compiled by the author.

rate franchise tax nor the sales tax on their services. In addition, as a public utility, the LECs are subject to the tangible personal property tax at the 88 percent listing rate. Private businesses are subject to both the corporate franchise tax and the general sales tax, (should their goods or services be defined as taxable,) but not to the gross receipts tax. Private businesses are not subject to the 88 percent listing rate.

Second, any company which is subject to the gross receipts tax will not have its services subject to the general sales tax.

Third, any company subject to the state corporate franchise tax will also be subject to the municipal income tax.

With these three general principles, the rationale for the system of taxation currently in place can be evaluated. First, the local telephone companies LECs are currently the only ones in the industry still strictly defined and fully treated as a public utility (i.e., subject to the gross receipts tax and the higher personal property tax listing rate.)

The interexchange and the cellular companies, since 1987, have not been subject to gross receipts tax but have been treated as a private company paying the Franchise Tax and a Sales Tax. However, a comparison of lines two with lines three and four shows the inconsistency in the treatment of private business and that of the IXCs and cellular. Specifically, these telecommunications firms can be subject to the 88 percent listing rate, unlike a true private business.

Third, the private communications firms, like the CAPS and paging systems, are generally treated much as this hybrid private business/telecommunications firm. However, there are two gray areas. First, the services provided by the CAPS are not subject to the sales tax on their services. Second, the CAPS and ALTS, strictly speaking, are subjected to the higher 88 percent listing rate for tangible personal property. However, there is some question as to the precise definitions of what legally constitutes a telecommunications firm and whether CAPS and paging systems fit under this definition. Also, the ability of the Department of Taxation to accurately identify all of these firms and subject them to the higher personal property tax is not a certainty. It is only very recently that the Department has become aggressive in identifying and taxing these firms as telecommunications firms. The administrative difficulties and legal problems in levying this tax lead one to speculate as to whether *all* firms of this type are universally and consistently subject to some type of taxation. Hence, the question mark in this box.

Fourth, cable television is not subject to the sales tax nor the state gross receipts tax although they are subject to local franchise taxes. As cable companies do not provide two-way service at this point, under Ohio law they are not classified as a telecommunications firm, and they are not subject to the 88 percent listing rate. However, once two-way telecommunications become possible, cable companies would technically become subject to the higher listing rate.

In summation, the State of Ohio continues to treat its LECs as it has for years, as a regulated franchise monopoly, not subject to the Corporate Franchise Tax but instead subject to a gross receipts tax. The State's general sales tax is not levied on local telecommunications services. The LECs are also levied a personal property tax with a differentially high listing rate of 88 percent versus 25 percent for private businesses. The interexchange companies, cellular companies and other actors in the industry are subject to the corporate franchise tax, have their sales subject to the general sales tax, and also pay the differentially higher personal property tax listing rate.

How Ohio's Telecommunications Tax Structure Differs From Other States

How does the State's tax system treatment of telecommunication firms compare to that of the other states? There are two sources of information on the methods of taxation used by other states: a recent survey of thirty-one states performed by the State of Ohio Department of Taxation, and a 1990 survey performed by Karl Case.[5] The Ohio Department of Taxation's survey obtained information on the structure of their tax system's treatment of telecommunications firms. The 31 states in the survey include neighboring states and states which Ohio considers as competitors in economic development.

There are three types of general state taxes to which a LEC may be liable to pay: a gross receipts tax (public utility excise tax), a corporate income (franchise) tax, and a sales tax. Some states very aggressively tax the LECs. In eight states, each of the three taxes is levied (Table 15-2).

The combination of taxes which is most frequently used is that which treats the LECs most like a private corporation; that is, they are subject to a corporate income tax and their output is taxed under the general sales tax. Two states only tax the LECs under the corporation income tax with no taxation of sales: Colorado and Oregon. The state of Oregon has no general sales tax so, in effect, this state also treats its LECs as any other a private business in the state.

Five states tax the LECs under both a gross receipts and a corporate income tax, while four tax the LECs under a gross receipts tax and a sales tax.

TABLE 15-2
Configuration of State Taxes of Local Exchange Companies

Corporate Income, Sales Tax, Gross Receipts:	
Florida	Pennsylvania
Kentucky	South Carolina
Illinois	Texas
North Carolina	Wisconsin
Corporate Income, Gross Receipts:	
California	Virginia
Delaware	West Virginia
Sales Tax, Gross Receipts:	
Maryland	New Jersey
Massachusetts	New York
Corporate Income, Sales Tax:	
Connecticut	Minnesota
Indiana	Missouri
Iowa	Nebraska
Georgia	Oklahoma
Kansas	Tennessee
Michigan	Washington
Corporate Income:	
Colorado	Oregon
Gross Receipts:	
Ohio	

Source: Ohio Department of Taxation.

Ohio is indeed unique. It is the only state among the 31 sampled states which only subject the LECs to one of the state taxes, the gross receipts tax.

Most states also subject telecommunications services to sales taxes. Of the 31 states, 26 subject some or all of telecommunications services to the general sales tax. Of these states, 22 tax both local services and long distance services. Two states, including Ohio, tax long distance services but not local services. Three, on the other hand, tax local service only, while exempting long distance services. Five states tax neither local nor long distance services. Of these five, Delaware and Oregon, do not have a state general sales tax at all (Table 15-3).

Telecommunications firms are also subject to local taxes. In all states, real property is subject to the property tax. In twelve states, the personal property tax is not levied on telecommunications firms. In eleven others, the personal property tax is levied at a higher rate than on normal businesses through the imposition of higher assessment (listing) rates. Ohio falls into this latter group (Table 15-4).

TABLE 15-3
Sales Taxation of Local Exchanges and Interexchange Carriers

Both Taxed:			
Connecticut Florida Illinois Indiana Kansas	Kentucky* Maryland Massachusetts Michigan Minnesota	Missouri Nebraska* New Jersey New York* North Carolina Oklahoma	Pennsylvania Tennessee Texas Washington Wisconsin
Interchange Only:			
Colorado Ohio			
Local Exchange Only:			
Georgia Iowa South Carolina			
Neither Taxed:			
California Delaware (No General State Tax) Oregon (No General State Tax) Virginia West Virginia			

Source: Ohio Department of Taxation.

TABLE 15-4
Assessment Levels of Real Property and Tangible Personal Property, 1992

	Levels as a Percentage of Market Value			
	Commercial/Industrial		Telecommunications Utility	
	Real	Property	Real	Property
Ohio*	35%	25%	35%	88%
Indiana*	33 1/3	33 1/3	33 1/3	33 1/3
Kentucky	100	100	100	100
Michigan*	50	50	50	50
Pennsylvania*	Max 100	X	Max 100	X
West Virginia*	60	60	60	60
Alabama*	20	20	30	30
Alaska	100	100	100	100
Arizona*	25	25	30	30
Arkansas*	20	20	20	20
California*	100	100	100	100
Colorado*	29	29	29	29
Connecticut*	70	70	X	X
Delaware	60	X	60	X
District of Columbia*	100	100	100	X
Florida*	100	100	Local	Local
Georgia	40	40	40	40
Hawaii*	100	X	100	X
Idaho*	100	100	100	100
Illinois*	33 1/3	X	33 1/3	X
Iowa	100	X	100	X
Kansas*	25	25	33	33
Louisiana*	15	15	10.25	25
Maine*	100	100	100	X
Maryland*	100	100	100	100
Massachusetts*	100	100	100	100
Minnesota*	3.1/4.75	X	4.75	X
Mississippi	15	15	30	30
Missouri*	32	33 1/3	32	33 1/3
Montana*	3.86	Max 9	12	12
Nebraska*	100	100	100	100
Nevada	35	35	35	35
New Hampshire*	100	X	X	X
New Jersey	100	50	100	50
New Mexico	33 1/3	33 1/3	33 1/3	33 1/3
New York	100	X	100	X
North Carolina	100	100	100	100
North Dakota*	10	X	10	10
Oklahoma*	11-14	10-20	24	24
Oregon	100	100	100	100
Rhode Island	100	100	100	100
South Carolina*	6	10.5	10.5	10.5
South Dakota*	100	X	100	100
Tennessee*	40	30	55	55
Texas	100	100	100	100
Utah*	95	100	100	100
Vermont*	1	1	1	1
Virginia*	100	100	100	100
Washington	100	100	100	100
Wisconsin*	100	100	X	X
Wyoming*	11.5	11.5	11.5	11.5

Source: Advisory Commission on Intergovernmental Relations, *Significant Features of Fiscal Federalism, 1993*.

MV - market value
X - exempt

[1] By assessment level unless otherwise noted.

One way to compare the degree of the difference in the taxation of telecommunications personal property relative to that of a regular business is to compare the ratios of the assessment or listing rates for the two types of businesses. Here, the degree of the difference in Ohio is seen more plainly. Of the twelve states which make the distinction in their personal property taxation, two do not tax commercial/industrial property but do tax telecommunications property. Of the remaining ten, differential in the assessment the ratio in the State of Ohio is significantly higher than in all others. The ratio in Ohio is 3.52, while that same ratio in the remainder of the states having a differential in assessment ratios is typically below 2.00 (Table 15-5).

AGGREGATE COLLECTIONS FROM TELECOMMUNICATIONS FIRMS

A tax system will differ among states, not only on the basis of its structure, but also on the level of collections. A logical question to ask is: What are the

TABLE 15-5
Assessment Rates on Telecommunications and Commercial/Industrial Personal Property

	Commercial/Industrial	Telecommunications	Ratio
Ohio	25%	88%	3.52
Alabama	20%	30%	1.50
Arizona	25%	30%	1.20
Kansas	25%	33%	1.33
Louisiana	15%	25%	1.40
Mississippi	15%	30%	2.00
Montana	9%	12%	1.33
North Dakota	X	10%	*
Oklahoma	10%-20%	24%	1.20-2.40
South Dakota	X	100%	*
Tennessee	30%	55%	1.83
Wisconsin	100%	X	0.00

Source: Advisory Commission on Intergovernmental Relations, *Significant Features of Fiscal Federation, 1993*; Policy Research Center, Georgia State University.

X-exempt

*Cannot be calculated.

differences in total tax collections from the taxation of telecommunications firms in the State of Ohio versus other states?

In Figure 15-1, from the work of Karl Case, the total amount of taxes paid as a proportion of total receipts of telecommunications firms in the two separate years, 1984 and 1990, are shown.

In 1984, and again in 1990, the state of Ohio was ranked sixteenth highest of the 50 states plus Washington D.C. with respect to total telecommunications taxes paid relative to operating revenues of the firms. When compared to its surrounding states, Ohio has had a higher ratio of taxes to operating revenues than any of its neighbors. Perhaps more significantly, the difference between Ohio and its neighboring states has widened considerably over these years. In 1984, the average rate of state and local tax collection to operating revenues was 9.5 percent in Ohio versus an average of eight percent in the surrounding states, an 18 percent difference in the ratio. By 1990, the tax collection ratio had grown to 10.0 percent in Ohio while falling to an average of 7.1 percent in the surrounding states. The divergence between the tax ratios in Ohio to that in the neighboring states had grown to 41 percent. In summation, although Ohio does not subject its telecommunications firms to as wide a variety of taxes as other states, it takes a greater than average proportion of the revenues of the firms in taxes than do most other states and all bordering states.

The reason for this high rate of collections is not the breadth of taxes but the relatively high nominal rate of taxation on telecommunications firms.

In Table 15-6, the gross receipts tax rate for the eighteen states currently imposing this tax on telecommunications firms is shown. Ohio ranks seventh with its 4.75 percent rate. On closer inspection, however, it can be seen that this ranking is artificially low. Two states with higher rates, Oregon and South Dakota, impose the tax only on rural phone companies, and compa-

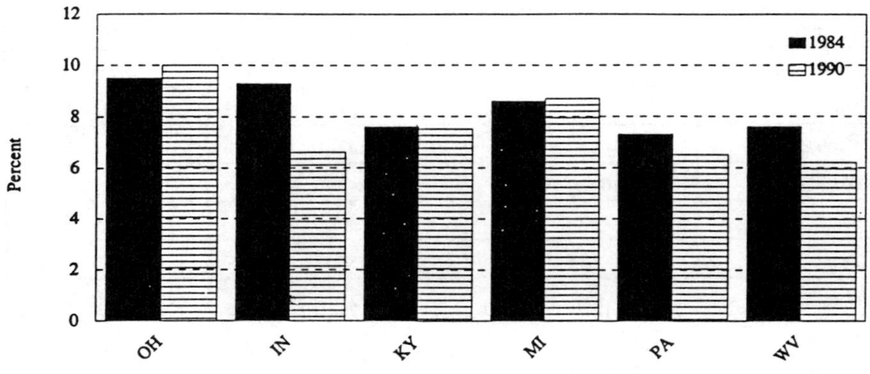

Source: Case (1992)

FIGURE 15-1. Telecommunications taxes as percent of operating revenue for Ohio and surrounding states.

TABLE 15-6
Gross Receipts Tax Rates

Washington, D.C.	9.70%	
Wisconsin	7.80%	(To be Repealed in 1996)
New Jersey	6.25%	
Oregon	6.00%	(Rural Phone Companies)
Rhode Island	6.00%	(Decrease to 5% in 1997)
South Dakota	2.00-5.00%	(Rural Phone Companies)
Ohio	4.75%	
Pennsylvania	4.40%	
West Virginia	4.00%	
New York	3.50%	
North Carolina	3.22%	
Florida	2.50%	
Alabama	2.50%	
Maryland	2.00%	
Montana	1.80%	
Indiana	1.20%	
South Carolina	0.30%	

Source: Case (1992).

nies can elect to pay the gross receipts tax in lieu of the local property tax. In terms of whether the state is and will continue to be out of line with the remainder of the country, two of the other states which have a higher gross receipts tax are now scheduled to reduce or eliminate the tax entirely in the near future.[6]

The relatively high rates of taxation on property are best exhibited in the information in Table 15-7. For this table, the effective personal property tax rate on a hypothetical investment has been calculated for telecommunications firms in Ohio, surrounding states, and several of its competitor states. The hypothetical investment is taken to be one with a usable life of ten years (for example, investment in central office equipment), and is depreciated in accordance with the property tax depreciation schedules for telecommunications firms in the state of Ohio. Given the listing rate in each of the states and the average nominal local millage rates in these states as reported by Levin and Driscoll[7], we are able to calculate the lifetime effective tax rates

TABLE 15-7
Personal Property Tax Rates on Investment in Telecommunications: Ohio and Selected States

Ohio	23.08%
California	4.40%
Florida	8.69%
Illinois	0.00%
Indiana	11.25%
Kentucky	6.18%
Massachusetts	6.87%
Michigan	11.89%
New Jersey	5.63%
New York	0.00%
Pennsylvania	0.00%
Texas	8.91%
West Virginia	8.26%

Source: Calculated by the author.

(discounted tax payments as a share of initial cost) from the personal property tax in each of these states.[8]

The very high rates imposed in the state of Ohio are evident. In Ohio, the effective personal property tax rate over the ten-year period is 23.08 percent, more than twice as high as any other state in the sample except for Michigan, which is just barely under one half as high as that imposed in the state of Ohio. Here, again, we see that the high rates of taxation on the telecommunications industry in the state of Ohio is not the result of a large number of taxes, but rather is a result of the high rates placed by the excise tax and by the personal property tax.

The high taxation on telecommunications can be attributed to the treatment of Ohio's telephone companies in a way which is different from other (non-utility) companies. In Figure 15-2, estimates of the amount of revenue which could be obtained from telephone companies, in particular the local exchange companies, in 1995 in a system which treats the LECs as a telephone company and as a private business are given. Here it can be seen that, as a result of its treatment as a telephone company, taxation in the utilities sector generates \$385 million in taxes, versus \$243 million were this sector to be treated as a non-utility. The big difference is primarily attributable to the personal property tax, where annual taxes are estimated to be \$273 mil-

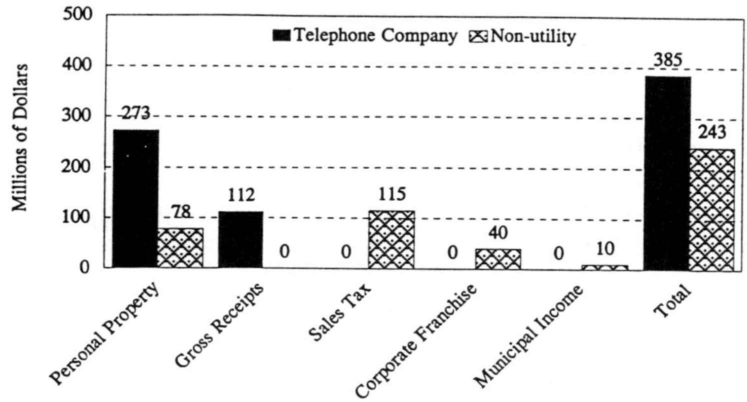

Source: Levin and Driscoll, *Telecommunications and Taxation in Ohio,* 1994; Ohio Department of Taxation

FIGURE 15-2. Estimated tax liability of Ohio Telephone companies in 1995 compared to estimated tax liability of the same companies taxed as non-utilities.

lion under the current regime, versus just $78 million were the companies to be treated as non-utilities. Under the current system, the local phone companies would pay approximately $112 million under the gross receipts tax, versus nothing were they to be taxed as businesses. Offsetting this non-revenue loss is the amount of sales tax revenues which would generate $115 million in state and local revenues.[9] The corporate franchise tax, currently not levied on telephone companies, would generate approximately $40 million in taxes were it placed on this sector.[10] An additional $10 million would be raised in the municipal income tax which on business, is the local version of the state's corporate franchise tax.

STRUCTURAL ISSUES REGARDING THE TAXATION OF TELECOMMUNICATIONS FIRMS

Although it is interesting and important to compare the treatment of an industry in one state relative to other (and competitor) states, the system itself should be subject to scrutiny relative to the standards set by the general principles of taxation.

The function of a tax system is, simply put, to raise revenue while imposing the least hardship or burden on the economy and those who are taxed. While the concepts of "hardship" or "burden" can be difficult to compare across different regions or systems, the general principle underlying these concepts is fairly easy. The system of taxation or revenue-raising should be one which does not unduly interfere with the economic behavior of individuals and institutions and one which does not unduly burden one or another segment of society or sector of the economy. People should be able to pay their taxes and otherwise go about their business as they would have in the absence of the tax. And individuals should be able to feel as though they are not unjustly singled-out to bear the burden of funding the public wheel. In short, the tax system should be efficient and equitable. In addition, the system should impose low costs in terms of administration and compliance, since these costs are also deadweight losses to the economy. Finally, the revenue system should be one which provides a stable and reliable source of revenue for the government since such a stable and reliable source of revenue ensures the delivery of needed public services with a minimum of changes in tax rates and rules.

In summation, a tax system should meet the following four criteria:

- Efficiency;
- Equity;
- Administrative ease; and
- Revenue adequacy and stability.

Each of these criteria, as they relate to the system of taxation in Ohio will discussed in turn.

Efficiency

The principle of efficiency, as it applies to taxation, is one which relates to the ways in which a tax system distorts the allocation of economic activity across goods and across regions. An efficient tax system would be one which treats separate goods or services in the same way so that it does not induce people to consume or producers to produce, certain goods simply on the basis of its tax treatment. If a perfectly operating market system allocates an economy's resources to the production and consumption of goods which lead to the greatest degree of welfare, then any system which distorts those decisions unnecessarily imposes a cost (an "excess burden") on the economy.

For example, a sales tax system which is efficient would tax all goods at the same rate so as to avoid making any good or service artificially more or less expensive relative to the other. A tax system which favored one particular good over another would cause the economy's resources to be used in ways that it would not have been used in the absence of the tax. Unless there is reason to believe that the market is not allocating resources efficiently in the absence of taxation, such a tax system would itself be inefficient.

The principle of efficiency in taxation is, in part, related to the popular concept of "the level playing field". Without "the level playing field", one sector or some businesses in a sector are treated differently than others. Higher taxes on a business causes them to artificially shrink either because of less consumer demand arising from tax-induced higher prices or a loss of investors owing to differentially higher taxation of returns to investment in the business.

In summation, by favoring one type of behavior of organization over another, the tax system would then induce behavior which was not determined by pure economic factor but, instead, was determined on the basis of artificial, tax-related, factors.[11]

In this regard, the current system of taxation of telecommunications in Ohio is inefficient in a number regards.

First, to the extent that the local exchange market has become competitive, the extraordinarily high tax rate on personal property in the State discriminates against investment in the local exchange market. Again, to the extent that the market is competitive, it is no longer a certainty that the LECs can blithely pass forward any and all tax increases to the customers. Consequently, extraordinarily high taxes can reduce the return to, and the desirability of, investment in the local network. As such, projects which would be economically justified on the basis of pure economic factors would be dissuaded by the tax treatment alone. This diversion of investment is a classic example of inefficiency in the tax system.

Second, to the extent that different "players" in the same market are treated differently, the tax system discriminates against one set of participants and induces inefficient allocation of an economy's resources. With regard to the Ohio tax system, the current imbalance in the treatment on the LEC's versus the cable companies; the IXC's versus the re-sellers and the LECs versus the CAPs (whether the inequity be "de jure" or "de facto") results in inequities which provides advantage to one sector over another or to one or another organizational structure versus another organizational structure.

Each of these "horizontal" inequities, and consequent inefficiencies, are attributable to the current tax treatment of tangible personal property in the current Ohio tax code.

First, it should be clear that the IXCs are currently operating in a competitive environment. As such, they must compete with other industries for investment funds. With the existing high tax rates on investment in this industry, it becomes *artificially* less profitable for firms to invest in this industry versus all other competitive firms. This is clearly an inefficiency, diverting capital funds from this market.

Second, to the extent that investment funds are demanded in the long-distance market and to the extent that the traditional relationship between the IXCs and the LECs (with access fees to the LECs for connection) is avoidable through the establishment of relationships which can "by-pass" this system, (e.g., CAPS, cellular), the tax system artificially grants a comparative advantage to activity in the "by-pass" market. Third, and most troublesome, is the evolving co-mingling of the services which are, or soon will be, offered by the LECs and the cable companies (and the PCS systems, the paging systems, etc.). By virtue of the current inequality in the treatment of investment in equipment which ultimately will provide similar service capabilities, differing only in the type of organization which makes the investment, the tax system is diverting resources from one type of organization to another.

Each of these represent textbook examples of the types of inefficiencies which can be brought about by a tax system. Although the arguments proceed about the degree and pace of advancement toward competition in this market, it is clear that the day will soon come when the distinctions between the service providers will disappear and the tax-related distinctions will cause inefficiencies.

Equity

The taxation of telecommunications in Ohio consists of two separate markets: the local market and the long-distance market. Each is confronted with two separate forms of taxation. The local market faces the gross receipts tax and the property tax. The long distance market faces the Corporate Franchise Tax, the sales tax and the property tax.

As in all forms of taxation, the incidence of the tax is ultimately determined by the ability of the taxed entity to pass the tax elsewhere. When a tax is placed upon a business, their response will be to protect their net rate of return by passing the tax forward in prices. Their ability to do this will be determined by the willingness of the consumers of these services, households or businesses, to pay the additional price. The willingness of the consumers to pay the additional price is measured by the price elasticity of demand for the good. If the quantity of the good or service demanded does not change in response to the higher price, then the demand is price inelastic and the firm can easily shift the burden of the taxes forward with no impact on the rate of return to investment in the industry. If demand is more price elastic, then consumers will adjust their buying habits in response to the tax-induced price increase, spending more on alternative means of communication, for example, or simply reducing the amount of telecommunications services they purchase. In this case, prices cannot increase by the full amount of the tax. To protect the rate of return to investment in this industry, the tax will be passed elsewhere, for example, to employees in the industry in the form of lower wages.

As indicated, there are two distinct and legally separated markets in the telecommunications industry: the local market and the long-distance market. In the case of local service, there are two taxes: the gross receipts tax and the personal property tax. To assess the incidence of these taxes, one should first consider the unique market of local telecommunications. Pricing and rates of return in the market are controlled by rate of return regulation. The Public Utility Commission of Ohio (PUCO) sets allowable rates of return in this industry. If taxes are increased, PUCO will permit the LECs to increase their prices to recover the higher taxes they pay. Since the demand for these local services by consumers has generally agreed to be price inelastic[12], the consumer bears the burden of the tax. Also, since at this point, there are few, if any, alternatives to the local network for households, the inability of household to choose alternative service providers insures that they will bear the ultimate burden of any tax change.

Businesses also pay for local service and can respond to changing prices for this service.

The price sensitivity is also low for businesses. As a result, it is still quite easy for the local exchange companies to pass forward taxes to consumers, whether they be households or businesses.

In the long distance market, we have a situation of more competitors and more price sensitive demand.[13] We also have a market which is subject to a different set of taxes: the corporate franchise tax, the sales tax and the property tax. With the price sensitivity and availability of alternative providers which can provide a service while locating much of its property and labor force out of the state, there is a strong potential for burden to be borne by the immobile factors within the state of Ohio. As consumers shift to long distance providers who can offer services at lower rates because of lower taxes, the telecommunications firms in the taxing state find that it is difficult to pass their own taxes forward to consumers and businesses. The telecommunications firms in the state would find that there is downward pressure on their net rate of return. The firms would then pass the residual burden to workers in the industry or the level of investment in the industry in the state will decrease, passing the burden further to other immobile factors in the state, such as land owners.

In summation, the burden of local service is largely borne by consumers. Households bear it in the higher price they pay for local service and businesses pay the higher price for service and subsequently attempt to pass on the cost to consumers of the goods or services which they provide. The long distance market is somewhat different in that higher state taxes do not affect all providers of long distance services in the state equally. In the case of the personal property tax and the corporation franchise tax, higher rates will only affect the cost of providing long distance service to the extent that the provider has personal property, employment and sales in the state. If a long distance provider can operate in Ohio with little physical presence, then an increase in personal property or corporate franchise tax rates will put them in a favorable position relative to alternative providers who do have a large physical presence. The firm with more employment and investment in the state will be less than fully able to pass the higher rates forward in taxes and the burden will be borne by local workers in the region or other immobile factors.

Administrative Ease

Administration requires the identification of local taxpayers and collection and auditing of tax collectors. All taxes require administration. In the field of telecommunications, the task is complicated by the fact that firms that are in this industry are difficult to define and identify. What constitutes a "telecommunications" firm can be a matter of interpretation, both technologically and legally.

This leads to much conflict between taxpayers and tax filers regarding their precise tax status. The conflicts ultimately involve a significant amount of staff and legal time on behalf of both the taxpayers and the Department of Taxation. For example, in the MCI case, the company alleged, and the Ohio Supreme Court found, that MCI was being treated differently, for tax purposes, than other firms providing similar services. This case, and the attempts to insure equal treatment of similar providers, represented a significant legal and administrative cost to the state and MCI. The response by the state, to identify all firms providing telecommunications services and taxes them as such, will engender future administrative and legal expenses, as the state attempts to demonstrate that firms are "telecommunications" firms and the firms attempt to demonstrate that they are not.

Take the case of the competitive access providers (CAPs). It may be argued that some of these providers do not strictly provide dial-tone service. Also, do paging companies strictly fall under the definition of a telecommunications firm? Does a large insurance company, or a retail firms which provides its own internal communications or access to the LXCs, fall under the definitions of a telecommunications company since they engage in the kinds of activities which are described in the law?

Finally, take the case of the cable industry. At this time, they are not categorized, or treated as, a telecommunications industry. Hence, investment in personal property which is currently made by the cable companies is taxed at the 25 percent listing rate. However, at the point that the cable companies begin to offer two-way telecommunications services and dial-tone service, then the property will become subject to the higher listing rate of 88 percent.

The task of administration is complicated by the fact that many firms operating in the industry provide more than telecommunications services. Again, consider a cable company. Once it provides the two-way voice communications, it will be doing so using the same equipment and personal property with which it is using to provide one-way video services. Should the entire company be subject to the higher listing rate of the telecommunications firms? If not, how should the Department of Taxation allocate the personal property of the cable company between that which should be subject to the regular listing rate versus the public utilities listing rate? If it is only the portion of personal property which is dedicated to telecommunications, how will this property be fairly and separately assessed, particularly since the property which is used in the provision of cable services is frequently the same as that used in the provision of the telecommunications services. What about a paging company which sometimes provides one-way and sometimes provides two-way transmissions? What proportion of their personal property should be subject to private versus public utility listing rates?

These are examples of difficulties in interpretation which have occurred or will soon occur. Given the pace of technological change which is occurring in the industry, it is likely that other examples of telecommunications-like services will be offered by firms. The task of the state will be to identify these firms, subject them to taxation as a telecommunications firm, engage in a legal dispute with the company, at which point the laws will need to be re-written, either before or after legal challenge. This process will continue as long as innovation in the industry occurs. As long as a distinction in tax treatment remains between telecommunications firms and all other firms, the difficulties in administrating the tax system will remain, regardless of how high the quality of the tax administrators and the administrative process.

Revenue Adequacy And Stability

In this section we will briefly overview the revenue stability and growth of the two major taxes applied to the telecommunications firms: the public utilities excise tax and the personal property tax on telecommunications. There has been little research done on the issues of the stability of these two general types of taxes. In this case, we will rely on historical trends in the state of Ohio and draw whatever inferences we might on the stability and growth potential of this revenue source.

Turning to the public utilities excise tax, the tax base, rate, and liabilities under the public utilities excise tax since 1981 are shown in Table 15-8. Here it can be seen that, while growing at a fairly strong rate through the middle of 1980s, the revenues obtained from this tax have fallen quite sharply since the middle 1980s. The decrease has been due to two major changes in the

TABLE 15-8
Telephone Company Utility Excise Taxes: Tax Base, Rate, Liabilities, and Credits for Fiscal Years 1981 through 1993
(Dollar Amount in Thousands)

Tax Year	Tax Base	Rate	Liability	Credits
1981	$1,884,322	5.00%	$94,216	$0
1982	2,117,865	4.75%	99,829	0
1983	2,425,457	5.28%	128,003	0
1984	2,540,031	4.75%	120,651	0
1985	2,841,935	4.75%	134,992	0
1986	2,994,901	4.75%	142,258	0
1987	2,967,077	4.75%	138,006	2,930
Long distance companies exempt:				
1988	2,534,109	4.75%	112,159	8,211
1989	2,672,945	4.75%	117,311	9,665
Access charges exempt:				
1990	2,258,213	4.75%	103,701	4,564
1991	2,235,743	4.75%	104,195	2,003
1992	2,273,938	4.75%	105,846	2,167
1993	2,327,971	4.75%	105,489	5,088

Source: Ohio Department of Taxation.

law: the exemption of long distance companies from the base in 1987, and the exemption of access charges paid by long distance companies in 1989. The rate of tax has stayed basically constant since 1982, with only a temporary increase in the rate in 1983. Two other changes in laws which would affect collections were the introduction of two credits; the credit for non-recurring 911 expenses, and the lifeline program described earlier.

In Table 15-9, a serious deterioration in the *real* (inflation-adjusted) revenues obtained from this tax is shown quite clearly. The actual collections from this tax were deflated by the GDP deflator for state and local government services. The decrease in real revenues has been substantial, falling by over 42 percent, or at a 7.5 percent annual rate since 1986. Obviously, some

TABLE 15-9
Telephone Public Utility Excise Tax Collections:
(Thousands of Constant 1987 Dollars)

Year	Collections
1981	$126,847
1982	126,928
1983	153,022
1984	138,361
1985	147,573
1986	149,785
1987	140,679
1988	109,771
1989	110,151
1990	93,678
1991	90,290
1992	89,454
1993	86,662

Source: Calculated by the author.

of this decrease has been a result of the changes in the tax laws, however, real revenues have continued to decrease since 1990. Real revenues in 1993 were 8 percent below their 1990 levels.

From Table 15-10, part of the reason for this decrease in the real base, in spite of the growing use of telecommunications services, can be seen. This table contains information on nominal revenues and real revenues, and information on what is referred to as the "real base." The real base is the base of the gross receipts tax deflated by the consumer price index for local telephone charges. What has happened over the last several years has been that the growth in the price of local telephone services has been substantially below the growth in the price of all other goods and services. Looking again at tax collections in the 1990s, we can see that, although real revenues have fallen in the 1990s, the real base has actually increased. In sum, the growth in the base of the real gross receipts tax has not been particularly strong, in part because of the decrease in the relative price of telecommunications services.

Turning to the personal property tax of telecommunications firms, historical information on the value of personal property in telecommunications, the base of the personal property, is reported on Table 15-11. The base of the tax grew very strongly in the mid-1980s, when much of the activity and growth in competition in the long distance market occurred. However, in the 1990s, the growth in the personal property tax base of these telecommunications firms has been very weak. Information is available separately for local exchange and interexchanges only since 1990. Looking at this data, we can see that the weaknesses largely come from the local exchange companies, where the growth in personal property has been minimal. Combined,

TABLE 15-10
Nominal Revenues, Real Revenues, and Real Base of the Telephone Public Utilities Excise Tax (Thousands of Dollars)

Year	Nominal Revenues	Real Revenues[1]	Real Base[2]
1981	$94,216	$126,848	$2,324,454
1982	$99,829	$126,928	$2,340,182
1983	$128,003	$153,022	$2,477,484
1984	$120,651	$138,361	$2,276,013
1985	$134,992	$147,573	$2,360,411
1986	$142,258	$149,785	$2,256,896
1987	$138,006	$140,679	$2,129,990
1988	$112,159	$109,771	$1,793,424
1989	$117,311	$110,151	$1,824,535
1990	$103,701	$93,678	$1,512,533
1991	$104,195	$90,290	$1,453,724
1992	$105,846	$89,454	$1,460,461
1993	$105,489	$86,662	$1,488,472

Source: Calculated by the author; Ohio Department of Taxation.

[1]Deflated by GDP Deflator for State and Local Government Purchases.
[2]Deflated by CPI for Local Telephone Charges.

the rate of growth in the personal property tax base has not been fast enough to keep up with inflation. Over this time period from 1990 to 1993, a period in which there was a significant amount of telecommunications investment nationally, the real personal property tax base declined by nearly 2 percent.

Here again, apart from structural changes in tax laws, the bases of these two major telecommunications taxes, the gross receipts tax and the personal property tax, have not provided a particularly adequate stream of revenue.

It is important to keep in mind that this information is a short-term analysis based simply on trends in one particular state during one particular period of time. The data does not exist to support a more sophisticated analysis of the long-term growth potential of these revenue sources. However, there are a few relevant observations which could be made. First, a priori, we might expect that the base of the gross receipts tax would not be very income elastic. With technological innovations and impending competition pushing down the relative price of telephone services, the revenue raising ability of this base would not be expected to keep pace with many other goods whose prices move more closely with the general price level. Second, the level of the gross receipts base is largely determined by the number of customers

TABLE 15-11
Value of Personal Property in Telecommunications in Ohio

Year	Local Exchange	Interexchange	Total	Percent Change
1981			$2,624,030	
1982			$2,844,355	8.4%
1983			$2,970,608	4.4%
1984			$3,116,233	4.9%
1985			$3,123,797	0.2%
1986			$3,298,680	5.6%
1987			$3,583,493	8.6%
1988			$3,777,347	5.4%
1989			$4,014,611	6.3%
1990	$3,272,742	$815,302	$4,088,044	1.8%
1991	$3,413,658	$848,915	$4,262,573	4.3%
1992	$3,437,817	$873,274	$4,311,091	1.1%
1993	$3,486,240	$931,709	$4,417,949	2.5%

Source: Ohio Department of Taxation.

and not the level of actual usage. Since the population or the number of households grows more slowly than the level of income, the base would not be expected to grow in an elastic fashion.

With regard to the base of the personal property tax, the experience of the last few years, with a surprisingly slow growth in the base, could be attributable to several factors. First, it simply may be that these years were an aberration and that the short term performance of the tax base in this period is not reflective of the long-term growth potential. Alternatively, the slow growth of the base during this period may be an indication of the high degree of sensitivity of the tax base to the high tax rates on investment in the State of Ohio. With high sensitivity of investment to these tax rates, the base would grow very slow in an area where rates are high. It could, indeed, be the case that a higher growth in the base may result from lower tax rates.

Summary

This section provided an overview of the system of telecommunications taxation in the state of Ohio and how it stands up relative to the principles of appropriate taxation. There are two areas of concern: the inefficiencies of the differential treatment of telecommunications firms and the economic development implications of this treatment, and revenue adequacy implications of changing the mode of taxation. The tax system, as it now stands, introduces disincentives to investment and development in the industry. These disincentives arise primarily from the differentially high taxation of personal property in telecommunications.

The mechanism to offset these disincentives would be the treatment of the firms in the industry, from LEC on upward or downward, as a normal business. This would require a reduction in taxes applied to the telecommunications firms and a switch in the base from a gross receipts tax to a corporate franchise tax. This switch may bring with it a change in the revenue raising capacity and stability of the revenues obtained from this sector. The trade-off is between a tax system which is, on its face, less inhibitive toward investment and one which provides significant and stable revenue. Given that the trade-off is between the economic development implications of the industry (real or imagined) and the revenues to support public functions, these two elements of reform deserve special consideration. In the next two sections of this chapter, the economic development implications of differential taxation of telecommunications firms and the revenue implications of a change in the system are evaluated in more detail.

TELECOMMUNICATIONS TAXATION AND ECONOMIC DEVELOPMENT

How Taxation Can Affect Economic Development

The level and structure of telecommunication taxation differs across states. Because of these differences in taxation and because telecommunications firms can respond to differentials in tax structures and levels across states, decisions concerning telecommunications taxation will have important economic development implications.

For a normal business, the tax system may interfere with the process of economic development primarily by reducing the potential rate of return to a business's investment in a community. The case of an industry like telecommunications is somewhat different. To the extent that the *output* of telecommunications firms is also an *input* into the production of other firms, the tax treatment of telecommunications can have external and secondary economic development implications. Over the past few decades many firms have grown to require telecommunications services to design, produce and market their output. By discouraging investment in this intermediate output, the disincentive effects of a tax system to investment in the industry can have implications for the productivity of other industries and the desirability of investment by other firms in the region.

The line of argument on the economic consequences of telecommunications taxation is:

- How does activity in the telecommunications industry itself affect the regional economy?
- How does the tax system affect telecommunications industry investment and employment?
- How does telecommunications investment affect the overall regional economic development potential of a region?

There are three ways the particular tax structure may hinder economic development in Ohio. First, the provisions of the tax laws on telecommunications, in particular, the high tax on personal property on public utilities, may reduce the after tax rate of return on investment by these firms relative to other states. For some types of new infrastructure investment, these firms have the option of making the investment in other states while still satisfying the service demands of Ohio residents. In other words, for some kinds of investment, where the facility is located is transparent for the Ohio resident or business. This is particularly the case for the IXC's. The losses to the state in such cases are the reduced revenue from the personal property tax, and the loss in allocations of profits of multi-state companies to the states.[14] Second, to the extent that the construction and operation of facilities require workers (for example in the laying of fiber cable or the modernization of central office equipment), the state loses income tax revenue, general sales tax revenues, and the real property tax revenue associated with the property holdings on employees. The level of employment in the industry itself in the state may be adversely affected by differentially high taxation.

The third type of loss incurred by the disincentive to invest are those associated with the potential deterioration of the state's infrastructure (e.g. the inability to keep up with current and competing technologies). Since the quality of a region's telecommunications infrastructure has become an important determinant of a firm's location decisions, any disincentive from the tax system that deters or redirects this investment can adversely influence the development of other industries in the state.

While each of these claims are certainly true in principle, it is essential that we place some empirical meat on the conceptual skeleton of the economic development argument. There is little work in the professional literature upon which to directly rely to address this issue. However, a number of studies have been performed which address the relevance and importance of the industry to the state and its role in the development of new and existing industries.

The studies that do exist are of three types:

- studies which measure the general economic consequences of the telecommunications industry on overall state economic development;
- studies which measure the economic importance of the telecommunications in a particular state; and
- surveys of the views of those involved in the economic development process on the importance of telecommunications infrastructure to economic development.

None of these types of studies fully addresses the question at hand, but each lends some evidence which help us to determine the full economic consequences of telecommunications tax policy on economic development.

THE IMPORTANCE OF THE INDUSTRY TO THE STATE

The first type of study quantitatively links telecommunications use to improved economic performance nationally and at a regional level. Cronin (1994) has shown that, over the past thirty years, the productivity of the telecommunications industry itself has grown very rapidly. In addition, the reduced price and increased use of telecommunications has allowed other industries to substitute telecommunications for other factors of production and to enjoy increased productivity. Taking into account that the price of telecommunications services fell rapidly relative to the price of other factors of production leading to a substitution of it for other factors of production, Cronin estimated that, in 1991, a dollar of expenditures on telecommunications saved a typical firm $2.30 in expenditures on other factors of production. The implication is that increased expenditures on telephonic infrastructure in a region will permit increased telecommunications usage by local producers, increasing productivity and the competitive position of the state relative to other states and to the rest of the world.[15] These are the "end user" benefits of the expenditures on telecommunications.

There are also benefits which accrue in a region from the simple process of making the telecommunications investment expenditures. The construction of these facilities provide direct benefits to the economy.

Overall, the estimates by Cronin show a potential gain of an average of 4,440 jobs and $144 million for the period 1993 through 1999 as a result of projected telecommunications industry activity in the state. The benefits come both from the construction and employment impacts of the industry and the gains to other industries from improved productivity. The tax revenues from these generated income increases are estimated at $16 million per year.

This evidence shows the powerful and growing role of telecommunications in economic development. It does not, however, directly bear on the question at hand: the impact of tax policy on infrastructure investment in a particular region, and the subsequent impact on that region's economic development.

Regional Growth in Employment in The Telecommunications Industry

Another indicator of economic activity in telecommunications is the level of employment. If facilities are located elsewhere because of tax levels, these facilities will carry with them jobs. Although there are other factors which may have stronger influence on the determination of the location of telecommunications employment, it would be useful to gauge the extent to which the recent trends in telecommunications employment are related to tax treatment.

To address this issue, we have obtained information on the trends in the level of employment in this industry over the past eighteen years. The Bureau of Labor Statistics, through the Current Establishment Survey Program, provides information on employment in the Communications sector (SIC 48) at the state level.

The level of employment change in any industry will be influenced by many features, such as the overall growth rate in a region's economy. For sectors like telecommunications, whose output is sold to the general population and to businesses in the region, the level of employment will be strongly correlated with overall level of population and employment. What is most important and interesting, in terms of the analysis of trends in employment is the degree to which employment in the industry diverges from that which could be easily explained by the general trend in the regional economy; that is, the degree to which the state is gaining or losing a specialization in the industry.

One such measure of the importance of an industry to a region is the Location Quotient (LQ). The location quotient is measured as the percentage of total regional employment in an industry relative to that same proportion for the nation. This is a measure of the specialization of the industry for the state or region and the concentration of that industry's employment in the state.

An industry which has a location quotient greater than one means that there is a particular concentration of employment in that industry in a state. For example, in the industrial state of Michigan, the LQ for manufacturing was 1.45 in 1993, indicating that there is 45 percent more employment in manufacturing in Michigan, in terms of percentage of total employment, than in the typical state.

In the following Tables 15-12 and 15-13, the location quotient for employment in this sector for Ohio and surrounding states is compared to the change in this measure of concentration over two periods of time: 1976 to 1993 and 1984 to 1993. The first table provides the longest time-trend on this behavior over time while the second provides a shorter, although more directly a post-divestiture comparison of trends in employment. Also, information for more states is available for the shorter time-span.

In general, this analysis shows that the communications sector has become more regionally concentrated in the United States over time. This can be seen by examining where on this matrix the majority of the states appear. The bulk of the states, in both tables, appear on the upper left and the lower right cells. The states on this diagonal are either the states which have had a specialization in the communications sector (LQ greater then 1.0) and have become more specialized in the industry over time (a rising LQ), or alternatively have not had a particular specialization in the industry and their reliance on the industry declined further. In the longer term comparison (1976 to 1993), 16 of the 24 states appear on this diagonal. This attests to the growing regional concentration of employment in this sector. The bulk of the states on this diagonal are those which have not specialized in this sector and which show less specialization over time. The State of Ohio is among this group.

Looking at the shorter, "post-divestiture" 1984-93 period, we see that over two-thirds of all states appear on the diagonal, which again indicates increased regional concentration of employment. States which have had a specialization in employment in this industry have become more specialized

TABLE 15-12
Location Quotient for Telecommunications Employment, 1976 to 1993

	Location Quotient - 1993		
	Greater than 1.0	**Less than 1.0**	
Rising: 1976-1993	Georgia Maryland New Jersey Texas Virginia	Illinois Pennsylvania	
Declining: 1976-1993	California Florida Hawaii Nebraska New York North Dakota	Idaho Indiana Iowa Kentucky Michigan Minnesota	Mississippi New Mexico Ohio Oregon South Carolina

Source: Calculated by the author.

TABLE 15-13
Location Quotient for Telecommunications Employment, 1984 to 1993

	Location Quotient - 1993		
	Greater than 1.0	**Less than 1.0**	
Rising: 1984-1993	Colorado (1988) Georgia Maryland Missouri (1988) New Jersey North Dakota Texas Virginia West Virginia	Connecticut Delaware Illinois Massachusetts (1988) Pennsylvania South Carolina	
Declining: 1984-1993	Alaska (1987) California Florida Hawaii Nebraska New York	Idaho Indiana Iowa Kentucky Louisiana Michigan Minnesota Mississippi Montana (1988)	New Mexico Ohio Oklahoma (1988) Oregon South Dakota Utah (1988) Washington (1988) Wisconsin (1988) Wyoming (1988)

Source: Calculated by the author.

while those that do not have a concentration of employment in this industry have continued to see the importance of the industry in the state decline. Again, Ohio is seen to be in the group with little concentration and declining concentration of employment in this industry.

In Figure 15-3, the trend in the Ohio location quotient for communications employment over the past 18 years. The LQ has been consistently below one, indicating a lack of specialization in this industry in the State. This is reasonable, since none of the headquarters for the Baby Bells (RBOCs) is in the state. However, what is interesting about the trend in the index of specialization is the sharp drop in the most recent four years, indicating a deterioration of the presence of the industry in Ohio.

In Figure 15-4, the location quotients for employment in this industry over time for each of the states surrounding Ohio are shown. Two points should be made. First, for the majority of the states in this group, the trend is the same as in Ohio, with low LQs which fall off further in the most recent years. Clearly, it is difficult, on the basis of these trends to attribute the decline in the LQ to the Ohio tax structure since the forces which are driving down the LQ in Ohio are also apparently at work in the rest of the region. Second, however, there are two states whose level and trend deviate from

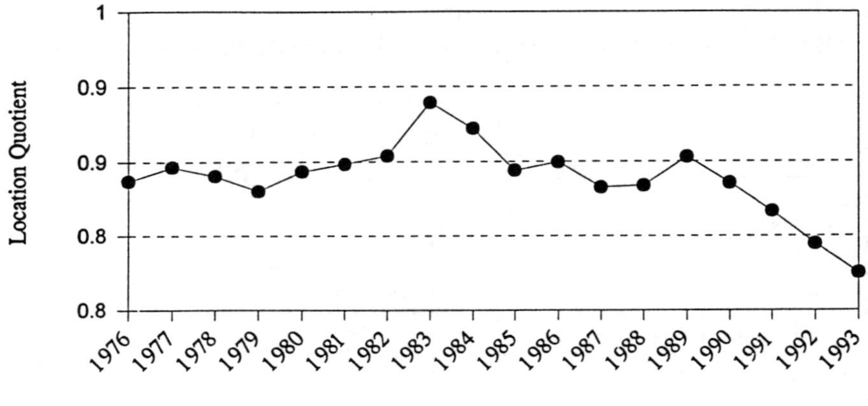

Source: Calculated by the author.

FIGURE 15-3. Location quotients for telecommunications employment for Ohio (1976–1993).

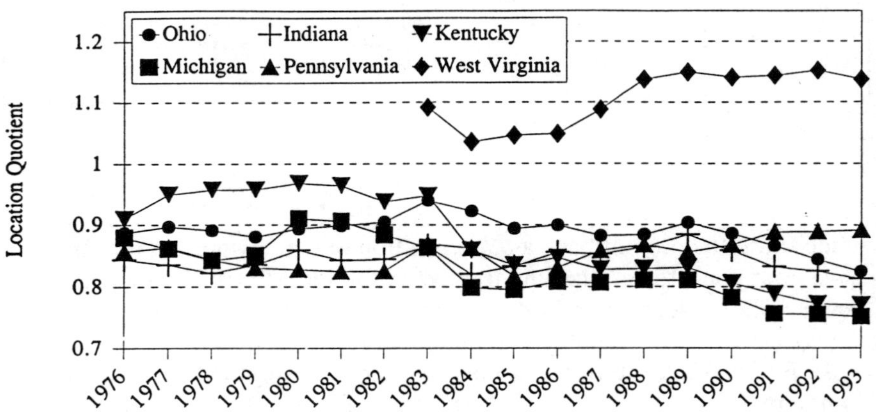

Source: Calculated by the author

FIGURE 15-4. Location quotients for telecommunications employment for Ohio and surrounding states (1976–1993).

the rest of the region. In Pennsylvania, the LQ has risen in the past few years. Recall that Pennsylvania is one of the states in the region which has no personal property tax on telecommunications. This does not provide any rigorous evidence, but it is worth noting. In West Virginia, where the LQ has been above 1.0 and rising, the aggregate state and local tax collection as a share of operating revenues (as calculated by Case (1992)) is ranked 43rd, indicating a very low comparative tax burden.

Any conclusion from this analysis, like the previous analysis, cannot be considered rigorously determined. Clearly, it is broader economic forces which are primarily driving the overall trends. But, in this limited analysis, an examination of the states in this region of the country which have deviated from this trend raises the possibility that tax levels and rates may not be benign when it comes to investment and employment trends.

How Does Telecommunications Infrastructure Affect Other Industries?

Perhaps the most important question relating to the economic development implications of infrastructure development is: what is the likely impact of telecommunications infrastructure on the location of industry in the United States.

One study which bears directly on this issue is one performed by Deloitte and Touche (1991), *New Jersey Telecommunications Infrastructure Study*. As a part of this study, two relevant surveys were performed, each of which addressed the issue of telecommunications infrastructure development and regional economic growth. The first survey was targeted at businesses involved in the location decision-making process, or which had recently made a relocation or site-selection decision. The second was a survey of the public utility commissions in the United States

In each of these surveys, questions were asked concerning the role which telecommunications infrastructure development currently plays, and may play in the future firm business location decisions and, by implication, the future economic health of a region.

Over 1,600 surveys were mailed to companies which had relocated in recent years. Since the study focused upon New Jersey, the mailings were targeted at firms which had relocated into New Jersey. However, of these 1,600 surveys, approximately 600 were sent to firms in other states. Among the questions which were asked was the extent to which these companies were becoming more telecommunications-intensive. Over 95 percent of the New Jersey firms and 85 percent of the responses from outside of New Jersey indicated that they had become more information-intensive.

A question was also asked concerning the extent to which the availability of technologically advanced telecommunications services was important to their company's ability of compete in the current business environment. As shown in Table 15-14 and Figure 15-5, the vast majority of those surveyed responded that these capabilities were either "Important" or "Critical" to their ability to compete.

TABLE 15-14
Proportion of Relocating Businesses Citing the Importance of Advanced Telecommunications Services to the Ability of Firms to be Competitive Currently and in the Future

	New Jersey Respondents	Other Respondents
Currently:		
Important	64%	52%
Critical	22%	26%
Future:		
Important	46%	47%
Critical	47%	38%

Source: Deloitte and Touche, *New Jersey Telecommunications Infrastructure Study*, Volume 3, Section VIII.

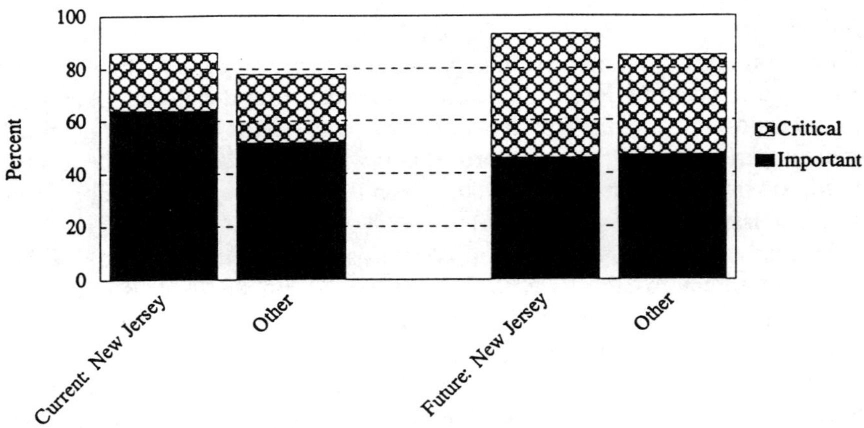

Source: Deloitte and Touche

FIGURE 15-5. Proportion of relocating businesses citing the importance of advanced telecommunications services to the ability of firms to be competitive currently and in the future.

Survey respondents were then asked the extent to which these capabilities would be important in the *future.* The responses provided further evidence of the potential growing importance. The responses even more strongly indicated that advanced telecommunications capabilities would be "Important" or "Critical" in the coming years.

Finally, firms were asked to rate the importance of 22 separate factors in their relocation decision. The respondents were asked to rate the importance of each factor to their relocation decision on a scale of 1 to 5, with a rating of 1 indicating that the factor was irrelevant to the location decision and 5 indicating it was very important. The ratings of these factors are given in Table 15-15.

The importance of telecommunications infrastructure is evident in these responses. Of the 22 factors, the availability of telecommunications services ranks seventh (fourth among the New Jersey respondents), above other factors which have traditionally been viewed as important to the location decision. For example, these services rank above the costs and availability of energy, the costs and availability of housing, and the proximity to suppliers, and just below a skilled labor force.

The second survey was sent to each of the fifty state public service commissions, 35 of which responded to the survey. Among the questions asked of these public service commissions were those pertaining to the importance of telecommunications and telecommunications infrastructure to the process of economic development.

Respondents were asked whether "the availability of a high-quality, technologically advanced, and reasonably priced telecommunications network was of equal importance with competitively priced energy services or low wage rates" in the business relocation decision. In this survey, 70 percent of the respondents (82 percent, when each commission's response was weighted by the proportion of total access lines which they represented), indicated that telecommunications services were just as important as energy and labor costs.

Respondents were then asked whether "telecommunications will play an even more important role regarding economic development in the future (i.e., next three to five years). Of the responses, 33 percent (24 percent on a weighted access line basis) indicated that telecommunications will play a "significantly increased role", while 55 percent (55 percent on a weighted access line basis) felt that telecommunications would play a "slightly increased" role. The regulatory agencies were also asked if they had been approached by a LEC with a request for customized service plans to specifically support economic development Twenty-seven percent (40 percent on a weighted access line basis) had already been approached with such a request, although the issue of telecommunications and economic development has only very recently become recognized as having some importance.

Finally, commissions were asked whether they would begin to compare the rate of telecommunications technology development relative to surrounding states in making regulatory rulings. Sixty-five percent (64 percent on a weighted access line basis) responded that they would. On the simpler question of whether they would now begin to simply monitor that rate of

TABLE 15-15
New Jersey Telecommunications Infrastructure Study Relocating Businesses
(Importance of Business Location Decision-Making Factors)

Factors	United States		New Jersey	
	Rating	Rank	Rating	Rank
Access to Major Airports	3.57	1	3.18	5
Availability of Land	2.60	14	2.85	10
Long-Term Financing	2.20	21	2.29	18
Skilled Labor Force	3.17	6	3.90	1
Availability of Telecommunications Services	**3.03**	**7**	**3.18**	**4**
Market Conditions	3.40	5	2.97	6
Cost of Land	2.77	9	2.59	15
Energy Availability and Costs	2.71	11	2.96	8
Environmental Regulations	2.34	20	2.74	11
Major Highway Access	3.53	3	3.86	2
Labor Costs	3.54	2	3.62	3
Strength of Labor Unions	2.52	18	2.67	12
Proximity to Major Markets	3.46	4	2.97	7
Proximity to Suppliers	2.77	10	2.59	13
Proximity to Technical Universities	2.18	22	2.13	20
Price of telecommunications Products or Services	**2.66**	**12**	**2.49**	**16**
Colleges and Universities in the Area	2.35	19	2.03	22
Cultural Opportunities	2.55	16	2.09	21
Housing Availability and Costs	2.88	8	2.59	14
Crime Rate	2.55	15	2.87	9
Rating of Public Schools	2.53	17	2.43	17
Recreational Opportunities	2.65	13	2.23	19

Source: Deloitte and Touche (1991).

technology deployment, ninety-one percent (95 percent on a weighted access line basis) indicated that they planned to begin such monitoring.

Telecommunications Industry And Regional Growth Prospects

One final way to evaluate the importance of the telecommunications industry to the future economic development of the state is to identify those industries which comprise the "telecommunications-intensive" industry and evaluate their expected performance in the future. These are the industries which would benefit most from the deployment of new technologies and where growth would be a function of the development of telecommunications infrastructure. It is those industries most likely to be drawn by adequate telecommunication infrastructure and whose economic success would be a function of this infrastructure development.

Based upon information on the cost structure of certain industries provided by the United States Department of Commerce's inter-industry (input-output) model, the top twenty-five telecommunications intensive industries have been identified.[16] These telecommunications-intensive industries are defined on the basis of their telecommunications as a share of total production expenses or costs. The economic outlook for this subset of industries was then compared to that for all other industries. Projections of employment and output growth, by industry, were obtained from the Bureau of Labor Statistics.[17]

As shown on Table 15-16, the projected rate of growth in employment in the telecommunications industry through the year 2005 is expected to be 0.2 percent per year. This compares unfavorably to the 1.2 percent per year rate of growth expected from all industries. The group of industries categorized as telecommunications-intensive are not expected to generate a tremendous amount of new jobs.

In addition to projecting the level of employment, the Bureau of Labor Statistics has also projected the level of output growth—the value of the output which these workers produce. The difference between the growth in output and the growth in employment is equivalent to the growth in the productivity of labor. The higher the difference between output growth and employment growth, the greater the increase the productivity. Looking at the output projections, we find that the projected rate of growth in output in the telecommunications-intensive industries is to be 2.63 percent per year versus just 2.20 percent for all industries. Although generating fewer jobs, the telecommunications-intensive industries will generate greater output, implying that this subset of industries will be those with a high rate of productivity growth. The rate of growth in labor productivity can be estimated by the difference between the rate of growth in output and the rate of

TABLE 15-16
Projected Growth of Telecommunication-Intensive Industries

Telecommunications-Intensive Industries	Employment (1990-2005)	Output (1990-2005)
Communications, Except Radio and TV	-1.8	2.8
Finance and Insurance, real Estate	1.3	2.1
Business Services	2.5	3.5
Wholesale Trade	1.0	2.2
Retail Trade	1.6	2.5
Hotels and other lodging places	1.9	1.8
Personal and Repair Services, Except Auto Repair	1.2	2.0
Printing and Publishing	1.3	2.4
Health Services	2.6	3.3
Social Services	3.1	3.7
Non-profit organizations	1.0	1.9
Automobile Repair and Services	2.0	2.0
Apparel	-1.8	1.8
Amusements	1.8	3.2
Trucking and Warehousing	1.5	3.0
Electronic Components and Accessories	-0.4	3.1
Misc. Manufacturing	-0.2	1.1
Computer Equipment	-0.9	7.6
Office and Accounting Machines	-1.9	0.1
Federal Government Enterprises	0.2	0.6
Ophthalmic goods	0.5	3.7
Photographic Equipment and supplies	-1.8	2.3
General Industrial Machinery and Equipment	-0.5	5.2
Radio, TV, and Communication Equipment	-1.1	2.6
Scientific, Controlling Instruments	-1.4	1.8
Radio and TV Broadcasting, Cable TV	0.9	3.1
	1.3	2.1
Total - Telecommunications Intensive Industries	0.20	2.63
Total - All Industries	1.20	2.20

Source: Bureau of Labor Statistics (1991).

growth in employment. Using this approximation, we see that labor productivity growth is expected to be 2.4 percent per year for the telecommunications-intensive group of industries while just 1.0 percent per year for all industries as a whole.

Industries which are characterized by high rates of growth in productivity are also generally high wage and high wage growth industries. To the extent that this holds true in the future, the growth in these telecommunication-intensive industries could directly provide high wage jobs, although not as many jobs in raw terms. These higher wage jobs could have a greater indirect impact on job growth, with one high wage job able to support greater numbers of additional, indirect jobs.

TELECOMMUNICATIONS TAXES AND INFRASTRUCTURE INVESTMENT: A PERSPECTIVE ON OHIO'S STRUCTURE

As indicated in other parts of this paper, the way in which the tax treatment of telecommunications firms in Ohio is out of line with other states is primarily attributable to the personal property tax. The rate of taxation on these assets is quite high. What makes this tax more troublesome for telecommunications firms as opposed to other firms which may be subject to this tax, and which may indicate that the tax system itself may have detrimental regional economic impacts, is the fact that the industry is very capital intensive and, moreover, the capital which is used by the telecommunications industry is, by and large, the highly taxed personal property.

In Table 15-17, it is shown that the telecommunications industry is the second most capital intensive of the 50 United States industrial groupings, with 38.4 percent of all costs going for capital services.

In Figure 15-6, the share of total real and personal property which is accounted for by personal property in the telecommunications industry and other utilities is shown. The utilities industry is one which is known to have large amounts of personal property relative to total property. Here, it can be seen that, even when compared to this subgroup of industries, the telecommunications firms have a very high share of total property in highly taxed personal property (83 percent of total market value and 94 percent of assessed value.)

The telecommunications industry is in a period of transition in a number of ways. The industry, once characterized as one with a few, very large players, now includes many smaller, start-up firms. The industry is very capital intensive, and high up-front costs of starting up in a very capital-intensive industry coupled with high taxation on this property can inhibit the development of the industry. Second, the industry is undergoing an explosion in new technologies which induces early obsolescence, high rates of economic de-

TABLE 15-17
Capital Intensity of Various Industries: Capital Cost as Share of Total Cost

Industry	Capital Intensity
Crude Petroleum	38.4
Telecommunications	36.3
Utilities	26.6
Mining	14.1
Transportation	10.5
Agriculture	10.0
Chemicals	7.3
Wholesale and Retail Trade	6.8
Rubber & Plastics	4.6
Motor Vehicles	3.5
Computers	3.1
Food & Beverages	2.5
Construction	1.3

Source: Cronin (1994).

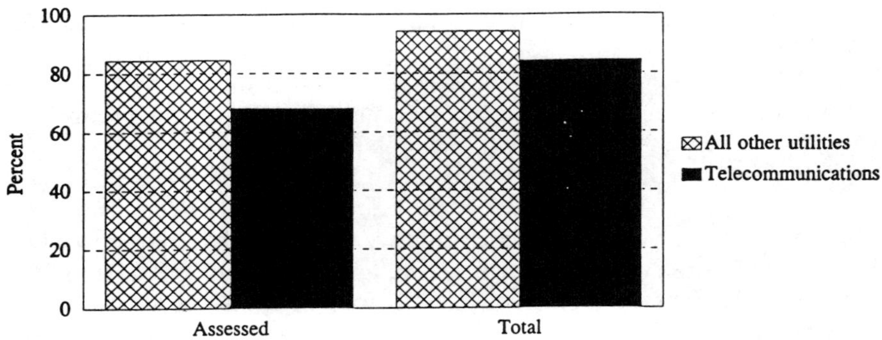

Source: Ohio Department of Taxation

FIGURE 15-6. Personal property as a share of total property of telecommunications and other utilities.

preciation and a higher required rate of replacement investment. In other words, not only is the industry highly capital intensive, but the high rates of obsolescence require a very high ratio of investment spending to other costs of doing business. In such an economic environment, a punitive tax system can seriously undermine the maintenance of a competitive telecommunications infrastructure.

REVENUE

To review, the levies placed directly on telecommunications firms include: the Public Utility Excise Tax (gross receipts) on LEC's, Corporate Franchise Taxation of IXCs and other private providers of telecommunications services, real and tangible personal property taxes, sales taxation of long distance services and the municipal income taxes.

The structural problems with the system of telecommunications suggests several options for tax reform. One important aspect of any proposal, however, is the implications of the tax reform for the ability of governments at all levels to raise revenue.

There are two types of reform to be considered. First, there is the issue of the 88 percent listing rate on telecommunications personal property. Second, there is the more general issue of whether all telecommunications firms, including the LECs, should be treated as normal businesses; that is, taxed under the Corporate Franchise Tax instead of the Gross Receipts Tax, with their services subject to the general sales tax. The decision to change the current treatment of all telecommunications firms as private businesses, including the reduction in the personal property tax listing rate, implies four distinct changes in taxation of telecommunications. They are:

- Repeal of the Gross Receipts Tax on local telephone companies;
- Imposition of a Corporate Franchise Tax on local telephone companies.
- Reduction of the listing rate on telecommunications personal property from its current 88 percent to the 25 percent rate applicable to all other personal property in the state. (There are two alternative methods of reducing the listing rate: reducing the listing for all new investments in personal property while retailing the higher listing rate on existing property, or, reducing the listing rate for all property immediately);
- Imposition of a retail sales tax on local telephone service, and other telecommunication services, such as paging services, cable services, etc.

Several other proposals have been made to increase revenues through the expansion of the sales tax base on telecommunications. They include the taxation of cable services, the services of CAPs and also the taxation of WATS and WATS-like services, which are currently exempt from the sales tax.

In this section, we evaluate this mix of reform for their revenue effects. (We choose the personal property tax listing rate reduction option in which new personal property is listed at the 25 percent rate with existing property kept at 88 percent.

Aggregate Effects

Estimates of the revenue implications of these proposals and variants of these proposals which take into account phase-in provisions have been made by two separate groups: the Ohio Department of Taxation and Levin-Driscoll, on behalf of the Ohio Telephone Association. The range of revenue estimates is narrow so those of the Department of Taxation are noted here, with exceptions noted in the text. A summary of the revenue implications for FY97 is given in Table 15-18.[18]

For the repeal of the gross receipts tax, the loss in revenue is expected to be approximately $105.4 million by 1997. The imposition of a sales tax on local business and household telephone services of the current 5.0 percent rate would raise $119.4 million. Thus, there seems to be agreement that the sales tax rate of 5.0 percent would largely replace the revenue lost through the 4.75 percent gross receipts tax.

There have been proposals to eliminate the current WATS and WATS-like exemption and taxation of cable services. This tax would be expected to pick up more than $40 million by 1997.

TABLE 15-18
Estimates of Change in Revenue Under Alternative Tax Law Changes, Fiscal Year 1997 (Millions of Dollars)

	Fiscal Year 1997
Repeal Public Utility Excise Tax:	(105.4)
Personal Property Tax:	
Old at 88%, New at 25%: OTA	(105.7)
Sales Tax:	
Local Telephone Companies:	119.4
WATS and 800; Cable and Other	43.3
Impose Corporate Franchise Tax:	49.4

Source: Ohio Department of Taxation; and Levin and Driscoll (1993).

The estimates of the losses from the reduction in the listing rate for tangible personal property from 88 percent to 25 percent on new personal property (a reduction in the listing rate on new personal property only, while keeping the listing rate at 88 percent for the old property) would cost $105.7 million by 1997.

The most problematic tax in terms of estimating the revenue effects is the Corporate Franchise Tax. There is a substantial divergence in estimates between the Department of Taxation and the Ohio Telephone Association on the revenue implications of reform. In 1997, the Ohio Telephone Association projects a 33 percent higher amount of revenue than does the Department of Taxation ($85.0 million versus $63.4 million).

One area of concern with regard to the corporate franchise tax is the uncertainty regarding future revenues from the LECs should they become subject to a tax on profits instead of gross receipts. The industry is entering a period during which, it is logically argued, the demands for new and replacement investment will grow rapidly. Under the current corporate tax policy, this will similarly increase the level of tax depreciation for these LECs, and in the short run, will increase tax depreciation more rapidly than revenues. The potential exists for a short-run erosion of the tax base (taxable profits). There are also a number of other issues regarding the ability of the corporate income tax to capture taxable profits.[19] It is for these reasons that there is uncertainty regarding the future revenues from this source.

One piece of evidence which supports this uncertainty is gained from the experience of the switch to a corporate franchise tax on the interexchange companies. Information was provided on the liabilities of telecommunications firms which had corporate liabilities above $100,000 for tax years 1991 and $200,000 for tax years 1987 through 1990. Under the Corporate Franchise Tax, firms pay either on the basis of their taxable income or, as a way of insuring minimal payment, on their net worth. From the sample of interexchange companies over that six year period only 46 percent of the Corporate Franchise Taxes paid were levied directly on profits, with the other 54 percent derived from the net worth tax. The net income tax component was in effect in just twenty percent of these cases. The fear that the local phone companies may not have taxable corporate income to the extent that they now do is not without justification, given the nature of the industry at this time and existing structural difficulties with the Corporate Franchise Tax.

Distribution of Revenue Change Across Governmental Levels

The proposed tax changes would affect all levels of government: state, county, school district and municipal. In Table 15-19, the impact of proposed

TABLE 15-19
Estimates of Change in Revenues Under Alternative Tax Law Changes, by Level of Government, FY97 (Millions of Dollars)

	State	School District	Counties	Townships	Municipalities
Repeal Gross Receipts	(105.4)	---	---	---	---
Personal Property Tax: 88%/25% phase-in	---	(74.1)	(20.4)	(3.6)	(7.6)
Sales Tax					
Local Telephone Co.	99.5	---	19.9	---	---
WATS and 800	35.9	---	7.4	---	---
Corporate Franchise	49.4	---	---	---	14.0
Local Government Funds	---	---	1.6	0.2	2.2
Net Impact	**79.4**	**(74.1)**	**8.5**	**(3.4)**	**8.6**

Source: Ohio Department of Taxation, Inter-Office Communication, September 2, 1993.

changes in the taxation of telecommunications on various levels of government are shown.

The repeal of the Gross Receipts tax takes $105.4 million from the State government but has no direct impact on any local government. On the other hand, the phased reduction of the personal property tax (taxing new personal property investment at a 25 percent listing rate while keeping the 88 percent listing rate on other already existing property) reduces the revenues of local government, with school districts bearing the bulk of the impact.

The elements of the proposed reform which raise revenues include the Corporate Franchise Tax and the expansion of the base of the sales tax to include local services. The Corporate Franchise Tax will bring nearly $50 million to the state government in FY97. Municipalities will gain $14 million through the municipal income tax, which taxes business income.

The sales tax would raise nearly as much money as the gross receipts tax loses for the state government, bringing in $99.5 million. County governments would also raise nearly $20 million at current rates through the introduction of a sales tax on telecommunications.

The taxation of WATS services and other telecommunications services such as cable services has also been proposed as well as taxation of the telecommunications services. The Ohio Department of Taxation estimates that these levies could raise $35.9 million for the state government and $7.4 million for the county government.

The net impacts of changes in the taxation of telecommunications clearly show that the state government is likely to be the clearest winner should a system of taxation be established which treats the telecommunications industry like a private industry, netting $79.4 million in FY97, ($43.5 million without the new taxation of WATS and WATS-like services). It is the school districts which would bear the biggest brunt of the reduction in the personal property tax listing rate.

Using information on the payments of personal property taxes to school districts by the telecommunications firms, it is possible to quantify the proportionate implications for school districts in the state by county. One important distributional implication of the elimination of the public utility listing rate on telecommunications property arises from the fact that it is the lower income areas of the state which have the highest concentrations of telecommunications taxable property as a part of their tax base. In Table 15-20, the fifteen counties with the highest proportion of their assessed value accounted for by telecommunications personal property are reported, along with their average personal income as a percentage of the statewide average. Only one of these fifteen counties had per capita income above the statewide average, and this was barely above that average. The concentra-

TABLE 15-20
Telecommunications Property as Share of Total Taxable Property and Income as Share of State Average

	Telecommunication Property	Personal Income
Vinton	8.44%	74.22%
Morrow	8.29%	78.88%
Henry	7.84%	90.57%
Hancock	7.60%	100.12%
Auglaize	7.29%	93.21%
Hardin	6.96%	79.25%
Fayette	6.84%	75.16%
Mergs	6.84%	75.84%
Clinton	6.75%	85.25%
Preble	6.55%	84.83%
Allen	6.53%	96.23%
Madison	6.50%	86.62%
Williams	6.43%	88.57%
Definance	6.42%	93.84%
Darke	6.39%	77.70%

Source: Ohio Department of Taxation.

tion of lower income counties among those standing to lose most as a result of a reduction in the listing rate for telecommunications property is clear.

In this section, we have provided an analysis of the change in revenue from several alterations in the tax treatment of telecommunications firms. It is important to keep in mind that these estimates are based upon the assumption that all other provisions of the tax code remain the same. Keep in mind that the changes proposed here deal with four separate types of taxes: sales taxes, gross receipts taxes, corporate franchise taxes and property taxes. In each case, there will be proposed changes in the structure of the tax system and, given that changing structures mean different revenue-raising capacity, it is likely that any comprehensive tax reform would entail changes in tax rates, as well. For this reason, any detailed discussion or investigation of revenue-neutrality with regard to this sector of the economy would become inoperative upon other changes. For example, should the commission recommend a change in the listing rate, a change in the sales tax rate or the elimination of the net worth provision of the corporate franchise tax, the revenue sensitivity analysis done to this point would change.

ISSUES IN THE SALES TAXATION OF TELECOMMUNICATIONS

Quite apart from the major issues of what form of taxation should be applied to telecommunications, there are a number of smaller issues which must be addressed in designing any system of taxation. Most of these issues surround the sales taxation of telecommunications. At this time, Ohio does not tax local service but does impose a tax on long distance service. For a review of the tax treatment of telecommunications services in other states, refer back to Table 15-3.

The first issue, and the major philosophical issue in the taxation of telecommunications, is how to define telecommunications services. As currently defined by Ohio statute, a firm is a telecommunications firm when it supplies two-way communications services. However, there are a number of one-way communications services such as paging services which, although not technically constituting telecommunications, do provide the a service which could be taxable. Should these services be subject to a general sales tax? This is an issue which must be addressed.

There is also the issue of "enhanced services". Enhanced services are those which are not provided by the telephone companies themselves but are alterations, adjustments or enhancements to the form or content of the signal which is transmitted. For example, there is the issue of the taxation of data transmitted over telecommunications infrastructure. The transmittal of the data *is not* itself taxable but the medium which is used to deliver this information is taxable. However, the price of such a service does not separately itemize the parts of the price. In the case of such services, the cost of the service (the telecommunications cost and the cost of the value-added) is bundled together in one bill. The administrative costs of unbundling these costs could be large.

Another issue in telecommunications taxation is one which blends the problems of the definition of a telecommunications service and the issue of how to treat enhanced services is that of e-mail, the depositing of information through someone's phone line. All states are currently grappling with the method of taxation of this and other similar services under the sales tax.

A related issue is that of the taxation of 900-services. An individual who accesses these services gets a bill for his full service—the cost of the telecommunications and the additional services, whether it be fortune-telling or sports scores. The problem of taxation, and unbundling the telecommunications portion from the added services, is one which should be addressed.

There are also smaller issues, such as the means of taxing receipts of pay phones. Although phone booths provide a similar service selling from a home or business, the administrative problems of imposing the tax have led most states to exempt pay phone services from taxation.

One issue, which is outside of the issue of defining a telecommunications service, is that of the treatment of WATS and WATS-like charges. Ohio currently exempts these charges from taxation. The rationale for the exemption is "economic development." Many firms which utilize WATS services (for retail or marketing purposes) may find it profitable to leave a state should the WATS service become taxable. These firms are typically very mobile firms and could very easily relocate to a state with a more favorable tax environment (e.g., one which exempts WATS services) without significant relocation costs. The exemption however has been criticized since it provides a tax advantage to larger firms which have a high enough phone volume to exploit the WATS exemption, while smaller firms with lower call volumes would pay taxes on their long-distance calls.

These are just a few of the technical, legal and economic development issues which have arisen around this developing industry. A full discussion of these issues is beyond the scope of this paper. However, suffice it to say that the principle of efficiency in taxation is one which dictates that services which are similar should be treated similarly in order to avoid tax induced changes in the way businesses and consumers act and organize. For this reason, it is important that, in the imposition of a truly general tax on telecommunications services, that the definition of the service be broad enough to capture all close-substitutes.

SUMMARY OF ISSUES

Issue #1—Should all telecommunications tangible personal property be subject to the 88 percent listing rate?

The most substantive issue, in terms of revenues, tax administration and economic effects, with regard to the current treatment of telecommunications firms in Ohio is the differentially high 88 percent listing rate for telecommunications personal property. The rate is established for all public utilities operating in the state.

There are two types of telecommunications firms which should be separately considered in the determination of the appropriate treatment of these firms. They are: the local exchange companies (LECs) and the interexchange companies (IXCs).

In 1987, the State of Ohio recognized the different markets within which the local exchanges and the interexchange companies then operated when they repealed the public utilities excise tax on the interexchange companies and other providers of telecommunications services, such as the cellular phone companies. It was clear even then that those in this market enjoyed none of the protection of a franchise monopoly, that the barriers to entry into the market—technological, economic and legal—had largely been eliminated and that the long distance carriers were engaged in competition with an increasingly large number of interexchange carriers. Recognizing that they were market competitors, they were then subject to the same set of taxes as other market participants.

However, these companies also were left subject to the telecommunications tangible personal property tax at the 88 percent listing rate—unlike other competitive industries. The decision to keep the higher listing rate, in large part, was a result of revenue considerations. So, although admitting the conceptual distinction between these firms and all other firms had virtually disappeared, the differential tax treatment remains. There is little remaining justification for the higher listing rate, other than revenue.

The consequences of the higher listing rate have grown more serious over the intervening years. The pace of technological change which drives much of the new investment in the industry has not waned. As the interexchange market becomes more price-competitive, the demands on these companies to carefully choose least-cost sites for facilities has also grown. Consequently, the economic development implications of the higher listing rate are as strong as ever. The economic cost of erring on the side of higher taxation may be high.

The issue of the taxation of the local exchange companies under the lower listing rate is more problematic. The elimination of this treatment for the IXCs was premised upon the disappearance of the monopoly status of the companies: the lack of a franchise monopoly and the growing competition in the market. Are these same factors at work in the local exchange market? Are they strong enough to justify the loss of revenue from a reduction in the listing rate?

The question now being asked is whether the state should drop its differential treatment of the telecommunications industry in light of current developments. The answer seems to bend in favor of treating the industry much as any other industry. Perhaps the result would be clearer if we were hypothetically to ask, if the industry were currently taxed as an ongoing private industry, would anyone recommend the imposition of differentially higher taxes on this industry? Particularly in an era during which the development of the infrastructure for this industry has become important, the differentially higher taxation of the industry under the personal property tax would be difficult to justify. More importantly, any argument to tax new investment higher under the personal property tax, when technological developments and the attendant increase in the demands for these new investments, would seem out of touch with current reality and out of resonance with the goals of a tax reform process which has as one of its goals, the development of a tax environment which is conducive to economic growth and development.

Issue #2—Should all telecommunications firms be treated as private businesses and subject to the corporate franchise tax?

One conceptual issue which must be resolved before arguing persuasively that local telephone companies be treated as any other general business is that concerning whether the local phone company is operating in the same kind of marketplace as any other business. That is, is the market now subject to the same kinds of competitive pressures as any other business? Traditionally, the justification for the special or unique treatment of the telecommunications industry has been that is was a *monopoly,* endowed with certain monopoly rights.

By the standards of most industries, it would difficult to characterize the market for local services as "competitive". The vast proportion of phone calls made in this country are routed through the local switching network. In the United States, approximately 99.6 percent of all calls go through the public switched network. Should a consumer of telephonic services provided by the local phone company decide that his service is not to his of her liking, very few households would have any readily available alternative.

Nonetheless, the primary underlying cause of this lack of alternatives, *barriers to entry,* are quickly being eroded. There no longer exists the insurmountable barriers to entry in the market that once existed. By-passing the local network to gain access to the long distance market can be obtained through the use of the services of a competitive access provider (CAP).

Many of these CAPS are very small companies. Clearly, the barriers to entry into this portion of the market cannot be considered overwhelming. Moreover, the availability of CAPs to large users allows the possibility of "skimming", or choosing only the most profitable elements or links in the telecommunications chain, heightening their impact on the monopoly position of the LECs.

For many companies, the alternative of using customer-premise equipment in a local office provides another easily available alternative to the local network, the traditional services provided by the LECs. This represents another encroachment upon the "monopoly" position of the LECs and another chink in the armor of the argument of "barriers to entry".

Also, cellular companies can provide a means of partially by-passing (competing with) the local network. With the growing use of cellular, the supposed monopoly position of the LECs is further undermined. Paging systems now provide another alternative to the local network. In some systems, which are currently available, messages can be sent back to the sender from the receiver, providing effective two-way communication. Although not currently available, the potential for Personal Communication Systems (PCS) also provides a powerful alternative to the local switched network.

The cable industry provides another example of the impending competition in this market. Very recently, Time Warner Inc., the nation's second largest cable television operator received permission from the Public Utilities Commission of Ohio (PUCO) to use its 13,000 mile network of fiber optic and coaxial cable to provide local services in 38 counties, representing nearly half of Ohio's population.

Even with electric utilities, fiber can be used in two-way transmission information for meter-reading, load management, etc. Here, too, the potential is emerging for encroachment on the local communications "monopoly".

In short, the competitiveness of the market is debatable at this point, but moving rapidly away from the monopoly position. Should the differential treatment of LECs be maintained or should the gross receipts Tax be replaced with the Corporate Franchise Tax? There is no absolutely right or wrong answer to this question, but the trends in the market put a higher weight on the side of the argument that the switch should be made. In terms of making these decisions, one must keep in mind that decisions on tax policy, particularly during an exercise in fundamental or basic tax reform, can be durable. Consequently, the decision should be made with an eye toward future developments, specifically whether the local exchange market will be more competitive over time than it is now.

Issue #3—How Important Is Tax Policy to the Future of the Telecommunications Industry and Telecommunications Infrastructure?

The telecommunications industry is one which provides a service which is expanding in its use, by both consumers and producers. The technological advances and productivity growth in the industry have helped drive down the real cost of phone service and cost of doing business for other firms.

Yet, the important questions remain: How important are tax rates to the decision to make an investment in telecommunications infrastructure in a particular state? How badly would the services and infrastructure deteriorate with a poorly structured tax system?

This field of study, the impact of telecommunications taxation on economic development, is one in which little professional and quantitative work has been done with *direct* relevance, particularly for a region within an already well-developed network of telecommunications infrastructure. The factors which give rise to this question have only very recently become important, and there is little historical evidence upon which to rely to extract an estimate of their quantitative importance.

One approach to address this issue is to "surmise" the potential impacts based upon pieces of this puzzle. What has been found is that, as new competitors in the industry have entered, and these firms grow, the location and timing of new investment in infrastructure becomes an important economic development factor for firms which use these technologies. The survey of site-selection professionals cited in the text clearly illustrates that the price and quality of telecommunications infrastructure is moving up the list of factors which are considered in site-selection and, hence, regional economic development potential. While for some types of investment, the location of the investment will not matter much for the quality of telecommunications services, for others it is clearly important. For example, the profitability of investment by the CAPS can be influenced by tax policy and the willingness of these firms to provide their services in one area versus another will be impacted. The decision by a "Baby Bell" on where to install fiber-optic lines next is another example of a decision in which the location of the investment can have important regional development implications. What the *strength* of this disincentive will mean for the pace of economic development and job growth remains a matter for speculation rather than a matter of quantification.

Issue #4—What Can Be Done to Ease the Administrative Difficulties Inherent in the Current Tax Treatment of Telecommunications Firms?

The issue of the administratibility of the system of telecommunications hinges on the important point of the need to distinguish between types of firms, with some taxed under the regular business and others taxed under the hybrid telecommunications/business system with the 88 percent listing rate.

Over time, the field of telecommunications services widens and the lines between a telecommunications firm and a regular business blurs. Firms which provide telephone service may also provide other services. Firms which currently do not provide telecommunications services may soon do so. High on that list of potential new entrants are the cable companies. How should these firms be treated? How would the separate values of these multi-product firms be assessed?

In terms of administration of the taxation of the industry, the current system is difficult to manage. The Department of Taxation is required to interpret a law which is written broadly to capture all of those firms providing the services and to find firms which are in the industry for the purpose of taxing them at differentially higher rates. These issues largely disappear with the elimination of the differences in tax treatment of telecommunications and other firms. Not only would the elimination of the current system remove the disincentives inherent in this taxation but it would alleviate the administrative costs of the tax system for both the government and the industry. Whatever justification for the differential taxation of telecommunications exists, it must be subject to a trade-off of those benefits against those to be gained through the reduction in administrative costs and the allocative impacts of reform.

Issue #5—What Types of Telecommunications Services Should be Included in a Telecommunications Sales Tax Base?

Currently, the state taxes long distance service provided by the IXCs but does not tax local service. The local service is exempt since the law prohibits taxation of any service which is subject to the gross receipts tax. Should the gross receipts tax be removed, local service could be taxed.

If that is done, then it is very important that the law be written to insure that the close substitutes to the traditional local phone service be taxed as well. The task of defining the base of this tax is daunting and many states are currently going through this process.

There are also the issues of taxing telecommunications-like services, such as computer data services. This issue is very troublesome and deals with questions concerning the uses of the service (personal versus business), pyramiding of taxes, location of the service-delivery and many other conceptual problems.

ENDNOTES

1. Case (1992).

2. A LATA is a "Local Access Transport Area" within which the LECs have exclusive rights to supply local services through their local switching network.

3. There are a number of deductions from gross receipts Among them are: $25,000 for all companies; amounts attributable to the sale of merchandise, sale to other public utilities for resale; receipts from business done with the Federal Government; and amounts billed on behalf of other entities by telephone companies.

4. In 1987, when the change went into effect, the personal property listing rate for non-public utility firms was 31 percent, but has since been ratcheted down to its current 25 percent level.

5. Case (1992).

6. The New York State gross receipts tax rate is temporarily higher than is reported in this table since a temporary rate increase was imposed in recent years.

7. Levin and Driscoll (1993).

8. The effective tax rate is calculated as: $\sum_t \frac{(r.l.d_t)}{(1+i)^t}$, where r is the state average property tax rate, l is the listing rate, d_t is the depreciated value of a dollar's worth of personal property in year t and I is the discount rate, which is assumed to be three percent in these calculations.

9. The gross receipts tax is generally paid on the receipts of the phone company for all telephonic services, excluding those for sales to government, and receipts of access charges. The sales tax base would be essentially the same, with government purchases excluded and access charges exempt from taxation. Business purchases are also taxed under both regimes.

10. The estimates of the potential revenue from this source is one in which there has been some disagreement between the industry estimates and those of the Ohio Department of Taxation. For example, the Levin and Driscoll estimates, prepared for the Ohio Telephone Association, show potential revenues of $45 million versus $40 million from the Department of Taxation estimates. The differences in estimated revenues from this source widens over time. The source of these differences in revenue estimates is discussed in more detail in Section V of this chapter.

11. The issue of the overall efficiency of a tax system is quite complex. The simple notion that a distortion in the tax system will lead to an inefficient allocation of resources presumes that there are no other existing distortions in the system. For example, an element of the tax system which leads to more activity in one sector rather than another may induce economic *efficiencies* if there already exists a distortion which lowered activity in that sector.

12. See Taylor (1980), Table 3-4, for a summary of existing elasticity estimates.

13. See Taylor (1980), Table 3-5.

14. This occurs since the allocation formula for state corporation income taxes includes factors which weight the share of a company's property and payroll in the state.

15. Although it can be demonstrated that telecommunications use is a catalyst for productivity growth, the fact remains that it is and has been the technology itself, not the location of the technology, which has been a spur to this growth. If new technologies are developed and installed elsewhere, there would be productivity gains enjoyed by Ohio residents and businesses, regardless of the location of the physical investment. Surely the extent of the gains would be lower than those enjoyed in the regions of the investment, but there would be some gains. The productivity gains estimated on the basis of national or aggregate studies overestimate the consequences of investment on growth within a particular region.

16. Deloitte and Touche (1991).

17. Bureau of Labor Statistics (1991).

18. These revenue impact estimates were made for a separate proposal which includes transition provisions. The revenue impact of these provisions have largely run their course by fiscal 1997, and a true picture of the pure revenue implications of the switch can be obtained from that year's estimates.

19. These issues are covered in more detail in Martinez and Grace (1994).

16 The Gross Receipts Tax

Richard McHugh

STRUCTURE OF THE TAX

The Public Utility Excise Tax in Ohio is an ad valorem levy on the gross receipts of electric, natural gas, waterworks, local telephone, pipe line, heating, telegraph and water transportation public utilities operating in the state of Ohio.[1] The current rate of the tax is 4.75 percent (6.75 percent on pipe line companies). Receipts of sales to both households and businesses are taxed. In Ohio, the gross receipts tax is levied on public utilities in lieu of the Corporate Franchise Tax.

There are several important exemptions from the base of this tax. First, municipally-owned utilities are exempt from the public utilities excise tax. Second, the receipts of private firms derived wholly from interstate business are exempted from the base of the gross receipts tax. Third, the receipts of the sales of utilities to government are exempt.

The Public Utilities Excise Tax raised $647.6 million in FY93. This accounts for slightly more than 6 percent of total own-source General Fund Revenues in the State. It is the fourth most important source of state government revenue in Ohio.

RECENT TRENDS IN COLLECTIONS

The revenues from the tax have grown quite slowly over the past few years. The total amount of revenue raised, by class of utility, over the years

1988 to 1993 is shown in Table 16-1. Over that five-year period, the growth rate in gross receipts taxes from all classes of utilities averaged just 1.9 percent per year. Over that same period, the growth in nominal personal income in the state averaged 5.4 percent. The slow growth in gross tax revenue was felt across *all* classes of public utilities. In no class of public utility was the rate of growth in the collections equal to the growth in personal income.

The slow growth in collections is attributable to several factors. First, the sluggish growth in these collections was, in part, due to legislated changes in the taxable base (e.g., the elimination of long distance carriers from the base of the telephone gross receipts tax and the deductibility of access charges from the taxable receipts of local exchange companies). Second, the slow growth in receipts has been the result of low-income elasticities of demand for the goods which are taxed: natural gas, electric, etc. That is, as income rises, the demand for these goods or services naturally rises less rapidly than income. Third, the slow growth of this ad valorem levy has also been the result of slow growth in the price of these goods in recent years. The price of these public utilities are regulated by the Public Utility Commission of Ohio (PUCO), and the number of requests for rate increases from PUCO has

TABLE 16-1
Collection from the Public Utilities Excise Tax, by Class of Utility: 1988 to 1993 (Money Amounts in Thousands)

Utility		1988	1989	1990	1991	1992	1993	1988-93
Electric	(Amount) (% Change)	345,682	355,225 (2.8)	374,752 (5.5)	379,502 (1.3)	401,672 (5.8)	399,914 (-0.4)	54,232 (3.0)
Nat'l Gas	(Amount) (% Change)	97,922	102,257 (4.4)	103,941 (1.6)	95,923 (-7.7)	93,615 (-2.4)	103,813 (10.9)	5,891 (1.2)
Telephone	(Amount) (% Change)	112,159	117,311 (4.6)	102,701 (-12.5)	104,195 (1.5)	105,846 (1.6)	105,489 (-0.3)	6,670 (-1.2)
Rural Ele.	(Amount) (% Change)	12,130	644 (-94.7)	13,244 (1956.5)	13,589 (2.6)	14,586 (7.3)	14,522 (-0.2)	2,392 (3.7)
Waterworks	(Amount) (% Change)	1,922	2,019 (5.0)	2,019 (0.0)	2,031 (0.6)	2,203 (8.5)	2,234 (1.4)	312 (3.1)
Pipe Line	(Amount) (% Change)	1,946	2,418 (24.3)	2,418 (0.0)	1,510 (-37.6)	1,215 (-19.5)	1,298 (6.8)	648 (-7.8)
Other	(Amount) (% Change)	7,527	20,536 (172.8)	5,551 (-73.0)	7,259 (30.7)	966 (-86.7)	8,776 (708.5)	1,249 (16.6)
Total	(Amount) (% Change)	579,288	600,410 (3.6)	604,626 (0.7)	604,009 (-0.1)	620,103 (2.7)	636,076 (2.6)	56,788 (1.9)

Source: Ohio Department of Taxation, *Annual Report*, (1994).

dwindled in recent years. Since the tax is based upon *value* of utility services instead of *quantity*, slow growth in prices will lead to slow growth in revenues unless the demand for the good is very sensitive to price. Finally and most importantly, structural problems in the design of the public utility excise tax have led to the erosion of the tax base over time. Specifically, the existence of specific exemptions from the base of the gross receipts tax has introduced incentives to provide these public utilities in ways which escape taxation. This last factor, the structural problems of the tax, deserves special attention, since not only will it impact revenues, but will also lead to the misallocation of resources in these sectors. These structural issues are discussed more fully in the next section.

STRUCTURAL ISSUES

The Public Utilities Excise Tax is levied in lieu of the Ohio Corporate Franchise Tax (corporate income tax). However, at existing rates, the tax raises significantly more revenues from these sectors than would be raised through the direct imposition of the Ohio Corporate Franchise Tax. The principle justification for this large public utilities excise tax is that it is imposed on industries which are granted a "franchise." By virtue of their franchise, they are theoretically protected from competition in their service are also given the special privileges associated with "eminent domain" and access to public right-of-ways. In short, the extra tax can be viewed as an implicit quid pro quo for these endowed privileges.

The structural equity and horizontal efficiency issues regarding the current Public Utility Excise Tax are ultimately attributable to the growing encroachment upon the presumed monopoly position of the utilities. These companies now face some competition as new providers of similar services have breached into the market. To understand this structural tax issue, a review of some of the new alternative methods of public utility service provisions and the interaction with the existing tax system would be useful.

Most significantly, many of the alternative providers are not subject to the Public Utilities Excise Tax. In the field of electricity there are several alternative sources of power to which users have access. For example, there is the possibility of obtaining power through the process of cogeneration, in which a non-utility may produce power for itself and sell its excess supply to other users, bypassing the traditional power company and without being subject to the gross receipts tax. In addition, large users of electricity may purchase their power from an out-of-state source, avoiding the burden of the gross receipts tax by virtue of the interstate business exemption provided by current law.

In the field of telecommunications, there are a whole host of new "by-pass" operators which provide access to long distance service—a service traditionally provided by the local exchange companies. A "by-pass" operator is a provider of telecommunications services who does not utilize the local exchange company's (local phone company) telecommunications infrastructure. These alternative providers introduce competition to the local exchange company and are not taxed under the public utility excise tax. Examples include the operators of privately owned networks (Competitive Access Providers), which provide direct access on their own systems to long distance carriers for large users of long distance services. Another type of encroachment on the market of the local exchange carriers comes from privately owned PBX's (Personal Business Exchange), which individual customers may install for their own internal use, thus avoiding the gross receipts tax. The paging services and the emerging personal communication systems (PCS) will also, to some extent, permit bypass of the local exchange.

In the realm of natural gas, FERC Order 636, issued in April of 1992, requires that natural gas companies "unbundle" the pricing of their services (that is, separating the pricing of the storage, transmission and sales of natural gas). In effect, this permitted customers to purchase their natural gas from one supplier and pay the pipeline companies only for the transmission or transport of the gas. The practical impact of this, from the standpoint of the gross receipts tax, is that local customers can purchase natural gas from an out-of-state source which is not subject to the gross receipts tax.In these cases, the only gross receipts taxes which would be collected would be those levied on the "wheeling charges" (those which the utility places charges for the transport of the natural gas). This provides another source of leakage from the gross receipts tax base and a source of an incentive to consider alternative providers of natural gas.

There are also inequities which arise from the combination of the exclusion of municipal electric utilities from taxation and the exemption of interstate business from taxation. While some municipal utilities produce their own power, others do not. Rather, some municipal utilities purchase power wholesale from another utility. This, in itself, does not represent any sort of *de facto* inefficiency or inequity. If a municipal utility purchase its power from another public utility in the state, then there is no purely tax-induced inequity since a gross receipts tax is paid by the in-state producer. However, since a municipal utility can purchase its electricity from an out-of-state provider, and all interstate business is exempt from taxation, and since municipal utilities are exempt from taxation, no gross receipts tax is paid on purchases either at the wholesale or the retail level. This activity not only reduces the revenues from the gross receipts tax but also imparts a cost (price) advantage to municipal utilities at the expense of the investor-owned utilities. This advantage, however, may be in part a well-defined policy of subsidizing power in communities served by municipal utilities which are disproportionately located in poorer rural communities and in central cities. There are approximately one hundred of these municipal electric companies, the vast majority being small and/or rural. However, there are several larger municipally-owned utilities in the state, such as these owned in Hamilton, Columbus and Cleveland.

Independent of the interaction between the municipal exclusion and interstate exemption, a municipal public utility is given an advantage by virtue of the simple fact that they are excluded from the tax. For example, a municipal telephone service can fully escape the gross receipts tax. The technology in the field of telecommunications has progressed to the point that now such a system could be built to serve a small community or to serve parts of larger areas and be competitive with the local exchange companies which ARE subject to the gross receipts tax. Here, too, the incentive exists to avoid the tax (through the availability of affordable alternatives) thus resulting in tax-induced changes in behavior which artificially alter the delivery of the service and which erode the tax base.

Although it is difficult to ascertain the precise role which the municipal exemption of the Public Utilities Excise Tax played in the development of municipal public utilities, it is surely the case that the exemption provides an option which "tilts the playing field" against the investor-owned companies.

In short, the availability of the alternative methods of obtaining public utility services which are not subject to gross receipts taxation represents a tax-induced incentive to alter the system of service delivery. These tax-induced changes in behavior lead to inefficiencies, are potential (and exploited) leakages from the gross receipts tax base, and present tax administrators with legal and compliance challenges. These problems will become more significant in revenue and allocative terms as the industries become more "competitive" and additional alternatives are made available to consumers. At this point, it is not possible to strictly quantify how much of this type of erosion has occurred, but it is clear that there is a strong potential that these problems will become increasingly significant over time.

ALTERNATIVES FOR REFORM

There are two fundamental alternatives for reform which could address the structural problems in the Public Utilities Excise Tax. These potential reforms are designed to improve efficiency and horizontal equity by treating providers of similar services in a similar fashion.

Option I: Eliminate the Gross Receipts Tax

One approach is to abandon the separate and distinct treatment of public utilities inherent in the Public Utilities Excise Tax by eliminating the tax altogether and subjecting the industry to the same taxes as any other private business.

Several states have, over the past decade, eliminated their gross receipts tax on some of their public utilities and replaced it with the corporate income tax and, in some cases, subjecting the service to the sales tax. This elimination has been the logical outcome of the view that these industries market structures have changed away from simple monopolies enough to warrant treatment as any other private business. That is, these markets are now more competitive. If the motivation for the elimination of the gross receipts tax is the growing competitiveness of the market, then it is clear that the corporate franchise tax should be imposed and sale taxes imposed where appropriate.

In terms of the Corporate Franchise Tax, the public utility would be viewed as any other investor-owned concern, operating and earning income in the state. This substitution would seem appropriate.

There is an issue regarding the appropriateness of imposing a sales tax on public utilities. The gross receipts tax and the sales tax are ad valorem levies on the production or consumption of the same item. The difference between the two levies is simply the point at which the tax is imposed: the gross receipts tax on the seller, the sales tax on the buyer.

In conceptual terms, however, the issue is whether utility services can be taxed under the provisions of the Ohio general sales tax. The sales tax in Ohio is currently levied on tangible goods, and also services, if they are specifically identified as taxable. There is also the issue of whether the sales of services to businesses should be taxed, since sales for resale should be exempt to avoid pyramiding of taxes.[2]

To implement a sales tax on these utilities, the state can specifically broaden the tax base to include utility services. As in the case of other items subject to a sales tax, one would then need to deal with the issue of sales to business (potential sales for resale). Alternatively, the state can implement a new and separate public utility tax on these sales regardless of to whom they are made or from where the utility services were produced. Should the state choose the second alternative, the sales to governments and to business can be taxed unless specifically exempt. This tax may be defined either as an ad valorem levy or a tax per unit of consumption.

An important difference between the two types of levies, the sales tax and the separate public utility tax, is that, should the state take the alternative of defining a new utility excise tax, these sales would not be subject to the permissive (local) sales tax. Broadening the sales tax base of the general sales tax to include utilities would also broaden the base for the local sales taxes. There are four policy issues here. First, will the substitution of a Corporate Franchise Tax and sales tax for the gross receipts tax yield revenues equivalent to the gross receipts tax? Second, will the substitution of the Corporate

Franchise Tax and sales tax eliminate the inequities and inefficiencies associated with the gross receipts tax? Third, will the gross price of utilities to consumers change upon the switch from the gross receipts tax to the Franchise/Sales tax package? Fourth, have the market conditions in these "public utilities" changed significantly enough in the past few years to warrant a switch from their treatment as a protected monopoly to one of a regular private business?

Issue 1—Revenue implications

The proposed switch of taxes imposed on these industries will have implications for the revenue which could be raised from these sectors. The Department of Taxation and relevant industry associations have estimated the amount of revenue which would be raised by the imposition of a Corporate Franchise tax on firms in some of the industries currently subject to the gross receipts tax.

Telecommunications firms paid $105 million in gross receipts taxes in 1993. Estimates of the amount which would be raised through a Corporation Franchise Tax are in the range of $40 million to $45 million, with the lower estimate provided by the Ohio Department of Taxation and the higher estimate provided by the industry association, the Ohio Telephone Association.[3]

Electric utilities currently contribute $400 million in gross receipts taxes. Estimates of the amount which would be raised from the imposition of a Corporate Franchise Tax on electric utilities range from $76 million to $133 million. Again, the lower estimate has been provided by the Ohio Department of Taxation and the higher estimate by the industry association.

No independent estimates of the revenue raising potential of a Corporate Franchise Tax on the other utilities have been made.

The simple replacement of the Gross Receipts Tax with the Corporate Franchise Tax will lose revenue. Based upon the two cases which have been specifically examined, the telecommunications sector and the electric utility sector, the Corporate Franchise Tax will raise approximately one-third the revenue of the gross receipts tax.

The situation, in terms of revenue from the imposition of the Corporate Franchise Tax on public utilities, may be even worse. There is the fear, expressed most vigorously by the Department of Taxation, that the franchise tax may be an unreliable source of revenue and the tax could produce even less than they have estimated. The franchise tax, particularly the tax placed simply upon corporate net income (ignoring the alternative net wealth element of the tax), can be subject to much accounting manipulation which reduces revenues.[4] The Department of Taxation views this tax as a potential "sieve", allowing much of what could be taxed to escape taxation.

Since the Corporate Franchise Tax will raise much less revenue than Gross Receipts Tax, it is essential that the Gross Receipts Tax be substituted with a combination of the franchise tax *and* a consumption or sales tax.

Would this yield a sufficient amount of revenue to leave the state with the revenues it would have without the gross receipts tax? Again, we are forced to rely upon the evidence obtained from just two of the sectors now taxed under the gross receipts tax: the telecommunications sector and the electric utilities.

For telecommunications, the imposition of a sales (or consumption tax) in combination with the franchise tax, would yield approximately the same amount of revenue as the gross receipts electric utilities, we do not have specific estimates of the revenues which could be raised by putting the electric services under the sales tax. However, the Department of Taxation estimated that the total amount which would be raised from the combination of a sales tax on water, natural gas and electric was $370 million. As an approximation to the amount which electric utilities alone might generate, the assumption can be made that these companies would generate the same proportion of water, gas and electric sales tax revenues as it paid in their combined gross receipts tax in 1993 (80.6 percent). Under this reasonable assumption, we estimate that the sales tax on electric would raise approximately $296 million. When combined with the estimates of potential revenues from the Corporate Franchise Tax on electric utilities of between $76 million to $133 million, we estimate that the full substitution of a sales\franchise tax for the gross receipts would yield a net change in revenues of –$27.0 million to +27.4 million. Again, as with telecommunications, the full swap could pretty evenly match revenue losses with revenue gains, with some potential for a small loss in total revenues.

Issue 2—Corporate/sales taxation and economic neutrality

The most troublesome aspect of the gross receipts tax is the non-neutrality which arises from two elements of the tax law:the exemption of receipts from interstate business from the base of the tax; and the exemption of municipal utilities from the tax. Would the imposition of a sales or separate consumption tax address these non-neutralities and "level the playing field"?

In the case of the exemption of municipal utilities, the switch to the sales or consumption tax would improve resource allocation. Since all consumption would be taxed, it would not matter what the form of organization the seller would be: municipal or investor-owned. The incentives to operate a utility through the government would be eliminated.

In the case of sales of utilities which were purchased out-of-state, the switch to a broad-based utilities consumption/sales tax would again eliminate non-neutralities. If a municipal power plant bought power from an out-of-state source or if a natural gas company purchased out-of-state power from a broker, or if a plant bought its power from a cogeneration source, the ultimate purchase of that power would be subject to a tax just as a sales tax is imposed on the purchase of an automobile, regardless of where it was manufactured. Such a switch to a consumption/sales tax, if broadly imposed, would improve the horizontal equity of the tax system and eliminate incentives to divert business to out-of-state sources.

Issue 3—The tax "swap" and the price of utilities

The third issue is that of what the switch from a gross receipts tax to the corporate franchise tax would do to the gross price of these utilities to the consumer of the service. On the one hand, the elimination of the gross receipts tax would reduce costs in this rate-of-return regulated industry. Prices, in principle, should fall by the full amount of the tax. The imposition of the equal yield sales and franchise tax would push the gross prices up to their original level. This would be the case since franchise taxes would represent a cost which the regulators would pass through to consumers while the sales tax paid by the consumers directly in their bills would be part of the gross price. In practice, the Public Utilities Commission of Ohio (PUCO) would need to request a rate hearing from all of those affected by the switch. There is the potential for a lag between the gross receipts tax elimination and consequent net price reductions. The legislation making the tax swap could, however, specifically request that the reductions take effect immediately.

Issue 4—Are all public utilities competitive?

The motivation for the switch from the gross receipts tax to a corporate franchise tax and sales/consumption tax is that the gross receipts tax puts the utilities at a disadvantage relative to competitors—something of which there were none when the original tax laws were written. In the past, "mistakes" (e.g., overly high or poorly designed) in taxation which existed mattered little since the public utility was guaranteed a fair rate of return anyway. Higher or inappropriate taxation was passed forward to consumers through the decisions of the utility regulators.

However, now that these "monopolies" become subject to competition, tax policy mistakes can have important allocative effects and may leave the public utility at a disadvantage relative to their competitors.

Are all of the industries currently subject to the gross receipts tax now "competitive"? This is a question which has no definitive answer, and we will not attempt to resolve this issue in this short chapter. However, some comments are in order.

There are two ways of viewing the issue of the competitiveness of these industries. On the one hand, it is certainly the case that the large bulk of the business done in these industries is still done by the traditional public utilities. There are very few (if any) options for getting power into a house without running electricity through the power lines of the local electric company. Likewise, in the natural gas industry, almost all gas is delivered using the public utilities' infrastructure. There is competition in the purchase of the electricity or the raw natural gas as discussed above. However, the amount of purchases from the alternative sources is still very small. If one wants to define a monopoly in terms of some measure of concentration of sales in a particular industry, then the utilities are still looking an awful lot like a monopoly and in many cases are the exclusive providers of the utility service.

However, if one takes the view that a monopoly no longer exists when the "monopolist" must make its pricing and production decision with an eye towards an alternative provider of the same service, then the monopoly no longer exists. This is what is termed "virtual competition". This situation exists to some degree in the electric and natural gas industries and it certainly exists in the telecommunications time, it seems clear that the market in electricity and natural gas could develop to the point that the pricing and service decisions of these monopolies will become very sensitive to the alternative sources of service which are available.

In short, there is no easy answer to the question of whether there is now competition in these industries. However, there is clearly encroachment on these markets, particularly in the telecommunications market. With this encroachment, bad tax policy is likely to have adverse allocative consequences.

Option II: "Tighten Up"the Gross Receipts Tax

Another option for the reform of the Public Utility Excise Tax would be to retain the tax but to deal directly with the current exemptions which have lead to the horizontal inequities and consequent inefficiencies. The two relevant exemptions are those for municipals and for interstate business. The elimination of the exemption of the sales of municipal utilities is not possible in light of the inability of one level of government to tax another. However, the exemption of interstate sales from the gross receipts tax arises on the basis of tax laws written in the early twentieth century, a time during which interstate sales were excluded on the basis of the commerce clause in part to avoid double taxation. This also was a time during which such interstate sales were not a significant factor in these industries. The state now could consider capturing this activity in the tax base by eliminating this exemption.

The state may also take a less ambitious approach to reform and address perceived abuses of the interstate exemption clause through increased auditing to guard against utility companies overstating their exemptions for interstate sales in order to minimize taxes.

CONCLUSION

The Ohio Public Utilities Excise Tax is a gross receipts tax levied on regulated utilities operating in the state. The tax has been a major source of revenue for the state.

As the tax is currently structured, there is the potential for it to introduce a number of distortions which may induce economically inefficient provision of these utility services. While these structural defects have always existed, recent technological innovations and changes in some important Federal regulations have introduced significant competitive elements into these markets which had previously been viewed as inviolable monopolies. These developments have made the inefficiencies and inequities from these structural problems more urgently in need of attention.

One obvious approach to reform of the Public Utility Excise Tax would be to scrap the tax entirely and begin to treat the public utility companies, for tax purposes, as any other firm. This approach raises many important issues. For example, as the fourth largest source of revenues in the state, a tremendous amount of revenue would need to be replaced. They can only be replaced if these utility services are subject to the general sales tax, or some alternative sales-type tax.

ENDNOTES

1. Throughout this chapter, this tax will alternately be referred to as the "gross receipts tax" or, as it is formally known in Ohio, the Public Utility Excise Tax.

2. Sales taxes are, in some states, not imposed when the sale is for "resale" (typically, the sale is to business). The rational for the elimination of business purchases from the sales tax is that the good or service would ultimately be taxed twice or more. However, in many states, the sales of these services ARE taxed, since the energy or Telecommunications service does not end up as a part of the final product: that is, it is truly "consumed" in the production of a good or service. The switch from gross receipts to general sales could remove business purchases from the tax base and, consequently, less revenue would be raised by the sales tax.

In many states which impose a tax on electricity and natural gas, businesses do pay sales taxes. The specifics of the rules of taxation differ from state to state but, in general, the exclusion is usually written into the law as an exemption for particular business activities (e.g., industrial use, agricultural use). Consequently, a fair bit of the sales tax on utilities is paid by businesses. It is too simplistic to say that the households DO pay while businesses DON'T pay. There is no *a priori* case to think that all businesses would be excluded were the sales tax to be imposed in Ohio and, therefore, the base of the tax may not fall substantially. The experience in Ohio on the tax on telecommunications is instructive. Long distance calls are subject to the sales tax. No distinction is made here on the basis of the type of user of the telecommunications service, business or personal.

3. Levin and Driscoll, *Telecommunications and Taxation in Ohio*, May 1994.

4. This is a major concern which is addressed more fully in Jorge Martinez-Vazquez and Martin Grace, *Business Taxation in Ohio: General Franchise Tax and Taxes on Financial Institutions and Insurance Companies*. Chapters 10, 11 and 12 in this volume.

5. Ohio Department of Taxation Inter-office Communication, September 2, 1993.

References

Aaron, Henry J. "Some Criticism of Tax Burden Indices." *National Tax Journal*, September 1965, 18, pp. 313-318.

______. "Some Observations on Property Tax Valuation and the Significance of Full Value Assessment." Arthur D. Lynn, Jr. ed., In *The Property Tax and Its Administration*, Madison: University of Wisconsin Press, 1969.

______. *Who Pays the Property Tax? A New View.* Washington D.C.: The Brookings Institution, 1975.

Adolphson, Donald L., Gary Cornia, and Larry Walters. "A New Method to Measure Obsolescence in a Regulated Electric Utility." *Proceedings of the 1988 Public Utilities Workshop*, Wichita: The Wichita State University, 1988, pp. 161-90.

______. "Railroad Property Valuation Using Data Envelopment Analysis." *Interfaces*, 1989, 19(3), pp. 18-26.

Advisory Commission on Intergovernmental Relations.*Changing Public Attitudes on Government and Taxes, 1993*. Washington, D.C.: ACIR, 1993.

______. *Financing Schools and Property Tax Relief - A State Responsibility.* Washington D.C.: ACIR, 1973.

______. *Fiscal Balance in the American Federal System*. Washington D.C.: ACIR, 1987.

______. *Significant Features of Fiscal Federalism, Volumes 1 and 2.* Washington D.C.: ACIR, various years.

______. *State Revenue Capacity and Tax Effort*. Washington, D.C.: ACIR, 1991.

______. *Taxation of Interstate Mail Order Sales: 1994 Revenue Estimates*. Washington, D.C.: Government Printing Office, May 1994.

______. *The Role of the States in Strengthening the Property Tax: Volume I.* Washington, D.C.: ACIR, 1963.

Agabian, Merritt. "Replacement Cost New Concepts." In *Appraising Machinery and Equipment*, Washington, D.C.: American Society of Appraisers, 1989, pp. 39-48.

Alico, John. "Depreciation Theory." In *Appraising Machinery and Equipment*, Washington, D.C.: The American Society of Appraisers, 1989, pp. 59-78.

American Federation of Federal, County and Municipal Employees. "Testimony of Marcia Howard." Columbus: AFL-CIO, June 1994.

American Gas Association. *The New Guide to Utility Rate Making*. Washington, D.C., American Gas Association, 1986.

Anderson, Gerald H. "Is the Rust Belt's Revival Real?" *Economic Commentary*, Federal Reserve Bank of Cleveland, March 1, 1992.

Anderson, John E. "Property Tax Base Income Elasticities: Pooled Estimation of Partial and Total Income Effects." *Property Tax Journal,* June 1992, pp. 157-74.

Aronson, J. Richard, and E. Schwartz. "Financing Public Goods and the Distribution of Population in a System of Local Governments." *National Tax Journal*, 1973, 26, pp. 137-160.

Association of American Railroads. *Railroad Facts: 1993*. Washington, D.C.: Association of American Railroads, 1993.

______. *Railroads and States*. Washington, D.C.: Association of American Railroads, 1994.

Atkinson, Scott E., and Robert Halvorsen. "The Relative Efficiency of Public and Private Firms in a Regulated Environment: The Case of U.S. Electric Utilities." *Journal of Public Economics*, 1986, 29(3), pp. 281-294.

Auerbach, A., and K. Hassett. "Tax Policy and Business Fixed Investment in the United States." *Journal of Public Economics*, 1992, 47, pp. 141-170.

Averch, H., and L. Johnson. "Behavior of the Firm under Regulatory Constraint." *American Economic Review*, December 1962, pp. 1052-1069.

Babcock, Michael W. *Efficiency and Adjustment: The Impact of Railroad Regulation.* Washington, D.C.: Cato Institute, 1984, Policy Paper No. 33.

Bahl, Roy, David L. Sjoquist, and Loren W. Williams. "School Finance Reform the Impact on Property Taxes." In *Proceedings of the 83rd Annual Conference on Taxation 1990*, by the National Tax Association - Tax Institute of America. Columbus: NTA-TIA, 1991, pp.163-171.

Bartik, Timothy J. "Economic Development and Black Economic Success." Draft Final Report prepared for the Economic Development Administration, U.S. Department of Commerce, Kalamazoo: W.E. Upjohn Institute for Employment Research, 1992.

______. "Small Business Start-ups in the United States: Estimates of the Effects of Characteristics of States." *Southern Economic Journal*, 1989, 55(4), pp. 1004-1018.

______. "Who Benefits From Local Job Growth?" *Regional Studies*, 1993, 27(4), pp. 297-311.

______. *Who Benefits from State and Local Economic Development Polices?* Kalamazoo: W.E. Upjohn Institute for Employment Research, 1992.

Bartik, Timothy J., et al. "Saturn and State Economic Development." *Forum for Applied Research and Public Policy*, Spring 1987, pp. 29-40.

Battelle Memorial Institute. *Taxation of Ohio Utilities, Its Effect on the Ohio Economy*. Columbus: Battelle, 1982.

Bergstrom, V., and E. Panas. "How Robust Is the Capital-Skill Complementarity Hypothesis?" *Review of Economics and Statistics*, August 1992, 74, pp. 540-546.

Berno, Donald, and Jack Whitmore. "Historical Review of Ohio State and Local Government Finances." *Commission to Study the Ohio Economy and Tax Structure*, Atlanta: Policy Research Center, Georgia State University, 8 November 1994, Staff Report Number 4.

Bhattacharyya, Arunava, Elliot Parker, and Kambiz Raffiee. "An Examination of The Effect of Ownership on the Relative Efficiency of Public and Private Water Utilities." *Land Economics*, 1994, 70(2), pp. 197-209.

Blanchard, O., and L. F. Katz. "Regional Evolutions." *Brookings Papers on Economic Activity,* 1992, 1, pp. 1-75.

Bland, Robert L. *A Revenue Guide for Local Government.* Washington, D.C.: International City Managers Association, 1989.

Bluefield Waterworks & Improvement Company v. Public Service Commission of W. Va. 262 U.S. 679, 1923.

Bohm Robert A., and Eleanor D. Craig. "Sales Tax Base Modification, Revenue Stability, and Equity." In *Proceedings of The 80th Annual Conference on Taxation 1987,* by the National Tax Association - Tax Institute of America. Columbus: NTA-TIA, 1988, pp. 167-173.

Bound, J., and H. J. Holzer. "Industrial Shifts, Skills Levels, and the Labor Market for White and Black Males." National Bureau of Economic Research Working Paper Number 3715, 1991.

Bosworth, B., and G. Burtless. "Effects of Tax Reform on Labor Supply, Investment, and Saving." *The Journal of Economic Perspectives*, Winter 1992, 6, pp. 3-25.

Bowman, John H. "Property Tax Law and Administration." In Robert D. Ebel, ed., *A Fiscal Agenda for Nevada*, Reno: University of Nevada Press, pp. 277-310.

______. "Recent Changes in Property Taxation and Their Implications for Balance in State and Local Revenue Systems." In Frederick D. Stocker, ed., *The Quest for Balance in State-local Revenue Structures*, Boston: Lincoln Institute of Land Policy, 1987, pp. 71-106.

Bowman, John, George E. Hoffer, and Michael D. Pratt. "Current Patterns and Trends in State and Local Intangibles Taxation." *National Tax Journal*, 1990, 33(4), pp. 439-450.

Brainard, Daniel C., and Thomas W. Kluth. "Charting the Great Lakes Economy: Employment Performance during Recessions." *REI Review*, Fall 1990.

Break, George. *Financing Government in a Federal System*. Washington, D.C.: The Brookings Institution, 1980.

Brealy, Richard, and Stewart Myers. *Principles of Corporate Finance*. New York: McGraw-Hill Book Company, 1981.

Brewer, Homer T. "Distribution of Railroad Valuation To Political Subdivisions." *Proceedings of the 39th International Conference on Assessment Administration*, 1972, pp. 98-105.

Brueckner, Jan K. "A Modern Analysis of the Effects of Site Value Taxation." *National Tax Journal,* March 1986, 39, pp. 49-58.

Buchanan, James M., and Marilyn R. Flowers. *The Public Finances: An Introductory Text*. 6th ed., Homewood: Irwin, 1987.

Buckeye Association of School Administrators. "A School Finance Concept Paper." Columbus, OH, 1994.

Callen, J.G., F. Mathewson, and H. Mohring. "The Benefits and Costs of Rate of Return Regulation." *American Economic Review*, 1967, 66, pp. 290-297.

Carlton, Dennis W. "The Location and Employment Choices of New Firms: An Econometric Model." In William C. Wheaton, ed., *Interregional Movements and Regional Growth*, Washington, D.C.: The Urban Institute, 1979.

______. "The Location and Employment Choices of New Firms: An Econometric Model with Discrete and Continuous Endogenous Variables." *Review of Economics and Statistics*, 1983, 65, pp. 440-49.

Carroll, Robert, and David Joulfaian. "Do Taxes Affect Corporate Financial Decisions?—The Choice of Organizational Form." Mimeo, Office of Tax Analysis, U.S. Department of the Treasury, September 1993.

Carroll, R., and M. Wasylenko. "Do State Business Climates Still Matter? Evidence of a Structural Change." *National Tax Journal*, March 1994, 47(1), pp. 19-38.

Case, Karl. "State and Local Tax Policy and the Telecommunications Industry." *Commission to Study the Ohio Economy and Tax Structure*, Atlanta: Policy Research Center, Georgia State University, 23 December 1994, Staff Report Number 10b.

______. *State and Local Tax Policy and the Telecommunications Industry*. Washington, D.C.: Council of Governors' Policy Advisors, 1992.

Center for Business and Economic Research, University of Tennessee. "An Economic Report to the Governor of the State of Tennessee on the State's Economic Outlook." Nashville: The Tennessee State Planning Office, January 1995.

Chapman, D., T. Tyrrell, and T. Maint. "Electricity Demand Growth and the Energy Crisis." *Science*, 1982, 178, pp. 703-708.

Citizens for Tax Justice. *A Far Cry From Fair*. Washington, D.C.: Citizens for Tax Justice, 1991.

Citizens Research Council of Michigan. "Proposal A: Questions Regarding School Property Taxes." Lansing: Citizens Research Council of Michigan, June 1994.

Clatanoff, Robert M. *Patterns of Property Tax Administration in the United States.* Chicago: International Association of Assessing Officers, Research and Information Series No. 5, 1986.

Coalson, John. "State and Local Corporate Tax Roundup." *Corporate Taxation*, May/June 1992, 3(1).

Coalson, John L., and Michael T. Ptrik. "Consolidated or Combined Returns and Alternative Corporate Reporting Methods: A Georgia Perspective." *Journal of State Taxation*, Fall 1989, 8(2), pp. 132-151.

Columbus Southern Power Company and Ohio Power Company. Statement to the Commission to Study the Ohio Economy and Tax Structure, 1994.

Commerce Clearing House. *State Income Taxes*. Chicago: CCH, 1994.

______. *State Tax Guide*. Property Taxation of Inventories, Chart 20-150, p. 2023.

Commission to Study the Ohio Economy and Tax Structure. "Taxation and Economic Development in Ohio: A Blueprint for the Future." Final Report. Atlanta: Policy Research Center, Georgia State University, 23 December 1994.

Coriell, Karen Bond. "Chaos, Contradiction and Confusion: Ohio's Real Property Tax Exemptions." *Ohio State Law Journal,* 1992, 53, pp. 264-317.

Cornell, Bradford. *Corporate Valuation: Tools for Effective Appraisal and Decision Making*. Homewood: Irwin, 1993.

Cornia, Gary. "Ohio Tangible Business Personal Property: Property Taxation." *Commission to Study the Ohio Economy and Tax Structure*, Atlanta: Policy Research Center, Georgia State University, 21 November 1994b, Staff Report Number 8b.

______. "Public Utility Taxation: Tangible Personal Property." *Commission to Study the Ohio Economy and Tax Structure*, Atlanta: Policy Research Center, Georgia State University, 18 November 1994a, Staff Report Number 8a.

Corporation for Enterprise Development. *Development Report Card for the States*. Corporation for Enterprise Development, 1994.

Costello, Kenneth, Robert E. Burns, and Youssef Hegazy. *Overview of Issues Relating to the Retail Wheeling of Electricity*. Columbus: The National Regulatory Research Institute, 1994.

Cronin, Francis J., et al. "Telecommunications and Growth: The Contribution of Telecommunications Infrastructure Investment to Aggregate Sectoral Productivity." *Telecommunications Policy*, December 1993.

Cronin, Francis J. "Telecommunications Network Modernization and the Ohio Economy." Paper presented at the Telecommunications Taxation Conference, Georgia State University, August 1994.

Cross, R. *Unemployment, Hysteresis and the Natural Rate*. New York: Basil Blackwell, 1988.

Cypress, David E. "Dual Use Property: The Reporting of Tangible Personal Property Used Partly for Business." Comptroller of the Treasury, Division of Local Government, Nashville, Tenn., 1989.

Dearborn, Philip. "Ohio Metropolitan Area Revenues." *Commission to Study the Ohio Economy and Tax Structure*, Atlanta: Policy Research Center, Georgia State University. 15 November 1994, Staff Report Number 7.

DeBoer, Larry. *The Taxation of Property in Indiana*. West Lafayette: Center for Tax Policy Studies, Purdue University, 1992.

Deloitte and Touche. *New Jersey Telecommunications Infrastructure Study*. Columbus: Deloitte and Touche, 1991.

DeLong, J. B., and L. Summers. "Equipment Investment and Economic Growth." *Quarterly Journal of Economics*, 1991, 106, pp. 445-502.

Dildine, L. "Measuring State Fiscal Incentives for Economic Development of High-Tech Industries." Paper presented at the *86th Annual Conference on Taxation 1993*, in St. Paul, by the National Tax Association - Tax Institute of America. Columbus: NTA-TIA, 1994.

Dorrian, Hugh J. CPA, *City of Columbus, Ohio General Operation Fund Resources*. Columbus: CPA, 1993.

Duchi, Mary Laird. "Ohio's Economic and Demographic Structure." *Commission to Study the Ohio Economy and Tax Structure,* Atlanta: Policy Research Center, Georgia State University, 15 November 1994, Staff Report Number 3.

Due, John F. "New Railroad Companies Formed to Take Over Abandoned or Spun-off Lines." *Transportation Journal*, 1984, pp. 30-42.

______. "Studies of State-Local Tax Influence on Location of Industry." *National Tax Journal*, 1961, 14(2), pp. 163-173.

Due, John F., and John L. Mikesell. *Sales Taxation: State and Local Tax Structure and Administration*. Washington: The Urban Institute Press, 1994.

Dun & Bradstreet Corporation, Economic Analysis Department. *New Business Incorporations*. New York, New Jersey: Dun & Bradstreet Corporation, various issues.

______. *Business Failure Record*, New York, New Jersey: Dun & Bradstreet Corporation, various issues.

Dye, Richard F., and Therese J. McGuire. "Growth and Variability of State and Individual Income and General Sales Taxes." *National Tax Journal*, March 1991, 44(1), pp. 55-66.

Ebel, Robert D. *A Fiscal Agenda for Nevada*. Reno: University of Nevada Press, 1990.

Ebel, Robert D., and Therese J. McGuire, eds. *Final Report of the Minnesota Tax Study Commission*. St Paul: Butterworths, 1986.

Ebel, Robert D., and James Ortbal. "Direct Residential Property Tax Relief." *Governmental Perspectives*, Spring 1989.

Economic Trends. Federal Reserve Bank of Cleveland, June 1993 through May 1994.

Eckert, Joseph K., and Jane H. Malme. *Assessment Administration Practices in the U.S. and Canada.* Chicago: International Association of Assessing Officers, September 1991.

Edison Electric Institute. *Statistical Yearbook of the Electric Utility: 1991.* Washington, D.C.: Edison Electric Institute, 1992.

______. *1992 Statistics Non-investor-owned Electric Utilities*. Washington, D.C.: Edison Electric Institute, 1993.

______. "Status of Retail Wheeling in the States." Washington, D.C.: Edison Electric Institute, 1994.

Edwards, Chris R., ed. *Facts & Figures on Government Finance*. 29th ed. Tax Foundation, 1994.

Eisinger, P. *"The Rise of the Entrepreneurial State: State and Local Economic Development Policy in the United States."* Madison: University of Wisconsin Press, 1988.

Energy Information Administration. *Financial Statistics of Selected Publicly Owned Electric Utilities: 1990*. Washington, D.C.: Energy Information Administration, 1992.

Farley, Jewette. "Personal Property—The Redheaded, Freckled-faced Stepchild of Assessment." *Journal of Property Tax Management*, 1991, 1(3), pp. 45-48.

Feenberg, Daniel, and Harvey S. Rosen. "The Interaction of State and Federal Tax Systems: The Impact of State and Local Tax Deductibility." *The American Economic Review*, May 1986, 76(2), pp. 126-137.

Feldstein, Martin S. "On the Theory of Tax Reform." *Journal of Public Economics*, 1976, 6, pp. 77-104.

Fisher, Ronald C. "Local Sales Taxes: Tax Rate Differentials, Sales Loss, and Revenue Estimation." *Public Finance Quarterly*, 1980, 8(2), pp. 171-188.

Fisher, Ronald, and Lawrence Martin. "Taxes and Telecommunications in an Era of Change."

In Robert D. Ebel and Therese J. McGuire, eds., *Final Report of the Minnesota Tax Study Commission*, *Volume 2, Staff Papers*, St. Paul: Butterworth Legal Publishers, pp. 223-250.

Fleeter, Howard B. "Equity, Adequacy, and Reliability in Ohio Education Finance." Report to the Governor's Education Management Council, School of Public Policy and Management, Ohio State University, 1992.

Fleisher, B. M., and G. Rhodes. "Unemployment and the Labor Force Participation Rate of Married Men and Women." *Review of Economics and Statistics*, 1976, 58, pp. 398-406.

Fletcher, Gregory G. "Significant Court Cases Concerning Ad Valorem Taxation of Public Utility and Railroad Property." *Assessment Journal*, 1994, 1(1), pp. 43-55.

Folkman, Gordon, and Carolyn MacDonald. "Property Tax Regressivity in Minnesota." *State Tax Notes,* 19 April 1993, pp. 928-934.

Fogarty, Michael, and Jar-Chi Lee. "Ohio's Telecommunications Infrastructure as a Source of Economic Development." REI Program Paper Series, Cleveland: Center for Regional Economic Issues, Case Western University, 1993.

Fosler, S. *The New Economic Role of American States: Strategies in a Competitive World Economy.* New York: Oxford University Press, 1988.

Fox, William. "Ohio's Sales Tax: Current Condition and Policy Options." *Commission to Study the Ohio Economy and Tax Structure*, Atlanta: Policy Research Center, Georgia State University, 2 November 1994, Staff Report Number 2.

______. "Japanese Investment in Tennessee: The Economic Effects of Nissan's Location in Smyrna." In E. Yanarella and W. Green, ed., *The Politics of Industrial Recruitment: Japanese Automobile Investment and Economic Development in the American States*, New York: Greenwood Press, 1990.

______. "Tax Structure and the Location of Economic Activity Along State Borders." *National Tax Journal*, 1986, 39, pp. 387-401.

______, ed. *Sales Taxation: Critical Issues in Policy and Administration*. Westport: Praeger Press, 1992.

Fox, William, and Charles Campbell. "Stability of the State Sales Tax Income Elasticity." *National Tax Journal*, 1984, 37(2), pp. 201-212.

Fox, William, H. Herzog, and A. Schlottman. "Metropolitan Fiscal Structure and Migration." *Journal of Regional Science*, November 1989, 29(4), pp. 523-536.

Fox, William, and Matthew N. Murray. "Economic Aspects of Taxing Services." *National Tax Journal*, 1988, 41(1), pp. 19-36.

______. "Local Public Policies and Interregional Business Development." *Southern Economic Journal*, 1990, 57(2), pp. 413-427.

Freeman, R.B. "Employment and Earnings of Disadvantaged Young Men in a Labor Shortage Economy." In C. Jencks and P.E. Peterson, eds., *The Urban Underclass*, Washington, D.C.: Brookings Institution, 1991, pp. 103-121.

Frey, W.H., and A. Speare, Jr. *Regional and Metropolitan Growth and Decline in the United States*. New York: Russell Sage Foundation, 1988.

Fullerton, Don, and Diane Linn Rogers. *Who Bears the Lifetime Tax Burden?* Washington, D.C.: Brookings Institution, 1993.

Gall, Maryann B., and Jeffrey B. Ellman. "Sales and Use Tax: Current Developments in State 'Packaging' Exemptions." *State Tax Notes*, 28 December 1992, pp. 967-974.

Galveston Electric Company v. Galveston. 258 U.S. 388 (1922).

Garippa, John E., and Seth I. Davenport. "Two States Battle for Manufacturing in the Northeast." *Journal of Property Tax Management*, 1991, 1(3), pp 45-48.

Garreau, Joel. *Edge City: Life on the New Frontier*. New York: Doubleday, 1991.

George, Henry. *Progress and Poverty*. New York: Robert Schalkenbach Foundation, 1879, reprint 1960.

Gold, Steven D. "Changes in State Government Finances in the 1980's." *National Tax Journal*, XLIV(1).

______. "Simplifying the Sales Tax : Credits or Exemptions." In William F. Fox, ed., *Sales Taxation: Critical Issues in Policy and Administration*, Westport: Praeger Press, 1992.

Goode, Richard. "The Economic Definition of Income." In Joseph Pechman, ed., *Comprehensive Income Taxation*, Washington, D.C.: The Brookings Institution, 1977, pp. 1-37.

Grace, Martin, and Julie Hotchkiss. "External Impacts on the Property-Liability Insurance Cycle." Center for Risk Management and Insurance, Georgia State University, 1994, Working Paper 93-2.

Graeser, Laird, and Allen Maury. "Sales Tax on Services: State Trends." In William F. Fox, ed., *Sales Taxation: Critical Issues in Policy and Administration*, Westport: Praeger, 1992.

Graham, David M. "Purposes of Appraisals." In *Appraising Machinery and Equipment*, Washington, D.C.: American Society of Appraisers, 1989, pp. 29-38.

Grant Thorton, Inc. *Manufacturing Climates Study*. Chicago: Grant Thorton, August 1990.

Gravelle, Jane. "Enterprise Zones: The Design of Tax Subsidies." Congressional Research Service Report for Congress, 3 June 1992.

Greater Columbus Economic Strategy. Prepared for the Greater Columbus Chamber of Commerce, no date, 114 pages.

Hatcher, David B., and Arlon Tussing. "State Regulatory Challenges for the Natural Gas Industry and the 1990s and Beyond." Columbus: The National Regulatory Research Institute, 1992.

Hellerstein, Walter. "Critical Issues in State Taxation of Telecommunications." In Thomas Pogue, ed., *State Taxation of Business: Issues and Policy Options*, Westport: Praeger, 1992.

______. "Florida's Sales Tax on Services." *National Tax Journal*, 1988, 61(1), pp. 1-18.

Herzog, Henry, and A. Schlottman. "State and Local Deductibility and Metropolitan Migration." *National Tax Journal*, 1986, 39 (2), pp. 189-200.

Hines, J.R., Jr. "Altered States: Taxes and the Location of Foreign Direct Investment in America." Mimeo, Harvard University, Cambridge, June 1993.

Hirschman, Carolyn. "Hated Business Tax Goes Under Microscope." *Business First*, 21 February 1994.

Hobart, Lisa A., and Dennis W. Platte. "Valuation of Fast-Food Restaurant Equipment." *Assessment Journal*, 1994, 1(1), pp. 39-41.

Hofman, C. A., and Gary R. Wells. "The Argument for Consistency in the Valuation of Public Utilities." *Assessor Journal*, 1980, 15(4), pp. 191-198.

Howe, Edward T., and Donald Reeb. "Major State and Local Taxes Imposed on U.S. Electric Utilities." *Journal of State Taxation*, 1987, 9(1), pp. 3-27.

Hyman, Leonard S. *America's Electric Utilities: Past, Present and Future*. Fourth Edition. Arlington: Public Utilities Reports, Inc., 1992.

Iannacito, Alan C. "Identification of Machinery and Equipment." In *Appraising Machinery and Equipment*, Washington, D.C.: American Society of Appraisers, 1989, pp. 17-28.

Ihlanfeldt, Keith, R. *Job Accessibility and the Employment and School Enrollment of Teenagers.* Kalamazoo: W.E. Upjohn Institute for Employment Research, 1992.

Ihlanfeldt, Keith, R., and David L. Sjoquist. "The Effect of Job Access on Black and White Youth Employment: A Cross-Sectional Analysis." *Urban Studies*, 1991, 28, pp. 255-65.

Internal Revenue Service. *Statistics of Income Bulletin*. Washington, D.C.: U.S. Government Printing Office, various years.

International Association of Assessing Officers. *Appraising Real Property*. Chicago: International Association of Assessing Officers, 1990a.

______. *Property Appraisal and Assessment Administration*. Chicago: International Association of Assessing Officers, 1990b.

______. *Standard on Valuation of Personal Property*. Chicago: International Association of Assessing Officers, 1990c.

______. *Property Tax Administration*. Chicago: International Association of Assessing Officers, 1992.

Jensen, Jens P. *Property Taxation in the United States*. Chicago: University of Chicago Press, 1931.

Joyce, Philip G., and Daniel R. Mullins. "The Changing Fiscal Structure of the State and Local Public Sector: The Impact of Tax and Expenditure Limitations." *Public Administration Review,* May/June 1991, 51(3), pp. 240-253.

Kahn, Alfred E. "New Challenges in Public Utility Regulation." National Conference of State Legislatures, Washington, D.C.: 1985, pp. 1-7.

______. *The Economics of Regulation: Principles and Institutions*. New York: John Wiley & Sons, 1971.

Karier, T. "Business Tax Incentives and Investments." Jerome Levy Institute of Bard College Working Paper Series, Number 103, February 1994.

Keeler, Theodore E. "Railroad Costs, Returns to Scale, and Excess Capacity." *The Review of Economics and Statistics*, 1974, 56(2), pp. 201-08.

Kesselman, J.R., S. H. Williamson, and E. R. Berndt. "Tax Credits for Employment Rather Than Investment." *American Economic Review*, June 1977, 67(3), pp. 339-349.

Ladd, Helen. "Spatially Targeted Economic Development Strategies: Do They Work?" *Cityscape: A Journal of Policy Development and Research,* Proceedings of the Regional Growth and Community Development Conference November 1993, Washington D.C.: August 1994, pp. 193-218.

Ladd, Helen F., and Dana Weist. "General Sales Taxation." In Therese J. McGuire and Dana Wolfe Naimark, eds., *State and Local Finance for the 1990s: A Case Study of Arizona*, Tempe: School of Public Affairs, Arizona State University, 1991, pp. 117-156.

______. "State and Local Tax Systems: Balance Among Taxes versus Balance Among Policy Goals." In Frederick D. Stocker, ed., *The Quest for Balance in State-Local Revenue Structures*, Lincoln Institute of Land Policy, Tax Policy Roundtable, 1987, Property Tax Papers Series, #TPR-16.

Ladd, Helen F., and John Yinger. *American Ailing Cities*. Baltimore: John Hopkins Press, 1989.

Ledebur, Larry C., and William R. Barnes. *All In It Together: Cities, Suburbs, and Local Economic Regions*. Washington, D.C.: National League of Cities, Research Report of the National League of Cities, 1993.

Levin, Richard A. "Property Tax Limits in Ohio." *Revenue Administration*, pp. 141-54.

Levin, Richard A., and William Driscoll. "Balancing Fairness and Growth: The Success of Ohio's Library Funding." Columbus: Levin and Driscoll, 1994a.

_____. "Limits to Growth in the Ohio Property Tax Base Since 1975 and the Consequences for School Funding." Columbus: Levin and Driscoll, 1994b.

_____. *Telecommunications and Taxation in Ohio*. Columbus: Levin and Driscoll, 1994c.

_____. *Ohio's Property Taxes on Retail Business: A 13-State Comparison*. Columbus: Levin and Driscoll, 1993.

Levine, G.J. "To Tax or Not To Tax." *International Journal of Urban and Regional Research*, 1990, 2(4), pp. 543-566.

Maize, Kennedy P. "Retail Wheeling Coming to Your Neighborhood Soon." *The Electricity Journal*, 1994, 7(3), pp. 7-8.

Martinez, Jorge, and Martin Grace. "Business Taxation in Ohio: General Franchise Tax and Taxes on Financial Institutions and Insurance Companies." *Commission to Study the Ohio Economy and Tax Structure*, Atlanta: Policy Research Center, Georgia State University, 14 November 1994, Staff Report Number 9.

Martson, S.T. "Two Views of the Geographic Distribution of Unemployment." *Quarterly Journal of Economics*, 1985, 100, pp. 57-79.

Marvel, M., and W. Shkurti. "The Economic Impact of Development: Honda in Ohio." *Economic Development Quarterly*, 1993, 7, pp. 50-62.

McGuire, Therese J. "Jobs and Taxes: Do State Taxes Affect Economic Development?" Institute of Government and Public Affairs, Policy Forum, University of Illinois, 1993, 6(2).

McGuire, Therese, and Dana Naimark, eds. *State and Local Finance for the 1990s: A Case Study of Arizona*. Tempe: Arizona State University, 1991.

McHugh, Richard. "The Setting for Fiscal Reform: Selected Tables." *Commission to Study the Ohio Economy and Tax Structure*, Atlanta: Policy Research Center, Georgia State University, 31 May 1994a, Staff Report Number 1.

_____. "The Taxation of Telecommunications in Ohio." *Commission to Study the Ohio Economy and Tax Structure*, Atlanta: Policy Research

Center, Georgia State University, 10 October 1994b, Staff Report Number 10a.

______. "Memorandum on the Gross Receipts Tax in Ohio." November 1994c.

______. "Memorandum on the Ohio Estate Tax." November 1994d.

McIntyre, Robert S., et al. *A Far Cry From Fair*. Washington, D.C.: Citizens for Tax Justice, 1991.

McMillian, Jim. "Primary Sources for Cost Data Used in Developing Commercial Real Property and Business Personal Property Appraisal Schedules." *Assessment Digest*, 1993, pp. 10-17.

Mikesell, John L. "Central Cities and Sales Tax Rate Differentials: The Border City Problem." *National Tax Journal*, 1970, 23(2), pp. 206-214.

______. "Patterns of Exclusion of Personal Property From American Property Tax Systems." *Public Finance Quarterly*, 1992, 20(4), pp. 528-542.

______. "Retail Sales and Use Taxation in Minnesota." In Robert D. Ebel and Therese J. McGuire, eds., *Final Report of the Minnesota Tax Study Commission*, St. Paul: Butterworths, 1986, pp. 155-188.

______. "Sales Taxation of Not-for-Profit Organizations: Purchases and Sales." In William F. Fox, ed., *Sales Taxation: Critical Issues in Policy and Administration*, Westport: Praeger Press, 1992, pp. 121-130.

______. "Selected Business Property Taxation Issues: Personal Property." In John H. Bowman, ed., *Taxation of Business Property: Is Uniformity Still a Valid Norm?* Westport: Praeger, forthcoming.

Mills, David E. "The Non-Neutrality of Land Value Taxation." *National Tax Journal,* March 1981, 34, pp. 125-129.

Mills, John S. *Principles of Political Economy*. London: Ashley, Longmans, Green & Co., 1921.

Minnesota Department of Revenue. "Minnesota Tax Incidence Study: Who Pays Minnesota's Household and Business Taxes?" November 1993.

Money, J. "Housing Segregation, Negro Employment, and Metropolitan Decentralization: An Alternative Perspective." *Quarterly Journal of Economics*, 1969, 83, pp. 299-311.

Moody's Public Utility Manual. New York: Moody's Investor Service, 1993.

Moore, T.S., and A. Laramore. "Industrial Change and Urban Joblessness: An Assessment of the Mismatch Hypothesis." *Urban Affairs Quarterly*, 1990, 25, pp. 640-58.

Morse, G., and M. Farmer. "Location and Investment Effects of a Tax Abatement Program." *National Tax Journal*, 1986, 39, pp. 229-236.

Mueller, Dennis. *Public Choice II*. New York: Cambridge University Press, 1989.

Multistate Tax Commission. *Hearing Officer's Report, Uniform Principles Governing State Transactional Taxation of Telecommunications*. Washington, D.C.: Multistate Tax Commission, 1993.

Munnell, Alicia H. "How Does Public Infrastructure Affect Regional Economic Performance?" *New England Economic Review*, 1990, pp. 11-33.

Murray, Matthew. "Using State Policies to Promote Economic Development." In *Proceedings of the 86th Annual Conference on Taxation 1993,* by the National Tax Association - Tax Institute of America. Columbus: NTA-TIA 1994, pp.158-163.

Musgrave, Richard. *The Theory of Public Finance*. New York: McGraw-Hill, 1959.

Musgrave, Richard A., and Peggy B. Musgrave. *Public Finance in Theory and Practice*. 5th ed., New York: McGraw-Hill Book Company, 1989.

Nathan, Richard P., and Charles F. Adams. "Understanding Central City Hardship." *Political Science Quarterly*, Spring 1976, 91, pp. 47-62.

Netzer, Dick. *Economics of Property Tax.* Washington D.C.: The Brookings Institution, 1966.

______. "Reforming Utility Taxation: Federal Intervention and Economic Realities." The Urban Research Center of New York University, 1986.

New York State, Office of Policy Analysis and Development. *Survey of Railroad Utility Taxation Practices Among the States*. Albany, 1993.

Oakland, William H. "How Should Businesses Be Taxed." In Thomas F. Pogue and Frederick D. Stocker, eds., *State Taxation of Business*, 1992, pp. 17-34.

______. "Income Redistribution in a Federal System." In G. Zodrow, ed., *Local Provision of Public Services: The Tiebout Model After Twenty-five Years*. New York: Academic Press, 1983.

Oates, Wallace. "The Theory of Public Finance in a Federal System." *Canadian Journal of Economics*, 1968, 1, 37-54.

Office of Management and Budget. *Economic Report of the President*. Washington, D.C.: Government Printing Office, 1994.

Ohio Bureau of Employment Services. *Labor Market Projections, Ohio Projections 1991-2000*. Columbus: Ohio Bureau of Employment Services, February 1993.

Ohio Chamber of Commerce. "Testimony of Daniel Navin." Columbus: Ohio Chamber of Commerce, April 1994.

Ohio Department of Development. *Ohio Economic Competitiveness Project*. Cleveland: Cleveland State University, May 1993.

Ohio Department of Education. *The CUPP Printout*. processed report, July 1994.

Ohio Department of Taxation. *Annual Report*. Columbus: Ohio Department of Taxation, various years.

______. *Ohio Taxes*. Columbus: Ohio Department of Taxation, 1994.

Ohio Office of Budget and Management. *State of Ohio Executive Budget for the Biennium July 1, 1993 to June 30, 1995. Book Two: Report on Tax Expenditures.* Columbus: State of Ohio, 1995.

Ohio Public Expenditure Council. "Brief Facts Concerning Michigan School Finance Reform Votes." Columbus: Ohio Public Expenditure Council, June 1994, Report 94-6.

Ohio Revised Code: Annotated. Cincinnati: Anderson Publishing Company, 1991.

Ohio Society of CPAs. "Ohio Municipal Income Tax Uniformity Guide." Testimony presented to *Commission to Study the Ohio Economy and Tax Structure*, 1994.

Ohio's Third Century: Meeting the Economic Challenge through Science and Technology. A Report of the Ohio Science and Technology Commission, 1993.

Ohio United Way, Ohio Citizens' Council. "Testimony of Judith Tieman Bird." Testimony presented to *Commission to Study the Ohio Economy and Tax Structure*, June 1994.

Ondrich, Jan, and Michael Wasylenko. *Foreign Direct Investment in the United States*. Kalamazoo: W.E. Upjohn Institute for Employment Research, 1993.

Papke, James and Papke, Leslie. "State-Local Tax Concessions as Urban Development Tools: Incentives, Subsidies, Windfalls?" In *Proceedings of the 83rd Annual Conference on Taxation 1991*, by the National Tax

Association-Tax Institute of America. Columbus: NTA-TIA, 1992, pp.215-225.

Papke, Leslie. "Interstate Business Tax Differentials and New Firm Location: Evidence from Panel Data." *Journal of Public Economics*, 1991, 45(1), pp. 47-68.

______. "Tax Policy and Urban Development: Evidence from an Enterprise Zone Program." National Bureau of Economic Research Working Paper Number 3945, 1991.

______. "Subnational Taxation and Capital Mobility: Estimates of Tax-Price Elasticities." *National Tax Journal*, 1987, 40(2), pp. 191-204.

______. "What Do We Know About Enterprise Zones?" National Bureau of Economic Research Working Paper No. 4251, January 1993.

Pauly, Mark. "Income Redistribution as a Local Public Good." *Journal of Public Economics*. February 1973, 2(1), pp. 35-58.

Pearson, Gerald N. "A Public Information Procedure for Personal Property Taxpayers." *Assessment Digest,* 1994, 1(1), pp. 71-73.

Pennsylvania Economy League. *Development, Equity and the Graded Tax in the City of Pittsburgh*. Pittsburgh: Pennsylvania Economy League, March 1985.

Phares, Donald. *Who Pays State and Local Taxes.* Cambridge: Oelegschlager, Gunn and Hann, 1980.

Phillips, Charles F. *The Regulation of Public Utilities*. Arlington: Public Utility Reports, Inc., 1993.

Phillips, J. "Buying Jobs? Iowa Ups the Ante with IPSCO," in *Economic Trends*, Department of Economics and Finance, College of Business Administration, Omaha: Creighton University, Spring, 1994.

Plaut, Thomas R., and Joseph E. Pluta. "Business Climate, Taxes and Expenditures, and State Industrial Growth in the United States." *Southern Economic Journal*, July 1983, 50(1), pp. 99-119.

Pollakowski, Henry O. *Adjustments Effects of a Tax on Land: The Pittsburgh Case*. Cambridge: Lincoln Institute of Land Policy, 1982, Lincoln Institute Monograph #82-8.

Pomp, Richard. "The Role of State Tax Incentives in Attracting and Retaining Business." *Economic Development Review*, Spring 1988, 6(2), pp. 53-62.

Pomp, R.D. "Modernization and Simplification of Tax Administration and the Tax Law." *Tax Notes*, November 1985.

Poterba, James M. "Lifetime Incidence and the Distributional Burden of Excise Taxes." *National Bureau of Economic Research,* Working Paper No. 2833, 1989.

Premus, Robert. "Long-Run Growth and Cyclical Behavior of Ohio's Economy." *Ohio Economic Trends Review*, Winter 1986, 1(2).

Price Waterhouse, and Levin and Driscoll. *Comparative Analysis of Taxation of the Insurance Industry in Ohio, 1987-1992*. 1994.

Property Tax Division. *Ohio Personal Property Audit Handbook*. Columbus: The Ohio Department of Taxation, undated.

R.W. Beckett Corporation. "Testimony of Don Brackenhoff." Columbus: R.W. Beckett Corporation, May 1994.

Rabe, James G., and Robert F. Reilly. "Valuation of Intangible Assets for Property Tax Purposes." *NPA*, 1994, pp. 26-30.

Reeves, Clyde. "The Property Tax Dilemma." *Property Tax Journal*, 1982, 1(1), pp. 51-62.

Regional Income Tax Agency. *Information Booklet*. Brecksville: Regional Income Tax Agency, 1994.

Remsha, Michael J. "Property Tax Reduction Opportunities for Personal Property." *Journal of Property Tax Management*, 1992, 2(2), pp. 55-59.

Rice, Paul. "Sources of Pricing and Reference Material." In *Appraising Machinery and Equipment*, Washington, D.C.: American Society of Appraisers, 1989, pp. 49-58.

Ring, Raymond J., Jr. "The Proportion of Consumers' and Producers Goods in the General Sales Tax." *National Tax Journal*, 1989, 42(2), pp. 167-179.

Roberts, Paul D. "Classification: Personal Property or Real Property." *Journal of Property Taxation*, 1988, 1(1), pp. 79-80.

Rosen, Harvey S. *Public Finance*. 4th ed., Chicago: Irwin, 1995.

Rubin, M. "Urban Enterprise Zones: Do They Work? Evidence from New Jersey." *Public Budgeting and Finance*, Winter 1990, 10(4), pp. 3-17.

Rupp, Daniel. "Letter to Commission Staff." Columbus: September 1994.

Rusk, David. *Cities Without Suburbs*. Washington, D.C.: The Woodrow Wilson Center Press, 1993.

Schmidt, Robert C. "Managing the Property Tax Function." *Journal of State Taxation*, 1982, 1(2), pp. 239-45.

Schroeder, Larry D., and David L. Sjoquist. "An Analysis of Circuit-Breaker Programs for the State of Georgia." Atlanta: Department of Economics, Georgia State University, 1976.

Seligman, Edwin R.A. *Essays in Taxation*. 10th ed. New York: MacMillan, 1925.

Sheridan, Richard, Michael Sobul, Mark Hoffman, and Wilbur Thompson. "Ohio's Changing Economy." *Ohio Economic Trends Review*, Summer 1985, 1(1).

Shooshan and Jackson, Inc. *Telecommunications Infrastructure and Economic Development in the Northeast-Midwest Region*. Washington, D.C.: Northeast-Midwest Institute, 1988.

Siegfried, John, and Paul Smith. "The Distributional Effects of a Sales Tax on Services." *National Tax Journal*, 1991, 44(1), pp. 41-53.

Simons, Henry C. *Personal Income Taxation*. Chicago, Illinois: University of Chicago Press, 1938.

Sjoquist, David. " Real Property Taxation in Ohio: Analysis and Policy Options." *Commission to Study the Ohio Economy and Tax Structure,* Atlanta: Policy Research Center, Georgia State University, 9 September 1994, Staff Report Number 6.

Sjoquist, David et al. "Local Income Taxes." paper prepared for the ASPA Annual Conference. Atlanta: Policy Research Center, Georgia State University, 1993.

Skipper, H.D. "State Taxation of Insurance Companies: Time for a Change." *Journal of Insurance Regulation*, 1987, 6, pp. 121-142.

Slemrod, Joel. "Optimal Progressivity." In Robert Ebel and Therese McGuire, eds., *Final Report of the Minnesota Tax Study Commission, Volume 2, Staff Papers*, 1986, pp. 127-138.

Slemrod, Joel, and Nikki Soren. "The Compliance Cost of the U.S. Individual Income Tax System." *National Tax Journal*, December 1984, 37, pp. 461-474.

Sobul, Mike. "Equity in School Finance: Local Funding Issues." In *Equity in School Finance Public Practice CLE*, Columbus: Ohio Department of Taxation, 1993.

______. "Issues in Property Taxation for Schools." In *Public Practice CLE, School Finance*, Columbus: Ohio Department of Taxation, 1992.

______. "Ohio's Local Option School District Income Tax: An Update." Paper presented at the *84th Annual Conference on Taxation 1990*, in

Williamsburg, by the National Tax Association—Tax Institute of America. Columbus: NTA-TIA, 1991.

Sommers, Dixie. "Recession and Recovery in Ohio's Industries." *Ohio Economic Trends Review*, Spring 1986, 1(3).

State Board of Equalization. *Survey of Railroad and Utility Taxation Practices Among The States.* Albany, 1993.

State of Ohio. *Executive Budget, for the Biennium July 1, 1993 to June 30, 1995, Book Two, Report on Tax Expenditures*. Prepared by the Department of Taxation and Submitted to the 120th Assembly by George V. Voinovich, Governor, January 1993.

State Policy Reports. June 1994, 12(11), Issue 1 of 2, p. 9.

Stewart, Barbara. "The Economics of the Underwriting Cycle." *Journal of Insurance*, 1984, 42, pp.2-6.

Sunley, Emil M., and Mary M. Walz. "Simplification of Minnesota's Personal Income Tax." In Robert Ebel and Therese McGuire, eds., *Final Report of the Minnesota Tax Study Commission, Volume 2, Staff Papers*, Minneapolis: Butterworths Legal Publishers, 1986, pp. 107-126.

Taylor, Lester P. *Telecommunications Demand: A Survey and Critique*. Cambridge: Ballinger Publisher, Company, 1980.

Thompson, Herbert G., and Lynda L. Wolf. "Regional Differences in Generation of Electricity." *Land Economics*, 1993, 69(3), pp. 234-248.

U.S. Department of Commerce. *Survey of Current Business*. Washington, D.C.: U.S. Department of Commerce, 1994, various issues.

U.S. Department of Commerce, Bureau of Economic Analysis. *National Income and Product Accounts of the United States, Volume 1: 1929-58*. Washington, D.C.: U.S. Department of Commerce, 1992.

______. *Regional Economic Information System* (CD-ROM). Washington, D.C.: U.S. Department of Commerce, 1994.

_____. *Regional Projections to 2040*. Washington D.C.: Bureau of Economic Analysis, June 1990.

U.S. Department of Commerce, Bureau of the Census. *1980 Census of Housing*. Washington, D.C.: U.S. Department of Commerce, 1980a.

______. *1980 Census of Population, Metropolitan Areas, Section 1*. Washington, D.C.: U.S. Department of Commerce, 1980b.

______. *1990 Census of Housing*. Washington, D.C.: U.S. Department of Commerce, 1990a.

______. *1990 Census of Population*. Washington, D.C.: U.S. Department of Commerce, 1990b.

______. *1990 Census of Population and Housing: Public Use Microdata Samples, Georgia*. ICPSR Edition. Ann Arbor: Inter-university Consortium for Political and Social Research, 1990c.

______. *Government Finances*. Washington, D.C.: U.S. Government Printing Office, various years.

______. *City Government Finances in 1977/78.*

______. *Statistical Abstract of the United States, 1994.*

U.S. Department of Defense. *Defense,* Arlington: U.S. Department of Defense, December 1992, Almanac issue.

U.S. Department of Labor. *Employment and Earnings*. Washington, D.C.: Bureau of Labor Statistics, 1994, various issues.

U.S. Department of Labor, Bureau of Labor Statistics. *Metropolitan Area Wage Comparisons 1990*. Washington, D.C.: U.S. Department of Labor, 1991.

______. "Outlook 1990-2004, Industry Output and Employment." *Monthly Labor Review*, November 1991.

U.S. General Accounting Office. *Enterprise Zones: Lessons from the Maryland Experience*. Washington, D.C.: U.S. General Accounting Office, 1988, GAO/PEMD-89-2.

Urbancic, Frank R. "Individual Income Tax Instructions of the Southern States: A Readability Study." *Southern Business & Economic Journal*, April 1992, pp. 154-159.

Vaughn, R. *State Taxation and Economic Development*. Council of State Planning Agencies, Washington, D.C.: 1979.

Vedder, Richard, David Klingaman, and Lowell Galloway. "The Economic Impact of Excise and Sales Taxation in Ohio." Mimeo, Pub, 5 February 1992.

Wallace, Sally. "Effects of State Income Taxes on Migration." Unpublished manuscript, Policy Research Center, Georgia State University, 1994.

______. "Memorandum on the Individual Income Tax Estimates," 21 December 1994b.

Wallace, Sally, and Barbara Edwards. "Ohio's State and Local Individual Income Taxes: Analysis and Options." *Commission to Study the Ohio Economy and Tax Structure*, Atlanta: Policy Research Center, Georgia State University, 30 November 1994a, Staff Report Number 5.

Wallace, W.A. *Auditing*. New York: Macmillan, 1986.

Walsh, Michael J., and Jonathan D. Jones. "More Evidence on the 'Border Tax' Effect: The Case of West Virginia, 1979-84." *National Tax Journal*, 1988, 41(2), pp. 261-265.

Wassmer, Robert. "The Use and Abuse of Economic Development Incentives in a Metropolitan Area." In *Proceedings of the 86th Annual Conference on Taxation 1993*, by the National Tax Association-Tax Institute of America. St. Paul: NTA-TIA, 11 November 1994, pp. 146-157.

______. "Property Tax Statements and the Simultaneous Determination of Local Fiscal Variables in a Metropolitan Area." *Land Economics*, August 1992, 68(3), pp. 268-282.

Wasylenko, Michael. "Empirical Evidence on Interregional Business Location Decisions and the Role of Fiscal Incentives in Economic Development." In H. Herzog and A. Schlottmann, *Industry Location and Public Policy*, Knoxville: University of Tennessee Press, 1991, pp.13-30.

______. "Has the Relationship Changed Between Taxes and Business Location Decisions?" In *Proceedings of the 86th Annual Conference on Taxation 1994,* by the National Tax Association-Tax Institute of America Columbus: NTA-TIA, 1995, pp. 107-112.

______. "The Role of Fiscal Incentives in Economic Development: How Ohio Stands Relative to Its Competitor States." *Commission to Study the Ohio Economy and Tax Structure.* Atlanta: Policy Research Center, Georgia State University, 5 November 1994, Staff Report Number 11.

Wasylenko, Michael, and Therese J. McGuire. "Jobs and Taxes: The Effect of Business Climate on States' Employment Growth Rates." *National Tax Journal*, December 1985, 36(4), pp. 497-512.

Welch, F. "The Employment of Black Men." *Journal of Labor Economics*, 1990, 8, pp. S26-74.

Western State Association of Tax Administrators. *Appraisal Handbook: Valuation of Utility and Railroad Property*, 1989.

Wheeler, Gloria, and Gary C. Cornia. "An Analysis of Self-Reporting Tangible Business Personal Property Process." *Property Tax Journal*, 1989, 8(3), pp. 171-182.

White, Fred C. "Trade-off in Growth and Stability in State Taxes." *National Tax Journal*, March 1983, pp. 103-114.

Williamson, O. E. "Managerial Discretion and Business Behavior." *American Economic Review*, 1963, 53(5), pp. 1032-57.

Wilson, George W. "The Relative Importance of Economic Regulation of Transportation Vis-a-Vis Everything Else." In Kenneth D. Boyer and William G. Shepherd, eds., *Economic Regulation: Essays in Honor of James R. Nelson*, East Lansing: Michigan State University Press, 1981, pp. 9-38.

Woolery, Arlo. *Valuation of Railroad and Utility Property*. Cambridge: Lincoln Institute of Land Policy, 1992, p. 778.

Yuskewick, J. Matthers, and Mable Kitchen. "Ohio Income Tax: A System in Disarray." *Ohio Law Review*, 1993, 8(1).

Index